JavaScript & jQuery

the missing manual®

The book that should have been in the box®

David Sawyer McFarland

O'REILLY®

Beijing | Cambridge | Farnham | Köln | Sebastopol | Tokyo

JavaScript & jQuery: The Missing Manual

by David Sawyer McFarland

Copyright © 2014 Sawyer McFarland Media, Inc. All rights reserved.
Printed in the United States of America.

Published by O'Reilly Media, Inc.,
1005 Gravenstein Highway North, Sebastopol, CA 95472.

O'Reilly books may be purchased for educational, business, or sales promotional use. Online editions are also available for most titles (*http://safaribooksonline.com*). For more information, contact our corporate/institutional sales department: (800) 998-9938 or *corporate@oreilly.com*.

July 2008:	First Edition.
October 2011:	Second Edition.
September 2014:	Third Edition.

Revision History for the Third Edition:

2014-09-10   First release

See *http://oreilly.com/catalog/errata.csp?isbn=9781491947074* for release details.

ISBN-13: 978-1-491-94707-4

[LSI]

Contents

Part One: Getting Started with JavaScript

Part Six: **Appendix**

The Missing Credits

ABOUT THE AUTHOR

 David Sawyer McFarland is president of Sawyer McFarland Media, Inc., a web development and training company in Portland, Oregon. He's been building websites since 1995, when he designed his first site—an online magazine for communication professionals. He's served as webmaster at the University of California at Berkeley and the Berkeley Multimedia Research Center, and oversaw a complete CSS-driven redesign of Macworld.com.

In addition to building websites, David is also a writer, trainer, and instructor. He's taught web design at UC Berkeley Graduate School of Journalism, the Center for Electronic Art, the Academy of Art College, Ex'Pressions Center for New Media, and Portland State University. He's written articles about the web for *Practical Web Design, MX Developer's Journal, Macworld* magazine, and CreativePro.com.

He welcomes feedback about this book by email: *missing@sawmac.com*. (If you're seeking technical help, however, please refer to the sources listed in Appendix A.)

ABOUT THE CREATIVE TEAM

Nan Barber (editor) is associate editor for the Missing Manual series. She lives in Massachusetts with her husband and various electronic devices. Email: *nanbarber@gmail.com*.

Melanie Yarbrough (production editor) works and plays in Cambridge, Massachusetts, where she bakes up whatever she can imagine and bikes around the city. Email: *myarbrough@oreilly.com*.

Jennifer Davis (technical reviewer) is an engineer with years of experience improving platform development efficiency. As a Chef Automation engineer, she helps companies discover their own best practices to improving workflow reducing mean time to deploy. She is an event organizer for Reliability Engineering, the Bay Area Chef user group.

Alex Stangl (technical reviewer) has developed software professionally for 25+ years, using a myriad of languages and technologies. He enjoys challenging problems and puzzles, learning new languages (currently Clojure), doing technical reviews, and being a good dad and husband. Email: *alex@stangl.us*.

Jasmine Kwityn (proofreader) is a freelance copyeditor and proofreader. She lives in New Jersey with her husband, Ed, and their three cats, Mushki, Axle, and Punky. Email: *jasminekwityn@gmail.com*.

Bob Pfahler (indexer) is a freelance indexer who indexed this book on behalf of Potomac Indexing, LLC, an international indexing partnership at *www.potomacindexing.com*. Besides the subject of computer technology, he specializes in business, management, biography, and history. Email: *bobpfahler@hotmail.com*.

ACKNOWLEDGMENTS

Many thanks to all those who helped with this book, including Jennifer Davis and Alex Stangl, whose watchful eyes saved me from potentially embarrassing mistakes. Thanks also to my many students at Portland State University who have sat through my long JavaScript lectures and struggled through my programming assignments—especially the members of Team Futzbit (Combination Pizza Hut and Taco Bell) for testing the tutorials: Julia Hall, Amber Brucker, Kevin Brown, Josh Elliott, Tracy O'Connor, and Blake Womack. Also, we all owe a big debt of gratitude to John Resig and the jQuery team for creating the best tool yet for making JavaScript fun.

Finally, thanks to David Pogue for getting me started; Nan Barber for making my writing sharper and clearer; my wife, Scholle, for putting up with an author's crankiness; and thanks to my kids, Graham and Kate, because they're just awesome.

—David Sawyer McFarland

THE MISSING MANUAL SERIES

Missing Manuals are witty, superbly written guides to computer products that don't come with printed manuals (which is just about all of them). Each book features a handcrafted index and cross-references to specific pages (not just chapters). Recent and upcoming titles include:

Access 2010: The Missing Manual by Matthew MacDonald

Access 2013: The Missing Manual by Matthew MacDonald

Adobe Edge Animate: The Missing Manual by Chris Grover

Buying a Home: The Missing Manual by Nancy Conner

Creating a Website: The Missing Manual, Third Edition by Matthew MacDonald

CSS3: The Missing Manual, Third Edition by David Sawyer McFarland

David Pogue's Digital Photography: The Missing Manual by David Pogue

Dreamweaver CS6: The Missing Manual by David Sawyer McFarland

Dreamweaver CC: The Missing Manual by David Sawyer McFarland and Chris Grover

Excel 2010: The Missing Manual by Matthew MacDonald

Excel 2013: The Missing Manual by Matthew MacDonald

Facebook: The Missing Manual, Third Edition by E. A. Vander Veer

FileMaker Pro 13: The Missing Manual by Susan Prosser and Stuart Gripman

Flash CS6: The Missing Manual by Chris Grover

Galaxy Tab: The Missing Manual by Preston Gralla

Galaxy S4: The Missing Manual by Preston Gralla

Galaxy S5: The Missing Manual by Preston Gralla

Google+: The Missing Manual by Kevin Purdy

HTML5: The Missing Manual, Second Edition by Matthew MacDonald

iMovie '11 & iDVD: The Missing Manual by David Pogue and Aaron Miller

iPad: The Missing Manual, Sixth Edition by J.D. Biersdorfer

iPhone: The Missing Manual, Seventh Edition by David Pogue

iPhone App Development: The Missing Manual by Craig Hockenberry

iPhoto '11: The Missing Manual by David Pogue and Lesa Snider

iPod: The Missing Manual, Eleventh Edition by J.D. Biersdorfer and David Pogue

Kindle Fire HD: The Missing Manual by Peter Meyers

Living Green: The Missing Manual by Nancy Conner

Microsoft Project 2010: The Missing Manual by Bonnie Biafore

Microsoft Project 2013: The Missing Manual by Bonnie Biafore

Motorola Xoom: The Missing Manual by Preston Gralla

NOOK HD: The Missing Manual by Preston Gralla

Office 2010: The Missing Manual by Nancy Conner and Matthew MacDonald

Office 2011 for Macintosh: The Missing Manual by Chris Grover

Office 2013: The Missing Manual by Nancy Conner and Matthew MacDonald

OS X Mountain Lion: The Missing Manual by David Pogue

OS X Mavericks: The Missing Manual by David Pogue

OS X Yosemite: The Missing Manual by David Pogue

Personal Investing: The Missing Manual by Bonnie Biafore

Photoshop CS6: The Missing Manual by Lesa Snider

Photoshop CC: The Missing Manual by Lesa Snider

Photoshop Elements 12: The Missing Manual by Barbara Brundage

PHP & MySQL: The Missing Manual, Second Edition by Brett McLaughlin

QuickBooks 2014: The Missing Manual by Bonnie Biafore

QuickBooks 2015: The Missing Manual by Bonnie Biafore

Switching to the Mac: The Missing Manual, Mavericks Edition by David Pogue

Switching to the Mac: The Missing Manual, Yosemite Edition by David Pogue

Windows 7: The Missing Manual by David Pogue

Windows 8: The Missing Manual by David Pogue

WordPress: The Missing Manual, Second Edition by Matthew MacDonald

Your Body: The Missing Manual by Matthew MacDonald

Your Brain: The Missing Manual by Matthew MacDonald

Your Money: The Missing Manual by J.D. Roth

For a full list of all Missing Manuals in print, go to *www.missingmanuals.com/library.html.*

Introduction

The Web was a pretty boring place in its early days. Web pages were constructed from plain old HTML, so they could display information, and that was about all. Folks would click a link and then wait for a new web page to load. That was about as interactive as it got.

These days, most websites are almost as responsive as the programs on a desktop computer, reacting immediately to every mouse click. And it's all thanks to the subjects of this book—JavaScript and its sidekick, jQuery.

■ What Is JavaScript?

JavaScript is a programming language that lets you supercharge your HTML with animation, interactivity, and dynamic visual effects.

JavaScript can make web pages more useful by supplying immediate feedback. For example, a JavaScript-powered shopping cart page can instantly display a total cost, with tax and shipping, the moment a visitor selects a product to buy. JavaScript can produce an error message immediately after someone attempts to submit a web form that's missing necessary information.

JavaScript also lets you create fun, dynamic, and interactive interfaces. For example, with JavaScript, you can transform a static page of thumbnail images into an animated slideshow. Or you can do something more subtle like stuff more information on a page without making it seem crowded by organizing content into bite-size panels that visitors can access with a simple click of the mouse (page 326). Or add something useful and attractive, like pop-up tooltips that provide supplemental information for items on your web page (page 321).

Another one of JavaScript's main selling points is its immediacy. It lets web pages respond instantly to actions like clicking a link, filling out a form, or merely moving the mouse around the screen. JavaScript doesn't suffer from the frustrating delay associated with server-side programming languages like PHP, which rely on communication between the web browser and the web server. Because it doesn't rely on constantly loading and reloading web pages, JavaScript lets you create web pages that feel and act more like desktop programs than web pages.

If you've visited Google Maps (*http://maps.google.com*), you've seen JavaScript in action. Google Maps lets you view a map of your town (or pretty much anywhere else for that matter), zoom in to get a detailed view of streets and bus stops, or zoom out to get a bird's-eye view of how to get across town, the state, or the nation. While there were plenty of map sites before Google, they always required reloading multiple web pages (usually a slow process) to get to the information you wanted. Google Maps, on the other hand, works without page refreshes—it responds immediately to your choices.

The programs you create with JavaScript can range from the really simple (like popping up a new browser window with a web page in it) to full-blown web applications like Google Docs (*http://docs.google.com*), which lets you create presentations, edit documents, and build spreadsheets using your web browser with the feel of a program running directly on your computer.

A Bit of History

Invented in 10 days by Brendan Eich at Netscape back in 1995, JavaScript is nearly as old as the Web itself. While JavaScript is well respected today, it has a somewhat checkered past. It used to be considered a hobbyist's programming language, used for adding less-than-useful effects such as messages that scroll across the bottom of a web browser's status bar like a stock ticker, or animated butterflies following mouse movements around the page. In the early days of JavaScript, it was easy to find thousands of free JavaScript programs (also called *scripts*) online, but many of those scripts didn't work in all web browsers, and at times even crashed browsers.

NOTE JavaScript has little to do with the Java programming language. JavaScript was originally named LiveScript, but a quick deal by marketers at Netscape eager to cash in on the success of Sun Microsystem's then-hot programming language led to this long-term confusion. Don't make the mistake of confusing the two...especially at a job interview!

In the early days, JavaScript also suffered from incompatibilities between the two prominent browsers, Netscape Navigator and Internet Explorer. Because Netscape and Microsoft tried to outdo each other's browsers by adding newer and (ostensibly) better features, the two browsers often acted in very different ways, making it difficult to create JavaScript programs that worked well in both.

NOTE After Netscape introduced JavaScript, Microsoft introduced jScript, their own version of JavaScript included with Internet Explorer.

Fortunately, the worst of those days is nearly gone and contemporary browsers like Firefox, Safari, Chrome, Opera, and Internet Explorer 11 have standardized much of the way they handle JavaScript, making it easier to write JavaScript programs that work for most everyone. (There are still a few incompatibilities among current web browsers, so you'll need to learn a few tricks for dealing with cross-browser problems. You'll learn how to overcome browser incompatibilities in this book.)

In the past several years, JavaScript has undergone a rebirth, fueled by high-profile websites like Google, Yahoo!, and Flickr, which use JavaScript extensively to create interactive web applications. There's never been a better time to learn JavaScript. With the wealth of knowledge and the quality of scripts being written, you can add sophisticated interaction to your website—even if you're a beginner.

> **NOTE** JavaScript is also known by the name ECMAScript. ECMAScript is the "official" JavaScript specification, which is developed and maintained by an international standards organization called Ecma International: *www. ecmascript.org.*

JavaScript Is Everywhere

JavaScript isn't just for web pages, either. It's proven to be such a useful programming language that if you learn JavaScript you can create Yahoo! Widgets and Google Apps, write programs for the iPhone, and tap into the scriptable features of many Adobe programs like Acrobat, Photoshop, Illustrator, and Dreamweaver. In fact, Dreamweaver has always offered clever JavaScript programmers a way to add their own commands to the program.

In the Yosemite version of the Mac OS X operating system, Apple lets users automate their Macs using JavaScript. In addition, JavaScript is used in many helpful front end web development tools like Gulp.js (which can automatically compress images and CSS and JavaScript files) and Bower (which makes it quick and easy to download common JavaScript libraries like jQuery, jQuery UI, or AngularJS to your computer).

JavaScript is also becoming increasingly popular for server-side development. The Node.js platform (a version of Google's V8 JavaScript engine that runs JavaScript on the server) is being embraced eagerly by companies like Walmart, PayPal, and eBay. Learning JavaScript can even lead to a career in building complex server-side applications. In fact, the combination of JavaScript on the *frontend* (that is, JavaScript running in a web browser) and the *backend* (on the web server) is known as *full stack JavaScript development.*

In other words, there's never been a better time to learn JavaScript!

■ What Is jQuery?

JavaScript has one embarrassing little secret: writing it can be hard. While it's simpler than many other programming languages, JavaScript is still a programming language. And many people, including web designers, find programming difficult.

To complicate matters further, different web browsers understand JavaScript differently, so a program that works in, say, Chrome may be completely unresponsive in Internet Explorer 9. This common situation can cost many hours of testing on different machines and different browsers to make sure a program works correctly for your site's entire audience.

That's where jQuery comes in. jQuery is a JavaScript library intended to make JavaScript programming easier and more fun. A JavaScript library is a complex set of JavaScript code that both simplifies difficult tasks and solves cross-browser problems. In other words, jQuery solves the two biggest JavaScript headaches: complexity and the finicky nature of different web browsers.

jQuery is a web designer's secret weapon in the battle of JavaScript programming. With jQuery, you can accomplish tasks in a single line of code that could take hundreds of lines of programming and many hours of browser testing to achieve with your own JavaScript code. In fact, an in-depth book solely about JavaScript would be at least twice as thick as the one you're holding; and, when you were done reading it (if you could manage to finish it), you wouldn't be able to do half of the things you can accomplish with just a little bit of jQuery knowledge.

That's why most of this book is about jQuery. It lets you do so much, so easily. Another great thing about jQuery is that you can add advanced features to your website with thousands of easy-to-use jQuery plug-ins. For example, the jQuery UI plug-in (which you'll meet on page 299) lets you create many complex user interface elements like tabbed panels, drop-down menus, pop-up date-picker calendars—all with a single line of programming!

Unsurprisingly, jQuery is used on millions of websites (*http://trends.builtwith.com/javascript/jQuery*). It's baked right into popular content management systems like Drupal and WordPress. You can even find job listings for "jQuery Programmers" with no mention of JavaScript. When you learn jQuery, you join a large community of fellow web designers and programmers who use a simpler and more powerful approach to creating interactive, powerful web pages.

■ HTML: The Barebones Structure

JavaScript isn't much good without the two other pillars of web design—HTML and CSS. Many programmers talk about the three languages as forming the "layers" of a web page: HTML provides the *structural* layer, organizing content like pictures and words in a meaningful way; CSS (Cascading Style Sheets) provides the *presentational* layer, making the content in the HTML look good; and JavaScript adds a *behavioral* layer, bringing a web page to life so it interacts with web visitors.

In other words, to master JavaScript, you need to have a good understanding of both HTML and CSS.

NOTE For a full-fledged introduction to HTML and CSS, check out *Head First HTML with CSS and XHTML* by Elisabeth Robson and Eric Freeman. For an in-depth presentation of the tricky subject of Cascading Style Sheets, pick up a copy of *CSS3: The Missing Manual* by David Sawyer McFarland (both from O'Reilly).

HTML (Hypertext Markup Language) uses simple commands called *tags* to define the various parts of a web page. For example, this HTML code creates a simple web page:

```
<!DOCTYPE html>
<html>
<head>
<meta charset=utf-8>
<title>Hey, I am the title of this web page.</title>
</head>
<body>
Hey, I am some body text on this web page.
</body>
</html>
```

It may not be exciting, but this example has all the basic elements a web page needs. This page begins with a single line—the document type declaration, or *doctype* for short—that states what type of document the page is and which standards it conforms to. HTML actually comes in different versions, and you use a different doctype with each. In this example, the doctype is for HTML5; the doctype for an HTML 4.01 or XHTML document is longer and also includes a URL that points the web browser to a file on the Internet that contains definitions for that type of file.

In essence, the doctype tells the web browser how to display the page. The doctype can even affect how CSS and JavaScript work. With an incorrect or missing doctype, you may end up banging your head against a wall as you discover lots of cross-browser differences with your scripts. If for no other reason, always include a doctype in your HTML.

Historically, there have been many doctypes—HTML 4.01 Transitional, HTML 4.01 Strict, XHTML 1.0 Transitional, XHTML 1.0 Strict—but they required a long line of confusing code that was easy to mistype. HTML5's doctype—<!DOCTYPE html>—is short, simple, and the one you should use.

How HTML Tags Work

In the example in the previous section, as in the HTML code of any web page, you'll notice that most instructions appear in pairs that surround a block of text or other commands. Sandwiched between brackets, these *tags* are instructions that tell a web browser how to display the web page. Tags are the "markup" part of the Hypertext Markup Language.

The starting (*opening*) tag of each pair tells the browser where the instruction begins, and the ending tag tells it where the instruction ends. Ending or *closing* tags always include a forward slash (/) after the first bracket symbol (<). For example, the tag

<p> marks the start of a paragraph, while </p> marks its end. Some tags don't have closing tags, like <img>, <input>, and <br> tags, which consist of just a single tag.

For a web page to work correctly, you must include at least these three tags:

- The <html> tag appears once at the beginning of a web page (after the doctype) and again (with an added slash) at the end. This tag tells a web browser that the information contained in this document is written in HTML, as opposed to some other language. All of the contents of a page, including other tags, appear between the opening and closing <html> tags.

  If you were to think of a web page as a tree, the <html> tag would be its root. Springing from the root are two branches that represent the two main parts of any web page—the *head* and the *body*.

- The *head* of a web page, surrounded by <head> tags, contains the title of the page. It may also provide other, invisible information (such as search keywords) that browsers and web search engines can exploit.

  In addition, the head can contain information that's used by the web browser for displaying the web page and for adding interactivity. You put Cascading Style Sheets, for example, in the head of the document. The head of the document is also where you often include JavaScript programming and links to JavaScript files.

- The *body* of a web page, as set apart by its surrounding <body> tags, contains all the information that appears inside a browser window: headlines, text, pictures, and so on.

Within the <body> tag, you commonly find tags like the following:

- You tell a web browser where a paragraph of text begins with a <p> (opening paragraph tag), and where it ends with a </p> (closing paragraph tag).

- The <strong> tag emphasizes text. If you surround some text with it and its partner tag, </strong>, you get boldface type. The HTML snippet <strong>Warning!</strong> tells a web browser to display the word "Warning!" in bold type.

- The <a> tag, or anchor tag, creates a *hyperlink* in a web page. When clicked, a hyperlink—or *link*—can lead anywhere on the Web. You tell the browser where the link points by putting a web address inside the <a> tags. For instance, you might type <a href="http://www.missingmanuals.com">Click here!</a>.

  The browser knows that when your visitor clicks the words "Click here!" it should go to the Missing Manuals website. The href part of the tag is called an *attribute* and the URL (the uniform resource locator or web address) is the *value*. In this example, *http://www.missingmanuals.com* is the *value* of the href attribute.

UP TO SPEED

Validating Web Pages

As mentioned on page xvii, a web page's doctype identifies which type of HTML or XHTML you used to create the web page. The rules differ subtly depending on type: For example, unlike HTML 4.01, XHTML doesn't let you have an unclosed <p> tag, and requires that all tag names and attributes be lowercase (<a> *not* <A>, for example). HTML5 includes new tags and lets you use either HTML or XHTML syntax. Because different rules apply to each variant of HTML, you should always *validate* your web pages.

An HTML validator is a program that makes sure a web page is written correctly. It checks the page's doctype and then analyzes the code in the page to see whether it matches the rules defined by that doctype. For example, the validator flags mistakes like a misspelled tag name or an unclosed tag. The World Wide Web Consortium (W3C), the organization that's responsible for many of the technologies used on the Web,

has a free online validator at *http://validator.w3.org*. You can copy your HTML and paste it into a web form, upload a web page, or point the validator to an already existing page on the Web; the validator then analyzes the HTML and reports back whether the page is valid or not. If there are any errors, the validator tells you what the error is and on which line of the HTML file it occurs.

Valid HTML isn't just good form—it also helps to make sure your JavaScript programs work correctly. A lot of JavaScript involves manipulating a web page's HTML: identifying a particular form field, for example, or placing new HTML (like an error message) in a particular spot. In order for JavaScript to access and manipulate a web page, the HTML must be in proper working order. Forgetting to close a tag, using the same ID name more than once, or improperly nesting your HTML tags can make your JavaScript code behave erratically or not at all.

■ CSS: Adding Style to Web Pages

At the beginning of the Web, HTML was the only language you needed to know. You could build pages with colorful text and graphics and make words jump out using different sizes, fonts, and colors. But today, web designers turn to Cascading Style Sheets to add visual sophistication to their pages. CSS is a formatting language that lets you make text look good, build complex page layouts, and generally add style to your site.

Think of HTML as merely the language you use to structure a page. It helps identify the stuff you want the world to know about. Tags like <h1> and <h2> denote headlines and assign them relative importance: A *heading 1* is more important than a *heading 2*. The <p> tag indicates a basic paragraph of information. Other tags provide further structural clues: for example, a <ul> tag identifies a bulleted list (to make a list of recipe ingredients more intelligible, for example).

CSS, on the other hand, adds design flair to well-organized HTML content, making it more beautiful and easier to read. Essentially, a CSS *style* is just a rule that tells a web browser how to display a particular element on a page. For example, you can create a CSS rule to make all <h1> tags appear 36 pixels tall, in the Verdana font, and in orange. CSS can do more powerful stuff, too, like add borders, change margins, and even control the exact placement of a page element.

When it comes to JavaScript, some of the most valuable changes you make to a page involve CSS. You can use JavaScript to add or remove a CSS style from an HTML tag, or dynamically change CSS properties based on a visitor's input or mouse clicks. You can even animate from the properties of one style to the properties of another (say, animating a background color changing from yellow to red). For example, you can make a page element appear or disappear simply by changing the CSS display property. To animate an item across the screen, you can change the CSS position properties dynamically using JavaScript.

Anatomy of a Style

A single style that defines the look of one element is a pretty basic beast. It's essentially a rule that tells a web browser how to format something—turn a headline blue, draw a red border around a photo, or create a 150-pixel-wide sidebar box to hold a list of links. If a style could talk, it would say something like, "Hey, Browser, make *this* look like *that*." A style is, in fact, made up of two elements: the web page element that the browser formats (the *selector*) and the actual formatting instructions (the *declaration block*). For example, a selector can be a headline, a paragraph of text, a photo, and so on. Declaration blocks can turn that text blue, add a red border around a paragraph, position the photo in the center of the page—the possibilities are endless.

> **NOTE** Technical types often follow the lead of the W3C and call CSS styles *rules*. This book uses the terms "style" and "rule" interchangeably.

Of course, CSS styles can't communicate in nice, clear English. They have their own language. For example, to set a standard font color and font size for all paragraphs on a web page, you'd write the following:

```
p { color: red; font-size: 1.5em; }
```

This style simply says, "Make the text in all paragraphs—marked with <p> tags—red and 1.5 ems tall." (An *em* is a unit or measurement that's based on a browser's normal text size.) As Figure I-1 illustrates, even a simple style like this example contains several elements:

- **Selector.** The selector tells a web browser which element or elements on a page to style—like a headline, paragraph, image, or link. In Figure I-1, the selector (p) refers to the <p> tag, which makes web browsers format all <p> tags using the formatting directions in this style. With the wide range of selectors that CSS offers and a little creativity, you can gain fine control of your pages' formatting. (Selectors are an important part of using jQuery, so you'll find a detailed discussion of them starting on page 119.)

- **Declaration block.** The code following the selector includes all the formatting options you want to apply to the selector. The block begins with an opening brace ({) and ends with a closing brace (}).

- **Declaration.** Between the opening and closing braces of a declaration, you add one or more *declarations*, or formatting instructions. Every declaration has two parts, a *property* and a *value*, and ends with a semicolon. A colon separates the property name from its value: `color : red;`.

- **Property.** CSS offers a wide range of formatting options, called *properties*. A property is a word—or a few hyphenated words—indicating a certain style effect. Most properties have straightforward names like `font-size`, `margin-top`, and `background-color`. For example, the `background-color` property sets—you guessed it—a background color.

> **NOTE** If you need to brush up on your CSS, grab a copy of *CSS3: The Missing Manual*.

- **Value**. Finally, you get to express your creative genius by assigning a *value* to a CSS property—by making a background blue, red, purple, or chartreuse, for example. Different CSS properties require specific types of values—a color (like red, or #FF0000), a length (like 18px, 2in, or 5em), a URL (like *images/ background.gif*), or a specific keyword (like top, center, or bottom).

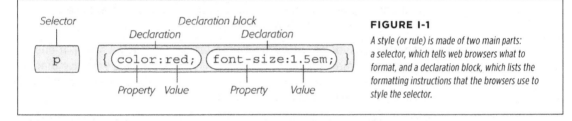

FIGURE I-1

A style (or rule) is made of two main parts: a selector, which tells web browsers what to format, and a declaration block, which lists the formatting instructions that the browsers use to style the selector.

You don't need to write a style on a single line as pictured in Figure I-1. Many styles have multiple formatting properties, so you can make them easier to read by breaking them up into multiple lines. For example, you may want to put the selector and opening brace on the first line, each declaration on its own line, and the closing brace by itself on the last line, like so:

```
p {
    color: red;
    font-size: 1.5em;
}
```

It's also helpful to indent properties, with either a tab or a couple of spaces, to visibly separate the selector from the declarations, making it easy to tell which is which. And finally, putting one space between the colon and the property value is optional, but adds to the readability of the style. In fact, you can put as much white space between the two as you want. For example, `color:red`, `color: red`, and `color : red` all work.

■ Software for JavaScript Programming

To create web pages made up of HTML, CSS, and JavaScript, you need nothing more than a basic text editor like Notepad (Windows) or TextEdit (Mac). But after typing a few hundred lines of JavaScript code, you may want to try a program better suited to working with web pages. This section lists some common editors—some free and some you can buy.

> **NOTE** There are literally hundreds of tools that can help you create web pages and write JavaScript programs, so the following is by no means a complete list. Think of it as a greatest-hits tour of the most popular programs that JavaScript fans are using today.

Free Programs

There are plenty of free programs out there for editing web pages and style sheets. If you're still using Notepad or TextEdit, give one of these a try. Here's a short list to get you started:

- **Brackets** (Windows, Mac, and Linux, *http://brackets.io*) is an open source code editor from Adobe. It's free (there is a commercial version with more features named Edge Code), has many great features including a great live browser preview, and is even written in JavaScript!

- **Notepad++** (Windows, *http://notepad-plus-plus.org*) is a coder's friend. It highlights the syntax of JavaScript and HTML code, and lets you save macros and assign keyboard shortcuts to them so you can automate the process of inserting the code snippets you use most.

- **HTML-Kit** (Windows, *www.chami.com/html-kit*) is a powerful HTML/XHTML editor that includes lots of useful features, like the ability to preview a web page directly in the program (so you don't have to switch back and forth between browser and editor), shortcuts for adding HTML tags, and a lot more.

- **CoffeeCup Free HTML Editor** (Windows, *www.coffeecup.com/free-editor*) is the free version of the commercial ($49) CoffeeCup HTML editor.

- **TextWrangler** (Mac, *www.barebones.com/products/textwrangler*) is free software that's actually a pared-down version of BBEdit, the sophisticated, well-known text editor for the Mac. TextWrangler doesn't have all of BBEdit's built-in HTML tools, but it does include syntax coloring (highlighting tags and properties in different colors so it's easy to scan a page and identify its parts), FTP support (so you can upload files to a web server), and more.

- **Eclipse** (Windows, Linux, and Mac, *www.eclipse.org*) is a free, popular choice among Java Developers, but includes tools for working with HTML, CSS, and JavaScript. A version specifically for JavaScript developers is also available (*www.eclipse.org/downloads/packages/eclipse-ide-javascript-web-developers/indigor*), as well as Eclipse plug-ins to add autocomplete for jQuery (*http://marketplace.eclipse.org/category/free-tagging/jquery*).

- **Aptana Studio** (Windows, Linux, and Mac, *www.aptana.org*) is a powerful, free coding environment with tools for working with HTML, CSS, JavaScript, PHP, and Ruby on Rails.

- **Vim** and **Emacs** are tried and true text editors from the Unix world. They're included with OS X and Linux, and you can download versions for Windows. They're loved by serious programmers, but have a steep learning curve for most people.

Commercial Software

Commercial website development programs range from inexpensive text editors to complete website construction tools with all the bells and whistles:

- **Atom** (Windows and Mac, *https://atom.io*) is a new kid on the block. It's not yet available for sale, but the beta version is free for now. Atom is developed by the folks at GitHub (a site for sharing and collaboratively working on projects), and offers a large array of features built specifically for the needs of today's developers. It features a modular design, which allows for lots of third-party plug-ins that enhance the program's functionality.

- **SublimeText** (Windows, Mac, and Linux, *https://www.sublimetext.com*) is a darling of many programmers. This text editor ($70) includes many timesaving features for JavaScript programmers, like "auto-paired characters," which automatically plops in the second character of a pair of punctuation marks (for example, the program automatically inserts a closing parenthesis after you type an opening parenthesis).

- **EditPlus** (Windows, *www.editplus.com*) is an inexpensive text editor ($35) that includes syntax coloring, FTP, autocomplete, and other wrist-saving features.

- **BBEdit** (Mac, *www.barebones.com/products/bbedit*). This much-loved Mac text editor ($99.99) has plenty of tools for working with HTML, XHTML, CSS, JavaScript, and more. It includes many useful web building tools and shortcuts.

- **Dreamweaver** (Mac and Windows, *www.adobe.com/products/dreamweaver.html*) is a visual web page editor ($399). It lets you see how your page looks in a web browser. The program also includes a powerful text editor for writing JavaScript programs and excellent CSS creation and management tools. Check out *Dreamweaver CC: The Missing Manual* for the full skinny on how to use this powerful program.

◼ About This Book

Unlike a piece of software such as Microsoft Word or Dreamweaver, JavaScript isn't a single product developed by a single company. There's no support department at JavaScript headquarters writing an easy-to-read manual for the average web developer. While you'll find plenty of information on sites like Mozilla.org (see, for example, https://developer.mozilla.org/en/JavaScript/Reference or www.ecmascript.org), there's no definitive source of information on the JavaScript programming language.

Because there's no manual for JavaScript, people just learning JavaScript often don't know where to begin. And the finer points regarding JavaScript can trip up even seasoned web pros. The purpose of this book, then, is to serve as the manual that should have come with JavaScript. In this book's pages, you'll find step-by-step instructions for using JavaScript to create highly interactive web pages.

Likewise, you'll find good documentation on jQuery at http://api.jquery.com. But it's written by programmers for programmers, and so the explanations are mostly brief and technical. And while jQuery is generally more straightforward than regular JavaScript programming, this book will teach you fundamental jQuery principles and techniques so you can start off on the right path when enhancing your websites with jQuery.

JavaScript & jQuery: The Missing Manual is designed to accommodate readers who have some experience building web pages. You'll need to feel comfortable with HTML and CSS to get the most from this book, because JavaScript often works closely with HTML and CSS to achieve its magic. The primary discussions are written for advanced-beginner or intermediate computer users. But if you're new to building web pages, special boxes called Up to Speed provide the introductory information you need to understand the topic at hand. If you're an advanced web page jockey, on the other hand, keep your eye out for similar shaded boxes called Power Users' Clinic. They offer more technical tips, tricks, and shortcuts for the experienced computer fan.

> **NOTE** This book periodically recommends *other* books, covering topics that are too specialized or tangential for a manual about using JavaScript. Sometimes the recommended titles are from Missing Manual series publisher O'Reilly Media—but not always. If there's a great book out there that's not part of the O'Reilly family, we'll let you know about it.

This Book's Approach to JavaScript

JavaScript is a real programming language: It doesn't work like HTML or CSS, and it has its own set of (often complicated) rules. It's not always easy for web designers to switch gears and start thinking like computer programmers, and there's no *one* book that can teach you everything there is to know about JavaScript.

The goal of *JavaScript & jQuery: The Missing Manual* isn't to turn you into the next great programmer (though it might start you on your way). This book is meant to familiarize web designers with the ins and outs of JavaScript and then move on to jQuery so that you can add really useful interactivity to a website as quickly and easily as possible.

In this book, you'll learn the basics of JavaScript and programming; but just the basics won't make for very exciting web pages. It's not possible in 500 pages to teach you everything about JavaScript that you need to know to build sophisticated, interactive web pages. Instead, much of this book will cover the wildly popular jQuery JavaScript library, which, as you'll soon learn, will liberate you from all of the minute, time-consuming details of creating JavaScript programs that run well across different browsers.

You'll learn the basics of JavaScript, and then jump immediately to advanced web page interactivity with a little help—OK, a *lot* of help—from jQuery. Think of it this way: You could build a house by cutting down and milling your own lumber, constructing your own windows, doors, and doorframes, manufacturing your own tile, and so on. That do-it-yourself approach is common to a lot of JavaScript books. But who has that kind of time? This book's approach is more like building a house by taking advantage of already-built pieces and putting them together using basic skills. The end result will be a beautiful and functional house built in a fraction of the time it would take you to learn every step of the process.

About the Outline

JavaScript & jQuery: The Missing Manual is divided into five parts, each containing several chapters:

- **Part One** starts at the very beginning. You'll learn the basic building blocks of JavaScript as well as get some helpful tips on computer programming in general. This section teaches you how to add a script to a web page, store and manipulate information, and add smarts to a program so it can respond to different situations. You'll also learn how to communicate with the browser window, store and read cookies, respond to various events like mouse clicks and form submissions, and modify the HTML of a web page.

- **Part Two** introduces jQuery—the Web's most popular JavaScript library. Here you'll learn the basics of this amazing programming tool that will make you a more productive and capable JavaScript programmer. You'll learn how to select and manipulate page elements, add interaction by making page elements respond to your visitors, and add flashy visual effects and animations.

- **Part Three** covers jQuery's sister project, jQuery UI. jQuery UI is a JavaScript library of helpful "widgets" and effects. It makes adding common user interface elements like tabbed panels, dialog boxes, accordions, drop-down menus really easy. jQuery UI can help you build a unified-looking and stylish user interface for your next big web application.

- **Part Four** looks at some advanced uses of jQuery and JavaScript. In particular, Chapter 13 covers the technology that single-handedly made JavaScript one of the most glamorous web languages to learn. In this chapter, you'll learn how to use JavaScript to communicate with a web server so your pages can receive information and update themselves based on information provided by a web server—without having to load a new web page. Chapter 14 guides you step by step in creating a to-do list application using jQuery and jQuery UI.

- **Part Five** takes you past the basics, covering more complex concepts. You'll learn more about how to use jQuery effectively, as well as delve into advanced

JavaScript concepts. This part of the book also helps you when nothing seems to be working: when your perfectly crafted JavaScript program just doesn't seem to do what you want (or worse, it doesn't work at all!). You'll learn the most common errors new programmers make as well as techniques for discovering and fixing bugs in your programs.

At the end of the book, an appendix provides a detailed list of references to aid you in your further exploration of the JavaScript programming language.

■ The Very Basics

To use this book, and indeed to use a computer, you need to know a few basics. This book assumes that you're familiar with a few terms and concepts:

- **Clicking**. This book gives you three kinds of instructions that require you to use your computer's mouse or trackpad. To *click* means to point the arrow cursor at something on the screen and then—without moving the cursor at all—to press and release the clicker button on the mouse (or laptop trackpad). To *right-click* means to do the same thing with the right mouse button. To *double-click*, of course, means to click twice in rapid succession, again without moving the cursor at all. And to *drag* means to move the cursor *while* pressing the button.

TIP If you're on a Mac and don't have a right mouse button, you can accomplish the same thing by pressing the Control key as you click with the one mouse button.

When you're told to ⌘-*click* something on the Mac, or *Ctrl-click* something on a PC, you click while pressing the ⌘ or Ctrl key (both of which are near the space bar).

- **Menus**. The *menus* are the words at the top of your screen or window: File, Edit, and so on. Click one to make a list of commands appear, as though they're written on a window shade you've just pulled down.

- **Keyboard shortcuts**. If you're typing along in a burst of creative energy, it's sometimes disruptive to have to take your hand off the keyboard, grab the mouse, and then use a menu (for example, to use the Bold command). That's why many experienced computer mavens prefer to trigger menu commands by pressing certain combinations on the keyboard. For example, in the Firefox web browser, you can press Ctrl-+ (Windows) or ⌘-+ (Mac) to make text on a web page get larger (and more readable). When you read an instruction like "press ⌘-B," start by pressing the ⌘-key; while it's down, type the letter B, and then release both keys.

- **Operating system basics**. This book assumes that you know how to open a program, surf the Web, and download files. You should know how to use the Start menu (Windows) and the Dock or Apple menu (Macintosh), as well as the Control Panel (Windows), or System Preferences (Mac OS X).

If you've mastered this much information, you have all the technical background you need to enjoy *JavaScript & jQuery: The Missing Manual*.

About→These→Arrows

Throughout this book, and throughout the Missing Manual series, you'll find sentences like this one: "Open the System→Library→Fonts." That's shorthand for a much longer instruction that directs you to open three nested folders in sequence, like this: "On your hard drive, you'll find a folder called System. Open that. Inside the System folder window is a folder called Library; double-click it to open it. Inside *that* folder is yet another one called Fonts. Double-click to open it, too."

Similarly, this kind of arrow shorthand helps to simplify the business of choosing commands in menus, as shown in Figure I-2.

FIGURE I-2

In this book, arrow notations help simplify menu instructions. For example, View→Text Size→Increase is a more compact way of saying, "From the View menu, choose Text Size; from the submenu that then appears, choose Increase."

◼ About the Online Resources

This book is designed to get your work onto the Web faster and more professionally; it's only natural, then, that much of the value of this book also lies on the Web. Online, you'll find example files so you can get some hands-on experience. You can also communicate with the Missing Manual team and tell us what you love (or hate) about the book. Head over to *www.missingmanuals.com*, or go directly to one of the following sections.

Living Examples

As you read the book's chapters, you'll encounter a number of *living examples*—step-by-step tutorials that you can build yourself, using raw materials (like graphics and

half-completed web pages) that you can download from either *https://github.com/
sawmac/js3e* or from this book's Missing CD page at *www.missingmanuals.com/
cds.* You might not gain very much from simply reading these step-by-step lessons
while relaxing in your porch hammock, but if you take the time to work through
them at the computer, you'll discover that these tutorials give you unprecedented
insight into the way professional designers build web pages.

You'll also find, in this book's lessons, the URLs of the finished pages, so that you
can compare your work with the final result. In other words, you won't just see
pictures of JavaScript code in the pages of the book; you'll find the actual, working
web pages on the Internet.

Registration

If you register this book at *http://oreilly.com*, you'll be eligible for special offers—like
discounts on future editions of *JavaScript & jQuery: The Missing Manual.* Register-
ing takes only a few clicks. To get started, type *www.oreilly.com/register* into your
browser to hop directly to the Registration page.

Feedback

Got questions? Need more information? Fancy yourself a book reviewer? On our
Feedback page, you can get expert answers to questions that come to you while
reading, share your thoughts on this Missing Manual, and find groups for folks who
share your interest in JavaScript and jQuery. To have your say, go to *www.missing-
manuals.com/feedback.*

Errata

In an effort to keep this book as up to date and accurate as possible, each time we
print more copies, we'll make any confirmed corrections you've suggested. We also
note such changes on the book's website, so you can mark important corrections
into your own copy of the book, if you like. Go to *http://tinyurl.com/jsjq3-mm* to
report an error and view existing corrections.

Safari® Books Online

Safari® Books Online is an on-demand digital library that lets you easily search over
7,500 technology and creative reference books and videos to find the answers you
need quickly.

With a subscription, you can read any page and watch any video from our library
online. Read books on your cellphone and mobile devices. Access new titles before
they're available for print, and get exclusive access to manuscripts in development
and post feedback for the authors. Copy and paste code samples, organize your
favorites, download chapters, bookmark key sections, create notes, print out pages,
and benefit from tons of other time-saving features.

PART

1

Getting Started with JavaScript

Writing Your First JavaScript Program

By itself, HTML doesn't have any smarts: It can't do math, it can't figure out if someone has correctly filled out a form, and it can't make decisions based on how a web visitor interacts with it. Basically, HTML lets people read text, look at pictures, watch videos, and click links to move to other web pages with more text, pictures, and videos. In order to add intelligence to your web pages so they can respond to your site's visitors, you need JavaScript.

JavaScript lets a web page react intelligently. With it, you can create smart web forms that let visitors know when they've forgotten to include necessary information. You can make elements appear, disappear, or move around a web page (see Figure 1-1). You can even update the contents of a web page with information retrieved from a web server—without having to load a new web page. In short, JavaScript lets you make your websites more engaging, effective, and useful.

NOTE Actually, HTML5 *does* add some smarts to HTML—including basic form validation. But because not all browsers support these nifty additions (and because you can do a whole lot more with forms and JavaScript), you still need JavaScript to build the best, most user-friendly and interactive forms. You can learn more about HTML5 and web forms in Ben Henick's *HTML5 Forms* (O'Reilly) and Gaurav Gupta's *Mastering HTML5 Forms* (Packt Publishing).

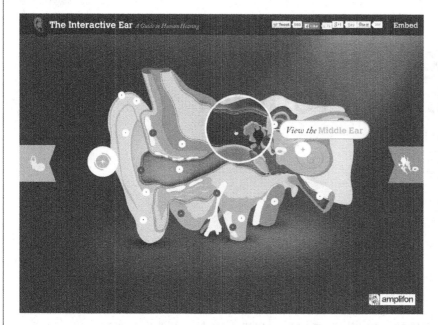

FIGURE 1-1

*The Interactive Ear
(http://www.amplifon.
co.uk/interactive-ear/),
an interactive guide to
human hearing, lets
visitors learn about and
explore the different
parts of the human ear.
New information appears
in response to mouse
movements and clicks.
With JavaScript, you can
create your own interac-
tive effects.*

■ Introducing Programming

For a lot of people, the term "computer programming" conjures up visions of super-intelligent nerds hunched over keyboards, typing nearly unintelligible gibberish for hours on end. And, honestly, some programming is like that. Programming can seem like complex magic that's well beyond the average mortal. But many programming concepts aren't difficult to grasp, and as programming languages go, JavaScript is a good first language for someone new to programming.

Still, JavaScript is more complex than either HTML or CSS, and programming often is a foreign world to web designers; so one goal of this book is to help you think more like a programmer. Throughout this book, you'll learn fundamental programming concepts that apply whether you're writing JavaScript, ActionScript, or even writing a desktop program using C++. More importantly, you'll learn how to approach a programming task so you'll know exactly what you want to do before you start adding JavaScript to a web page.

Many web designers are immediately struck by the strange symbols and words used in JavaScript. An average JavaScript program is sprinkled with symbols ({ } [ ] ; , () !=) and full of unfamiliar words (var, null, else if). In many ways, learning a programming language is a lot like learning another language. You need to learn new words, new punctuation, and understand how to put them together so you can communicate successfully.

Every programming language has its own set of keywords and characters, and its own set of rules for putting those words and characters together—the language's *syntax*. You'll need to memorize the words and rules of the JavaScript language (or at least keep this book handy as a reference). When learning to speak a new language, you quickly realize that placing an accent on the wrong syllable can make a word unintelligible. Likewise, a simple typo or even a missing punctuation mark can prevent a JavaScript program from working, or trigger an error in a web browser. You'll make plenty of mistakes as you start to learn to program—that's just the nature of programming.

At first, you'll probably find JavaScript programming frustrating—you'll spend a lot of your time tracking down errors you made when typing the script. Also, you might find some of the concepts related to programming a bit hard to follow at first. But don't worry: If you've tried to learn JavaScript in the past and gave up because you thought it was too hard, this book will help you get past the hurdles that often trip up folks new to programming. (And if you do have programming experience, this book will teach you JavaScript's idiosyncrasies and the unique concepts involved in programming for web browsers.)

In addition, this book isn't just about JavaScript—it's also about jQuery, the world's most popular JavaScript library. jQuery makes complex JavaScript programming easier...*much* easier. So with a little bit of JavaScript knowledge and the help of jQuery, you'll be creating sophisticated, interactive websites in no time.

FREQUENTLY ASKED QUESTION

Compiled vs. Scripting Languages

JavaScript is called a scripting language. *I've heard this term used for other languages like PHP and ColdFusion as well. What's a scripting language?*

Most of the programs running on your computer are written using languages that are *compiled*. Compiling is the process of creating a file that will run on a computer by translating the code a programmer writes into instructions that a computer can understand. Once a program is compiled, you can run it on your computer, and because a compiled program has been converted directly to instructions a computer understands, it will run faster than a program written with a scripting language. Unfortunately, compiling a program is a time-consuming process: You have to write the program, compile it, and then test it. If the program doesn't work, you have to go through the whole process again.

A scripting language, on the other hand, is only compiled when an *interpreter* (another program that can convert the script into something a computer can understand) reads it. In the case of JavaScript, the interpreter is built into the web browser. So when your web browser reads a web page with a JavaScript program in it, the web browser translates the JavaScript into something the computer understands. As a result, a scripting language operates more slowly than a compiled language, because every time it runs, the program must be translated for the computer. Scripting languages are great for web developers: Scripts are generally much smaller and less complex than desktop programs, so the lack of speed isn't as important. In addition, because they don't require compiling, creating and testing programs that use a scripting language is a much faster process.

What's a Computer Program?

When you add JavaScript to a web page, you're writing a computer program. Granted, most JavaScript programs are much simpler than the programs you use to read email, retouch photographs, and build web pages. But even though JavaScript programs (also called *scripts*) are simpler and shorter, they share many of the same properties of more complicated programs.

In a nutshell, any computer program is a series of steps that are completed in a designated order. Say you want to display a welcome message using the web-page visitor's name: "Welcome, Bob!" There are several things you'd need to do to accomplish this task:

1. **Ask the visitor's name.**

2. **Get the visitor's response.**

3. **Print (that is, display) the message on the web page.**

While you may never want to print a welcome message on a web page, this example demonstrates the fundamental process of programming: Determine what you want to do, then break that task down into individual steps. Every time you want to create a JavaScript program, you must go through the process of determining the steps needed to achieve your goal. Once you know the steps, you'll translate your ideas into programming *code*—the words and characters that make the web browser behave how you want it to.

■ How to Add JavaScript to a Page

Web browsers are built to understand HTML and CSS and convert those languages into a visual display on the screen. The part of the web browser that understands HTML and CSS is called the *layout* or *rendering* engine. But most browsers also have something called a *JavaScript interpreter*. That's the part of the browser that understands JavaScript and can execute the steps of a JavaScript program. The web browser is usually expecting HTML, so you must specifically tell the browser when JavaScript is coming by using the <script> tag.

The <script> tag is regular HTML. It acts like a switch that in effect says "Hey, web browser, here comes some JavaScript code; you don't know what to do with it, so hand it off to the JavaScript interpreter." When the web browser encounters the closing </script> tag, it knows it's reached the end of the JavaScript program and can get back to its normal duties.

Much of the time, you'll add the <script> tag in the web page's <head> section, like this:

```
<!DOCTYPE HTML PUBLIC "-//W3C//DTD HTML 4.01//EN" "http://www.w3.org/TR/
html4/strict.dtd">
<html>
```

```
<head>
<title>My Web Page</title>
<script type="text/javascript">
</script>
</head>
```

The `<script>` tag's `type` attribute indicates the format and the type of script that follows. In this case, `type="text/javascript"` means the script is regular text (just like HTML) and that it's written in JavaScript.

If you're using HTML5, life is even simpler. You can skip the type attribute entirely:

```
<!doctype html>
<html>
<head>
<meta charset="UTF-8">
<title>My Web Page</title>
<script>
</script>
</head>
```

In fact, web browsers let you leave out the type attribute in HTML 4.01 and XHTML 1.0 files as well—the script will run the same; however, your page won't validate correctly without the type attribute (see the box on page xix for more on validation). This book uses HTML5 for the doctype, but the JavaScript code will be the same and work the same for HTML 4.01, and XHTML 1.

You then add your JavaScript code between the opening and closing `<script>` tags:

```
<!doctype html>
<html>
<head>
<meta charset="UTF-8">
<title>My Web Page</title>
<script>
  alert('hello world!');
</script>
</head>
```

You'll find out what this JavaScript does in a moment. For now, turn your attention to the opening and closing `<script>` tags. To add a script to your page, start by inserting these tags. In many cases, you'll put the `<script>` tags in the page's `<head>` in order to keep your JavaScript code neatly organized in one area of the web page.

However, it's perfectly valid to put `<script>` tags anywhere inside the page's HTML. In fact, as you'll see later in this chapter, there's a JavaScript command that lets you write information directly into a web page. Using that command, you place the `<script>` tags in the location on the page (somewhere inside the body) where you want the script to write its message. In fact, it's common to put `<script>` tags just below the closing </body> tag—this approach makes sure the page is loaded and the visitor sees it before running any JavaScript.

The Client Side vs. the Server Side

JavaScript was originally created as a *client-side* language. Client-side JavaScript is delivered to web browsers by a web server. The people visiting your site download your web page and its JavaScript, and then their web browser—the client—processes the JavaScript and makes the magic happen.

An alternative type of web programming language is called a *server-side* language, which you'll find in pages built around PHP, .NET, ASP, ColdFusion, Ruby on Rails, and other web server technologies. Server-side programming languages, as the name suggests, run on a web server. They can exhibit a lot of intelligence by accessing databases, processing credit cards, and sending email around the globe. The problem with server-side languages is that they require the web browser to send requests to the web server, forcing visitors to wait until a new page arrives with new information.

Client-side languages, on the other hand, can react immediately and change what a visitor sees in his web browser without the need to download a new page. Content can appear or disappear, move around the screen, or automatically update based on how a visitor interacts with the page. This responsiveness lets you create websites that feel more like desktop programs than static web pages. But JavaScript isn't the only client-side technology in town. You can also use plug-ins to add programming smarts to a web page. Java applets are one example. These are small programs, written in the Java programming language, that run in a web browser. They also tend to start up slowly and have been known to crash the browser.

Flash is another plug-in based technology that offers sophisticated animation, video, sound, and lots of interactive potential.

In fact, it's sometimes hard to tell if an interactive web page is using JavaScript or Flash. For example, Google Maps could also be created in Flash (in fact, Yahoo! Maps was at one time a Flash application, until Yahoo! re-created it using JavaScript). A quick way to tell the difference: Right-click on the part of the page that you think might be Flash (the map itself, in this case); if it is, you'll see a pop-up menu that includes "About the Flash Player."

Ajax, which you'll learn about in Part Four of this book, brings the client side and server side together. Ajax is a method for using JavaScript to talk to a server, retrieve information from the server, and update the web page without the need to load a new web page. Google Maps uses this technique to let you move around a map without forcing you to load a new web page.

These days, JavaScript is finding a lot of use outside of the web browser. Node.js is a server-side version of JavaScript that can connect to databases, access the web server's filesystem, and perform many other tasks on a web server. This book doesn't discuss that aspect of JavaScript programming, but for a great video introduction to Node.js, check out *www.youtube.com/watch?v=hKQr2DGJjUQ/*.

In addition, some relatively new databases even use JavaScript as the language for creating, retrieving, and updating database records. MongoDB and CouchDB are two popular examples. You may hear the term full-stack JavaScript, which means using JavaScript as the language for the client-side browser, the web server, and database control. One language to rule them all!

External JavaScript Files

Using the <script> tag as discussed in the previous section lets you add JavaScript to a single web page. But many times you'll create scripts that you want to share with all of the pages on your site. For example, you might add a panel of additional navigation options that slides onto the page in response to a visitor's mouse movements (see Figure 1-2). You'll want that same fancy slide-in panel on every page of your site, but copying and pasting the same JavaScript code into each page is a really bad idea for several reasons.

First, it's a lot of work copying and pasting the same code over and over again, especially if you have a site with hundreds of pages. Second, if you ever decide to change or enhance the JavaScript code, you'll need to locate every page using that JavaScript and update the code. Finally, because all of the code for the JavaScript program would be located in every web page, each page will be that much larger and slower to download.

A better approach is to use an external JavaScript file. If you've used external CSS files for your web pages, this technique should feel familiar. An external JavaScript file is a text file containing JavaScript code and ending with the file extension *.js*—*navigation.js*, for example. The file is linked to a web page using the <script> tag. For example, to add this JavaScript file to your home page, you might write the following:

```
<!doctype html>
<html>
<head>
<meta charset="UTF-8">
<title>My Web Page</title>
<script src="navigation.js"></script>
</head>
```

The src attribute of the <script> tag works just like the src attribute of an <img> tag, or an <a> tag's href attribute. In other words, it points to a file either in your website or on another website (see the box on page 11).

NOTE   When adding the src attribute to link to an external JavaScript file, don't add any JavaScript code between the opening and closing <script> tags. If you want to link to an external JavaScript file and add custom JavaScript code to a page, use a second set of <script> tags. For example:

```
<script src="navigation.js"></script>
<script>
  alert('Hello world!');
</script>
```

You can (and often will) attach multiple external JavaScript files to a single web page. For example, you might have created one external JavaScript file that controls a drop-down navigation panel, and another that lets you add a nifty slideshow to a page of photos. On your photo gallery page, you'd want to have both JavaScript programs, so you'd attach both files.

In addition, you can attach external JavaScript files and add a JavaScript program to the same page like this:

```
<!doctype html>
<html>
<head>
<meta charset="UTF-8">
<title>My Web Page</title>
<script src="navigation.js"></script>
<script src="slideshow.js"></script>
<script>
  alert('hello world!');
</script>
</head>
```

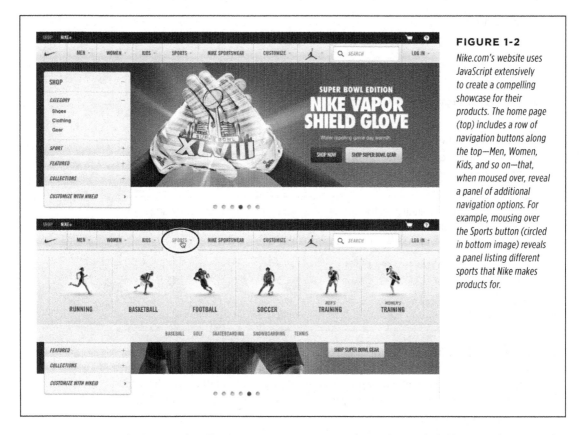

FIGURE 1-2

Nike.com's website uses JavaScript extensively to create a compelling showcase for their products. The home page (top) includes a row of navigation buttons along the top—Men, Women, Kids, and so on—that, when moused over, reveal a panel of additional navigation options. For example, mousing over the Sports button (circled in bottom image) reveals a panel listing different sports that Nike makes products for.

Just remember that you must use one set of opening and closing <script> tags for each external JavaScript file. You'll create an external JavaScript file in the tutorial that starts on page 15.

You can keep external JavaScript files anywhere inside your website's root folder (or any subfolder inside the root). Many web developers create a special directory for external JavaScript files in the site's root folder: common names are *js* (meaning JavaScript) or *libs* (meaning libraries).

UP TO SPEED

URL Types

When attaching an external JavaScript file to a web page, you need to specify a *URL* for the src attribute of the <script> tag. A URL or *Uniform Resource Locator* is a path to a file—like another web page, a graphic, or a JavaScript file—located on the Web. There are three types of paths: *absolute path, root-relative path*, and *document-relative path*. All three indicate where a web browser can find a particular file.

An *absolute path* is like a postal address—it contains all the information needed for a web browser located anywhere in the world to find the file. An absolute path includes *http://*, the hostname, and the folder and name of the file. For example: *http://www.uptospeedguides.com/scripts/site.js.*

A *root-relative* path indicates where a file is located relative to a site's top-level folder—the site's root folder. A root-relative path doesn't include *http://* or the domain name. It begins with a / (slash) indicating the site's root folder—the folder the home page is in. For example, */scripts/site.js* indicates that the file *site.js* is located inside a folder named *scripts*, which is itself located in the site's top-level folder. An easy way to create a root-relative path is to take an absolute path and strip off the *http://* and the host name. For example, *http://www.uptospeedguides.com/index.html* written as a root-relative URL is */index.html.*

A *document-relative* path specifies the path from the web page to the JavaScript file. If you have multiple levels of folders on your website, you'll need to use different paths to point to the same JavaScript file. For example, suppose you have a JavaScript file named *site.js* located in a folder named *scripts* in your website's main directory. The document-relative path to that file will look one way for the home page—*scripts/site.js*—but for a page located inside a folder named *about*, the path to the same file would be different; *../scripts/site.js*—the *../* means climb up *out* of the

about folder, while the */scripts/site.js* means go to the *scripts* folder and get the file *site.js.*

Here are some tips on which URL type to use:

* If you're pointing to a file that's not on the same server as the web page, you *must* use an absolute path. It's the only type that can point to another website.

* Root-relative paths are good for JavaScript files stored on your own site. Because they always start at the root folder, the URL for a JavaScript file will be the same for every page on your website, even when web pages are located in folders and subfolders on your site. However, root-relative paths don't work unless you're viewing your web pages through a web server—either your web server out on the Internet, or a web server you've set up on your own computer for testing purposes. In other words, if you're just opening a web page off your computer using the browser's File→Open command, the web browser won't be able to locate, load, or run JavaScript files that are attached using a root-relative path.

* Document-relative paths are the best when you're designing on your own computer without the aid of a web server. You can create an external JavaScript file, attach it to a web page, and then check the JavaScript in a web browser simply by opening the web page off your hard drive. Document-relative paths work fine when moved to your actual, living, breathing website on the Internet, but you'll have to rewrite the URLs to the JavaScript file if you move the web page to another location on the server. This book uses document-relative paths, which will let you follow along and test the tutorials on your own computer without a web server.

NOTE Sometimes the order in which you attach external JavaScript files matters. As you'll see later in this book, sometimes scripts you write depend upon code that comes from an external file. That's often the case when using JavaScript libraries (JavaScript code that simplifies complex programming tasks). You'll see an example of a JavaScript library in action in the tutorial on page 16.

■ Your First JavaScript Program

The best way to learn JavaScript programming is by actually programming. Throughout this book, you'll find hands-on tutorials that take you step by step through the process of creating JavaScript programs. To get started, you'll need a text editor (see page xxii for recommendations), a web browser, and the exercise files located at *https://github.com/sawmac/js3e* (see the following Note for complete instructions).

NOTE The tutorials in this chapter require the example files from this book's website, *www.missingmanuals. com/cds/jsjq3emm*. (The tutorial files are stored as a single Zip file.)

In Windows, download the Zip file and double-click it to open the archive. Click the Extract All Files option, and then follow the instructions of the Extraction Wizard to unzip the files and place them on your computer. If you have trouble opening the Zip file, the free 7-Zip utility can help: *www.7-zip.org.*

On a Mac, simply double-click the file to decompress it. After you've downloaded and decompressed the files, you should have a folder named *MM_JAVASCRIPT3E* on your computer, containing all of the tutorial files for this book.

To get your feet wet and provide a gentle introduction to JavaScript, your first program will be very simple:

1. **In your favorite text editor, open the file *hello.html*.**

    This file is located in the *chapter01* folder in the *MM_JAVASCRIPT3E* folder you downloaded as described in the note above. It's a very simple HTML page, with an external cascading style sheet to add a little visual excitement.

2. **Click in the empty line just *before* the closing </head> tag and type:**

    ```
    <script>
    ```

    This code is actually HTML, not JavaScript. It informs the web browser that the stuff following this tag is JavaScript.

3. **Press the Return key to create a new blank line, and type:**

    ```
    alert('hello world');
    ```

    You've just typed your first line of JavaScript code. The JavaScript alert() function is a command that pops open an Alert box and displays the message that appears inside the parentheses—in this case, *hello world*. Don't worry about all of the punctuation (the parentheses, quotes, and semicolon) just yet. You'll learn what they do in the next chapter.

4. **Press the Return key once more, and type `</script>`. The code should now look like this:**

```
<link href="../_css/site.css" rel="stylesheet">
<script>
  alert('hello world');
</script>
</head>
```

In this example, the stuff you just typed is shown in boldface. The two HTML tags are already in the file; make sure you type the code exactly where shown.

5. **Launch a web browser and open the *hello.html* file to preview it.**

A JavaScript Alert box appears (see Figure 1-3). Notice that the page is blank when the alert appears. (If you don't see the Alert box, you probably mistyped the code listed in the previous steps. Double-check your typing and read the following Tip.)

TIP When you first start programming, you'll be shocked at how often your JavaScript programs don't seem to work...at all. For new programmers, the most common cause of nonfunctioning programs is simple typing mistakes. Always double-check to make sure you spelled commands (like `alert` in the first script) correctly. Also, notice that punctuation frequently comes in pairs (the opening and closing parentheses, and single-quote marks from your first script, for example). Make sure you include both opening and closing punctuation marks when they're required.

---

6. **Click the Alert box's OK button to close it.**

When the Alert box disappears, the web page appears in the browser window.

Although this first program isn't earth-shatteringly complex (or even that interesting), it does demonstrate an important concept: A web browser will run a JavaScript program the moment it reads in the JavaScript code. In this example, the `alert()` command appeared *before* the web browser displayed the web page, because the JavaScript code appeared *before* the HTML in the `<body>` tag. This concept comes into play when you start writing programs that manipulate the HTML of the web page—as you'll learn in Chapter 3.

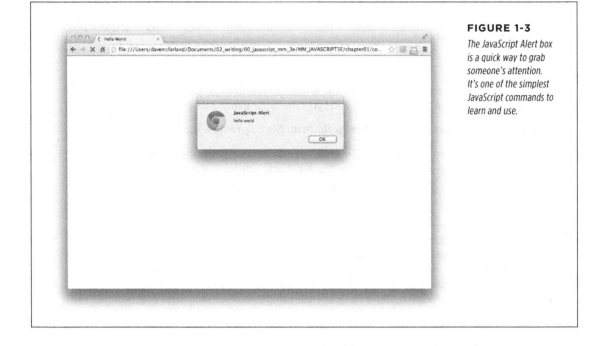

FIGURE 1-3

The JavaScript Alert box is a quick way to grab someone's attention. It's one of the simplest JavaScript commands to learn and use.

NOTE   Some versions of Internet Explorer (IE) don't like to run JavaScript programs in web pages that you open directly off your hard drive, for fear that the code might do something harmful. So when you try to preview the tutorial files for this book in Internet Explorer, you might see a message saying that IE has blocked the script. Click "Allow blocked content."

This annoying behavior only applies to web pages you preview from your computer, not to files you put up on a web server. To avoid hitting the "Allow blocked content" button over and over, preview pages in a different web browser, like Chrome or Firefox.

■ Writing Text on a Web Page

The script in the previous section popped up a dialog box in the middle of your monitor. What if you want to print a message directly onto a web page using JavaScript? There are many ways to do so, and you'll learn some sophisticated techniques later in this book. However, you can achieve this simple goal with a built-in JavaScript command, and that's what you'll do in your second script:

1. **In your text editor, open the file *hello2.html*.**

   While <script> tags usually appear in a web page's <head>, you can put them and JavaScript programs directly in the page's body.

2. **Directly below <h1>Writing to the document window</h1>, type the following code:**

   ```
   <script>
   document.write('<p>Hello world!</p>');
   </script>
   ```

   Like the alert() function, document.write() is a JavaScript command that literally writes out whatever you place between the opening and closing parentheses. In this case, the HTML <p>Hello world!</p> is added to the page: a paragraph tag and two words.

3. **Save the page and open it in a web browser.**

   The page opens and the words "Hello world!" appear below the headline (see Figure 1-4).

NOTE The tutorial files you downloaded also include the completed version of each tutorial. If you can't seem to get your JavaScript working, compare your work with the file that begins with *complete_* in the same folder as the tutorial file. For example, the file *complete_hello2.html* contains a working version of the script you added to file *hello2.html*.

The two scripts you just created may leave you feeling a little underwhelmed with JavaScript...or this book. Don't worry—this is only the beginning. It's important to start out with a full understanding of the basics. You'll be doing some very useful and complicated things using JavaScript in just a few chapters. In fact, in the remainder of this chapter you'll get a taste of some of the advanced features you'll be able to add to your web pages after you've worked your way through the first two parts of this book.

■ Attaching an External JavaScript File

As discussed on page 8, you'll usually put JavaScript code in a separate file if you want to use the same scripts on more than one web page. You then instruct your web pages to load that file and use the JavaScript inside it. External JavaScript files also come in handy when you're using someone else's JavaScript code. In particular, there are collections of JavaScript code called *libraries*, which provide useful JavaScript programming. Usually, these libraries make it easy to do something that's normally quite difficult. You'll learn more about JavaScript libraries on page 105, and, in particular, the JavaScript library this book (and much of the Web) uses—jQuery.

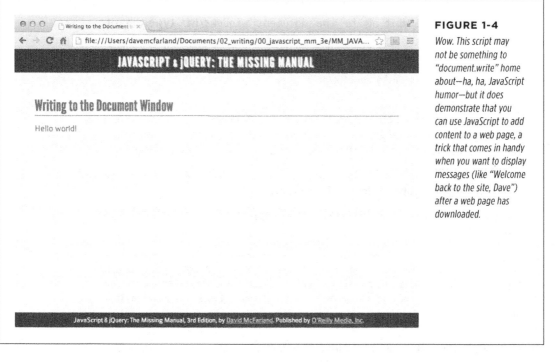

FIGURE 1-4

Wow. This script may not be something to "document.write" home about—ha, ha, JavaScript humor—but it does demonstrate that you can use JavaScript to add content to a web page, a trick that comes in handy when you want to display messages (like "Welcome back to the site, Dave") after a web page has downloaded.

But for now, you'll get experience attaching an external JavaScript file to a page, and writing a short program that does something cool:

1. **In your text editor, open the file *fadeIn.html*.**

   This page contains just some simple HTML—a few <div> tags, a headline, and a couple of paragraphs. You'll be adding a simple visual effect to the page, which causes all of the content to slowly fade into view.

2. **Click in the blank line between the** <link> **and closing** </head> **tags near the top of the page, and type:**

   ```
   <script src="../_js/jquery.min.js"></script>
   ```

   This code links a file named *jquery.min.js*, which is contained in a folder named *_js*, to this web page. When a web browser loads this web page, it also downloads the *jquery.min.js* JavaScript file and runs the code inside it.

   Next, you'll add your own JavaScript programming to this page.

NOTE The min part means that the file is *minimized*—a process that removes unneeded whitespace and condenses the code to make the file smaller so that it downloads faster.

3. **Press Return to create a new blank line, and then type:**

   ```
   <script>
   ```

   HTML tags usually travel in pairs—an opening and closing tag. To make sure you don't forget to close a tag, it helps to close the tag immediately after typing the opening tag, and then fill in the stuff that goes between the tags.

4. **Press Return twice to create two blank lines, and then type:**

   ```
   </script>
   ```

   This ends the block of JavaScript code. Now you'll add some programming.

5. **Click the empty line between the opening and closing script tags and type:**

   ```
   $(document).ready(function() {
   ```

   You're probably wondering what the heck that is. You'll find out all the details of this code on page 112, but in a nutshell, this line takes advantage of the programming that's inside the *jquery.min.js* file to make sure that the browser executes the next line of code at the right time.

6. **Hit return to create a new line, and then type:**

   ```
   $('header').hide().slideDown(3000);
   ```

   This line does something magical: It makes the "JavaScript & jQuery The Missing Manual" header first disappear and then slowly slide down onto the page over the course of 3 seconds (or 3,000 milliseconds). How does it do that? Well, that's part of the magic of jQuery, which makes complex effects possible with just a single line of code.

7. **Hit Return one last time, and then type:**

   ```
   });
   ```

   This code closes up the JavaScript code, much as a closing `</script>` tag indicates the end of a JavaScript program. Don't worry too much about all those weird punctuation marks—you'll learn how they work in detail later in the book. The main thing you need to make sure of is to type the code exactly as it's listed here. One typo, and the program may not work.

   The final code you added to the page should look like the bolded text in the following:

   ```
   <link href="../_css/site.css" rel="stylesheet">
   <script src="../_js/jquery.min.js"></script>
   <script>
   $(document).ready(function() {
     $('header').hide().slideDown(3000);
   });
   </script>
   </head>
   ```

TIP To make your programming easier to read, it's a good idea to indent code. Much as you indent HTML tags to show which tags are nested inside of other tags, you can indent lines of code that are inside another block of code. For example, the line of code you added in step 6 is nested inside the code for steps 5 and 7, so hitting Tab or pressing the spacebar a couple of times before typing the code for step 6 can make your code easier to understand (as pictured in the final code listed at the end of step 7).

8. **Save the HTML file, and open it in a web browser.**

   You should see the headline—Sliding Down—plus a paragraph and the footer at the bottom of the browser window, followed by the boxes containing "JavaScript & jQuery: The Missing Manual" slowly slide down into place. Change the number 3000 to different values (like 250 and 10000) to see how that changes the way the page works.

NOTE If you try to preview this page in Internet Explorer and it doesn't seem to do anything, you'll need to click the "Enable blocked content" box that appears at the bottom of the page (see the Note on page 14).

As you can see, it doesn't take a whole lot of JavaScript to do some amazing things to your web pages. Thanks to jQuery, you'll be able to create sophisticated, interactive websites even if you're not a programming wizard. However, you'll find it helps to know the basics of JavaScript and programming. Chapters 2 and 3 will cover the basics of JavaScript to get you comfortable with the fundamental concepts and syntax that make up the language.

■ Tracking Down Errors

The most frustrating moment in JavaScript programming comes when you try to view your JavaScript-powered page in a web browser...and nothing happens. It's one of the most common experiences for programmers. Even experienced programmers often don't get it right the first time they write a program, so figuring out what went wrong is just part of the game.

Most web browsers are set up to silently ignore JavaScript errors, so you usually won't even see a "Hey, this program doesn't work!" dialog box. (Generally, that's a good thing, as you don't want a JavaScript error to interrupt the experience of viewing your web pages.)

So how do you figure out what's gone wrong? There are many ways to track errors in a JavaScript program. You'll learn some advanced *debugging* techniques in Chapter 17, but the most basic method is to consult the web browser. Most web browsers keep track of JavaScript errors and record them in a separate window called an *error console*. When you load a web page that contains an error, you can then view the console to get helpful information about the error, like which line of the web page it occurred in and a description of the error.

Often, you can find the answer to the problem in the error console, fix the JavaScript, and then the page will work. The console helps you weed out the basic typos you make when you first start programming, like forgetting closing punctuation, or mistyping the name of a JavaScript command. You can use the error console in your favorite browser, but because scripts sometimes work in one browser and not another, this section shows you how to turn on the JavaScript console in all major browsers, so you can track down problems in each.

The Chrome JavaScript Console

Google's Chrome browser is beloved by many a web developer. Its DevTools feature gives you many ways to troubleshoot HTML, CSS, and JavaScript problems. Also, its JavaScript console is a great place to begin tracking down errors in your code. It not only describes the errors it finds, it also identifies the line in your code where each error occurred.

To open the JavaScript console, click the Customize menu button (circled in Figure 1-5) and choose Tools→JavaScript Console. Or use the keyboard shortcut Ctrl+Shift+J (Windows) or ⌘-Option-J (Mac).

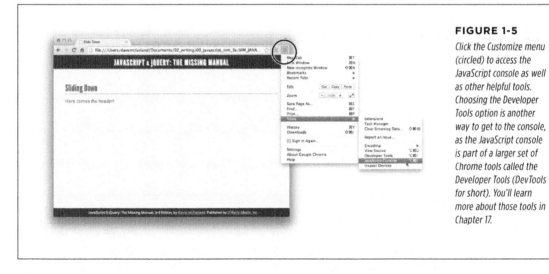

FIGURE 1-5

Click the Customize menu (circled) to access the JavaScript console as well as other helpful tools. Choosing the Developer Tools option is another way to get to the console, as the JavaScript console is part of a larger set of Chrome tools called the Developer Tools (DevTools for short). You'll learn more about those tools in Chapter 17.

After you open the console, you can examine any errors that appear in the current page. For example, in Figure 1-6, the console identifies the error as an "Uncaught SyntaxError: Unexpected token ILLEGAL." OK, it may not be immediately obvious what that means, but as you encounter (and fix) more errors you'll get used to these terse descriptions. Basically, a syntax error points to some kind of typographical error—an error with the syntax or language of the program. The "Unexpected token ILLEGAL" part just means that the browser has encountered an illegal character, or (and here's the tricky part) that there's a missing character. In this case, looking closely at the code you can see there's an opening single quote mark before "slow" but no final quote mark.

The console also identifies the name of the file the error is in (*complete_slide.html,* in this case) and the line number the error occurs (line 10). Click the filename, and Chrome opens the file above the console and briefly highlights the line (see Figure 1-5).

> **TIP** Because the error console displays the line number where the error occurred, you may want to use a text editor that can show line numbers. That way, you can easily jump from the error console to your text editor and identify the line of code you need to fix.

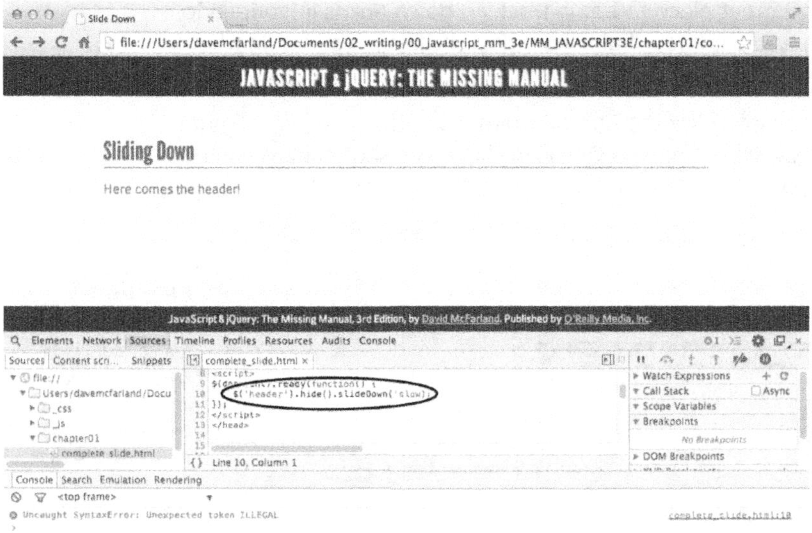

FIGURE 1-6

Chrome's JavaScript console identifies errors in your programs. Click the filename listed to the right of the error, and Chrome briefly highlights the page with the error (circled).

Unfortunately, there's a long list of things that can go wrong in a script, from simple typos to complex errors in logic. When you're just starting out with JavaScript programming, many of your errors will be the simple typographic sort. For example, you might forget a semicolon, quote mark, or parenthesis, or misspell a JavaScript command. You're especially prone to typos when following examples from a book (like this one). Here are a few common mistakes you might make and the (not-so obvious) error messages you may encounter:

- **Missing punctuation.** As mentioned earlier, JavaScript programming often involves lots of symbol pairs like opening and closing parentheses and brackets. For example, if you type `alert('hello';`—leaving off the closing parenthesis— you'll probably get the: "Unexpected token ;" message, meaning that Chrome was expecting something other than the character it's showing. In this case, it encountered the semicolon instead of the closing parenthesis.

- **Missing quote marks**. A *string* is a series of characters enclosed by quote marks (you'll learn about these in greater detail on page 27). For example, *'hello'* is a string in the code alert('hello');. It's easy to forget either the opening or closing quote mark. It's also easy to mix up those quote marks; for instance, by pairing a single-quote with a double quote like this: alert('hello");. In either case, you'll probably see an "Uncaught SyntaxError: Unexpected token ILLEGAL" error.

- **Misspelling commands**. If you misspell a JavaScript command—aler('hello');—you'll get an error saying that the misspelled command isn't defined: for example, "Uncaught ReferenceError: aler is not defined ," if you misspell the alert command. You'll also encounter problems when you misspell jQuery functions (like the .hide() and .slideDown() functions in the previous tutorial). In this case, you'll get a different error. For example, if you mistyped "hide" as "hid" in step 6 on page 17, Chrome will give you this error: "Uncaught TypeError: Object [object Object] has no method 'hid'".

- **Syntax error**. Occasionally, Chrome has no idea what you were trying to do and provides this generic error message. A syntax error represents some mistake in your code. It may not be a typo, but you may have put together one or more statements of JavaScript in a way that isn't allowed. In this case, you need to look closely at the line where the error was found and try to figure out what mistake you made. Unfortunately, these types of errors often require experience with and understanding of the JavaScript language to fix.

As you can see from the preceding list, many errors you'll make simply involve forgetting to type one of a pair of punctuation marks—like quote marks or parentheses. Fortunately, these are easy to fix, and as you get more experience programming, you'll eventually stop making them almost completely (no programmer is perfect).

The Internet Explorer Console

Internet Explorer provides a sophisticated set of developer tools for not only viewing JavaScript errors, but also analyzing CSS, HTML, and transfers of information over the network. When open, the developer tool window appears in the bottom half of the browser window. Press the F12 key to open the developer tools, and press it again to close them. You'll find JavaScript errors listed under the Console tab (circled in Figure 1-7).

NOTE If you first open a web page and then open the Internet Explorer console, you won't see any errors (even if there are some). You need to reload the page to see any errors. Once the console is open, you'll see errors on the pages you visit as they load.

IE's Console displays error messages similar to those described earlier for Chrome. However, sometimes they're very different. For example, IE's "Unterminated string constant" is an "Unexpected token ILLEGAL" error in Chrome. Like Chrome, Internet Explorer identifies the line of code in the HTML file where the error occurred, which you can click to see the actual code where the error occurs.

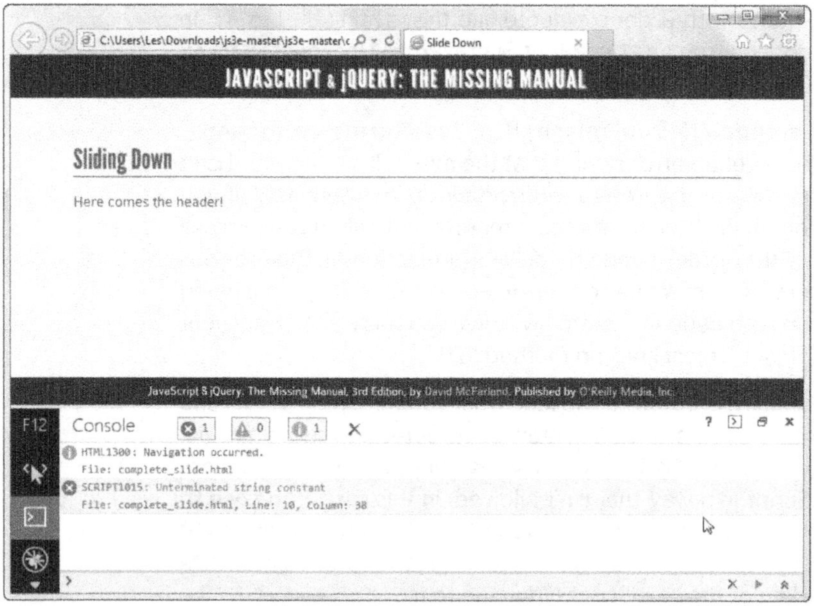

FIGURE 1-7

The Internet Explorer developer tools provide access to JavaScript errors that occur on a page, as well as a whole lot of other information.

The Firefox JavaScript Web Console

Mozilla's Firefox browser also gives you a console to view JavaScript errors. To open the JavaScript console, on Windows click the Firefox tab in the top left of the browser window and choose Web Developer→Web Console. On a Mac, select Tools→Web Developer→Web Console. Or use the keyboard shortcuts Ctrl+Shift+I (Windows) or ⌘-Option-K (Mac).

Once the console opens, you'll see any JavaScript errors on the page. Unfortunately, Firefox's Web Console is more like a fire hose of data than a simple JavaScript error reporter (Figure 1-8). That's because it provides information on all sorts of things: files downloaded, CSS and HTML errors, and more.

NOTE The Firebug plug-in (*http://getfirebug.com*) greatly expands on Firefox's Error Console. In fact, it provided the model for the developer tools in Internet Explorer, Chrome, and Safari (discussed next).

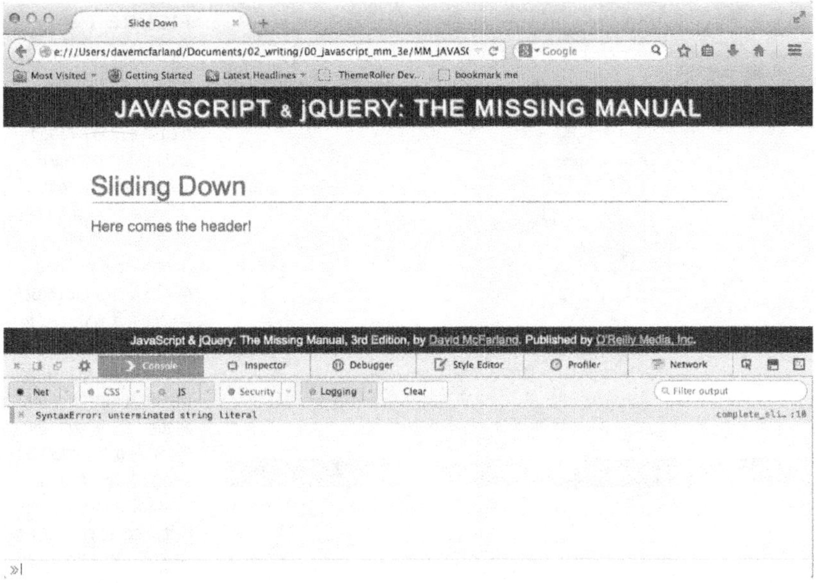

FIGURE 1-8

If you don't want to see all of the messages in Firefox's Web Console, just click the button for the type of message you wish to hide. For example, click the CSS button to hide CSS error messages, the Security button to hide security warnings, and so on. You'll know if the button is disabled because it looks lighter gray, like the CSS and Security buttons here. A button is enabled when it's darker and looks like it has been pressed "in," like the Net, JS (short for JavaScript), and Logging buttons here.

The Safari Error Console

Safari's error console is available from the Develop menu: Develop→Show Error Console (or, if you're on a Mac, use the Option-⌘-C keyboard shortcut). However, the Develop menu isn't normally turned on when Safari is installed, so there are a couple of steps to get to the JavaScript console.

To turn on the Develop menu, you need to first access the Preferences window. Choose Safari→Preferences. Once the Preferences window opens, click the Advanced button. Turn on the "Show Develop menu in menu bar" box and close the Preferences window.

When you restart Safari, the Develop menu will appear between the Bookmarks and Window menus in the menu bar at the top of the screen. Select Develop→Show Error Console to open the console (see Figure 1-9).

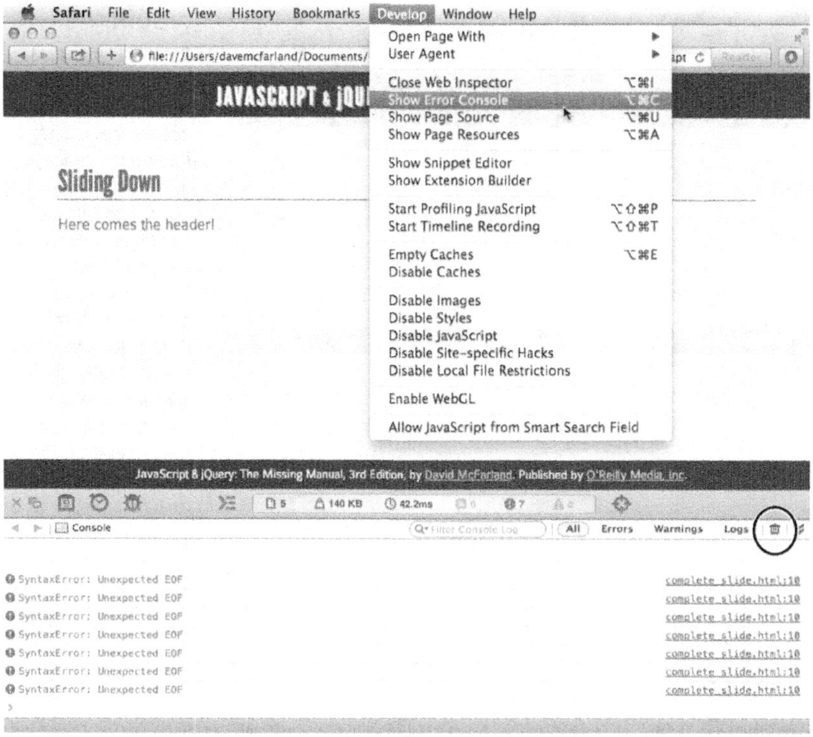

FIGURE 1-9

The Safari Error Console displays the name of the JavaScript error, the filename (and location), and the line on which Safari encountered the error. Each tab or browser window has its own error console, so if you've already opened the console for one tab, you need to choose Develop→Show Error Console again if you wish to see an error for another tab or window. In addition, if you reload a page, Safari doesn't clear any prior errors on that page, so you can end up with a long list of old, fixed errors as you work on a page and reload it. The answer: click the Trash icon (circled) to remove the list of old errors, and then reload the page.

NOTE If you're on Windows, you may have an old version of the Safari browser. Apple has stopped updating Safari for Windows, so the Safari information shown here may not apply to you.

The Grammar of JavaScript

L earning a programming language is a lot like learning any new language: you need to learn new words and punctuation, as well as master a new set of rules. And just as you need to learn the grammar of French to speak French, you must become familiar with the grammar of JavaScript to program JavaScript. This chapter covers the concepts that all JavaScript programs rely on.

If you've had any experience with JavaScript programming, many of these concepts may be old hat, so you might just skim this chapter. But if you're new to JavaScript, or you're still not sure about the fundamentals, this chapter introduces you to basic (but crucial) topics.

Statements

A JavaScript *statement* is a basic programming unit, usually representing a single step in a JavaScript program. Think of a statement as a sentence: Just as you string sentences together to create a paragraph (or a chapter, or a book), you combine statements to create a JavaScript program. In the previous chapter, you saw several examples of statements. For example:

```
alert('Hello world!');
```

This single statement opens an alert window with the message "Hello World!" In many cases, a statement is a single line of code. Each statement ends with a semicolon—it's like a period at the end of a sentence. The semicolon makes it clear that the step is over and that the JavaScript interpreter should move on to the next action. When you're writing a JavaScript program, you generally type a statement, enter a semicolon, press Return to create a new line, type another statement, followed by a semicolon, and so on until the program is complete.

NOTE As you see more advanced examples of JavaScript (like later in this book), you'll realize that semicolons don't always go at the end of every *line*. A semicolon sometimes won't appear until after many lines of code. Nonetheless, those multiple lines still form a single *statement*—just think of them as one, really long statement with lots of different punctuation (kind of like this sentence).

Officially, putting a semicolon even at the end of every *statement* is optional, and some programmers leave it out to make their code shorter. Don't be one of them. Leaving off the semicolon makes reading your code more difficult and, in some cases, causes JavaScript errors. If you want to make your JavaScript code more compact so that it downloads more quickly, see page 585.

Built-In Functions

JavaScript (and web browsers) lets you use various commands to make things happen in your programs and on your web pages. These commands, called *functions*, are like verbs in a sentence. They get things done. For example, the alert() function you encountered earlier makes the web browser open a dialog box and display a message.

Some functions, like alert() or document.write(), which you encountered on page 15, are specific to web browsers. In other words, they only work with web pages, so you won't find them when programming in other environments that use JavaScript (like Node.js, Adobe Photoshop, or Flash's JavaScript-based ActionScript).

Other functions are universal to JavaScript and work anywhere JavaScript works. For example, isNaN() is a function that checks to see whether a particular value is a number—this function comes in handy when you want to see if a visitor has correctly supplied a number for a question that requires a numerical answer (for example, "How many widgets would you like?"). You'll learn more about how to use isNaN()on page 564.

You'll learn many JavaScript functions throughout this book. One quick way to identify a function is by the parentheses. For example, you can tell isNaN() is a function because of the parentheses following isNaN.

In addition, JavaScript lets you create your own functions, so you can make your scripts do things beyond what the standard JavaScript commands offer. You'll learn about functions in Chapter 3, starting on page 85.

NOTE Sometimes you'll hear people refer to a JavaScript function as a *method*.

Types of Data

You deal with different types of information every day. Your name, the price of food, the address of your doctor's office, and the date of your next birthday are all information that is important to you. You make decisions about what to do based on this information. Computer programs are no different. They also rely on information to get things done. For example, to calculate the total for a shopping cart, the program needs to know the price and quantity of each item ordered. To customize a web page with a visitor's name ("Welcome Back, *Kotter*"), the program needs to know the name.

Programming languages usually categorize information into different types, and treat each type in a different way. In JavaScript, the three most basic types of data are number, string, and Boolean.

Numbers

Numbers are used for counting and calculating; you can keep track of the number of days until summer vacation, or calculate the cost of buying two tickets to a movie. Numbers are very important in JavaScript programming: You can use numbers to keep track of how many times a visitor has visited a web page, to specify the exact pixel position of an item on a web page, or to determine how many products a visitor wants to order.

In JavaScript, a number is represented by a numeric character; *5*, for example, is the number five. You can also use fractional numbers with decimals, like 5.25 or 10.3333333. JavaScript even lets you use negative numbers, like –130 or -459.67.

Because numbers are frequently used for calculations, your programs will often include mathematical operations. You'll learn about *operators* on page 33, but just to provide an example of using JavaScript with numbers, say you wanted to print the total value of 5 plus 15 on a web page; you could do that with this line of code:

```
document.write(5 + 15);
```

This snippet of JavaScript adds the two numbers together and prints the total (20) onto a web page. There are many different ways to work with numbers, and you'll learn more about them starting on page 33.

Strings

To display a name, a sentence, or any series of letters, you use strings. A *string* is just a series of characters (letters and other symbols) enclosed inside of quote marks. For example, 'Welcome, Hal', and "You are here" are both examples of strings. You used a string in Chapter 1 with the alert command—alert('Hello World!').

A string's opening quote mark tells the JavaScript interpreter that what follows is a string—just a series of symbols. The interpreter accepts the symbols literally, rather than trying to interpret the string as anything special to JavaScript like a command. When the interpreter encounters the final quote mark, it understands that it has reached the end of the string and continues onto the next part of the program.

You can use either double quote marks (`"hello world"`) or single quote marks (`'hello world'`) to enclose the string, but you must make sure to use the *same type* of quote mark at the beginning and end of the string (for example, `"this is not right'` isn't a valid string because it begins with a double-quote mark and ends with a single-quote).

So, to pop-up an alert box with the message *Warning, warning!* you could write:

```
alert('Warning, warning!');
```

or

```
alert("Warning, warning!");
```

You'll use strings frequently in your programming—when adding alert messages, when dealing with user input on web forms, and when manipulating the contents of a web page. They're so important that you'll learn a lot more about using strings starting on page 36.

FREQUENTLY ASKED QUESTION

Putting Quotes into Strings

When I try to create a string with a quote mark in it, my program doesn't work. Why?

In JavaScript, quote marks indicate the beginning and end of a string, even when you don't want them to. When the JavaScript interpreter encounters the first quote mark, it says to itself, "Ahh, here comes a string." When it reaches a matching quote mark, it figures it has come to the end of the string. That's why you can't create a string like this: `"He said, "Hello.""`. In this case, the first quote mark (before the word "He") marks the start of the string, but as soon as the JavaScript interpreter encounters the second quote mark (before the word "Hello"), it figures that the string is over, so you then end up with the string "*He said,*" then the *Hello.* part, and then another, empty string created by the two quote marks at the end. This code creates a JavaScript error, and your program won't work.

There are a couple of ways to get around this conundrum. The easiest method is to use single quotes to enclose a string that has one or more double quotes inside it. For example, `'He said, "Hello."'` is a valid string—the single quotes create the string, and the double quotes inside are a *part* of the string.

Likewise, you can use double quotes to enclose a string that has a single quote inside it: `"This isn't fair"`, for example.

Another method is to tell the JavaScript interpreter to just treat the quote mark inside the string literally—that is, treat the quote mark as part of the string, not the end of the string. You do this using an *escape character*. If you precede the quote mark with a backward slash (`\`), JavaScript treats the quote as part of the string. So, you could rewrite the example like this: `"He said, \"Hello.\""`. In some cases, an escape character is the only choice. For example: `'He said, "This isn\'t fair."'`. Because the string is enclosed by single quotes, the lone single quote in the word "isn't" has to have a backward slash before it: *isn\'t*.

You can even escape quote marks when you don't necessarily have to—as a way to make it clear that the quote mark should be taken literally. For example, `'He said, \"Hello.\"'`. Even though you don't need to escape the double quotes (because single quotes surround the entire string), some programmers do it anyway so it's clear to them that the quote mark is just a quote mark.

Booleans

Whereas numbers and strings offer almost limitless variations, the Boolean data type is simple. It is either one of two values: *true* or *false*. You'll encounter Boolean data types when you create JavaScript programs that respond intelligently to user input and actions. For example, if you want to make sure a visitor supplied an email address before submitting a form, you can add logic to your page by asking the simple question: "Did the user type a valid email address?" The answer to this question is a Boolean value: Either the email address is valid (true) or it's not (false). Depending on the answer to the question, the page could respond in different ways. For example, if the email address is valid (true), then submit the form; if it is not valid (false), then display an error message and prevent the form from being submitted.

In fact, Boolean values are so important that JavaScript includes two special keywords to represent those values:

```
true
```

and

```
false
```

You'll learn how Boolean values come into play when adding logic to your programs in the box on page 66.

■ Variables

You can type a number, string, or Boolean value directly into your JavaScript program, but these data types work only when you already have the information you need. For example, you can make the string "Hi, Bob" appear in an alert box like this:

```
alert('Hi, Bob');
```

But that statement only makes sense if everyone who visits the page is named Bob. If you want to present a personalized message for different visitors, the name needs to be different depending on who is viewing the page: "Hi, Mary," "Hi, Joseph," "Hi, Ezra," and so on. Fortunately, all programming languages provide a tool called a *variable* to deal with just this kind of situation.

A variable is a way to store information so you can later use and manipulate it. For example, imagine a JavaScript-based pinball game where the goal is to get the highest score. When a player first starts the game, her score will be 0, but as she knocks the pinball into targets, the score will get bigger. In this case, the score is a variable because it starts at 0 but changes as the game progresses—in other words, a variable holds information that can *change* with the circumstances. See Figure 2-1 for an example of another game that uses variables.

Think of a variable as a kind of basket: You can put an item into a basket, look inside the basket, dump out the contents of a basket, or even replace what's inside the basket with something else. However, even though you might change what's inside the basket, the basket itself remains the same.

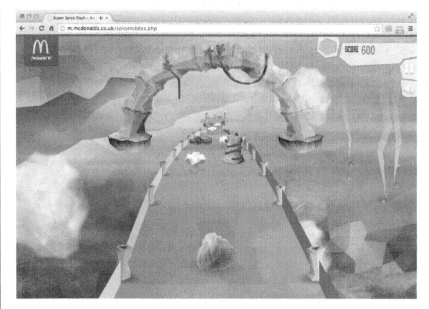

Creating a Variable

In JavaScript, to create a variable named score, you would type:

```
var score;
```

The first part, var, is a JavaScript keyword that creates, or, in programming-speak, *declares* the variable. The second part of the statement, score, is the variable's name.

What name you use is up to you, but there are a few rules you must follow when naming variables:

- **Variable names must begin with a letter, $, or _.** In other words, you can't begin a variable name with a number or punctuation: so 1thing, and &thing won't work, but score, $score, and _score are fine.

- **Variable names can only contain letters, numbers, $, and _.** You can't use spaces or any other special characters anywhere in the variable name: fish&chips and fish and chips aren't legal, but fish_n_chips and plan9 are.

- **Variable names are case-sensitive.** The JavaScript interpreter sees uppercase and lowercase letters as distinct, so a variable named SCORE is different from a variable named score, which is also different from variables named sCoRE and Score.

- **Avoid keywords.** Some words in JavaScript are specific to the language itself: var, for example, is used to create a variable, so you can't name a variable var. In addition, some words, like alert, document, and window, are considered special properties of the web browser. You'll end up with a JavaScript error if you try to use those words as variable names. You can find a list of some reserved words in Table 2-1. Not all of these reserved words will cause problems in all browsers, but it's best to steer clear of these names when naming variables.

TABLE 2-1 *Some words are reserved for use by JavaScript and the web browser. Avoid using them as variable names.*

JAVASCRIPT KEYWORDS	RESERVED FOR FUTURE USE	RESERVED FOR BROWSER
break	abstract	alert
case	boolean	blur
catch	byte	closed
continue	char	document
debugger	class	focus
default	const	frames
delete	double	history
do	enum	innerHeight
else	export	innerWidth
false	extends	length
finally	final	location
for	float	navigator
function	goto	open
if	implements	outerHeight
in	import	outerWidth
instanceof	int	parent
new	interface	screen
null	let	screenX
return	long	screenY
switch	native	statusbar
this	package	window
throw	private	
true	protected	
try	public	
typeof	short	
var	static	

JAVASCRIPT KEYWORDS	RESERVED FOR FUTURE USE	RESERVED FOR BROWSER
void	super	
while	synchronized	
with	throws	
	transient	
	volatile	
	yield	

In addition to these rules, aim to make your variable names clear and meaningful. Naming variables according to what type of data you'll be storing in them makes it much easier to look at your programming code and immediately understand what's going on. For example, score is a great name for a variable used to track a player's game score. The variable name s would also work, but the single letter "s" doesn't give you any idea about what's stored in the variable.

Likewise, make your variable names easy to read. When you use more than one word in a variable name, either use an underscore between words or capitalize the first letter of each word after the first. For example, imagepath isn't as easy to read and understand as image_path or imagePath.

Using Variables

Once you declare a variable, you can store any type of data you'd like in it. To do so, you use the = sign. For example, to store the number 0 in a variable named score, you could type this code:

```
var score;
score = 0;
```

The first line of this code creates the variable; the second line stores the number 0 in that variable. The equals sign is called an *assignment operator*, because it's used to assign a value to a variable. You can also create a variable and store a value in it with a single JavaScript statement like this:

```
var score = 0;
```

You can store strings, numbers, and Boolean values in a variable:

```
var firstName = 'Peter';
var lastName = 'Parker';
var age = 22;
var isSuperHero = true;
```

NOTE To save typing, you can declare multiple variables with a single `var` keyword, like this:

```
var x, y, z;
```

You can even declare and store values into multiple variables in one JavaScript statement:

```
var isSuperHero=true, isAfraidOfHeights=false;
```

Once you've stored a value in a variable, you can access that value simply by using the variable's name. For example, to open an alert dialog box and display the value stored in the variable `score`, you'd type this:

```
alert(score);
```

Notice that you don't use quotes with a variable—that's just for strings; so the code `alert('score')` will display the word "score" and not the value stored in the variable `score`. Now you can see why strings have to be enclosed in quote marks: The JavaScript interpreter treats words without quotes as either special JavaScript objects (like the `alert()` command) or as variable names.

NOTE You should only use the `var` keyword once for each variable—when you first create the variable. After that, you're free to assign new values to the variable without using `var`.

■ Working with Data Types and Variables

Storing a particular piece of information like a number or string in a variable is usually just a first step in a program. Most programs also manipulate data to get new results. For example, you can add a number to a score to increase it, multiply the number of items ordered by the cost of the item to get a sub total, or personalize a generic message by adding a name to the end: "Good to see you again, Igor." JavaScript provides various *operators* to modify data. An operator is a symbol or word that can change one or more values into something else. For example, you use the + sign—the addition operator—to add numbers together. There are different types of operators for the different data types.

Basic Math

JavaScript supports basic mathematical operations such as addition, division, subtraction, and so on. Table 2-2 shows the most basic math operators and how to use them.

TABLE 2-2 *Basic math with JavaScript*

OPERATOR	WHAT IT DOES	HOW TO USE IT
+	Adds two numbers	5 + 25
-	Subtracts one number from another	25 - 5
*	Multiplies two numbers	5 * 10
/	Divides one number by another	15/5

FREQUENTLY ASKED QUESTION

Spaces, Tabs, and Carriage Returns in JavaScript

JavaScript seems so sensitive about typos. How do I know when I'm supposed to use space characters, and when I'm not allowed to?

In general, JavaScript is pretty relaxed about spaces, carriage returns, and tabs. You can often leave out spaces or even add extra spaces and carriage returns without a problem. JavaScript interpreters ignore extra spaces, so you're free to insert extra spaces, tabs, and carriage returns to format your code. For example, you don't need a space on either side of an assignment operator, but you can add them if you find it easier to read. Both of the following lines of code work:

```
var formName='signup';
var formRegistration = 'newsletter' ;
```

In fact, you can insert as many spaces as you'd like, and even insert carriage returns within a statement. So both of the following statements also work:

```
var formName      =         'signup';
var formRegistration

                  =

        'newsletter';
```

Of course, just because you can insert extra space, doesn't mean you should. The last two examples are actually harder to read and understand because of the extra space. So the general rule of thumb is to add extra space if it makes your code easier to understand. For example, extra carriage returns help make code easier to read when declaring and setting the value of multiple variables at once. The following code is a single line:

```
var score=0, highScore=0, player='';
```

However, some programmers find it easier to read if each variable is on its own line:

```
var score=0,
    highScore=0,
    player='';
```

Whether you find this spacing easier to read is up to you; the JavaScript interpreter just ignores those line breaks. You'll see examples of how space can make code easier to read with JavaScript object literals (page 136) and with arrays (page 44).

There are a couple of important exceptions to these rules. For example, you can't insert a carriage return inside a string; in other words, you can't split a string over two lines in your code like this:

```
var name = 'Bob
          Smith';
```

Inserting a carriage return (pressing the Enter or Return key) like this produces a JavaScript error and your program won't run.

In addition, you must put a space between keywords: `varscore=0`, for example, is not the same as `var score=0`. The latter example creates a new variable named "score," while the former stores the value 0 in a variable named "varscore." The JavaScript interpreter needs the space between var and score to identify the var keyword: `var score=0`. However, a space isn't necessary between keywords and symbols like the assignment operator (=) or the semicolon that ends a statement.

You may be used to using an x for multiplication (4 x 5, for example), but in JavaScript, you use the * (asterisk) to multiply two numbers.

You can also use variables in mathematical operations. Because a variable is only a container for some other value like a number or string, using a variable is the same as using the contents of that variable. Here's an example:

```
var price = 10;
var itemsOrdered = 15;
var totalCost = price * itemsOrdered;
```

The first two lines of code create two variables (`price` and `itemsOrdered`) and store a number in each. The third line of code creates another variable (`totalCost`) and stores the results of multiplying the value stored in the `price` variable (10) and the value stored in the `itemsOrdered` variable. In this case, the total (150) is stored in the variable `totalCost`.

This sample code also demonstrates the usefulness of variables. Suppose you write a program as part of a shopping cart system for an e-commerce website. Throughout the program, you need to use the price of a particular product to make various calculations. You could code the actual price throughout the program (for example, say the product cost $10, so you'd type 10 in each place in the program that price is used). However, if the price ever changes, you'd have to locate and change each line of code that uses the price. By using a variable, on the other hand, you can set the price of the product somewhere near the beginning of the program. Then, if the price ever changes, you only need to modify the one line of code that defines the product's price to update the price throughout the program:

```
var price = 20;
var itemsOrdered = 15;
var totalCost = price * itemsOrdered;
```

There are lots of other ways to work with numbers (you'll learn a bunch starting on page 562), but you'll find that you most frequently use the basic math operators listed in Table 2-2.

The Order of Operations

If you perform several mathematical operations at once—for example, if you add up several numbers and then multiply them all by 10—you need to keep in mind the order in which the JavaScript interpreter performs its calculations. Some operators take precedence over other operators, so they're calculated first. This fact can cause some unwanted results if you're not careful. Take this example:

```
4 + 5 * 10
```

You might think this is simply calculated from left to right: 4 + 5 is 9 and 9 * 10 is 90. It's not. The multiplication actually goes first, so this equation works out to 5 * 10 is 50, plus 4 is 54. Multiplication (the * symbol) and division (the / symbol) take precedence over addition (+) and subtraction (−).

To make sure that the math works out the way you want it, use parentheses to group operations. For example, you could rewrite the equation above like this:

```
(4 + 5) * 10
```

Any math that's performed inside parentheses happens first, so in this case the 4 is added to 5 first and the result, 9, is then multiplied by 10. If you want the multiplication to occur first, it would be clearer to write that code like this:

```
4 + (5*10);
```

Combining Strings

Combining two or more strings to make a single string is a common programming task. For example, if a web page has a form that collects a person's first name in one form field and his last name in a different field, you need to combine the two fields to get his complete name. What's more, if you want to display a message letting the user know his form information was submitted, you need to combine the generic message with the person's name: "John Smith, thanks for your order."

Combining strings is called *concatenation*, and you accomplish it with the + operator. Yes, that's the same + operator you use to add number values, but with strings it behaves a little differently. Here's an example:

```
var firstName = 'John';
var lastName = 'Smith';
var fullName = firstName + lastName;
```

In the last line of the code above, the contents of the variable firstName are combined (or concatenated) with the contents of the variable lastName. The two are literally joined together and the result is placed in the variable fullName. In this example, the resulting string is "JohnSmith"—there isn't a space between the two names, as concatenating just fuses the strings together. In this case (and many others), you need to add an empty space between strings that you intend to combine:

```
var firstName = 'John';
var lastName = 'Smith';
var fullName = firstName + ' ' + lastName;
```

The ' ' in the last line of this code is a single quote, followed by a space, followed by a final single quote. This code is simply a string that contains an empty space. When placed between the two variables in this example, it creates the string "John Smith". This last example also demonstrates that you can combine more than two strings at a time; in this case, three strings.

NOTE Remember that a variable is just a container that can hold any type of data, like a string or number. So when you combine two variables with strings (firstName + lastName), it's the same as joining two strings like this: 'John' + 'Smith'.

Combining Numbers and Strings

Most of the mathematical operators only make sense for numbers. For example, it doesn't make any sense to multiply 2 and the string "eggs". If you try this example, you'll end up with a special JavaScript value NaN, which stands for "not a number." However, there are times when you may want to combine a string with a number. For example, say you want to present a message on a web page that specifies how many times a visitor has been to your website. The number of times she's visited is a *number*, but the message is a *string*. In this case, you use the + operator to do two things: convert the number to a string and concatenate it with the other string. Here's an example:

```
var numOfVisits = 101;
var message = 'You have visited this site ' + numOfVisits + ' times.';
```

In this case, *message* contains the string "You have visited this site 101 times." The JavaScript interpreter recognizes that there is a string involved, so it realizes it won't be doing any math (no addition). Instead, it treats the + as the concatenation operator, and at the same time realizes that the number should be converted to a string as well.

This example may seem like a good way to print words and numbers in the same message. In this case, it's obvious that the number is part of a string of letters that makes up a complete sentence, and whenever you use the + operator with a string value and a number, the JavaScript interpreter converts the number to a string.

That feature, known as *automatic type conversion*, can cause problems, however. For example, if a visitor answers a question on a form ("How many pairs of shoes would you like?") by typing a number (2, for example), that input is treated like a string—'2'. So you can run into a situation like this:

```
var numOfShoes = '2';
var numOfSocks = 4;
var totalItems = numOfShoes + numOfSocks;
```

You'd expect the value stored in totalItems to be 6 (2 shoes + 4 pairs of socks). Instead, because the value in numOfShoes is a string, the JavaScript interpreter converts the value in the variable numOfSocks to a string as well, and you end up with the string '24' in the totalItems variable. There are a couple of ways to prevent this error.

First, you add + to the beginning of the string that contains a number like this:

```
var numOfShoes = '2';
var numOfSocks = 4;
var totalItems = +numOfShoes + numOfSocks;
```

Adding a + sign before a variable (making sure there's no space between the two) tells the JavaScript interpreter to try to convert the string to a number value—if the string only contains numbers, like '2', you'll end up with the string converted to a number. In this example, you end up with 6 (2 + 4). Another technique is to use the Number() command like this:

```
var numOfShoes = '2';
var numOfSocks = 4;
var totalItems = Number(numOfShoes) + numOfSocks;
```

Number() converts a string to a number if possible. (If the string is just letters and not numbers, you get the NaN value to indicate that you can't turn letters into a number.)

In general, you'll most often encounter numbers as strings when getting input from a visitor; for example, when retrieving a value a visitor entered into a form field. So, if you need to do any addition using input collected from a form or other source of visitor input, make sure you run it through the Number() command first.

NOTE This problem only occurs when adding a number to a string that contains a number. If you try to multiply the numOfShoes variable with a variable containing a number—shoePrice, for example—the JavaScript interpreter will convert the string in numOfShoes to a number and then multiply it by the shoePrice variable.

Changing the Values in Variables

Variables are useful because they can hold values that change as the program runs—a score that changes as a game is played, for example. So how do you change a variable's value? If you just want to replace what's contained inside a variable, assign a new value to the variable. For example:

```
var score = 0;
score = 100;
```

However, you'll frequently want to keep the value that's in the variable and just add something to it or alter it in some way. For example, with a game score, you never just set a new score—you add or subtract from the current score. To add to the value of a variable, you use the variable's name as part of the operation, like this:

```
var score = 0;
score = score + 100;
```

That last line of code may appear confusing at first, but it uses a very common technique. Here's how it works: All of the action happens to the right of the = sign first; that is, the *score + 100* part. Translated, it means "take what's currently stored in score (0) and then add 100 to it." The result of that operation is *then* stored back into the variable score. The final outcome of these two lines of code is that the variable score now has the value of 100.

The same logic applies to other mathematical operations like subtraction, division, and multiplication:

```
score = score - 10;
score = score * 10;
score = score / 10;
```

In fact, performing math on the value in a variable and then storing the result back into the variable is so common that there are shortcuts for doing so with the main mathematical operations, as pictured in Table 2-3.

TABLE 2-3 *Shortcuts for performing math on a variable*

OPERATOR	WHAT IT DOES	HOW TO USE IT	THE SAME AS
+=	Adds value on the right side of equals sign to the variable on the left.	score += 10	score = score + 10
-=	Subtracts value on the right side of the equals sign from the variable on the left.	score -= 10	score = score - 10
*=	Multiplies the variable on the left side of the equals sign and the value on the right side of the equals sign.	score *= 10	score = score * 10
/=	Divides the value in the variable by the value on the right side of the equals sign.	score /= 10	score = score / 10
++	Placed directly after a variable name, ++ adds 1 to the variable.	score++	score = score + 1
--	Placed directly after a variable name, -- subtracts 1 from the variable.	score--	score = score - 1

The same rules apply when concatenating a string to a variable. For example, say you have a variable with a string in it and want to add another couple of strings onto that variable:

```
var name = 'Franklin';
var message = 'Hello';
message = message + ' ' + name;
```

As with numbers, there's a shortcut operator for concatenating a string to a variable. The += operator adds the string value to the right of the = sign to the end of the variable's string. So you could rewrite the last line of the above code like this:

```
message += ' ' + name;
```

You'll see the += operator frequently when working with strings, and throughout this book.

■ Tutorial: Using Variables to Create Messages

In this tutorial, you'll use variables to print (that is, write) a message onto a web page.

> **NOTE** To follow along with the tutorials in this chapter, you need to download the tutorial files from this book's companion website. See the Note on page 12 for details.

1. **In a text editor, open the file *use_variable.html* in the *chapter02* folder.**

   This page is just a basic HTML file with a simple CSS-enhanced design. It doesn't yet have any JavaScript. You'll use variables to write a message onto a web page.

2. **Locate the `<h1>` tag (a little over half way down the file) and add the opening and closing `<script>` tags, so that the code looks like this:**

   ```
   <h1>Using a Variable</h1>
   <script>

   </script>
   ```

   This HTML should be familiar by now: It simply sets the page up for the script you're about to write.

> **NOTE** This page uses the HTML5 doctype. If you're using XHTML 1.0 or HTML 4.01, add `type="javascript"` to the `<script>` tag like this: `<script type="text/javascript">`. This step isn't needed for the script to work, only for the page to pass the W3C Validator (see page xix for more on validation).

3. **In between the `<script>` tags, type:**

   ```
   var firstName = 'Cookie';
   var lastName = 'Monster';
   ```

   You've just created your first two variables—`firstName` and `lastName`—and stored two string values into them. Next, you'll add (or concatenate) the two strings together, and print the results to the web page.

4. **Below the two variable declarations, type:**

   ```
   document.write('<p>');
   ```

   As you saw in Chapter 1, the `document.write()` command inserts text directly to a web page. In this case, you're using it to write HTML tags to your page. You supply the command a string—`'<p>'`—and it outputs that string just as if you had typed it into your HTML code. It's perfectly OK to supply HTML tags as part of the `document.write()` command. In this case, the JavaScript is adding the opening tag for a paragraph to hold the text you're going to print on the page.

NOTE The document.write() command provides a simple way to get used to JavaScript programming, but it's not the most efficient way to insert HTML in a web page. As you get more comfortable with programming, you can move on to more advanced techniques including some really useful functions courtesy of jQuery (page 127).

5. **Press Return and type the following JavaScript:**

   ```
   document.write(firstName + ' ' + lastName);
   ```

   Here you use the values stored in the variables you created in step 3. The + operator lets you put several strings together to create one longer string, which the document.write() command then writes to the HTML of the page. In this case, the value stored in firstName—'Cookie'—is added to a space character, and then added to the value of lastName—'Monster'. The results are one string: 'Cookie Monster'.

6. **Press Return again and type document.write('</p>');.**

   The finished script should look like this:

   ```html
   <script type="text/javascript">
   var firstName = 'Cookie';
   var lastName = 'Monster';
   document.write('<p>');
   document.write(firstName + ' ' + lastName);
   document.write('</p>');
   </script>
   ```

7. **Preview the page in a web browser to enjoy the fruits of your labor (see Figure 2-2).**

   The words "Cookie Monster" should appear below the headline "Using a Variable." If you don't see anything, there's probably a typo in your code. Compare the script above with what you typed and check page 18 for tips on debugging a script using Firefox, Safari, Chrome, or IE 9.

8. **Return to your text editor and change the second line of the script to read:**

   ```
   var lastName = 'Jar';
   ```

   Save the page and preview it in a web browser. Voilà! The message now reads: Cookie Jar. (The file *complete_use_variable.html* has a working copy of this script.)

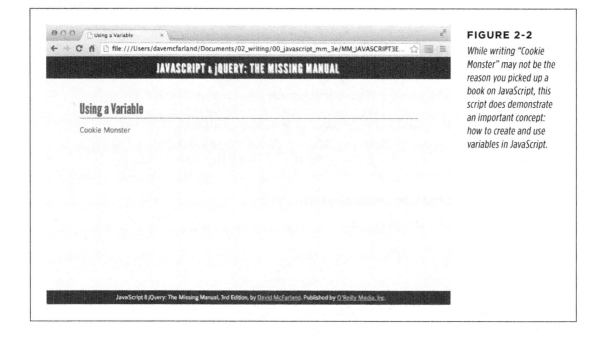

FIGURE 2-2

While writing "Cookie Monster" may not be the reason you picked up a book on JavaScript, this script does demonstrate an important concept: how to create and use variables in JavaScript.

■ Tutorial: Asking for Information

In the last script, you saw how to create variables, but you didn't get to experience how variables let a program respond to the user and produce unique, customized content. In this next tutorial, you'll learn how to use the prompt() command to gather input from a user and change the display of the page based on that input.

1. **In a text editor, open the file *prompt.html* in the *chapter02* folder.**

   To make your programming go faster, the file already has the <script> tags you're going to need. There are two sets of <script> tags: one in the head and one in the body. The JavaScript you're about to add will do two things. First, it will open up a dialog box that asks the user to type an answer to a question. Second, in the body of the web page, a customized message will appear using the user's response.

2. **Between the first set of <script> tags in the document head, type the bolded code:**

   ```
   <script>
   var name = prompt("What is your name?", "");
   </script>
   ```

The prompt() function produces a dialog box similar to one from the alert() function. However, instead of just displaying a message, the prompt() function can also retrieve an answer. In addition, to use the prompt() function, you supply two strings separated by a comma between the parentheses. Figure 2-3 shows what happens to those two strings: The first string appears as the dialog box's question (in this example, "What is your name?").

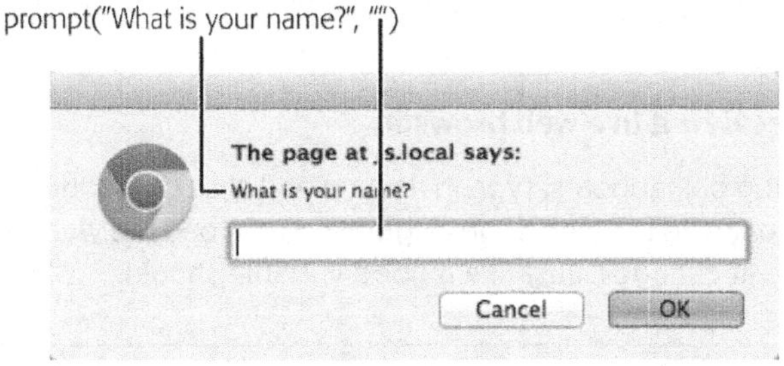

prompt("What is your name?", "")

FIGURE 2-3
The prompt() function is one way to retrieve user input. It works by providing two strings to the function—one to appear as the question, and another that pre-fills the prompt box with text.

The page at js.local says:
What is your name?

Cancel   OK

The second string appears in the field the visitor types into. This example uses what's called an *empty string*, which is just two double quote marks ("") and results in a blank text field (as discussed on page 28, you can use either single or double quote marks for strings). However, you can supply a useful instruction like "Please type both your first and last names" for the second string, and it will appear in the field. Unfortunately, a visitor must first delete that text from the text field before entering his own information.

The prompt() function returns a string containing whatever the visitor types into the dialog box. In this line of JavaScript code, that result is stored into a new variable named name.

NOTE Many functions *return* a value. In other words, the function supplies some information after it's done. You can choose to ignore this information or store it into a variable for later use. In this example, the prompt() function returns a string that you store in the variable name.

3. **Save the page and preview it in a web browser.**

When the page loads, you'll see a dialog box. Notice that nothing else happens—you don't even see the web page—until you fill out the dialog box and click OK. You'll also notice that nothing much happens after you click OK—that's because, at this point, you've merely collected and stored the response; you haven't used that response on the page. You'll do that next.

4. **Return to your text editor. Locate the second set of `<script>` tags and add the code in bold:**

```
<script>
document.write("<p>Welcome, " + name + "</p>");
</script>
```

Here you take advantage of the information supplied by the visitor. As with the script on page 41, you're combining several strings—an opening paragraph tag and text, the value of the variable, and a closing paragraph tag—and printing the results to the web page.

5. **Save the page and preview it in a web browser.**

When the Prompt dialog box appears, type in a name and click OK. Notice that the name you type appears in the web page (Figure 2-4). Reload the web page and type a new name—it changes! Just like a good variable should.

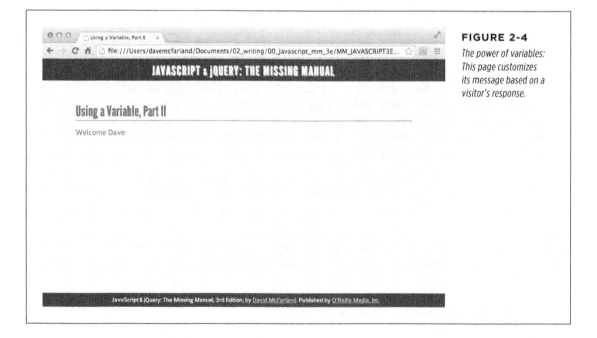

FIGURE 2-4

The power of variables: This page customizes its message based on a visitor's response.

Arrays

Simple variables, like the ones you learned about in the previous section, hold only one piece of information, such as a number or a string value. They're perfect when you only need to keep track of a single thing like a score, an age, or a total cost. However, if you need to keep track of a bunch of related items—like the names of all of the days in a week, or a list of all of the images on a web page—simple variables aren't very convenient.

For example, say you've created a JavaScript shopping cart system that tracks items a visitor intends to buy. If you wanted to keep track of all of the items the visitor adds to her cart using simple variables, you'd have to write code like this:

```
var item1 = 'Xbox 360';
var item2 = 'Tennis shoes';
var item3 = 'Gift certificate';
```

But what if she wanted to add more items than that? You'd have to create more variables—*item4, item5,* and so on. And, because you don't know how many items the visitor might want to buy, you really don't know how many variables you'll have to create.

Fortunately, JavaScript provides a better method of tracking a list of items, called an *array*. An array is a way of storing more than one value in a single place. Think of an array like a shopping list. When you need to go to the grocery store, you sit down and write a list of items to buy. If you just went shopping a few days earlier, the list might only contain a few items, but if your cupboard is bare, your shopping list might be quite long. Regardless of how many items are on the list, though, there's still just a single list.

Without an array, you have to create a new variable for each item in the list. Imagine, for example, that you couldn't make a list of groceries on a single sheet of paper, but had to carry around individual slips of paper—one for each item that you're shopping for. If you wanted to add another item to buy, you'd need a new slip of paper; then you'd need to keep track of each slip as you shopped (see Figure 2-5). That's how simple variables work. But with an array, you can create a single list of items, and even add, remove, or change items at any time.

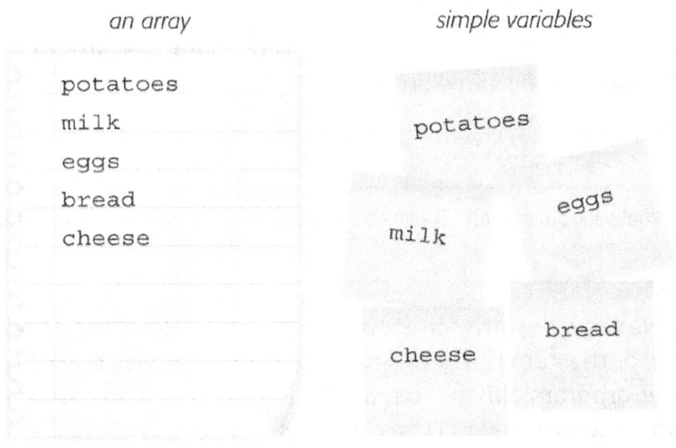

an array simple variables

an array
potatoes
milk
eggs
bread
cheese

potatoes

eggs

milk

bread

cheese

FIGURE 2-5

An array provides a simple, organized way to track a list of related items. Adding another item to the list is just like writing a new item at the bottom of the list.

Creating an Array

To create and store items in an array, you first declare the array's name (just as you would a variable) and then supply a list of comma-separated values: each value represents one item in the list. As with variables, what you name your array is up to you, but you need to follow the same naming rules listed on page 38. To create an array, you put the list of items between opening and closing brackets: [ ]. For example, to create an array containing abbreviations for the seven days of the week, you could write this code:

```
var days = ['Mon', 'Tues', 'Wed', 'Thurs', 'Fri', 'Sat', 'Sun'];
```

The brackets are very important—they tell the JavaScript interpreter that it's dealing with an array. You can create an empty array without any elements like this:

```
var playList = [];
```

Creating an empty array is the equivalent of declaring a variable, as described on page 29. You'll create an empty array when you don't add items to the array until the program is running. For example, the above array might be used to track songs that someone selects from a list on a web page. You don't know ahead of time which songs the person will choose, so you declare an empty array and later fill it with items as the person selects music. (Adding items to an array is described on page 48.)

NOTE When looking through other people's JavaScript programs (or other JavaScript books), you may encounter another way to create an array using the *Array* keyword, like this:

```
var days = new Array('Mon', 'Tues', 'Wed');
```

This method is valid, but the method used in this book (called an *array literal*) is preferred by the pros because it requires less typing, less code, and is considered more "elegant."

You can store any mix of values in an array. In other words, numbers, strings, and Boolean values can all appear in the same array:

```
var prefs = [1, -30.4, 'www.oreilly.com', false];
```

NOTE You can even store arrays and other objects as elements inside an array. This technique can help store complex data.

The array examples above show the array created on a single line. However, if you've got a lot of items to add, or the items are long strings, trying to type all of that on a single line can make your program difficult to read. Another option many programmers use is to create an array over several lines, like this:

```
var authors = [ 'Ernest Hemingway',
                'Charlotte Bronte',
                'Dante Alighieri',
                'Emily Dickinson'
              ];
```

As mentioned in the box on page 34, a JavaScript interpreter skips extra space and line breaks, so even though this code is displayed on five lines, it's still just a single statement, as indicated by the final semicolon on the last line.

TIP   To make the names line up as above, you'd type the first line—var authors = ['Ernest Hemingway',—hit Return, then press the space key as many times as it takes to line up the next value, 'Charlotte Bronte'.

Accessing Items in an Array

You can access the contents of a simple variable just by using the variable's name. For example, alert(lastName) opens an alert box with the value stored in the variable lastName. However, because an array can hold more than one value, you can't just use its name alone to access the items it contains. A number, called an *index*, indicates the position of each item in an array. To access a particular item in an array, you use that item's index number. For example, say you've created an array with abbreviations for the days of the week, and want to open an alert box that displayed the first item. You could write this:

```
var days = ['Mon', 'Tues', 'Wed', 'Thurs', 'Fri', 'Sat', 'Sun'];
alert(days[0]);
```

This code opens an alert box with 'Mon' in it. Arrays are *zero-indexed*, meaning that the *first* item in an array has an index value of 0, and the *second* item has an index value of 1. In other words, subtract one from the item's spot in the list to get its index value—the fifth item's index is 5 minus 1 (that is, 4). Zero-indexing is pretty confusing when you first get started with programming, so Table 2-4 shows how the array days (from the above example) is indexed, as well as the values it contains and how to access each value.

TABLE 2-4 *Items in an array must be accessed using an index number equivalent to their place in the list minus 1*

INDEX VALUE	ITEM	TO ACCESS ITEM
0	Mon	days[0]
1	Tues	days[1]
2	Wed	days[2]
3	Thurs	days[3]
4	Fri	days[4]
5	Sat	days[5]
6	Sun	days[6]

You can change the value of an item in an array by assigning a new value for that index position. For example, to put a new value into the first item in the array days, you could write this:

```
days[0] = 'Monday';
```

Because the index number of the last item in an array is always one less than the total number of items in an array, you only need to know how many items are in an array to access the last item. Fortunately, this is an easy task because every array has a length property, which contains the total number of items in the array. To access the length property, add a period followed by length after the array's name: For example, days.length returns the number of items in the array named days (if you created a different array, playList, for example, you'd get its length like this: playList.length). So you can use this tricky bit of JavaScript to access the value stored in the last item in the array:

```
days[days.length-1]
```

This last snippet of code demonstrates that you don't have to supply a literal number for an index (for example, the 0 in days[0]). You can also supply an equation that returns a valid number. In this case, days.length – 1 is actually a short equation: It first retrieves the number of items in the days array (that's 7 in this example) and subtracts 1 from it. So, in this case, days[days.length-1] translates to days[6].

You can also use a variable containing a number as the index:

```
var i = 0;
alert(days[i]);
```

The last line of code is the equivalent of alert(days[0]);. You'll find this technique particularly useful when working with loops, as described in the next chapter (page 80).

Adding Items to an Array

Say you've created an array to track items that a user clicks on a web page. Each time the user clicks the page, an item is added to the array. JavaScript supplies several ways to add contents to an array.

■ ADDING AN ITEM TO THE END OF AN ARRAY

To add an item to the end of an array, you can use the index notation from page 47, using an index value that's one greater than the last item in the list. For example, say you've created an array named properties:

```
var properties = ['red', '14px', 'Arial'];
```

At this point, the array has three items. Remember that the last item is accessed using an index that's one less than the total number of items, so in this case, the last item in this array is properties[2]. To add another item, you could do this:

```
properties[3] = 'bold';
```

This line of code inserts 'bold' into the fourth spot in the array, which creates an array with four elements: ['red', '14px', 'Arial', 'bold']. When you add the new item, you use an index value that's equal to the total number of elements currently in the array, so you can be sure you're always adding an item to the end of an array by using the array's `length` property as the index. For example, you can rewrite the last line of code like this:

```
properties[properties.length] = 'bold';
```

You can also use an array's `push()` command, which adds whatever you supply between the parentheses to the end of the array. As with the `length` property, you apply `push()` by adding a period to the array's name followed by `push()`. For example, here's another way to add an item to the end of the `properties` array:

```
properties.push('bold');
```

Whatever you supply inside the parentheses (in this example, the string `'bold'`) is added as a new item at the end of the array. You can use any type of value, like a string, number, Boolean, or even a variable.

One advantage of the `push()` command is that it lets you add more than one item to the array. For example, say you want to add three values to the end of an array named `properties`, you could do that like this:

```
properties.push('bold', 'italic', 'underlined');
```

ADDING AN ITEM TO THE BEGINNING OF AN ARRAY

If you want to add an item to the beginning of an array, use the `unshift()` command. Here's an example of adding the `bold` value to the beginning of the `properties` array:

```
var properties = ['red', '14px', 'Arial'];
properties.unshift('bold');
```

After this code runs, the array `properties` contains four elements: `['bold', 'red', '14px', 'Arial']`. As with `push()`, you can use `unshift()` to insert multiple items at the beginning of an array:

```
properties.unshift('bold', 'italic', 'underlined');
```

> **NOTE** Make sure you use the *name* of the array followed by a period and the method you wish to use. In other words, `push('new item')` won't work because the JavaScript interpreter doesn't know which array it should add that item to. You must first use the array's name (whatever name you gave the array when you created it) followed by a period, and then the method, like this: `authors.push('Stephen King');`.

CHOOSING HOW TO ADD ITEMS TO AN ARRAY

So far, this chapter has shown you three ways to add items to an array. Table 2-5 compares these techniques. Each of these commands accomplishes similar tasks, so the one you choose depends on the circumstances of your program. If the order that the items are stored in the array doesn't matter, then any of these methods work. For example, say you have a page of product pictures, and clicking one picture adds the product to a shopping cart. You use an array to store the cart items. The order the items appear in the cart (or the array) doesn't matter, so you can use any of these techniques.

However, if you create an array that keeps track of the order in which something happens, then the method you choose does matter. For example, say you've created a page that lets visitors create a playlist of songs by clicking song names on the page. Because a playlist lists songs in the order they should be played, the order is important. So if each time the visitor clicks a song, the song's name should go at the end of the playlist (so it will be the last song played), then use the push() method.

TABLE 2-5 *Various ways of adding elements to an array*

METHOD	ORIGINAL ARRAY	EXAMPLE CODE	RESULTING ARRAY	EXPLANATION
.length property	var p = [0,1,2,3]	p[p.length]=4	[0,1,2,3,4]	Adds one value to the end of an array.
push()	var p = [0,1,2,3]	p.push(4,5,6)	[0,1,2,3,4,5,6]	Adds one or more items to the end of an array.
unshift()	var p = [0,1,2,3]	p.unshift(4,5)	[4,5,0,1,2,3]	Adds one or more items to the beginning of an array.

The push() and unshift() commands return a value. To be specific, once push() and unshift() complete their tasks, they supply the number of items that are in the array. Here's an example:

```
var p = [0,1,2,3];
var totalItems = p.push(4,5);
```

After this code runs, the value stored in totalItems is 6, because there are six items in the p array.

Deleting Items from an Array

If you want to remove an item from the end or beginning of an array, use the pop() or shift() commands. Both commands remove one item from the array: The pop() command removes the item from the end of the array, while shift() removes one item from the beginning. Table 2-6 compares the two methods.

TABLE 2-6 *Two ways of removing an item from an array*

METHOD	ORIGINAL ARRAY	EXAMPLE CODE	RESULTING ARRAY	EXPLANATION
pop()	var p = [0,1,2,3]	p.pop()	[0,1,2]	Removes the last item from the array.
shift()	var p = [0,1,2,3]	p.shift()	[1,2,3]	Removes the first item from the array.

Once they've completed their tasks of removing an item from an array, pop() and shift() return a value. In fact, they return the value that they just removed. So, for example, this code removes a value and stores that value in the variable removedItem:

```
var p = [0,1,2,3];
var removedItem = p.shift();
```

The value of removedItem after this code runs is 0 and the array *p* now contains [1,2,3].

POWER USERS' CLINIC

Creating a Queue

The methods used to add items to an array—push() and unshift()—and the methods used to remove items from an array—pop() and shift()—are often used together to provide a way of accessing items in the order they were created. A classic example is a music playlist. You create the list by adding songs to it; then, as you play each song, it's removed from the list. The songs are played in the order they appear in the list, so the first song is played and then removed from the list. This arrangement is similar to a line at the movies. When you arrive at the movie theater, you take your place at the end of the line; when the movie's about to begin, the doors open and the first person in line is the first to get in.

In programming circles, this concept is called FIFO for "First In, First Out." You can simulate this arrangement using arrays and the push() and shift() commands. For example, say you had an array named playlist. To add a new song to the end of the list, you'd use push(), like this:

```
playlist.push('Yellow Submarine');
```

To get the song that's supposed to play next, you get the first item in the list like this:

```
nowPlaying = playlist.shift();
```

This code removes the first item from the array and stores it in a variable named nowPlaying. The FIFO concept is useful for creating and managing queues such as a playlist, a to-do list, or a slideshow.

NOTE This chapter's files include a web page that lets you interactively test the different array commands. It's named *array_methods.html* and it's in the *testbed* folder. Open the file in a web browser and click the various buttons on the web page to see how the array methods work. (By the way, all the cool interactivity of that page is thanks to JavaScript and jQuery.)

■ Tutorial: Writing to a Web Page Using Arrays

You'll use arrays in many of the scripts in this book, but to get a quick taste of creating and using arrays, try this short tutorial.

NOTE See the note on page 12 for information on how to download the tutorial files.

---

1. **In a text editor, open the file *arrays.html* in the *chapter02* folder.**

   You'll start by simply creating an array containing four strings. As with the previous tutorial, this file already contains <script> tags in both the head and body regions.

2. **Between the first set of** <script> **tags, type the bolded code:**

```
<script>
var authors = [ 'Ernest Hemingway',
                'Charlotte Bronte',
                'Dante Alighieri',
                'Emily Dickinson'
              ];
</script>
```

   This code comprises a single JavaScript statement, but it's broken over five lines. To create it, type the first line—var authors = ['Ernest Hemingway',—hit Return, then press the Space bar until you line up under the first ' (16 spaces), and then type 'Charlotte Bronte', hit Return and continue.

NOTE Most HTML editors use a *monospaced* font like Courier or Courier New for your HTML and JavaScript code. In a monospaced font, each character is the same width as every other character, so it's easy to line up columns (like all the author names in this example). If your text editor doesn't use Courier or something similar, you may not be able to line up the names perfectly.

   As mentioned on page 46, when you create an array with lots of elements, you can make your code easier to read if you break it over several lines. You can tell it's a single statement because there's no semicolon until the end of line 5.

   This line of code creates an array named authors and stores the names of four authors (four string values) into the array. Next, you'll access an element of the array.

3. **Locate the second set of** <script> **tags, and add the code in bold:**

```
<script>
document.write('<p>The first author is <strong>');
document.write(authors[0] + '</strong></p>');
</script>
```

   The first line starts a new paragraph with some text and an opening <strong> tag—just plain HTML. The next line prints the value stored in the first item of the authors array and prints the closing </strong> and </p> tags to create a complete HTML paragraph. To access the first item in an array, you use a 0 as the index—authors[0]—instead of 1.

   At this point, it's a good idea to save your file and preview it in a web browser. You should see "The first author is Ernest Hemingway" printed on the screen.

If you don't, you may have made a typo when you created the array in either step 2 or 3.

NOTE Remember to use the error console in your browser (described on page 18) to help you locate the source of any JavaScript errors.

4. **Return to your text editor and add these two lines of code below to your script:**

```
document.write('<p>The last author is <strong>');
document.write(authors[4] + '</strong></p>');
```

This step is pretty much the same as the previous one, except that you're printing a different array item. Save the page and preview it in a browser. You'll see "undefined" in place of an author's name (see Figure 2-6). Don't worry; that's intentional. Can you figure out why it's not working?

Remember that an array's index values begin at 0, so the last item is actually the total number of items in the array minus 1. In this case, there are four strings stored in the authors array, so that last item would actually be accessed with authors[3].

NOTE If you try to read the value of an item using an index value that doesn't exist, you'll end up with the JavaScript "undefined" value. All that means is that there's no value stored in that index position.

Fortunately, there's an easy technique for retrieving the last item in an array no matter how many items are stored in the array.

5. **Return to your text editor and edit the code you just entered. Erase the 4 and add the bolded code in its place:**

```
document.write('<p>The last author is <strong>');
document.write(authors[authors.length-1] + '</strong></p>');
```

As you'll recall from "Adding Items to an Array" on page 48, an array's length property stores the number of items in the array. So the total number of items in the authors array can be found with this code: authors.length. At this point in the script, that turns out to be 4.

Knowing that the index value of the last item in an array is always 1 less than the total number of items in an array, you just subtract one from the total to get the index number of the last item: authors.length-1. You can provide that little equation as the index value when accessing the last item in an array: authors[authors.length-1].

You'll finish up by adding one more item to the beginning of the array.

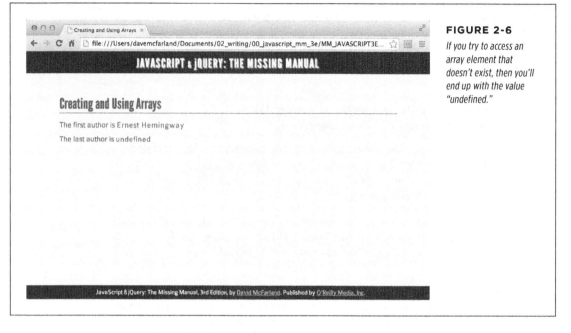

FIGURE 2-6

If you try to access an array element that doesn't exist, then you'll end up with the value "undefined."

6. **Add another line of code after the ones you added in step 5:**

   ```
   authors.unshift('Stan Lee');
   ```

   As you read on page 49, the unshift() method adds one or more items to the beginning of an array. After this line of code runs, the authors array will now be ['Stan Lee', 'Ernest Hemingway', 'Charlotte Bronte', 'Dante Alighieri','Emily Dickinson'].

   Finally, you'll print out the newly added item on the page.

7. **Add three more lines (bolded below) so that your final code looks like this:**

   ```
   document.write('<p>The first author is <strong>');
   document.write(authors[0] + '</strong></p>');
   document.write('<p>The last author is <strong>');
   document.write(authors[authors.length-1] + '</strong></p>');
   authors.unshift('Stan Lee');
   document.write('<p>I almost forgot <strong>');
   document.write(authors[0]);
   document.write('</strong></p>');
   ```

   Save the file and preview it in a web browser. You should see something like Figure 2-7. If you don't, remember that the error console in your web browser can help you locate the error (page 18).

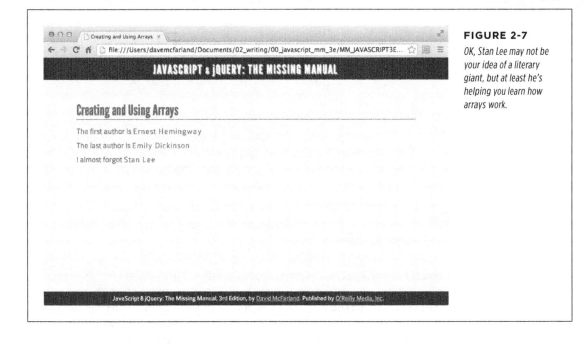

FIGURE 2-7

OK, Stan Lee may not be your idea of a literary giant, but at least he's helping you learn how arrays work.

A Quick Object Lesson

So far in this book, you've learned that you can write something to a web page with the document.write() command, and to determine how many items are in an array, you type the name of the array followed by a period and the word "length," like so: days.length. You're probably wondering what those periods are about. You've made it through three chapters without learning the particulars of this feature of JavaScript syntax, and it's time to address them.

You can conceptualize many of the elements of the JavaScript language, as well as elements of a web page, as *objects*. The real world, of course, is filled with objects too, such as a dog or a car. Most objects are made up of different parts: A dog has a tail, a head, and four legs; a car has doors, wheels, headlights, a horn; and so on. An object might also do something—a car can transport passengers, a dog can bark. In fact, even a part of an object can do something: For example, a tail can wag, and a horn can honk. Table 2-7 illustrates one way to show the relationships between objects, their parts, and actions.

TABLE 2-7 *A simplified view of the world*

OBJECT	PARTS	ACTIONS
dog		bark
	tail	wag
car		transport
	horn	honk

The world of JavaScript is also filled with objects: a browser window, a document, and a date are just a few examples. Like real-world objects, JavaScript objects are also made up of different parts. In programming-speak, the parts of an object are called *properties*. The actions an object can perform are called *methods*, which are functions (like the built-in alert() function) that are specific to an object (see Table 2-8).

> **NOTE** You can always tell a method from a property because when you use a method, the name ends in parentheses: write(), for example.

Each object in JavaScript has its own set of properties and methods. For example, the array object has a property named length, and the document object has a method named write(). To access an object's property or execute one of its methods, you use *dot syntax*—those periods! The dot (period) connects the object with its property or method. For example, document.write() means "run the write() method of the document object." If the real world worked like that, you'd have a dog wag his tail like this: dog.tail.wag(). (Of course, in the real world, a doggy treat works a lot better.)

TABLE 2-8 *Some methods and properties of two JavaScript objects: the document object and an array*

OBJECT	PROPERTY	METHOD
document	title	
	url	
		write()
['Kate','Graham','Sam']	length	
		push()
		pop()
		unshift()

And just as you might own several dogs in the real world, your JavaScript programs can have multiple versions (called *instances*) of the same kind of object. For example, say you create two simple variables like this:

```
var first_name = 'Jack';
var last_name = 'Hearts';
```

You've actually created two different *string* objects. Strings have their own set of properties and methods, which are different from the methods and properties of other objects, like dates (you'll learn some of these properties and methods on page 568). When you create an object (also called creating an *instance* of that object), you can access all of the properties and methods for that object.

> **NOTE** You've already encountered another object—called the window object—which represents the browser window itself. It's basically the container object for a web page and everything else on the page. For example, `alert()` and `prompt()` are both methods of the window object and can be written like this: `window.alert()` and `window.prompt()`. However, because the window object is always present in a web page, you can leave its name out, so `alert('hello')` and `window.alert('hello')` do the same thing.

Whenever you create a new variable and store a value into it, you're really creating a new instance of a particular type of object. So each of these lines of JavaScript create different types of JavaScript objects:

```
var first_name = 'Bob'; // a string object
var age = 32; // a number object
var valid = false; // a Boolean object
```

In fact, when you change the type of information stored in a variable, you change the type of object it is as well. For example, if you create a variable named data that stores an array, then store a number in the variable, you've changed that variable's type from an array to a number object:

```
var data = false; // a Boolean object
data = 32; //changes to number object
```

The concepts of objects, properties, methods, and dot syntax may seem a little weird at first glance. However, they are fundamental parts of how JavaScript works, and integral to using jQuery as well, so you'll get used to them pretty quickly.

> **TIP** JavaScript includes a special keyword for determining the type of an object (string, number, Boolean, and so on). It's called the `typeof` operator and is placed before a variable to determine the type of object inside that variable. For example:
>
> ```
> var data = 32;
> alert(typeof data); // "number" appears in alert window
> data = 'Roger roger';
> alert(typeof data); // "string" appears in the alert window
> ```

As you continue reading this book, keep these few facts in mind:

- The world of JavaScript is populated with lots of different types of objects.

- Each object has its own properties and methods.

- You access an object's property or activate an object's method using dot syntax: document.write(), for example.

■ Comments

When you're in the midst of programming, you feel like you understand everything that's going on in your program. Every line of code makes sense, and better yet, it works! But a month or two later, when your boss or a client asks you to make a change or add a new feature to that cool script you wrote, you might find yourself scratching your head the moment you look at your once-familiar JavaScript: What's that variable for? Why'd I program it like that? What's going on in this section of the program?

It's easy to forget how a program works and why you wrote your code the way you did. Fortunately, most programming languages provide a way for programmers to leave notes for themselves or other programmers who might look through their code. JavaScript lets you leave *comments* throughout your code. If you've used HTML or CSS comments, these should feel familiar. A comment is simply a line or more worth of notes: The JavaScript interpreter ignores them, but they can provide valuable information on how your program works.

To create a single line comment, precede the comment with double forward slashes:

```
// this is a comment
```

You can also add a comment after a JavaScript statement:

```
var price = 10; // set the initial cost of the widget
```

The JavaScript interpreter ignores everything after the // until the end of the line.

You can also add several lines worth of comments by beginning the comments with /* and ending them with */. (These are the same type of comments CSS uses.) The JavaScript interpreter ignores all of the text between these two sets of symbols. For example, say you want to give a description of how a program works at the beginning of your code. You can do that like this:

```
/*
    JavaScript Slideshow:
    This program automates the display of
    images in a pop-up window.
*/
```

You don't need to leave the /* and */ on their own lines, either. In fact, you can create a single line JavaScript comment with them:

```
/* this is a single line comment */
```

In general, if you want to just write a short, one-line comment, use //. For several lines of comments, use the /* and */ combination.

When to Use Comments

Comments are an invaluable tool for a program that's moderately long or complex and that you want to keep using (and perhaps changing) in the future. While the simple scripts you've learned so far are only a line or two of code, you'll eventually be creating longer and much more complex programs. To make sure you can quickly figure out what's going on in a script, it's a good idea to add comments to help you understand the overall logic of the program and to explain any particularly confusing or complex bits.

> **NOTE** Adding lots of comments to a script makes the script larger (and slower to download). In general, the amount of comments you'll add to a script won't add significantly to the size of the file. But if you want to squeeze every unnecessary byte out of your files, page 585 shows you ways to make JavaScript files smaller and faster.

Many programmers add a block of comments at the beginning of an external JavaScript file. These comments can explain what the script is supposed to do, identify the date the script was created, include a version number for frequently updated scripts, and provide copyright information.

For example, at the beginning of the jQuery library's JavaScript file, you'll find this comment:

```
/*!
 * jQuery JavaScript Library v1.11.0
 * http://jquery.com/
 *
 * Includes Sizzle.js
 * http://sizzlejs.com/
 *
 * Copyright 2005, 2014 jQuery Foundation, Inc. and other contributors
 * Released under the MIT license
 * http://jquery.org/license
 *
 * Date: 2014-01-23T21:02Z
 */
```

At the beginning of the script, you might also include instructions on how to use the script: variables that might need to be set, anything special you might need to do to your HTML to make the script work, and so on.

You should also add a comment before a series of complex programming steps. For example, say you write a script that animates an image across a visitor's browser window. One part of that script is determining the image's current position in the browser window. This can take several lines of programming; it's a good idea to place a comment before that section of the program, so when you look at the script later, you'll know exactly what that part of the program does:

```
// determine x and y positions of image in window
```

The basic rule of thumb is to add comments anywhere you'll find them helpful later. If a line of code is painfully obvious, you probably don't need a comment. For example, there's no reason to add a comment for simple code like alert('hello'), because it's pretty obvious what it does (opens an alert box with the word "hello" in it).

Comments in This Book

Comments are also very helpful when explaining JavaScript. In this book, comments frequently explain what a line of programming does or indicate the results of a particular statement. For example, you might see a comment like the following to show the results of an alert statement:

```
var a = 'Bob';
var b = 'Smith';
alert(a + ' ' + b); // 'Bob Smith';
```

The third line ends with a comment that indicates what you should see when you preview this code in a web browser. If you want to test the code that you read in this book by adding it to a web page and viewing it in a web browser, you can leave out comments like these when typing the code into a web page. These types of comments are intended simply to help you understand what's happening in the code as you read along with the book.

Likewise, as you start to learn some of the more complex commands available in JavaScript, you'll begin to manipulate the data in variables. You'll often see comments in this book's code to display what should be stored in the variable after the command is run. For example, the charAt() command lets you select a character at a specific point in a string. When you read about how to use that command in this book, you might see code like this:

```
var x = "Now is the time for all good programmers.";
alert(x.charAt(2)); // 'w'
```

The comment // 'w' that appears at the end of the second line indicates what you should see in an alert dialog box if this code were actually run in a web browser. (And, yes, 'w' is correct. When counting the letters in a string, the first letter is counted as character 0, because strings are really arrays of characters. So charAt(2) retrieves the *third* character from the string. Sometimes programming just hurts your brain.)

Adding Logic and Control to Your Programs

So far you've learned about some of JavaScript's basic building blocks. But simply creating a variable and storing a string or number in it doesn't accomplish much. And building an array with a long list of items won't be much help unless you have an easy way to work your way through the items in the array. In this chapter, you'll learn how to make your programs react intelligently and work more efficiently by using conditional statements, loops, and functions.

■ Making Programs React Intelligently

Our lives are filled with choices: "What should I wear today?", "What should I eat for lunch?", "What should I do Friday night?", and so on. Many choices you make depend on the situation. For example, say you decide you want to go to the movies on Friday night. You'll probably ask yourself a bunch of questions like "Are there any good movies playing?", "Is there a movie starting at the right time?", "Do I have enough money to go to the movies (and buy a $17 bag of popcorn)?"

Suppose there *is* a movie that's playing at just the time you want to go. You then ask yourself a simple question: "Do I have enough money?" If the answer is yes, you'll head out to the movie. If the answer is no, you won't go. But on another Friday, you do have enough money, so you go to the movies. This scenario is just a simple example of how the circumstances around us affect the decisions we make.

JavaScript has the same kind of decision-making feature called *conditional statements*. At its most basic, a conditional statement is a simple yes or no question. If the answer to the question is yes, your program does one thing; if the answer is no, it does something else. Conditional statements are one of the most useful programming concepts: They let your programs react to different situations and behave intelligently. You'll use them countless times in your programming. To get a clear picture of their usefulness, here are a few examples of how they can come in handy:

- **Form validation.** When you want to make sure someone filled out all of the required fields in a form ("Name," "Address," "Email," and so on), you'll use conditional statements. For example, if the Name field is empty, don't submit the form.

- **Drag and drop.** If you add the ability to drag elements around your web page, you might want to check where the visitor drops the element on the page. For example, if he drops a picture onto an image of a trash can, you make the photo disappear from the page.

- **Evaluating input.** Suppose you pop up a window to ask a visitor a question like, "Would you like to answer a few questions about how great this website is?" You'll want your script to react differently depending on how the visitor answers the question.

Figure 3-1 shows an example of an application that uses conditional statements.

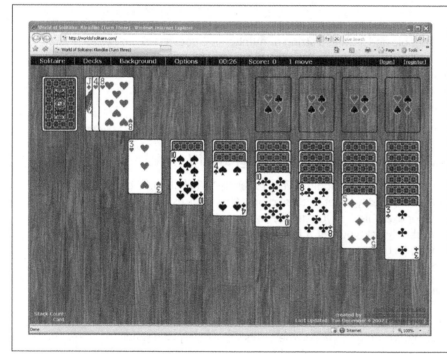

FIGURE 3-1

It takes a lot of work to have fun. A JavaScript-based game like Solitaire (http://worldofsolitaire. com) demonstrates how a program has to react differently based on the conditions of the program. For example, when a player drags and drops a card, the program has to decide if the player dropped the card in a valid location or not, and then perform different actions in each case.

Conditional Statement Basics

Conditional statements are also called if/then statements, because they perform a task only if the answer to a question is true: "*If* I have enough money, *then* I'll go to the movies." The basic structure of an if/then conditional statement looks like this:

```
if ( condition ) {
    // some action happens here
}
```

There are three parts to the statement: if indicates that the programming that follows is a conditional statement; the parentheses enclose the yes or no question, called the *condition* (more on that in a moment); and the curly braces ({ }) mark the beginning and end of the JavaScript code that should execute if the condition is true.

> **NOTE** In the code listed above, the // some action happens here is a JavaScript *comment*. It's not code that actually runs; it's just a note left amidst the code. In this case, the comment points out to you, the reader, what's supposed to go in that part of the program. See page 58 for more on comments.

In many cases, the condition is a comparison between two values. For example, say you create a game that the player wins when the score is over 100. In this program, you'll need a variable to track the player's score and, at some point, you need to check to see if that score is more than 100 points. In JavaScript, the code to check if the player won could look like this:

```
if (score > 100) {
  alert('You won!');
}
```

The important part is score > 100. That phrase is the condition, and it simply tests whether the value stored in the score variable is greater than 100. If it is, then a "You won!" dialog box appears; if the player's score is less than or equal to 100, then the JavaScript interpreter skips the alert and moves onto the next part of the program. Figure 3-2 provides a visualization of this process.

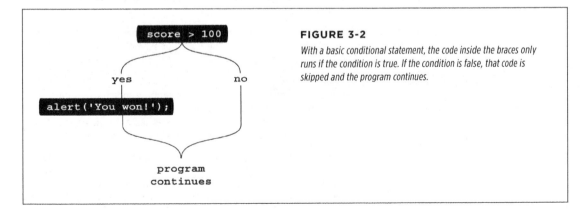

FIGURE 3-2

With a basic conditional statement, the code inside the braces only runs if the condition is true. If the condition is false, that code is skipped and the program continues.

In addition to > (greater than), there are several other conditional operators used to compare numbers (see Table 3-1).

> **TIP** Type two spaces (or press the Tab key once) before each line of JavaScript code contained within a pair of braces. The spaces (or tab) indent those lines and make it easier to see the beginning and ending brace, and to figure out what code belongs inside the conditional statement. Two spaces is a common technique, but if four spaces make your code easier for you to read, then use four spaces. The examples in this book indent code inside braces.

TABLE 3-1 *Use these comparison operators to test values as part of a conditional statement*

COMPARISON OPERATOR	WHAT IT MEANS
==	**Equal to.** Compares two values to see if they're the same. Can be used to compare numbers or strings.
!=	**Not equal to.** Compares two values to see if they're not the same. Can be used to compare numbers or strings.
===	**Strict equal to.** Compares not only the values but also the type of the value. In other words, the two values must also share the same type—string, number, or Boolean—in order for the condition to be true. For example, while '2' == 2 is true, '2' === 2 is not true, because the first value is inside quote marks (a string) and the second is a number. Many programmers prefer this strict equality operator because it ensures you're comparing like types of information. However, when retrieving a number value from a form (or a prompt() dialog box), you'll get a string value like '2', and not an actual number. You should convert the string to a number before comparing using a comparison—see page 37 for more on converting strings to numbers.
!==	**Strict not equal to.** Like strict equal to compare values and type. For example, while '2' != 2 is false, '2' ! = = 2 is true, because although the values are the same, the types are not.
>	**Greater than.** Compares two numbers and checks if the number on the left side is greater than the number on the right. For example, 2 > 1 is true, since 2 is a bigger number than 1, but 2 > 3 is false, because 2 isn't bigger than 3.
<	**Less than.** Compares two numbers and checks if the number on the left side is less than the number on the right. For example, 2 < 3 is true, because 2 is a smaller number than 3, but 2 < 1 is false, because 2 isn't less than 1.
>=	**Greater than or equal to.** Compares two numbers and checks if the number on the left side is greater than or the same value as the number on the right. For example, 2 >= 2 is true, because 2 is the same as 2, but 2 >= 3 is false, because 2 isn't a bigger number 3, nor is it equal to 3.
<=	**Less than or equal to.** Compares two numbers and checks if the number on the left side is less than or the same value as the number on the right. For example, 2 <= 2 is true, because 2 is the same as 2, but 2 <= 1 is false, because 2 isn't a smaller number than 1, nor is 2 equal to 1.

You'll frequently test to see if two values are equal or not. For example, say you create a JavaScript-based quiz, and one of the questions asks, "How many moons does Saturn have?" The person's answer is stored in a variable named answer. You might then write a conditional statement like this:

```
if (answer == 31) {
  alert('Correct. Saturn has 31 moons.');
}
```

The double set of equals signs (==) isn't a typo; it instructs the JavaScript interpreter to compare two values and decide whether they're equal. As you learned in Chapter 2, in JavaScript, a single equals sign is the *assignment operator* that you use to store a value into a variable:

```
var score = 0; //stores 0 into the variable score
```

Because the JavaScript interpreter already assigns a special meaning to a single equals sign, you need to use two equals signs whenever you want to compare two values to determine if they're equal or not.

You can also use the == (called the *equality operator*) to check to see if two strings are the same. For example, say you let the user type a color into a form, and if he types *red*, then you change the background color of the page to red. You could use the conditional operator for that:

```
if (enteredColor == 'red') {
  document.body.style.backgroundColor='red';
}
```

NOTE In the code above, don't worry right now about how the page color is changed. You'll learn how to dynamically control CSS properties using JavaScript on page 134.

You can also test to see if two values aren't the same using the *inequality* operator:

```
if (answer != 31) {
  alert("Wrong! That's not how many moons Saturn has.");
}
```

The exclamation mark translates to "not", so != means "not equal to." In this example, if the value stored in answer is not 31, then the poor test taker would see the insulting alert message.

The code that runs if the condition is true isn't limited to just a single line of code as in the previous examples. You can have as many lines of JavaScript between the opening and closing curly braces as you'd like. For example, as part of the JavaScript quiz example, you might keep a running tally of how many correct answers the test taker gets.

So, when the Saturn question is answered correctly, you also want to add 1 to the test taker's total. You would do that as part of the conditional statement:

```
if (answer == 31) {
  alert('Correct. Saturn has 31 moons.');
  numCorrect += 1;
}
```

NOTE As described on page 39, the line of code above—numCorrect += 1—simply adds 1 to the value currently in the variable numCorrect.

And you could add additional lines of JavaScript code between the braces as well—any code that should run if the condition is true.

POWER USERS' CLINIC

The Return of the Boolean

On page 29, you learned about the Boolean values—true and false. Booleans may not seem very useful at first, but they're essential when you start using conditional statements. In fact, because a condition is really just a yes or no question, the answer to that question is a Boolean value. For example, check out the following code:

```
var x = 4;
if ( x == 4 ) {
    //do something
}
```

The first line of code stores the number 4 into the variable x. The condition on the next line is a simple question: Is the value stored in x equal to 4? In this case, it is, so the JavaScript between the curly braces runs. But here's what really happens in between the parentheses: The JavaScript interpreter converts the condition into a Boolean value. (In programming-speak, the interpreter *evaluates* the condition.) If the condition evaluates to true (meaning the answer to the question is yes), then the code between the braces runs. However, if the condition evaluates to false, then the code in the braces is skipped.

One common use of Booleans is to create what's called a *flag*—a variable that marks whether something is true. For example,

when validating a form full of visitor-submitted information, you might start by creating a valid variable with a Boolean value of true—this means you're assuming, at first, that she filled out the form correctly. Then, you'd run through each form field, and if any field is missing information or has the wrong type of information, you'd change the value in valid to false. After checking all of the form fields, you'd test what's stored in *valid*, and if it's still true, you submit the form. If it's not true (meaning one or more form fields were left blank), you'd display some error messages and prevent the form from submitting:

```
var valid = true;
// lot of other programming gunk happens
in here
// if a field has a problem then you set
valid to false
if (valid) {
 //submit form
} else {
 //print lots of error messages
}
```

Adding a Backup Plan

But what if the condition is false? The basic conditional statement in the previous section doesn't have a backup plan for a condition that turns out to be false. In the real world, if you're deciding what to do Friday night and you don't have enough money for the movies, you'd want to do something else. An if statement has its own kind of backup plan, called an *else clause*. For example, say as part of the JavaScript testing script, you want to notify the test taker if he gets the answer right, or if he gets it wrong. Here's how you can do that:

```
if (answer == 31) {

  alert('Correct. Saturn has 31 moons.');

  numCorrect = numCorrect + 1;

} else {

  alert("Wrong! That's not how many moons Saturn has.");

}
```

This code sets up an either/or situation; only one of the two messages will appear (Figure 3-3). If the number 31 is stored in the variable answer, then the "correct" alert appears; otherwise, the "wrong" alert appears.

To create an else clause, just add else after the closing brace for the conditional statement followed by another pair of braces. You add the code that should execute if the condition turns out to be false in between the braces. Again, you can have as many lines of code as you'd like as part of the else clause.

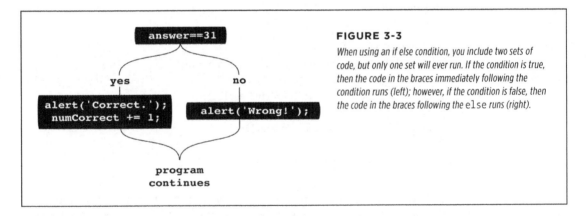

FIGURE 3-3

When using an if else condition, you include two sets of code, but only one set will ever run. If the condition is true, then the code in the braces immediately following the condition runs (left); however, if the condition is false, then the code in the braces following the else *runs (right).*

Testing More Than One Condition

Sometimes you'll want to test several conditions and have several possible outcomes: Think of it like a game show where the host says, "Would you like the prize behind door #1, door #2, or door #3?" You can only pick one. In your day-to-day activities, you also are often faced with multiple choices like this one.

For example, return to the "What should I do Friday night?" question. You could expand your entertainment options based on how much money you have and are willing to spend. For example, you could start off by saying, "If I have $50 or more,

I'll go out to a nice dinner and a movie (and have some popcorn too)." If you don't have $50, you might try another test: "If I have $35 or more, I'll go to a nice dinner." If you don't have $35, then you'd say, "If I have $12 or more, I'll go to the movies." And finally, if you don't have $12, you might say, "Then I'll just stay at home and watch TV." What a Friday night!

JavaScript lets you perform the same kind of cascading logic using else if statements. It works like this: You start with an if statement, which is option number 1; you then add one or more else if statements to provide additional questions that can trigger additional options; and finally, you use the else clause as the fallback position. Here's the basic structure in JavaScript:

```
if (condition) {
  // door #1
} else if (condition2) {
  // door #2
} else {
  // door #3
}
```

This structure is all you need to create a JavaScript "Friday night planner" program. It asks visitors how much money they have, and then determines what they should do on Friday (sound familiar?). You can use the prompt() command that you learned about on page 42 to collect the visitor's response and a series of if/else if statements to determine what he should do:

```
var fridayCash = prompt('How much money can you spend?', '');
if (fridayCash >= 50) {
  alert('You should go out to dinner and a movie.');
} else if (fridayCash >= 35) {
  alert('You should go out to a fine meal.');
} else if (fridayCash >= 12) {
  alert('You should go see a movie.');
} else {
  alert('Looks like you will be watching TV.');
}
```

Here's how this program breaks down step by step: The first line opens a prompt dialog box asking the visitor how much he can spend. Whatever the visitor types is stored in a variable named fridayCash. The next line is a test: Is the value the visitor typed 50 or more? If the answer is yes, then an alert appears, telling him to go get a meal and see a movie. At this point, the entire conditional statement is done. The JavaScript interpreter skips the next else if statement, the following else if statement, and the final else clause. With a conditional statement, only one of the outcomes can happen, so once the JavaScript interpreter encounters a condition that evaluates to true, it runs the JavaScript code between the braces for that condition and skips everything else within the conditional statement (Figure 3-4).

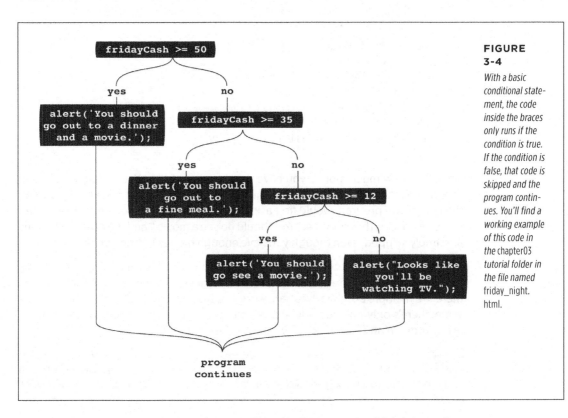

FIGURE 3-4

With a basic conditional statement, the code inside the braces only runs if the condition is true. If the condition is false, that code is skipped and the program continues. You'll find a working example of this code in the chapter03 tutorial folder in the file named friday_night.html.

Suppose the visitor typed *25*. The first condition, in this case, wouldn't be true because 25 is a smaller number than 50. So the JavaScript interpreter skips the code within the braces for that first condition and continues to the else if statement: "Is 25 greater than or equal to 35?" Because the answer is no, it skips the code associated with that condition and encounters the next else if. At this point, the condition asks if 25 is greater than or equal to 12; the answer is yes, so an alert box with the message, "You should go see a movie" appears and the program ends, skipping the final else clause.

The order in which you place your conditional statements can affect how the program runs. For example, say you switched the order of the conditional statements in the above example:

```
var fridayCash = prompt('How much money can you spend?', '');
if (fridayCash >= 12) {
  alert('You should go see a movie.');
} else if (fridayCash >= 35) {
  alert('You should go out to a fine meal.');
} else if (fridayCash >= 50) {
  alert('You should go out to dinner and a movie.');
} else {
  alert('Looks like you will be watching TV.');
}
```

No matter how much money you have you'll never get the "You should go out to a fine meal" or "You should go out to dinner and a movie" message. If you have $100, then the above program would first ask "Is 100 >= 12?" Of course, the answer to that is Yes, so you see the message, "You should go see a movie," and the other conditions are simply skipped, even though you have enough money for the two other options.

You'll encounter this problem when comparing numeric values using the < or > operators. Because lots of different numbers can be larger or smaller than another number, there are multiple possible "yes" answers. For testing if a variable is equal to some value, there's only one possible answer, so you can put those types of comparison in any order in an if / else if / then series of statements.

> **TIP** There's another way to create a series of conditional statements that all test the same variable, as in the fridayCash example. Switch statements do the same thing, and you'll learn about them on page 579.

More Complex Conditions

When you're dealing with many different variables, you'll often need even more complex conditional statements. For example, when validating a required email address field in a form, you'll want to make sure both that the field isn't empty and that the field contains an email address (and not just random typed letters). Fortunately, JavaScript lets you do these kinds of checks as well.

■ MAKING SURE MORE THAN ONE CONDITION IS TRUE

You'll often need to make decisions based on a combination of factors. For example, you may only want to go to a movie if you have enough money *and* there's a movie you want to see. In this case, you'll go only if two conditions are true; if either one is false, then you won't go to the movie. In JavaScript, you can combine conditions using what's called the *logical AND operator*, which is represented by two ampersands (&&). You can use it between the two conditions within a single conditional statement. For example, if you want to check if a number is between 1 and 10, you can do this:

```
if (a > 1 && a < 10) {
  //the value in a is between 1 and 10
  alert("The value " + a + " is between 1 and 10");
}
```

In this example, there are two conditions: a > 1, is the same as "Is the value in a greater than 1?"; a < 10 asks if the value stored in the variable a is less than 10. The JavaScript contained between the braces will run only if *both* conditions are true. So if the variable a has the number 0 stored in it, the first condition (a < 10) is true (0 is less than 10), but the second condition is false (0 is not greater than 1).

You're not limited to just two conditions. You can connect as many conditions as you need with the && operator:

```
if (b>0 && a>0 && c>0) {
  // all three variables are greater than 0
}
```

This code checks three variables to make sure all three have a value greater than 0. If just one has a value of 0 or less, then the code between the braces won't run.

■ MAKING SURE AT LEAST ONE CONDITION IS TRUE

Other times you'll want to check a series of conditions, but you only need one to be true. For example, say you've added a keyboard control for visitors to jump from picture to picture in a photo gallery. When the visitor presses the N key, the next photo appears. In this case, you want her to go to the next picture when she types either *n* (lowercase), or if she has the Caps Lock key pressed, *N* (uppercase). You're looking for a kind of either/or logic: Either this key *or* that key was pressed. The *logical OR operator*, represented by two pipe characters (||), comes in handy:

```
if (key == 'n' || key == 'N') {
  //move to the next photo
}
```

> **NOTE** To type a pipe character, press Shift-\. The key that types both backslashes and pipe characters is usually located just above the Return key.

With the OR operator, only one condition needs to be true for the JavaScript that follows between the braces to run.

As with the AND operator, you can compare more than two conditions. For example, say you've created a JavaScript racing game. The player has a limited amount of time, a limited amount of gas, and a limited number of cars (each time he crashes, he loses one car). To make the game more challenging, you want it to come to an end when any of these three things runs out:

```
if (gas <= 0 || time <= 0 || cars <= 0) {
  //game is over
}
```

When testing multiple conditions, it's sometimes difficult to figure out the logic of the conditional statement. Some programmers group each condition in a set of parentheses to make the logic easier to grasp:

```
if ((key == 'n') || (key == 'N')) {
  //move to the next photo
}
```

To read this code, simply treat each grouping as a separate test; the results of the operation between parentheses will always turn out to be either true or false.

◼ NEGATING A CONDITION

If you're a Superman fan, you probably know about Bizarro, an anti-hero who lived on a cubical planet named Htrae (Earth spelled backwards), had a uniform with a backwards S, and was generally the opposite of Superman in every way. When Bizarro said "Yes," he really meant "No," and when he said "No," he really meant "Yes."

JavaScript programming has an equivalent type of character called the NOT operator, which is represented by an exclamation mark (!). You've already seen the NOT operator used along with the equals sign to indicate "not equal to": !=. But the NOT operator can be used by itself to completely reverse the results of a conditional statement; in other words, it can make false mean true, and true mean false.

You use the NOT operator when you want to run some code based on a negative condition. For example, say you've created a variable named valid that contains a Boolean value of either true or false (see the box on page 66). You use this variable to track whether a visitor correctly filled out a form. When the visitor tries to submit the form, your JavaScript checks each form field to make sure it passes the requirements you set up (for example, the field can't be empty and it has to have an email address in it). If there's a problem, like the field is empty, you could then set valid to false (valid = false).

Now if you want to do something like print out an error and prevent the form from being submitted, you can write a conditional statement like this:

```
if (! valid) {
  //print errors and don't submit form
}
```

The condition ! valid can be translated as "if not valid," which means if valid is false, then the *condition* is true. To figure out the results of a condition that uses the NOT operator, just evaluate the condition without the NOT operator, then reverse it. In other words, if the condition results to true, the ! operator changes it to false, so the conditional statement doesn't run.

As you can see, the NOT operator is very simple to understand (translated from Bizarro-speak: It's very confusing, but if you use it long enough, you'll get used to it).

Nesting Conditional Statements

In large part, computer programming entails making decisions based on information the visitor has supplied or on current conditions inside a program. The more decisions a program makes, the more possible outcomes and the "smarter" the program seems. In fact, you might find you need to make further decisions *after* you've gone through one conditional statement.

Suppose, in the "What to do on Friday night?" example, you want to expand the program to include every night of the week. In that case, you need to first determine what day of the week it is, and then figure out what to do on that day. So you might have a conditional statement asking if it's Friday, and if it is, you'd have another series of conditional statements to determine what to do on that day:

```
if (dayOfWeek == 'Friday') {
  var fridayCash = prompt('How much money can you spend?', '');
  if (fridayCash >= 50) {
    alert('You should go out to dinner and a movie.');
  } else if (fridayCash >= 35) {
    alert('You should go out to a fine meal.');
  } else if (fridayCash >= 12) {
    alert('You should go see a movie.');
  } else {
    alert('Looks like you will be watching TV.');
  }
}
```

In this example, the first condition asks if the value stored in the variable dayOfWeek is the string 'Friday'. If the answer is yes, then a prompt dialog box appears, gets some information from the visitor, and another conditional statement is run. In other words, the first condition, (dayOfWeek == 'Friday'), is the doorway to another series of conditional statements. However, if dayOfWeek isn't 'Friday', then the condition is false and the nested conditional statements are skipped.

Tips for Writing Conditional Statements

The example of a nested conditional statement in the last section may look a little scary. There are lots of (), {}, elses, and ifs. And if you happen to mistype one of the crucial pieces of a conditional statement, your script won't work. There are a few things you can do as you type your JavaScript that can make it easier to work with conditional statements.

- **Type both of the curly braces before you type the code inside them.** One of the most common mistakes programmers make is forgetting to add a final brace to a conditional statement. To avoid this mistake, type the condition and the braces first, then type the JavaScript code that executes when the condition is true. For example, start a conditional like this:

```
if (dayOfWeek=='Friday') {

}
```

In other words, type the `if` clause and the first brace, hit Return twice, and then type the last brace. Now that the basic syntax is correct, you can click in the empty line between the braces and add JavaScript.

- **Indent code within braces.** You can better visualize the structure of a conditional statement if you indent all of the JavaScript between a pair of braces:

```
if (a < 10 && a > 1) {
  alert("The value " + a + " is between 1 and 10");
}
```

By using several spaces (or pressing the Tab key) to indent lines within braces, it's easier to identify which code will run as part of the conditional statement. If you have nested conditional statements, indent each nested statement:

```
if (a < 10 && a > 1) {
  //first level indenting for first conditional
  alert("The value " + a + " is between 1 and 10");
  if (a==5) {
    //second level indenting for 2nd conditional
    alert(a + " is half of ten.");
  }
}
```

- **Use == for comparing equals.** When checking whether two values are equal, don't forget to use the equality operator, like this:

```
if (name == 'Bob') {
```

A common mistake is to use a single equals sign, like this:

```
if (name = 'Bob') {
```

A single equals sign stores a value into a variable, so in this case, the string `'Bob'` would be stored in the variable `name`. Frustratingly, the JavaScript interpreter treats this step as true, so the code following the condition will always run.

■ Tutorial: Using Conditional Statements

Conditional statements will become part of your day-to-day JavaScript toolkit. In this tutorial, you'll try out conditional statements to control how a script runs.

NOTE See the note on page 12 for information on how to download the tutorial files.

1. **In a text editor, open the file *conditional.html* in the *chapter03* folder.**

   You'll start by simply prompting the visitor for a number. This file already contains `<script>` tags in both the head and body regions.

2. **Between the first set of \<script\> tags, in the page's** \<head\> **section, type the bolded code shown here:**

```
<script>
var luckyNumber = prompt('What is your lucky number?','');
</script>
```

This line of code opens a JavaScript prompt dialog box, asks a question, and stores whatever the visitor typed into the luckyNumber variable (remember: the = sign stores a value in a variable). Next, you'll add a conditional statement to check what the visitor typed into the prompt dialog box.

3. **Locate the second set of \<script\> tags down in the body of the page, and add the code in bold:**

```
<script>
if (luckyNumber == 7 ) {
</script>
```

Don't forget the double equals signs (==), which compare two values. Here's the beginning of the conditional statement; it simply checks to see if the visitor typed 7.

4. **Press Return twice and type the closing brace, so the code looks like this:**

```
<script>
if (luckyNumber == 7 ) {

}
</script>
```

The closing brace ends the conditional statement. Any JavaScript you add between the two braces will run only if the condition is true.

> **NOTE** As mentioned on page 73, it's a good idea to add the closing brace before writing the code that runs as part of the conditional statement.

5. **Click into the empty line above the closing brace. Hit the space bar twice and type:**

```
document.write("<p>Hey, 7 is my lucky number too!</p>");
```

The two spaces before the code indent the line so you can easily see that this code is part of the conditional statement. The actual JavaScript here should feel familiar by now—it simply writes a message to the page.

6. **Save the file and preview it in a web browser. Type** 7 **when the prompt dialog box appears.**

You should see the message "Hey, 7 is my lucky number too!" below the headline when the page loads. If you don't, go over your code and make sure you typed it correctly (see page 18 for tips on dealing with a broken script). Reload the page, but this time type a different number. This time, nothing appears underneath the headline. You'll add an `else` clause to print another message.

7. **Return to your text editor, and add the bolded text to your page:**

```
<script>
if (luckyNumber == 7 ) {
  document.write("<p>Hey, 7 is my lucky number too!</p>");
} else {
  document.write("<p>The number " + luckyNumber + " is lucky for you!</p>");
}
</script>
```

The `else` clause provides a backup message, so if the visitor doesn't type 7, she'll see a different message that includes her lucky number. To round out this exercise, you'll add an `else if` statement to test more values and provide another message.

FREQUENTLY ASKED QUESTION

Seeing Double <script> Tags

Why do <script> *tags appear in two places—in both the head and body of the page?*

When using the document.write( ) method to add content to a page, you have to place the document.write( ) code in the exact position on the page you want the message to appear—in this case, in the body below the <h1> tag. The first set of script tags appears in the head, because you want the prompt window to appear earlier. If you move the prompt( ) method down in the body (go ahead and try it), you'll see that when the page loads, only a part of the page gets displayed when the prompt appears. Because the JavaScript at that point

runs immediately, before any of the other parts of the pages displays, the web browser has to wait until the visitor fills out the prompt window before it can display the rest of the page. In other words, the page looks weird.

However, by putting the prompt up in the <head> section, the page starts off blank, when the prompt window appears—it just looks a little better. In the next chapter, you'll learn how to add content to any spot on a page without having to use the document.write( ) method. Once you know that technique, you can keep all of your JavaScript code together in one location on the page.

---

8. **Add the two bolded lines below to your script:**

```
<script>
if (luckyNumber == 7 ) {
  document.write("<p>Hey, 7 is my lucky number too!</p>");
} else if (luckyNumber == 13 || luckyNumber == 24) {
  document.write("<p>Wooh. " + luckyNumber + "? That's an unlucky number!<
p>");
} else {
  document.write("<p>The number " + luckyNumber + " is lucky for you!</
p>");
}
</script>
```

At this point, the script first checks to see if 7 is stored in the variable luckyNumber; if luckyNumber holds a value other than 7, then the else if kicks in. This conditional statement is made up of two conditions, luckyNumber == 13 and luckyNumber == 24. The ||, called the logical OR operator, makes the entire conditional statement turn out to be true if either of the conditions are true. So if the visitor types in 13 *or* 24, a "That's an unlucky number" message is printed to the page.

> **NOTE** You add the logical OR operator by typing Shift-\ twice to get ||.

Preview the page in a web browser, and type 13 when the prompt dialog box appears. Press the browser's reload button, and try different numbers as well as letters or other characters. You'll notice that if you type a word or other non-number character, the final else clause kicks in, printing a message like, "The number asdfg is lucky for you!" That doesn't make a lot of sense, so you'll pop up another prompt dialog box if your visitor enters a non-number the first time.

9. **Return to your text editor, and locate the first set of <script> tags in the <head> of the page. Add the bolded code shown below:**

```
<script>
var luckyNumber = prompt('What is your lucky number?','');
luckyNumber = parseInt(luckyNumber, 10);
</script>
```

This line of code runs the value of luckyNumber through a function named parseInt(). This JavaScript command takes a value and tries to convert it to an integer, which is a whole number like -20, 0, 1, 5, or 100. You can learn about this command on page 562, but for now just realize that if the visitor types in text like "ha ha," the parseInt() command won't be able to convert that to a number; instead, the command will provide a special JavaScript value, NaN, which stands for "not a number." You can use that information to pop up another prompt dialog box if a number isn't entered the first time.

10. **Add the bolded code to your script:**

```
<script>
var luckyNumber = prompt('What is your lucky number?','');
luckyNumber = parseInt(luckyNumber);
if (isNaN(luckyNumber)) {
 luckyNumber = prompt('Please, tell me your lucky number.','');
}
</script>
```

Here again, a conditional statement comes in handy. The condition isNaN(luckyNumber) uses another JavaScript command that checks to see if something is a number. Specifically, it checks to see if the value in luckyNumber is *not* a number. If the value isn't a number (for example, the visitor types asklsdkl), a second prompt appears and asks the question again. If the visitor did type a number, the second prompt is skipped.

Save the page and preview it in a web browser again. This time, type a word and click OK when the prompt dialog box appears. You should then see a second prompt. Type a number this time. Of course, this script assumes the visitor made an honest mistake by typing a word the first time, but won't make the same mistake twice. Unfortunately, if the visitor types a word in the second prompt, you end up with the same problem—you'll learn how to fix that in the next section.

NOTE You'll find a completed version of this tutorial in the *chapter03* tutorial folder: *complete_conditional. html.*

Handling Repetitive Tasks with Loops

Sometimes a script needs to repeat the same series of steps over and over again. For example, say you have a web form with 30 text fields. When the user submits the form, you want to make sure that none of the fields are empty. In other words, you need to perform the same set of actions—check to see if a form field is empty—30 times. Computers are good at performing repetitive tasks, so it makes sense that JavaScript includes the tools to quickly do the same thing repeatedly.

In programming-speak, performing the same task over and over is called a *loop*, and because loops are so common in programming, JavaScript offers several different types. All do the same thing, just in slightly different ways.

While Loops

A *while loop* repeats a chunk of code as long as a particular condition is true; in other words, *while* the condition is true. The basic structure of a while loop is this:

```
while (condition) {
  // javascript to repeat
}
```

The first line introduces the while statement. As with a conditional statement, you place a condition between the set of parentheses that follow the keyword while. The condition is any test you'd use in a conditional statement, such as x > 10 or answer == 'yes'. And just like a conditional statement, the JavaScript interpreter runs all of the code that appears between the opening and closing braces *if* the condition is true.

However, unlike a conditional statement, when the JavaScript interpreter reaches the closing brace of a while statement, instead of continuing to the next line of the program, it jumps back to the top of the while statement and tests the condition a second time. If the condition is again true, the interpreter runs the JavaScript between the braces a second time. This process continues until the condition is no longer true; then the program continues to the next statement following the loop (Figure 3-5).

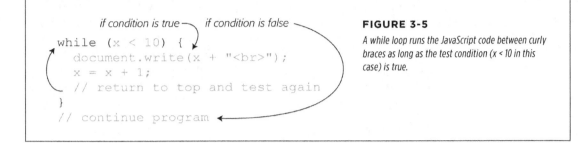

FIGURE 3-5

A while loop runs the JavaScript code between curly braces as long as the test condition (x < 10 in this case) is true.

Say you want to print the numbers 1 to 5 on a page. One possible way to do that is like this:

```
document.write('Number 1 <br>');
document.write('Number 2 <br>');
document.write('Number 3 <br>');
document.write('Number 4 <br>');
document.write('Number 5 <br>');
```

Notice that each line of code is nearly identical—only the number changes from line to line. In this situation, a loop provides a more efficient way to achieve the same goal:

```
var num = 1;
while (num <= 5) {
   document.write('Number ' + num + ' <br>');
   num += 1;
}
```

The first line of code—var num = 1;—isn't part of the while loop: Instead, it sets up a variable to hold the number to be printed to the page. The second line is the start of the loop. It sets up the test condition. As long as the number stored in the variable num is less than or equal to 5, the code between the braces runs. When the test condition is encountered for the first time, the value of num is 1, so the test is true (1 is less than 5), and the *document.write()* command executes, writing "Number 1
" to the page (the <br> is just an HTML line break to make sure each line prints onto a separate line on the web page).

> **NOTE** A more compact way to write num += 1 (which just adds one to the current number stored in the variable num) is like this:
>
>   num++
>
> This shorthand method also adds one to the variable *num* (see Table 2-3 on page 39 for more information.)

The last line of the loop—num += 1—is very important. Not only does it increase the value of num by 1 so the next number (2, for example) will print, but it also makes it possible for the test condition to eventually turn out to be false (if the += operator looks weird, turn back to page 39 for an explanation of how it works). Because the JavaScript code within a while statement repeats as long as the condition is true, you must change one of the elements of the condition so the condition eventually becomes false in order to stop the loop and move onto the next part of the script. If the test condition never turns out to be false, you end up with what's called an *infinite loop*—a program that never ends. Notice what would happen if you left that line out of the loop:

```
var num = 1;
while (num <= 5) { // this is an endless loop
  document.write('Number ' + num + ' <br>');
}
```

The first time through this loop, the test would ask: Is 1 less than or equal to 5? The answer is yes, so document.write() runs. At the end of the loop (the last brace), the JavaScript interpreter goes back to the beginning of the loop and tests the condition again. At this point, num is still 1, so the condition is true again and the document.write() executes. Again, the JavaScript interpreter returns to the beginning of the loop and tests the condition a third time. You can see where this goes: an endless number of lines that say "Number 1."

This simple example also shows some of the flexibility offered by loops. Say, for example, you wanted to write the numbers 1–100, instead of just 1–5. Instead of adding lots of additional lines of document.write() commands, you just alter the test condition like this:

```
var num = 1;
while (num <= 100) {
  document.write('Number ' + num + ' <br>');
  num = num + 1;
}
```

Now the loop will execute 100 times, writing 100 lines to the web page.

Loops and Arrays

You'll find loops come in handy when dealing with a common JavaScript element—an array. As you recall from page 44, an array is a collection of data. You can think of an array as a kind of shopping list. When you go shopping, you actually perform a kind of loop: You walk around the store looking for an item on your list and, when you find it, you put it into your cart; then you look for the next item on your list, put it into the cart, and so on, until you've gone through the entire list. Then you're done (this is the same as exiting the loop) and you can go to the checkout counter (in other words, move to the next step of your "program").

You can use loops in JavaScript to go through items in an array and perform a task on each item. For example, say you're building a program that generates a calendar. The calendar is completely generated using JavaScript, and you want to print the name of each day of the week on the calendar. You might start by storing the names of the days into an array like this:

```
var days = ['Monday', 'Tuesday', 'Wednesday', 'Thursday', ↵
    'Friday', 'Saturday', 'Sunday'];
```

> **NOTE**   The ↵ symbol that appears in the code above indicates that this line of JavaScript code belongs on a single line. The width of this book's pages sometimes prevents a single line of code from fitting on a single printed line, the ↵ symbol is used to indicate code that should appear together on a single line. If you were going to type this code into a text editor, you'd type it as one long line (and leave out the ↵).

You can then loop through each item in the array and print it to the page. Remember that you access one item in an array using the item's index value. For example, the first item in the days array above (Monday) is retrieved with days[0]. The second item is days[1], and so on.

Here's how you can use a while loop to print each item in this array:

```
var counter = 0;
while (counter < days.length) {
  document.write(days[counter] + ', ');
  counter++;
}
```

The first line—var counter = 0—sets up (or *initializes*) a counter variable that's used both as part of the test condition, and as the index for accessing array items. The condition—counter < days.length—just asks if the current value stored in the counter variable is less than the number of items in the array (remember, as described on page 48, the number of items in an array is stored in the array's length property). In this case, the condition checks if the counter is less than 7 (the number of days in the week). If counter is less than 7, then the loop begins: The day of the week is written to the page (followed by a comma and a space), and the counter is incremented by 1 (counter++ is the same as counter += 1, or counter = counter + 1 [see page 39]). After the loop runs, it tries the test again; the loop continues to run until the test turns out to be false. This process is diagrammed in Figure 3-6.

```
var counter = 0;
while (counter < days.length) {
    document.write(days[counter] + ', ');
    counter++;
}
```

FIGURE 3-6

For this loop, the condition is tested 8 times. The last test asks if 7 is less than 7. It isn't, so the while statement is completed, and the JavaScript interpreter skips the loop and continues with the next part of the script. The final result of this script will be "Monday, Tuesday, Wednesday, Thursday, Friday, Saturday, Sunday,." Notice that there's a comma after Sunday as well. To avoid this extra comma, you could use the array object's join() *method; this advanced technique is described on page 582*

counter *value* before test	condition	loop?	days[counter]	counter *value* after counter++
0	0 < 7	yes	days[0]	1
1	1 < 7	yes	days[1]	2
2	2 < 7	yes	days[2]	3
3	3 < 7	yes	days[3]	4
4	4 < 7	yes	days[4]	5
5	5 < 7	yes	days[5]	6
6	6 < 7	yes	days[6]	7
7	7 < 7	no		

For Loops

JavaScript offers another type of loop, called a *for loop*, that's a little more compact (and a little more confusing). For loops are usually used for repeating a series of steps a certain number of times, so they often involve some kind of counter variable, a conditional test, and a way of changing the counter variable. In many cases, a for loop can achieve the same thing as a while loop, with fewer lines of code. For example, here's the while loop shown on page 79:

```
var num = 1;
while (num <= 100) {
    document.write('Number ' + num + ' <br>');
    num += 1;
}
```

You can achieve the same effect using a for loop with only three lines of code:

```
for (var num = 1; num <= 100; num++) {
    document.write('Number ' + num + ' <br>');
}
```

At first, for loops might look a little confusing, but once you figure out the different parts of the for statement, they aren't hard. Each for loop begins with the keyword for, followed by a set of parentheses containing three parts, and a pair of curly braces. As with while loops, the stuff inside curly braces (document.write('Number' + num + '
'); in this example) is the JavaScript code that executes as part of the loop.

Table 3-2 explains the three parts inside the parentheses, but in a nutshell, the parts are: initialize a counter, test a condition, and change the counter. The first part (var num=1;) initializes a counter variable. This step only happens once at the very beginning of the statement. The second part is the condition, which is tested to see if the loop is run; the third part is an action that happens at the end of each loop—it usually changes the value of the counter, so the test condition eventually turns out to be false and the loop ends.

TABLE 3-2 *Understanding the parts of a for loop*

PARTS OF LOOP	WHAT IT MEANS	WHEN IT'S APPLIED
for	Introduces the for loop.	
var num = 1;	Set variable num to 1.	Only once; at the very beginning of the statement.
num <= 100;	Is num less than or equal to 100? If yes, then loop again. If not, then skip loop and continue script.	Before each time through the loop.
num++	Add 1 to variable num. Same as num=num + 1 and num+=1.	At end of each time through loop.

Because for loops provide an easy way to repeat a series of steps a set number of times, they work really well for working through the elements of an array. The while loop in Figure 3-5, which writes each item in an array to the page, can be rewritten using a for loop, like this:

```
var days = ['Monday', 'Tuesday', 'Wednesday', 'Thursday', ↵
    'Friday', 'Saturday', 'Sunday'];
for (var i=0; i<days.length; i++) {
  document.write(days[i] + ', ');
}
```

> **TIP** Seasoned programmers often use a very short name for counter variables in for loops. In the code above, the letter i acts as the name of the counter. A one-letter name (i, j, and z are common) is fast to type; and because the variable isn't used for anything except running the loop, there's no need to provide a more descriptive name like counter.

The examples so far have counted up to a certain number and then stopped the loop, but you can also count backwards. For example, say you want to print the items in an array in reverse order (in other words, the last item in the array prints first). You can do this:

```
var example = ['first','second','third','last'];
for (var j = example.length - 1 ; j >= 0; j--) {
    document.write(example[j] + '<br>');
}
```

In this example, the counter variable j starts with the total number of items in the array minus 1 (4-1=3). (Why minus 1? Because accessing an item in an array is always one less than the item's place in the array: the first item's index is 0, the second's is 1, and the last item is the length of the array minus 1. In other words, to access the last item in this array, you'd type example[3]).

Each time through the loop, you test to see if the value in j is greater than or equal to 0; if it is, the code between the curly braces runs. Then, 1 is subtracted from j (j--), and the test is run again. So this loop moves backwards from the end of the array (the item with an index of 3) to the beginning of the array (the item with an index of 0).

Do/While Loops

There's another, less common type of loop, known as a *do/while loop*. This type of loop works nearly identically to a while loop. Its basic structure looks like this:

```
do {
 // javascript to repeat
} while (condition) ;
```

In this type of loop, the conditional test happens at the *end*, after the loop has run. As a result, the JavaScript code within the curly braces always run *at least once*. Even if the condition isn't ever true, the test isn't performed until after the code runs once.

There aren't too many cases where this comes in handy, but it's very useful when you want to prompt the user for input. The tutorial you did earlier in this chapter (page 74) is a good example. That script asks visitors to type in a number. It includes a bit of a fail-safe system, so if they don't type a number, the script asks them one more time to type a number. Unfortunately, if someone's really stubborn and types something other than a number the second time, a nonsensical message is printed to the page.

However, with a do/while loop, you can continually prompt the visitor for a number until she types one in. To see how this works, you'll edit the page you completed on page 77:

1. **In a text editor, open the *conditional.html* page you completed on page 77.**

   (If you didn't complete that tutorial, you can just open the file *complete_conditional.html*.) You'll replace the code near the top of the page with a do/while loop.

2. **Locate the code between the <script> tags in the <head> of the page, and delete the bolded code shown here:**

   ```
   var luckyNumber = prompt('What is your lucky number?','');
   luckyNumber = parseInt(luckyNumber, 10);
   if (isNaN(luckyNumber)) {
    luckyNumber = prompt('Please, tell me your lucky number.','');
   }
   ```

The code you deleted provided the second prompt dialog box. You won't need that anymore. Instead, you'll wrap the code that's left inside a do/while loop.

3. **Place the cursor before the first line of code (the line that begins with var luckyNumber) and type:**

```
do {
```

This code creates the beginning of the loop. Next, you'll finish the loop and add the test condition.

4. **Click at the end of the last line of JavaScript code in that section and type: } while (isNaN(luckyNumber));. The completed code block should look like this:**

```
do {
  var luckyNumber = prompt('What is your lucky number?','');
  luckyNumber = parseInt(luckyNumber, 10);
} while (isNaN(luckyNumber));
```

Save this file and preview it in a web browser. Try typing text and other non-numeric symbols in the prompt dialog box. That annoying dialog box continues to appear until you actually type a number.

Here's how it works: The do keyword tells the JavaScript interpreter that it's about to enter a do/while loop. The next two lines are then run, so the prompt appears and the visitor's answer is converted to a whole number. It's only at this point that the condition is tested. It's the same condition as the script on page 77: It just checks to see if the input retrieved from the visitor is "not a number." If the input isn't a number, the loop repeats. In other words, the prompt will keep reappearing as long as a non-number is entered. The good thing about this approach is that it guarantees that the prompt appears at least once, so if the visitor does type a number in response to the question, there is no loop.

You can find the completed, functioning tutorial in the file *complete_do-while.html* in the *Chapter03* folder.

Functions: Turn Useful Code Into Reusable Commands

Imagine that at work you've just gotten a new assistant to help you with your every task (time to file this book under "fantasy fiction"). Suppose you got hungry for a slice of pizza, but because the assistant was new to the building and the area, you had to give him detailed directions: "Go out this door, turn right, go to the elevator, take the elevator to the first floor, walk out of the building..." and so on. The assistant follows your directions and brings you a slice. A couple hours later, you're hungry again, and you want more pizza. Now, you don't have to go through the whole set of directions again—"Go out this door, turn right, go to the elevator..." By this time, your assistant knows where the pizza joint is, so you just say, "Get me a slice of pizza," and he goes to the pizza place and returns with a slice.

In other words, you only need to provide detailed directions a *single time*; your assistant memorizes those steps and with the simple phrase "Get me a slice," he instantly leaves and reappears a little while later with a piece of pizza. JavaScript has an equivalent mechanism called a *function*. A function is a series of programming steps that you set up at the beginning of your script—the equivalent of providing detailed directions to your assistant. Those steps aren't actually run when you create the function; instead, they're stored in the web browser's memory, where you can call upon them whenever you need those steps performed.

Functions are invaluable for efficiently performing multiple programming steps repeatedly. For example, say you create a photo gallery web page filled with 50 small thumbnail images. When someone clicks one of the small photos, you might want the page to dim, a caption to appear, and a larger version of that image to fill the screen. Each time someone clicks an image, the process repeats; so on a web page with 50 small photos, your script might have to do the same series of steps 50 times. Fortunately, you don't have to write the same code 50 times to make this photo gallery work. Instead, you can write a function with all the necessary steps, and then, with each click of the thumbnail, you run the function. You write the code once, but you run it any time you like.

The basic structure of a function looks like this:

```
function functionName() {
  // the JavaScript you want to run
}
```

The keyword `function` lets the JavaScript interpreter know you're creating a function—it's similar to how you use `if` to begin an if/else statement or `var` to create a variable. Next, you provide a function name; as with a variable, you get to choose your own function name. Follow the same rules listed on page 30 for naming variables. In addition, it's common to include a verb in a function name like `calculateTax`, `getScreenHeight`, `updatePage`, or `fadeImage`. An active name makes it clear that it does something and makes it easier to distinguish between function and variable names.

Directly following the name, you add a pair of parentheses, which are another characteristic of functions. After the parentheses, there's a space followed by a curly brace, one or more lines of JavaScript and a final, closing curly brace. As with `if` statements, the curly braces mark the beginning and end of the JavaScript code that makes up the function.

> **NOTE** As with if/else statements, functions are more easily read if you indent the JavaScript code between the curly braces. Two spaces (or a tab) at the beginning of each line are common.

Here's a very simple function to print out the current date in a format like "Sun May 12 2008":

```
function printToday() {
  var today = new Date();
  document.write(today.toDateString());
}
```

The function's name is printToday. It has just two lines of JavaScript code that re-trieve the current date, convert the date to a format we can understand (that's the toDateString() part), and then print the results to the page using our old friend the document.write() command. Don't worry about how all of the date stuff works—you'll find out about dates later in this book, on page 568.

Programmers usually put their functions at the beginning of a script, which sets up the various functions that the rest of the script will use later. Remember that a function doesn't run when it's first created—it's like telling your assistant how to get to the pizza place without actually sending him there. The JavaScript code is merely stored in the browser's memory, waiting to be run later, when you need it.

But how do you run a function? In programming-speak, you *call* the function when-ever you want the function to perform its task. Calling the function is just a matter of writing the function's name, followed by a pair of parentheses. For example, to make our printToday function run, you'd simply type:

```
printToday();
```

As you can see, making a function run doesn't take a lot of typing—that's the beauty of functions. Once they're created, you don't have to add much code to get results.

NOTE When calling a function, don't forget the parentheses following the function. That's the part that makes the function run. For example, printToday won't do anything, but printToday() executes the function.

Mini-Tutorial

Because functions are such an important concept, here's a series of steps for you to practice creating and using a function on a real web page:

1. **In a text editor, open the file *print_date.html*.**

   You'll start by adding a function in the head of the document.

2. **Locate the empty line between the <script> tags in the <head> of the page, and type the following code:**

   ```
   function printToday() {
     var today = new Date();
     document.write(today.toDateString());
   }
   ```

   The basic function is in place, but it doesn't do anything yet.

3. **Save the file and preview it in a web browser.**

   Nothing happens. Well, actually something does happen; you just don't see it. The web browser read the function statements into memory, and was waiting for you to actually call the function, which you'll do next.

4. **Return to your text editor and the *print_date.html* file. Locate the <p> tag that begins with "Today is", and between the two <strong> tags, add the following bolded code:**

```
<p>Today is <strong>
<script>
 printToday();
</script>
</strong></p>
```

   Save the page and preview it in a web browser (Figure 3-7). The current date is printed to the page. If you wanted to print the date at the bottom of the web page as well, all you'd need to do is call the function a second time.

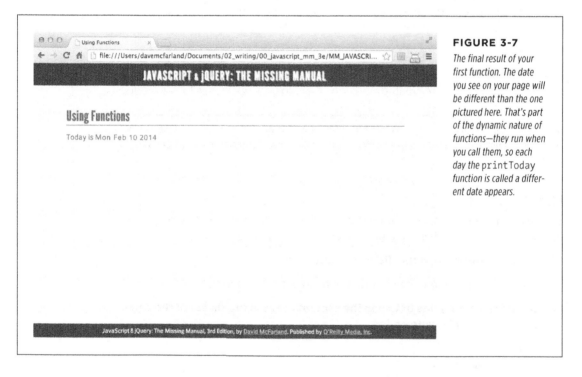

FIGURE 3-7

The final result of your first function. The date you see on your page will be different than the one pictured here. That's part of the dynamic nature of functions—they run when you call them, so each day the printToday *function is called a different date appears.*

Giving Information to Your Functions

Functions are even more useful when they receive information. Think back to your assistant—the fellow who fetches you slices of pizza. The original "function" described on page 85 was simply directions to the pizza parlor and instructions to buy a slice and return to the office. When you wanted some pizza, you "called" the function by telling your assistant "Get me a slice!" Of course, depending on how you're feeling, you might want a slice of pepperoni, cheese, or olive pizza. To make your instructions more flexible, you can tell your assistant what type of slice you'd like. Each time you request some pizza, you can specify a different type.

JavaScript functions can also accept information, called *parameters*, which the function uses to carry out its actions. For example, if you want to create a function that calculates the total cost of a person's shopping cart, then the function needs to know how much each item costs, and how many of each item was ordered.

To start, when you create the function, place the name of a new variable inside the parentheses—this is the *parameter*. The basic structure looks like this:

```
function functionName(parameter) {
  // the JavaScript you want to run
}
```

The parameter is just a variable, so you supply any valid variable name (see page 30 for tips on naming variables). For example, say you want to save a few keystrokes each time you print something to a web page. You create a simple function that lets you replace the web browser's document.write() function with a shorter name:

```
function print(message) {
  document.write(message);
}
```

The name of this function is print and it has one parameter, named message. When this function is called, it receives some information (the message to be printed) and then it uses the document.write() function to write the message to the page. Of course, a function doesn't do anything until it's called, so somewhere else on your web page, you can call the function like this:

```
print('Hello world.');
```

When this code is run, the print function is called and some text—the string 'Hello world.'—is sent to the function, which then prints "Hello world." to the page. Technically, the process of sending information to a function is called "passing an argument." In this example, the text—'Hello world.'—is the *argument*. Arguments are the values you pass to a function, and correspond to the parameters defined when you create the function.

Even with a really simple function like this, the logic of when and how things work can be a little confusing if you're new to programming. Here's how each step breaks down, as shown in the diagram in Figure 3-8:

1. **The function is read by the JavaScript interpreter and stored in memory. This step just prepares the web browser to run the function later.**

2. **The function is called and information—"Hello world."—is passed to the function.**

3. **The information passed to the function is stored in a new variable named** message. **This step is equivalent to** var message = 'Hello world.';.

4. **Finally, the function runs, printing the value stored in the variable** message **to the web page.**

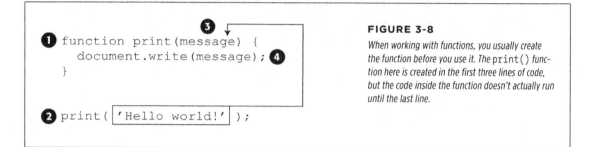

FIGURE 3-8

When working with functions, you usually create the function before you use it. The print() *function here is created in the first three lines of code, but the code inside the function doesn't actually run until the last line.*

A function isn't limited to a single parameter, either. You can pass any number of arguments to a function. You just need to specify each parameter in the function, like this:

```
function functionName(parameter1, parameter2, parameter3) {
  // the JavaScript you want to run
}
```

And then call the function with the same number of arguments in the same order:

```
functionName(argument1, argument2, argument3);
```

In this example, when functionName is called, argument1 is stored in parameter1, argument2 in parameter2, and so on. Expanding on the print function from above, suppose in addition to printing a message to the web page, you want to specify an HTML tag to wrap around the message. This way, you can print the message as a headline or a paragraph. Here's what the new function would look like:

```
function print(message,tag) {
  document.write('<' + tag + '>' + message +'</' + tag + '>');
}
```

The function call would look like this:

```
print('Hello world.', 'p');
```

In this example, you're passing two arguments—'Hello world.' and 'p'—to the function. Those values are stored in the function's two parameters—*message* and *tag*. The result is a new paragraph—<p>Hello world.</p>—printed to the page.

You're not limited to passing just strings to a function either: You can send any type of JavaScript variable or value to a function. For example, you can send an array, a variable, a number, or a Boolean value as an argument.

Retrieving Information from Functions

Sometimes a function simply does something like write a message to a page, move an object across the screen, or validate the form fields on a page. Other times, you'll want to get something back from a function: after all, the "Get me a slice of pizza" function wouldn't be much good if you didn't end up with some tasty pizza at the end. Likewise, a function that calculates the total cost of items in a shopping cart isn't very useful unless the function lets you know the final total.

Some of the built-in JavaScript functions we've already seen return values. For example, the prompt() command (page 42) pops up a dialog box with a text field, and whatever the user types into the box is returned. As you've seen, you can then store that return value into a variable and do something with it:

```
var answer = prompt('What month were you born?', '');
```

The visitor's response to the prompt dialog box is stored in the variable answer; you can then test the value inside that variable using a conditional statement or do any of the many other things JavaScript lets you do with variables.

To return a value from your own functions, you use return followed by the value you wish to return:

```
function functionName(parameter1, parameter2) {
  // the JavaScript you want to run
  return value;
}
```

For example, say you want to calculate the total cost of a sale including sales tax. You might create a script like this:

```
var TAX = .08; // 8% sales tax
function calculateTotal(quantity, price) {
  var total = quantity * price * (1 + TAX);
  var formattedTotal = total.toFixed(2);
  return formattedTotal;
}
```

The first line stores the tax rate into a variable named TAX (which lets you easily change the rate simply by updating this line of code). The next three lines define the function. Don't worry too much about what's happening inside the function—you'll learn more about working with numbers on page 562. The important part is the fourth line of the function—the return statement. It returns the value stored in the variable formattedTotal.

To make use of the return value, you usually store it inside a variable. So in this example, you could call the function like this:

```
var saleTotal = calculateTotal(2, 16.95);
document.write('Total cost is: $' + saleTotal);
```

In this case, the values 2 and 16.95 are passed to the function. The first number represents the number of items purchased, and the second their individual cost. The function determines the total cost plus tax and returns the total: That result is then stored into a new variable—saleTotal—which is then used as part of a document. write() command to print the total cost of the sale including tax.

NOTE The return keyword should be the last statement in a function, because as soon as a browser's JavaScript interpreter encounters the return statement, it exits the function. Any lines of code following the return statement in the function are never executed.

You don't have to store the return value into a variable, however. You can use the return value directly within another statement like this:

```
document.write('Total: $' + calculateTotal(2, 16.95));
```

In this case, the function is called and its return value is added to the string 'Total: $', which is then printed to the document. At first, this way of using a function may be hard to read, so you might want to take the extra step of just storing the function's results into a variable and then using that variable in your script.

NOTE A function can only return one value. If you want to return multiple items, store the results in an array, and return the array. See page 44 for more on arrays.

Keeping Variables from Colliding

One great advantage of functions is that they can cut down the amount of programming you have to do. You'll probably find yourself using a really useful function time and time again on different projects. For example, a function that helps calculate shipping and sales tax could come in handy on every order form you create, so you might copy and paste that function into other scripts on your site or on other projects.

One potential problem arises when you just plop a function down into an already-created script, however. What happens if the script uses the same variable names as the function? Will the function overwrite the variable from the script, or vice versa? For example:

```
var message = 'Outside the function';
function warning(message) {
  alert(message);
}
warning('Inside the function'); // 'Inside the function'
alert(message); // 'Outside the function'
```

Notice that the variable message appears both outside the function (the first line of the script) and as a parameter in the function. A parameter is really just a variable that's filled with data when the function's called. In this case, the function call—warning('Inside the function');—passes a string to the function and the function stores that string in the variable message. It looks like there are now two versions of the variable message. So what happens to the value in the original message variable that's created in the first line of the script?

You might think that the original value stored in message is overwritten with a new value, the string 'Outside the function'; it's not. When you run this script, you'll see two alert dialog boxes: The first will say "Inside the function" and the second "Outside the function." There are actually two variables named message, but they exist in separate places (Figure 3-9).

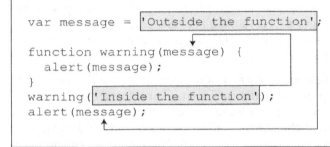

FIGURE 3-9

A function parameter is only visible inside the function, so the first line of this function—function warning(message)—creates a new variable named message that can only be accessed inside the function. Once the function is done, that variable disappears.

The JavaScript interpreter treats variables inside of a function differently than variables declared and created outside of a function. In programming-speak, each function has its own *scope*. A function's scope is like a wall that surrounds the function—variables inside the wall aren't visible to the rest of the script outside the wall. Scope is a pretty confusing concept when you first learn about it, but it's very useful. Because a function has its own scope, you don't have to be afraid that the names you use for parameters in your function will overwrite or conflict with variables used in another part of the script.

So far, the only situation we've discussed is the use of variables as parameters. But what about a variable that's created inside the function, but not as a parameter, like this:

```
var message = 'Outside the function';
function warning() {
  var message ='Inside the function';
  alert( message );
}
warning(); // 'Inside the function'
alert( message ); //'Outside the function'
```

Here, the code creates a message variable twice—in the first line of the script, and again in the first line inside the function. This situation is the same as with parameters—by typing var message inside the function, you've created a new variable inside the function's scope. This type of variable is called a *local variable*, as it's only visible within the walls of the function—the main script and other functions can't see or access this variable.

However, variables created in the main part of a script (outside a function) exist in *global scope*. All functions in a script can access variables that are created in its main body. For example, in the code below, the variable message is created on the first line of the script—it's a *global variable*, and it can be accessed by the function:

```
var message = 'Global variable';
function warning() {
  alert( message );
}
warning(); // 'Global variable'
```

This function doesn't have any parameters and doesn't define a message variable, so when the alert(message) part is run, the function looks for a global variable named message. In this case, that variable exists, so an alert dialog with the text "Global variable" appears.

There's one potential gotcha with local and global variables—a variable only exists within the function's scope if it's a parameter, or if the variable is created inside the function with the var keyword. Figure 3-9 demonstrates this situation. The top chunk of code demonstrates how both a global variable named message and a function's local variable named message can exist side-by-side. The key is the first line inside the function—var message ='Inside the function';. To create a local variable, you must use var to declare the variable inside the function.

Compare that to the code in the bottom half of Figure 3-10. In this case, the function doesn't use the var keyword. Instead, the line of code message='Inside the function'; doesn't create a new local variable; it simply stores a new value inside the global variable message. The result? The function clobbers the global variable, replacing its initial value.

The notion of variable scope is pretty confusing, so the preceding discussion may not make a lot of sense for you right now. But just keep one thing in mind: If the variables you create in your scripts don't seem to be holding the values you expect, you might be running into a scope problem. If that happens, come back and reread this section.

■ Tutorial: A Simple Quiz

Now it's time to bring together the lessons from this chapter and create a complete program. In this tutorial, you'll create a simple quiz system for asking questions and evaluating the quiz taker's performance. First, this section will look at a couple of ways you could solve this problem, and discuss efficient techniques for programming.

As always, the first step is to figure out what exactly the program should do. There are a few things you want the program to accomplish:

- **Ask questions.** If you're going to quiz people, you need a way to ask them questions. At this point, you know one simple way to get feedback on a web page: the prompt() command. In addition, you'll need a list of questions; because arrays are good for storing lists of information, you'll use an array to store your quiz questions.

- **Let the quiz taker know if she's right or wrong.** After you get the answer from the quiz taker, you need to determine if it's the right answer: A conditional statement can take care of that. Then, to let the quiz taker know if she's right or wrong, you can use the alert()command.

- **Print the results of the quiz.** You need a way to track how well the quiz taker's doing—a variable that keeps track of the number of correct responses will work. Then, to announce the final results of the quiz, you can either use the alert() command or the document.write() method.

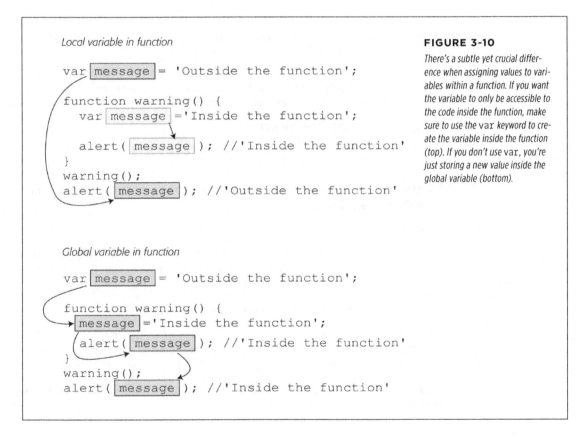

Local variable in function

```
var  message  = 'Outside the function';

function warning() {
   var  message ='Inside the function';

   alert( message ); //'Inside the function'
}
warning();
alert( message ); //'Outside the function'
```

Global variable in function

```
var message = 'Outside the function';

function warning() {
   message ='Inside the function';
   alert( message ); //'Inside the function'
}
warning();
alert( message ); //'Inside the function'
```

FIGURE 3-10

There's a subtle yet crucial difference when assigning values to variables within a function. If you want the variable to only be accessible to the code inside the function, make sure to use the var keyword to create the variable inside the function (top). If you don't use var, you're just storing a new value inside the global variable (bottom).

There are many ways to solve this problem. Some beginning programmers might take a brute-force approach and repeat the same code to ask each question. For example, the JavaScript to ask the first two questions in the quiz might look like this:

```
var answer1=prompt('How many moons does Earth have?','');
if (answer1 == 1 ) {
  alert('Correct!');
} else {
  alert('Sorry. The correct answer is 1');
}
var answer2=prompt('How many moons does Saturn have?','');
if (answer2 == 31) {
  alert('Correct!');
} else {
  alert('Sorry. The correct answer is 31');
}
```

This kind of approach seems logical because the goal of the program is to ask one question after another. However, it's not an efficient way to program. Whenever you see the same steps written multiple times in a program, it's time to consider using a loop or a function instead. We'll create a program that does both: uses a loop to go through each question in the quiz, and a function that performs the question asking tasks:

1. **In a text editor, open the file *quiz.html*.**

   You'll start by setting up a few variables that can track the number of correct answers and the questions for the quiz.

2. **Locate the code between the `<script>` tags in the `<head>` of the page, and type the following code:**

   ```
   var score = 0;
   ```

   This variable stores the number of answers the quiz taker gets right. At the beginning of the quiz, before any questions have been answered, you set the variable to 0. Next, you'll create a list of questions and their answers.

3. **Hit Return to add a new line and type `var questions = [`.**

   You'll be storing all of the questions inside an array, which is really just a variable that can hold multiple items. The code you just typed is the first part of an array statement. You'll be typing the array over multiple lines as described on page 46.

4. **Press Return twice to add two new lines and type `];`. Your code should now look like this:**

   ```
   var score = 0;
   var questions = [

   ];
   ```

The quiz is made up of a bunch of questions, so it makes sense to store each question as one item in an array. Then, when you want to ask the quiz questions, you simply go through each item in the list and ask the question. However, every question also has an answer, so you need a way to keep track of the answers as well.

One solution is to create another array—answers[ ], for example—that holds all of the answers. To ask the first question, look for the first item in the questions array, and to see if the answer is correct, look in the first item of the answers array. However, this has the potential drawback that the two lists might get out of sync: For example, you add a question in the middle of the questions array, but mistakenly put the answer at the beginning of the answers array. At that point, the first item in the questions array no longer matches the first item in the answers array.

A better alternative is to use a *nested array* or (if you really want to sound scary and out-of-this-world) a *multidimensional array.* All this really means is that you create an array that includes the question *and* the answer, and you store that array as one item in the questions array. In other words, you create a list where each item in the list is another list.

5. **Click in the empty line between the [and]; and add the code in bold below:**

   ```
   var questions = [ ['How many moons does Earth have?', 1],
     ];
   ```

   The code ['How many moons does Earth have?', 1] is an array of two items. The first item is a question, and the second item is the answer. This array is the first item in the array *questions*. You don't give this new array a name because it's nested inside another array. The comma at the end of the line marks the end of the first item in the questions array and indicates that another array item will follow.

6. **Hit Return to create a new, empty line and add the following two bolded lines to the script:**

   ```
   var questions = [
     ['How many moons does Earth have?', 1],
     ['How many moons does Saturn have?',31],
     ['How many moons does Venus have?', 0]
     ];
   ```

   These are two more questions for the quiz. Note that after the last item in an array, you *don't* type a comma. Setting up all of your questions in a single array provides for a lot of flexibility. If you want to add another question to the list, just add another nested array containing a new question and answer.

Now that the basic variables for the quiz are set up, it's time to figure out how to ask each question. The questions are stored in an array, and you want to ask each question in the list. As you'll recall from page 80, a loop is a perfect way to go through each item in an array.

7. **Click after the]; (the end of the questions array) and hit Return to create a new, empty line. Then add the following code:**

```
for (var i=0; i<questions.length; i++) {
```

This line is the first part of a *for* loop (page 82). It does three things: First, it creates a new variable named i and stores the number 0 in it. This variable is the counter that keeps track of the number of times through the loop. The second part—i<questions.length—is a condition, as in an if/else statement. It tests to see if the value in i is less than the number of items in the questions array—if that's true, the loop runs again. As soon as i is equal to or greater than the total number of items in the array, the loop is over. Finally, i++ changes the value of i each time through the loop—it adds 1 to the value of i.

Now it's time for the core of the loop—the actual JavaScript that's performed each time through the loop.

8. **Hit Return to create a new, empty line and add the following line of code:**

```
askQuestion(questions[i]);
```

Instead of putting all of the programming code for asking the question in the loop, you'll merely run a function that asks the questions. The function (which you'll create in a moment) is named askQuestion(). Each time through the loop, you'll send one item from the questions array to the function—that's the questions[i] part. Remember that you access an item in an array using an index value, so questions[0] is the first item in the array, questions[1] is the second item, and so on.

By creating a function that asks the questions, you make a more flexible program. You can move and reuse the function to another program if you want. Finally, you'll finish the loop code.

9. **Hit Return to create a new, empty line and type } to indicate the end of the loop. The finished loop code should look like this:**

```
for (var i=0; i<questions.length; i++) {
 askQuestion(questions[i]);
 }
```

Yes, that's all there is to it—just a simple loop that calls a function with every question in the quiz. Now, you'll create the heart of the quiz, the askQuestion() function.

10. **Create an empty line before the for loop you just added.**

In other words, you'll add the function between the two statements that define the basic variables at the beginning of the script and the loop you just added. It's OK to define functions anywhere in your script, but most programmers place functions near the beginning of the program. In many scripts, global vari-ables—like `score` and `questions` in this script—are defined first, so you can see and change those easily; functions appear next, as they usually form the core of most scripts; and finally, the step-by-step actions (like the loop) appear last.

11. **Add the following code:**

```
function askQuestion(question) {

}
```

This code indicates the body of the function—it's always a good idea to type both the beginning and ending curly braces of a function and then add the script within them. That way, you won't accidentally forget to add the closing curly brace.

This function receives a single argument and stores it in a parameter named `question`. Note that this isn't the same as the `questions[]` array you created in step 6. In this case, the `question` variable will actually be filled by one item from the `questions[]` array. As you saw in step 8, one item from that array is actually another array containing two items, the question and the answer.

12. **Add the line in bold below:**

```
function askQuestion(question) {
  var answer = prompt(question[0],'');
}
```

This should look familiar—your old friend the `prompt()` command. The only part that might feel new is `question[0]`. That's how you access the first element in the array `question`. In this example, the function receives one array, which includes a question and answer. For example, the first array will be `['How many moons does Earth have?', 1]`. So `question[0]` accesses the first item—'How many moons does Earth have'—which is passed to the `prompt()` command as the question that will appear in the prompt dialog box.

Your program stores whatever the quiz taker types into the prompt dialog box in the variable `answer`. Next, you'll compare the quiz taker's response with the question's actual answer.

13. **Complete the function by adding the code in bold below:**

```
function askQuestion(question) {
  var answer = prompt(question[0],'');
  if (answer == question[1]) {
   alert('Correct!');
   score++;
  } else {
   alert('Sorry. The correct answer is ' + question[1]);
  }
}
```

This code is just a basic *if/else* statement. The condition—answer == question[1]—checks to see if what the user entered (answer) is the same as the answer, which is stored as the second item in the array (question[1]). If they match, then the quiz taker was right: An alert appears to let her know she got it right, and her score is increased by one (score++). Of course, if she doesn't answer correctly, an alert appears displaying the correct answer.

At this point, the quiz is fully functional. If you save the file and load it into a web browser, you'll be able to take the quiz. However, you haven't yet provided the results to the quiz taker so she can see how many she got correct. You'll add a script in the <body> of the web page to print out the results.

14. **Locate the second pair of <script> tags near the bottom of the web page and type:**

```
var message = 'You got ' + score;
```

Here, you create a new variable and store the string 'You got ' plus the quiz taker's score. So if she got all three right, the variable message would be 'You got 3'. To make the script easier to read, you'll build up a longer message over several lines.

15. **Press Return and type:**

```
message += ' out of ' + questions.length;
```

This adds ' out of ' and the total number of questions to the message string, so at this point, the message will be something like "You got 3 out of 3". Now to finish up the message and print it to the screen.

16. **Add the bolded lines of code to your script:**

```
var message = 'You got ' + score;
message += ' out of ' + questions.length;
message += ' questions correct.';
document.write('<p>' + message + '</p>');
```

Save the page, and open it in a web browser. Take the quiz and see how well you do (Figure 3-11). If the script doesn't work, remember to try some of the troubleshooting techniques mentioned on page 18. You can also compare your script with a completed, functional version in the file *complete_quiz.html*.

Try adding additional questions to the questions[] array at the beginning of the script to make the quiz even longer.

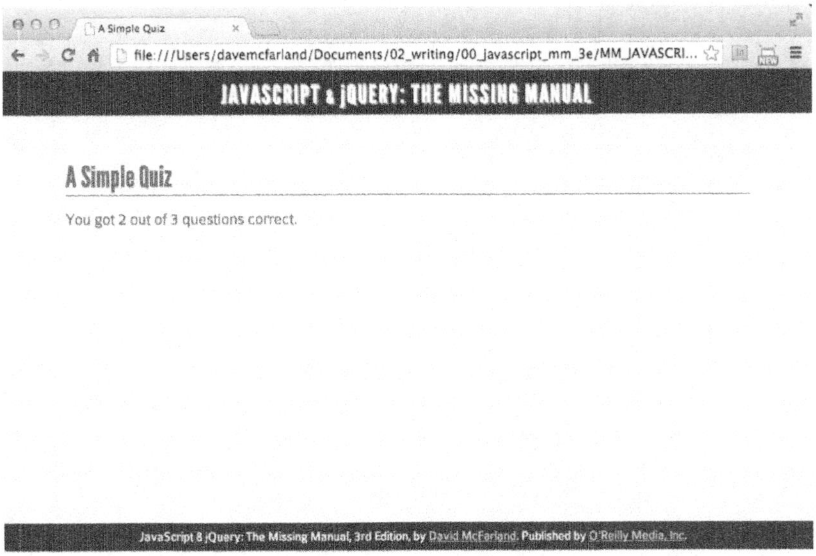

FIGURE 3-11

The results of your simple quiz program. After you learn more about how to manipulate a web page on page 127, respond to events on page 152, and work with web forms on page 251, try to rewrite this quiz program so the questions appear directly within the web page, and the score is dynamically updated after each answer. In other words, you'll soon learn how to ditch that clunky prompt( ) *command.*

Now that you've grasped some of the brain-stretching details of JavaScript, it's time to turn your attention to the real fun. In the next section, you'll learn about jQuery—what it is, how to use it, and, most importantly, how to have a lot of fun and get a lot done with JavaScript programming.

Getting Started with jQuery

Introducing jQuery

The first chapters of this book covered many of the fundamentals of the JavaScript programming language—the keywords, concepts, and syntax of JavaScript. Many of these concepts were fairly straightforward ("a variable is like a box in which you put a value"), but some topics may have had you scratching your head or reaching for a bottle of aspirin (like the for loops discussed on page 78). The truth is, for most people, JavaScript programming is difficult. In fact, a 1,000-page book on JavaScript programming won't cover everything there is to know about JavaScript and how it works in the many different web browsers out in the wild.

Programming is hard. That's why this book covers both JavaScript and jQuery. As you'll see in the first section of this chapter, jQuery is a JavaScript library that lets you jump-start your programming by handling many of the messy details of JavaScript programming for you. jQuery—whose motto is "write less, do more"—makes programming fun, fast, and rewarding. With jQuery, you can achieve in a single line of code what could take dozens (if not more) lines of pure JavaScript programming. After you go through this and the following chapter, you'll be able to achieve more with your web pages than if you studied that 1,000-page book on JavaScript alone.

About JavaScript Libraries

Many JavaScript programs have to deal with the same set of web page tasks again and again: selecting an element, adding new content, hiding and showing content, modifying a tag's attributes, determining the value of form fields, and making programs react to different user interactions. The details of these basic actions can be quite complicated—especially if you want the program to work in all major browsers. Fortunately, JavaScript *libraries* offer a way to leap-frog past many time-consuming programming details.

A JavaScript library is a collection of JavaScript code that provides simple solutions to many of the mundane, day-to-day details of JavaScript. Think of it as a collection of prewritten JavaScript functions that you add to your web page. These functions make it easy to complete common tasks. Often, you can replace many lines of your own JavaScript programming (and the hours required to test them) with a single function from a JavaScript library. There are lots of JavaScript libraries out there, and many of them help create major websites like Yahoo!, Amazon, CNN, Apple, and Twitter.

This book uses the popular jQuery library (*www.jquery.com*). There are other JavaScript libraries (see the box on the page 107), but jQuery has many advantages:

- **Relatively small file size.** A compressed version of the library is only around 96k for version 1.11 and 83k for version 2.1. (If your web server uses "gzip" compression, you can bring the file size down to less than 38k!)

- **Friendly to web designers.** jQuery doesn't assume you're a computer scientist. It takes advantage of CSS knowledge that most web designers already have.

- **It's tried and true.** jQuery is used on millions of sites, including many popular, highly trafficked websites like Pinterest, MSN.com, Amazon, Microsoft.com, Craigslist, and ESPN. In fact, it's used in over 57 percent of sites worldwide (*http://w3techs.com/technologies/details/js-jquery/all/all*). The fact that jQuery is so popular is a testament to how good it is.

- **It's free.** Hey, you can't beat that!

- **Large developer community.** As you read this, scores of people are working on the jQuery project—writing code, fixing bugs, adding new features, and updating the website with documentation and tutorials. A JavaScript library created by a single programmer (or one supplied by a single author) can easily disappear if the programmer (or author) grows tired of the project. jQuery, on the other hand, should be around for a long time, supported by the efforts of programmers around the world. Even big companies like Microsoft and Adobe are pitching in and supplying engineers and programming code. It's like having a bunch of JavaScript programmers working for you for free.

- **Plug-ins, plug-ins, plug-ins.** jQuery lets other programmers create *plug-ins*—add-on JavaScript programs that work in conjunction with jQuery to make certain tasks, effects, or features incredibly easy to add to a web page. In this book, you'll learn about plug-ins that make validating forms, adding drop-down navigation menus, and building interactive slideshows a half-hour's worth of work, instead of a two-week project. There are literally thousands of other plug-ins available for jQuery.

You've actually used jQuery in this book already. In the tutorial for Chapter 1 (page 15), you added just a few lines of JavaScript code to create the header that slid into view from the top of the page.

Other Libraries

jQuery isn't the only JavaScript library in town. There are many, many others. Some are designed to perform specific tasks, and others are all-purpose libraries aimed at solving every JavaScript task under the sun. Here are a few of the most popular:

- **Yahoo! User Interface Library** (*http://yuilibrary.com*) is a Yahoo! project, and indeed the company uses it throughout its site. Programmers are constantly adding to and improving the library, and they provide very good documentation on the YUI site.

- **Dojo Toolkit** (*http://dojotoolkit.org/*) is another library that has been around a long time. It's a very powerful and very large collection of JavaScript files that tackle nearly every JavaScript task around. It's used by lots of big enterprise companies including ADP, IBM, and VMware. But it's complex and aimed at programmers with lots of web application programming experience.

- **Mootools** (*http://mootools.net/*) is another popular library geared toward slick animation and visual effects.

Other libraries aim to provide frameworks for building web applications as well. Ember.js (*http://emberjs.com*), AngularJS (*http://angularjs.org*), and Backbone.js (*http://backbonejs.org*) are popular examples.

Some libraries are small and provide simple but useful utilities for JavaScript programming. Underscore.js (*http://underscorejs.org*), for example, is a very small library that offers a lot of additions to the JavaScript programming language without providing any of the visual effects, AJAX, or HTML-manipulation power of jQuery.

Then there are libraries with very specific purposes, like Raphaël (*http://raphaeljs.com*) whose sole purpose is to make drawing vector images in a browser easier.

In other words, you could swing a bat and hit about 10 different JavaScript libraries. Even so, jQuery is the best place for you to start on your exploration of JavaScript libraries. Then, as your skills increase, you may find a need for the options provided by some of these other libraries.

Getting jQuery

jQuery is simply a bunch of JavaScript code in an external JavaScript file. Like any external JavaScript file (page 15), you need to link it to your web page. However, because jQuery is so popular, you have a few choices when it comes to adding it to a web page: You can either use a version hosted at Google, Microsoft, or jQuery.com (Figure 4-1), or you can download the jQuery file to your own computer and add it to your website.

The first method uses a *CDN* or content distribution network—that is, another website hosts the jQuery file and sends it out to anyone who requests it. There are a couple of benefits to this approach: First, you can save your web server a few milliseconds by letting Google, Microsoft, or jQuery handle distributing the file to your site's visitors. In addition, CDNs have the added benefit of having servers located around the globe. So if someone in Singapore, for example, visits your site, he'll receive the jQuery file from a server that's probably a lot closer to him than your web server, which means he'll get the file faster and your site will appear to run more quickly.

Lastly, and most importantly, because other designers use these CDNs as well, there's a pretty good chance that someone visiting your site already has the jQuery file saved in their browser's cache. Because he's already downloaded the jQuery file from Google while visiting another site, he doesn't need to download it again when visiting your site, resulting in a substantial speed increase.

There are a couple of downsides to using a CDN: First, visitors need to be connected to the Internet for this method to work. That becomes an issue if you need to make sure your site works offline—for example, in a kiosk at a museum or during a programming demonstration in an Internet-free classroom. In that case, you need to download the jQuery file from jQuery.com (you'll learn how below) and add it to your website. Adding your own jQuery file also ensures that your website will continue to work if the CDN servers go down. (Of course, if Google's servers ever go down, then there may be bigger problems in the world than whether your website works.)

FIGURE 4-1

The jQuery.com home page is your jumping-off point for downloading jQuery and learning jQuery's API (a kind of dictionary listing all the functions built into jQuery). The row of icons at the top left of the page take you to jQuery's other projects: jQuery UI (which you'll see in Part Three), jQuery Mobile (for building websites to be viewed on mobile devices), Sizzle (a JavaScript library built into jQuery that makes it easier to select and change parts of a web page), and QUnit (for testing your JavaScript programs).

Linking to the jQuery File on a CDN Server

Microsoft, jQuery, and Google all let you include the jQuery file on one of your web pages using their servers. For example, to link to version 1.11.0 of jQuery using Microsoft's CDN, you would add this line of code in the <head> of your web page (just before the closing </head> tag), like this:

```
<script src="http://ajax.aspnetcdn.com/ajax/jQuery/jquery-1.11.0.min.js">
</script>
```

Using the jQuery CDN, you'd use this code:

```
<script src="http://code.jquery.com/jquery-1.11.0.min.js"></script>
```

And the code using Google's CDN looks like this:

```
<script src="//ajax.googleapis.com/ajax/libs/jquery/1.11.0/jquery.min.js">
</script>
```

You only need to use one of these lines on your page, based on the CDN you prefer to use. The Google CDN seems to be the most popular, so if you're unsure of which to use, use the Google servers.

If you choose to use jQuery 2 (see the box below), just change the `1.11.0` in the above lines to `2.1.0` (or whatever number is the current version of jQuery, which you can find listed at *http://jquery.com/download/*). For example, to use Google's CDN to download version 2.1.0 of jQuery you'd add this line of code:

```
<script src="//ajax.googleapis.com/ajax/libs/jquery/2.1.0/jquery.min.js">
</script>
```

FREQUENTLY ASKED QUESTION

jQuery Version 1 or 2?

There are two versions of jQuery on jQuery.com—1 and 2. Which should I use?

At this writing, jQuery version 1.11 and jQuery 2.1 are functionally the same. The big difference—and the reason the jQuery team released jQuery 2—is that jQuery 2 has stripped out all support for Internet Explorer 6, 7, and 8. Older versions of Internet Explorer often work differently from newer browsers and therefore require extra JavaScript programming to get new features to work. Supporting those browsers requires more code, expanding the size of the jQuery library file.

In the hopes that IE 6, 7, and 8 will one day vanish from the world, the jQuery team created a leaner version of jQuery that removes all support for those browsers. However, IE 6, 7, and 8 are still in use, so jQuery version 1 is still being maintained. In fact, IE8 is still the most commonly used version of Internet

Explorer. Because of that, you'll be using jQuery version 1.11 in this book. It has all the same features as jQuery 2, but still supports older versions of Internet Explorer. Until the audience who visits your site no longer use Internet Explorer 8, you should stick with the latest release of version 1 (version 1.11 as of this writing).

Going forward, any new features that the jQuery team adds to jQuery will only go into the version 2 branch of jQuery. Version 1 will only change to incorporate bug fixes. Rest assured, though, everything you learn in this book will work in both versions. However, if, after reading this book, some fantastic, new, gotta-have-it feature is added to jQuery 2, you may consider switching to that version.

Downloading Your Own jQuery File

You can easily download the jQuery file and add it to your site along with all your other web pages and files. The tutorial files you downloaded for this book as described in the note on page 12 include the jQuery library file, but since the jQuery team updates the library on a regular basis, you can find the latest version at *http://jquery.com/download/.*

To download the latest version of jQuery:

1. **Visit *http://jquery.com/download/.***

   This page has information about the code, a list of the CDNs mentioned above, and previous versions of jQuery.

2. **Select version 1.x or 2.x.**

   This book uses version 1.11, but read the box on page 109 for more information. In a nutshell, if your site needs to work in the still widely used Internet Explorer 8, then use version 1.11.

   The jQuery file comes in two versions on the download site—compressed and uncompressed. The uncompressed file is very large (over 280 k), and is only provided so you can learn more about jQuery by looking at its code. The code includes lots of comments (page 58) that help make clear what the different parts of the file do. (But in order to understand the comments, you need to know *a lot* about JavaScript.)

   You should use the compressed version for your websites. The compressed version is a *minified* file, meaning that it's much smaller than a regular JavaScript file: All JavaScript comments and unnecessary spaces (tabs, line breaks, and so on) are removed, making the file hard-to-read but faster to download.

NOTE You can usually identify a minified JavaScript file by the appearance of *.min* in the filename; for example, *jquery-1.11.0.min.js* indicates that this file contains the minified version of version 1.11.0 of jQuery.

3. **Right-click the link for the compressed file and from the menu that appears, choose Save Link As.**

   If you just click the link, you won't download the file. Instead, the web browser displays all the code in a browser window, so you need to use this "Save as" method.

4. **Navigate to the folder on your computer where you keep your website and save the file.**

   You can save the jQuery file anywhere you want on your site, but many web designers keep their external JavaScript files in a folder that's dedicated to the purpose. Usually the folder has a name like *scripts, libs, js, or _js*.

FREQUENTLY ASKED QUESTION

The jQuery Version Used in This Book

I see that this book uses version 1.11.0 of jQuery, but the current version on the jQuery site is 1.11.x. Is this a problem?

jQuery is always evolving. New bugs are often discovered, and the jQuery team works diligently to fix them. In addition, as new versions of web browsers come out with new capabilities and better support for current standards, the jQuery team updates jQuery to work most efficiently with those browsers. Finally, new features are sometimes added to jQuery to make it more useful for web programmers. For these reasons, it's likely that you can find a newer version of jQuery than the one that's used in this book. If there is a newer version, then by all means use it.

jQuery has matured over the years and its core functionality changes very little. While the jQuery programmers are often tinkering under the hood to make jQuery faster, work better across browsers, and fix bugs, the way you use jQuery doesn't usually change that much. In other words, while programmers might alter a jQuery function to perform better, the way you *use* that function—the function name, the arguments you give it, and the values it returns—don't often change. This means that what you learn in this book will most probably work with a newer version of jQuery, but only faster and better.

This isn't always the case, however. For example, six months after the last edition of this book came out, jQuery 1.9 was released. That version eliminated a jQuery command used in some of the examples in this book, so readers who tried to use the latest version of jQuery found that a couple tutorials no longer worked.

You can often tell how much different one version of jQuery is from another by the numbering scheme. The first number points to a very significant new version, like jQuery version 1 or version 2. (As discussed in the box on page 109, version 2 has the same features as version 1.11 but doesn't support Internet Explorer 8 or earlier.)

Then there are the dot releases—jQuery 1.1, 1.2, 1.3 and so on. Each of those numbers usually offers new functions, rewriting of older functions to work better, and so on. Finally, the last number, like the final 0 in jQuery 1.11.0, usually refers to some sort of bug fix (for jQuery 1.11 in this case). So if you're using version 1.11.0 of jQuery and version 1.11.3 comes out, it's usually a good idea to upgrade, as this will probably include fixes from problems discovered in 1.11.0.

To find out what's changed in a new version, just visit the Download page (*http://jquery.com/download/*)—and look for the link to the Release Notes for the current version. For example, the page *http://blog.jquery.com/2014/01/24/jquery-1-11-and-2-1-released/* discusses the release of versions 1.11.0 and 2.1. The Release Notes list changes made to that version. After reading the list of changes, you can decide for yourself if it seems worthwhile to upgrade. For example, if the changes relate to features you don't use on your site, you can probably skip that upgrade; however, if the changes are bug fixes related to features you do use, it's a good idea to upgrade. If you use jQuery plug-ins on your site, you'll need to be a bit more cautious about upgrading to the latest version of jQuery, unless you're sure the plug-in works with the new version of jQuery.

◼ Adding jQuery to a Page

If you're using one of the CDN versions of jQuery (page 108), you can point to it using one of the code snippets listed on page 109. For example, to use the Google CDN version of jQuery, you'd add <script> tags to the head of the page like this:

```
<script src="//ajax.googleapis.com/ajax/libs/jquery/1.11.0/jquery.min.js">
</script>
```

> **TIP** When using the Google CDN, you can leave off parts of the version number. If you use 1.11 instead of 1.11.0 in the link (`<script src="ajax.googleapis.com/ajax/libs/jquery/1.11/jquery.min.js"></script>`), then Google loads the latest version in the 1.11 family—1.11.2, for example. If jQuery is updated to 1.11.9, then Google loads that version. This technique is smart since (as mentioned in the box on page 111) the minor version changes 1.11.0 to 1.11.2 are often bug fixes that will improve the functioning of your site.

Once you've downloaded jQuery to your computer, you tell the web page you wish to use it on where the browser can find the file. The jQuery file is simply an external *.js* file, so you attach it just like any external JavaScript file, as described on page 15. For example, say you've stored the *jquery.js* file in a folder named *js* in your site's root folder. To attach the file to your home page, you'd add the following script tag to the head of the page:

```
<script src="js/jquery-1.11.0.min.js"></script>
```

Once you've attached the jQuery file, you're ready to add your own scripts that take advantage of jQuery's advanced functions. The next step is to add a second set of <script> tags with a little bit of jQuery programming in it:

```
<script src="js/jquery-1.11.0.min.js"></script>
<script>
$(document).ready(function() {
  // your programming goes here
});
</script>
```

The second set of <script> tags holds any programming you want to add to the particular web page; however, you're probably wondering what that $(document).ready() business is all about. The $(document).ready() function is a built-in jQuery function that waits until the HTML for a page loads before it runs your script.

Why would you want to do that? Because a lot of JavaScript programming is about manipulating the contents of a web page: for example, animating a div, fading an image into view, making a menu drop down when a visitor moves over a link, and so on. To do something fun and interactive with a page element, JavaScript needs to select it. However, JavaScript can't select an HTML tag until the web browser downloads it. A web browser immediately runs any JavaScript it encounters, so the rest of the page doesn't download immediately. (You can see this effect in the quiz tutorial from the last chapter. When you load that quiz, the page is blank. Only after you finish the quiz does the content appear—that's because the JavaScript for the quiz runs first, before the web browser displays the HTML tags.)

In other words, in order to do cool stuff to the HTML on your page, you need to wait until the page loads. That's what the $(document).ready() function does: It waits until the HTML is finished loading and then runs the JavaScript code. If all that seems confusing, just keep in mind that when putting your JavaScript in the page's <head> (before the main HTML loads) you should always do two things: include a .ready() function and put your code inside that function between $(document).ready(function() { and the final });.

In addition, here are a few things to keep in mind:

- The link to the jQuery file must precede any programming that relies on jQuery. In other words, don't put any other script tags before the <script> tag that loads jQuery.

- Put your JavaScript programming *after* any CSS style sheets (both linked, external style sheets and internal style sheets). Because jQuery programming often references styles from a style sheet, you should put your JavaScript programming after the web browser has loaded any styles. A good rule of thumb is to put your JavaScript programming (all your <script> tags) after any other content inside the <head> tag, but before the closing </head> tag.

- Add a JavaScript comment—for example, //end ready—after the }); that marks the end of the ready() function. For example:

```
$(document).ready(function() {
  // your programming goes here
}); // end ready
```

Putting a comment at the end of the function makes it easy to identify the end of the program. As you'll see later, jQuery often requires lots of little collections of this brace, parenthesis, and semicolon trio. By adding a comment after them, it'll be much easier to identify which group of punctuation belongs to which part of your program.

TIP jQuery provides a shortcut method for writing $(document).ready(function() { }:

```
$(function() {
  // your programming goes here
}); // end ready
```

Modifying Web Pages: An Overview

JavaScript gives you the power to change a web page before your very eyes. Using JavaScript, you can add pictures and text, remove content, or change the appearance of an element on a page instantly. In fact, dynamically changing a web page is the hallmark of the all JavaScript-powered websites. For example, Google Maps (*http://maps.google.com*) provides access to a map of the world; when you zoom into the map or scroll across it, the page gets updated without the need to load a new web page. Similarly, when you mouse over a movie title at Netflix (*www.netflix. com*), an information bubble appears on top of the page providing more detail about the movie (see Figure 4-2). In both of these examples, JavaScript is changing the HTML that the web browser originally downloaded.

In this chapter, you'll learn how to alter a web page using JavaScript. You'll add new content, HTML tags and HTML attributes, and also alter content and tags that are already on the page. In other words, you'll use JavaScript to generate new HTML and change the HTML that's already on the page.

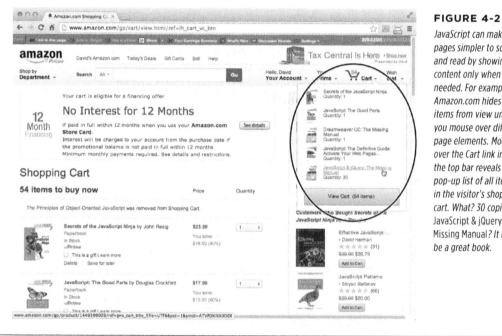

FIGURE 4-2

JavaScript can make web pages simpler to scan and read by showing content only when it's needed. For example, Amazon.com hides some items from view until you mouse over different page elements. Mousing over the Cart link in the top bar reveals a pop-up list of all items in the visitor's shopping cart. What? 30 copies of JavaScript & jQuery: The Missing Manual? It must be a great book.

It may seem hard to believe, but, if you know how to create web pages with HTML and CSS, you already know a lot of what you need to effectively use JavaScript to create interactive websites. For example, the popular Datepicker plug-in for the jQuery UI project makes it easy for visitors to select a date on a form (for instance, as part of a flight or event scheduler). When a visitor clicks into a specially marked text field, a calendar pops up (Figure 4-3). While the effect is really cool, and the calendar makes it especially easy to pick a date, JavaScript provides only the interactivity—the actual calendar is created with the same old HTML and CSS that you're familiar with.

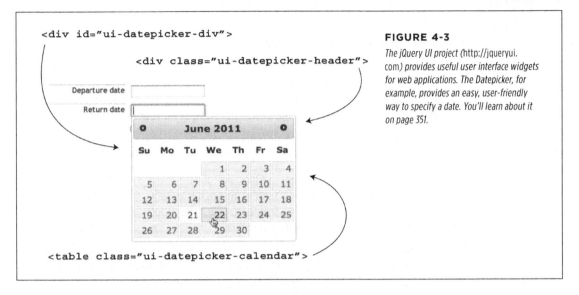

```
<div id="ui-datepicker-div">

              <div class="ui-datepicker-header">
```

Departure date

Return date

○		June 2011				○
Su	Mo	Tu	We	Th	Fr	Sa
			1	2	3	4
5	6	7	8	9	10	11
12	13	14	15	16	17	18
19	20	21	22	23	24	25
26	27	28	29	30		

```
<table class="ui-datepicker-calendar">
```

FIGURE 4-3

The jQuery UI project (http://jqueryui. com) provides useful user interface widgets for web applications. The Datepicker, for example, provides an easy, user-friendly way to specify a date. You'll learn about it on page 351.

If you look under the calendar's hood, you'll find a series of HTML tags such as divs, a table, and <td> tags, with special classes and IDs (ui-datepicker-month, ui-datepicker-div, and so on) applied to them. A style sheet with class and ID styles adds color, typography, and formatting. In other words, you could create this same calendar yourself with HTML and CSS. JavaScript just makes the presentation interactive by making the calendar appear when a visitor clicks on a form field and disappear when the visitor selects a date.

One way of thinking about modern JavaScript programming—especially as it applies to user interface design—is as a way to automate the creation of HTML and the application of CSS. In the Amazon example in Figure 4-2, JavaScript makes the pop-up information appear when a visitor mouses over a button, but the really fun part (the design of that info bubble) is simply a good use of HTML and CSS...stuff you probably already know how to do!

So a lot of what you'll use JavaScript for is manipulating a web page by adding new content, changing the page's HTML, or applying CSS to an element. Whenever you change the content, HTML, or CSS on a page—whether you're adding a navigation bar complete with pop-up menus, creating a JavaScript-driven slide show, or simply making a headline slide into view (as you did in the tutorial in Chapter 1)—you'll perform two main steps:

1. **Select an element on a page.**

   An element is any existing tag, and before you can do anything with that element, you need to *select* it using JavaScript (which you'll learn how to do in this chapter). For example, to make a page fade into view, you first must select the page's content (the `<body>` tag); to make a pop-up menu appear when you mouse over a button, you need to select that button. Even if you simply want to use JavaScript to add text to the bottom of a web page, you need to select a tag to insert the text inside, before, or after.

2. **Do something with the element.**

OK, "do something" isn't a very specific instruction. That's because there's nearly an endless number of things you can *do* with an element to alter the way your web page looks or acts. In fact, most of this book is devoted to teaching you different things to do to page elements. Here are a few examples:

- **Change a property of the element.** When animating a `<div>` across a page, for example, you change that element's position on the page.

- **Add new content.** If, while filling out a web form, a visitor incorrectly fills out a field, it's common to make an error message appear—"Please supply an email address," for example. In this case, you're adding content somewhere in relation to that form field.

- **Remove the element.** In the Amazon.com example pictured in Figure 4-2, the pop-up box disappears when you mouse off the Cart link. In this case, JavaScript is removing that box from the page.

- **Extract information from the element.** Other times, you'll want to know something about the tag you've selected. For example, to validate a text field, you need to select that text field, then find out what text was typed into that field—in other words, you need to get the value of that field.

- **Add/remove a class attribute.** Sometimes you'll want an element on a page to change appearance: the text in a paragraph to turn blue, or the background color of a text field to turn red to indicate an error. While JavaScript can make these visual changes, often the easiest way is to simply apply a class and let a web browser make those visual changes based on a CSS style from a style sheet. To change the text of a paragraph to blue, for example, you can simply create a class style with blue text color, and use JavaScript to apply the class to the paragraph dynamically.

Many times, you'll do several of the things listed above at the same time. For example, say you want to make sure a visitor doesn't forget to type her email address into a form field. If she tries to submit the form without her email address, you can notify her. This task might involve first finding out if she's typed anything into that text field (extracting information from the element), printing an error message (adding new content) if she doesn't, and highlighting that form field (by adding a class to the text field).

Selecting a page element is the first step. To understand how to identify and modify a part of a page using JavaScript, you first need to get to know the Document Object Model.

Understanding the Document Object Model

When a web browser loads an HTML file, it displays the contents of that file on the screen (appropriately styled with CSS, of course). But that's not all the web browser does with the tags, attributes, and contents of the file: It also creates and memorizes a "model" of that page's HTML. In other words, the web browser remembers the HTML tags, their attributes, and the order in which they appear in the file—this representation of the page is called the *Document Object Model,* or DOM for short.

The DOM provides the information JavaScript needs to communicate with the elements on the web page. The DOM also provides the tools necessary to navigate through, change, and add to the HTML on the page. The DOM itself isn't actually JavaScript—it's a standard from the World Wide Web Consortium (W3C) that most browser manufacturers have adopted and added to their browsers. The DOM lets JavaScript communicate with and change a page's HTML.

To see how the DOM works, take a look at this very simple web page:

```
<!DOCTYPE HTML>
<html>
<head>
  <meta charset="UTF-8">
  <title>A web page</title>
</head>
<body class="home">
  <h1 id="header">A headline</h1>
  <p>Some <strong>important</strong> text</p>
</body>
</html>
```

On this and all other websites, some tags wrap around other tags—like the <html> tag, which surrounds all other tags, or the <body> tag, which wraps around the tags and contents that appear in the browser window. You can represent the relationship between tags with a kind of family tree (Figure 4-4). The <html> tag is the "root" of the tree—like the great-great-great granddaddy of all of the other tags on the page—while other tags represent different "branches" of the family tree; for example, the <head> and <body> tags, which each contain their own set of tags.

In addition to HTML tags, web browsers also keep track of the text that appears inside a tag (for example, "A headline" inside the <h1> tag in Figure 4-4), as well as the *attributes* that are assigned to each tag (the class attribute applied to the <body> tag and the ID attribute applied to the <h1> tag in Figure 4-4). In fact, the DOM treats each of these—tags (also called *elements*), attributes, and text—as individual units called *nodes.*

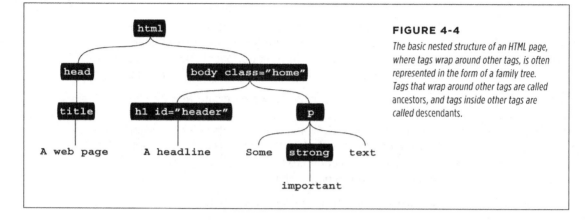

FIGURE 4-4

The basic nested structure of an HTML page, where tags wrap around other tags, is often represented in the form of a family tree. Tags that wrap around other tags are called ancestors, *and tags inside other tags are called* descendants.

JavaScript provides several ways to select elements on a page so you can do something to them—like make them fade out of view or move across the page. The `document.getElementById()` method lets you select an element with a particular ID applied to its HTML. So if you have a `<div>` tag with the ID banner applied to it—`<div id="banner">`—you could select that div like this:

```
document.getElementById('banner');
```

Likewise, the `document.getElementsByTagName()` method selects every instance of a particular tag—`document.getElementsByTagName('a')`, for example, selects all anchor tags (links) on a page; and some browsers support methods for selecting all elements with a particular class or using a CSS selector to select page elements.

More recent browser versions offer a way to select DOM elements based on CSS selectors. For example, the `document.getElementsByClassName( )` retrieves all elements that share a particular class name. To select all elements with a class of author, you could use this code:

```
document.getElementsByClassName('author');
```

A more comprehensive function is the `querySelectorAll( )` method, which lets you use any CSS selector to select page elements. For example, to select only `<span>` tags with the author class, you could write the following:

```
document.querySelectorAll('span.author');
```

As you'll see in the next section, jQuery uses the CSS selector approach to selecting HTML page elements, and does it in a way that supports the most browsers.

◼ Selecting Page Elements: The jQuery Way

jQuery offers a very powerful technique for selecting and working on a collection of elements—CSS selectors. That's right, if you're used to using Cascading Style Sheets to style your web pages, you're ready to use jQuery. A CSS selector is simply the instruction that tells a web browser which tag the style applies to. For example, h1 is a basic element selector, which applies a style to every <h1> tag, while .copyright is a class selector, which styles any tag that has a class attribute of copyright like this:

```
<p class="copyright">Copyright, 2011</p>
```

With jQuery, you select one or more elements using a special command called the *jQuery object*. The basic syntax is like this:

```
$('selector')
```

You can use nearly all CSS 2.1 and many CSS 3 selectors when you create a jQuery object (even if the browser itself doesn't understand the particular selector—like certain CSS3 selectors in older versions of IE). For example, if you want to select a tag with a specific ID of banner in jQuery, you can write this:

```
$('#banner')
```

The #banner is the CSS selector used to style a tag with the ID name banner—the # part indicates that you're identifying an ID. Of course, once you select one or more elements, you'll want to do something with them—and jQuery provides many tools for working with elements. For example, say you want to change the HTML inside an element. You can write the following line:

```
$('#banner').html('<h1>JavaScript was here</h1>');
```

You'll learn more about how to work with page elements using jQuery starting on page 127, and throughout the rest of this book. But first, you need to learn more about using jQuery to select page elements.

Basic Selectors

Basic CSS *selectors* like IDs, classes, and element selectors make up the heart of CSS. They're a great way to select a wide range of elements using jQuery.

Because reading about selectors isn't the best way to gain an understanding of them, this book includes an interactive web page so you can test selectors. In the *testbed* folder of this chapter's tutorial files, you'll find a file named *selectors.html*. Open the file in a web browser. You can test various jQuery selectors by typing them into the selector box and clicking Apply (Figure 4-5).

> **NOTE** See page 12 for information on where to find the tutorial files for this book.

ID SELECTORS

You can select any page element that has an ID applied to it using jQuery and a CSS ID selector. For example, say you have the following HTML in a web page:

```
<p id="message">Special message</p>
```

To select that element using jQuery looks like this:

```
var messagePara = $('#message');
```

You don't just use the ID name ('message'); you have to use the CSS-syntax for defining an ID selector ('#message'). In other words, you include the pound sign before the ID name, just as if creating a CSS style for that ID.

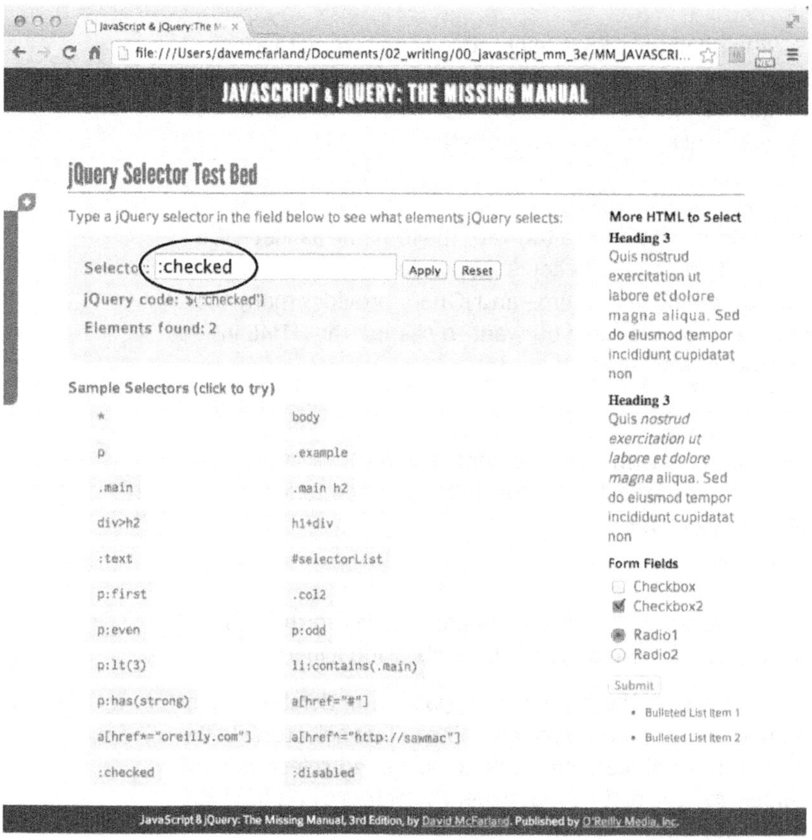

FIGURE 4-5

The selectors.html file, provided with this book's tutorial files, lets you try out jQuery selectors. Type a selector in the Selector form field (circled), and then click Apply. The page converts your selector into a jQuery object, and any elements that match the selector you typed turn red. Below the field is the jQuery code used to select the item, as well as the total number or elements selected. In this case, :checked is the selector, and radio buttons and checkboxes that are selected on the page (you can see two at bottom right) are highlighted in red.

ELEMENT SELECTORS

jQuery also has its own replacement for the getElementsByTagName() method. Just pass the tag's name to jQuery. For example, using the old DOM method to select every <a> tag on the page, you'd write this:

```
var linksList = document.getElementsByTagName('a');
```

With jQuery, you'd write this:

```
var linksList = $('a');
```

> **TIP** jQuery supports an even wider range of selectors than are listed here. Although this book lists many useful ones, you can find a complete list of jQuery selectors at *http://api.jquery.com/category/selectors/*.

CLASS SELECTORS

Another useful way of selecting elements is by class name. For example, suppose you want to create a navigation bar that includes drop-down menus; when a visitor mouses over one of the main navigation buttons, you want a drop-down menu to appear. You need to use JavaScript to control those menus, and you need a way to program each of the main navigation buttons to open a drop-down menu when someone mouses over the button.

> **NOTE** Because finding all elements with a particular class name is such a common task, the latest version of most browsers support a method to do that. But since not all browsers have a built-in way to find elements of a specific class (like IE8 and earlier), a library like jQuery, which takes the different browsers into account, is invaluable.

One technique is to add a class—like navButton—to each of the main navigation bar links, and then use JavaScript to search for links with *just* that class name and apply all of the magical menu-opening power to those links. This scheme may sound confusing, but the important point for now is that to make this navigation bar work, you need a way to select only the links with a specific class name.

Fortunately, jQuery provides an easy method to select all elements with the same class name. Just use a CSS class selector like this:

```
$('.submenu')
```

Again, notice that you write the CSS class selector just like, well, a CSS class selector, with the period before the class name. Once you select those tags, you can manipulate them using jQuery. For example, to hide all tags with the class name of .submenu, you'd write this:

```
$('.submenu').hide();
```

You'll learn more about the jQuery hide() function on page 184, but for now, this example gives you a bit of an idea of how jQuery works.

Understanding CSS

Cascading Style Sheets are a big topic in any discussion of JavaScript. To get the most out of this book, you need to have at least some background in web design and know a bit about CSS and how to use it. CSS is the most important tool a web designer has for creating beautiful websites, so if you don't know much about it, now's the time to learn. Not only will CSS help you use jQuery, but you'll find that you can use JavaScript in combination with CSS to easily add interactive visual effects to a web page.

If you need some help getting up to speed with CSS, there are plenty of resources at your disposal.

For a basic overview on CSS, try the HTML Dog CSS Tutorials (*http://www.htmldog.com/guides/css/*). You'll find basic, intermediate, and advanced tutorials at the site.

You can also pick up a copy of *CSS3: The Missing Manual*, which provides thorough coverage of CSS (including many hands-on tutorials just like the ones in this book).

Most of all, when working with jQuery, it's very important to understand *CSS selectors*—the instructions that tell a web browser which tag a CSS rule applies to. To get a handle on selectors, the resources in this box are very good. There are also a few places to go if you just want a refresher on the different selectors that are available:

- *http://css.maxdesign.com.au/selectutorial/*
- *https://developer.mozilla.org/en-US/docs/Web/Guide/ CSS/Getting_started/Selectors/*

Advanced Selectors

jQuery also lets you use more complicated CSS selectors to accurately pinpoint the tags you wish to select. Don't worry too much about mastering these right now: Once you've read a few more chapters and gained a better understanding of how jQuery works and how to use it to manipulate a web page, you'll probably want to turn back to this section and take another look.

- **Descendant selectors** provide a way to target a tag inside another tag. For example, say you've created an unordered list of links and added an ID name of navBar to the list's <ul> tag like this: <ul id="navBar">. The jQuery expression $('a') selects all <a> tags on the page. However, if you want to select only the links inside the unordered list, you use a descendant selector like this:

    $('#navBar a')

  Again, this syntax is just basic CSS: a selector, followed by a space, followed by another selector. The selector listed last is the target (in this case, a), while each selector to the left represents a tag that wraps around the target.

- **Child selectors** target a tag that's the child of another tag. A child tag is the direct descendant of another tag. For example, in the HTML diagrammed in Figure 4-4, the <h1> and <p> tags are children of the <body> tag, but the <strong> tag is not (because it's wrapped by the <p> tag). You create a child selector by first listing the parent element, followed by a >, and then the child element. For example, to select <p> tags that are the children of the <body> tag, you'd write this:

```
$('body > p')
```

- **Adjacent sibling** selectors let you select a tag that appears directly after another tag. For example, say you have an invisible panel that appears when you click a tab. In your HTML, the tab might be represented by a heading tag (say <h2>), while the hidden panel is a <div> tag that follows the header. To make the <div> tag (the panel) visible, you'll need a way to select it. You can easily do so with jQuery and an adjacent sibling selector:

```
$('h2 + div')
```

To create an adjacent sibling selector, just add a plus sign between two selectors (which can be any type of selector: IDs, classes, or elements). The selector on the right is the one to select, but only if it comes directly after the selector on the left.

- **Attribute selectors** let you select elements based on whether the element has a particular attribute, and even check to make sure the attribute matches a specific value. With an attribute selector, you can find <img> tags that have the alt attribute set, or even match an <img> tag that has a particular alt text value. Or you could find every link tag that points outside your site, and add code to just those links, so they'll open in new windows.

You add the attribute selector after the name of the element whose attribute you're checking. For example, to find <img> tags that have the alt attribute set, you write this:

```
$('img[alt]')
```

There are a handful of different attribute selectors:

- [attribute] selects elements that have the specified attribute assigned in the HTML. For example, $('a[href]') locates all <a> tags that have an href attribute set. Selecting by attribute lets you exclude named anchors—<a name="placeOnPage"></a>—that are simply used as in-page links.

- [attribute="value"] selects elements that have a particular attribute with a specific value. For example, to find all text boxes in a form, you can use this:

```
$('input[type="text"]')
```

Because most form elements share the same tag—<input>—the only way to tell the type of form element is to check its type attribute (selecting form elements is so common that jQuery includes specific selectors just for that purpose, as described on page 253).

- [attribute^="value"] matches elements with an attribute that *begins* with a specific value. For example, if you want to find links that point outside your site, you can use this code:

```
$('a[href^="http://"]')
```

Notice that the entire attribute value doesn't have to match, just the beginning. So href^=http:// matches links that point to *http://www.yahoo.com, http://www.google.com,* and so on. Or you could use this selector to identify mailto: links like this:

```
$('a[href^="mailto:"]')
```

- [attribute$="value"] matches elements whose attribute ends with a specific value, which is great for matching file extensions. For example, with this selector, you can locate links that point to PDF files (maybe to use JavaScript to add a special PDF icon, or dynamically generate a link to Adobe.com so your visitor can download the Acrobat Reader program). The code to select links that point to PDF files looks like this:

```
$('a[href$=".pdf"]')
```

- [attribute*="value"] matches elements whose attribute contains a specific value anywhere in the attribute. For example, you can find any type of link that points to a particular domain. For example, here's how to find a link that points to *http://missingmanuals.com*:

```
$('a[href*="missingmanuals.com"]')
```

This selector provides the flexibility to find not only links that point to *http://www.missingmanuals.com,* but also *http://missingmanuals.com* and *http://www.missingmanuals.com/library.html.*

> **NOTE** jQuery has a set of selectors that are useful when working with forms. They let you select elements such as text fields, password fields, and selected radio buttons. You'll learn about these selectors on page 253.

jQuery Filters

jQuery also provides a way to filter your selections based on certain characteristics. For example, the :even filter lets you select every even element in a collection. In addition, you can find elements that contain particular tags, specific text, elements that are hidden from view, and even elements that do *not* match a particular selector. To use a filter, you add a colon followed by the filter's name after the main selector. For example, to find every even row of a table, write your jQuery selector like this:

```
$('tr:even')
```

This code selects every even <tr> tag. To narrow down the selection, find every even table row in a table with class name of striped. You can do that like this:

```
$('.striped tr:even')
```

Here's how :even and other filters work:

- :even and :odd select every *other* element in a group. These filters work a little counter-intuitively; just remember that a jQuery selection is a list of all elements that match a specified selector. In that respect, they're kind of like arrays (page 44). Each element in a jQuery selection has an index number—remember that index values for arrays always start at 0 (page 47). So, since :even filters on even index values (like 0, 2, and 4), this filter actually returns the first, third, and fifth items (and so on) in the selection—in other words, it's really selecting every other odd element! The :odd filter works the same except it selects every odd index number (1, 3, 5, and so on).

- :first and :last select the first or the last element in a group. For example, if you wanted to select the first paragraph on a web page, you'd type this:

  ```
  $('p:first');
  ```

  And to select the last paragraph on a page, you'd type this:

  ```
  $('p:last');
  ```

- You can use :not() to find elements that *don't* match a particular selector type. For example, say you want to select every <a> tag except ones with a class of navButton. Here's how to do that:

  ```
  $('a:not(.navButton)');
  ```

  You give the :not() function the name of the selector you wish to ignore. In this case, .navButton is a class selector, so this code translates to "does not have the class of .navButton." You can use :not() with any of the jQuery filters and with most jQuery selectors; so, for example, to find every link that doesn't begin with http://, you can write this:

  ```
  $('a:not([href^="http://"])')
  ```

- :has() finds elements that contain another selector. For example, say you want to find all <li> tags, but only if they have an <a> tag inside them. You'd do that like this:

  ```
  $('li:has(a)')
  ```

  This setup is different from a descendant selector because it doesn't select the <a>; it selects <li> tags, but only those <li> tags with a link inside them.

- :contains() finds elements that contain specific text. For example, to find every link that says "Click Me!" you can create a jQuery object like this:

  ```
  $('a:contains(Click Me!)')
  ```

- :hidden locates elements that are hidden, which includes elements that either have the CSS display property set to none (which means you won't see them on the page), elements you hide using jQuery's hide() function (discussed on page 184), elements with width and height values set to 0, and hidden form fields. (This selector doesn't apply to elements whose CSS visibility property is set to invisible.) For example, say you've hidden several <div> tags; you can find them and then make them visible using jQuery, like this:

```
$('div:hidden').show();
```

This line of code has no effect on <div> tags that are currently visible on the page. (You'll learn about jQuery's show() function on page 184.)

• :visible is the opposite of :hidden. It locates elements that are visible on the page.

Understanding jQuery Selections

When you select one or more elements using the jQuery object—for example, $('#navBar a')—you don't end up with a traditional list of DOM nodes, like the ones you get if you use getElementById() or getElementsByTagName(). Instead, you get a special jQuery-only selection of elements. These elements don't understand the traditional DOM methods; so, if you learned about the DOM in another book, you'll find that none of the methods you learned there works with the jQuery object as is. That may seem like a major drawback, but nearly all of the properties and methods of a normal DOM node have jQuery equivalents, so you can do anything the traditional DOM can do—only usually much faster and with fewer lines of code.

There are, however, two big conceptual differences between how the DOM works and how jQuery selections work. jQuery was built to make JavaScript easier and faster to program. One of the goals of the library is to let you do a lot of stuff with as few lines of code as possible. To achieve that, jQuery uses two unusual principles: *automatic loops* and *chaining functions*.

■ AUTOMATIC LOOPS

Normally, when you're using the DOM and you select a bunch of page elements, you then need to create a loop (page 78) to go through each selected node and then do something to that node. For example, if you want to select all the images in a page and then hide them—something you might do if you want to create a JavaScript-driven slideshow—you must first select the images and then create a loop to go through the list of images.

Because looping through a collection of elements is so common, jQuery functions have that feature built right in. In other words, when you apply a jQuery function to a selection of elements, you don't need to create a loop yourself, since the function does it automatically.

For example, to select all images inside a <div> tag with an ID of slideshow and then hide those images, you write this in jQuery:

```
$('#slideshow img').hide();
```

The list of elements created with $('#slideshow img') might include 50 images. The hide() function automatically loops through the list, hiding each image individually.

This setup is so convenient (imagine the number of `for` loops you won't have to write) that it's surprising that this great feature isn't just part of JavaScript.

■ CHAINING FUNCTIONS

Sometimes you'll want to perform several operations on a selection of elements. For example, say you want to set the width and height of a `<div>` tag (with an ID of popUp) using JavaScript. Normally, you'd have to write at least two lines of code. But jQuery lets you do it with a single line:

```
$('#popUp').width(300).height(300);
```

jQuery uses a useful principle called *chaining*, which lets you add functions one after the other. Each function is connected to the next by a period, and operates on the same jQuery collection of elements as the previous function. So the code above changes the width of the element with the ID popUp, *and* changes the height of the element. Chaining jQuery functions lets you concisely carry out a large number of actions. For example, say you not only want to set the width and height of the `<div>` tag, but also want to add text inside the `<div>` and make it fade into view (assuming it's not currently visible on the page). You can do so very succinctly like this:

```
$('#popUp').width(300).height(300).text('Hi!').fadeIn(1000);
```

This code applies four jQuery functions—`width()`, `height()`, `text()`, and `fadeIn()`—to the tag with an ID name of popUp.

> **NOTE** A long line of chained jQuery functions can be hard to read, so some programmers break it up over multiple lines like this:
>
> ```
> $('#popUp').width(300)
>            .height(300)
>            .text('Message')
>            .fadeIn(1000);
> ```
>
> As long as you only add a semicolon on the *last line* of the chain, the JavaScript interpreter treats the lines as a single statement.

The ability to chain functions is built into jQuery. Chaining is not a regular part of JavaScript, so you can't just add non-jQuery functions (either ones you create or built-in JavaScript functions) in the chain, without some specific programming on your part.

■ Adding Content to a Page

jQuery provides many functions for manipulating elements and content on a page, from simply replacing HTML, to precisely positioning new HTML in relation to a selected element, to completely removing tags and content from the page.

NOTE An example file, *content_functions.html*, located in the *testbed* tutorial folder, lets you take each of these jQuery functions for a test drive. Just open the file in a web browser, type some text in the text box, and then click any of the boxes to see how each function works.

To study the following examples of these functions, assume you have a page with the following HTML:

```
<div id="container">
  <div id="errors">
    <h2>Errors:</h2>
  </div>
</div>
```

Here are the five most useful jQuery functions for manipulating content on a page:

- `.html()` can both read the current HTML inside an element and replace the current contents with some other HTML. You use the `html()` function in conjunction with a jQuery selection.

  To retrieve the HTML currently inside the selection, just add `.html()` after the jQuery selection. For example, you can run the following command using the HTML snippet at the beginning of this section:

  ```
  alert($('#errors').html());
  ```

  This code creates an alert box with the text `"<h2>Errors:</h2>"` in it. When you use the `html()` function in this way, you can make a copy of the HTML inside a specific element and paste it into another element on a page.

  If you supply a string as an argument to `.html()`, you replace the current contents inside the selection:

  ```
  $('#errors').html('<p>There are four errors in this form</p>');
  ```

  This line of code replaces all of the HTML inside an element with an ID of `errors`. It would change the example HTML snippet to:

  ```
  <div id="container">
    <div id="errors">
      <p>There are four errors in this form</p>
    </div>
  </div>
  ```

  Notice that it replaces the `<h2>` tag that was previously there. You can avoid replacing that HTML using other functions listed below.

NOTE If you use the `html()` or `text()` functions to retrieve the HTML or text from a jQuery selection containing multiple elements, only the HTML or text from the *first* element in the selection is retrieved. For example, if you had a page with 10 div tags on it and you ran this code—`var divContents = $('div').html();`—only the HTML from the first div on the page would be stored in the `divContents` variable.

However, when using `html()` or `text()` to insert HTML or text into a jQuery selection, *all* selected elements will be affected by the insertion. For example, this code—`$('div').html('<p>Hello</p>');`—will replace the HTML in every div on the page with a single paragraph and the word "Hello."

- `.text()` works like `.html()` but it doesn't accept HTML tags. It's useful when you want to replace the text within a tag. For example, in the code at the beginning of this section, you'll see an `<h2>` tag with the text "Errors:" in it. Say, after running a program to check to see if there were any errors in the form, you wanted to replace the text "Errors:" with "No errors found", you could use this code:

  ```
  $('#errors h2').text('No errors found');
  ```

  The `<h2>` tag stays in place; only the text inside changes. jQuery encodes any HTML tags that you pass to the `text()` function, so `<p>` is translated to `&lt;p&gt;`. This fact can come in handy if you want you to actually display the brackets and tag names *on* the page. For example, you can use it to display example HTML code for other people to view.

- `.append()` adds HTML as the last child element of the selected element. For example, say you select a `<div>` tag, but instead of replacing the contents of the `<div>`, you just want to add some HTML before the closing `</div>` tag. The `.append()` function is a great way to add an item to the end of a bulleted (`<ul>`) or numbered (`<ol>`) list. As an example, say you run the following code on a page with the HTML listed at the beginning of this section:

  ```
  $('#errors').append('<p>There are four errors in this form</p>');
  ```

  After this function runs, you end up with HTML like this:

  ```
  <div id="container">
    <div id="errors">
      <h2>Errors:</h2>
      <p>There are four errors in this form</p>
    </div>
  </div>
  ```

  Notice that the original HTML inside the `<div>` remains the same, and the new chunk of HTML is added after it.

- `.prepend()` is just like `.append()`, but adds HTML directly *after* the opening tag for the selection. For example, say you run the following code on the same HTML listed previously:

  ```
  $('#errors').prepend('<p>There are four errors in this form</p>');
  ```

  After this `prepend()` function, you end up with the following HTML:

```
<div id="container">
  <div id="errors">
    <p>There are four errors in this form</p>
    <h2>Errors:</h2>
  </div>
</div>
```

Now the newly added content appears directly after the <div>'s opening tag.

- If you want to add HTML just *outside* of a selection, either before the selected element's opening tag or directly after the element's closing tag, use the .before() or .after() functions. For example, it's common practice to check a text field in a form to make sure that the field isn't empty when your visitor submits the form. Assume that the HTML for the field looks like the following before the form is submitted:

```
<input type="text" name="userName" id="userName">
```

Now suppose that when the visitor submits the form, this field is empty. You can write a program that checks the field and then adds an error message after the field. To add the message after this field (don't worry right now about how you actually check that the contents of form fields are correct—you'll find out on page 273), you can use the .after() function like this:

```
$('#userName').after('<span class="error">User name required</span>');
```

That line of code makes the web page show the error message, and the HTML component would look like this:

```
<input type="text" name="userName" id="userName">
<span class="error">User name required</span>
```

The .before() function simply puts the new content before the selected element. So this line of code:

```
$('#userName').before('<span class="error">User name required</span>');
```

would generate this HTML:

```
<span class="error">User name required</span>
<input type="text" name="userName" id="userName">
```

NOTE The functions listed in this section—html(), text(), and so on—are the most popular ways of adding and altering content on a page but they're not the only ones. You can find more functions at *http://api. jquery.com/category/manipulation/*.

Replacing and Removing Selections

At times you may want to completely replace or remove a selected element. For example, say you've created a pop-up dialog box using JavaScript (not the old-fashioned alert() method, but a more professional-looking dialog box that's actually just an absolutely positioned <div> floating on top of the page). When the visitor clicks the "Close" button on the dialog box, you naturally want to remove the dialog box from the page. To do so, you can use the jQuery remove() function. Say the pop-up dialog box had an ID of popup; you can use the following code to delete it:

```
$('#popup').remove();
```

The .remove() function isn't limited to just a single element. Say you want to remove all <span> tags that have a class of error; you can do this:

```
$('span.error').remove();
```

You can also completely replace a selection with new content. For example, suppose you have a page with photos of the products your company sells. When a visitor clicks on an image of a product, it's added to a shopping cart. You might want to replace the <img> tag with some text when the image is clicked ("Added to cart," for example). You'll learn how to make particular elements react to events (like an image being clicked) in the next chapter, but for now just assume there's an <img> tag with an ID of product101 that you wish to replace with text. Here's how you do that with jQuery:

```
$('#product101').replaceWith('<p>Added to cart</p>');
```

This code removes the <img> tag from the page and replaces it with a <p> tag.

NOTE jQuery also includes a function named clone() that lets you make a copy of a selected element. You'll see this function in action in the tutorial on page 145.

Setting and Reading Tag Attributes

Adding, removing, and changing elements isn't the only thing jQuery is good at, and it's not the only thing you'll want to do with a selection of elements. You'll often want to change the value of an element's attribute—add a class to a tag, for example, or change a CSS property of an element. You can also get the value of an attribute—for instance, what URL does a particular link point to?

Classes

Cascading Style Sheets are a very powerful technology, letting you add all sorts of sophisticated visual formatting to your HTML. One CSS rule can add a colorful background to a page, while another rule might completely hide an element from view. You can create some really advanced visual effects simply by using JavaScript to remove, add, or change a class applied to an element. Because web browsers process and implement CSS instructions very quickly and efficiently, simply adding a class to a tag can completely change that tag's appearance—even make it disappear from the page.

Skip View Source

One problem with using JavaScript to manipulate the DOM by adding, changing, deleting, and rearranging HTML code is that it's hard to figure out what the HTML of a page looks like when JavaScript is finished. For example, the View Source command available in every browser only shows the web page file as it was downloaded from the web server. In other words, you see the HTML *before* it was changed by JavaScript, which can make it very hard to figure out whether the JavaScript you're writing is really producing the HTML you're after. For example, if you could see what the HTML of your page looks like after your JavaScript adds 10 error messages to a form page, or after your JavaScript program creates an elaborate pop-up dialog box complete with text and form fields, it would be a lot easier to see if you're ending up with the HTML you want.

Fortunately, all major browsers offer a set of developer tools that let you view the *rendered HTML*—the HTML that the browser displays after JavaScript has done its magic. Usually, the tools appear as a pane at the bottom of the browser window, below the web page. Different tabs let you access JavaScript code, HTML, CSS, and other useful resources. The exact name of the tab and method for turning on the tools panel varies from browser to browser:

- In Chrome, select View→Developer→Developer Tools and click the Elements tab in the panel at the bottom of the browser window.

- In Firefox, choose Tools→Developer→Inspector. This opens a panel at the bottom of the browser window showing the JavaScript-affected (or is that infected?) HTML.

- In Internet Explorer, press F12 to open the Developer Tools panel, then click the HTML tab to see the page's HTML. In the case of IE, the HTML tab starts by showing the downloaded HTML (the same as the View Source command). But if you click the refresh icon (or press F5), the HTML tab shows the rendered HTML complete with any JavaScript-created changes.

- In Safari, make sure the Developer menu is on (choose Safari→Preferences, click the Advanced button, and make sure the "Show Develop menu in menu bar" is checked). Then open the page you're interested in looking at, and choose Develop→Show Web Inspector. Click the Elements tab in the panel that appears at the bottom of the browser window.

- In Opera, choose Tools→Advanced→Opera Dragonfly. (Dragonfly is the name of Opera's built-in set of developer tools.) In the panel that appears at the bottom of the browser window, click the Documents tab.

jQuery provides several functions for manipulating a tag's class attribute:

- addClass() adds a specified class to an element. You add the addClass() after a jQuery selection and pass the function a string, which represents the class name you wish to add. For example, to add the class externalLink to all links pointing outside your site, you can use this code:

```
$('a[href^="http://"]').addClass('externalLink');
```

This code would take HTML like this:

```
<a href="http://www.oreilly.com/">
```

And change it to the following:

```
<a href="http://www.oreilly.com/" class="externalLink">
```

For this function to be of any use, you'll need to create a CSS class style before-hand and add it to the page's style sheet. Then, when the JavaScript adds the class name, the web browser can apply the style properties from the previously defined CSS rule.

NOTE When using the addClass() and removeClass() functions, you only supply the class name—leave out the period you normally use when creating a class selector. For example, addClass('externalLink') is correct, but addClass('.externalLink') is wrong.

This jQuery function also takes care of issues that arise when a tag already has a class applied to it—the addClass() function doesn't eliminate the old classes already applied to the tag; the function just adds the new class as well.

NOTE Adding multiple class names to a single tag is perfectly valid and frequently very helpful. Check out *www.cvwdesign.com/txp/article/177/use-more-than-one-css-class* for more information on this technique.

- removeClass() is the opposite of addClass(). It removes the specified class from the selected elements. For example, if you wanted to remove a class named highlight from a <div> with an ID of alertBox, you'd do this:

```
$('#alertBox').removeClass('highlight');
```

- Finally, you may want to *toggle* a particular class—meaning add the class if it doesn't already exist, or remove the class if it does. Toggling is a popular way to show an element in either an on or off state. For example, when you click a radio button, it's checked (on); click it again, and the checkmark disappears (off).

Say you have a button on a web page that, when clicked, changes the <body> tag's class. By so doing, you can add a complete stylistic change to a web page by crafting a second set of styles using descendant selectors. When the button is clicked again, you want the class removed from the <body> tag, so the page reverts back to its previous appearance. For this example, assume the button the visitor clicks to change the page's style has an ID of changeStyle and you want to toggle the class name altStyle off and on with each click of the button. Here's the code to do that:

```
$('#changeStyle').click(function() {
  $('body').toggleClass('altStyle');
});
```

At this point, don't worry about the first and third lines of code above; those have to do with events that let scripts react to actions—like clicking the button—that happen on a page. You'll learn about events in the next chapter. The bolded line of code demonstrates the toggleClass() function; it either adds or removes the class altStyle with each click of the button.

Reading and Changing CSS Properties

jQuery's css() function also lets you directly change CSS properties of an element, so instead of simply applying a class style to an element, you can immediately add a border or background color, or set a width or positioning property. You can use the css() function in three ways: to find the current value for an element's CSS property, to set a single CSS property on an element, or to set multiple CSS properties at once.

To determine the current value of a CSS property, pass the name of the property to the css() function. For example, say you want to find the background color of a <div> tag with an ID of main:

```
var bgColor = $('#main').css('background-color');
```

After this code runs, the variable bgColor will contain a string with the element's background color value.

> **NOTE** jQuery may not always return CSS values the way you expect. In the case of colors (like the CSS background color, or color properties), jQuery always returns either an rgb value like rgb(255, 0, 10) or, if there is any transparency in the color, an rgba color value like rgba(255,10,10,.5). jQuery returns RGB values regardless of whether the color in the style sheet was defined using hexadecimal notation (#F4477A), RGB using percentages (rgb(100%,10%,0%), or HSL (hsl(72,100%,50%). In addition, jQuery translates all unit values to pixels, so even if you use CSS to set the <body> tag's font-size to 150%, jQuery returns a pixel value when checking the font-size property.

The css() function also lets you set a CSS property for an element. To use the function this way, you supply two arguments to the function: the CSS property name and a value. For example, to change the font size for the <body> tag to 200%, you can do this:

```
$('body').css('font-size', '200%');
```

The second argument you supply can be a string value, like '200%', or a numeric value, which jQuery translates to pixels. For example, to change the padding inside all of the tags with a class of .pullquote to 100 pixels, you can write this code:

```
$('.pullquote').css('padding',100);
```

In this example, jQuery sets the padding property to 100 pixels.

> **NOTE** When you set a CSS property using jQuery's .css() function, you can use the CSS shorthand method. For example, here's how you could add a black, one-pixel border around all paragraphs with a class of highlight:
>
> ```
> $('p.highlight').css('border', '1px solid black');
> ```

It's often useful to change a CSS property based on its current value. For example, say you want to add a "Make text bigger" button on a web page, so when a visitor clicks the button, the page's font-size value doubles. To make that happen, you read the value, and then set a new value. In this case, you first determine the current font-size and then set the font-size to twice that value. It's a little trickier than you might think. Here's the code, and a full explanation follows:

```
var baseFont = $('body').css('font-size');
baseFont = parseInt(baseFont);
$('body').css('font-size',baseFont * 2);
```

The first line retrieves the <body> tag's font-size value—the returned value is in pixels and is a string like this: '16px'. Because you want to double that size—multiplying it by 2—you must convert that string to a number by removing the "px" part of the string. The second line accomplishes that using the JavaScript parseInt() method discussed on page 562. That function essentially strips off anything following the number, so after line 2, baseFont contains a number, like 16. Finally, the third line resets the font-size property by multiplying the baseFont value by 2.

NOTE This code affects the page's type size only if the other tags on the page—paragraphs, headlines, and so on—have their font-size set using a relative value like ems or percentages. If the other tags use absolute values like pixels, changing the <body> tag's font size won't affect them.

Changing Multiple CSS Properties at Once

If you want to change more than one CSS property on an element, you don't need to resort to multiple uses of the .css() function. For example, if you want to dynamically highlight a <div> tag (perhaps in reaction to an action taken by a visitor), you can change the <div> tag's background color *and* add a border around it, like this:

```
$('#highlightedDiv').css('background-color','#FF0000');
$('#highlightedDiv').css('border','2px solid #FE0037');
```

Another way is to pass what's called an *object literal* to the .css() function. Think of an object literal as a list containing pairs of property names and values. After each property name, you insert a colon (:) followed by a value; each name/value pair is separated by a comma, and the whole shebang is surrounded by braces ({}). Thus, an object literal for the two CSS property values above looks like this:

```
{ 'background-color' : '#FF0000', 'border' : '2px solid #FE0037' }
```

Because an object literal can be difficult to read if it's crammed onto a single line, many programmers break it up over multiple lines. The following is functionally the same as the previous one-liner:

```
{
  'background-color' : '#FF0000',
  'border' : '2px solid #FE0037'
}
```

The basic structure of an object literal is diagrammed in Figure 4-6.

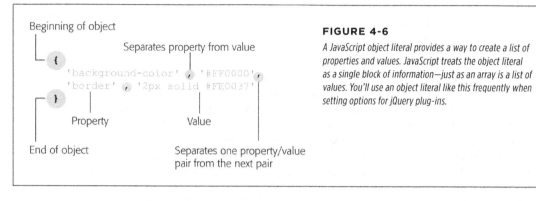

Beginning of object

Separates property from value

Property

Value

End of object

Separates one property/value
pair from the next pair

FIGURE 4-6

A JavaScript object literal provides a way to create a list of properties and values. JavaScript treats the object literal as a single block of information—just as an array is a list of values. You'll use an object literal like this frequently when setting options for jQuery plug-ins.

To use an object literal with the css() function, just pass the object to the function like this:

```
$('#highlightedDiv').css({
    'background-color' : '#FF0000',
    'border' : '2px solid #FE0037'
});
```

Study this example closely, because it looks a little different from what you've seen so far, and because you'll be encountering lots of code that looks like it in future chapters. The first thing to notice is that this code is merely a single JavaScript statement (essentially just one line of code)—you can tell because the semicolon that ends the statement doesn't appear until the last line. The statement is broken over four lines to make the code easier to read.

Next, notice that the object literal is an argument (like one piece of data) that's passed to the css() function. So in the code css({, the opening parenthesis is part of the function, while the opening { marks the beginning of the object. The three characters in the last line break down like this: } is the end of the object literal and the end of the argument passed to the function;) marks the end of the function, the last parenthesis in css(); and ; marks the end of the JavaScript statement.

And if all this object literal stuff is hurting your head, you're free to change CSS properties one line at a time, like this:

```
$('#highlightedDiv').css('background-color','#FF0000');
$('#highlightedDiv').css('border','2px solid #FE0037');
```

Or, a better method is to use jQuery's built-in chaining ability (page 127). Chaining is applying several jQuery functions to a single collection of elements by adding that function to the end of another function, like this:

```
$('#highlightedDiv').css('background-color','#FF0000')
                    .css('border','2px solid #FE0037');
```

This code can be translated as: find an element with an ID of highlightedDiv and change its background color, then change its border color. Chaining provides better performance than making the selection–$('#highlightedDiv')—twice as in the code above, because each time you make a selection you make the web browser run all of the jQuery code for selecting the element. Thus, this code is not optimal:

```
$('#highlightedDiv').css('background-color','#FF0000');
$('#highlightedDiv').css('border','2px solid #FE0037');
```

This code forces the browser to select the element, change its CSS, select the element a second time (wasting processor time), and apply CSS again. Using the chaining method, the browser only needs to select the element a single time and then run the CSS function twice; selecting the element once is faster and more efficient.

Reading, Setting, and Removing HTML Attributes

Because changing classes and CSS properties using JavaScript are such common tasks, jQuery has built-in functions for them. But the addClass() and css() functions are really just shortcuts for changing the HTML class and style attributes. jQuery includes general-purpose functions for handling HTML attributes—the attr() and removeAttr() functions.

The attr() function lets you read a specified HTML attribute from a tag. For example, to determine the current graphic file a particular <img> points to, you pass the string 'src' (for the <img> tag's src property) to the function:

```
var imageFile = $('#banner img').attr('src');
```

The attr() function returns the attribute's value as it's set in the HTML. This code returns the src property for the first <img> tag inside another tag with an ID of banner, so the variable imageFile would contain the path set in the page's HTML: for instance, 'images/banner.png' or 'http://www.thesite.com/images/banner.png'.

> **NOTE** When passing an attribute name to the .attr() function, you don't need to worry about the case of the attribute name—href, HREF, or even HrEf will work.

If you pass a second argument to the attr() function, you can set the tag's attribute. For example, to swap in a different image, you can change an <img> tag's src property like this:

```
$('#banner img').attr('src','images/newImage.png');
```

If you want to completely remove an attribute from a tag, use the removeAttr() function. For example, this code removes the bgColor property from the <body> tag:

```
$('body').removeAttr('bgColor');
```

■ Acting on Each Element in a Selection

As discussed on page 126, one of the unique qualities of jQuery is that most of its functions automatically loop through each item in a jQuery selection. For example, to make every `<img>` on a page fade out, you only need one line of JavaScript code:

```
$('img').fadeOut();
```

The `.fadeOut()` function causes an element to disappear slowly, and when attached to a jQuery selection containing multiple elements, the function loops through the selection and fades out each element. There are plenty of times when you'll want to loop through a selection of elements and perform a series of actions on each element. jQuery provides the `.each()` function for just this purpose.

For example, say you want to list of all of the external links on your page in a bibliography box at the bottom of the page, perhaps titled "Other Sites Mentioned in This Article." (OK, you may not ever want to do that, but just play along.) Anyway, you can create that box by:

1. **Retrieving all links that point outside your site.**

2. **Getting the HREF attribute of each link (the URL).**

3. **Adding that URL to the other list of links in the bibliography box.**

jQuery doesn't have a built-in function that performs these exact steps, but you can use the each() function to do it yourself. It's just a jQuery function, so you slap it on at the end of a selection of jQuery elements like this:

```
$('selector').each();
```

Anonymous Functions

To use the each() function, you pass a special kind of argument to it—an *anonymous function*. The anonymous function is simply a function containing the steps that you wish to perform on each selected element. It's called *anonymous* because, unlike the functions you learned to create on page 85, you don't give it a name. Here's an anonymous function's basic structure:

```
function() {
  //code goes here
}
```

Because there's no name, you don't have a way to call the function. For example, with a regular named function, you use its name with a set of parentheses like this: calculateSalesTax();. Instead, you use the anonymous function as an argument that you pass to another function (strange and confusing, but true!). Here's how you incorporate an anonymous function as part of the each() function:

```
$('selector').each(function() {
  // code goes in here
});
```

Figure 4-7 diagrams the different parts of this construction. The last line is particularly confusing because it includes three different symbols that close up three parts of the overall structure. The } marks the end of the function (that's also the end of the argument passed to the each() function); the) is the last part of the each() function; and ; indicates the end of a JavaScript statement. In other words, the JavaScript interpreter treats all of this code as a single statement.

Now that the outer structure's in place, it's time to put something inside the anonymous function: all of the stuff you want to happen to each element in a selection. The each() function works like a loop—meaning the instructions inside the anonymous function will run once for each element you've retrieved. For example, say you have 50 images on a page and add the following JavaScript code to one of the page's scripts:

```
$('img').each(function() {
  alert('I found an image');
});
```

Fifty alert dialog boxes with the message "I found an image" would appear. (That'd be really annoying, so don't try this at home.)

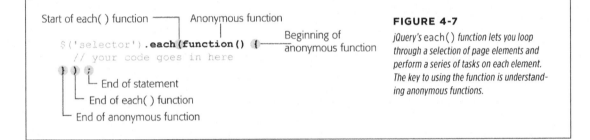

FIGURE 4-7

jQuery's each() function lets you loop through a selection of page elements and perform a series of tasks on each element. The key to using the function is understanding anonymous functions.

NOTE This may look somewhat familiar. As you saw on page 112, when you add jQuery to a page, you should use the document.ready() function to make sure a page's HTML has loaded before the browser executes any of the JavaScript programming. That function also accepts an anonymous function as an argument:

```
$(document).ready(function() {
  // programming goes inside this
  // anonymous function
});
```

this and $(this)

When using the each() function, you'll naturally want to access or set attributes of each element—for example, to find the URL for each external link. To access the current element through each loop, you use a special keyword called this. The this keyword refers to whatever element is calling the anonymous function. So the first time through the loop, this refers to the first element in the jQuery selection, while the second time through the loop, this refers to the second element.

The way jQuery works, this refers to a traditional DOM element, so you can access traditional DOM properties. But, as you've read in this chapter, the special jQuery selection lets you tap into all of the wonderful jQuery functions. So to convert this to its jQuery equivalent, you write $(this).

At this point, you're probably thinking that all of this *this* stuff is some kind of cruel joke intended to make your head swell. It's not a joke, but it sure is confusing. To help make clear how to use $(this), take another look at the task described at the beginning of this section—creating a list of external links in a bibliography box at the bottom of a page.

Assume that the page's HTML already has a <div> tag ready for the external links. For example:

```
<div id="bibliography">
<h3>Web pages referenced in this article</h3>
<ul id="bibList">
</ul>
</div>
```

The first step is to get a list of all links pointing outside your site. You can do so using an attribute selector (page 123):

```
$('a[href^="http://"]')
```

Now to loop through each link, add the each() function:

```
$('a[href^="http://"]').each()
```

Then add an anonymous function:

```
$('a[href^="http://"]').each(function() {

});
```

The first step in the anonymous function is to retrieve the URL for the link. Because each link has a different URL, you must access the current element each time through the loop. The $(this) keyword lets you do just that:

```
$('a[href^=http://]').each(function() {
  var extLink = $(this).attr('href');
});
```

The code in the middle, bolded line does several things: First, it creates a new variable (extLink) and stores the value of the current element's href property. Each time through the loop, $(this) refers to a different link on the page, so each time through the loop, the extLink variable changes.

After that, it's just a matter of appending a new list item to the <ul> tag (see the HTML above), like this:

```
$('a[href^=http://]').each(function() {
  var extLink = $(this).attr('href');
  $('#bibList').append('<li>' + extLink + '</li>');
});
```

You'll use the $(this) keyword almost every time you use the each() function, so in a matter of time, $(this) will become second nature to you. To help you practice this concept, you'll try it out in a tutorial.

NOTE The example script used in this section is a good way to illustrate the use of the $(this) keyword, but it probably isn't the best way to accomplish the task of writing a list of external links to a page. First, if there are no links, the <div> tag (which was hardcoded into the page's HTML) will still appear, but it'll be empty. In addition, if someone visits the page without JavaScript turned on, he won't see the links, but will see the empty box. A better approach is to use JavaScript to create the enclosing <div> tag as well. You can find an example of that in the file *bibliography.html* accompanying the tutorials for this chapter.

■ Automatic Pull Quotes

In the final tutorial for this chapter, you'll create a script that makes it very easy to add pull quotes to a page (like the one pictured in Figure 4-8). A *pull quote* is a box containing an interesting quote from the main text of a page. Newspapers, magazines, and websites all use these boxes to grab readers' attention and emphasize an important or interesting point. But adding pull quotes manually requires duplicating text from the page and placing it inside a <div> tag, <span> tag, or some other container. Creating all that HTML takes time and adds extra HTML and duplicate text to the finished page. Fortunately, with JavaScript, you can quickly add any number of pull quotes to a page, adding just a small amount of HTML.

Overview

The script you're about to create will do several things:

1. **Locate every <span> tag containing a special class named pq (for pull quote).**

   The only work you have to do to the HTML of your page is to add <span> tags around any text you wish to turn into a pull quote. For example, suppose there's a paragraph of text on a page and you want to highlight a few words from that paragraph in pull quote box. Just wrap that text in the <span> tag like this:

   ```
   <span class="pq">...and that's how I discovered the Loch Ness monster.
   </span>
   ```

2. **Duplicate each <span> tag.**

   Each pull quote box is essentially another span tag with the same text inside it, so you can use JavaScript to just duplicate the current <span> tag.

3. **Remove the** pq **class from the duplicate <span> and add a new class** pullquote.

The formatting magic—the box, larger text, border, and background color—that makes up each pull quote box isn't JavaScript's doing. The page's style sheet contains a CSS class selector, .pullquote, that does all of that. So by simply using JavaScript to change the duplicate tags' class name, you completely change the look of the new <span> tags.

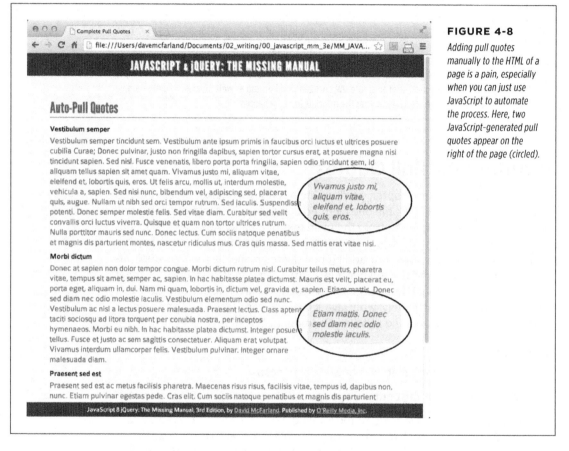

FIGURE 4-8

Adding pull quotes manually to the HTML of a page is a pain, especially when you can just use JavaScript to automate the process. Here, two JavaScript-generated pull quotes appear on the right of the page (circled).

4. **Add the duplicate <span> tag to the page.**

Finally, you add the duplicate <span> tag to the page. (Step 2 just makes a copy of the tag in the web browser's memory, but doesn't actually add that tag to the page yet. This gives you the opportunity to further manipulate the duplicated tag before displaying it for the person viewing the page.)

Programming

Now that you have an idea of what you're trying to accomplish with this script, it's time to open a text editor and make it happen.

NOTE See the note on page 12 for information on how to download the tutorial files.

1. **In a text editor, open the file *pull-quote.html* in the *chapter04* folder.**

   You'll start at the beginning by adding a link to the jQuery file.

2. **Click in the empty line just above the closing </head> tag and type:**

   ```
   <script src="../_js/jquery.min.js"></script>
   ```

   This loads the jQuery file from the site. Note that the name of the folder containing the jQuery file is *_js* (don't forget the underscore character at the beginning). Next, you'll add a set of <script> tags for your programming.

NOTE You'll see that no version name is used when linking to the jQuery file, although page 112 suggested that you use the version number, like this:

```
<script src="../_js/jquery.1.11.0.min.js"></script>
```

The version number is left off in this book to make it easier to update the tutorial files with new versions of jQuery. For example, as of this writing jQuery 1.11.0 is the latest version of jQuery 1—see the box on page 109 for the difference between versions 1 and 2. But by the time you're reading this, it might be version 1.11.1 or 1.12.0. The tutorial files will have the latest version of jQuery, so you'll always be using the latest version.

3. **Press Enter (or Return) to create a new line below the jQuery code and add the code listed in bold below:**

   ```
   <script src="../_js/jquery.min.js"></script>
   <script>

   </script>
   ```

NOTE The line numbers to the left of each line of code are just for your reference. Don't actually type them as part of the script on the web page.

Now add the document.ready() function.

4. **Click on the empty line between the <script> tags and add the code in bold:**

   ```
   1   <script src="../_js/jquery.min.js"></script>
   2   <script>
   3   $(document).ready(function() {
   4
   5   }); // end ready
   6   </script>
   ```

   The JavaScript comment // end ready is particularly helpful as your programs get longer and more complicated. On a long program, you'll end up with lots of }); scattered throughout, each marking the end of an anonymous function and a function call. Putting a comment that identifies what the $\}$); matches makes it much easier to later return to your code and understand what is going on.

Steps 1–4 cover the basic setup for any program you'll write using jQuery, so make sure you understand what it does. Next, you'll get into the heart of your program by selecting the <span> tags containing the text that should appear in the pullquote boxes.

5. **Add the bolded code on line 4:**

```
1   <script src="../_js/jquery.min.js"></script>
2   <script>
3   $(document).ready(function() {
4   $('span.pq')
5   }); // end ready
6   </script>
```

The $('span.pq') is a jQuery selector that locates every <span> tag with a class of pq applied to it. Next you'll add the code needed to loop through each of these <span> tags and do something to them.

6. **Add the bolded code on lines 4 and 6:**

```
1   <script src="../_js/jquery.min.js"></script>
2   <script>
3   $(document).ready(function() {
4     $('span.pq').each(function() {
5
6     }); // end each
7   }); // end ready
8   </script>
```

As discussed on page 138, .each() is a jQuery function that lets you loop through a selection of elements. The function takes one argument, which is an anonymous function.

Next you'll start to build the function that will apply to each matching <span> tag on this page. Get started by creating a copy of the <span>.

7. **Add the code listed in bold on line 5 below to the script:**

```
1   <script src="../_js/jquery-1.6.2.min.js"></script>
2   <script >
3   $(document).ready(function() {
4     $('span.pq').each(function() {
5       var quote=$(this).clone();
6     }); // end each
7   }); // end ready
8   </script>
```

This function starts by creating a new variable named quote, which contains a *clone* (just a copy) of the current <span> (see page 139 if you forgot what $(this) means). The jQuery .clone() function duplicates the current element, including all of the HTML within the element. In this case, it makes a copy of the <span> tag, including the text inside the <span> that will appear in the pull quote box.

Cloning an element copies everything, including any attributes applied to it. In this instance, the original <span> had a class named pq. You'll remove that class from the copy.

8. **Add the two lines of code listed in bold on lines 6 and 7 below to the script:**

```
1    <script src="../_js/jquery.min.js"></script>
2    <script>
3    $(document).ready(function() {
4      $('span.pq').each(function() {
5        var quote=$(this).clone();
6        quote.removeClass('pq');
7        quote.addClass('pullquote');
8      }); // end each
9    }); // end ready
10   </script>
```

As discussed on page 131, the removeClass() function removes a class name from a tag, while the addClass() function adds a class name to a tag. In this case, we're replacing the class name on the copy, so you can use a CSS class named .pullquote to format the <span> as a pull quote box.

Finally, you'll add the <span> to the page.

9. **Add the bolded line of code (line 8) to the script:**

```
1    <script src="../_js/jquery.min.js"></script>
2    <script>
3    $(document).ready(function() {
4      $('span.pq').each(function() {
5        var quote=$(this).clone();
6        quote.removeClass('pq');
7        quote.addClass('pullquote');
8        $(this).before(quote);
9      }); // end each
10   }); // end ready
11   </script>
```

This line is the final piece of the function—up until this line, you've just been manipulating a copy of the <span> in the web browser's memory. No one viewing the page would see it until the copy is actually added to the DOM.

In this case, you're inserting the copy of the <span> tag, just before the one in your HTML. In essence, the page will end up with HTML sort of like this:

```
<span class="pullquote">...and that's how I discovered the Loch Ness monster.
</span> <span class="pq">...and that's how I discovered the Loch Ness
monster.</span>
```

Although the text looks like it will appear duplicated side by side, the CSS formatting makes the pull quote box float to the right edge of the page.

> **NOTE** To achieve the visual effect of a pull quote box, the page has a CSS style that uses the CSS float property. The box is moved to the right edge of the paragraph in which the text appears, and the other text in the paragraph wraps around it. If you're unfamiliar with this technique, you can learn about the CSS float property at *http://css.maxdesign.com.au/floatutorial/*. If you wish to examine the .pullquote style, just look in the head of the tutorial file. That style and all its properties are listed there.

At this point, all of the JavaScript is complete. However, you won't see any pull quote boxes until you massage the HTML a bit.

10. **Find the first <p> tag in the page's HTML. Locate a sentence and wrap <span class="pq"> </span> around it. For example:**

```
<span class="pq">Nullam ut nibh sed orci tempor rutrum.</span>
```

You can repeat this process to add pull quotes to other paragraphs as well.

11. **Save the file and preview it in a web browser.**

The final result should look something like Figure 4-8. If you don't see a pull quote box, make sure you added the <span> tag in step 10 correctly. Also, check out the tips on page 18 for fixing a malfunctioning program. You can find a completed version of this tutorial in the file *complete_pull-quote.html*.

Action/Reaction: Making Pages Come Alive with Events

When you hear people talk about JavaScript, you usually hear the word "interactive" somewhere in the conversation: "JavaScript lets you make interactive web pages." What they're really saying is that JavaScript lets your web pages react to something a visitor does: moving a mouse over a navigation button produces a menu of links; selecting a radio button reveals a new set of form options; clicking a small photo makes the page darken and a larger version of the photo pop onto the screen.

All the different visitor actions that a web page can respond to are called *events*. JavaScript is an *event-driven* language: Without events, your web pages wouldn't be able to respond to visitors or do anything really interesting. It's like your desktop computer. Once you start it up in the morning, it doesn't do you much good until you start opening programs, clicking files, making menu selections, and moving your mouse around the screen.

▪ What Are Events?

Web browsers are programmed to recognize basic actions like the page loading, someone moving a mouse, typing a key, or resizing the browser window. Each of the things that happens to a web page is an event. To make your web page interactive, you write programs that respond to events. In this way, you can make a `<div>` tag appear or disappear when a visitor clicks the mouse, a new image appear when she mouses over a link, or check the contents of a text field when she clicks a form's Submit button.

An event represents the precise moment when something happens. For example, when you click a mouse, the precise moment you release the mouse button, the web browser signals that a click event has just occurred. The moment that the web browser indicates that an event has happened is when the event *fires*, as programmers put it.

Web browsers actually fire several events whenever you click the mouse button. First, as soon as you press the mouse button, the mousedown event fires; then, when you let go of the button, the mouseup event fires; and finally, the click event fires (Figure 5-1).

> **NOTE** Understanding when and how these events fire can be tricky. To let you test out different event types, this chapter includes a demo web page with the tutorial files. Open *events.html* (in the *testbed* folder) in a web browser. Then move the mouse, click, and type to see some of the many different events that constantly occur on a web page (Figure 5-1).

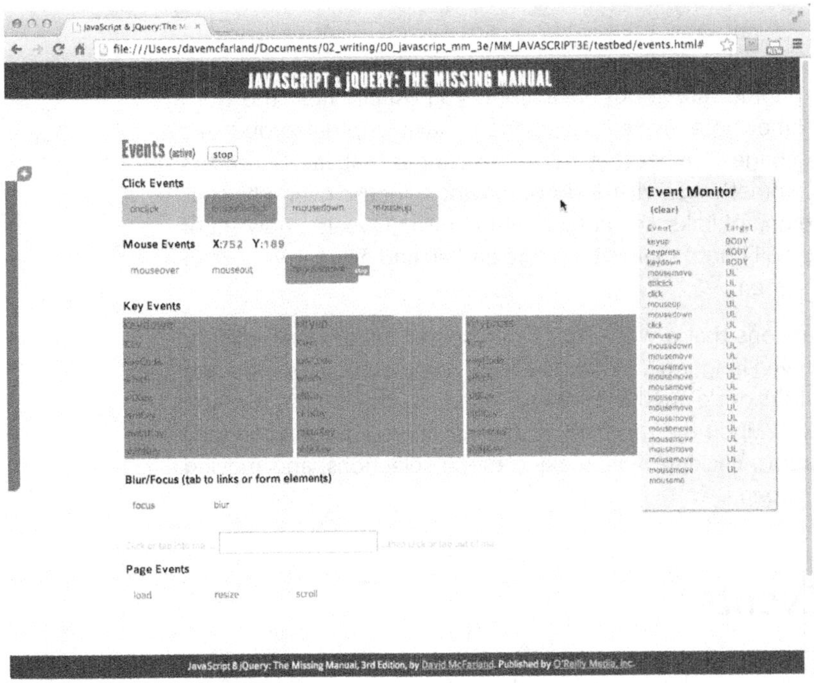

FIGURE 5-1

While you may not be aware of it, web browsers are constantly firing off events whenever you type, mouse around, or click. For example, double-clicking the mouse triggers two mouse-down, mouseup, and onclick events, as well as the doubleclick event itself. The events.html file (included with the tutorial files in the testbed folder) shows you many of these events in action.

Mouse Events

Ever since Steve Jobs introduced the Macintosh in 1984, the mouse has been a critical device for all personal computers (as has the trackpad for laptops). Folks use it to open applications, drag files into folders, select items from menus, and even to draw. Naturally, web browsers provide lots of ways of tracking how a visitor uses a mouse to interact with a web page:

- **click.** The click event fires after you click and release the mouse button. You'll commonly assign a click event to a link: For example, a link on a thumbnail image can display a larger version of that image when clicked. However, you're not limited to just links. You can also make any tag on a page respond to an event—even just clicking anywhere on the page.

NOTE   The click event can also be triggered on links via the keyboard. If you tab to a link, then press the Enter (Return) key, the click event fires.

- **dblclick.** When you press and release the mouse button twice quickly, a double-click (dblclick) event fires. It's the same action you use to open a folder or file on your desktop. Double-clicking a web page isn't a usual web-surfer action, so if you use this event, you should make clear to visitors where they can double-click and what will happen after they do. Also note each click in a double-click event also fires two click events, so don't assign click and dblclick events to the same tag. Otherwise, the function for the click will run twice before the dblclick function runs.

- **mousedown.** The mousedown event is the first half of a click—the moment when you click the button before releasing it. This event is handy for dragging elements around a page. You can let visitors drag items around your web page just like they drag icons around their desktop—by clicking on them (without releasing the button) and moving them, and then releasing the button to drop them (you'll learn how to do this with jQuery UI on page 399).

- **mouseup.** The mouseup event is the second half of a click—the moment when you release the button. This event is handy for responding to the moment when you drop an item that has been dragged.

- **mouseover.** When you move your mouse over an element on a page, a mouseover event fires. You can assign an event handler to a navigation button using this event and have a submenu pop up when a visitor mouses over the button. (If you're used to the CSS :hover pseudo-class, then you know how this event works.)

- **mouseout.** Moving a mouse off an element triggers the mouseout event. You can use this event to signal when a visitor has moved her mouse off the page, or to hide a pop-up menu when the mouse travels outside the menu.

- **mousemove.** Logically enough, the mousemove event fires when the mouse moves—which means this event fires all of the time. You use this event to track the current position of the cursor on the screen. In addition, you can assign this event to a particular tag on the page—a <div>, for example—and respond only to movements within that tag.

Document/Window Events

The browser window itself understands a handful of events that fire from when the page loads to when the visitor leaves the page:

- **load.** The load event fires when the web browser finishes downloading all of a web page's files: the HTML file itself, plus any linked images, Flash movies, and external CSS and JavaScript files. Web designers have traditionally used this event to start any JavaScript program that manipulated the web page. However, loading a web page and all its files can take a long time if there are a lot of graphics or other large linked files. In some cases, this meant the JavaScript didn't run for quite some time after the page was displayed in the browser. Fortunately, jQuery offers a much more responsive replacement for the load event, as described on page 160.

- **resize.** When you resize your browser window by clicking the maximize button, or dragging the browser's resize handle, the browser triggers a resize event. Some designers use this event to change the layout of the page when a visitor changes the size of his browser. For example, after a visitor resizes his browser window, you can check the window's width—if the window is really wide, you could change the design to add more columns of content to fit the space.

- **scroll.** The scroll event is triggered whenever you drag the scroll bar, or use the keyboard (for example, the up, down, home, end, and similar keys) or mouse scroll wheel to scroll a web page. If the page doesn't have scrollbars, no scroll event is ever triggered. Some programmers use this event to help figure out where elements (after a page has scrolled) appear on the screen.

- **unload.** When you click a link to go to another page, close a browser tab, or close a browser window, a web browser fires an unload event. It's like the last gasp for your JavaScript program and gives you an opportunity to complete one last action before the visitor moves on from your page. Nefarious programmers have used this event to make it very difficult to ever leave a page. Each time a visitor tries to close the page, a new window appears and the page returns. But you can also use this event for good: For example, a program can warn a visitor about a form he's started to fill out but hasn't submitted, or the program could send form data to the web server to save the data before the visitor exits the page.

Form Events

In the pre-JavaScript days, people interacted with websites mainly via clicking links and filling out forms created with HTML. Entering information into a form field was really the only way for visitors to provide input to a website. Because forms are still such an important part of the web, you'll find plenty of form events to play with:

- **submit.** Whenever a visitor submits a form, the submit event fires. A form might be submitted by clicking the Submit button, or simply by hitting the Enter (Return) key while the cursor is in a text field. You'll most frequently use the submit event with form validation—to make sure all required fields are correctly filled out *before* the data is sent to the web server. You'll learn how to validate forms on page 273.

- **reset.** Although not as common as they used to be, a Reset button lets you undo any changes you've made to a form. It returns a form to the state it was when the page was loaded. You can run a script when the visitor tries to reset the form by using the reset event. For example, if the visitor has made some changes to the form, you might want to pop up a dialog box that asks "Are you sure you want to delete your changes?" The dialog box could give the visitor a chance to click a No button and prevent the process of resetting (erasing) the form.

- **change.** Many form fields fire a change event when their status changes: for instance, when someone clicks a radio button, or makes a selection from a drop-down menu. You can use this event to immediately check the selection made in a menu, or which radio button was selected.

- **focus.** When you tab or click into a text field, it gives the field focus. In other words, the browser's attention is now focused on that page element. Likewise, selecting a radio button, or clicking a checkbox, gives those elements focus. You can respond to the focus event using JavaScript. For example, you could add a helpful instruction inside a text field—"Type your full name." When a visitor clicks in the field (giving it focus), you can erase these instructions, so he has an empty field he can fill out.

- **blur.** The blur event is the opposite of focus. It's triggered when you exit a currently focused field, by either tabbing or clicking outside the field. The blur event is another useful time for form validation. For example, when someone types her email address in a text field, then tabs to the next field, you could immediately check what she's entered to make sure it's a valid email address.

> **NOTE** Focus and blur events also apply to links on a page. When you tab to a link, a focus event fires; when you tab (or click) off the link, the blur event fires.

Keyboard Events

Web browsers also track when visitors use their keyboards, so you can assign commands to keys or let your visitors control a script by pressing various keys. For example, pressing the space bar could start and stop a JavaScript animation.

Unfortunately, the different browsers handle keyboard events differently, even making it hard to tell which letter was entered! (You'll find one technique for identifying which letter was typed on a keyboard in the Tip on page 165.)

- **keypress.** The moment you press a key, the keypress event fires. You don't have to let go of the key, either. In fact, the keypress event continues to fire, over and over again, as long as you hold the key down, so it's a good way to see if a visitor is holding down the key. For example, if you created a web racecar game you could assign a key to the gas pedal. The player only has to press the key down and hold it down to make the car move.

- **keydown.** The keydown event is like the keypress event—it's fired when you press a key. Actually, it's fired right *before* the keypress event. In Opera, the keydown event only fires once. In other browsers, the keydown event behaves just like the keypress event—it fires over and over as long as the key is pressed.

- **keyup.** Finally, the keyup event is triggered when you release a key.

■ Using Events the jQuery Way

Traditionally, programming with events has been tricky. For a long time, Internet Explorer had a completely different way of handling events than other browsers, requiring two sets of code (one for IE and one for all other browsers) to get your code to work. Fortunately, IE9 and later use the same method for handling events as other browsers, so programming is a lot easier. However, there are still a lot of people using IE8, so a good solution that makes programming with events easy and cross-browser compatible is needed. Fortunately, you have jQuery.

As you learned in the last chapter, JavaScript libraries like jQuery solve a lot of the problems with JavaScript programming—including pesky browser incompatibilities. In addition, libraries often simplify basic JavaScript-related tasks. jQuery makes assigning events and *event helpers* (the functions that deal with events) a breeze.

As you saw on page 113, jQuery programming involves (a) selecting a page element and then (b) doing something with that element. In fact, because events are so integral to JavaScript programming, it's better to think of jQuery programming as a three-step process:

1. **Select one or more elements.**

   The previous chapter explained how jQuery lets you use CSS selectors to choose the parts of the page you want to manipulate. When assigning events, you want to select the elements that the visitor will interact with. For example, what will a visitor click—a link, a table cell, an image? If you're assigning a mouseover event, what page element does a visitor mouse over to make the action happen?

2. **Assign an event.**

   In jQuery, most DOM events have an equivalent jQuery function. So to assign an event to an element, you just add a period, the event name, and a set of parentheses. So, for example, if you want to add a mouseover event to every link on a page, you can do this:

   ```
   $('a').mouseover();
   ```

   To add a click event to an element with an ID of menu, you'd write this:

   ```
   $('#menu').click();
   ```

   You can use any of the event names listed on pages page 148–152 (and a couple of jQuery-only events discussed on page 162).

   After adding the event, you still have some work to do. In order for something to happen when the event fires, you must provide a function for the event.

3. **Pass a function to the event.**

   Finally, you need to define what happens when the event fires. To do so, you pass a function to the event. The function contains the commands that will run when the event fires: for example, making a hidden <div> tag visible or high-lighting a moused-over element.

   You can pass a previously defined function's name like this:

   ```
   $('#start').click(startSlideShow);
   ```

   When you assign a function to an event, you omit the ( ) that you normally add to the end of a function's name to call it. In other words, the following won't work:

   ```
   $('#start').click(startSlideShow());
   ```

   However, the most common way to add a function to an event is to pass an *anonymous function* to the event. You read about anonymous functions on page 138—they're basically a function without a name. The basic structure of an anonymous function looks like this:

   ```
   function() {
   // your code here
   }
   ```

The basic structure for using an anonymous function with an event is pictured in Figure 5-2.

NOTE   To learn more about how to work with jQuery and events, visit *http://api.jquery.com/category/events/*.

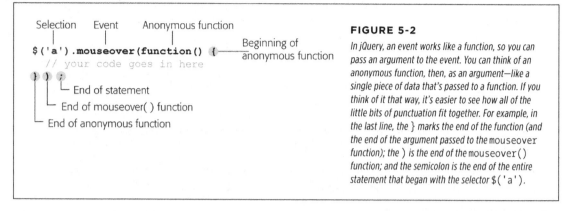

Selection   Event   Anonymous function

```
$('a').mouseover(function() {
    // your code goes in here
});
```

Beginning of
anonymous function

End of statement

End of mouseover( ) function

End of anonymous function

FIGURE 5-2

In jQuery, an event works like a function, so you can pass an argument to the event. You can think of an anonymous function, then, as an argument—like a single piece of data that's passed to a function. If you think of it that way, it's easier to see how all of the little bits of punctuation fit together. For example, in the last line, the } marks the end of the function (and the end of the argument passed to the mouseover *function); the) is the end of the* mouseover( ) *function; and the semicolon is the end of the entire statement that began with the selector* $('a').

Here's a simple example. Assume you have a web page with a link that has an ID of menu. When a visitor moves his mouse over that link, you want a hidden list of additional links to appear—assume that the list of links has an ID of submenu. So what you want to do is add a mouseover event to the menu, and then call a function that shows the submenu. The process breaks down into four steps:

1. **Select the menu:**

   ```
   $('#menu')
   ```

2. **Attach the event:**

   ```
   $('#menu').mouseover();
   ```

3. **Add an anonymous function:**

   ```
   $('#menu').mouseover(function() {


   }); // end mouseover
   ```

   You'll encounter lots of collections of closing brace, closing parenthesis, and semicolons—});—which frequently mark the end of an anonymous function inside a function call. You see them everywhere, so it's always a good idea to add a JavaScript comment—in this example, // end mouseover—to specify what that trio of punctuation means.

4. **Add the necessary actions (in this case, it's showing the submenu):**

   ```
   $('#menu').mouseover(function() {
     $('#submenu').show();
   }); // end mouseover
   ```

A lot of people find the crazy nest of punctuation involved with anonymous functions very confusing (that last }); is always a doozy). And it *is* confusing, but the best way to get used to the strange world of JavaScript is through lots of practice, so the following hands-on tutorial should help reinforce the ideas just presented.

NOTE The show( ) function is discussed in the next chapter on page 184.

■ Tutorial: Introducing Events

This tutorial gives you a quick introduction to using events. You'll make the page react to several different types of events so you can get a handle on how jQuery events work and how to use them.

NOTE See the note on page 12 for information on how to download the tutorial files.

1. **In a text editor, open the file *events_intro.html* in the *chapter05* folder.**

   You'll start at the beginning by adding a link to the jQuery file.

2. **Click in the empty line just above the closing </head> tag and type:**

   ```
   <script src="../_js/jquery.min.js"></script>
   ```

   This line loads the jQuery file from the site. Note that the name of the folder containing the jQuery file is *_js* (don't forget the underscore character at the beginning). Next, you'll add a set of <script> tags for your programming.

3. **Press Enter (or Return) to create a new line below the jQuery code and add another set of opening and closing script tags:**

   ```
   <script src="../_js/jquery.min.js"></script>
   <script>

   </script>
   ```

   Now add the document.ready() function.

4. **Click in the empty line between the <script> tags and add the code in bold:**

   ```
   <script src="../_js/jquery.min.js"></script>
   <script>
   $(document).ready(function() {

   }); // end ready
   </script>
   ```

   Don't forget the JavaScript comment after the }); . Even though adding comments requires a little extra typing, they'll be very helpful in identifying the different parts of a program. At this point, you've completed the steps you'll follow whenever you use jQuery on your web pages.

Next, it's time to add an event. Your first goal will be simple: have an alert box appear when a visitor double clicks anywhere on the page. To begin, you need to select the element (the page in this case) that you wish to add the event to.

5. **Click in the empty line inside the .ready() function and add the bolded code below:**

   ```
   <script src="../_js/jquery.min.js"></script>
   <script>
   $(document).ready(function() {
     $('html')
   }); // end ready
   </script>
   ```

   The $('html') selects the HTML element; basically, the entire browser window. Next, you'll add an event.

6. **Type .dblclick(); // end double click after the jQuery selector so your code looks like this:**

   ```
   <script src="../_js/jquery.min.js"></script>
   <script>
   $(document).ready(function() {
     $('html').dblclick(); // end double click
   }); // end ready
   </script>
   ```

   .dblclick() is a jQuery function that gets the browser ready to make something happen when a visitor double-clicks on the page. The only thing missing is the "make something happen" part, which requires passing an anonymous function as an argument to the dblclick() function (if you need a recap on how functions work and what "passing an argument" means, turn to page 85).

7. **Add an anonymous function by typing the code in bold below:**

   ```
   <script src="../_js/jquery.min.js"></script>
   <script>
   $(document).ready(function() {
     $('html').dblclick(function() {

     }); // end double click
   }); // end ready
   </script>
   ```

   Don't worry, the rest of this book won't crawl through every tutorial at this glacial pace, but it's important for you to understand what each piece of the code is doing. The function() { } is just the outer shell; it doesn't do anything until you add programming inside the { and }. That's the next step.

8. **Finally, add an alert statement:**

```
<script src="../_js/jquery.min.js"></script>
<script>
$(document).ready(function() {
  $('html').dblclick(function() {
    alert('ouch');
  }); // end double click
}); // end ready
</script>
```

If you preview the page in a web browser and double-click anywhere on the page, a JavaScript alert box with the word "ouch" should appear. If it doesn't, double-check your typing to make sure you didn't miss anything.

> **NOTE** After that long build-up, having "ouch" appear on the screen probably feels like a let-down. But keep in mind that the alert() part of this script is unimportant—it's all the other code you typed that demonstrates the fundamentals of how to use events with jQuery. As you learn more about programming and jQuery, you can easily replace the alert box with a series of actions that (when a visitor double-clicks the page) moves an element across the screen, displays an interactive photo slideshow, or starts a car-racing game.

Now that you've got the basics, you'll try out a few other events.

1. **Add the code in bold below so your script looks like this:**

```
<script src="../_js/jquery.min.js"></script>
<script>
$(document).ready(function() {
  $('html').dblclick(function() {
    alert('ouch');
  }); // end double click
  $('a').mouseover(function() {

  }); // end mouseover
}); // end ready
</script>
```

This code selects all links on a page (that's the $('a') part), then adds an anonymous function to the mouseover event. In other words, when someone mouses over any link on the page, something is going to happen.

2. Add two JavaScript statements to the anonymous function you added in the last step:

```
<script src="../_js/jquery.min.js"></script>
<script>
$(document).ready(function() {
  $('html').dblclick(function() {
    alert('ouch');

  }); // end double click
  $('a').mouseover(function() {
    var message = "<p>You moused over a link</p>";
    $('.main').append(message);
  }); // end mouseover
}); // end ready
</script>
```

The first line here—var message = "<p>You moused over a link</p>";—creates a new variable named message and stores a string in it. The string represents an HTML paragraph tag with some text. The next line selects an element on the page with a class name of main (that's the $('.main')) and then appends (or adds to the end of that element) the contents of the message variable. The page contains a <div> tag with the class of main, so this code simply adds "You moused over a link" to the end of that div each time a visitor mouses over a link on the page. (See page 129 for a recap of jQuery's append() function.)

3. Save the page, preview it in a browser, and mouse over any link on the page.

Each time you mouse over a link, a paragraph is added to the page (Figure 5-3). Now you'll add one last bit of programming: when a visitor clicks on the form button on the page, the browser will change the text that appears on that button.

4. Lastly, add the code in bold below so your finished script looks like this:

```
<script src="../_js/jquery.min.js"></script>
<script>
$(document).ready(function() {
  $('html').dblclick(function() {
    alert('ouch');
  }); // end double click
  $('a').mouseover(function() {
    var message = '<p>You moused over a link</p>';
    $('.main').append(message);
  }); // end mouseover
  $('#button').click(function() {
   $(this).val("Stop that!");
  }); // end click
}); // end ready
</script>
```

You should understand the basics here: $('#button')$ selects an element with the ID button (the form button in this case), and adds a click event to it, so when someone clicks the button, something happens. In this example, the words "Stop that!" appear on the button.

On page 139, you saw how to use $(this) inside of a loop in jQuery. It's the same idea inside of an event: $(this) refers to the element that is responding to the event—the element you select and attach the event to. In this case, this is the form button. (You'll learn more about the jQuery val() function on page 253, but basically you use it to read the value from or change the value of a form element. In this example, passing the string "Stop that!" to the val() function sets the button's value to "Stop that!")

5. **Save the page, preview it in a browser, and click the form button.**

The button's text should instantly change (Figure 5-3). For an added exercise, add the programming to make the text field's background color change to red when a visitor clicks or tabs into it. Here's a hint: You need to (a) select the text field; (b) use the focus() event (page 259); (c) use $(this) (as in step 12) to address the text field inside the anonymous function; and (d) use the .css() function (page 134) to change the background color of the text field. You can find the answer (and a complete version of the page) in the *complete_events_intro.html* file in the *chapter05* folder.

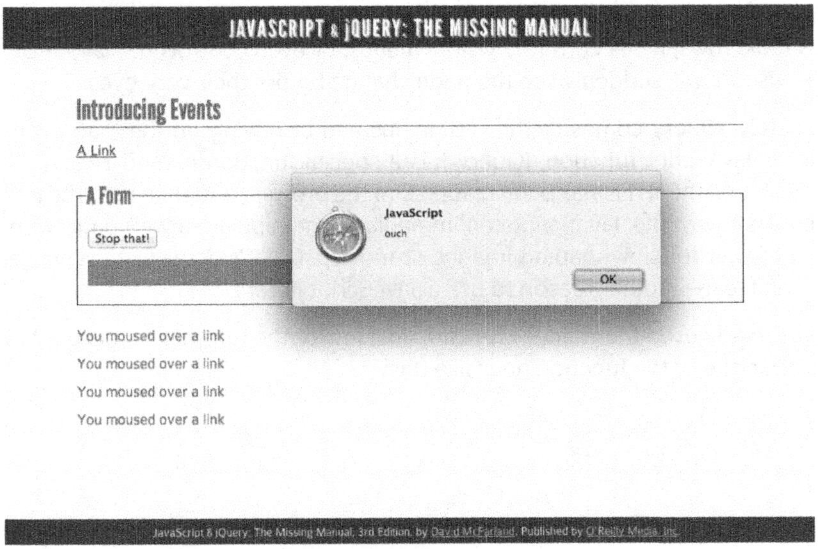

FIGURE 5-3

jQuery makes it easy for your web pages to respond to user interaction, such as opening an alert box when the page is clicked twice, adding text to the page in response to mousing over a link, or clicking a form button.

■ More jQuery Event Concepts

Because events are a critical ingredient for adding interactivity to a web page, jQuery includes some special jQuery-only functions that can make your programming easier and your pages more responsive.

Waiting for the HTML to Load

When a page loads, a web browser tries immediately to run any scripts it encounters. So scripts in the head of a page might run before the page fully loads—you saw this in the Moon Quiz tutorial on page 94, where the page was blank until the script asking the questions finished. Unfortunately, this phenomenon often causes problems. Because a lot of JavaScript programming involves manipulating the contents of a web page—displaying a pop-up message when a particular link is clicked, hiding specific page elements, adding stripes to the rows of a table, and so on—you'll end up with JavaScript errors if your program tries to manipulate elements of a page that haven't yet been loaded and displayed by the browser.

The most common way to deal with that problem has been to use a web browser's onload event to wait until a page is fully downloaded and displayed before executing any JavaScript. Unfortunately, waiting until a page fully loads before running JavaScript code can create some pretty strange results. The onload event only fires *after* all of a web page's files have downloaded—meaning all images, movies, external style sheets, and so on. As a result, on a page with lots of graphics, the visitor might actually be staring at a page for several seconds while the graphics load *before* any JavaScript runs. If the JavaScript makes a lot of changes to the page—for example, styles table rows, hides currently visible menus, or even controls the layout of the page—visitors will suddenly see the page change before their very eyes.

Fortunately, jQuery comes to the rescue. Instead of relying on the load event to trigger a JavaScript function, jQuery has a special function named ready() that waits just until the HTML has been loaded into the browser and then runs the page's scripts. That way, the JavaScript can immediately manipulate a web page without having to wait for slow-loading images or movies. (That's actually a complicated and useful feat—another reason to use a JavaScript library.)

You've already used the ready() function in a few of the tutorials in this book. The basic structure of the function goes like this:

```
$(document).ready(function() {
  //your code goes here
});
```

Basically, all of your programming code goes inside this function. In fact, the ready() function is so fundamental, you'll probably include it on every page on which you use jQuery. You only need to include it once, and it's usually the first and last line of a script. You must place it within a pair of opening and closing <script> tags (it is JavaScript, after all) and after the <script> and </script> tags that adds jQuery to the page.

So, in the context of a complete web page, the function looks like this:

```
<!DOCTYPE html>
<html>
<head>
<meta charset="UTF-8">
<title>Page Title</title>
<script src="js/jquery.js"></script>
<script>
$(document).ready(function() {
    // all of your JavaScript goes in here.
}); // end of ready() function
</script>
</head>
<body>
The web page content...
</body>
</html>
```

TIP Because the ready() function is used nearly anytime you add jQuery to a page, there's a shorthand way of writing it. You can remove the $(document).ready part, and just type this:

```
$(function() {
  // do something on document ready
});
```

■ AN ALTERNATIVE TO $(DOCUMENT).READY()

Putting the $(document).ready() function in the <head> of an HTML document serves to delay your JavaScript until your HTML loads. But there's another way to do the same thing: put your JavaScript code after the HTML. For example, many web developers simply put their JavaScript code directly before the closing </body> tag, like this:

```
<!DOCTYPE html>
<html>
<head>
<meta charset="UTF-8">
<title>Page Title</title>
</head>
<body>
The web page content...
<script src="js/jquery.js"></script>
<script>
    // all of your JavaScript goes in here.
</script>
</body>
</html>
```

In this case, there's no need for $(document).ready(), because by the time the scripts load, the document is ready. This approach can have some major benefits. First, you don't need to type that extra bit of code to include the .ready() function. Second, loading and running JavaScript freezes the web browser until the scripts load and finish running. If you include a lot of external JavaScript files and they take a while to download, your web page won't display right away. For your site's visitors, it will look like it's taking a long time for your page to load.

You may read on web design blogs that putting your scripts at the bottom of the page is the proper way to add JavaScript. However, there are also downsides to this approach. In some cases, the JavaScript code you add to a page has dramatic effects on the page's appearance. For example, you can use JavaScript to completely re-draw a complex HTML table so it's easier to view and navigate. Or you might take the basic typography of a page and make it look really cool (*http://letteringjs.com*).

In these cases, if you wait until the HTML loads and displays before downloading jQuery and running your JavaScript code, your site's visitors may see the page one way (before it's transformed by JavaScript) and then watch it change right before their eyes. This "quick change act" can be disconcerting. In addition, if you're building a web application that doesn't work without JavaScript, there's no point in showing your visitors the page's HTML, until after the JavaScript loads—after all, the buttons, widgets, and JavaScript-powered interface tools of your web app are just useless chunks of HTML until the JavaScript powers them.

So the answer to where to put your JavaScript is "it depends." In some cases, your site will appear more responsive if you put the JavaScript after the HTML, and sometimes when you put it before. Thankfully, due to browser-caching, once one page on your site downloads the necessary JavaScript files, the other pages will have instant access to the files in the browser cache and won't need to waste time downloading them again. In other words, don't sweat it: if you feel like your web page isn't displaying fast enough, then you can try moving the scripts down to the end of the page. If it helps, then go for it. But, in many cases, whether you use the .ready() function at the top of the page won't matter at all.

NOTE When building a web page on your computer and testing it directly in your web browser, you won't encounter the problems discussed in this section. It's only when you put your site on a web server and have to download the script and page files over a sometimes slow Internet connection that you can see whether you have any problems with the time it takes to load and display a web page.

Mousing Over and Off an Element

The mouseover and mouseout events are frequently used together. For example, when you mouse over a button, a menu might appear; move your mouse off the button, and the menu disappears. Because coupling these two events is so common, jQuery provides a shortcut way of referring to both. jQuery's hover() function works just like any other event, except that instead of taking one function as an argument, it accepts two functions. The first function runs when the mouse travels over the element, and the second function runs when the mouse moves off the element. The basic structure looks like this:

```
$('#selector').hover(function1, function2);
```

You'll frequently see the hover() function used with two anonymous functions. That kind of code can look a little weird; the following example will make it clearer. Suppose when someone mouses over a link with an ID of menu, you want a (currently invisible) DIV with an ID of submenu to appear. Moving the mouse off of the link hides the submenu again. You can use hover() to do that:

```
$('#menu').hover(function() {
    $('#submenu').show();
}, function() {
    $('#submenu').hide();
}); // end hover
```

To make a statement containing multiple anonymous functions easier to read, move each function to its own line. So a slightly more readable version of the code above would look like this:

```
$('#menu').hover(
  function() {
    $('#submenu').show();
  }, // end mouseover
  function() {
    $('#submenu').hide();
  } // end mouseout
); // end hover
```

Figure 5-4 diagrams how this code works for the mouseover and mouseout events.

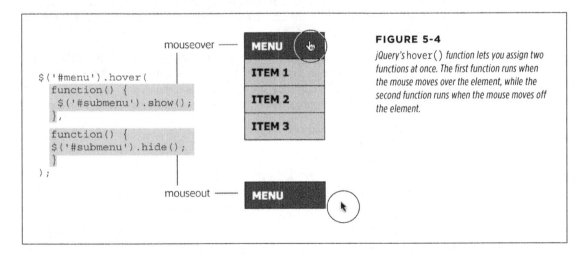

FIGURE 5-4

jQuery's hover() function lets you assign two functions at once. The first function runs when the mouse moves over the element, while the second function runs when the mouse moves off the element.

If the anonymous function method is just too confusing, you can still use plain old named functions (page 85) to get the job done. First, create a named function to run when the mouseover event triggers; create another named function for the mouseout event; and finally, pass the names of the two functions to the hover() function. In other words, you could rewrite the code above like this:

```
function showSubmenu() {
  $('#submenu').show();
}
function hideSubmenu() {
  $('#submenu').hide();
}
$('#menu').hover(showSubmenu, hideSubmenu);
```

If you find this technique easier, then use it. There's no real difference between the two, though some programmers like the fact that by using anonymous functions you can keep all of the code together in one statement, instead of spread out among several different statements.

> **NOTE** Versions of jQuery prior to 1.9 included a very useful toggle() function. This function worked like hover() except for click events. You could run one set of code on the first click, and a second set of code on the second click. In other words, you could "toggle" between clicks—great for showing a page item on the first click, then closing that item on the second click. Because toggle() is no longer part of jQuery, you'll learn how to replicate that functionality in the tutorial starting on page 174.

The Event Object

Whenever a web browser fires an event, it records information about the event and stores it in an *event object*. The event object contains information that was collected when the event occurred, like the vertical and horizontal coordinates of the mouse, the element on which the event occurred, or whether the Shift key was pressed when the event was triggered.

In jQuery, the event object is available to the function assigned to handling the event. In fact, the object is passed as an argument to the function, so to access it, you just include a parameter name with the function. For example, say you want to find the X and Y position of the cursor when the mouse is clicked anywhere on a page:

```
$(document).click(function(evt) {
  var xPos = evt.pageX;
  var yPos = evt.pageY;
  alert('X:' + xPos + ' Y:' + yPos);
}); // end click
```

The important part here is the evt variable. When the function is called (by clicking anywhere in the browser window), the event object is stored in the evt variable. Within the body of the function, you can access the different properties of the event object using dot syntax—for example, evt.pageX returns the horizontal location of the cursor (in other words, the number of pixels from the left edge of the window).

NOTE In this example, evt is just a variable name supplied by the programmer. It's not a special JavaScript keyword, just a variable used to store the event object. You could use any name you want such as event or simply e.

The event object has many different properties, and (unfortunately) the list of properties varies from browser to browser. Table 5-1 lists some common properties.

TABLE 5-1 *Every event produces an event object with various properties that you can access within the function handling the event*

EVENT PROPERTY	DESCRIPTION
pageX	The distance (in pixels) of the mouse pointer from the left edge of the browser window.
pageY	The distance (in pixels) of the mouse pointer from the top edge of the browser window.
screenX	The distance (in pixels) of the mouse pointer from the left edge of the monitor.
screenY	The distance (in pixels) of the mouse pointer from the top edge of the monitor.
shiftKey	Is true if the shift key is down when the event occurs.
which	Use with the keypress event to determine the numeric code for the key that was pressed (see tip, next).
target	The object that was the "target" of the event—for example, for a click event, the element that was clicked.
data	A jQuery object used with the on() function to pass data to an event handling function (page 167).

TIP If you access the event object's which property with the keypress event, you'll get a numeric code for the key pressed. If you want the specific key that was pressed (a, K, 9, and so on), you need to run the which property through a JavaScript method that converts the key number to the actual letter, number, or symbol on the keyboard:

```
String.fromCharCode(evt.which)
```

Stopping an Event's Normal Behavior

Some HTML elements have preprogrammed responses to events. A link, for example, usually loads a new web page when clicked; a form's Submit button sends the form data to a web server for processing when clicked. Sometimes you don't want the web browser to go ahead with its normal behavior. For example, when a form is submitted (the submit() event), you might want to stop the form data from being sent if the person filling out the form left out important data.

You can prevent the web browser's normal response to an event with the preventDefault() function. This function is actually a part of the event object (see the previous section), so you'll access it within the function handling the event. For example, say a page has a link with an ID of menu. The link actually points to another menu page (so visitors with JavaScript turned off will be able to get to the menu page). However, you've added some clever JavaScript, so when a visitor clicks the link, the menu appears right on the same page. Normally, a web browser would follow the link to the menu page, so you need to prevent its default behavior, like this:

```
$('#menu').click(function(evt){
  // clever javascript goes here
 evt.preventDefault(); // don't follow the link
});
```

Another technique is simply to return the value false at the end of the event function. For example, the following is functionally the same as the code above:

```
$('#menu').click(function(evt){
  // clever javascript goes here
  return false; // don't follow the link
});
```

Removing Events

At times, you might want to remove an event that you had previously assigned to a tag. jQuery's off() function lets you do just that. To use it, first create a jQuery object with the element you wish to remove the event from. Then add the off() function, passing it a string with the event name. For example, if you want to prevent all tags with the class tabButton from responding to any click events, you can write this:

```
$('.tabButton').off('click');
```

Take a look at a short script to see how the off() function works.

```
1   $('a').mouseover(function() {
2     alert('You moved the mouse over me!');
3   });
4   $('#disable').click(function() {
5     $('a').off('mouseover');
6   });
```

Lines 1–3 add a function to the mouseover event for all links (<a> tags) on the page. Moving the mouse over the link opens an alert box with the message "You moved your mouse over me!" However, because the constant appearance of alert messages would be annoying, lines 4–6 let the visitor turn off the alert. When the visitor clicks a tag with an ID of *disable* (a form button, for example), the mouseover events are unbound from all links, and the alert no longer appears.

If you want to remove all events from an element, don't give the off() function any arguments. For example, to remove all events—mouseover, click, dblclick, and so on—from a submit button, you could write this code:

```
$('input[type="submit"]').off();
```

This is a pretty heavy-handed approach, however, and in most cases you won't want to remove all event handlers from an element.

NOTE For more information on jQuery's off() function, visit *http://api.jquery.com/off/*.

POWER USERS' CLINIC

Stopping an Event in Its Tracks

The event model lets an event pass beyond the element that first receives the event. For example, say you've assigned an event handler for click events on a particular link; when you click the link, the click event fires and a function runs. The event, however, doesn't stop there. Each ancestor element (a tag that wraps around the element that's clicked) can also respond to that same click. So if you've assigned a click event helper for a <div> tag that the link is inside, the function for that <div> tag's event will run as well.

This concept, known as *event bubbling*, means that more than one element can respond to the same action. Here's another example: Say you add a click event to an image so when the image is clicked, a new graphic replaces it. The image is inside a <div> tag to which you've also assigned a click event. In this case, an alert box appears when the <div> is clicked. Now when you click the image, both functions will run. In other words, even though you clicked the image, the <div> also receives the click event.

You probably won't encounter this situation too frequently, but when you do, the results can be disconcerting. Suppose in the example in the previous paragraph, you don't want the <div> to do anything when the image is clicked. In this case, you have to stop the click event from passing on to the <div> tag without stopping the event in the function that handles the click event on the image. In other words, when the image is clicked, the function assigned to the image's click event should swap in a new graphic, but then stop the click event.

The stopPropagation() function prevents an event from passing onto any ancestor tags. The function is a method of the event object (page 164), so you access it within an event-handling function:

```
$('#theLink').click(function(evt) {
  // do something
  evt.stopPropagation(); // stop event
from continuing
});
```

■ Advanced Event Management

You can live a long, happy programming life using just the jQuery event methods and concepts discussed on the previous pages. But if you really want to get the most out of jQuery's event-handling techniques, then you'll want to learn about the on() function.

NOTE If your head is still aching from the previous section, you can skip ahead to the tutorial on page 174 until you've gained a bit more experience with event handling.

The on() method is a more flexible way of dealing with events than jQuery's event-specific functions like click() or mouseover(). It not only lets you specify an event and a function to respond to the event, but also lets you pass additional data for the event-handling function to use. This lets different elements and events (for example, a click on one link, or a mouseover on an image) pass different information to the same event-handling function—in other words, one function can act differently based on which event is triggered.

NOTE As jQuery has evolved, the names used to add and remove events to elements have changed quite a bit. If you're reading older books or blog posts, you might run into function names like bind(), live(), and delegate(). Those have all been replaced with the on() function to add events to elements. In addition, the off() function replaces the older unbind() function for removing events from elements.

The basic format of the on() function is the following:

```
$('#selector').on('click', selector, myData, functionName);
```

The first argument is a string containing the name of the event (like click, mouseover, or any of the other events listed on pages 148–152).

The second argument is optional, so you don't have to provide a value for this argument when you use the on() function. If you do supply the argument, it must be a valid selector like tr, .callout, or #alarm.

NOTE You can use that second argument to apply the event to a different element within the selected element. That technique is called *event delegation,* and you'll learn about it in a bit on page 171.

The third argument is the data you wish to pass to the function—either an object literal or a variable containing an object literal. An object literal (discussed on page 136) is basically a list of property names and values:

```
{
    firstName : 'Bob',
    lastName : 'Smith'
}
```

You can store an object literal in a variable like so:

```
var linkVar = {message:'Hello from a link'};
```

The fourth argument passed to the on() function is another function—the one that does something when the event is triggered. The function can either be an anonymous function or named function—in other words, this part is the same as when using a regular jQuery event, as described on page 152.

NOTE Passing data using the on( ) function is optional. If you want to use on( ) merely to attach an event and function, then leave the data variable out:

```
$('selector').on('click', functionName);
```

This code is functionally the same as:

```
$('selector').click(functionName);
```

Suppose you wanted to pop up an alert box in response to an event, but you wanted the message in the alert box to be different based on which element triggered the event. One way to do that would be to create variables with different object literals inside, and then send the variables to the on() function for different elements. Here's an example:

```
var linkVar = { message:'Hello from a link'};
var pVar = { message:'Hello from a paragraph'};
function showMessage(evt) {
    alert(evt.data.message);
}
$('a').on('mouseover',linkVar,showMessage);
$('p').on('click',pVar,showMessage);
```

Figure 5-5 breaks down how this code works. It creates two variables, linkVar on the first line and pVar on the second line. Each variable contains an object literal, with the same property name, message, but different message text. A function, showMessage(), takes the event object (page 164) and stores it in a variable named evt. That function runs the alert() command, displaying the message property (which is itself a property of the event object's data property). Keep in mind that message is the name of the property defined in the object literal.

Other Ways to Use the on() Function

jQuery's on() function gives you a lot of programming flexibility. In addition to the techniques listed in the previous section, it also lets you tie two or more events to the same function. For example, say you write a program that makes a large image appear on the screen when a visitor clicked a thumbnail image (the common "lightbox" effect found on thousands of websites). You want the larger image to disappear when the visitor either clicks anywhere on the page or hits any key on the keyboard (providing both options makes your program respond to people who prefer the keyboard over the mouse and vice versa). Here's some code that does that:

```
$(document).on('click keypress', function() {
  $('#lightbox').hide();
}); // end on
```

The important part is 'click keypress'. By providing multiple event names, each separated by a space, you're telling jQuery to run the anonymous function when *any* of the events in the list happen. In this case, when either the click or keypress event fires on the document.

FIGURE 5-5

jQuery's on() *function lets you pass data to the function responding to the event. That way, you can use a single named function for several different elements (even with different types of events), while letting the function use data specific to each event helper.*

In addition, if you want to attach several events that each trigger different actions, you don't need to use the on() function multiple times. In other words, if you want to make one thing happen when a visitor clicks an element, and another when a visitor mouses over that same element, you might be tempted to write this:

```
$('#theElement').on('click', function() {
  // do something interesting
}); // end on
$('#theElement').on('mouseover', function() {
  // do something else interesting
}); // end on
```

You can do the same thing by passing an object literal (page 136) to the on() function that is composed of an event name, followed by a colon, followed by an anonymous function. Here's the code above rewritten, calling the on() function only once and passing it an object literal (in bold):

```
$('#theElement').on({
  'click' : function() {
    // do something interesting
  }, // end click function
  'mouseover' : function() {
    // do something interesting
  } // end mouseover function
}); // end on
```

Delegating Events with on()

As mentioned on page 167, the on() method can accept a second argument, which is another selector:

```
$('#selector').on('click', selector, myData, functionName);
```

That second argument can be any valid jQuery selector, like an ID, class, element, or any of the selectors discussed on page 119. Passing a selector to the on() function significantly changes how on() works. Without passing a selector, the event is applied to the initial selector—$('#selector')—in the example above. Say you added this code to a page:

```
$('li').on('click', function() {
  $(this).css('text-decoration': 'line-through');
}); // end on
```

This code adds a line through the text in every <li> tag that a visitor clicks. Remember that, in this case, $(this) refers to the element that's handling the event—the clicked <li> tag. In other words, the click event is "bound" to the <li> tag. In most cases, that's exactly what you want to do—define a function that runs when the visitor interacts with a specific element. You can have the function run when a visitor clicks a link, mouses over a menu item, submits a form, and so on.

NOTE Still not sure what $(this) stands for? See page 139 for an in-depth discussion, and page 159 for details on how $(this) works with event handlers.

However, there's one problem with this method of attaching event handlers to elements: it only works if the element is already on the page. If you dynamically add HTML after you add an event handler like click(), mouseover(), or on(), those new elements won't have any event handlers attached to them. OK, that's a mindful. Here's an example to make it clearer.

Imagine you've created a To-Do List application that lets a visitor manage a list of tasks. When the application first loads, there's nothing in the list (#1 in Figure 5-6). A visitor can fill out a text field and click an Add Task button to add more tasks to the list (#2 in Figure 5-6). After the visitor finishes a task, she can click that task to mark it done (#3 in Figure 5-6).

To mark a task done, you know you need to add a click event to each <li> tag so when it's clicked, the <li> is marked as done in some way. In Figure 5-6, a completed task is grayed-out and has a line through it. The problem is that when the page loads there are no <li> tags, so adding a click event handler to every <li> tag won't have any effect. In other words, the code on page 171 won't work.

NOTE Note: You can learn more about jQuery event delegation at *http://api.jquery.com/on/*.

Instead, you have to *delegate* the events, which means applying an event to a parent element higher up in the chain (an element that already exists on the page) and then listening for events on particular child elements. Because the event is applied to an already existing element, adding new children won't interfere with this process. In other words, you're *delegating* the task of listening to events to an already existing parent element. For a more detailed explanation, see the box on page 175. Meanwhile, here's how you can use the on() function to make this particular example work:

```
$('ul').on('click', 'li', function() {
  $(this).css('text-decoration': 'line-through');
}); // end on
```

When you created the page, you added an empty <ul> tag as a container for adding each new task inside an <li> tag. As a result, when the page loads, one empty <ul> tag is already in place. Then, running the above code adds the on() function to that tag. The visitor hasn't yet added any to-do list items, so there are no <li> tags. However, when you add the selector 'li' as the second argument in the on() function, you're saying that you want to listen to click events *not* on the <ul> tag but on any <li> tags inside that unordered list. It doesn't matter when the <li> tags are added to the page because the <ul> tag is the one doing the event listening.

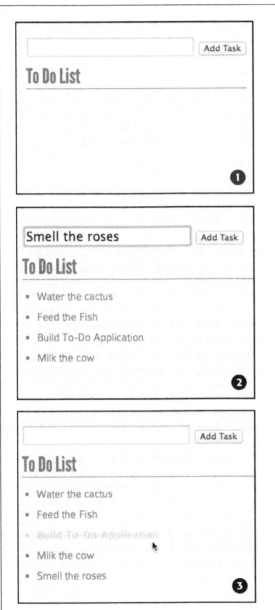

FIGURE 5-6

Sometimes you'll write JavaScript code that dynamically adds new HTML to a page. In this example, visitors can add new items (tasks, in this example) to an unordered list. When the page first loads there are no items in the list, just an empty pair of `<ul>` `</ul>` *tags (top). As a visitor types in new tasks and clicks the Add Task button, new* `<li>` *tags are added to the page (middle). To mark a task done, just click the task in the list (bottom). You'll find this working example in the tutorial file to-do-list.html in the* chapter05 *folder.*

■ HOW EVENT DELEGATION AFFECTS THE $(THIS) OBJECT

As mentioned earlier, the $(this) object refers to the element that's currently being handled within a loop (page 139) or by an event handler (page 159). Normally, in an event handler, $(this) refers to the initial selector. For example:

```
$('ul').on('click', function() {
  $(this).css('text-decoration': 'line-through');
}
```

In the above code, $(this) refers to the <ul> tag the visitor clicks. However, when you use event delegation, the initial selector is no longer the element that's being interacted with—it's the element that contains the element the visitor clicks on (or mouses over, tabs to, and so on). Take a look at the event delegation code one more time:

```
$('ul').on('click', 'li', function() {
  $(this).css('text-decoration': 'line-through');
}); // end on
```

In this case, the <li> tag is the one the visitor will click, and it's the element that needs to respond to the event. In other words, <ul> is just the container, and the function needs to be run when the <li> tag is clicked. So, in this example, $(this) is going to refer to the <li> tag, and the function above will add a line through each <li> tag the visitor clicks.

For many tasks, you won't need event delegation at all. However, if you ever need to add events to HTML that isn't already on the page when it loads, then you'll need to use this technique. For example, when you use Ajax (Chapter 13), you may need to use event delegation to apply events to HTML content that's dynamically added to a web page from a web server.

NOTE In some cases, you may want to use event delegation simply to improve JavaScript performance. If you're adding lots and lots of tags to the same event handler, for example, hundreds of table cells in a large table, it's often better to delegate the event to the <table> tag like this:

```
$('table').on('click', 'td', function () {
  // code goes here
});
```

By adding the event to the table, you're avoiding having to apply event handlers directly to hundreds or even thousands of individual elements, a task that can consume browser memory and processing power.

■ Tutorial: A One-Page FAQ

"Frequently Asked Questions" pages are a common sight on the Web. They can help improve customer service by providing immediate answers 24/7. Unfortunately, most FAQ pages are either one very long page full of questions and complete answers, or a single page of questions that link to separate answer pages. Both solutions slow down the visitors' quest for answers: in the first case, forcing a visitor to scroll down a long page for the question and answer he's after, and in the second case, making the visitor wait for a new page to load.

In this tutorial, you'll solve this problem by creating a JavaScript-driven FAQ page. All of the questions will be visible when the page loads, so it's easy to locate a given question. The answers, however, are hidden until the question is clicked—then the desired answer fades smoothly into view (Figure 5-7).

Overview of the Task

The JavaScript for this task will need to accomplish several things:

- When a question is clicked, the corresponding answer will appear.

- When a question whose answer is visible is clicked, then the answer should disappear.

FREQUENTLY ASKED QUESTION

Is Event Delegation Voodoo?

OK, I understand the basics of event delegation, but how does it actually work?

As you read in the box on page 167, event "bubbles" up through the HTML of a page. When you click on a link inside a paragraph, the click event is first triggered on that link; then, the parent element—the paragraph—gets the click event, followed by the <body> and then the <html>. In other words, an event that's triggered on one HTML element passes upwards to each of its parents.

This fact can be really helpful in the case of event delegation. As mentioned on page 171, sometimes you want to apply events to HTML that doesn't yet exist—like an item in a to-do list—that only comes into existence after the page loads and a visitor adds a list item. Although you can't add a click event to a <li> tag that isn't there yet, you can add the click event to an already existing parent like a <ul> tag, or even a <div> tag that holds that <ul> tag.

As discussed on page 164, every event has an event object that keeps track of lots of different pieces of information. In this case, the most important piece of information is the target property. This property specifies the exact HTML tag receiving the event. For example, when you click a link, that link is the target of the click. Because of event bubbling, a parent tag can "hear" the event and then determine which child element was the target.

So, with event delegation, you can have a parent element listen for events—like a <ul> tag listening for a click event. Then, it can check to see which tag was the actual target. For example, if the <li> tag was the target, then you can run some specific code to handle that situation—like crossing off the list item as in the to-do list example.

In addition, you'll want to use JavaScript to hide all of the answers when the page loads. Why not just use CSS to hide the answers to begin with? For example, setting the CSS display property to none for the answers is another way to hide the answers. The problem with this technique is what happens to visitors who don't have JavaScript turned on: They won't see the answers when the page loads, nor will they be able to make them visible by clicking the questions. To make your pages viewable to both those with JavaScript enabled and those with JavaScript turned off, it's best to use JavaScript to hide any page content.

NOTE   See the note on page 12 for information on how to download the tutorial files.

The Programming

1. **In a text editor, open the file *faq.html* in the *chapter05* folder.**

   This file already contains a link to the jQuery file, and the $(document).ready() function (page 160) is in place. First, you'll hide all of the answers when the page loads.

2. **Click in the empty line after the $(document).ready() function, and then type $('.answer').hide();.**

   The text of each answer is contained within a <div> tag with the class of answer. This one line of code selects each <div> and hides it (the hide() function is discussed on page 184). Save the page and open it in a web browser. The answers should all be hidden.

NOTE   The elements are hidden with JavaScript instead of CSS, because some visitors may not have JavaScript turned on. If that's the case, they won't get the cool effect you're programming in this tutorial, but they'll at least be able to see all of the answers.

The next step is determining which elements you need to add an event listener to. The answer appears when a visitor clicks the question, therefore you must select every question in the FAQ. On this page, each question is a <h2> tag in the page's main body.

3. **Press Return to create a new line and add the code in bold below to the script:**

   ```
   <script src="../_js/jquery.min.js></script>
   <script>
   $(document).ready(function() {
     $('.answer').hide();
    $('.main h2')
   }); // end of ready()
   </script>
   ```

   That's a basic descendant selector used to target every <h2> tag inside an element with a class of main (so it doesn't affect any <h2> tags elsewhere on the page). Now it's time to add an event handler. The click event is a good candidate, but you'll need to do something more to make it work. For this example, each click will either show the answer or hide it. That sounds like a job for a conditional statement. Essentially, you want to check whether the answer <div> that's placed after the <h2> tag is hidden: if it is, then show it, if not, then hide it.

4. **Add the following bolded code to attach an event handler to the `<h2>` tags:**

```
$(document).ready(function() {
  $('.answer').hide();
  $('.main h2').click(function() {

  }); // end click
}); // end of ready()
```

This code adds a `click` event to those `<h2>` tags. The `// end click` comment isn't required, but, as mentioned on page 58, a comment can really help you figure out what code a set of `});` characters belongs to. With this code in place, whatever you put inside the anonymous function here will run each time a visitor clicks one of those `<h2>` tags.

5. **On the empty line inside the function, type:**

```
var $answer = $(this).next('.answer');
```

Here, you're creating a variable—$answer—that will hold a jQuery object. As discussed on page 159, `$(this)` refers to the element currently responding to the event—in this case, a particular `<h2>` tag. jQuery provides several functions to make moving around a page's structure easier. The `.next()` function finds the tag immediately following the current tag. In other words, it finds the tag following the `<h2>` tag. You can further refine this search by passing an additional selector to the `.next()` function—the code `.next('.answer')` finds the first tag following the `<h2>` that also has the class `answer`.

In other words, you're storing a reference to the `<div>` immediately following the `<h2>` tag, That `<div>` holds the answer to the question. You're storing it in a variable, because you'll need to access that element several times in the function: to see whether the answer is hidden, to show the answer if it is hidden, and to hide it if it's visible. Every time you access jQuery using the `$( )`, you're telling the browser to fire off a bunch of programming code inside jQuery. So the code `$('this').next('.answer')` makes jQuery do some work. Instead of repeating those same steps over and over, you can just store the results of that work in a variable, and use that variable again and again to point to the `<div>` you wish to hide or show.

When you need to use the same jQuery results over and over and over again, it's a good idea to store the results a single time in a variable you can use repeatedly. This makes the program more efficient, saves the browser from having to unnecessarily do extra work, and make your web page more responsive.

The variable begins with a $ symbol (as in $answer) to show that you're storing a jQuery object (the result of running the `$( )` function). It's not a requirement that you add the $ in front of the variable name; it's just a common convention jQuery programmers use to let them know that they can use all the wonderful jQuery functions—like `.hide()`—with that variable.

NOTE The .next() function is just one of the many jQuery functions (also called *methods*) that help you navigate through a page's DOM. To learn about other helpful functions, visit *http://docs.jquery.com/Traversing*. You can also read more in "Traversing the DOM" on page 531.

6. **Add an empty if/else clause to your code, like this:**

```
$(document).ready(function() {
  $('.answer').hide();
  $('.main h2').click(function() {
  var $answer = $(this).next('.answer');
  if ( ) {

  } else {

  }
}); // end click
}); // end of ready()
```

Experienced programmers don't usually type an empty if/else statement like this, but as you're learning it can be really helpful to build up your code one piece at a time. Now, why not test to see whether the answer is currently hidden.

7. **Type $(answer.is(':hidden') inside the parentheses of the conditional statement:**

```
$(document).ready(function() {
  $('.answer').hide();
  $('.main h2').click(function() {
  var $answer = $(this).next('.answer');
  if ($answer.is(':hidden')) {

  } else {

  }
}); // end click
}); // end of ready()
```

You're using the $answer variable you created in step 5. That variable contains the element with the class answer that appears immediately after the <h2> tag the visitor clicks. Remember, that's a <div> containing the answer to the question inside the <h2> tag.

You're using jQuery's is() method to see whether that particular element is hidden. The is() method checks to see whether the current element matches a particular selector. You give the function any CSS or jQuery selector, and that function tests whether the object matches the given selector. If it does, the function returns a true value; if not, it returns a false value. That's perfect! As you know, a conditional statement needs either a true or false value to work (page 66).

The :hidden selector used here is a special, jQuery-only selector that identifies hidden elements. In this case, you're checking to see whether the answer is currently hidden. If not, then you can show it.

8. **Add line 6 below to your program:**

```
$(document).ready(function() {
  $('.answer').hide();
$('.main h2').click(function() {
 var $answer = $(this).next('.answer');
 if ($answer.is(':hidden')) {
  $answer.slideDown();
 } else {

 }
}); // end click
}); // end of ready()
```

The slideDown() function is one of jQuery's animation functions (you'll learn more about animation in the next chapter). It reveals a hidden element by sliding it down onto the page. At this point, you can check out your hard work. Save the page and check it out in a web browser. Click one of the questions on the page. The answer below it should open (if it doesn't, double-check your typing and refer to the troubleshooting tips on page 18).

If you look at the page, you'll see a blue + symbol to the left of each headline. The plus sign is a common icon used to mean, "Hey, there's more here." To indicate that a visitor can click to hide the answer, replace the plus sign with a minus sign. You can do it easily by adding a class to the <h2> tag.

9. **After the line of code you added in the last step, type the following:**

```
$(this).addClass('close');
```

Remember that $(this) applies to the element that's receiving the event (page 159). In this case, that's the <h2> tag. Thus, this new line of code adds a class named close when the answer is shown. The minus sign icon is defined within the style sheet as a background image. (Once again, CSS makes JavaScript programming easier.)

In the next step, you'll complete the second half of the toggling effect—hiding the answer when the question is clicked a second time.

10. **In the else section of the conditional statement, add two more lines of code (bolded below). The finished code should look like this:**

```
<script src="../_js/jquery.min.js></script>
<script>
$(document).ready(function() {
  $('.answer').hide();
 $('.main h2').click(function() {
  var $answer = $(this).next('.answer');
  if ($answer.is(':hidden')) {
   $answer.slideDown();
   $(this).addClass('close');
  } else {
   $answer.fadeOut();
   $(this).removeClass('close');
  }
 }); // end click
}); // end of ready()
</script>
```

This part of your program hides the answer. You could have used the slideUp() function, which hides the element by sliding it up and out of view, but to add interest and variation, in this case you'll fade the answer out of view using the fadeOut() function (about which you'll learn more on page 185).

Finally, you'll remove the close class from the <h2> tag: this makes the + sign reappear at the left of the headline.

Save the page and try it out. Now when you click a question, not only does the answer appear, but the question icon changes (Figure 5-7).

> **TIP** Once you're done, try replacing the slideDown() function with fadeIn() and the fadeOut() function with slideUp(). Which of these animation functions do you prefer?

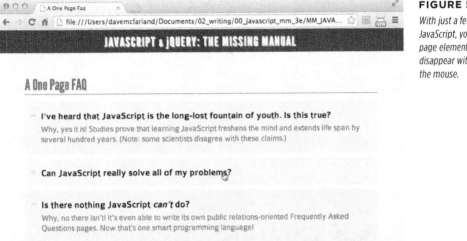

FIGURE 5-7

With just a few lines of JavaScript, you can make page elements appear or disappear with a click of the mouse.

Animations and Effects

I n the last two chapters, you learned the basics of using jQuery: how to load the jQuery library, select page elements, and respond to events like a visitor clicking on a button or mousing over a link. Most jQuery programs involve three steps: selecting an element on the page, attaching an event handler to that element, and then responding to that event by doing something. In this chapter, you'll start learning about the "doing something" part with jQuery's built-in effect and animation functions. You'll also get a little CSS refresher covering a few important CSS properties related to creating visual effects. In addition, you'll also learn how to combine CSS3 animations with jQuery's tools for super-smooth (and easy) animation effects.

■ jQuery Effects

Making elements on a web page appear and disappear is a common JavaScript task. Drop-down navigation menus, pop-up tooltips, and automated slideshows all rely on the ability to show and hide elements when you want to. jQuery supplies a handful of functions that achieve the goal of hiding and showing elements.

To use each of these effects, you apply them to a jQuery selection, like any other jQuery function. For example, to hide all tags with a class of submenu, you can write this:

```
$('.submenu').hide();
```

Each effect function also can take an optional speed setting and a *callback* function. The speed represents the amount of time the effect takes to complete, while a callback is a function that runs when the effect is finished. (See page 194 for details on callbacks.)

To assign a speed to an effect, you supply one of three string values—'fast', 'normal', or 'slow'—or a number representing the number of milliseconds the effect takes (1,000 is 1 second, 500 is half of a second, and so on). For example, the code to make an element fade out of view slowly would look like this:

```
$('element').fadeOut('slow');
```

Or if you want the element to fade out *really* slowly, over the course of 10 seconds:

```
$('element').fadeOut(10000);
```

When you use an effect to make an element disappear, the element isn't actually removed from the web browser's understanding of the page. The element still exists in the DOM, or Document Object Model (page 117). The element's code is still in the browser's memory, but its display setting (same as the CSS display setting) is set to none. Because of that setting, the element no longer takes up any visual space, so other content on the page may move into the position previously filled by the hidden element. You can see all of the jQuery effects in action on the *effects.html* file included in the *testbed* tutorial folder, as shown in Figure 6-1.

> **NOTE** The keywords used for setting the speed of an effect—'fast', 'normal', and 'slow'—are the same as 200 milliseconds, 400 milliseconds, and 600 milliseconds. So
>
> ```
> $('element').fadeOut('slow');
> ```
>
> is the same as
>
> ```
> $('element').fadeOut(600);
> ```

Basic Showing and Hiding

jQuery provides three functions for basic hiding and showing of elements:

- **show()** makes a hidden element visible. It doesn't have any effect if the element is already visible on the page. If you don't supply a speed value, the element appears immediately. However, if you supply a speed value—show(1000), for example—the element animates from the top-left corner down to the bottom-left corner.

- **hide()** hides a visible element. It doesn't have any effect if the element is already hidden, and as with the show() function, if you don't supply a speed value, the element immediately disappears. However, with a speed value the element animates out of view in a kind of shrinking motion.

- **toggle()** switches an element's current display value. If the element is currently visible, toggle() hides the element; if the element is hidden, then toggle() makes the element appear. This function is ideal when you want to have a single control (like a button) alternately show and hide an element.

In the tutorial on page 176 in Chapter 5, you saw the hide() function in action. That script uses hide() to make all of the answers on an FAQ page disappear when the page's HTML loads.

Fading Elements In and Out

For a more dramatic effect, you can fade an element out or fade it in—in either case, you're just changing the opacity of the element over time. jQuery provides four fade-related functions:

- **fadeIn()** makes a hidden element fade into view. First, the space for the element appears on the page (this may mean other elements on the page move out of the way); then the element gradually becomes visible. This function doesn't have any effect if the element is already visible on the page. If you don't supply a speed value, the element fades in using the *'normal'* setting (400 milliseconds).

- **fadeOut()** hides a visible element by making it fade out of view like a ghost. It doesn't have any effect if the element is already hidden, and like the fadeIn() function, if you don't supply a speed value, the element fades out over the course of 400 milliseconds. The FAQ tutorial on page 176 used this function to make the answers disappear.

- **fadeToggle()** combines both fade in and fade out effects. If the element is currently hidden, it fades into view; if it's currently visible, the element fades out of view. You could use this function to make an instruction box appear or disappear from a page. For example, say you have a button with the word "instructions" on it. When a visitor clicks the button, a div with instructions fades into view; clicking the button a second time fades the instructions out of view. To make the box fade in or out over the course of half a second (500 milliseconds), you could write this code:

```
$('#button').click(function() {
    $('#instructions').fadeToggle(500);
}); // end click
```

- **fadeTo()** works slightly differently than other effect functions. It fades an image to a specific opacity. For example, you can make an image fade so that it's semitransparent. Unlike other effects, you must supply a speed value. In addition, you supply a second value from 0 to 1 that indicates the opacity of the element. For example, to fade all paragraphs to 75% opacity, you'd write this:

```
$('p').fadeTo('normal',.75);
```

This function changes an element's opacity regardless of whether the element is visible or invisible. For example, say you fade a currently hidden element to 50% opacity, the element fades into view at 50% opacity. If you hide a semi-transparent element and then make it reappear, its opacity setting is recalled.

If you fade an element to 0 opacity, the element is no longer visible, but the space it occupied on the page remains. In other words, unlike the other disappearing effects, fading to 0 will leave an empty spot on the page where the element is.

In addition, if you fade an element and then hide it, that element disappears from the page. If you then show the element, it remembers its opacity setting, so the browser makes the element visible on the page again, but only at 50% opacity.

Sliding Elements

For a little more visual action, you can also slide an element in and out of view. The functions are similar to the fading elements in that they make page elements appear and disappear from view, and may have a speed value:

- **slideDown()** makes a hidden element slide into view. First, the top of the element appears and anything below the element is pushed down as the rest of the element appears. It doesn't have any effect if the element is already visible on the page. If you don't supply a speed value, the element slides in using the 'normal' setting (400 milliseconds). The tutorial on page 179 used this function to make an answer appear on the FAQ page.

- **slideUp()** removes the element from view by hiding the bottom of the element and moving anything below the element up until the element disappears. It doesn't have any effect if the element is already hidden, and as with the `slideDown()` function, if you don't supply a speed value, the element slides out over the course of 400 milliseconds.

- **slideToggle()** applies the `slideDown()` function if the element is currently hidden, and the `slideUp()` function if the element is visible. This function lets you have a single control (like a button) both show and hide an element.

UP TO SPEED

Absolute Positioning with CSS

Normally, when you hide an element on a web page, other elements move to fill the space. For example, if you hide an image on a page, the image disappears, and content below that image moves up the page. Likewise, making an element appear forces other content to move to make room for the newly displayed element. You may not want content on your page to jump around like that. In that case, you can turn to CSS and *absolute positioning* to place an element outside the flow of normal page content. In other words, you can have a div, image, or paragraph appear on top of the page, as if sitting on its own separate layer, using the CSS position property.

To make an element appear above the page, give it a position value of absolute. You can then specify the placement for that element on the page using the left, right, top, and/or bottom properties. For example, say you have a `<div>` tag containing a login form. The login form won't normally be visible, but when a visitor clicks a link, that form slides into place, sitting above other content on the page. You could position that div like this:

```
#login {
    position: absolute;
    left: 536px;
    top: 0;
    width: 400px;
}
```

This style places the div at the top of the browser window and 536px from the left edge. You can also place an element from the right edge of the browser window using the right property, or in relationship to the bottom edge of the browser window using the bottom property.

Of course, you may want to place an element in relation to something other than the browser window. For example, pop-up tooltips are usually positioned in relation to some other element: A word on the page might have a ? next to it, that when clicked, opens a small box with a definition for that word. In this case, the tooltip needs to be positioned not in relationship to the top, left, right, or bottom of the browser window, but next to the word. To achieve this, you need to supply a position that's relative to an element that surrounds the absolutely positioned item. For example, look at this HTML:

```
<span class="word">Heffalump
<span class="definition">An  imaginary,
elephant-like creature from Winnie the
Pooh</span>
</span>
```

To make the definition span appear below the word, you first need to position the word span relatively, and then position the definition absolutely like this:

```
.word { position: relative; }
.definition {
    position: absolute;
    bottom: -30px;
    left: 0;
    width: 200px;
}
```

For more information on absolute positioning, visit *www.elated.com/articles/css-positioning/* or pick up a copy of *CSS3: The Missing Manual.*

■ Tutorial: Login Slider

In this tutorial, you'll get a little practice with using jQuery effects by creating a common user interface element: a panel that slides into and out of view with a click of the mouse (see Figure 6-2).

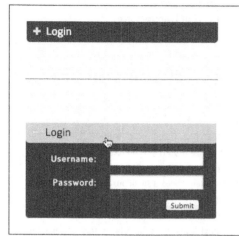

FIGURE 6-2

Now you don't see it, now you do. The login form is normally hidden from view (top), but a simple mouse click reveals the form, ready for the visitor to fill out and log on.

The basic task is rather simple:

1. **Select the paragraph with the "Login" message on it.**

   Remember that a lot of jQuery programming first begins with selecting an element on the page. In this case, the "Login" paragraph will receive clicks from a visitor.

2. **Attach a click event handler to that paragraph.**

   JavaScript isn't interactive without events: The visitor needs to interact with the selection (the Login paragraph) to make something happen.

3. **Toggle the display of the form on and off.**

   The previous two steps are just review (but necessary for so much of jQuery programming). This last step is where you'll use the effects you've learned about. You can make the form instantly appear (the show() function), slide into view (the slideDown() function), or fade into view (the fadeIn() function.)

> **NOTE** See the note on page 12 for information on how to download the tutorial files.

The Programming

1. **In a text editor, open the file *login.html* in the *chapter06* folder.**

   This file already contains a link to the jQuery file, and the $(document).ready() function (page 160) is in place. First, you'll select the paragraph with the "Login" text.

2. **Click in the empty line after the $(document).ready() function, and then type $('#open').**

The "Login" text is inside a paragraph tag that's surrounded by a link: `<a href="form.html"><p id="open">Login</p></a>`. The link will direct users to another page that has the login form in it. The link is there so if a visitor doesn't have JavaScript turned on in her browser, she won't be able to see the hidden login form. By adding a link, you assure that even people without JavaScript turned on have an alternative way to reach a login form.

The `$('#open')` you just typed selects the paragraph. Now, it's time to add an event handler.

NOTE The `<p>` tag mentioned in step 2 is wrapped in an `<a>` tag. If you've been building websites for a while, you may think that's invalid HTML. And it was—in HTML 4 and earlier. When you use the HTML5 doctype (page xvii), it's valid to wrap block-level elements like `<p>`, `<h1>`, and even `<div>` tags with links. Doing so is an easy way to create a large, clickable link target.

---

3. **Add the bolded code below, so the script looks like this:**

```
$(document).ready(function() {
  $('#open').click(function(evt) {

  }); // end click
}); // end ready
```

This code adds a click handler, so each time a visitor clicks on the paragraph, something happens. In this case, the form should appear when clicked once and then disappear when clicked again, appear on the next click, and so on. In other words, the form toggles between visible and invisible. jQuery offers three functions that will serve this purpose: `toggle()`, `fadeToggle()`, and `slideToggle()`. The difference is merely in how the effect looks.

You're also adding an argument to the anonymous function inside the `click()` method. As discussed on page 164, every event automatically gets passed an event object, which contains different properties and methods. You'll need this object to tell jQuery to stop the browser from following the link to the form page.

4. **Click in the empty line inside the click() function and type:**

```
evt.preventDefault();
```

The `preventDefault()` method stops the browser from following the link that surrounds the paragraph. Remember, the link is there to give visitors whose browsers don't have JavaScript turned on a way to reach a login form. But for browsers with JavaScript, you must tell the browser to stay on the page and run some more JavaScript.

5. **After the last line you added, type:**

```
$('#login form').slideToggle(300);
```

This code selects the login form, slides it into view if it currently isn't visible, and then slides it back out of view. Finally, you'll change the class of the paragraph, so that the "Login" paragraph can change appearance using a CSS class style.

6. **Add the code in bold below, so the finished script looks like this:**

```
$(document).ready(function() {
  $('#open').click(function(evt) {
    evt.preventDefault();
    $('#login form').slideToggle(300);
    $(this).toggleClass('close');
  }); // end click
}); // end ready
```

As you'll recall from page 159, when you're inside of an event handler, you can use $(this) to refer to the element that responds to the event. In this case, $(this) refers to the paragraph the visitor clicks on—the $('#open') in line 2 above. The toggleClass() function simply adds or removes a class from the element. Like the other toggle functions, toggleClass() adds the specified class if it's missing or removes the class if it's present. In this example, there's a class style—.close—in a style sheet on the page. This style simply adds a different background image to indicate that the visitor can close the login slider. (Look in the <head> and you can see the style and what it does.)

7. **Save the page and preview it in a web browser.**

Make sure you click the "Login" paragraph several times to see how it works. You'll find a finished version of the tutorial—*complete_login.html*—in the *chapter06* folder. Try out the other toggle effects as well, by replacing slideToggle() with toggle() or fadeToggle().

But what if you want two different effects? One for making the form appear—slide the form down into view, for example—and a different effect to make it disappear— fade out of view, for example. The code in step 5 won't work because the click() function doesn't let you choose between two different actions. You'll need to use the same trick you used in the FAQ tutorial in the previous chapter (page 174): when the visitor clicks the "Login" link, you need to check if the form is hidden. If it is, then show it; if it's visible then hide it.

To make the form slide into view then fade out of view on alternating clicks, you use this code:

```
$(document).ready(function() {
  $('#open').click(function(evt) {
    evt.preventDefault();
    if ($('#login form').is(':hidden')) {
      $('#login form').fadeIn(300);
```

```
      $(this).addClass('close');
    } else {
      $('#login form').slideUp(600);
      $(this).removeClass('close');
    }
  }); // end click
}); // end ready
```

> **NOTE** You'll find the above code in the *completed_login2.html* file in this chapter's tutorial folder.

Animations

You aren't limited to just the built-in effects jQuery supplies. Using the `animate()` function, you can animate any CSS property that accepts numeric values such as pixel, em, or percentage values. For example, you can animate the size of text, the position of an element on a page, the opacity of an object, or the width of a border.

> **NOTE** jQuery, by itself, can't animate color—for example, the color of text, background color, or border color. However, jQuery UI has many additional animation effects including the ability to animate color. You'll learn about jQuery UI's animation tools in Chapter 12.

To use this function, you must pass an object (page 136) containing a list of CSS properties you wish to change and the values you wish to animate to. For example, say you want to animate an element by moving it 650 pixels from the left edge of the page, changing its opacity to 50%, and enlarging its font size to 24 pixels. The following code creates an object with those properties and values:

```
{
  left: '650px',
  opacity: .5,
  fontSize: '24px'
}
```

Note that you only have to put the value in quotes if it includes a measurement like px, em, or %. In this example, you need quotes around `'650px'` because it contains px, but not around the opacity value because .5 is simply a number and doesn't contain any letters or other characters. Likewise, putting quotes around the property (`left`, `opacity`, and `fontSize`) is optional.

> **NOTE** JavaScript doesn't accept hyphens for CSS properties. For example, `font-size` is a valid CSS property, but you can't use it in the name of key in an object literal. The hyphen has a special meaning in JavaScript (it's the minus operator). When using CSS properties as a key in an object literal, remove the hyphen and capitalize the first letter of the word following the hyphen. For example, `font-size` becomes `fontSize`, and `border-left-width` becomes `borderLeftWidth`.

NOTE However, if you want to stick with the true CSS property names (to prevent confusion), put the property name in quotes like this:

```
{
  'font-size': '24px',
  'border-left-width': '2%'
}
```

Suppose you want to animate an element with an ID of message using these settings. You can use the animate() function like this:

```
$('#message').animate(
  {
    left: '650px',
    opacity: .5,
    fontSize: '24px'
  },
  1500
);
```

The animate() function can take several arguments. The first is an object literal containing the CSS properties you wish to animate. The second is the duration (in milliseconds) of the animation. In the above example, the animation lasts 1,500 milliseconds, or 1.5 seconds.

NOTE In order to animate a position of an element using the CSS left, right, top, or bottom properties, you must set that element's CSS position property to either absolute or relative. Those are the only two positioning properties that let you assign positioning values to them (see the box on page 187).

You can also set a property relative to its current value using += or -= as part of the animation options. For example, say you want to animate an element by moving it 50 pixels to the right each time you click on it. Here's how:

```
$('#moveIt').click(function() {
  $(this).animate(
    {
      left:'+=50px'
    },
    1000); // end animate
}); // end click
```

Easing

The jQuery effects functions (slideUp(), fadeIn(), an so on) and the animation() function accept another argument that controls the speed during the animation: *easing*, which refers to the speed during different points of the animation. For example, while moving an element across the page, you could have the element's movement start slowly, then get really fast, and finally slow down as the animation completes. Adding easing to an animation can make it more visually interesting and dynamic.

jQuery includes only two easing methods: swing and linear. The linear method provides a steady animation so each step of the animation is the same (for example, if you're animating an element across the screen, each step will be the same distance as the previous one). Swing is a bit more dynamic, as the animation starts off a bit more quickly, then slows down. Swing is the normal setting, so if you don't specify any easing, jQuery uses the swing method.

The easing method is the second argument for any jQuery effect, so to make an element slide up using the linear method, you'd write code like this:

```
$('#element').slideUp(1000,'linear');
```

When using the animate() function, the easing method is the third argument after the object containing the CSS properties you wish to animate, and the overall speed of the animation. For example, to use the linear easing method with the animation code from page 192, you'd write:

```
$('#message').animate(
{
  left: '650px',
  opacity: .5,
  fontSize: '24px'
},
1500,
'linear'
);
```

You're not limited to the two easing methods jQuery supplies, however. Thanks to the industrious work of other programmers, you can add a whole bunch of other easing methods—some quite dramatic and fun to watch. In fact, the jQueryUI library includes many additional easing methods. You'll learn more about jQuery UI in Part Three, but there's no reason not to start using it now to add a little fun to your animations.

To use the jQueryUI (which is an external JavaScript file), you attach the file to your page after the code that links to the jQuery library. Once you've linked to the jQueryUI file, you can use any of the easing methods available (see *http://api.jqueryui.com/easings/* for a complete list). For example, say you want to make a div tag grow in size when a visitor clicks on it, and you want to make the animation more interesting by using the easeInBounce method. Assuming the div has an ID of animate, your code may look like this:

```
1 <script src="_js/jquery.min.js"></script>
2 <script src="_js/jquery-ui.min.js"></script>
3 <script>
4 $(document).ready(function() {
5   $('#animate').click(function() {
6     $(this).animate(
```

```
 7      {
 8         width: '400px',
 9         height: '400px'
10      },
11      1000,
12      'easeInBounce'); // end animate
13   }); // end click
14 }); // end ready
15 </script>
```

Lines 1 and 2 load jQuery and jQueryUI. Line 4 is the ever-present ready() function (page 160), and line 5 adds a click handler to the div. The heart of the action is in lines 6–12. As you'll recall from page 159, when you're inside of an event, $(this) refers to the element that's responding to the event—in this case, the <div> tag. In other words, by clicking the div, you also animate that div by changing its width and height (lines 8 and 9). Line 11 makes the animation occur over 1 second (1,000 milliseconds), and line 12 sets the easing method to easeInBounce (you can substitute any easing method, like easeInOutSine, easeInCubic, and so on).

> **NOTE** You can find an example of this code in action in the *chapter06* folder of the tutorial files. Open the file *easing_example1.html* in a web browser. The file *easing_example2.html* shows how to toggle between clicks: animate a <div> one way on the first click, and another way on the next.

■ Performing an Action After an Effect Is Completed

Sometimes you want to do something once an effect is complete. For example, suppose when a particular photo fades into view, you want a caption to appear. In other words, the caption must pop onto the page after the photo finishes fading into view. Normally, effects aren't performed one after the other; they all happen at the same time they're called. So if your script has one line of code to fade the photo into view, and another line of code to make the caption appear, the caption will appear while the photo is still fading in.

To do something after the effect is finished you can pass a *callback function* to any effect. That's a function that runs only after the effect is completed. The callback function is passed as the second argument to most effects (the third argument for the fadeTo() function).

For example, say you have an image on a page with an ID of photo, and a paragraph below it with an ID of caption. To fade the photo into view and then make the caption fade into view, you can use a callback function like this:

```
$('#photo').fadeIn(1000, function() {
  $('#caption').fadeIn(1000);
});
```

Of course, if you want to run the function when the page loads, you'd want to hide the photo and caption first, and then do the fadeIn effect:

```
$('#photo, #caption').hide();

$('#photo').fadeIn(1000, function() {

    $('#caption').fadeIn(1000);

});
```

If you use the animate() function, then the callback function appears after any other arguments—the object containing the CSS properties to animate, the animation duration, and the easing setting. The easing setting is optional, however, so you can also just pass the animate() function, property list, duration, and callback function. For instance, say you want to not only fade the photo into view but also increase its width and height from zero to full size (a kind of zooming effect). You can use the animate() function to do that, and then display the caption like this:

```
1 $('#photo').width(0).height(0).css('opacity',0);
2 $('#caption').hide();
3 $('#photo').animate(
4   {
5       width: '200px',
6       height: '100px',
7       opacity: 1
8   },
9   1000,
10  function() {
11      $('#caption').fadeIn(1000);
12  }
13 ); // end animate
```

Line 1 of the code above sets the width, height, and opacity of the photo to 0. (This hides the photo and gets it ready to be animated.) Line 2 hides the caption. Lines 3–13 are the animation function in action and the callback occurs on lines 10–12. This probably looks a little scary, but, unfortunately, the callback function is the only way to run an action (including an effect on a different page element) at the completion of an effect.

NOTE The file *callback.html* in the *chapter06* folder shows the above code in action.

Callback functions can get tricky when you want to animate several elements in a row: for example, to make an image move into the center of the screen, followed by a caption fading into view, and then having both the image and caption fade out. To make that happen, you need to pass a callback function to a callback function like this:

```
$('#photo').animate(
    {
        left: '+=400px'
    },
    1000,
    function() { // first callback function
        $('#caption').fadeIn(1000,
            function() { // second callback function
                $('#photo, #caption').fadeOut(1000);
            } // end second callback
        ); // end fadeIn
    } // end first callback function
); // end animate
```

NOTE The file *multiple-callbacks.html* in the *chapter06* folder shows this code in action.

However, you don't need to use a callback function if you want to add additional animations to the same page element. For example, say you want to move a photo onto the screen, then make it fade out of view. In this case, you simply use the animate() function to move the photo and then fade the image out of view. You can do that like this:

```
$('#photo').animate(
    {
        left: '+=400px',
    },
    1000
); // end animate
$('#photo').fadeOut(3000);
```

In this case, although the browser executes the code immediately, jQuery places each effect into a queue, so that first the animation runs and then the fadeOut() function runs. Using jQuery chaining (page 127), you could rewrite the code above like this:

```
$('#photo').animate(
    {
        left: '+=400px',
    },
    1000).fadeOut(3000);
```

If you want a photo to fade in, fade out, and then fade in again, you can use chaining like this:

```
$('#photo').fadeIn(1000).fadeOut(2000).fadeIn(250);
```

NOTE For more information on how the effects queue works visit the jQuery website: *http://api.jquery.com/jQuery.queue/*.

One additional jQuery function that can come in handy when queuing up effects on an element is the delay(). This function simply waits the specified number of milliseconds before beginning the next effect in the queue. For example, say you want to fade an image into view, wait 10 seconds, and then fade it out of view. You can use the delay() function like this:

```
$('#photo').fadeIn(1000).delay(10000).fadeOut(250);
```

Tutorial: Animated Dashboard

In this tutorial, you'll use the animate() function to move a <div> tag right from off the left edge of the page into view. The div is absolutely positioned (see the box on page 187 for more on absolute positioning) so that most of the box hangs off the left edge of the page outside the boundaries of the browser window (Figure 6-3, left). When a visitor mouses over the visible edge of the div, that div moves completely into view (Figure 6-3, right). To make this effect more fun, use the jQueryUI library to animate the background color of the div and to use a couple of different easing methods.

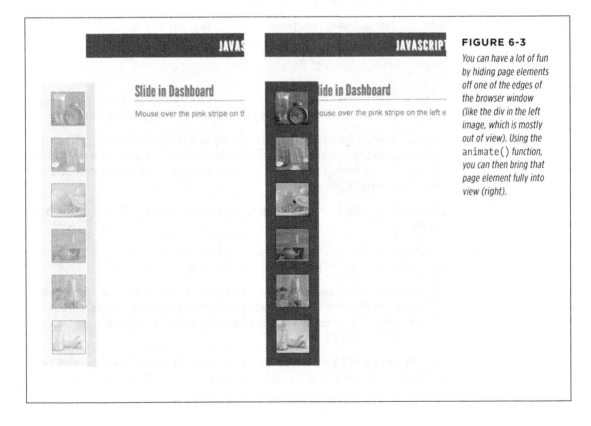

FIGURE 6-3

You can have a lot of fun by hiding page elements off one of the edges of the browser window (like the div in the left image, which is mostly out of view). Using the animate() *function, you can then bring that page element fully into view (right).*

NOTE   See the note on page 12 for information on how to download the tutorial files.

The basic task is rather simple:

1. **Select the <div> tag.**

   Remember that a lot of jQuery programming begins with selecting an element on the page—in this case, the <div> tag that a visitor mouses over.

2. **Attach a hover event.**

   The hover event (described on page 162) is a special jQuery function, not a real JavaScript event, that lets you perform one set of actions when a visitor mouses over an element, then a second set of actions when the visitor mouses off the element (the hover event is really just a combination of the mouseEnter and mouseLeave events).

3. **Add the animate function for the mouseEnter event.**

   When a visitor mouses over the div, you'll animate the left position of the div, moving it from out of view on the left edge of the browser window. In addition, you'll animate the background color of the div.

4. **Add another animate function for the mouseLeave event.**

   When a visitor moves the mouse off the div, you'll animate the div back to its original position and with its original background color.

The Programming

1. **In a text editor, open the file *animate.html* in the *chapter06* folder.**

   This file already contains a link to the jQuery file, and the $(document).ready() function (page 160) is in place. However, because you'll be animating the background color of the div and using a couple of interesting easing methods, you need to attach the jQueryUI file.

2. **Click in the empty line after the first <script> tag and add the code in bold below:**

   ```
   <script src="../_js/jquery-1.7.2.min.js"></script>
   <script src="../_js/jquery-ui.min.js"></script>
   ```

   jQueryUI is a jQuery *plug-in*. In the jQuery world, a plug-in is simply an external JavaScript file that lets you add complex effects and features to your site without a lot of programming on your part. Next you'll select the div and add the hover() function to it.

3. **Click in the empty line inside the $(document).ready() function and type $('#dashboard').hover(); // end hover so your code looks like this:**

   ```
   $(document).ready(function() {
     $('#dashboard').hover(); // end hover
   }); // end ready
   ```

`$('#dashboard')` selects the `<div>` tag (which has the ID dashboard applied to it). The `hover()` function takes two arguments—two functions (page 162)—that describe what to do when a visitor moves his mouse over the div, and then moves his mouse off the div. Instead of typing all of the code at once, you'll build it up piece by piece, first adding the `hover()` function, then adding the "shell" for two anonymous functions. This approach is helpful because the nest of parentheses, braces, commas, and semicolons can overwhelm you if you're not careful.

4. **Click between the parentheses of the hover() function and add two empty, anonymous functions:**

```
$(document).ready(function() {
  $('#dashboard').hover(
    function() {

    },
    function() {

    }
  ); // end hover
}); // end ready
```

jQuery's `.hover()` function is a bit wild looking when you've finished adding all of its programming (see step 12). However, it's really just a function that accepts two functions as arguments. It's a good idea to add the "shells" of the anonymous functions first—so you can make sure you've set it up correctly—before adding all of the programming inside the functions.

TIP Test your code frequently to make sure you haven't made any typos. In step 4, you can type `console.log('mouseEnter')` inside the first anonymous function and `console.log('mouseLeave')` inside the second anonymous function, and then preview the page in a web browser. You'll need to open the browser's console to see the results: F12 for Internet Explorer; Ctrl+Shift+J (Win) or ⌘-Option-J (Mac) for Chrome; Ctrl+Shift+K (Win) or ⌘-Option-K (Mac) for Firefox; and, ⌘-Option-C for Safari. The console should spit out the message "mouseEnter" when you mouse over the div, and "mouseLeave" when you mouse out. If no message appears in the console, you've made a typo. Double-check your code against these steps, or use the steps on page 18 to find errors using the browser's error console.

---

5. **Inside the first anonymous function, type `$(this).animate(); // end animate`.**

   As discussed on page 159, inside an event, `$(this)` refers to the page element to which you've attached the event. In this case, `$(this)` refers to the `<div>` tag with the ID dashboard. In other words, mousing over this div will also animate this div.

6. **Add an object literal with the CSS properties you wish to animate:**

```
$(document).ready(function() {
  $('#dashboard').hover(
    function() {
```

```
    $(this).animate(
  {
    left: '0',
    backgroundColor: 'rgb(27,45,94)'
  }
    ); // end animate
  },
  function() {

  }
  ); // end hover
}); // end ready
```

The first argument to the animate() function is an object (page 136) containing CSS properties. In this case, the div currently has a left value of -92px, so that most of the div is hidden, hanging off the left edge of the browser window. By animating its left value to 0, you're essentially moving it completely into view on the left edge. Likewise, thanks to jQueryUI, you're changing its background color from pink to dark blue. Next, you'll set a duration for the animation.

7. **Type a comma after the closing } of the object literal, press Return and then type** 500.

The comma marks the end of the first argument passed to the animate() function, while the 500 sets the length of the animation to half a second or 500 milliseconds. Lastly, you'll set an easing method.

8. **Type a comma after the 500, hit Return, and type 'easeInSine' so your code looks like this:**

```
$(document).ready(function() {
  $('#dashboard').hover(
    function() {
      $(this).animate(
        {
          left: '0',
          backgroundColor: 'rgb(27,45,94)'
        },
        500,
      'easeInSine'
      ); // end animate
    },
    function() {

    }
  ); // end hover
}); // end ready
```

The last argument to the animate() function here—'easeInSine'—tells the function to use an easing method that starts off somewhat slowly and then speeds up.

9. **Save the file. Preview it in a browser and mouse over the div.**

   The div should scoot into view. If it doesn't, troubleshoot using the techniques described on page 18. Of course, when you mouse off the div, nothing happens. You have to add the animate function to the second anonymous function.

10. **Add the code below to the second anonymous function:**

```
$(this).animate(
    {
        left: '-92px',
        backgroundColor: 'rgb(255,211,224)'
    },
    1500,
    'easeOutBounce'
); // end animate
```

   This code reverses the process of the first animation, moving the div back off the left edge of the window and reverting the background color to pink. The timing is a bit different—1.5 seconds instead of half a second—and the easing method is different.

11. **Save the file. Preview it in a browser and move your mouse over and off of the div.**

   You'll see the div move into view and then out of view. However, if you move the mouse over and off the div repeatedly and quickly, you'll notice some strange behavior: The div will keep sliding in and out of view long after you've finished moving the mouse. This problem is caused by how jQuery queues up animations on an element. As described on page 194, any animation you add to an element gets put into a sort of queue for that element. For example, if you have an element fade into view, fade out of view, and then fade back into view, jQuery performs each effect in order, one after the other.

   What's happening in the code for this tutorial is that each time you mouse onto and off of the div, an animation is added to the queue; so, rapidly mousing over the div creates a long list of effects for jQuery to perform: Animate the div into view, animate the div out of view, animate the div into view, animate the div out of view, and so on. The solution to this problem is to stop all animations on the div before performing a new animation. In other words, when you mouse over the div, and that div is in the process of being animated, then jQuery should stop the current animation, and proceed with the animation required by the mouseEnter event. Fortunately, jQuery supplies a function—the stop() function—for just such a problem.

12. Add `.stop()` between `$(this)` and `.animate` in the two anonymous functions. The finished code should look like this (additions are in bold):

```
$(document).ready(function() {
  $('#dashboard').hover(
    function() {
      $(this).stop().animate(
        {
          left: '0',
          backgroundColor: 'rgb(27,45,94)'
        },
        500,
        'easeInSine'
      ); // end animate
    },
    function() {
      $(this).stop().animate(
        {
          left: '-92px',
          backgroundColor: 'rgb(255,211,224)'
        },
        1500,
        'easeOutBounce'
      ); // end animate
    }
  ); // end hover
}); // end ready
```

The `.stop()` function here simply ends any animations on the div before starting a new one, and prevents multiple animations from building up in the queue.

Save the page and try it out in a web browser. You can find a finished version of this tutorial—*complete_animate.html*—in the *chapter06* folder.

■ jQuery and CSS3 Transitions and Animations

If you're keeping up with the latest and greatest in Cascading Style Sheets techniques, you may be wondering why even bother with jQuery? After all, CSS transitions let you use CSS alone to produce animations between two different CSS styles, and CSS animations let you produce complex animated effects (see Figure 6-4).

The new CSS animation effects are awesome, but not all browsers can enjoy them. Two still widely used versions of Internet Explorer—8 and 9—don't support either CSS transitions or animations. So, if you need to include those browsers in your website building plans, you'll need another way to add animation. In this instance, the jQuery animations discussed earlier in this chapter are your best bet for cross-browser animations.

> **NOTE** Browsers can't animate all CSS properties. For example, you can't animate the `font-family` property by morphing text from one font to another. But you can use many CSS properties in transitions and animations. For a complete list, visit *https://developer.mozilla.org/en-US/docs/Web/CSS/CSS_animated_properties*.

FIGURE 6-4

Cartoonist, JavaScript expert, and animator Rachel Nabors brings together CSS3 animations and jQuery to create a complete, animated adventure story at http:// codepen.io/rachelnabors/ full/lqswg. She uses jQuery to trigger animations created with CSS. Unfortunately, this cutting-edge example doesn't work in all browsers.

However, even if you want to use CSS transitions and animations, jQuery can still be a big asset. Unlike JavaScript, CSS doesn't really have any events. There's the `:hover` pseudo-class that lets you apply one style on `mouseEnter` and return to the previous style on `mouseLeave`. And the `:active` pseudo-class can sort of simulate a click. But for many events like double-clicks, scrolling, keyboard taps, there are no CSS equivalents. This means you can't use CSS alone to start an animation when a visitor types in a text field or double-clicks a button. In addition, there's no way, with just CSS, to trigger an animation on one element, when a visitor interacts with another element elsewhere on the page: for example, clicking a "Show settings" button at the top of the page to reveal a `<div>` elsewhere on the page.

NOTE This book doesn't cover CSS transitions and animations in much detail. If you want to learn more, pick up a copy of *CSS3: The Missing Manual*. For a quick primer on CSS transitions, visit *www.css3files.com/transition/*. For a primer on CSS animations, check out *www.css3files.com/animation/*.

jQuery and CSS Transitions

A CSS transition animates changes in CSS properties. An easy way to do this is just by applying a new style to an element and then animating that change. For example, you might create a class style for a button—.button, for example—that has a blue background. With a :hover pseudo-class—.button:hover—you can change that button to yellow. By adding a transition property to the .button style, you're telling the browser to animate the change from blue to yellow when the visitor mouses over the button, and animate the change from yellow to blue when the visitor mouses off of button.

You can add a transition to animate the change from one CSS property to another. For example, say you want to make all images on a page fade out of view using CSS transitions. You'd start by giving the images a style, like this:

```
img {
  opacity: 1;
}
```

The CSS opacity property controls the transparency of an element. A value of 1 means fully opaque and a value of 0 means completely transparent. You could then create a CSS class that sets the opacity to 0, like this:

```
img.faded {
  opacity: 0;
}
```

To add an animation between these two styles you use the CSS transition property. You should add this property to the original style (the one applied first to the element on the page). In this case, that's the img style. In addition, to make sure this works with all browsers that support CSS transitions, you'll need to use vendor prefixes, like this:

```
img {
  opacity: 1;
  -webkit-transition: opacity 1s;
  -moz-transition: opacity 1s;
  -o-transition: opacity 1s;
  transition: opacity 1s;
}
```

In this example, you're specifying that you want to animate any changes in opacity. You also want the animation to last for 1 second—that's the 1s in the code.

Now that the transition is added, if the faded class is added to an image, it will animate from 100% opacity to 0% opacity over the course of 1 second. In other words, it's like using jQuery's fadeOut() function with a 1 second duration. The key is getting that new class—faded—onto an image. Here's where jQuery can help you out. If you want to apply the style when the visitor clicks an image, use the click() event function like this:

```
$('img').click(function() {
  $(this).addClass('faded');
}
```

This way, when the visitor clicks the image, jQuery simply adds a class to it; the web browser then does all the heavy lifting by animating the opacity change (see Figure 6-5). If you want to fade the image back when it's clicked on again, you can use the toggleClass() function:

```
$('img').click(function() {
  $(this).toggleClass('faded');
}
```

The toggleClass() function adds a class if it's not already applied to the element, and removes it if it is. Because CSS doesn't have a selector for when a visitor clicks something, jQuery offers a simple way to trigger CSS transitions.

jQuery and CSS Animations

CSS animations provide much more control than simple transitions. With a CSS animation, you define *keyframes* that define CSS properties at certain steps in the animation. For example, you can make a button change color many times—from blue to red to orange to green—or move a <div> tag to the top of the screen, bottom of the screen to the left, and then to the right. In other words, while CSS transitions let you specify the beginning and ending styles of an animation, CSS animations let you specify any number of intermediate styles from the start of the animation to the end.

CSS animations can get pretty complex, pretty fast, and you can find resources beyond this book where you can learn more about how to create them. To get you started, this section will step you through a quick example of using jQuery to trigger an animation. Say you want to make a <div> change color and grow wider when a visitor presses the play button. (You may want to do this to highlight and reveal hidden text inside that box.)

JAVASCRIPT & jQUERY: THE MISSING MANUAL

CSS Transition Triggered By jQuery

Click a photo to make it fade out. Click the empty spot where the photo was to bring it back.

Click anywhere else on the page to fade the photos back into view.

FIGURE 6-5

jQuery and CSS transitions play well together. Using jQuery's event handlers, you can trigger CSS transition animations. In this example, clicking an image fades it out of view; clicking the empty space left behind fades the image back. This code won't work on Internet Explorer 9 or earlier, however—those browsers don't understand CSS transitions. You'll find the finished version of this page, jquery-trigger-css-animation.html, in the ch06 tutorial folder.

The first step is creating the animation. You do that with the @keyframes directive:

```
@keyframes growProgressBar{
  0% {
    width: 0%;
    background-color: red;
  }
  50% {
    background-color: yellow;
  }
  100% {
    width:88%;
    background-color: green;
  }
}
```

This kind of code may look unfamiliar to you, but it simply sets up an animation with a name—growProgressBar, in this case—and a series of keyframes. Each keyframe identifies one or more CSS properties that will change as the animation progresses. For example, the first keyframe above—0%—is the beginning of the animation and indicates that the element should be 0% wide and have a red background color.

The element will change color between keyframes from red to yellow to green. The percentage value used for each keyframe indicates when the specified CSS value should appear. Now imagine this animation will last 10 seconds (you'll specify the animation time separately, as you'll see in a moment). So at 0% of 10 seconds, the background color is red and the element is 0% wide. At 50% of 10 seconds, or half way through the animation at 5 seconds, the color will be yellow. Finally, when the animation is over at 100% of the time or 10 seconds, the element will be green and 88% wide.

Because in the example above the width is specified only in the first and last keyframes, that width will change from 0% to 88% over the entire duration of the animation.

Once you create the keyframes, you can add that animation to any number of elements. For example, say you had the following HTML: <div class="progressBar">. You could add this animation to that div like this:

```
.progressBar {
  animation-name: growProgessBar;
  animation-duration 10s;
  animation-fill-mode: forwards;
}
```

This code applies the animation to this element and makes it run for 10 seconds. The last CSS line—animation-fill-mode: forwards;—just makes sure that when the animation is finished, the element keeps the end keyframe properties. That is, the div should be 88% wide with green background. (Without this setting, the element will revert back to the styles it had before the animation ever happened.)

However, the animation in this code would begin immediately, as soon as the web page loads. What you want to do is start the animation when the visitor clicks a button. You can "pause" an animation (that is, stop it before it ever starts), using another animation property: animation-play-state. To prevent the animation from starting immediately, add that property to the style, with a value of paused:

```
.progressBar {
  animation-name: growProgessBar;
  animation-duration 10s;
  animation-fill-mode: forwards;
  animation-play-state: paused;
}
```

Adding the jQuery to trigger this animation is the easy part. All you need to do is change the animation-play-state property to running to start the animation. You can do that easily with the css() function. For example, you could create a button with an ID of start that, when clicked, would begin the animation. Here's how the jQuery code would look:

```
$('#start').click(function() {
  $('.progressBar').css('animation-play-state', 'running');
});
```

If you had a pause button with an ID of pause, you could use that to pause the animation as well:

```
$('#pause').click(function() {
  $('.progressBar').css('animation-play-state', 'paused');
});
```

Fortunately, jQuery is savvy about vendor prefixes. When you set the value of a CSS property that requires vendor prefixes, jQuery will set each of the vendor-prefixed versions of the CSS properties as well. Thank you, jQuery!

Another approach is to create the keyframes and a separate class style that has all of the animation properties defined in it. It looks something like this:

```
.animateDiv {
  animation-name: growProgessBar;
  animation-duration 10s;
  animation-fill-mode: forwards;
}
```

The element you want to animate won't have this .animateDiv class style applied to it when the page loads; as a result, that element won't start animating yet, which is exactly what you want. Then, you use jQuery to add this class to the element. As soon as the element receives this new class, the animation will begin. This approach lets you skip the animation-play-state property:

```
$('#start').click(function() {
  $('.progressBar').addClass('animateDiv');
});
```

You'll find examples of both approaches in this chapter's tutorial folder: *jquery-trigger-css-animation1.html* and *jquery-trigger-css-animation2.html*.

At this point, there are some drawbacks to using CSS animations. As mentioned earlier, IE 9 and earlier don't understand them at all. In addition, it's not as easy to keep track of the progress of a CSS animation as it is in jQuery.

NOTE Eventually, developers will probably all end up using CSS animations in combination with JavaScript. The W3C and browser vendors are working on lots of ways to control CSS animations with JavaScript by adding new events that detect the progress of CSS animations. If you do want to run jQuery code when a CSS animation is finished running, check out this article: *http://blog.teamtreehouse.com/using-jquery-to-detect-when-css3-animations-and-transitions-end*.

Common jQuery Tasks

In web design, you constantly work with a reliable handful of elements: Images can enhance a page's design and highlight web page elements. Links form the foundation of the Web, letting people jump from one piece of information to another, and you can control how those links work, whether in the same browser window or a new one. And when you've got lots of links, it's good to know how to collect them in a top-notch navigation bar. jQuery can make all of these page elements more interactive and exciting. In this chapter, you'll see how to use jQuery to make your images, links, windows, and navigation bars work better than ever.

Swapping Images

One of the most common uses of JavaScript is the simple *image rollover*. When you move your mouse over an image, it changes to another image. This basic technique has been used since the dawn of JavaScript to create interactive navigation bars whose buttons change appearance when the mouse hovers over them.

But in the past couple of years, more and more designers have turned to CSS to achieve this same effect. However, even if you're using CSS to create interactive navigation bars, it's still useful to understand how to use JavaScript to swap one image for another if you want to create slide shows, image galleries, and add other types of interactive graphic effects to a web page.

Changing an Image's src Attribute

Every image displayed on a web page has a src (short for *source*) attribute that indicates a path to a graphic file; in other words, it points to an image on a web server. If you change this property to point to a different graphic file, the browser displays the new image instead. Using jQuery, you can dynamically change the src attribute for an image.

For example, suppose you have an image on a page and that you've assigned it an ID of photo. The HTML might look something like this:

```
<img src="images/image.jpg" width="100" height="100" id="photo">
```

To swap in another image file, you just use the attr() function (page 137) to set the tag's src property to a new file, like this:

```
$('#photo').attr('src','images/newImage.jpg');
```

> **NOTE** When you change the src property of an image using JavaScript, the path to the image file is based on the page location, *not* the location of the JavaScript code. This point can be confusing when you use an external JavaScript file (page 15) located in a different folder. In the example above, the web browser would try to download the file *newImage.jpg* from a folder named *images*, which is located in the same folder as the web page. That method works even if the JavaScript code is included in an external file located in another folder elsewhere on the site. Accordingly, it's often easier to use root-relative links inside external JavaScript files (see the box on page 11 for more information on the different link types).

Changing an image's src attribute doesn't change any of the <img> tag's other attributes, however. For example, if the alt attribute is set in the HTML, the swapped-in image has the same alt text as the original. In addition, if the width and height attributes are set in the HTML, changing an image's src property makes the new image fit inside the same space as the original. If the two graphics have different dimensions, then the swapped-in image will be distorted.

In a situation like rollover images in a navigation bar, the two images will most likely be the same size and share the same alt attribute, so you don't get that problem. But you can avoid the image distortion problem entirely by simply leaving off the original image's width and height properties. Then when the new image is swapped in, the web browser displays the image at the dimensions set in the file.

Another solution is to first download the new image, get its dimensions, and then change the src, width, height, and alt attributes of the <img> tag:

```
1    var newPhoto = new Image();
2    newPhoto.src = 'images/newImage.jpg';
3    var photo = $('#photo');
4    photo.attr('src',newPhoto.src);
5    photo.attr('width',newPhoto.width);
6    photo.attr('height',newPhoto.height);
```

> **NOTE** The line numbers on the left aren't part of the code, so don't type them. They're just to make the code easier to read.

The key to this technique is line 1, which creates a new image object. To a web browser, the code new Image() says, "Browser, I'm going to be adding a new image to the page, so get ready." The next line tells the web browser to actually download the new image. Line 3 gets a reference to the current image on the page, and lines 4-6 swap in the new image and change the width and height to match the new image.

> **TIP** The jQuery attr() function can set multiple HTML attributes at once. Just pass an object (page 136) that contains each attribute name and new value. You could write the jQuery code from above more succinctly, like this:
>
> ```
> var newPhoto = new Image();
> newPhoto.src = 'images/newImage.jpg';
> $('#photo').attr({
>    src: newPhoto.src,
>    width: newPhoto.width,
>    height: newPhoto.height
> });
> ```

Normally, you'd use this image swap technique in conjunction with an event handler. For example, you can make an image change to another image when a visitor mouses over the image. This rollover effect is commonly used for navigation bars. However, you can change an image in response to any event: For example, you can make a new photo appear each time an arrow on a page is clicked, as in a slideshow.

Swapping Images with jQuery

There's another way to swap images that doesn't involve altering the src attribute or futzing around by individually changing other image attributes. As you read on page 127, jQuery is great at making quick changes to a page's HTML. You can use jQuery to add, remove, and change HTML. A straightforward way to swap one image with another is to replace the original image's <img> tag with a new <img> tag using jQuery's replaceWith() method.

For example, say you had the following image on your page:

```
<img src="sad.png" alt="Sad Face" height="50" width="50" id="swap">
```

You could replace that image with another <img> tag like this:

```
$('#swap').replaceWith('<img src="happy.png" alt="Happy Face" height="100" width="150" id="swap">');
```

jQuery's replaceWith() method replaces the current selection with whatever HTML you give it. Using this method you can set different src, alt, width, and height attributes in the string you provide to replaceWith()—for example: <img src="happy. png" alt="Happy Face" height="100" width="150" id="swap">. This is usually easier than changing each of those attributes separately as described in the previous section.

TIP The `replaceWith()` method returns the HTML that jQuery replaces. In other words, you can save the HTML you're removing. For example, if you wanted to replace an image but save its HTML for later use, you could do this:

```
var oldImage = $('#swap').replaceWith('<img src="happy.png" alt="Happy Face"
height="100" width="150" id="swap">');
```

Now, that `oldImage` variable contains the HTML that was replaced. Using the example from above, that variable would now hold:

```
<img src="sad.png" alt="Sad Face" height="50" width="50" id="swap">
```

You could then use that `oldImage` variable again—for example, to swap that image back into place later.

Preloading Images

There's one problem with swapping in a new image using the techniques listed above: When you swap the new file path into the `src` attribute, the browser has to download the image. If you wait until someone mouses over an image before downloading the new graphic, there'll be an unpleasant delay before the new image appears. In the case of a navigation bar, the rollover effect will feel sluggish and unresponsive.

To avoid that delay, *preload* any images that you want to immediately appear in response to an action. For example, when a visitor mouses over a button on a navigation bar, the rollover image should appear instantly. Preloading an image simply means forcing the browser to download the image *before* you plan on displaying it. When the image is downloaded, it's stored in the web browser's cache so any subsequent requests for that file are served from the visitor's hard drive instead of downloaded a second time from the web server.

Preloading an image is as easy as creating a new image object and setting the object's `src` property. In fact, you already know how to do that:

```
var newPhoto = new Image();
newPhoto.src = 'images/newImage.jpg';
```

What makes this preloading is that you do it before you need to replace an image currently on the web page. One way to preload is to create an array (page 44) at the beginning of a script containing the paths to all graphics you wish to preload, then loop through that list, creating a new image object for each one:

```
var preloadImages = ['images/roll.png',
                     'images/flower.png',
                     'images/cat.jpg'];
for (var i=0; I < preloadImages.length; i++) {
  new Image().src = preloadImages[i];
}
```

Lines 1–3 are a single JavaScript statement that creates an array named `preloadImages`, containing three values—the path to each graphic file to preload. (As mentioned on page 46, it's often easier to read an array if you place each array item on its own line.) Lines 4–6 show a basic JavaScript for loop (see page 82), which runs once for each item in the preloadImages array. Line 5 creates a new image object and sets its src attribute to a file path from the preloadImages array—that's the magic that causes the image to download.

You can use jQuery to achieve the same effect, and skip the new Image() function like this:

```
var preloadImages = ['images/roll.png',
                     'images/flower.png',
                     'images/cat.jpg'];
for (var i=0; i < preloadImages.length; i++) {
  $('<img>').attr('src',preloadImages[i]);
}
```

In line 5, you create a new <img> element using jQuery. This technique is new to you and a little tricky. By giving jQuery an actual tag <img> (including the < and > symbols), you create a new HTML element. Normally in jQuery, you leave out the < and >—as in $('img')—which tells jQuery to select existing image tags on the page. As you can see, jQuery can not only select existing HTML tags, but also *create* brand new ones.

The rest of the code—.attr('src', preloadImages[i])—uses the attr() function (which you saw on page 137). It sets the src property to the path of the new image file, which forces the web browser to download and preload the graphic.

Either technique for preloading images—the jQuery and non-jQuery method—works fine, so feel free to use whichever one makes the most sense to you.

Rollover Images

A *rollover image* is just an image swap (as discussed on page 209) triggered by the mouse moving over an image. In other words, you simply assign the image swap to the mouseover event. For example, say you have an image on the page with an ID of photo. When the mouse rolls over that image, you want the new image to appear. You can accomplish that with jQuery like this:

```
1   <script src="js/jquery.min.js"></script>
2   <script >
3   $(document).ready(function() {
4     var newPhoto = new Image();
5     newPhoto.src = 'images/newImage.jpg';
6     $('#photo').mouseover(function() {
7         $(this).attr('src', newPhoto.src);
8     }); // end mouseover
9   }); // end ready
10  </script>
```

Line 3 waits until the HTML has loaded, so the JavaScript can access the HTML for the current photo. Lines 4 and 5 preload the image that you want to swap in. The rest of the code assigns a mouseover event handler to the image, with a function that changes the image's src attribute to match the new photo.

Rollover images usually revert back to the old image once you move the mouse off the image, so you need to also add a mouseout event to swap back the image. As discussed on page 162, jQuery provides its own event, called hover(), which takes care of both the mouseover and mouseout events:

```
1   <script src="js/jquery.min.js"></script>
2   <script>
3   $(document).ready(function() {
4       var newPhoto = new Image();
5       newPhoto.src = 'images/newImage.jpg';
6       var oldSrc=$('#photo').attr('src');
7       $('#photo').hover(
8       function() {
9       $(this).attr('src', newPhoto.src);
10      },
11      function() {
12      $(this).attr('src', oldSrc);
13      }); // end hover
14  }); // end ready
15  </script>
```

The hover() function takes two arguments: The first argument is an anonymous function telling the browser what to do when the mouse moves over the image; the second argument is a function telling the browser what to do when the mouse moves off the image. This code also adds a variable, oldSrc, for tracking the original src attribute—the path to the file that appears when the page loads.

You aren't limited to rolling over just an image, either. You can add a hover() function to any tag—a link, a form element, even a paragraph. In this way, any tag on a page can trigger an image elsewhere on the page to change. For example, say you want to make a photo swap out when you mouseover a page's <h1> tag. Assume that the target image is the same as the previous example. You just change your code as shown here in bold:

```
1   <script src="js/jquery.min.js"></script>
2   <script>
3   $(document).ready(function() {
4       var newPhoto = new Image();
5       newPhoto.src = 'images/newImage.jpg';
6       var oldSrc=$('#photo').attr('src');
7       $('h1').hover(
8         function() {
9           $('#photo').attr('src', newPhoto.src);
10        },
11        function() {
```

```
12          $('#photo').attr('src', oldSrc);
13      }); //  end hover
14    }); // end ready
15  </script>
```

■ Tutorial: Adding Rollover Images

In this tutorial, you'll add a rollover effect to a series of images (see Figure 7-1). You'll also add programming to preload the rollover images in order to eliminate any delay between mousing over an image and seeing the rollover image. In addition, you'll learn a new technique to make the process of preloading and adding the rollover effect more efficient.

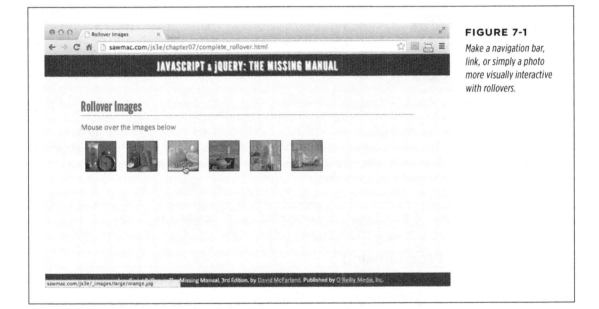

FIGURE 7-1

Make a navigation bar, link, or simply a photo more visually interactive with rollovers.

Overview of the Task

The tutorial file *rollover.html* (located in the *chapter07* tutorial folder) contains a series of six images (see Figure 7-2). Each image is wrapped by a link that points to a larger version of the photo, and all of the images are wrapped in a <div> tag with an ID of gallery. Basically, you're trying to achieve two things:

- Preload the rollover image associated with each of the images inside the <div>.

- Attach a hover() function to each image inside the <div>. The hover() function swaps the rollover image when the mouse moves over the image, then swaps back to the original image when the mouse moves off.

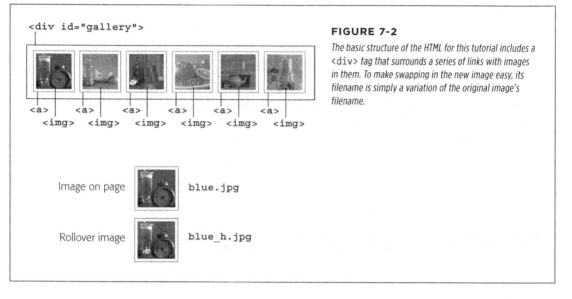

FIGURE 7-2

*The basic structure of the HTML for this tutorial includes a
<div> tag that surrounds a series of links with images
in them. To make swapping in the new image easy, its
filename is simply a variation of the original image's
filename.*

From this description, you can see that both steps are tied to the images inside
the <div>, so one way to approach this problem is to first select the images inside
the <div>, then loop through the selection, preloading each image's rollover and
attaching a hover() function.

> **NOTE** See the note on page 12 for information on how to download the tutorial files.

The Programming

1. **In a text editor, open the file *rollover.html* in the *chapter07* folder.**

   This file already contains a link to the jQuery file, and the $(document).ready()
   function (page 160). The first step is to select all of the images within the <div>
   tag and set up a loop with the jQuery each() function discussed on page 138.

2. **Click in the empty line after the $(document).ready() function and type
   $('#gallery img').each(function() {.**

   The selector #gallery img selects all <img> tags within a tag that has the ID
   gallery. jQuery's each() function provides a quick way to loop through a bunch
   of page elements, performing a series of actions on each element. The each()
   function takes an anonymous function (page 138) as its argument. It's a good
   idea to close (end) the anonymous and each functions before writing the code
   that runs inside the function, so you'll do that next.

3. **Press Return twice, and then type }); // end each to close the anonymous function, end the call to the each() function, and terminate the JavaScript statement. Your code should now look like this:**

```
1   <script src="../_js/jquery.min.js"></script>
2   <script>
3   $(document).ready(function() {
4     $('#gallery img').each(function() {
5
6     }); // end each
7   }); // end ready
```

At this point, the script loops through each of the images in the gallery, but doesn't do anything with them yet. The first order of business is to capture the image's src property and store it in a variable that you'll use later on in the script.

> **NOTE** The JavaScript comments—// end each and // end ready—aren't required for this script to work. However, they do make it easier to identify what part of the script the line goes with.

4. **Click inside the empty line (line 5 in step 3) and type:**

```
var imgFile = $(this).attr('src');
```

As described on page 139, you can use $(this) to refer to the current element in the loop; in other words, $(this) will refer to each of the image elements in turn. The jQuery attr() function (page 137) retrieves the specified HTML attribute. In this case, it retrieves the src property of the image and stores it in a variable named imgFile. For example, for the first image, the src property is _images/small/blue.jpg, which is the path to the image that appears on the page.

You can use that very src value to preload the image.

5. **Hit Return to create a blank line, and then add the following three lines of code:**

```
var preloadImage = new Image();
var imgExt = /(\.\w{3,4}$)/;
preloadImage.src = imgFile.replace(imgExt,'_h$1');
```

To preload an image you must first create an image object. In this case, you created the variable preloadImage to store the image object. Next, you'll preload the image by setting the Image object's src property.

One way to preload images (as discussed on page 212) is to create an array of paths to the image files you wish to preload, and then loop through each item in the array, creating an image object and adding the image's source to the object. However, that approach can require a lot of work because you need to know the path to each of the rollover images and type those paths into the array.

In this example, you'll use a more creative (and less labor-intensive method) to preload images. You just have to make sure you store the rollover image in the same location as the original image and name it similarly. For this web page, each image on the page has a corresponding rollover image with an _h added to the end of the image name. For example, for the image *blue.jpg*, there's a rollover image named *blue_h.jpg*. Both files are stored in the same folder, so the path to both files is the same.

Here's the creative part: Instead of manually typing the src of the rollover to preload it like this, preloadImage.src='_images/small/blue_h.jpg', you can let JavaScript figure out the *src* by simply changing the name of the original image's source so it reflects the name of the rollover. In other words, if you know the path to the image on the page, then its rollover image simply has an h added directly before the .jpg in that path. So *_images/small/blue.jpg* becomes *_images/small/blue_h.jpg*, and *_images/small/orange.jpg* becomes *_images/small/orange_h.jpg*.

That's what the other two lines of code do. The first line—var imgExt = /(\.\w{3,4}$)/;—creates a *regular expression*. A regular expression (which you'll learn about on page 546) is a pattern of characters that you can search for in a string: for example, three numbers in a row. Regular expressions can be tricky, but essentially this one matches a period followed by three or four characters at the end of a string. For example, it will match both *.jpeg* in */images/small/blue.jpeg* and *.png* in */images/orange.png*.

The next line—preloadImage.src = imgFile.replace(imgExt,'_h$1');—uses the replace() method (see page 560) to replace the matched text with something else. Here a *.jpg* in the path name will be replaced with *_h.jpg*, so *images/small/blue.jpg* is changed to *images/small/blue_h.jpg*. This technique is a little tricky because it uses a regular expression subpattern (see the box on page 561 for full details), so don't worry if you don't exactly understand how it works.

Now that the rollover image is preloaded, you can assign the hover() event to the image.

6. **Hit Return and then add the code listed on lines 9–11 below:**

```
1   <script src="../_js/jquery.min.js"></script>
2   <script>
3   $(document).ready(function() {
4   $('#gallery img').each(function() {
5     var imgFile = $(this).attr('src');
6     var preloadImage = new Image();
7     var imgExt = /(\.\w{3,4}$)/;
8     preloadImage.src = imgFile.replace(imgExt,'_h$1');
9     $(this).hover(
10
11    ); // end hover
12  }); // end each
13  }); // end ready
```

jQuery's hover() function is just a shortcut method of applying a mouseenter and mouseleave event to an element. To make it work, you pass two functions as arguments. The first function runs when the mouse moves over the element—in this case, the image changes to the rollover. The second function runs when the mouse moves off the element—here, the rollover image swaps back to the original image.

7. **In the empty line (line 10 in step 6), add the following three lines of code:**

```
function() {
  $(this).attr('src', preloadImage.src);
},
```

This first function simply changes the src property of the current image to the src of the rollover image. The comma at the end of the last line is required because the function you just added is acting as the first argument in a call to the hover() function—a comma separates each argument passed to a function.

8. **Finally, add the second function (lines 13–15 below). The finished script should look like this:**

```
1    <script src="../_js/jquery.min.js"></script>
2    <script>
3    $(document).ready(function() {
4    $('#gallery img').each(function() {
5      var imgFile = $(this).attr('src');
6      var preloadImage = new Image();
7      var imgExt = /(\.\w{3,4}$)/;
8      preloadImage.src = imgFile.replace(imgExt,'_h$1');
9      $(this).hover(
10       function() {
11         $(this).attr('src', preloadImage.src);
12       },
13       function() {
14         $(this).attr('src', imgFile);
15       }
16     ); // end hover
17   }); // end each
18 }); // end ready
```

This second function simply changes the src attribute back to the original image. In line 5, the path to the image originally on the page is stored in the variable imgFile. In this function (line 14), you access that value again to set the src back to its original value. Save the page, view it in a web browser, and mouse over each of the black and white images to see them pop into full color.

NOTE You can achieve the same rollover effect using CSS. This article explains how: *http://kyleschaeffer.com/ development/pure-css-image-hover/*. However, it's still good to understand how to swap one image for another with JavaScript. Because CSS is limited to just a few different states like `:hover`, or `:active`, using JavaScript opens up the possibility for using different events like double-clicks or key presses to trigger an image swap. Likewise, you might want to trigger an image swap using an element other than the image itself. For example, you might have a button labeled Flip Images that, when clicked, swaps every image on the page with new images.

◼ Tutorial: Photo Gallery with Effects

Now you'll expand on the last tutorial to create a single-page photo gallery. You'll be able to load a larger image onto the page when a visitor clicks a thumbnail image (see Figure 7-3). In addition, you'll use a couple of jQuery's effect functions to make the transition between larger images more visually interesting.

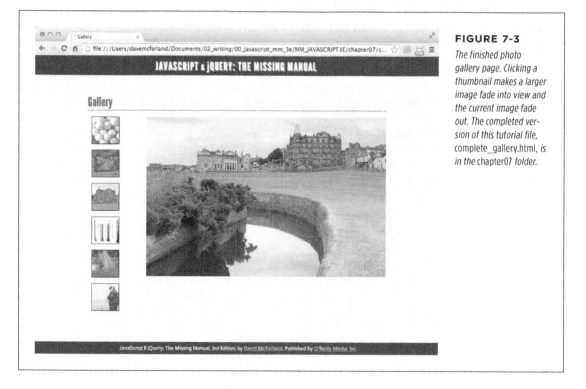

FIGURE 7-3

The finished photo gallery page. Clicking a thumbnail makes a larger image fade into view and the current image fade out. The completed version of this tutorial file, complete_gallery.html, *is in the* chapter07 *folder.*

Overview of the Gallery

The way the gallery works is pretty straightforward—click a thumbnail to see a larger image. However, this tutorial shows you how to add a few features that make the presentation more interesting by using fade effects to swap larger images in and out of the page.

Another important technique you'll use here is *unobtrusive JavaScript*. That simply means that users who have JavaScript turned off will still be able to access the larger versions of the photos. To achieve that, each thumbnail image is wrapped in a link that points to the larger image file (see Figure 7-4). For those without JavaScript, clicking the link exits the current web page and follows the link to load the larger image file. It won't look fantastic—the visitor has to exit the gallery page and will see just the single larger image, but the photos will at least be accessible. For folks who have JavaScript turned on, clicking a link will make the larger image fade into view on the page.

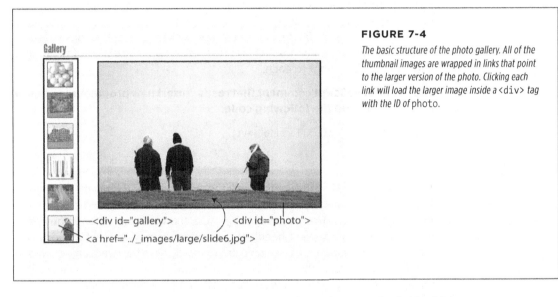

FIGURE 7-4

The basic structure of the photo gallery. All of the thumbnail images are wrapped in links that point to the larger version of the photo. Clicking each link will load the larger image inside a <div> tag with the ID of photo.

All of the action occurs when the link is clicked, so this script uses the link's click event to achieve the following steps:

- **Stop the default behavior of the link.** Normally, clicking a link takes you to another page. On this page, clicking the link around a thumbnail exits the web page and displays a larger image. Because you'll use JavaScript to display the image, you can add some JavaScript code to prevent the browser from following that link.

- **Get the href value of the link.** The link actually points to the larger image, so by retrieving the link's href, you also get the path to the larger image file.

- **Create a new image tag to insert into the page.** This image tag will include the path from the href value.

- **Fade the old image out while fading the new image in.** The current image fades out of view as the large version of the clicked thumbnail fades into view.

The tutorial includes a few additional nuances, but these four steps cover the basic process.

The Programming

This tutorial expands on the previous one, but the starting web page has been reorganized a little: There's a new set of thumbnails and they are now in a left column, and a <div> tag with an ID of photo has been added to the page (see Figure 7-4).

> **NOTE** See the note on page 12 for information on how to download the tutorial files.

1. **In a text editor, open the file *gallery.html* in the *chapter07* folder.**

   This file contains the programming from the previous tutorial, plus a new <div> tag to display the large version of each thumbnail image. Because the process of displaying a gallery image is triggered by clicking one of the links wrapped around the thumbnail images, the first step is to create a selection of those links and add the click event to each.

2. **Locate the JavaScript comment that reads "insert new programming below this line" and add the following code:**

   ```
   $('#gallery a').click(function(evt) {

   }); // end click
   ```

   The selector #gallery a selects all link tags inside another tag with the ID gallery. The .click is a jQuery function for adding a click event handler (see page 152 if you need a refresher on events). Also, the code passes an anonymous function to the click event handler (as mentioned on page 149, functions that are executed in response to an event automatically have the event object passed to them). In this case, the variable evt stores that event object. You'll use it in the next step to stop the browser from following the clicked link.

3. **Between the two lines of code you added in step 2, type the following:**

   ```
   evt.preventDefault();
   ```

   Normally, clicking a link makes the web browser load whatever the link points to (a web page, graphic file, PDF document, and so on). In this case, the link is just there so that people who don't have JavaScript turned on will be able to go to a larger version of the thumbnail image. To prevent the web browser from following the link for those who have JavaScript enabled, you run the event object's preventDefault() function (page 165).

   Next, you'll get the link's href attribute.

4. **Hit Return to create a new, blank line, and then add the bolded line of code below:**

   ```
   $('#gallery a').click(function(evt) {
     evt.preventDefault();
     var imgPath = $(this).attr('href');
   }); // end click
   ```

Here, $(this) refers to the element that's clicked—a link. A link's href attribute points to the page or resource the link goes to. In this case, each link contains a path to the larger image. That's important information, since you can use it to add an image tag that points to the image file. But before you do that, you need to get a reference to the large image that's currently displayed on the page. After all, you need to know what it is before you can fade it out of view.

TIP You'll see that each line of code inside the click() event in step 4 is indented. That's optional, but it helps make the code more readable, as described in the box on page 34. Many programmers use two spaces (or a tab) for each level of indentation.

---

5. **Hit Return and type:**

    ```
    var oldImage = $('#photo img');.
    ```

    The variable oldImage holds a jQuery selection containing the <img> element inside the photo <div> (see Figure 7-4). Now it's time to create a tag for the new image.

6. **Hit Return again and add the following to the script:**

    ```
    var newImage = $('<img src="' + imgPath +'">');
    ```

    There are quite a few things going on here. jQuery lets you select an element that's in the page's HTML. For example, $('img') selects all images on the page. In addition, the jQuery object can add a *new* element to the page. For example, $('<p>Hello</p>') creates a new paragraph tag containing the word Hello. This line creates a new <img> tag and stores it in a variable named newImage.

    Because the jQuery object expects a string as an argument ('<p>Hello</p>', for example), this line of code *concatenates* or *combines* several strings to make one. The first string (surrounded by single quotes) is <img src="; the second string is stored in the variable imgPath (which you created in step 4) and is the path to the image file (for example, ../_images/large/slide1.jpg); the third string (also surrounded by single quotes) is ">. Taken altogether, they add up to an HTML tag: <img src="../_images/large/slide1.jpg">. When the script passes it to the jQuery object like this, $('<img src="../_images/large/slide2.jpg">'), the browser creates a page element. It isn't displayed on the page yet, but the browser is ready to add it to the page at any time.

7. **Add the code listed below on lines 6–8 so the code you've added so far looks like this:**

    ```
    1  $('#gallery a').click(function(evt) {
    2    evt.preventDefault();
    3    var imgPath = $(this).attr('href');
    4    var oldImage = $('#photo img');
    5    var newImage = $('<img src="' + imgPath + '">');
    6    newImage.hide();
    ```

```
7     $('#photo').prepend(newImage);
8     newImage.fadeIn(1000);
9   }); // end click
```

In line 6, the newly created image (which is stored in the variable newImage) is hidden using the hide() function described on page 184. This step is necessary because if you just added the image tag created in line 5, the image would be immediately visible on the page—no cool fade-in effect. So you first hide the image, and then add it to the page inside the photo <div> (line 7). The prepend() function (described on page 129) adds HTML inside a tag. Specifically, it adds the HTML at the very beginning of the tag. At this point, there are two images on the page inside the photo <div>—Figure 7-5 shows how one image can sit on top of the other. The image on top is invisible, but in line 8, the fadeIn() function makes the image slowly fade in over the course of 1,000 milliseconds (1 second).

Now it's time to make the original image fade out.

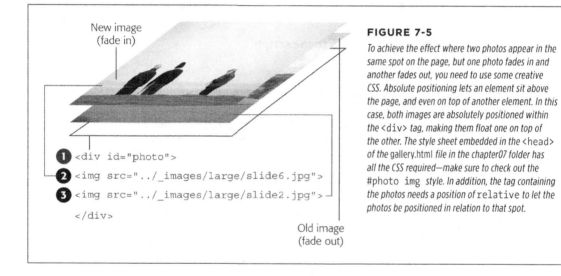

FIGURE 7-5

To achieve the effect where two photos appear in the same spot on the page, but one photo fades in and another fades out, you need to use some creative CSS. Absolute positioning lets an element sit above the page, and even on top of another element. In this case, both images are absolutely positioned within the <div> tag, making them float one on top of the other. The style sheet embedded in the <head> of the gallery.html file in the chapter07 folder has all the CSS required—make sure to check out the #photo img style. In addition, the tag containing the photos needs a position of relative to let the photos be positioned in relation to that spot.

8. **Press Return and then add these three lines of code:**

```
oldImage.fadeOut(1000,function(){
  $(this).remove();
}); // end fadeout
```

In step 5, you created a variable named oldImage and stored a reference to the original image on the page into it. That's the image you want to fade out, so you apply the fadeOut() function. You pass two arguments to the function: The first is the duration of the effect—1,000 milliseconds (1 second); the second is a callback function (as described on page 194 in Chapter 6). The callback function runs *after* the fade out effect finishes, and removes the <img> tag for that image.

NOTE The remove() function is discussed on page 130. It actually removes the tag from the DOM, which erases the HTML from the browser's memory, freeing up computer resources. If you didn't take this step, each time your visitor clicks a thumbnail, a new <img> tag would be added (see step 7), but the old one would simply be hidden, not deleted. You'd end up with lots and lots of unnecessary hidden <img> tags still embedded in the web page, slowing down the responsiveness of the web browser.

There's one final step—loading the first image. Currently the <div> tag where the photo goes is empty. You could type an <img> tag in that spot, so when the page loads there'd be a larger image for, say, the first thumbnail. But why bother—you've got JavaScript!

9. **Add one last line after the end of the `click()` function (line 13 below), so your completed code looks like this:**

```
1    $('#gallery a').click(function(evt) {
2      evt.preventDefault();
3      var imgPath = $(this).attr('href');
4      var oldImage = $('#photo img');
5      var newImage = $('<img src="' + imgPath + '">');
6      newImage.hide();
7      $('#photo').prepend(newImage);
8      newImage.fadeIn(1000);
9      oldImage.fadeOut(1000,function(){
10        $(this).remove();
11     }); // end fadeout
12   }); // end click
13   $('#gallery a:first').click();
```

This last statement has two parts. First the selector—#gallery a:first—selects just the first link only in the gallery <div>. Next is the click() function. So far, you've used jQuery's click() function to assign a function that runs when the event occurs. However, if you don't pass any arguments to an event function, jQuery simply triggers that event, causing any previously defined event handlers to run. So, this line triggers a click on the first link that makes the web browser run the function that you created earlier in lines 1–11. That is, it makes the larger image for the first thumbnail fade into view when the page loads.

Save the page and preview it in a web browser. Not only do the thumbnails change color when you mouse over them, clicking a thumbnail makes its associated large image fade into view. (If you're having trouble with your code, the file *complete_gallery.html* contains a working copy of the script.)

Controlling How Links Behave

Links make the web go around. Without the instant access to information provided by linking from page to page and site to site, the Web wouldn't have gotten very far. In fact, it wouldn't be a *web* at all. Links are one of the most common and powerful pieces of HTML—there are lots of JavaScript techniques for enhancing how links work. In this section, you'll learn the basics of using JavaScript to control links and how to open links in new windows.

You undoubtedly know a lot about links already. After all, they're the heart of the web, and the humble <a> tag is one of the first pieces of HTML a web designer learns. Adding JavaScript to a page can turn a basic link into a supercharged gateway of interactivity...but only if you know how to use JavaScript to control your links. Once you've got the basics, the latter part of this section will give you real-world techniques for controlling links with JavaScript.

Selecting Links with JavaScript

To do anything with a link on a web page, you must first select it. You can select all of the links on a page, just one, or a particular group of related links—for example, links that are grouped together in the same part of a page, or that share a certain characteristic such as external links that point to other websites.

jQuery gives you great flexibility in selecting document elements. For example, the code $('a') creates a jQuery selection of all links on a page. Furthermore, jQuery lets you refine your selections, so you can quickly select all the links within a particular area of a page. For example, you can select all of the links contained inside a bulleted list with an ID of mainNav like this: $('#mainNav a'). Likewise, you can use attribute selectors (page 123) to select links whose href values (the paths to the files they point to) match a certain pattern such as links that point to other sites, or that point to PDF files (see page 124 for an example).

And once you've used jQuery to select those links, you can use the jQuery functions to work with those links. For example, you can loop through each link using the each() function (page 138), apply a class to those links with the addClass() function (page 131), or add event functions to them (page 152). You'll see many examples of what you can do with links in this chapter.

Determining a Link's Destination

After you've selected one or more links, you may be interested in where they lead. For example, in the the photo gallery you built on page 220, each link pointed to a larger image; by retrieving the path, you used JavaScript to display that larger image. In other words, you extracted the link's href value and used that path to create a new <img> tag on the page. Likewise, you can retrieve the href value that leads to another web page and, instead of going to that page when you click the link, you can actually display the new web page on top of the current page.

In each case, you need to access the href attribute, which is an easy process using jQuery's attr() function (page 137). For example, say you've applied an ID to the link that leads back to a site's home page. You can retrieve that link's path like this:

```
var homePath = $('#homeLink').attr('href');
```

You'll find this information handy in many instances. For example, say you want to add the full URL of a link pointing outside of your site next to the link text itself. In other words, suppose you have a link with the text "Learn more about bark beetles" that points to *http://www.barkbeetles.org/*. Now suppose you'd like to change the text on the page to read, "Learn more about bark beetles (*www.barkbeetles.org*)", so when people print the page they'll know where that link leads to.

You can do that easily with the following JavaScript:

```
1    $('a[href^="http://"]').each(function() {
2      var href = $(this).attr('href');
3      href = href.replace('http://','');
4      $(this).after(' (' + href + ')');
5    });
```

> **NOTE** The line numbers at left aren't part of the code, so don't type them. They're just to help with examining the code line by line.

Line 1 selects all external links then runs the each() function (page 138), which simply applies a function to each link (in other words, it "loops" through the list of links). In this case, lines 2–4 make up the function body. Line 2 retrieves the link's href of the link (for example, *http://www.barkbeetles.org*). Line 3 is optional—it just simplifies the URL for display purposes by removing the http://, so the href variable now holds something like *www.barkbeetles.org* (you can learn about JavaScript's replace() method on page 560). Finally, line 4 adds the contents of the variable href (wrapped in parentheses) after the link: (*www.barkbeetles.org*), and line 5 closes the function.

You can take this basic premise even further by creating a bibliography at the bottom of the page listing all the links mentioned in the article. Instead of adding each web address after each link, you list each web address at the bottom of the page in a separate div. Try it!

Don't Follow That Link

When you add a click event to a link, you may not want the web browser to follow its normal behavior of exiting the current page and loading the link's destination. For example, in the image gallery on page 220, when you click a link on a thumbnail image, the page loads a larger image. Normally, clicking that link would exit the page and show the larger image by itself on a blank page. However, in this case, instead of following the link to the image, you stay on the same page, where the larger image is loaded.

There are a couple of ways you can stop a link in its tracks—you can return a false value or use jQuery's preventDefault() function (page 165). For example, say you have a link that takes a visitor to a login page. To make your site feel more responsive, you want to use JavaScript to show a login form when the visitor clicks that link. In other words, if the visitor's browser has JavaScript turned on, when he clicks that link, a form will appear on the page; if the browser has JavaScript turned off, clicking the link will take him to the login page.

There are several steps to achieve this goal:

1. **Select the login link.**

   See the first part of this section, if you need ideas for how to do this.

2. **Attach a `click` event handler.**

   You can use jQuery's `click()` function to do so. The `click()` function takes another function as an argument. That function contains the steps that happen when a user clicks the link. In this example, only two steps are required.

3. **Show the login form.**

   The login form might be hidden from view when the page loads—perhaps an absolutely positioned `<div>` tag directly under the link. You can show the form using the `show()` function or one of jQuery's other show effects (see page 184).

4. **Stop the link!**

   This step is the most important. If you don't stop the link, the web browser will simply leave the current page and go to the login web page.

Here's how to stop the link using the "return false" method. Assume that the link has an ID of `showForm` and the hidden `<div>` tag with the login form has an ID of `loginForm`:

```
1   $('#showForm').click(function() {
2       $('#loginForm').fadeIn('slow');
3       return false;
4   });
```

Line 1 accomplishes both steps 1 and 2 above; line 2 displays the hidden form. Line 3 is the part that tells the web browser "Stop! Don't follow that link." You must put the `return false;` statement as the last line of the function, because once the JavaScript interpreter encounters a return statement, it exits the function.

You can also use jQuery's `preventDefault()` function, like this:

```
1   $('#showForm').click(function(evt) {
2       $('#loginForm').fadeIn('slow');
3       evt.preventDefault();
4   });
```

The basic details of this script are the same as the one before it. The main difference is that the function assigned to the click event now accepts an argument—evt—which represents the event itself (the event object is described on page 164). The event has its own set of functions (methods) and properties—the `preventDefault()` function simply stops any default behavior associated with the event (for a click on a link, that's loading a new web page).

■ Opening External Links in a New Window

Losing visitors is one of the great fears for any site that depends on readership. On-line magazines that make money from ad revenue don't want to send people away from their site if they can help it; an e-commerce site doesn't want to lose a potential customer by letting a shopper click a link that leaves the site behind; and while displaying a portfolio of completed websites, a web designer might not want to let a potential client leave her site while viewing one of the designer's finished projects.

Many sites deal with these fears by opening a new window whenever a link to another site is clicked. That way, when the visitor finishes viewing the other site and closes its window, the original site is still there. HTML has long provided a method of doing that using a link's `target` attribute—if you set that attribute to _blank, a web browser knows to open that link in a new window (or, with browsers that use tabs, open the link a new tab).

NOTE There's quite a bit of debate among web usability experts about whether the strategy of opening new windows is a good or bad idea. For example, see *www.useit.com/alertbox/990530.html.*

Manually adding `target="_blank"` to each link that points outside your site takes a long time and is easy to forget. Fortunately, using JavaScript and jQuery, there's a quick, easy method to force web browsers to open external links (or any links you want) in a new window or browser tab. The basic process is simple:

1. **Identify the links you wish to open in a new window.**

   In this chapter, you'll use a jQuery selector (page 119) to identify those links.

2. **Add the `target` attribute with a value of _blank to the link.**

   You might be thinking, "Hey, that's invalid HTML. I can't do that." Well, first, it's only invalid for the strict versions of HTML 4.01 and XHTML 1.0, so it's fine for any other document type, including the HTML5 doctype. Second, your page will still validate since an HTML validator (for example, *http://validator.w3.org/*) analyzes only the actual HTML code in the web page file and not any HTML that JavaScript adds. And, lastly, every browser understands the `target` attribute, so you know that the link will open in a new window, regardless of the standards for strict document types.

In jQuery, you can complete the previous two steps in one line of code:

```
$('a[href^="http://"]').attr('target','_blank');
```

The jQuery selector—`$('a[href^="http://"]')`—uses an attribute selector (page 123) to identify <a> tags that begin with *http://* (for example, *http://www.yahoo.com*). The selector identifies all of these types of links and then uses the jQuery `attr()` function (page 137) to set the `target` attribute to _blank for each link. And that's it!

If you think you'll also be linking to secure web addresses—ones that begin with *https://*—then you should use this code instead:

```
$('a[href^="http://"], a[href^="https://"]').attr('target','_blank');
```

This uses a group selector to choose URLs that begin with either *http://* or *https://*.

Finally, if you use absolute paths to specify links to files on your own site, you need one more step. For example, if your site's address is *www.your_site.com*, and you link to other pages or files on your site like this: *http://www.your_site.com/a_page.html*, then the previous code also forces those links to open in a new window. If you don't want to open up a new window for every page of your site (your poor visitors), you need code like the following:

```
var myURL = location.protocol + '//' + location.hostname;
$('a[href^="http://"], a[href^="https://"]') ↵
.not('[href^="'+myURL+'"]').attr('target','_blank');
```

> **NOTE** The ↵ symbol at the end of a line of code indicates that the next line should really be typed as part of the first line. A *really* long line of JavaScript code won't fit on this book's page, so it's broken up over two lines.

This code first specifies the URL for your site and assigns it to a variable—myURL. The URL of your site is accomplished with a little bit of help from the browser's window object. A browser knows the protocol used for accessing a URL—http:, or for secured sites, https:. It's stored in the location object's protocol property. Likewise, the name of the site—*www.sawmac.com*, for example—is stored in the hostname property. So the JavaScript location.protocol + '//' + location.hostname generates a string that looks like *http://www.sawmac.com*. Of course, the hostname in this case changes depending upon where the page with this JavaScript code comes from. For example, if you put this code on a page that comes from *http://www.your_site.com*, then when someone views the page from that site, location.hostname would be *www.your_site.com*.

The second line of code starts with a jQuery selector, which retrieves all links that start with *http://*. Then, the not() function removes any links start with your URL—in this example, links that point to *http://www.sawmac.com*. (The not() function is a useful way of excluding some elements from a jQuery selection—to learn more about it, visit *http://api.jquery.com/not*.)

So to actually use this code on a page, you just link to the jQuery file, add the $(document).ready() function (page 160), and then insert the previous code inside like this:

```
<script src="js/jquery.min.js"></script>
<script>
$(document).ready(function() {
  var myURL = location.protocol + '//' + location.hostname;
  $('a[href^="http://"], a[href^="https://"]')↵
.not('[href^="'+myURL+'"]').attr('target','_blank');
});
</script>
```

Another approach would be to create an external JavaScript file (see page 15); in that file, create a function that runs the code to make external links open in a new window; attach that file to the page; and then call the function on that page.

For example, you could create a file named *open_external.js* with the following code:

```
function openExt() {
  var myURL = location.protocol + '//' + location.hostname;
  $('a[href^="http://"], a[href^="https://"]')↵
.not('[href^="'+myURL+'"]').attr('target','_blank');
}
```

Then add the following code to each page on your site that you'd like to apply this function to:

```
<script src="js/jquery.min.js"></script>
<script src="js/open_external.js"></script>
<script>
$(document).ready(function() {
  openExt();
  // add any other JavaScript code to the page
});
</script>
```

The benefit of using an external file is that if you've used this function throughout your site on hundreds of pages, you can easily update the script so it's fancier—for example, you can later change the openExt() function to open external pages in a frame within the current page. In other words, an external *.js* file makes it easier for you to keep your scripts consistent across your entire site.

■ Creating New Windows

Web browsers let you open new windows and customize many of their properties, like width and height, onscreen placement, and even whether they display scrollbars, menus, or the location (address) bar. The basic technique uses the open() method, which follows this basic structure:

```
open(URL, name, properties)
```

The open() method takes three arguments. The first is the URL of the page you wish to appear in the new open window—the same value you'd use for the href attribute for a link (*http://www.google.com, /pages/map.html,* or *../../portfolio.html,* for example). The second argument is a name for the window, which can be any name you'd like to use; follow the same naming rules used for variables as described on page 30. Finally, you can pass a string containing the settings for the new window (its height and width, for example).

In addition, when opening a new window, you usually create a variable to store a reference to that window. For example, if you want to open Google's home page in a new window that's 200 pixels tall and 200 pixels wide, you can write this code:

```
var newWin= open('http://www.google.com/', ↵
'theWin','height=200,width=200');
```

This code opens a new window and stores a reference to that window in the variable newWin. The section "Use the Window reference" on page 234 describes how to use this reference to control the newly opened window.

> **NOTE** The name you provide for the new window (theWin in this example) doesn't do much. However, once you've provided a name, if you try to open another window using the same name, you won't get a new window. Instead, the web page you request with the open() method just loads in the previously created window with the same name.

Window Properties

Browser windows have many different components: scroll bars, resize handles, toolbars, and so on, as shown in Figure 7-6. In addition, windows have a width and height and a position on the screen. You can set most of these properties when you create a new window by creating a string containing a comma-separated list of each property and its setting as the third argument for the open() method. For example, to set the width and height of a new window and to make sure the location bar appears, you can write this:

```
var winProps = 'width=400,height=300,location=yes';
var newWin = open('about.html','aWin',winProps);
```

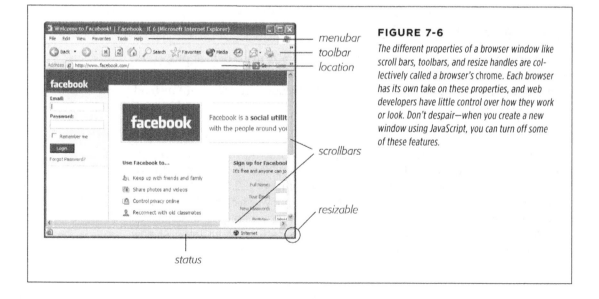

FIGURE 7-6

The different properties of a browser window like scroll bars, toolbars, and resize handles are collectively called a browser's chrome. Each browser has its own take on these properties, and web developers have little control over how they work or look. Don't despair—when you create a new window using JavaScript, you can turn off some of these features.

You set the properties that control the size or position of the window using pixel values, while the other properties take either the value yes (to turn on that property) or no (to turn off that property). In the case of any of the yes/no properties (like toolbar or location), if you don't specify a property value, the web browser turns that property off (for example, if you don't set the location property, the web browser hides the location field that normally appears at the top of the window). Only height, width, left, top, and toolbar work consistently across browsers. As noted in the following list, some browsers ignore some of these properties entirely, so if you create pop-up windows with JavaScript, make sure to test on every browser you can:

- **height** dictates the height of the window, in pixels. You can't specify percentage values or any other measurement beside pixels. If you don't specify a height, the web browser matches the height of the current window.

- **width** specifies the width of the window. As with height, you can only use pixels, and if you leave this property out, the web browser matches the width of the current window.

- **left** is the position, in pixels, from the left edge of the monitor.

- **top** is the position, in pixels, from the top edge of the monitor.

- **scrollbars** appear at the right and bottom edges of a browser window whenever a page is larger than the window itself. To completely hide the scrollbar, set this property to no. You can't control which scrollbar is hidden (it's either both or neither), and some browsers, like Chrome and Safari, won't let you hide scrollbars.

- **status** controls the appearance of the status bar at the bottom of the window. Firefox and Internet Explorer normally don't let you hide the status bar, so it's always visible in those browsers.

- **toolbar** sets the visibility of the toolbar containing the navigation buttons, bookmark button, and other controls available to the particular browser. On Safari, the toolbar and location settings are the same: Turning on either one displays both the toolbar buttons and the location field.

- **location** specifies whether the location field is visible. Also known as the address bar, this field displays the page's URL and lets visitors go to another page by typing a new URL. Opera, Internet Explorer, and Firefox don't let you hide a page's location entirely. This feature is supposed to stop nefarious uses of JavaScript like opening a new window and sending you off to another site that looks like the site you just left. Also, Safari displays the toolbars as well as the location field with this property turned on.

- **menubar** applies to browsers that have a menu at the top of their windows (for example, the common File and Edit menus that appear on most programs). This setting applies only to Windows browsers—Macs have the menu at the top of the screen, not the individual window. And it doesn't apply to IE 7 and later, which doesn't normally display a menu bar.

NOTE For amazing examples of JavaScript programming that use the `window.open()` method, check out *http://experiments.instrum3nt.com/markmahoney/ball/* and *http://thewildernessdowntown.com/*.

USE THE WINDOW REFERENCE

Once you open a new window, you can use the reference to that window to control it. For example, say you open a new window with the following code:

```
var newWin = open('products.html','theWin','width=300,height=300');
```

The variable `newWin`, in this case, holds a reference to the new window. You can then apply any of the browser's window methods to that variable to control the window. For example, if you want to close that window, you could use the `close()` method like this:

```
newWin.close();
```

Browsers support many different methods for the window object, but here are some of the most commonly used to control the window itself:

- **close()** closes the specified window. For example, the command `close()` closes the current window. But you can also apply this to a window reference: `newWin.close()`, for example. You can use any event to trigger this close, like a mouse click on a button that says, "Close this window."

NOTE If you use any one of these commands by itself, it applies to the window running the script. For example, adding the statement `close();` to a script closes the window the script is in. However, if you've opened a window and have a reference to that window (for example, a variable that you created when the window was opened, like `newWin`), then you can close that window from the page that originally created the window using the reference like this: `newWin.close()`.

- **blur()** forces the window to "lose focus." That is, the window moves behind any already opened windows. It's a way to hide an opened window, and web advertisers use it to create "pop under" ads—windows that open underneath any current windows, so when the visitor closes all of his windows, there's an annoying ad waiting for him.

- **focus()** is the opposite of `blur()` and forces the window to come to the top of the stack of other windows.

- **moveBy()** lets you move the window a set number of pixels to the right and down. You provide two arguments to the method—the first specifies the number of pixels to move to the right, and the second specifies how many pixels to move the window down. For example, `newWin.moveBy(200,300);` moves the window that's referenced by the `newWin` variable 200 pixels to the right and 300 pixels down on the screen. You can also use negative numbers so to move the window up 100 pixels and to the left 300 pixels you could write this code:

```
newWin.moveBy(-100,-300);
```

- **moveTo()** moves the window to a specific spot on the monitor specified by left and top values. This command is the same as setting the `left` and `top` properties (page 233) when opening a new window. For example, to move a window to the top-left corner of the monitor, you can run this code: `moveTo(0,0);`.

- **resizeBy()** changes the width and height of the window. It takes two arguments: The first specifies how many pixels wider to make the window; the second specifies how many pixels taller the window should be. For example, `resizeBy(100,200);` makes the current window 100 pixels wider and 200 pixels taller. You use negative numbers to make the window smaller.

- **resizeTo()** changes the windows dimensions to a set width and height. For example, `resizeTo(200,400);` changes the current window so it's 200 pixels wide and 400 pixels tall.

- **scrollBy()** scrolls the document inside the window by the specified number of pixels to the right and down. For example, `scrollBy(100,200);` scrolls the current document down 200 pixels and 100 pixels to the right. If the document can't scroll (in other words, the document fits within the window without scrollbars or the document has been scrolled to the end), then this function has no effect.

- **scrollTo()** scrolls the document inside the window to a specific pixel location to the right and from the top of the page. For example, `scrollTo(100,200);` scrolls the current document down 200 pixels from its top and 100 pixels from its left edge. If the document can't scroll (in other words, the document fits within the window without scrollbars or the document has been scrolled to the end), then this function has no effect.

TIP   The jQuery `scrollTo` plug-in provides a simple way to control document scrolling using JavaScript. Find out more about this plug-in at *https://github.com/flesler/jquery.scrollTo*.

■ EVENTS THAT CAN OPEN A NEW WINDOW

In the short history of the web, pop-up windows have gotten a bad name. Unfortunately, many websites have abused the `open()` method to force unwanted pop-up ads on unsuspecting visitors. These days, most browsers have a pop-up blocking feature that prevents unwanted pop-up windows, so even though you can add the JavaScript code to make a new window open as soon as a page loads, or when the visitor closes a window, most browsers won't let it happen. The visitor will either see a message letting her know that the browser prevented a new window from opening, or maybe get no indication at all that a pop-up window was blocked.

In fact, many browsers won't let you open a browser window using most events like `mouseover`, `mouseout`, or `keypress`. The only reliable way to use JavaScript to open windows is to trigger the action when the user clicks a link or submits a form. To do so, you add a `click` event to any HTML element (it doesn't have to be a link) and open a new window. For example, say you want some links on a page to open in a new window that's 300 pixels square, has scrollbars, and is resizable, but doesn't have any of the other browser chrome like toolbars. You can add a class name—popup, for example—to each of those special links, and then add this jQuery code to your page:

```
$('.popup').click(function() {
  var winProps='height=300,width=300,resizable=yes,scrollbars=yes';
  var newWin=open($(this).attr('href'),'aWin',winProps);
}
```

■ Introducing jQuery Plug-ins

With JavaScript and jQuery, you're already capable of adding useful interactivity to your web pages with just a few lines of code. But you may be hungry for more interesting and complex user interface add-ons. For example, how about a *slider*? That's a popular front page element that lets you display multiple slides, one after the other, on a large area of the page, as shown in Figure 7-7. The slides can be photos, videos, or just <div> tags full of HTML content. Visitors can navigate the slides by clicking buttons, or click a slide to jump off to another page on the site.

Programming sliders (also called *carousels*) can be difficult and complex. Fortunately, one of the benefits of jQuery is the large eco-system of *plug-ins*. A jQuery plug-in is a JavaScript file that works in conjunction with jQuery. Plug-ins do cool things like add sliders to a web page, help validate form input, and more. jQuery UI, which you'll read about in Part Three, is a large and complex plug-in that lets you add all the controls needed to build large-scale web applications. Most plug-ins, however, are small JavaScript files that do a single task really well.

The Wow Slider pictured in Figure 7-7 is a commercial plug-in (that is, it costs money if you put it on a business website). But many plug-ins are free and open source, which means you can use them without paying, and, even better, you can open the JavaScript files and see how they're written. Examining other developers' code is a great way to learn how to program plug-ins, and also gives you the possibility of improving on the plug-in by changing the code.

In this book, you'll learn about a few useful plug-ins, but there are literally thousands more scattered across the web. To begin with, the jQuery website hosts a directory of plug-ins at *http://plugins.jquery.com*. You'll find still more by visiting sites like Sitepoint.com or WebDesignerDepot.com, or just searching the Web. For example, searching for something like *google maps jquery plug-in* will result in a listing of possibly useful plug-ins to help you add a Google Map to your site.

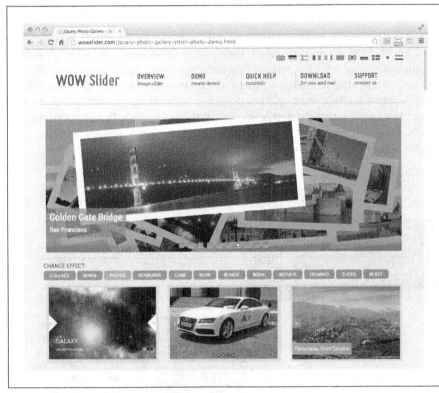

FIGURE 7-7

*Wow Slider (http://
wowslider.com) is a full-
featured jQuery plug-in
that makes it very easy to
create animated sliders.
It has many options for
displaying slides and can
animate the transition
between slides in some
cool and beautiful ways.*

What to Look for in a jQuery Plug-in

Before you download and use the first plug-in you stumble upon, you should think
about whether you really need it. You'll come across lots of cool plug-ins that do
fun things, and it's easy to be tempted by a plug-in because it looks great and does
something really cool. The problem is that it's very easy to add dozens of plug-ins
to a site, which forces your site's visitors to download dozens of plug-ins. All that
downloading slows your site's download speed and potentially slows down your
visitors' web browsers as they chug through multiple JavaScript programs to display
your web pages.

In addition, when you add a plug-in, you become dependent upon that plug-in's
programmer. If there was an undiscovered bug when the plug-in was released,
either you or the developer will need to fix it, or you'll have to remove the plug-in
from your site.

So it's good to limit your plug-ins to just the ones you really need and look for plug-
ins that have a good track record. If the plug-in was posted on a website just today,
and it's version 0.0.0.1, think twice before using it. You can determine how mature

a plug-in is by its version number—something like 0.0.1 means it's brand new, while version 4.1.10 has gone through multiple revisions.

Likewise, look at the plug-in's release date. jQuery's plug-in site provides this information for each plug-in. For example, the Chosen plug-in (whose listing is pictured in Figure 7-8) made its first appearance on the jQuery site on March 5, 2013. Sites like Github (*http://github.com*), which hosts many open source projects, including thousands of jQuery plug-ins, also show when the project was first created. It's also important to see when the plug-in was last updated. A plug-in that shows a long history of upgrades, bug fixes, and new features will probably be around for a while and continue to be updated if problems arise. If the plug-in was last updated 4 years ago, steer clear—it might not work with the latest version of jQuery, and certainly won't have been tested on the latest browsers.

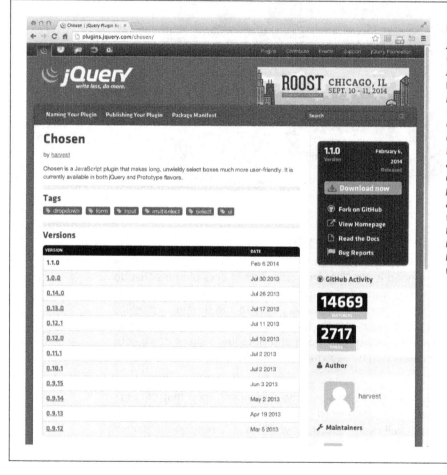

FIGURE 7-8

jQuery.com hosts its own public listing of free jQuery plug-ins at http:// plugins.jquery.com. Each plug-in has its own page, which shows a history of its development (the dates for when it was first added, each revision, and latest update). You can also see how many people (called watchers*) are following it. The more watchers a plug-in has the more popular it is. For example, the plug-in listed here has 14,669 watchers!*

You can also search for the plug-in on Google or Bing and read reviews or discussions on developer forums. If you find lots of search results saying things like "I can't get the XYZ plug-in to work in WordPress" or "Help! The XYZ plug-in makes my site unusable," then you may also have trouble.

jQuery Plug-in Basics

While jQuery plug-ins vary in complexity and quality, they usually have similar setup requirements. When you download a plug-in, you'll get the plug-in file itself—a *.js* file. In addition, there's frequently a CSS file that handles the visual formatting of any HTML that the plug-in adds to the page. For example, jQuery UI's super-useful Datepicker plug-in (page 351), which adds a pop-up calendar menu to a form field, making it very easy for a visitor to select a date, is formatted by an accompanying CSS file. In addition, plug-ins often include graphic files, which add visual components to the plug-in's HTML.

The basic process is as follows:

1. **Download the files.**

   You can get the files from the plug-in's website or, very often, from Github. The download often includes extra files that were used in developing the plug-in, like demonstration pages, special tests, and supplemental files. For now, you only need the *.js* file, the *.css* file, and any graphics the plug-in uses.

2. **Move the required files to your site's folder.**

   You can do this in a few ways. You can move the plug-in's *.js* file into the same directory you keep your other JavaScript files, and move the *.css* file into the directory where you keep your other CSS files. It's often best, however, to keep the graphic files for the plug-in with the *.css* file, because it's common for a plug-in's CSS file to reference those graphics.

   Another approach—one that makes it a lot easier to keep track of (and remove) plug-ins—is to put all the plug-in components in a folder with that plug-in's name, and then put that folder in the folder where you keep your JavaScript files, or in another folder simply named *plugins* in the root of your site. For example, say you download a plug-in named Super Plugin: it might include a file named *jquery.super-plugin.min.js*, a CSS file named *super-plugin.css*, and a folder named images with some graphics in it. You could create a folder named *super_plugin* and put all of those files inside it. Then take the *super_plugin* folder and place it in your site (for example, in a folder named *scripts* or a dedicated plug-in folder named *plugins*).

3. **Attach the plug-in's CSS file to a web page.**

   This code will go in the <head> of the web page, and should go directly below the link to other style sheets you use:

```
<link href="css/site.css" rel="stylesheet">
<link href="plugins/super_plugin/super-plugin.css" rel="stylesheet">
```

4. Link to the plug-in's JavaScript file.

jQuery plug-ins are dependent on jQuery, so you first need to link to the jQuery file, then link to any plug-in files, like this:

```
<script src="js/jquery.min.js"></script>
<script src="plugins/super_plugin/jquery.super-plugin.min.js"></script>
```

5. Modify your page's HTML.

Yes, that instruction is a little vague. However, each plug-in is different and has different rules governing its use. In most cases, to get a plug-in to work, you need to get into the page's HTML and add some content. That could be as simple as adding a few classes to already existing tags. These classes act as the plug-in's "handles," indicating which chunks of HTML the plug-in should select and modify.

Other times, you'll need to add specifically structured HTML. For example, jQuery UI's Accordion widget (page 338) needs you to create a particular structure: a HTML tag that acts as the accordion's "container," and a series of HTML header tags followed by divs, like this:

```
<div id="accordion">
  <h3>First header</h3>
  <div>First content panel</div>
  <h3>Second header</h3>
  <div>Second content panel</div>
</div>
```

The plug-in will modify the presentation of the HTML in some way: display it as an accordion with areas that a visitor can hide and show; create a moving set of sliders (like the Wow Slider pictures in Figure 7-6); or display a pop-up tooltip.

6. Call the plug-in function.

The exact method varies from plug-in to plug-in. However, many plug-ins follow a similar pattern: make a jQuery selection and then call the plug-in function. The jQuery selection is often an ID or a class selector that you added to your page's HTML. For example, with the jQuery UI Accordion it's as simple as selecting the HTML tag that contains the accordion elements and calling the accordion() function, like this:

```
$('#accordion').accordion();
```

Yes, it is often as simple as one line of code. Most plug-ins also let you modify how the plug-in works by passing additional instructions to it, often in the form of a JavaScript object literal. You can customize jQuery UI's Datepicker widget in many different ways, just by passing different information to the plug-in. For example, to show three months worth of calendars side by side and a panel below them that includes a button for selecting the current date, you'd provide an object literal to the plug-in like this:

```
$('#date').datepicker({
  numberOfMonths: 3,
  showButtonPanel: true
});
```

Each plug-in is different, but most follow the general pattern described in these steps. In the next section, you'll get some experience working with a specific plug-in in detail.

Build a Responsive Navigation Bar

As a website grows in size, it gets harder and harder to provide access to every part of the site without overwhelming the page (and its visitors) with links. To make navigating a site more manageable, many web designers use drop-down menu systems to keep links hidden until they're called for (see Figure 7-9). While there are CSS-only solutions to this problem, they aren't always ideal. First, CSS-only pop-up menus are temperamental: If you roll off the menu for just a split second, the menu disappears. In addition, the CSS code is often pretty complex, and if you're not a CSS master, you may prefer a JavaScript solution.

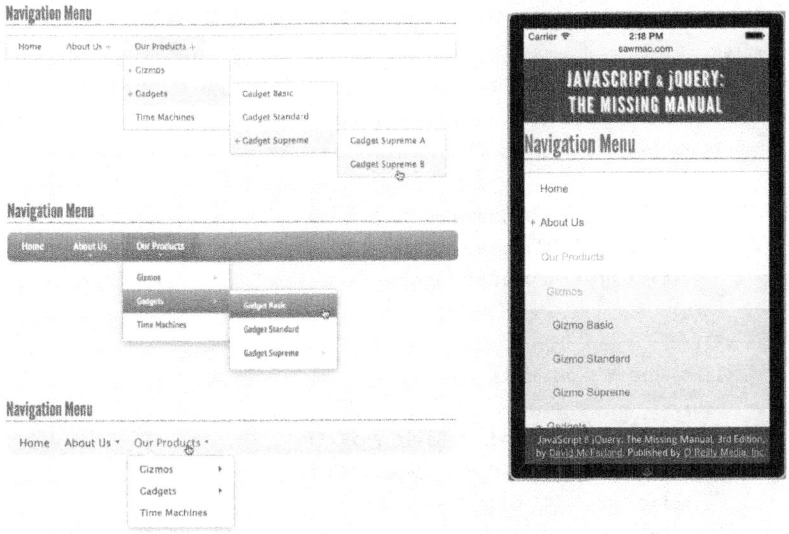

FIGURE 7-9

Navigating a website filled with many pages and sections can be confusing. A navigation bar with drop-down menus is an elegant way to simplify the presentation of your site's links (left). The jQuery SmartMenus plug-in (www.smart-menus.org) makes it easy for you to include many navigation options and include several already created visual themes: simple (left, top), blue (left, middle), and clean (left, bottom). And, when viewed on a phone, the menu collapses to an easy-to-navigate list of links (right).

Fortunately, with just a little JavaScript, you can create an animated menu system that works smoothly for your visitors in all browsers. This section uses a jQuery plug-in (jQuery SmartMenus) that simplifies the process of making a drop-down menu. In addition, this plug-in creates a *responsive* navigation bar—one that automatically adjusts to the size of the browser window, collapsing to a smaller size for mobile phones (Figure 7-9, right).

This navigation menu relies a lot more on HTML and CSS than other JavaScript techniques you've learned in this book so far. You'll use HTML to create a nested set of links, and CSS to format those links to look like a navigation bar and position and hide any submenus. But sit tight—you'll then add some JavaScript to animate the display of menus as the mouse moves over the navigation bar's buttons.

The HTML

The HTML for your navigation menu is a bulleted list created with the <ul> tag. Each of the top-level <li> tags represents one of the main buttons on the navigation bar. To create a submenu, you add a nested <ul> tag within the <li> tag the menu belongs to. For example, the HTML for the menu pictured in Figure 7-9 looks like this:

```html
<ul id="navigation" >
  <li><a href="#">Home</a></li>
  <li><a href="#">About Us </a>
    <ul>
      <li><a href="#">Our History</a></li>
      <li><a href="#">Driving Directions</a></li>
      <li><a href="#">Hours</a></li>
    </ul>
  </li>
  <li><a href="#">Our Products </a>
    <ul>
      <li><a href="#">Gizmos </a>
        <ul>
          <li><a href="#">Gizmo Basic</a></li>
          <li><a href="#">Gizmo Standard</a></li>
          <li><a href="#">Gizmo Supreme</a></li>
        </ul>
      </li>
      <li><a href="#">Gadgets </a>
        <ul>
          <li><a href="#">Gadget Basic</a></li>
          <li><a href="#">Gadget Standard</a></li>
          <li><a href="#">Gadget Supreme</a>
            <ul>
              <li><a href="#">Gadget Supreme A</a></li>
              <li><a href="#">Gadget Supreme B</a></li>
            </ul>
          </li>
        </ul>
      </li>
```

```
         <li><a href="#">Time Machines</a></li>
      </ul>
   </li>
</ul>
```

NOTE To keep this example visually simple, the HTML uses a # symbol in place of an actual URL for the `href` property on each `<a>` tag—`<a href="#">`, for example. In an actual navigation bar, each `<a>` tag would point to a real web page, like this: `<a href="products/gadgets/basic.html">`.

The three main navigation buttons are Home, About Us, and Our Products. Under About Us is a menu, represented by a nested list that includes the options Our History, Driving Directions, and Hours. The Our Products button contains another menu with the options Gizmos, Gadgets, and Time Machines. Both Gizmo and Gadgets have their own menus (two other nested lists); and under the Gadget Supreme option found under the Gadget menu), there are two more options (yet another nested list). A nested list is just another list that's indented one more level. Visually, the HTML above translates to a list like the following:

- Home
- About Us
  - Our History
  - Driving Directions
  - Hours
- Our Products
  - Gizmos
    - Gizmo Basic
    - Gizmo Standard
    - Gizmo Supreme
  - Gadgets
    - Gadget Basic
    - Gadget Standard
    - Gadget Supreme
      - Gadget Supreme A
      - Gadget Supreme B
  - Time Machines

As always, a nested list goes within the `<li>` tag of its parent item. For example, the `<ul>` tag containing the list items Gizmos, Gadgets, and Time Machines is contained within the `<li>` tag for the Our Products list item (if you need a refresher on creating HTML lists, check out *www.htmldog.com/guides/htmlbeginner/lists/*).

NOTE Make sure that the top-level links (Home, About Us, and Our Products in this example) always point to a page that links to the subpages in its section (for example, the Our History, Driving Directions, and Hours links under About Us). That way, if the browser doesn't have JavaScript turned on, it can still access the links in the submenus.

The CSS

The jQuery SmartMenus plug-in by Vasil Dinkov (*www.smartmenus.org*) does most of the work of placing the list items so you don't need to worry about creating the CSS necessary to create the side-by-side button or the drop-down and flyout menus. The main CSS file is named *sm-core.css*, and it handles the basics of placing the navigation buttons.

You can then create your own styles to customize the appearance of the buttons, or use one of the supplied design themes. Each theme comes in its own CSS file: *sm-simple.css*, *sm-clean.css*, *sm-blue.css*. You'll learn how to use a theme in the upcoming tutorial and how to customize the menu's appearance on page 248.

The JavaScript

The basic concept behind using JavaScript to control the display of menus is simple. When someone mouses over a list item, and if it has a nested list (a pop-up menu), then the JavaScript shows that nested list; it hides any nested lists when the mouse moves off.

There are a few subtleties that make this basic idea a bit more complicated. For example, pop-up menus that disappear the very instant the mouse moves off of its parent list item require precise mouse technique. It's easy for someone to mouse off a list item when trying to navigate to a pop-up menu. If the menu suddenly disappears, your visitor is forced to move the mouse back over the original list item to open the menu again. And when there are a couple of levels of pop-up menus, it's frustratingly easy to miss the target and lose the menus.

To deal with this problem, most navigation menu scripts add a timer feature that delays the disappearance of pop-up menus. This timer accommodates not-so-precise mouse technique and makes the pop-up menus feel less fragile.

The Tutorial

Now that you understand the basics of creating a navigation menu, here's how to make it happen. In these steps, you'll add CSS and JavaScript to transform the basic HTML menu list shown on page 243 into a navigation bar.

NOTE See the note on page 12 for information on how to download the tutorial files.

---

1. **In a text editor, open the file *menu.html* in the *chapter07* folder.**

   This file contains the bulleted list of links that you'll turn into a navigation bar. To see what it looks like without any JavaScript, open the page in a web browser. The first step in creating your smart menu is to attach a CSS file, which is supplied for you in this case.

2. **Click in the empty line after `<link href="../_css/site.css" rel="stylesheet">`, and type:**

   ```
   <link href="smartmenus/sm-core-css.css" rel="stylesheet" >
   <link href="smartmenus/sm-simple.css" rel="stylesheet" >
   ```

   The first `<link>` tag adds the core style sheet—this style sheet is always required because it provides basic formatting regardless of the color scheme or fonts you want. The second links to one of the three supplied themes. This file contains styles for the "simple" theme pictured in Figure 7-9.

   Now you need to make a small modification to the HTML.

3. **Locate the `<ul>` tag that marks the beginning of the navigation bar (it's just below the `<h1>` tag) and add a class attribute with two values so it looks like this:**

   ```
   <ul class="sm sm-simple">
   ```

   The sm class name is required for all SmartMenus. The plug-in requires this class to help it do its magic and apply its base CSS styles to the menu. The second class name—`sm-simple`—indicates which of the supplied themes you're using. If you had attached one of the other CSS files—*sm-clean.css* or *sm-blue.css*—in step 2, then you'd use a corresponding class name. In other words, replace the `sm-simple` with either `sm-clean` or `sm-blue`.

   Now it's time to add the JavaScript.

4. **Click in the empty line after `<script src="../_js/jquery.min.js"></script>` and type:**

   ```
   <script src="smartmenus/jquery.smartmenus.min.js"></script>
   ```

   This loads the SmartMenus plug-in. Remember, because the plug-in needs jQuery to work, you have to place this line after the `<script>` tag pointing to jQuery. In addition, notice that the JavaScript file and the two CSS files in the last step are inside a folder named *smartmenus*. As mentioned on page 239, it's a good idea to keep all of the files required by a plug-in in a separate folder named after that plug-in. That way, it's easy to find all of the plug-in files if you need to update the plug-in (when a new version comes out, say) or remove the plug-in files (if you get tired of the plug-in or it no longer works).

   Now you'll add the programming. The working file already contains a set of `<script>` tags with the `$(document).ready()` function in place.

5. **Click in the empty line inside the $(document).ready() function and add the following bolded code:**

```
$(document).ready(function() {
  $('.sm').smartmenus();
}); // end ready
```

To activate the menu, you first use jQuery to select the <ul> tag used for the main navigation bar—in this example, that tag has a class of sm applied to it, so the code $('.sm') selects that tag. The .smartmenus() function applies the jQuery SmartMenu plug-in programming to the menu. And, yes, it really is that easy!

6. **Save the file and preview it in a web browser. Mouse over the menu options, and resize the browser window so that it's as thin as you can make it.**

You'll notice that you now have drop-down menus on the main buttons, and fly-out buttons on the submenus. Pretty cool.

But you can do more. By passing the plug-in an object literal (page 136) filled with options, you can control how the plug-in works. For example, currently the submenus fade in when you mouse over a button and fade out when you mouse off. But by adding some code, you can make the submenus slide in and out. The code's a bit complex, so just take it step by step.

7. **Edit the code you just added by adding curly brackets (shown here in bold):**

```
$(document).ready(function() {
  $('.sm').smartmenus({ });
}); // end ready
```

The curly brackets pass an empty object literal to the function. As you read on page 136, an object literal is just a way to send one or more name/value pairs to a function. For example, here's a simple object that holds the author's name:

```
{ name : 'Dave' }
```

In this example, name is the name (also called a key) and 'Dave' is the value. Time to make some room for the values you're going to add.

8. **Add an empty line in between the { and } of the object literal, and then add a comment at the end, like this:**

```
$(document).ready(function() {
  $('.sm').smartmenus({

  }); // end smartmenus
}); // end ready
```

The comment will help you keep track of where the smart menu ends. Now add the first name/value pair.

9. **Add the code in lines 3–5 below:**

```
$(document).ready(function() {
  $('.sm').smartmenus({
    showFunction: function($ul, complete) {
      $ul.slideDown(250, complete);
    }
  }); // end smartmenus
}); // end ready
```

In this case, the name (or *key*) is showFunction. The SmartMenus plug-in has lots of pre-programmed settings, and showFunction is one of them. If the plug-in gets this name passed to it, the function that's sent as the value is used to animate the appearance of submenus. There's a lot of stuff going on here, but you should recognize the slideDown() function on line 4. (You first read about this jQuery animation effect on page 186.) You can replace slideDown with any of the jQuery animation effects you read about on page 183—for example, .hide() or .fadeIn()—or create your own animation entirely using the .animate() function discussed on page 191.

The number is the time the animation takes—in this case, 250 milliseconds. You can make this number smaller to make the slide-in action faster, or make the number bigger to slow the action down.

Now it's time to make the submenus slide up when the visitor mouses off them.

10. **Edit the code so it looks like the code below (additions are in bold):**

```
$(document).ready(function() {
  $('.sm').smartmenus({
    showFunction: function($ul, complete) {
      $ul.slideDown(250, complete);
    },
    hideFunction: function($ul, complete) {
      $ul.slideUp(250, complete);
    }
  }); // end smartmenus
}); // end ready
```

Don't forget the comma after the } on line 5. The comma is used to separate name/value pairs in an object literal. In this case, you're sending a second option to the SmartMenus plug-in: hideFunction.

NOTE The SmartMenus plug-in provides many ways to control how it works. For more information on using the plug-in, visit *www.smartmenus.org/docs/*.

11. **Save the page and preview it in a browser.**

You should now have a fully functional navigation bar. Check out the CSS in the file to see how the buttons are formatted, and try different CSS properties to customize the appearance of the menu. A completed version of the tutorial *complete_menu.html* is in the *chapter07* folder.

To see what the other themes look like, replace the link to the *sm-simple.css* style sheet, and change the sm-simple class on the <ul> tag of the navigation bar. For example, to use the blue theme, change the CSS link to:

```
<linkhref="smartmenus/sm-blue.css" rel="stylesheet" >
```

And update the <ul> tag to look like this:

```
<ul class="sm sm-blue">
```

You'll find a completed version of the tutorial in the *complete_menu.html* file. In addition, you can view examples of the two other SmartMenu themes in the *complete_menu_blue.html* and *complete_menu_clean.html* files.

Customizing the Look of the SmartMenus Plug-in

The simplest way to change the look of a SmartMenus navigation bar is to edit the CSS file. The supplied CSS files have lots of useful comments in them, making it clear what the styles do. For example, in the *sm-simple.css* file there's a group selector sm-simple, .sm-simple ul. This rule formats the appearance of the overall navigation bar (the outer <ul> tag) and each submenu (that is each <ul> tag inside the nav bar.

You can even create your own styles. Here's how:

1. **Save a copy of one of the style sheets whose formatting you like best and give it a new name.**

For example, save the *sm-simple.css* file as *sm-mymenu.css*.

2. **Replace the style sheet's prefix—.sm-simple, for example—with your own prefix.**

For example, replace .sm-simple with .sm-mymenu (or whatever you'd like to call it). Using a text editor with a find-and-replace tool will make this step quick work. Also, this step is optional; you can stick with the class name—.sm-simple, for example—that's already in the style sheet if you'd like.

3. **Make your style changes.**

Edit the styles any way you want. The .sm-simple a style controls how each of the buttons look, while the .sm-simple a span.sub-arrow style dictates the look of the indicator that appears next to buttons that have attached submenus.

4. **Attach your new style sheet to the web page.**

This step involves changing the link to point to your new style sheet:

```
<link rel="stylesheet" href="smartmenus/sm-mymenu.css">
```

5. **If you changed the prefix used in the style sheet—for example, you changed `.sm-simple` to `.sm-mymenu`—then edit the class name in the nav bar's `<ul>` tag. For example:**

```
<ul class="sm sm-mymenu">
```

The SmartMenus plug-in is easy to use and makes adding responsive drop-down menus a breeze.

PLUG-IN ALERT

Other jQuery Plug-ins for Enhancing Page Navigation

The jQuery SmartMenus plug-in is simple and effective, but there are a ton of other jQuery plug-ins for creating more advanced navigation.

- The jPanel plug-in (*http://jpanelmenu.com*) creates panel-style menus—those sidebar menus that slide into place when you click an icon. Facebook, Google, and many smartphone apps use this style of navigation.

- The Multi-level Push Menu plug-in (*http://multi-level-push-menu.make.rs*) is another menu system that hangs

out on the side of your screen. It provides multiple levels of navigation represented by small tabs that a visitor can open and close. It's a great way to organize and access a very large collection of links.

If neither of these plug-ins tickle your fancy, check out this list of 15 responsive jQuery navigation plug-ins at *http://speckyboy.com/2013/08/01/15-responsive-navigation-jquery-plugins/*.

CHAPTER

8

Enhancing Web Forms

S ince the earliest days of the web, forms have made it possible for websites to collect information from their visitors. Forms can gather email addresses for a newsletter, collect shipping information to complete an online sale, or simply receive visitor feedback. Forms also require your site's visitors to *think*: read labels, type information, make selections, and so on. Because some sites depend entirely on receiving form data—Amazon wouldn't be in business long if people couldn't use forms to order books—web designers need to know how to make their forms as easy to use as possible. Fortunately, JavaScript's ability to inject interactivity into forms can help you build forms that are easier to use and ensure more accurate visitor responses.

■ Understanding Forms

HTML provides a variety of tags to build a web form like the one pictured in Figure 8-1. The most important tag is the `<form>` tag, which defines the beginning (the opening `<form>` tag) and the end (the closing `</form>` tag) of the form. It also indicates what type of method the form uses to send data (*post* or *get*), and specifies where on the web the form data should be sent.

251

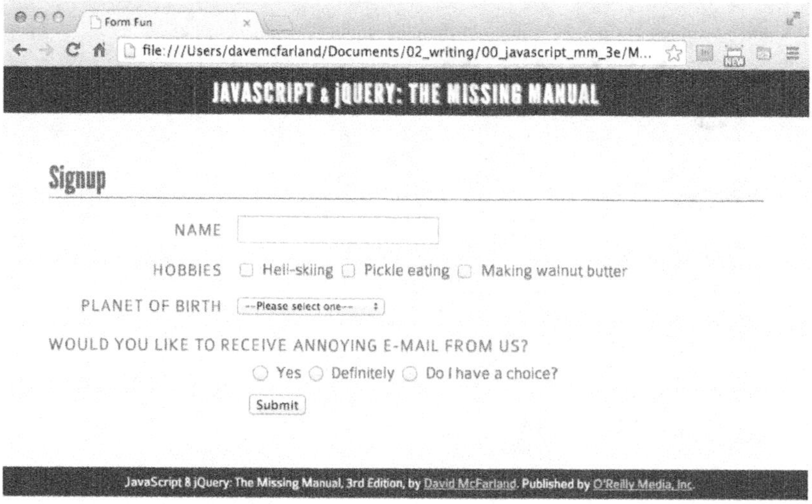

FIGURE 8-1

A basic form can include many different types of controls, including text fields, radio buttons, checkboxes, menu lists, submit buttons, and so on. For a list of HTML form fields and articles on how to use them, visit https://developer.mozilla.org/en-US/docs/Web/Guide/HTML/Forms.

You create the actual form controls—the buttons, text fields, and menus—using either the <input>, <textarea>, or <select> tags. Most of the form elements use the <input> tag. For example, text fields, password fields, radio buttons, checkboxes, and submit buttons all share the <input> tag, and you specify which one with the type attribute. For example, you create a text field by using the <input> tag and setting the type attribute to text like this:

```
<input name="user" type="text">
```

Here's the HTML that creates the form pictured in Figure 8-1; the <form> tag and form elements are shown in bold:

```
<form action="process.php" method="post" name="signup" id="signup">
  <div>
    <label for="username" class="label">Name</label>
    <input name="username" type="text" id="username" size="36">
  </div>
  <div><span class="label">Hobbies</span>
    <input type="checkbox" name="hobby" id="heliskiing" value="helisking">
    <label for="heliskiing">Heli-skiing</label>
    <input type="checkbox" name="hobby" id="pickle" value="pickle">
    <label for="pickle">Pickle eating</label>
    <input type="checkbox" name="hobby" id="walnut" value="walnut">
    <label for="walnut">Making walnut butter</label>
  </div>
  <div>
```

```
      <label for="planet" class="label">Planet of Birth</label>
      <select name="planet" id="planet">
      <option>Earth</option>
      <option>Mars</option>
      <option>Alpha Centauri</option>
      <option>You've never heard of it</option>
      </select>
      </div>
      <div class="labelBlock">Would you like to receive annoying e-mail from us?
  </div>
      <div class="indent">
      <input type="radio" name="spam" id="yes" value="yes" checked="checked">
       <label for="yes">Yes</label>
      <input type="radio" name="spam" id="definitely" value="definitely">
       <label for="definitely">Definitely</label>
      <input type="radio" name="spam" id="choice" value="choice">
       <label for="choice">Do I have a choice?</label>
      </div>
      <div>
        <input type="submit" name="submit" id="submit" value="Submit">
      </div>
  </form>
```

NOTE   The <label> tag in this sample is another tag commonly used in forms. It doesn't create a form control like a button, though. It lets you add a text label, visible on the page, that explains the purpose of the form control.

Selecting Form Elements

As you've seen repeatedly in this book, working with elements on the page first requires selecting those elements. To determine the value stored in a form field, for example, you must select that field. Likewise, if you want to hide or show form elements, you must use JavaScript to identify those elements.

As you've read, jQuery can use almost any CSS selector to select page elements. The easiest way to select a single form element is to assign an ID to it, like this:

```
<input name="user" type="text" id="user">
```

You can then use jQuery's selection function:

```
var userField = $('#user');
```

Once you select a field, you can do something with it. For example, say you want to determine the value in a field—to check what a visitor has typed into the field, for instance. If the form field has an ID of user, you can use jQuery to access the field's value, like this:

```
var fieldValue = $('#user').val();
```

NOTE The jQuery `val()` function is discussed on page 255.

But what if you wanted to select all `form` elements of a particular type? For example, you might want to add a click event to every radio button on a page.

Because the `<input>` tag is used for radio buttons, text fields, password fields, checkboxes, submit buttons, reset buttons, and hidden fields, you can't just select the `<input>` tag. Instead, you need to be able to find a particular type of input tag.

You could use a CSS attribute selector like this:

```
$('input[type="radio"]')
```

But jQuery offers an even easier way of selecting specific types of form fields (see Table 8-1). Using one of the jQuery form selectors, you can easily identify and work with all fields of a particular type. For example, suppose when the visitor submits the form, you want to check to make sure all text fields hold some value. You need to select those text fields and then check each to see if each field holds a value. jQuery lets you complete the first step like this:

```
$(':text')
```

Then, you simply loop through the results using the `.each()` function (page 138) to make sure there's a value in each field. (You'll learn a lot more about validating form fields on page 273).

TABLE 8-1 *jQuery includes lots of selectors to make it easy to work with specific types of form fields*

SELECTOR	EXAMPLE	WHAT IT DOES
`:input`	`$(':input')`	Selects all input, textarea, select, and button elements. In other words, it selects all form elements.
`:text`	`$(':text')`	Selects all text fields.
`:password`	`$(':password')`	Selects all password fields.
`:radio`	`$(':radio')`	Selects all radio buttons.
`:checkbox`	`$(':checkbox')`	Selects all checkboxes.
`:submit`	`$(':submit')`	Selects all submit buttons.
`:image`	`$(':image')`	Selects all image buttons.
`:reset`	`$(':reset')`	Selects all reset buttons.
`:button`	`$(':button')`	Selects all fields with type `button`.
`:file`	`$(':file')`	Selects all file fields (used for uploading a file).
`:hidden`	`$(':hidden')`	Selects all hidden fields.

You can combine the form selectors with other selectors as well. For example, say you have two forms on a page, and you want to select the text fields in just one of the forms. Assuming that the form with the fields you're after has an ID of `signup`, you can select text fields in that form only like this:

```
$('#signup :text')
```

In addition, jQuery provides a few very useful filters that find form fields matching a particular state:

- :checked selects all fields that are checkmarked or turned on—that is, check-boxes and radio buttons. For example, if you want to find all checkboxes and radio buttons that are turned on, you can use this code:

  ```
  $(':checked')
  ```

  Even better, you can use this filter to find which radio button within a group has been selected. For example, say you have a group of radio buttons ("Pick a delivery method") with different values (UPS, USPS, and FedEx, for instance) and you want to find the value of the radio button that your visitor has selected. A group of related radio buttons all share the same HTML name attribute; assume that you have a group of radio buttons that share the name shipping. You can use an attribute selector (page 123) in conjunction with the :checked filter to find the value of the checked radio button, like this:

  ```
  var checkedValue = $('input[name="shipping"]:checked').val();
  ```

  The selector—$('input[name="shipping"]')—selects all input elements with the name shipping, but adding the :checked—$('input[name="shipping"] :checked')—selects only the one that's checked. The val() function returns the value stored in that checkbox—USPS, for example.

- :selected selects all selected *option* elements within a list or menu, which lets you find which selection a visitor makes from a menu or list (<select> tag). For example, say you have a <select> tag with an ID of state, listing all 50 U.S. states. To find which state the visitor has selected, you can write this:

  ```
  var selectedState=$('#state :selected').val();
  ```

  Notice that unlike in the example for the :checked filter, there's a space between the ID name and the filter ('#state :selected'). That's because this filter se-lects the <option> tags, not the <select> tag. To put it in English, this jQuery selection means "find all selected options that are inside the <select> tag with an ID of state." The space makes it work like a CSS descendant selector: First it finds the element with the proper ID, and then searches inside that for any elements that have been selected.

NOTE You can enable multiple selections for a <select> menu. This means that the :selected filter can potentially return more than one element.

Getting and Setting the Value of a Form Element

At times you'll want to check the value of a form element. For example, you may want to check a text field to make sure an email address was typed into it. Or you may want to determine a field's value to calculate the total cost of an order. On the other hand, you may want to set the value of a form element. Say, for example, you have an order form that asks for both billing and shipping information. It would be helpful to give your visitors a "Same as billing" checkbox and have the shipping information fields automatically filled out using the information from the billing fields.

jQuery provides a simple function to accomplish both tasks. The val() function can both set and read the value of a form field. If you call the function without passing any arguments, it reads the field's value; if you pass a value to the function, it sets the form field's value. For example, say you have a field for collecting a user's email address with an ID of email. You can find the contents of that field like this:

```
var fieldValue = $('#email').val();
```

You can set the value of a field simply by passing a value to the val() function. For example, say you have a form for ordering products and you wanted to automatically calculate the total cost of a sale based on the quantity a visitor specifies (Figure 8-2). You can get the quantity the visitor supplies, multiply it by the cost of the products, and then set the value in the total field.

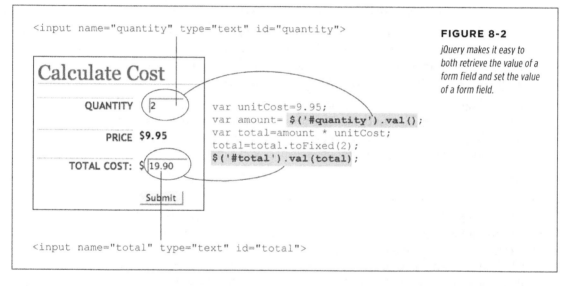

FIGURE 8-2

jQuery makes it easy to both retrieve the value of a form field and set the value of a form field.

The code to retrieve the quantity and set the total cost for the form in Figure 8-2 looks like this:

```
1    var unitCost=9.95;
2    var amount=$('#quantity').val(); // get value
3    var total=amount * unitCost;
4    total=total.toFixed(2);
5    $('#total').val(total); // set value
```

The first line of code creates a variable that stores the cost for the product. The second line creates another variable and retrieves the amount the visitor entered into the field with an ID of quantity. Line 3 determines the total cost by multiplying the order amount by the unit cost, and line 4 formats the result to include two decimal places (see page 565 for a discussion of the toFixed() method). Finally, line 5 sets the value in the field with ID total to the total cost. (You'll learn how to trigger this code using an event on page 260.)

Determining Whether Buttons and Boxes Are Checked

While the val() function is helpful for getting the value of any form element, for some fields, the value is important only if the visitor has selected the field. For example, radio buttons and checkboxes require visitors to make a choice by selecting a particular value. You saw on page 254 how you can use the :checked filter to find checked radio buttons and checkboxes, but once you find it, you need a way to determine the status of a particular button or box.

In HTML, the checked attribute determines whether a particular element is checked. For example, to turn on a box when the web page is loaded, you add the checked attribute like this for XHTML:

```
<input type="checkbox" name="news" id="news" checked="checked" />
```

And this for HTML5:

```
<input type="checkbox" name="news" id="news" checked>
```

Although in the first example—checked="checked"—it looks like checked is an HTML attribute, it's actually a property of the DOM (page 117). That is, it's a property of the checkbox element that can dynamically change when a visitor checks or unchecks the checkbox. Lots of other form elements also have dynamic properties: for example, text boxes have a property called disabled, which determines if a text box can be typed into (disabled is false) or not (disabled is true).

For DOM properties, you use jQuery's prop() method, like this:

```
if ($('#news').prop('checked')) {
  // the box is checked
} else {
  // the box is not checked
}
```

The code $('#news').prop('checked') returns the value true if the box is checked. If it's not, it returns the value false. So this basic conditional statement lets you perform one set of tasks if the box is turned on or a different set of tasks if the box is turned off. (If you need a refresher on conditional statements, turn to page 61.)

The checked property applies to radio buttons as well. You can use the prop() function in the same way to check whether the radio button's checked attribute is set.

Form Events

As you read in Chapter 5, events let you add interactivity to your page by responding to different visitor actions. Forms and form elements can react to many different events, so you can tap into a wide range of events to make your forms respond intelligently to your visitors' actions.

■ SUBMIT

Whenever a visitor submits a form by clicking a submit button or pressing Enter or Return when typing into a text field, the submit event is triggered. You can tap into this event to run a script when the form is submitted. That way, JavaScript can validate form fields to make sure they're correctly filled out. When the form is submitted, a JavaScript program checks the fields, and if there's a problem, JavaScript can stop the form submission and let the visitor know what's wrong; if there are no problems, then the form is submitted as usual.

To run a function when the form's submit event is triggered, first select the form, then use jQuery's submit() function to add your script. For example, say you want to make sure that the name field on the form pictured in Figure 8-1 has something in it when the form is submitted—in other words, a visitor can't leave the field blank. You can do so by adding a submit event to the form, and checking the value of the field before the form is submitted. If the field is empty, you want to let the visitor know and stop the submission process; otherwise, the form will be allowed to go through.

If you look at the HTML for the form on page 252, you can see that the form has an ID of signup and the name field has an ID of username. So you can validate this form using jQuery like this:

```
1   $(document).ready(function() {
2       $('#signup').submit(function() {
3           if ($('#username').val() == '') {
4               alert('Please supply a name in the Name field.');
5               return false;
6           }
7       }); // end submit()
8   }); // end ready()
```

Line 1 sets up the required $(document).ready() function so the code runs only after the page's HTML has loaded (page 160). Line 2 attaches a function to the form's submit event. Lines 3–6 are the validation routine. Line 3 checks to see if the value of the field is an empty string (' '), meaning the field is empty. If the field has nothing in it, then an alert box appears letting the visitor know what he did wrong.

Line 5 is very important: It stops the form from being submitted. If you omit this step, then the form will be submitted anyway, without the visitor's name. Line 6 completes the conditional statement, and line 7 is the end of the submit() function.

NOTE You can also stop the form from submitting by using the event object's `preventDefault()` function (page 165):

```
$('form').submit(function(evt) {
  // stop form submisssion
  evt.preventDefault();
}
```

The `submit` event only applies to forms, so you must select a form and attach the `submit` event function to it. You can select the form either by using an ID name that's supplied in the `<form>` tag of the HTML, or, if there's just a single form on the page, you can use a simple element selector like this:

```
$('form').submit(function() {
    // code to run when form is submitted
});
```

■ FOCUS

Whenever someone either clicks into a text field on a form or tabs into a text field, that field receives what's called *focus*. Focus is an event that the browser triggers to indicate that a visitor's cursor is on or in a particular field; you can be sure that that's where your visitor's attention is focused. You probably won't use this event very often, but some designers use it to erase any text that's already present in a field. For example, say you have the following HTML inside a form:

```
<input name="username" type="text" id="username"
  value="Please type your user name">
```

This code creates a text field on the form with the text "Please type your user name" inside it. This technique lets you provide instructions as to how the visitor is supposed to fill out the field. Then instead of forcing the visitor filling out the form to erase all that text herself, you can erase it when she focuses on the field, like this:

```
1  $('#username').focus(function() {
2    var field = $(this);
3    if (field.val()==field.prop('defaultValue')) {
4      field.val('');
5    }
6  });
```

Line 1 selects the field (which has an ID of username) and assigns a function to the focus event. Line 2 creates a variable, `field`, that stores a reference to the jQuery selection; as discussed on page 139, `$(this)` refers to the currently selected element within a jQuery function—in this case, the form field.

Line 4 is what actually erases the field. It sets the value of the field to an empty string—represented by the two single quote marks—thus removing any value from the field. But you don't want to erase this field every time the field gets the focus. For example, say someone comes to the form and clicks in the form field; the first time, that erases the "Please type your user name" text. However, if the visitor then types his name in the field, clicks outside the field, and then clicks back into the field, you don't want his name to suddenly disappear. That's where the conditional statement in line 3 comes into play.

Text fields have a property called defaultValue, which represents the text inside the field when the page first loads. Even if you erase that text, the web browser still remembers what was in the field when the page was loaded. The conditional statement checks to see if what is currently inside the field (field.val()) is the same as what was originally inside the field (field.prop('defaultValue')). If they are the same, then the JavaScript interpreter erases the text in the field.

Here's an example that explains the entire process. When the HTML on the previous page first loads, the text field has the value "Please type your user name." That's the field's defaultValue. So when a visitor first clicks into that field, the conditional statement asks the question "Is what's currently in the field the same as what was first in the field when the page loaded?" In other words, is "Please type your user name" equal to "Please type your user name"? The answer is yes, that field is erased.

However, say you typed *helloKitty* as your username, then tabbed into another field, and then realized that you mistyped your username. When you click back into the field to fix the mistake, the focus event is triggered again, and the function assigned to that event runs again. This time the question is "Is 'helloKitty' equal to 'Please type your username.'" The answer is no, so the field isn't erased and you can fix your typo.

> **NOTE** HTML5 forms support the placeholder attribute, which lets you put a temporary message in a text field. When a visitor begins typing, the placeholder is erased:
>
> ```
> <input name="username" type="text" id="username" placeholder="Please type your
> user name">
> ```
>
> This technique is easier than using the jQuery trick above, but the placeholder attribute doesn't work in Internet Explorer 9 or earlier.

■ BLUR

When you tab out of a field or click outside of the currently focused field, the browser triggers a blur event. This event is commonly used with text and textarea fields to run a validation script when someone clicks or tabs out of a field. For example, say you have a long form with a lot of questions, many of which require particular types of values (for example, email address, numbers, Zip codes, and so on). Say a visitor doesn't fill out any of those fields correctly, but hits the Submit button—and is faced with a long list of errors pointing out how she failed to fill out the form correctly. Rather than dumping all of those errors on her at once, you can also check fields as she fills out the form. That way, if she makes a mistake along the way, she'll be notified immediately and can fix the mistake right then.

Say, for instance, that you have a field for collecting the number of products the visitor wants. The HTML for that might look like this:

```
<input name="quantity" type="text" id="quantity">
```

You want to make sure that the field contains numbers only (for example, 1, 2, or 9, but not One, Two, or Nine). You can check for that after the visitor clicks out of the field like this:

```
1  $('#quantity').blur(function() {
2    var fieldValue=$(this).val();
3    if (isNaN(fieldValue)) {
4      alert('Please supply a number');
5    }
6  });
```

Line 1 assigns a function to the blur event. Line 2 retrieves the value in the field and stores it in a variable named `fieldValue`. Line 3 checks to make sure that the value is numeric using the `isNaN()` method (page 564). If it's not a number, then line 4 runs and an alert appears.

If you had a form with many fields that required numeric values, you could assign each of those fields the same class name—`class="numOnly"`, for example—and check each of those with code, like this:

```
1  $('.numOnly').blur(function() {
2    var fieldValue=$(this).val();
3    if (isNaN(fieldValue)) {
4      alert('Please supply a number');
5    }
```

This method lets you use just a few lines of code to check every one of the numeric fields.

■ CLICK

The `click` event is triggered when any form element is clicked. This event is particularly useful for radio buttons and checkboxes because you can add functions that alter the form based on the buttons a visitor selects. For example, say you have an order form that provides separate fields for both billing and shipping information. To save visitors whose shipping and billing information are the same from having to type their information twice, you can provide a checkbox—"Same as billing information," for example—that, when checked, hides the shipping information fields and makes the form simpler and more readable. (You'll see this example in action on page 271.)

Like other events, you can use jQuery's `click()` function to assign a function to a form field's `click` event:

```
$(':radio').click(function() {
  //function will apply to every radio button when clicked
});
```

CHANGE

The *change* event applies to form menus (Figure 8-3). Whenever you make a selection from the menu, the change event is triggered. You can use this event to run a validation function: For example, many designers commonly add an instruction as the first option in a menu, like "Please choose a country." To make sure a visitor doesn't pick a country, then accidentally change the menu back to the first option ("Please choose a country"), you can check the menu's selected value each time someone makes a new selection from the menu.

Or, you could program the form to change based on a menu selection. For example, you can run a function so whenever an option is selected from a menu, the options available from a second menu change. For example, Figure 8-3 shows a form with two menus; selecting an option from the top menu changes the list of available colors from the bottom menu.

To apply a change event handler to a menu, use jQuery's change() function. For example, say you have a menu listing the names of countries; the menu has an ID of country, and each time a new selection is made, you want to make sure the new selection isn't the instruction text "Please choose a country." You could do so like this:

```
$('#country').change(function() {
  if ($(this).val()=='Please choose a country') {
    alert('Please select a country from this menu.');
  }
}
```

Adding Smarts to Your Forms

Web forms demand a lot from your site's visitors: Text fields need to be filled out, selections made, checkboxes checked, and so on. If you want people to fill out your forms, it's in your interest to make the forms as simple as possible. Fortunately, JavaScript can do a lot to make your web forms easier to use. For example, you can hide form fields until they're needed, disable form fields that don't apply, and calculate totals based on form selections. JavaScript gives you countless ways to improve the usability of forms.

Focusing the First Field in a Form

Normally, to begin filling out a form, you have to click into the first text field and start typing. On a page with a login form, why make your visitors go to the extra trouble of moving their mouse into position and clicking into the login field before they can type? Why not just place the cursor in the field, ready to accept their login information immediately? With JavaScript, that's a piece of cake.

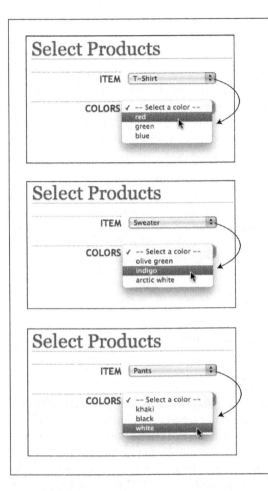

FIGURE 8-3

A form menu's change event lets you do interesting things when a visitor selects an option from a menu. In this case, selecting an option from the top menu dynamically changes the options presented in the second menu. Choose a product from the top menu, and the second menu displays the colors that product is available in.

The secret lies in focus, which isn't just an event JavaScript can respond to but a command that you can issue to place the cursor inside a text field. You simply select the text field, and then run the jQuery focus() function. Say, for example, that you'd like the cursor to be inside the name field pictured in Figure 8-1 when the page loads. If you look at the HTML for this form on page 252, you'll see that field's ID is username. So the JavaScript to place the focus on—that is, place the cursor in—that field looks like this:

```
$(document).ready(function() {
 $('#username').focus();
});
```

In this example, the text field has the ID username. However, you can also create a generic script that always focuses the first text field of a form, without having to assign an ID to the field:

```
$(document).ready(function() {
  $(':text:first').focus();
});
```

As you read on page 254, jQuery provides a convenient method of selecting all text fields—$(':text'). In addition, by adding :first to any selector, you can select the first instance of that element, so the jQuery selector $(':text:first') selects the first text field on the page. Adding .focus() then places the cursor in that text field, which waits patiently for the visitor to fill out the field.

If you have more than one form on a page (for example, a "search this site" form, and a "sign up for our newsletter" form), you need to refine the selector to identify the form whose text field should get focus. For example, say you want the first text field in a sign up form to have the cursor blinking in it, ready for visitor input, but the first text field is in a search form. To focus the sign up form's text field, just add an ID (signup, for example) to the form, and then use this code:

```
$(document).ready(function() {
  $('#signup :text:first').focus();
});
```

Now, the selector—$('#signup :text:first')—only selects the first text field inside the sign up form.

Disabling and Enabling Fields

Form fields are generally meant to be filled out—after all, what good is a text field if you can't type into it? However, there are times when you might *not* want a visitor to be able to fill out a text field, check a checkbox, or select an option from a menu. Say you have a field that should only be filled out if a previous box was turned on. For example, on the 1040 form used for determining U.S. income tax, there's a field for entering your spouse's Social Security number. You'd fill out that field only if you're married.

To "turn off" a form field that shouldn't be filled out, you can *disable* it using JavaScript. Disabling a field means it can't be checked (radio buttons and checkboxes), typed into (text fields), selected (menus), or clicked (submit buttons).

To disable a form field, simply set the field's disabled property to *true*. For example, to disable all input fields on a form, you can use this code:

```
$(':input').prop('disabled', true);
```

You'll usually disable a field in response to an event. Using the 1040 form example, for instance, you can disable the field for collecting a spouse's Social Security number when the "single" button is clicked. Assuming that the radio button for declaring yourself as single has an ID of `single`, and the field for a spouse's SSN has an ID of `spouseSSN`, the JavaScript code will look like this:

```
$('#single').click(function() {
  $('#spouseSSN').prop('disabled', true);
});
```

Of course, if you disable a field, you'll probably want a way to enable it again. To do so, simply set the `disabled` property to `false`. For example, to enable all fields on a form:

```
$(':input').prop('disabled', false);
```

> **NOTE** When disabling a form field, make sure to use the Boolean values (page 29) *true* or *false* and not the strings *'true'* or *'false'*. For example, this is wrong:
>
> ```
> $(':input').prop('disabled', 'false');
> ```
>
> And this is correct:
>
> ```
> $(':input').prop('disabled', false);
> ```

Back to the tax form example: If the visitor selects the "married" option, then you need to make sure that the field for collecting the spouse's Social Security number is active. Assuming the radio button for the married option has an ID of married, you can add the following code:

```
$('#married').click(function() {
  $('#spouseSSN').prop('disabled', false);
});
```

You'll run through an example of this technique in the tutorial on page 269.

Hiding and Showing Form Options

In addition to disabling a field, there's another way to make sure visitors don't waste time filling out fields unnecessarily—just hide the unneeded fields. For instance, using the tax form example from the last section, you may want to hide the field for a spouse's Social Security number when the "single" option is selected and show the field when the "married" option is turned on. You can do so like this:

```
$('#single').click(function() {
  $('#spouseSSN').hide();
});
$('#married').click(function() {
  $('#spouseSSN').show();
});
```

> **NOTE** jQuery's hide() and show() functions (as well as other functions for revealing and concealing elements) are discussed on page 184.

One usability benefit of hiding a field (as opposed to just disabling it) is that it makes the layout of the form simpler. After all, a disabled field is still visible and can still attract (or more accurately, distract) a person's attention.

In many cases, you'll want to hide or show more than just the form field: You'll probably want to hide that field's label and any other text associated with it. One strategy is to wrap the code you wish to hide (field, labels, and whatever other HTML) in a <div> tag, add an ID to that <div>, and then hide the <div>. You'll see an example of this technique in the following tutorial.

FREQUENTLY ASKED QUESTION

Stopping Multiple Submissions

Sometimes I get the same form information submitted more than once. How can I prevent that from happening?

Web servers aren't always the fastest creatures...and neither is the Internet. Often, there's a delay between the time a visitor presses a form's submit button, and when a new "We got your info" page appears. Sometimes this delay can be pretty long, and impatient web surfers hit the submit button a second (or third, or fourth) time, thinking that the first time they submitted the form, it simply didn't work.

This phenomenon can lead to the same information being submitted multiple times. In the case of an online sale, it can also mean a credit card is charged more than once! Fortunately, with JavaScript, there's an easy way to disable a submit button once the form submission process has begun. Using the submit button's disabled property, you can "turn it off" so it can't be clicked again.

Assume the form has an ID of formID, and the submit button has an ID of submit. First, add a submit() function to the form, and then, within the function, disable the submit button, like this:

```
$('#formID').submit(function() {
  $('#submit').prop('disabled',true);
});
```

If the page has only a single form, you don't even need to use IDs for the tags:

```
$('form').submit(function() {
  $('input[type=submit]')
prop('disabled',true);
});
```

In addition, you can change the message on the submit button by changing the button's value. For example, the button says Submit at first, but when the form is submitted, the button changes to say "...sending information". You could do that like this:

```
$('#formID').submit(function() {
  var subButton = $(this).find(':submit');
  subButton.prop('disabled',true);
  subButton.val('...sending information');
});
```

Make sure to put this code inside a $(document).ready() function, as described on page 160.

■ Tutorial: Basic Form Enhancements

In this tutorial, you'll add three usability improvements to a basic ordering form composed of fields for collecting billing and shipping information. First, you'll place the text cursor in the first field of the form when the page loads. Second, you'll

---

disable or re-enable form fields based on selections a visitor makes. Finally, you'll hide an entire section of the form when it's not needed (Figure 8-4).

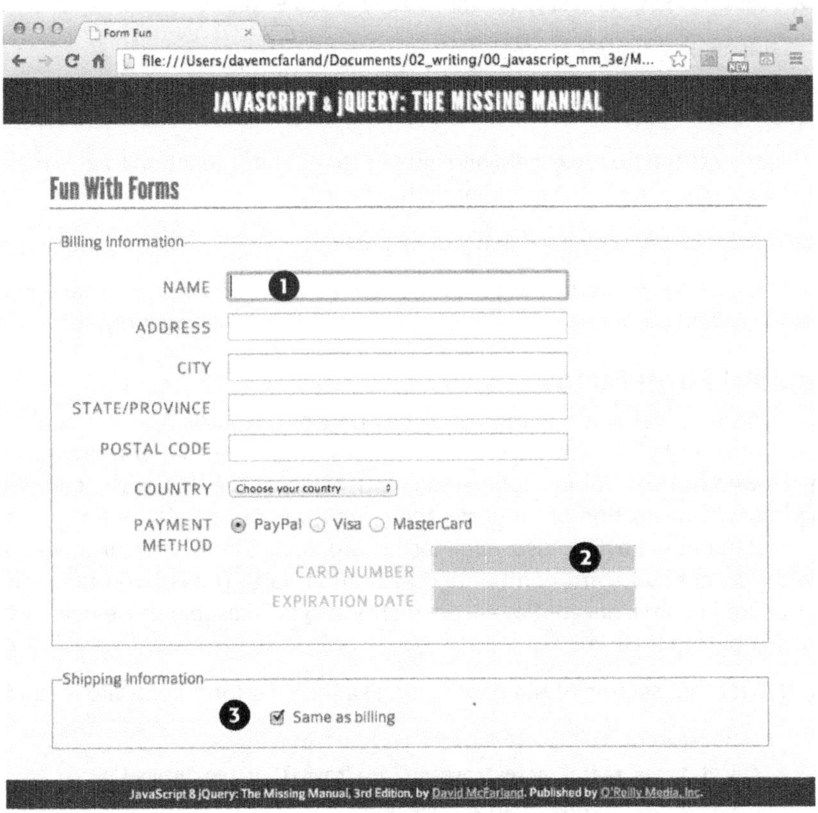

FIGURE 8-4

Using JavaScript, you can increase the usability of your web forms and add interactive features, like hiding fields that aren't needed and disabling fields that shouldn't be filled out.

> **NOTE** See the note on page 12 for information on how to download the tutorial files.

Focusing a Field

The first field on this tutorial's order form page collects the name of the person placing the order (Figure 8-4). To make using the form easier to fill out, you'll place the cursor in this field when the page loads:

1. **In a text editor, open the file *form.html* in the *chapter08* folder.**

   This file already contains a link to the jQuery file and the $(document).ready() function (page 160). There's a form that includes two sections—one for collecting billing information and another for collecting shipping information. (Check the page out in a web browser before continuing.)

The first step (actually, the only step for this part of the tutorial) is to focus the field.

2. **Click in the empty line after the $(document).ready() function and type $(':text:first').focus(); so the code looks like this:**

```
$(document).ready(function() {
  $(':text:first').focus();
}); // end ready()
```

This selects the first text field and applies the focus() function to it to make a browser place the insertion point in that field.

Save the file and preview it in a web browser.

When the page loads, the first field should have a blinking insertion bar—meaning that field has focus, and you can immediately start filling it out.

Disabling Form Fields

That last section was just a warm-up. In this part of the tutorial, you'll disable or enable two form fields in response to selections on the form. If you preview the form in a web browser (or just look at Figure 8-4), you'll see that at the end of the billing information section of the form, there are three radio buttons for selecting a payment method: PayPal, Visa, and MasterCard. In addition, there are two fields below for collecting a card number and expiration date. Those two options only apply for credit cards, not for PayPal payments, so you'll disable those fields when the PayPal button is clicked.

The HTML for that section of the page looks like this (the form fields are in bold):

```
1   <div><span class="label">Payment Method</span>
2   <input type="radio" name="payment" id="paypal" value="paypal">
3     <label for="paypal">PayPal</label>
4   <input type="radio" name="payment" id="visa" value="visa">
5     <label for="visa">Visa</label>
6   <input type="radio" name="payment" id="mastercard" value="mastercard">
7     <label for="mastercard">MasterCard</label>
8   </div>
9   <div id="creditCard" class="indent">
10    <div>
11      <label for="cardNumber" class="label">Card Number</label>
12    <input type="text" name="cardNumber" id="cardNumber">
13    </div>
14    <div>
15      <label for="expiration" class="label">Expiration Date</label>
16    <input type="text" name="expiration" id="expiration">
17    </div>
18  </div>
```

3. **Return to your text editor and the file _form.html._**

   You'll add to the code you created in the previous section. First, assign a function to the click event for the PayPal radio button.

4. **To the script at the top of the page, add the code in bold below:**

```
$(document).ready(function() {
  $(':text:first').focus();
  $('#paypal').click(function() {

  }); // end click
}); // end ready()
```

   The radio button for the PayPal option has an ID of paypal (see line 2 in the HTML code at the beginning of this section), so selecting that field is just a matter of typing $('#paypal'). The rest of the code assigns an anonymous function to the click event (if this isn't clear, check out the discussion on assigning functions to events on page 152). In other words, not only does clicking the PayPal radio button select it (that's normal web browser behavior), but it also triggers the function you're about to create.

   Next, you'll disable the credit card number and expiration date fields because they don't apply when the PayPal option is selected.

5. **Inside the anonymous function you added in the previous step, add a new line of code (line 4):**

```
1   $(document).ready(function() {
2     $(':text:first').focus();
3     $('#paypal').click(function() {
4       $('#creditCard input').prop('disabled', true);
5     }); // end click
6   }); // end ready()
```

   Although you want to disable two form fields, there's a simple way to do that with just one line of code. Both of the form fields are inside a <div> tag with an ID of creditCard (see line 9 of the HTML code above). So, the jQuery selector $('#creditCard input') translates to "select all <input> tags inside of an element with the ID creditCard." This flexible approach makes sure you select all of the input fields, so if you add another field, such as a CVV field, it gets selected as well (CVVs are those three numbers on the back of your credit card that web forms often request to enhance the security of online orders).

   To disable the fields, all you have to do is set the disabled property to true (page 264). However, this doesn't do anything to the text labels ("Card Number" and "Expiration Date"). Even though the fields themselves are disabled, those text labels remain bright and bold, sending the potentially confusing signal that the visitor can fill out the fields. To make the disabled status clearer, you'll change the labels to a light shade of gray. While you're at it, you'll also add a gray color to the background of the fields to make them _look_ disabled.

6. Add the bolded code below to your script:

```
$(document).ready(function() {
  $(':text:first').focus();
  $('#paypal').click(function() {
    $('#creditCard input').prop('disabled', true) ↵
      .css('backgroundColor','#CCC');
    $('#creditCard label').css('color','#BBB');
  }); // end click
}); // end ready()
```

NOTE The ↵ symbol at the end of a line of code in this book indicates that you should type the next line as part of the previous line. Because a *really* long line of JavaScript code won't fit on this book's page, it's broken up over two lines. However, as described on page 34, JavaScript is rather flexible when it comes to line breaks and spacing, so it's actually perfectly acceptable (and sometimes easier to read) if you break a single JavaScript statement over multiple lines like this:

```
$('#creditCard input').prop('disabled',true)
                      .css('backgroundColor','#CCC');
```

Note that some programmers indent code formatted over multiple lines—in this case, indenting the `.css()` function so it lines up with the `.prop()` function.

First, you use the jQuery's `css()` function to alter the background color of the text fields (note that the code is part of line 4, because it acts on the same selection as the `prop()` function). Next, you use the `css()` function to adjust the font color of any `<label>` tags inside the `<div>` tag (the `css()` function is described on page 134).

If you preview the page in a web browser at this point, you'll see that clicking the PayPal button does indeed disable the credit card number and expiration date fields and dims the label text. However, if you click either the Visa or MasterCard buttons, the fields stay disabled! You need to re-enable the fields when either of the other radio buttons is selected.

7. After the `click()` function, add a new blank line (you're adding new code between lines 7 and 8 in step 6) and then add the following:

```
$('#visa, #mastercard').click(function() {
  $('#creditCard input').prop('disabled', false) ↵
    .css('backgroundColor','');
  $('#creditCard label').css('color','');
}); // end click
```

The selector `$('#visa, #mastercard')` selects both of the other radio buttons (see lines 4 and 6 of the HTML on page 268). Notice that to remove the background color and text colors added by clicking the PayPal button, you simply pass an empty string as the color value: `$('#creditCard label')`.

`css('color','');`. That removes the color for that element, but leaves in place the color originally defined in the style sheet.

You're nearly done with this tutorial. In the final section, you'll completely hide a part of the page based on a form selection.

Hiding Form Fields

As is common on many product order forms, this tutorial's form includes separate fields for collecting billing and shipping information. In many cases, this information is exactly the same, so there's no need to make someone fill out both sets of fields if they don't have to. You'll frequently see a "Same as billing" checkbox on forms like these to indicate that the information is identical for both sets of fields. However, wouldn't it be even more useful (not to mention cooler) if you could completely hide the shipping fields when they aren't needed? With JavaScript, you can:

1. **Open the file *form.html* in a text editor.**

   You'll expand on the code you've been writing in the last two sections of this tutorial. First, add a function to the click event for the checkbox that has the label "Same as billing." The HTML for that checkbox looks like this:

   ```
   <input type="checkbox" name="hideShip" id="hideShip">
   ```

2. **Add the following code after the code you added in step 4 on page 269, but before the end of the script (the last line of code, which reads }); // end ready()):**

   ```
   $('#hideShip').click(function() {

   }); // end click
   ```

   Because the checkbox has the ID `hideShip`, the code above selects it and adds a function to the click event. In this case, instead of hiding just a single field, you want the entire group of fields to disappear when the box is checked. To make that easier, the HTML that makes up the shipping information fields is wrapped in a `<div>` tag with the ID of `shipping`: To hide the fields, you just need to hide the `<div>` tag.

   However, you'll only want to hide those fields when the box is checked. If someone clicks the box a second time to uncheck it, the `<div>` tag and its form fields should return. So the first step is to find out whether the box is checked.

3. **Add the code in bold below:**

   ```
   $('#hideShip').click(function() {
     if ($(this).prop('checked')) {

     }
   }); // end click
   ```

A simple conditional statement (page 61) makes it easy to test the state of the checkbox and either hide or show the form fields. The $(this) refers to the object being clicked—the checkbox in this case. The element's checked property lets you know if the box is checked or not. If it's checked, then this attribute returns true; otherwise, it returns false. To finish this code, you just need to add the steps for hiding and showing the form fields.

4. **Add the bolded code below (lines 16–18) to your script. The completed script should look like this:**

```
1   <script>
2   $(document).ready(function() {
3     $(':text:first').focus();
4     $('#paypal').click(function() {
5       $('#creditCard input').prop('disabled', true) ↵
6         .css('backgroundColor','#CCC');
7       $('#creditCard label').css('color','#BBB');
8     }); // end click
9     $('#visa, #mastercard').click(function() {
10      $('#creditCard input').prop('disabled', false) ↵
11        .css('backgroundColor','');
12      $('#creditCard label').css('color','');
13    }); // end click
14    $('#hideShip').click(function() {
15      if ($(this).prop('checked')) {
16        $('#shipping').slideUp('fast');
17      } else {
18        $('#shipping').slideDown('fast');
19      }
20    }); // end click
21  }); // end ready()
22  </script>
```

The $('#shipping') refers to the <div> tag with the form fields, while the slideUp() and slideDown() functions (described on page 186) hide and show the <div> tag by sliding the <div> up and out of view or down and into view. You can try out some of the other jQuery effects like fadeIn() and fadeOut(), or even create your own custom animation using the animate() function (page 191).

A finished version of this tutorial—*complete_form.html*—is in the *chapter08* folder. If your version isn't working, compare your code with the finished tutorial and refer to the troubleshooting steps on page 18.

◼ Form Validation

It can be frustrating to look over feedback that's been submitted via a form on your website, only to notice that your visitor failed to provide a name, email address, or some other piece of critical information. That's why, depending on the type of form you create, you might want to make certain information mandatory.

For instance, a form used for subscribing to an email newsletter isn't much use if the would-be reader doesn't type in an email address for receiving the newsletter. Likewise, if you need a shipping address to deliver a brochure or product, you'll want to be sure that the visitor includes her address on the form.

In addition, when receiving data from a web form, you want to make sure the data you receive is in the correct format—a number, for example, for an order quantity, or a correctly formatted URL for a web address. Making sure a visitor inputs information correctly is known as *form validation*, and with JavaScript, you can identify any errors before the visitor submits incorrect information.

Basically, form validation requires checking the form fields before the form is submitted to make sure required information is supplied and that information is properly formatted. The form's submit event—triggered when the visitor clicks a submit button or presses Return when the cursor's in a text field—is usually where the validation occurs. If everything is fine, the form information travels, as it normally would, to the web server. However, if there's a problem, the script stops the submission process and displays errors on the page—usually next to the problem form fields (Figure 8-5).

Checking to make sure a text field has been filled out is easy. As you read on page 255, you can simply access the form's value property (using the jQuery val() function, for example) and if the value is an empty string, then the field is empty. But it gets trickier when you're checking other types of fields, like checkboxes, radio buttons, and menus. In addition, you need to write some complicated JavaScript when you want to check to make sure the visitor submits particular *types* of information, like email addresses, Zip codes, numbers, dates, and so on. Fortunately, you don't need to write the code yourself; there's a wealth of form validation scripts on the web, and one of the best is a plug-in for the jQuery library.

> **NOTE**   HTML5 includes many built-in functions for form validation that let you skip JavaScript. Unfortunately, while many of the latest web browsers support HTML-only form validation, Internet Explorer 9 and earlier don't. In addition, at the time of this writing, the mobile iOS versions of Safari and Android don't, and desktop Safari has trouble as well.

jQuery Validation Plug-in

The Validation plug-in (*http://jqueryvalidation.org*) is a powerful but easy-to-use jQuery plug-in created by Jörn Zaefferer. It can check a form to make sure all required fields have been filled out, and check to make sure that visitor input meets particular requirements. For example, a quantity field must contain a number, and an email field must contain an email address. If a visitor doesn't fill out a form correctly, the plug-in will display error messages describing the problems.

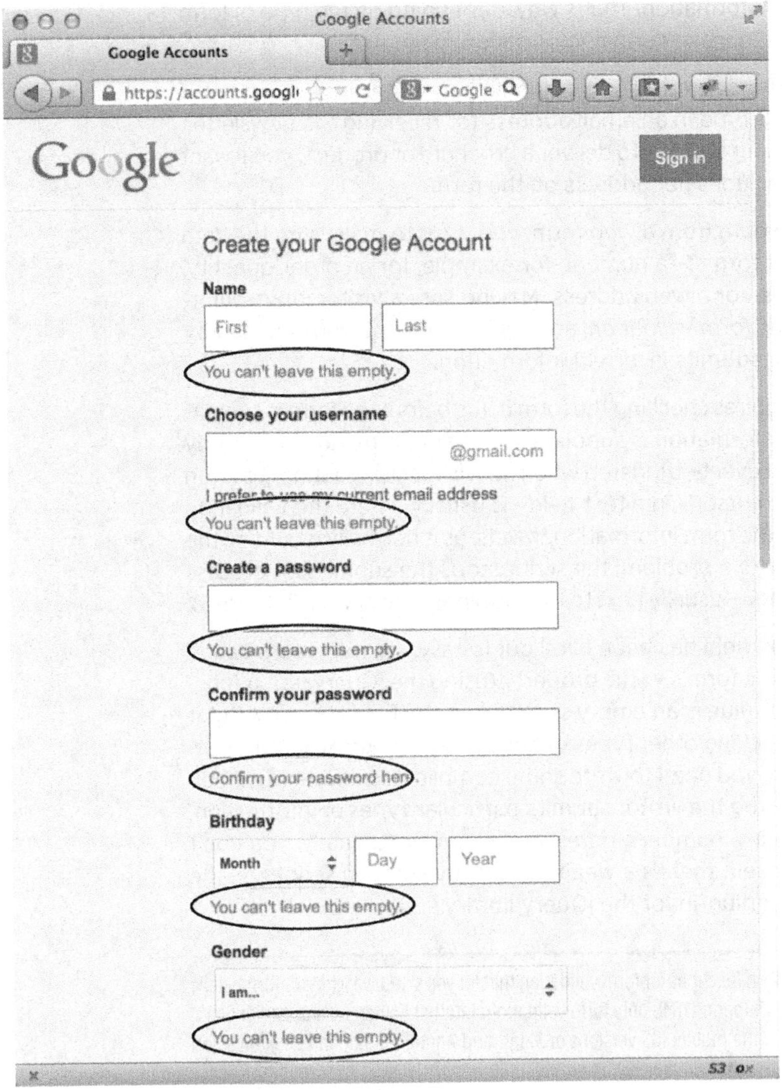

FIGURE 8-5

When you sign up for a Google account, you're faced with a sea of red error messages (circled) if you fail to fill out the form properly.

Here's the basic process of using the Validation plug-in:

1. **Download and attach the *jquery.js* file to the web page containing the form you wish to validate.**

   Read on page 107 for more info on downloading the jQuery library. The Validation plug-in uses the jQuery library, so you need to attach the jQuery file to the page first.

2. **Download and attach the Validation plug-in.**

   You can find the plug-in at *http://jqueryvalidation.org*. The download includes lots of extra stuff, including a demo, tests, and more. You really only need the *jquery.validate.min.js* file. (You'll also find this plug-in in the tutorial files in the *jquery_validate* folder located in the *chapter08* folder. The file is named *jquery.validate.min.js*—see the tutorial on page 286). This file is just an external JavaScript file, so follow the instructions on page 15 for linking the file to your page.

3. **Add validation rules.**

   Validation rules are just the instructions that say "make this field required, make sure that field gets an email address," and so on. In other words, this step is where you specify which fields get validated and how. There are a couple of methods for adding validation rules: a simple way using just HTML (page 276), and a more flexible but slightly more complicated way (page 279).

4. **Add error messages.**

   This step is optional. The Validation plug-in comes with a predefined set of error messages, like "This field is required," "Please enter a valid date," "Please enter a valid number," and so on. These basic messages are fine and to the point, but you may want to customize them for your form, so the errors provide more definite instruction for each form field—for example, "Please type your name," or "Please tell us your date of birth."

   There are two methods for adding error messages—the simple way is discussed on page 278, and the more flexible method on page 283.

> **NOTE** You can also control the style and placement of error messages as described on page 294.

5. **Apply the `validate()` function to the form.**

   The plug-in includes a function that makes all of the magic happen: `validate()`. To apply it, you first use jQuery to select the form, and then attach the function to that selection. For example, say you have a form with an ID of `signup` applied to it. The HTML might look like this:

   ```
   <form action="process.php" method="post" name="signup" id="signup">
   ```

   The simplest way to apply validation would be like this:

   ```
   $('#signup').validate();
   ```

The validate() function can accept many different pieces of information that affect how the plug-in works. For example, while you can specify validation rules and error messages in the HTML of the form (see the next section), you can also specify rules and errors when you call the validate() function. (You'll learn about this method on page 279.)

The entire JavaScript code for a very basic form validation (including the two steps already described in this section) could be as simple as this:

```
<script src="js/jquery.min.js"></script>
<script src="js/jquery.validate.min.js"></script>
<script>
$(document).ready(function() {
  $('#signup').validate();
}); // end ready
</script>
```

NOTE Remember to always wrap your script in jQuery's document.ready() function to make sure the script runs after the page's HTML is loaded (page 160).

Basic Validation

Using the Validation plug-in can be as simple as attaching the plug-in's JavaScript file, adding a few class and title attributes to the form elements you want to validate, and applying the validate() method to the form. The basic validate() method is the easiest way to validate a form, and may be all you need for most forms. (However, if you need to control where error messages are placed on a page, or apply more than one rule to a form field, or set a minimum or maximum number of characters for a text field, you'll need to use the advanced method described on page 279).

To add validation, follow the basic steps outlined in the previous sections (attaching the jQuery and Validation plug-in files, and so on), but in addition, you can embed rules and error messages in your form fields' HTML.

■ ADDING VALIDATION RULES

The simplest way to validate a field using the Validation plug-in is to assign one or more of the class names listed in Table 8-2 to the form element. The plug-in is cleverly programmed to scan the class names for each form element to determine if one of the validation terms is present, and if so, to apply the particular validation rule to that field.

For example, say you have a text field to collect a person's name. The basic HTML might look like this:

```
<input name="name" type="text">
```

To tell the plug-in that the field is mandatory—in other words, the form can't be submitted unless the visitor types something into this field—add a required class to the tag. For example, to make this text field required, add a class attribute to the tag like this:

```
<input name="name" type="text" class="required">
```

Adding a class in this way actually has nothing to do with CSS, even though usually you assign a class to a tag to provide a way of formatting that tag by creating a CSS class style. In this case, you're using a class name to provide the plug-in the information it needs to determine what kind of validation you're applying to that field.

> **NOTE** JavaScript validation is a great way to provide friendly feedback to visitors who accidentally skip a field or provide the wrong type of information, but it's not a good way to prevent malicious input. JavaScript validation is easy to circumvent, so to make absolutely sure that you don't receive bad data from visitors, you'll need to implement a server-side validation solution as well.

Requiring visitors to fill out a field is probably the most common validation task, but often you also want to make sure the data supplied matches a particular format. For example, if you're asking how many widgets someone wants, you're expecting a number. To make a field both mandatory *and* contain a specific type of value, you add both the *required* class plus one of the other classes listed in Table 8-2.

TABLE 8-2 *The Validation plug-in includes methods that cover the most common validation needs*

VALIDATION RULE	EXPLANATION
required	The field won't be submitted unless this field is filled out, checked, or selected.
date	Information must be in the format MM/DD/YYYY. For example, 10/30/2014 is considered valid, but 10-30-2014 is not.
url	Must be a full, valid web address like *http://www.chia-vet.com*. Partial URLs like *www.chia-vet.com* or chia-vet.com (*http://chia-vet.com*) are considered invalid.
email	Must be formatted like an email address: *bob@chia-vet.com*. This class doesn't actually check to make sure the email address is real, so someone could still enter *nobody@noplace.com* and the field would pass validation.
number	Must be a number like 32 or 102.50 or even –145.5555. However, the input can't include any symbols, so $45.00 and 100,000 are invalid.
digits	Can only include positive integers. So 1, 20, 12333 are valid, but 10.33 and –12 are not valid.
creditcard	Must be a validly formatted credit card number.

For example, say you have a field asking for someone's date of birth. This information is not only required, but should also be in a date format. The HTML for that field could look like this:

```
<input name="dob" type="text" class="required date">
```

Notice that the class names—required and date—are separated by a space.

If you exclude the required class and just use one of the other validation types—for example, class="date"—then that field is optional, but if someone does type something into the field, it must be in the proper format (a date).

> **TIP** When you require a specific format for field information, make sure to include specific instructions in the form so your visitors know how they should add their information. For example, if you require a field to be a date, add a message near the field that says something like "Please enter a date in the format MM/DD/YYYY, like 01/25/2015."

■ ADDING ERROR MESSAGES

The Validation plug-in supplies generic error messages to match the validation problems it checks for. For example, if a required field is left blank, the plug-in displays the message "This field is required." If the field requires a date, then the message "Please enter a valid date" appears. You can, however, override these basic messages and supply your own.

The easiest way is to add a title attribute to the form field and supply the error message as the title's value. For example, say you're using the required class to make a field mandatory, like this:

```
<input name="name" type="text" class="required">
```

To supply your own message, just add a *title* attribute:

```
<input name="name" type="text" class="required"
title="Please give us your name.">
```

Normally, web designers use the title attribute to increase a form field's accessibility by providing specific instructions that appear when someone mouses over the field, or for screen-reading software to read aloud. But with the Validation plug-in, you use the title attribute to supply the error message you wish to appear. The plug-in scans all validated fields and sees if there's a title attribute. If there is, then the plug-in uses the attribute's value as the error-message text.

If you use more than one validation method, you should supply a title that makes sense for either situation. For example, if you have a field that's required and that also must be a date, a message like "This field is required" doesn't make much sense if the visitor enters a date in the wrong format. Here's an example of an error message that makes sense whether the visitor leaves the field blank or enters the date the wrong way:

```
<input name="dob" type="text" class="required date"
title="Please enter your birthdate in the format 01/28/2014.">
```

Adding validation rules and error messages by adding class names and titles to fields is easy, and it works great. But sometimes you may have more complicated validation needs; the Validation plug-in offers a second, more advanced method of adding validation to a form. For example, you may want to have different error messages based on the type of error—like one message when a field is left blank and another when the visitor enters the wrong type of information. You can't do that using the basic validation method described in this section. Fortunately, the Validation plug-in offers a second, more advanced method that lets you implement a wider range of validation rules.

For example, you must use the advanced method if you want to make sure a minimum number of characters is entered into a field. When setting a password, for instance, you might want to make sure the password is at least six characters long.

Advanced Validation

The Validation plug-in provides another way of adding validation to a form that doesn't require changing the fields' HTML. In addition, the plug-in supports a wide variety of additional options for controlling how the plug-in works. You set these options by passing an object literal (page 136) to the `validate()` function, containing separate objects for each option. For example, to specify a validation rule, you pass one object containing the code for the rule. First, you include an opening brace directly after the first parenthesis for the validation function and a closing brace directly before the closing parenthesis:

```
$('idOfForm').validate({
    // options go in here
}); // end validate();
```

These braces represent an object literal, which will contain the option settings. Using the Validation plug-in in this way gets a little confusing, and the best way to understand how the plug-in's author intended it to work is to look at a simple example, like the one in Figure 8-6.

FIGURE 8-6

Even with a simple form like this one, you can use the Validation plug-in's advanced options for greater control.

TIP You can combine the basic validation method described on page 276 and the advanced method described here on the same form. For fields that have just one validation rule and error message, you can use the simple method because it's fast, and just use the advanced method for more complicated validation. The tutorial on page 286, for instance, uses both methods for validating a single form.

The HTML for the form in Figure 8-6 is as follows:

```
<form action="process.php" method="post" id="signup">
    <div>
```

```
      <label for="name">Name</label>
    <input name="name" type="text">
    </div>

    <div>
      <label for="email">E-mail Address</label>
    <input name="email" type="text">
    </div>
    <div>
      <input type="submit" name="submit" value="Submit">
    </div>
  </form>
```

This form contains two text fields, shown in bold: one for a person's name and one for an email address. This section walks through the process of validating both of these fields using advanced rules to make sure the name field is filled and the email field is both filled in and correctly formatted.

NOTE   You can find a complete list of options for the Validation plug-in at *http://jqueryvalidation.org/ validate.*

▦ ADVANCED RULES

The advanced way to specify validation rules involves passing an object containing the names of the form fields and the validation rule or rules you want to apply to the field. The basic structure of that object looks like this:

```
rules : {
  fieldname : 'validationType'
}
```

The object is named `rules`, and inside it you specify the fields and validation types you want to apply to the field. The entire object is then passed to the `validate()` function. For example, in the form pictured in Figure 8-6, to make the name field mandatory, you apply the `validate()` function to the form as described on the previous page, and then pass the `rules` object to the function like this:

```
$('#signup').validate({
  rules : {
    name : 'required'
  }
}); // end validate()
```

In this case, the field is named `name`, and the rule specifies that the field is required. To apply more than one validation rule to a form field, you must create another object for that field. For example, to expand the validation rules for the form in Figure 8-6, you can add a rule that would not only make the email field required, but also specify that the email address must be validly formatted:

```
1   $('#signup').validate({
2     rules : {
3       name : 'required',
4     email : {
5     required : true,
6     email : true
7     }
8     }
9   }); // end validate()
```

> **NOTE** According to the rules of JavaScript object literals, you must end each name/value pair except the last one with a comma. For example, in line 3 above, name : 'required' must have a comma after it, because another rule (for the email field) follows it. Turn to page 136 for a refresher on how object literals work.

Lines 4–7, shown in bold, specify the rules for the email field. The field's name is *email*, as specified in the HTML (see the HTML code on page 280); required : true make the field required; and email : true makes sure the field contains an email address.

You can use any of the validation types listed in Table 8-2. For example, say you add a field named "birthdate" to the form used in this example. To ensure that a date is entered into the field, you can expand the list of rules like this:

```
$('#signup').validate({
  rules : {
    name : 'required',
    email : {
      required : true,
      email : true
    },
  birthdate : 'date'
  }
}); // end validate()
```

If you also want the birthdate field to be a required field, adjust the code as follows:

```
$('#signup').validate({
  rules : {
    name : 'required',
    email : {
      required : true,
      email : true
    },
  birthdate : {
   date : true,
   required : true
  }
  }
}); // end validate()
```

As mentioned earlier, one of the most powerful and useful things you can do with advanced validation rules is require visitors' entries to be a certain minimum or maximum length. For example, on a complaint report form, you may want to limit comments to, say, 200 characters in length, so your customers will get to the point instead of writing *War and Peace*. There are also rules to make sure that numbers entered are within a certain range; for example, unless you're accepting information from mummies or vampires, you won't accept birth years earlier than 1900.

- **minlength.** The field must contain *at least* the specified number of characters. For example, the rule to make sure that at least six characters are entered into a field is this:

  ```
  minlength:6
  ```

- **maxlength.** The field must contain *no more* than the specified number of characters. For example, the rule to ensure that no more than 100 characters are entered into the field looks like this:

  ```
  maxlength:100
  ```

- **rangelength.** A combination of both `minlength` and `maxlength`. Specifies both the minimum and maximum number of characters allowed in a field. For example, the rule to make sure a field contains at least six characters but no more than 100 is as follows:

  ```
  rangelength:[6,100]
  ```

- **min.** Requires that the field contain a number that's greater than or equal to the specified number. For example, the following rule requires that the field both contains a number and that the number is greater than or equal to 10.

  ```
  min:10
  ```

  In this example, if the visitor enters *8*, the field won't validate because 8 is less than 10. Likewise, if your visitor types a word—*eight*, for example—the field won't validate and she'll get an error message.

- **max.** Like `min`, but specifies the largest number the field can contain. To make sure a field contains a number less than 1,000, for example, use the following:

  ```
  max:1000
  ```

- **range.** Combines `min` and `max` to specify both the smallest and largest numbers that the field must contain. For example, to make sure a field contains at least 10 but no more than 1,000, use this:

  ```
  range:[10,1000]
  ```

- **equalTo.** Requires that a field's contents match another field. For example, on a sign-up form, it's common to ask a visitor to enter a password and then verify that password by typing it a second time. This way, the visitor can make sure he didn't mistype the password the first time. To use this method, you must specify a string containing a valid jQuery selector. For example, say the first password field has an ID of `password` applied to it. If you want to make sure the "verify password" field matches the first password field, you use this code:

```
equalTo: '#password'
```

You can use these advanced validation rules in combination. Just take it one field at a time. Here's an example of how they work together: Assume you have a form that includes two fields, one for creating a password, and another for confirming that password. The HTML for those two fields might look like this:

```
<input name="password" type="password" id="password">
<input name="confirm_password" type="password" id="confirm_password">
```

NOTE The jQuery Validation plug-in has a second plug-in file named *additional-method.js,* which includes more validation rules including minimum number of words, US vehicle identification numbers, Dutch Bank account numbers, and other obscure (but potentially useful) validation rules. There isn't any documentation for these extra types, so you'll need to look in the code of *additional-method.js.* If you find ones you like, you should save a copy of the file—name it something like *my-rules.js*—and delete all of the other rules that you don't need. That way, you'll have a much smaller JavaScript file.

Both fields are required, and the password must be at least 8 characters but no more than 16. And finally, you want to make sure the "confirm password" field matches the other password field. Assuming the form has an ID of `signup`, you can validate those two fields with the following code:

```
$('#signup').validate({
  rules: {
    password: {
      required:true,
      rangelength:[8,16]
    },
    confirm_password: {
      equalTo:'#password'
    }
  }
}); // end validate()
```

■ ADVANCED ERROR MESSAGES

As you read on page 278, you can easily add an error message for a field by adding a title with the error message text. However, this approach doesn't let you create separate error messages for each type of validation error. For example, say a field is required and must have a number in it. You might want two different messages for each error: "This field is required", and "Please enter a number." You can't do that using the `title` attribute. Instead, you must pass a JavaScript object to the `validate()` function containing the different error messages you wish to display.

The process is similar to creating advanced rules, as described in the previous section. The basic structure of the messages object is as follows:

```
Messages : {
 Fieldname : {
  methodType : 'Error message'
  }
}
```

Validating with the Server

While JavaScript validation is great for quickly checking user input, sometimes you need to check in with the server to see if a field is valid. For example, say you have a signup form that lets visitors create their own usernames for use on your website's forums. No two people can share the same username, so it would be helpful if you could inform the person filling out the form if the username she wants is already taken before submitting the form. In this case, you have to consult with the server to find out whether the username is available.

The Validation plug-in provides an advanced validation method, called remote, that lets you check in with the server. This method lets you pass both the field name and the value the visitor has typed into that field to the web server, which can use a server-side language like PHP, Ruby, .NET, Java, or Node.js). The server can then take that information and do something with it, like check to see if a username is available, and then respond to the form with a value of either true (passed validation) or false (failed validation).

Assume you have a field named "username" that's both required and must not be a name currently in use on your

site. To create a rule for the field (using the advanced rules method described on page 280), you can add the following to the rules object:

```
username : {
  required: true,
  remote: 'check_username.php'
}
```

The remote method takes a string containing the path from the current page to a page on the web server. In this example, the page is named *check_username.php*. When the validation plug-in tries to validate this field, it sends the field's name (username) and the visitor's input to *check_username.php*, which then determines if the username is available. If the name is available, the PHP page returns the word 'true'; if the username is already taken, the page returns the word 'false', and the field won't validate.

All of this magic takes place via the power of Ajax, which you'll learn about in Part Four. To see a working example of this validation method, visit *http://jquery.bassistance.de/validate/demo/captcha/*.

In the preceding example, replace fieldname with the field you're validating, and methodType with one of the assigned validation methods. For example, to combine the validation methods for the password fields and messages for each of those errors, add the following code shown in bold:

```
$('#signup').validate({
  rules : {
    password : {
      required : true,
      rangelength : [8,16]
    },
    confirm_password : {
```

```
        equalTo : '#password'
      }
  }, // end of rules
  messages : {
    password : {
      required : "Please type the password you'd like to use.",
      rangelength : "Your password must be between 8 and 16 characters long."
    },
    confirm_password : {
      equalTo : "The two passwords don't match."
    }
  } // end of messages
}); // end validate()
```

TIP As you can see, using the advanced method can require a lot of object literals, and the number of {
and } characters required can often make the code confusing to understand. A good approach when using the
Validation plug-in's advanced method is to go slow and test often. Instead of trying all your rules and messages
in one furious typing session, add one rule, then test the page. If the validation doesn't work, you've probably
made a typo somewhere, so fix it before continuing on and adding a second rule. Once the rules are finished and
they work, add the object literal for any error messages. Again, go slow, add the messages one at a time, and
test often. And don't forget to check your browser's error console (page 18) to identify any JavaScript errors you
might make.

Styling Error Messages

When the Validation plug-in checks a form and finds an invalid form field, it does two
things: First, it adds a class to the form field; then it adds a <label> tag containing an
error message. For example, say your page has the following HTML for an email field:

```
<input name="email" type="text" class="required">
```

If you add the Validation plug-in to the page with this form and your visitor tries
to submit the form without filling out the email field, the plug-in would stop the
submission process and change the field's HTML, adding an additional tag. The new
HTML would look like this:

```
<input name="email" type="text" class="required error">
<label for="email" generated="true" class="error">This field is required.
</label>
```

In other words, the plug-in adds the class name error to the form field. It also inserts
a <label> tag with a class named error containing the error-message text.

To change the appearance of the error messages, you simply need to add a style
to your style sheet defining the look for that error. For example, to make the error
text bold and red, you can add this style to your style sheet:

```
label.error {
  color: #F00;
  font-weight: bold;
}
```

Because the Validation plug-in also adds an error class to the invalid form field, you can create CSS styles to format those as well. For example, to place a red border around invalid fields, you can create a style like this:

```
input.error, select.error, textarea.error {
  border: 1px red solid;
}
```

■ Validation Tutorial

In this tutorial, you'll take a form and add both basic and advanced validation options to it (Figure 8-7).

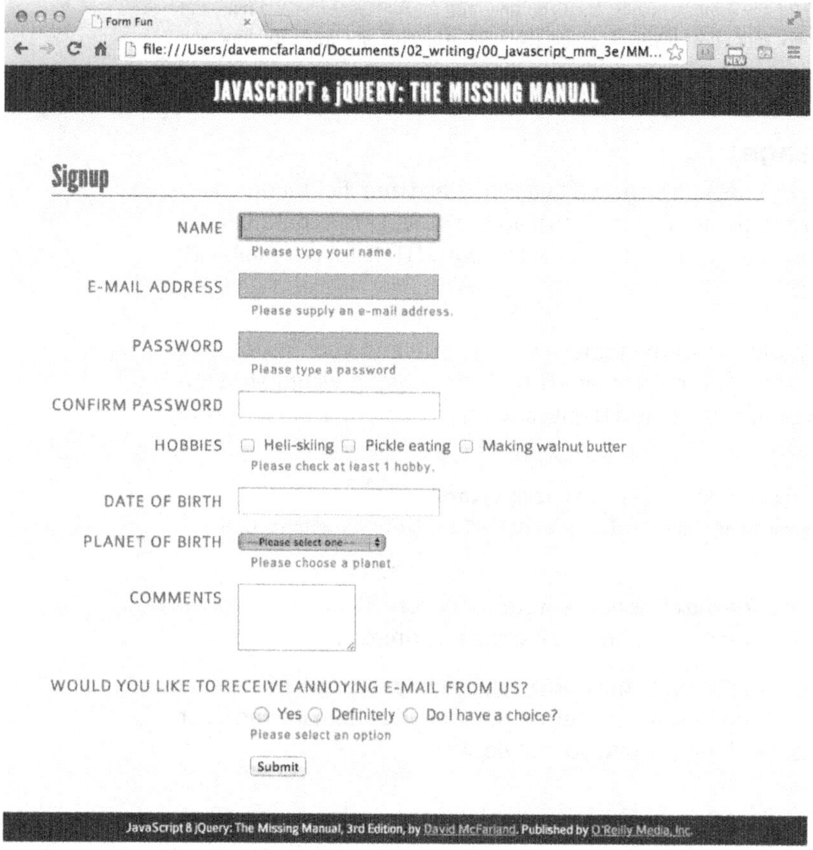

FIGURE 8-7

Don't let visitors submit your forms incorrectly! With a little help from the jQuery Validation plug-in, you can make sure that you get the information you're after.

NOTE   See the note on page 12 for information on how to download the tutorial files.

VALIDATION
TUTORIAL

Basic Validation

In this tutorial, you'll get started with the Validation plug-in by applying the basic validation methods described on page 276. Then you'll learn more complex validation procedures using the advanced method discussed on page 279. As you'll see, it's perfectly OK to mix and match the two approaches on the same form:

1. **In a text editor, open the file *validation.html* in the *chapter08* folder.**

   This file contains a form with a variety of form fields, including text fields, checkboxes, radio buttons, and menus. You'll add validation to this form, but first you need to attach the validation plug-in to the page.

2. **On the blank line immediately after the <script> tag that attaches the jQuery file to this page, type:**

   ```
   <script src="jquery_validate/jquery.validate.min.js"></script>
   ```

   The validation plug-in is contained in a folder named *jquery_validate*, which is in the same folder as the web page you're working on.

   This page already has another <script> tag, complete with the jQuery ready() function. You just need to add the validate() function to this page's form.

3. **In the blank line directly below $(document).ready(function(), type:**

   ```
   $('#signup').validate();
   ```

   The form has an ID of signup:

   ```
   <form action="process.html" method="post" name="signup" id="signup">
   ```

   So $('#signup') uses jQuery to select that form, and validate() applies the validation plug-in to the form. However, the form won't get validated until you specify some validation rules. So first, you'll make the name field required and supply a custom error message.

4. **Locate the HTML for the name field—<input name="name" type="text" id="name">—and add class and title attributes, so the tag looks like this (changes are in bold):**

   ```
   <input name="name" type="text" id="name"
   class="required" title="Please type your name.">
   ```

   The class="required" part of the code lets the Validation plug-in know that this field is mandatory, while the title attribute specifies the error message that the visitor will see if she doesn't fill out this field.

5. **Save the page, open it in a web browser, and click Submit.**

   Because the name field isn't filled out, an error message appears to the right of the field (circled in Figure 8-8).

Congratulations—you've just added validation to your form using the basic method discussed on page 276. Next, you'll add another validation rule for the "date of birth" field.

NOTE If you don't see an error message and instead get a page with the headline "Form Processed," the validation didn't work and the form was submitted anyway. Go over steps 1–4 again to make sure you didn't make any typos.

FIGURE 8-8

Don't worry about the appearance of the error message just yet. You'll learn how to format errors on page 295.

6. **Locate the HTML for the date of birth field—<input name="dob" type="text" id="dob">—and add class and title attributes so the tag looks like this (changes are in bold):**

    ```
    <input name="dob" type="text" id="dob" class="date"
    title="Please type your date of birth using this format: 01/19/2000">
    ```

    Because you didn't add the required class, filling out this field is optional. However, if the visitor does type anything into the field, the class="date" tells the plug-in that the input must be formatted like a date. You use the title attribute again to hold the error message if this field isn't valid. Save the page and try it out in a web browser—type something like *kjsdf* in the date of birth field and try to submit the form.

NOTE If you did want to require that the visitor fill out the date of birth field *and* enter a valid date, just add required to the class attribute. Just make sure date and required are separated by a space:

    class="date required"

    You can use the same technique for validating a menu (<select> tag).

7. **Locate the HTML for the opening select tag—<select name="planet" id="planet">—and add class and title attributes so the tag looks like this (changes are in bold):**

    ```
    <select name="planet" id="planet" class="required"
    title="Please choose a planet.">
    ```

You can validate menus just like text fields by adding a validation `class` and `title` attribute.

Now it's time to try the advanced validation method.

Advanced Validation

As mentioned on page 279, there are some things you can't do with the basic validation methods, like assign different error messages for different validation problems, or require a specific number of characters for input. In these cases, you need to use the Validation plug-in's advanced approach for creating validation rules and error messages.

To start, you'll add two validation rules and two different error messages for the form's email field:

1. **In the JavaScript code near the top of the file, locate the line $('#signup').** **validate(); and edit it to look like this:**

   ```
   $('#signup').validate({

   }); // end validate()
   ```

   In other words, add opening and closing braces between the parentheses in `validate()`, add an empty line between the braces, and add a JavaScript comment at the end. The comment is a note to identify the end of the `validate()` function. You'll soon be filling the script with braces and parentheses, so it can get tricky to remember which brace goes with what. This comment can help keep you from getting confused, but like all comments in code, it's optional.

   Next, you'll create the basic skeleton for adding validation rules.

2. **In the empty line (between the braces) you added in the last step, type:**

   ```
   rules: {

   } //end rules
   ```

   To make the code easier to read, you might also want to put two spaces before the `rules` and `}`. Indenting those lines makes it more visually obvious that these lines of code are part of the `validate()` function.

   This code creates an empty object, which you'll fill with specific field names and validation methods. In addition, a JavaScript comment identifies the end of the `rules` object. Next, you'll add rules for the email field.

3. **Edit the `validate()` function so it looks like this (changes are in bold):**

```
$('#signup').validate({
  rules: {
  email: {
   required: true,
   email: true
  }
  } // end rules
}); // end validate()
```

Here, you've added another object literal. The first part, `email`, is the name of the field you wish to validate and matches the field's name in the HTML. Next, two validation methods are specified—the field is required (meaning visitors must fill it in if they want to submit the form), and the input must match the form of an email address. "Test early and often" is a good motto for any programmer. Before moving on, you'll test to make sure the script is working.

4. **Save the file; preview it in a web browser and try to submit the form.**

You'll see the plug-in's default error message for missing information: "This field is required." Click in that field and type a couple letters. The error message changes to "Please enter a valid email address" (that's the standard message the plug-in prints when a visitor types something other than an email address into an email field). If you don't see any error messages, then go over your code and compare it to step 3 above.

Now you'll add custom error messages for this field.

5. **Return to your text editor. Type a comma after the closing brace for the rules object (but before the // end rules comment), and then type:**

```
messages: {

} // end messages
```

This code represents yet another object literal, named `messages`. This object will contain any error messages you wish to add to your form fields. Again, the comment at the end—`// end messages`—is optional. Now you'll add the actual error messages for the email field.

6. **Edit the `validate()` function so it looks like this (the additions are in bold):**

```
1    $('#signup').validate({
2      rules: {
3        email: {
4          required: true,
5          email: true
6        }
7      }, //end rules
8      messages: {
```

```
9    email: {
10   required: "Please supply your e-mail address.",
11   email: "This is not a valid e-mail address."
12   }
13    } // end messages
14   }); // end validate(),
```

Save the page and preview it in a web browser again. Try to submit the form without filling out the email address field. You should now see your custom error message: "Please supply your email address." Now, type something like *hello* into the email field. This time you should get the "This is not a valid email address" error.

If you don't get any error messages and, instead, end up on the "Form Processed!" page, there's a JavaScript error somewhere in your code. The most likely culprit is a missing comma after the `rules` object (see line 7), or in the `email` message object (see line 10).

Now it's time to add validation rules for the two password fields.

7. **Edit the rules object so it looks like this (changes are in bold):**

```
1    rules: {
2       email: {
3          required: true,
4          email: true
5       },
6    password: {
7    required: true,
8    rangelength:[8,16]
9    },
10   confirm_password: {
11   equalTo:'#password'
12   }
13    }, //end rules
```

Don't miss the comma on line 5—it's necessary to separate the email rules from the password rules.

The first set of rules applies to the first password field. It makes the field mandatory and requires the password to be at least 8 but not more than 16 characters long. The second rule applies to the email confirmation field and requires that its contents match the value in the first password field (details on how these rules work can be found on page 282).

TIP It's a good idea to save the file and test it after each step in this tutorial. That way, if the validation stops working, you know which step you made the error in.

These rules also need accompanying error messages.

8. **Edit the** messages **object so it looks like this (changes in bold):**

```
1   messages: {
2     email: {
3       required: "Please supply an e-mail address.",
4       email: "This is not a valid email address."
5     },
6     password: {
7     required: 'Please type a password',
8     rangelength: 'Password must be between 8 and 16 characters long.'
9     },
10    confirm_password: {
11    equalTo: 'The two passwords do not match.'
12    }
13    } // end messages
```

Don't forget the comma on line 5.

At this point, you should be feeling comfortable adding rules and error messages. Next, you'll add validation for the checkboxes and radio buttons.

Validating Checkboxes and Radio Buttons

Checkboxes and radio buttons usually come in groups, and typically, adding validation to several checkboxes or radio buttons in a single group is a tricky process of finding all boxes or buttons in a group. Fortunately, the Validation plug-in takes care of the hard parts, and makes it easy for you to quickly validate these types of form fields:

1. **Locate the HTML for the first checkbox—<input name="hobby" type="checkbox" id="heliskiing" value="heliskiing">—and add class and title attributes so the tag looks like this (changes are in bold):**

```
<input name="hobby" type="checkbox" id="heliskiing"
value="heliskiing" class="required" title="Please check at least 1 hobby.">
```

Here, you're using the basic validation technique described on page 276. You could also use the advanced technique and include the rules and error messages as part of the validate() function, but if you only require one validation rule and error message, the basic technique is more straightforward and less error-prone.

In this case, all three checkboxes share the same name, so the Validation plug-in treats them as a group. In other words, this validation rule applies to *all three boxes*, even though you've only added the class and title attributes to one box. In essence, you've required that visitors checkmark at least one box before they can submit the form.

You'll do the same thing for the radio buttons at the bottom of the form.

2. **Locate the HTML for the first radio button—`<input type="radio" name="spam" id="yes" value="yes">`—and add `class` and `title` attributes so the tag looks like this (changes are in bold):**

```
<input type="radio" name="spam" id="yes" value="yes"
class="required" title="Please select an option">
```

A related group of radio buttons always shares the same name (spam, in this case), so even though you've added a rule and error message to just one button, it will apply to all three. Because the field is required, visitors must select one of the three radio buttons to submit the form.

3. **Save the file, preview it in a web browser, and click Submit.**

You may notice something looks a bit odd: When the error messages for the checkbox and radio buttons appear, they come directly after the first checkbox and radio button (circled in Figure 8-9). Even worse, the messages appear between the form field and its label (for example, between the checkbox and the label "Heli-skiing").

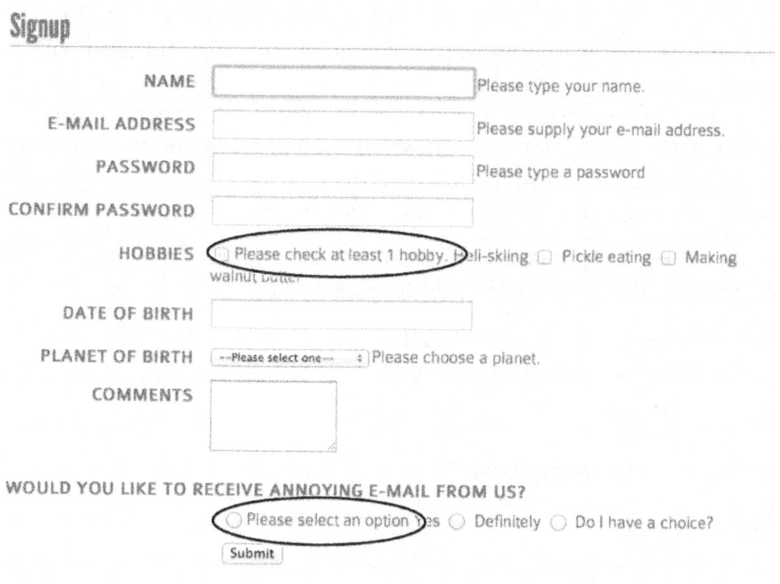

FIGURE 8-9

The Validation plug-in places error messages after the invalid form field. In the case of checkboxes and radio buttons, that looks awful. In order to place the error message elsewhere, you need to provide some instruction to the plug-in's `validate()` function.

The Validation plug-in places the error message directly after the form field that you apply the validation rule to. Normally, that's OK: When the message appears directly after a text field or menu, it looks fine (as in the earlier examples in this tutorial). But in this case, the message should go somewhere else, preferably after all of the checkboxes or radio buttons.

Fortunately, the Validation plug-in has a way to control the placement of error messages. You can create your own rules for error-message placement by passing another object literal to the validate() function.

4. **Locate the validation script you added earlier, and type a comma after the closing brace for the messages object (but before the // end messages comment). Insert a blank line after the messages object, and then type:**

```
errorPlacement: function(error, element) {
    if ( element.is(":radio") || element.is(":checkbox")) {
        error.appendTo( element.parent());
    } else {
        error.insertAfter(element);
    }
} // end errorPlacement
```

The Validation plug-in is programmed to accept an optional errorPlacement object, which is just an anonymous function (page 138) that determines where an error message is placed. Every error is sent through this function, so if you only want to change the placement of some error messages, you'll need to use a conditional statement to identify the form elements whose errors you wish to place. The function receives both the error message and the form element the error applies to, so you can use a conditional statement (page 61) to check whether the form field is either a radio button of a checkbox. If it is, the error message is added to the end of the element containing the button or checkbox. In this page's HTML, a <div> tag wraps around the group of checkboxes, and another <div> tag wraps the radio buttons. So the error message is placed just before the closing </div> tag using jQuery's appendTo() function (page 127).

You're done with all of the JavaScript programming for this form. Here's the complete script, including the $(document).ready() function:

```
1    $(document).ready(function() {
2      $('#signup').validate({
3        rules: {
4          email: {
5              required: true,
6              email: true
7          },
8          password: {
9              required: true,
10             rangelength:[8,16]
11         },
12         confirm_password: {equalTo:'#password'}
13       }, //end rules
14       messages: {
15         email: {
16             required: "Please supply an e-mail address.",
```

```
17              email: "This is not a valid email address."
18          },
19          password: {
20            required: 'Please type a password',
21            rangelength: 'Password must be between 8 and 16 characters long.'
22          },
23          confirm_password: {
24            equalTo: 'The two passwords do not match.'
25          }
26       }, // end messages
27       errorPlacement: function(error, element) {
28          if ( element.is(":radio") || element.is(":checkbox")) {
29             error.appendTo( element.parent());
30          } else {
31             error.insertAfter(element);
32          }
33       } // end errorPlacement
34    }); // end validate
35  }); // end ready()
```

Formatting the Error Messages

Now the page has working form validation, but the error messages don't look very good. Not only are they spread around the page, but they don't stand out the way they should. They'd look a lot better if they were bold, red, and appeared underneath the form field they apply to. You can make all of those formatting changes with a little simple CSS:

1. **Near the top of the validation.html file, click on the blank line between the opening <style> and closing </style> tags.**

    This page has an empty style sheet into which you'll add the styles. In a real-world situation, you'd probably use an external style sheet—either the main style sheet used by the other pages of the site, or a specific style sheet intended just for forms (*forms.css*, for example). But to keep things simpler for this tutorial, you'll just add the new styles to this page.

2. **Add the following CSS rule inside the <style> tags:**

    ```css
    #signup label.error {
      font-size: 0.8em;
      color: #F00;
      font-weight: bold;
      display: block;
      margin-left: 215px;
    }
    ```

    The CSS selector #signup label.error targets any <label> tag with a class of error that appears inside another element with the ID signup. In this case, the

<form> tag has an ID signup, and the Validation plug-in puts error messages inside a <label> tag and adds the class error (page 285). In other words, this CSS rule only applies to the error message inside this form.

The CSS properties themselves are pretty basic: First, the font size is reduced to .8 em; next, the color is changed to red, and the text is bolded. The display: block instruction informs the browser to treat the <label> tag as a block-level element. That is, instead of putting the error message *next* to the form field, the browser treats the error like a paragraph of its own, with line breaks above and below. Finally, to make the error message line up with the form fields (which are indented 215 pixels from the left edge of the main content area), you need to add a left margin.

To make it even clearer which fields have validation problems, you can add CSS rules to change the look of invalid form fields.

3. **Add one final rule to the *form.css* file:**

```
#signup input.error, #signup select.error {
  background: #FFA9B8;
  border: 1px solid red;
}
```

This rule highlights an invalid form field by adding a red border around its edges and a background color to the field.

That's all there is to it. Save the CSS file and preview the *validation.html* page in a web browser to see how the CSS affects the error messages (you may need to hit the browser's reload button to see the changes you made to the CSS file).

The final form should look like Figure 8-7 (page 286). You can find a completed version of the tutorial (*complete_validation.html*) in the *chapter08* folder.

Getting Started with jQuery UI

Expanding Your Interface

With jQuery and a little programming, you've seen how to add enhancements to forms, images, and links. You've added animations to your pages and created simple user interface elements like the login slider on page 188 and the animated dashboard on page 197. But perhaps you're ready for more complex user interface elements like pop-up dialog boxes, tabbed panels, or tooltips. You could learn to program that stuff from scratch, but as you read on page 236, there's a wide range of jQuery plug-ins that have them all figured out for you. jQuery UI is a plug-in that's solved a lot of user interface problems and wrapped those solutions into an easy to use package.

■ What Is jQuery UI?

jQuery UI (*http://jqueryui.com*) is an advanced jQuery plug-in and a sister-project to jQuery (Figure 9-1). jQuery UI provides a large set of effects, user interactions, and interface elements (called *widgets*) that simplify the process of building an interactive web application. In fact, in Chapter 14, you'll use jQuery UI and some custom programming to build a basic (but useful) web application.

jQuery UI is made up of many different parts which can be grouped into three categories:

- **Widgets.** A widget is a chunk of JavaScript that provides one useful interface element. For example, the dialog widget lets you display pop-up dialog boxes—they're like custom alert boxes (page 305), but let you control how they look and work. You could use this dialog box to show your visitor a login form, for example, or display your website's terms and conditions text. You could pop up a dialog to present an important message each time someone visits your site or display information about a photo each time a visitor mouses over it.

For another example, the datepicker widget provides an easy way for visitors to select a date. It opens a pop-up window with a calendar; the user can simply click a date on the calendar to select it. You could use this widget as part of a vacation rental form ("Begin your stay on what date?") or as a way to navigate through a listing of upcoming events.

jQuery UI is brimming with widgets, and you'll learn about some of them in this and the next chapter.

- **Interactions.** jQuery UI includes some very useful tools for letting visitors interact with your web pages. For example, you can make any element on a page draggable. Imagine an online shopping page where visitors can literally drag an item for sale into a shopping cart of the page. Or build an online checkers game where players can drag pieces to move them. You can also make page elements resizable—for example, say you pop up a dialog widget with a form for writing a blog post. A visitor viewing the dialog box can drag the corner of the box to make it larger or smaller. In other words, you can make a regular <div> act like a browser window, complete with resize handles. jQuery UI includes several interactions, as you'll see in Chapter 12.

- **Effects.** jQuery offers some types of animations, like fade in (page 185), fade out (page 185), slide down (page 186), and the animate() function. But jQuery UI offers many more—it lets you animate changes in color, changes between two different CSS classes, and many more. You'll read about these jQuery UI effects starting on page 438.

■ Why Use jQuery UI?

You may be wondering, with the thousands of available plug-ins, why you should use jQuery UI. Even without it, you can find all kinds of fancy plug-ins that offer tooltips, tabs, and dialog boxes. In fact, you can find plain old jQuery plug-ins that offer everything and more than jQuery UI does. You can learn more about these options in the box on page 302. Despite that, there are a few reasons why jQuery UI is a great choice:

- It's part of the jQuery Foundation. The jQuery Foundation (*https://jquery.org*) is a non-profit organization dedicated to promoting the development of jQuery, jQuery UI, and a few other projects. In other words, jQuery and jQuery UI are like siblings, and the teams responsible for the two projects work closely together, so as jQuery changes, jQuery UI will be fast to adapt.

- It's a complete package. If you wanted to, you could piece together, bit by bit, a set of plug-ins that duplicate everything that jQuery UI offers. But then you'd end up with dozens of different plug-ins by different authors, requiring dozens of CSS and JavaScript files. Keeping up with all of those different plug-ins would be a time-consuming challenge. jQuery UI is packaged in a single JavaScript file with two CSS files. When changes to jQuery UI arrive, updating those files is fast and simple.

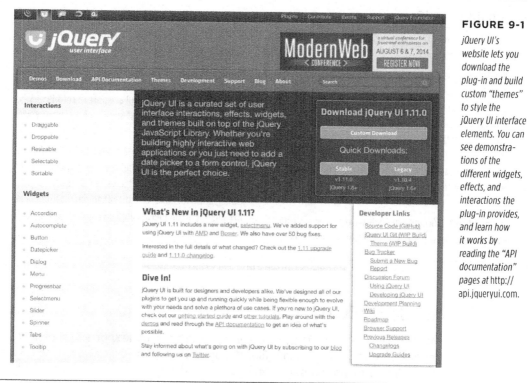

FIGURE 9-1
jQuery UI's website lets you download the plug-in and build custom "themes" to style the jQuery UI interface elements. You can see demonstrations of the different widgets, effects, and interactions the plug-in provides, and learn how it works by reading the "API documentation" pages at http://api.jqueryui.com.

- It offers a unified look. jQuery UI has a consistent look among all of its widgets. The tabbed panels look similar to the dialog boxes and the date picker, so you don't need to spend hours trying to get various plug-ins to look like they all belong on the same site. In addition, jQuery UI's ThemeRoller (which you'll see in Chapter 11) gives you an online tool for customizing the fonts, colors, shape, and design of jQuery UI's look. This makes it much easier to get jQuery UI's widgets to match the color scheme, fonts, and overall appearance of your existing website.

- It's a well-supported project. Many jQuery plug-ins are a labor of love by a single programmer—two or three at best. If the programmer loses interest, gets a new job, or becomes a monk, that plug-in may never be updated again, and any bugs it has won't be fixed. jQuery UI is built by a large team of individuals. It's routinely updated and bugs are fixed quickly. Because so many people are involved in the project, you can trust that it will be around for a while. (How many? If you look at the list of contributors—*https://github.com/jquery/jquery-ui/blob/master/AUTHORS.txt*—you'll see that over 270 people have had a hand in building jQuery UI.)

Alternatives to jQuery UI

jQuery UI isn't the only user interface library around. Here are some popular alternatives.

- **Kendo UI** (*www.telerik.com/kendo-ui*) is a complete set of plug-ins for building web (and mobile) apps. It includes some of the features of jQuery UI like a date picker and tooltips, but it also includes more advanced features like data visualization tools for presenting different types of charts and diagrams. Like jQuery, it includes a theme builder and extensive documentation. Unfortunately, while jQuery UI is free, Kendo UI costs anywhere from $399 to $699.

- **Wijmo UI** (*http://wijmo.com*) is a set of advanced user interface widgets. It's based on jQuery UI and jQuery Mobile, and provides over 40 different widgets that include charts, grids, spreadsheets, and so on. It's a superb set of plug-ins that provides everything a web application would need (and more) and works well on mobile as well as desktop. But at a price tag of $495–$1195 *per web developer*, it's best suited for a company with some cash to spend.

- **jQWidgets** (*www.jqwidgets.com*) is another set of plug-ins with a custom theme builder and a wide selection of widgets including data tables, grids, sliders, a color picker, and a lot more. Like the other options listed here, jQWidgets is a commercial product and costs $199 and up.

Using jQuery UI

You'll find jQuery UI at *http://jqueryui.com*. The home page sports a prominent box for downloading the necessary files (Figure 9-1). Skip the Quick Downloads links— these files are for programmers who want to work on or study jQuery UI's underlying JavaScript code. (If you do click this link, you'll find dozens of files used in building jQuery UI, many of which are for automating the process of creating jQuery UI and are useless for actually using jQuery UI on your website.)

Instead, click the big Custom Download button or click the Download button in the navigation bar near the top of the page. This leads to the Download Builder (Figure 9-2), which lets you pick the components you'd like to use and leave out the ones you don't. For example, you may find that the progressbar, slider, and spinner widgets aren't useful for you, so you can uncheck those boxes to exclude them from the download. In this way, you can make the jQuery UI plug-in file as small as possible, by only including the components you really need.

After you select the components you're interested in, you'll see a section called Theme at the bottom of the page. This area lets you select different design themes to use with jQuery UI and even access the ThemeRoller that lets you design a custom color, font, and design scheme for jQuery UI (just click "design a custom theme." You'll learn about themes and how to build your own in Chapter 11.

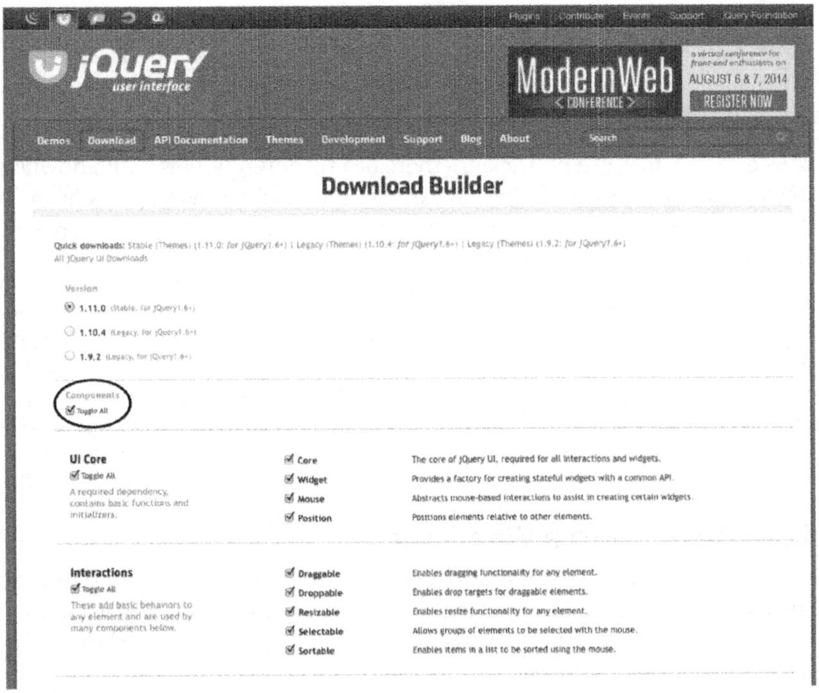

FIGURE 9-2

jQuery UI's download builder lets you customize jQuery UI to meet your needs. You can choose only the widgets, interactions, and effects you'll use, by turning off the boxes next to any items you don't want. If you only want to choose a few, click the first Toggle All button (circled) to uncheck all the boxes, and then just turn on the ones you'd like. Some widgets are dependent upon other components in the plug-in—fortunately, the download builder is smart enough to automatically turn on any necessary additional items for you. For example, if you deselect all components and then select the accordion widget, the download builder automatically checkmarks the Core and Widget boxes, because the accordion requires those to work.

To get the jQuery UI files, just click the Download button at the bottom of the Download Builder page. This downloads a Zip file containing a folder named something like *jquery-ui-1.11.1.custom*. Inside that are two other folders (see left image in Figure 9-3). You're only interested in the *images* folder, which contains graphics used by jQuery UI. You can ignore the external folder: it contains jQuery, which you've probably already downloaded and added to your site.

To use jQuery UI, you need the jQuery UI JavaScript file, which contains the programming required to make jQuery UI's cool widgets, effects, and interactions possible. You also need the CSS file, which applies the styles to the widgets and effects. As you can see in Figure 9-3, however, there are a lot of CSS and JavaScript files, so you need to figure out which to use.

As you read on page 110, jQuery files that include *min* in their name—like *jquery-ui. min.js*—are "minified" files, meaning that unnecessary white space (like extra spaces and carriage returns) has been removed and other optimizations made to make the file smaller. Minified files are the best to use on your website because they'll download quickly. However, the minification process makes them unreadable, so you can't really make changes to these types of files. You don't generally need to read the jQuery UI JavaScript file unless you want to learn how it's programmed, so you should use the *jquery-ui.min.js* file in your site.

The choice of CSS files is a bit trickier—there are six different files in the download! You really only need the *jquery-ui.min.css* file because it has all the CSS necessary for jQuery UI to work. The right image in Figure 9-3 demonstrates a good way to organize your jQuery and jQuery UI files.

> **NOTE** Why so many CSS files? In addition to the *jquery-ui.min.css* file, you'll find *jquery-ui.theme.min.css* and a *jquery-ui.structure.min.css* files. The *structure* file provides all CSS required for the "structure" of the CSS widgets, such as information about the placement of elements on the page, while the *theme* file contains only information about colors, fonts, font sizes, padding, and other visual aspects. In other words, to get the same effect as the *jquery-ui.min.css* file, you'd need to attach both the theme and structure files. Don't bother.

Adding jQuery UI to a Web Page

jQuery UI is simply a jQuery plug-in, so it follows the basic plug-in rules you read about on page 236. You attach a CSS file, attach jQuery, attach the jQuery UI JavaScript file, adjust your HTML a bit, and then call the plug-in function. Here are the steps in detail, so you'll have them in one place:

1. **Download jQuery UI as described in the previous section.**

    Once you have the files, you need to move the files and folders that make jQuery UI work into your own site, as pictured in Figure 9-3. Place the *jquery-ui.min. css* file and the *images* folder in the folder for your site's CSS files, and place the *jquery-ui.min.js* file in the folder you place JavaScript files. Always use the minified files—the ones with min in their names. Their smaller size means they'll download faster. To use jQuery UI, you need only the jquery—*ui.min.js* and jquery—*ui.min.css* files as well as the folder of images. Put the images folder in the same folder as the CSS file (Figure 9-3, right).

2. **Attach the jQuery UI CSS file to your web page, like this:**

    ```
    <link href="css/jquery-ui.min.css" rel="stylesheet">
    ```

    It's also a good idea to link the theme style sheet *before* your site's style sheet like this:

    ```
    <link href="css/jquery-ui.min.css" rel="stylesheet">
    <link href="css/site.css" rel="stylesheet">
    ```

    This way, if you want to make any small tweaks to the theme, you can include CSS rules in your site's style sheet that override ones in the theme style sheet.

In general, you don't want to change the CSS in the jQuery UI style sheet, as you may need to replace it with a newer style sheet when a new version of jQuery UI comes out. (You'll learn about theming and the CSS used in jQuery UI in depth in Chapter 11.)

3. **Attach the jQuery and the jQuery UI JavaScript files:**

```
<script src="js/jquery-1.11.0.min.js"></script>
<script src="js/jquery-ui.min.js"></script>
```

The jQuery UI file won't work without jQuery, so you need to make sure the jQuery file loads before the jQuery UI file.

After you've added the files to your site and linked them to your web pages, you're ready to start using jQuery UI. Because each effect, interaction, and widget is different, there's no one set of instructions to follow. The rest of this chapter will walk you through some of the most useful widgets in the jQuery UI plug-in.

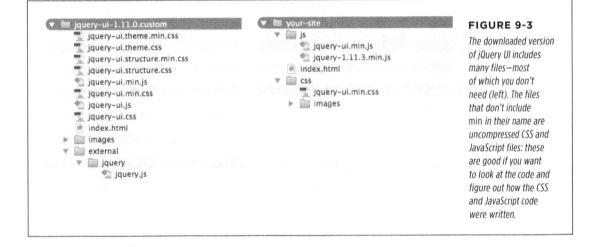

FIGURE 9-3

The downloaded version of jQuery UI includes many files—most of which you don't need (left). The files that don't include min in their name are uncompressed CSS and JavaScript files: these are good if you want to look at the code and figure out how the CSS and JavaScript code were written.

Adding Messages with Dialog Boxes

A web browser's normal alert box is pretty disruptive (flip back to Figure 1-3): it doesn't look anything like your web page design, and you can't change the text's color or font. It may even have warning messages you don't want your visitors to see; for example, Chrome adds a checkbox to alert boxes that says, "Prevent this page from creating additional dialogs." Fortunately, jQuery UI provides a dialog widget that lets you create your own dialog boxes, like the one shown in Figure 9-4. You can add text, forms, and images to jQuery UI dialogs, format them to look like the rest of your site, and even program them to do things when a visitor interacts with them.

Using the Dialog widget (like using most jQuery plug-ins) is astonishingly simple:

1. **Follow the steps above on page 304 to attach the CSS and JavaScript files.**

   You've got to start somewhere!

2. **Add a <div> tag with the content you want to appear inside the dialog box and a title attribute containing the words you want to appear as the title of the dialog.**

   For example, here's the HTML for the dialog shown in Figure 9-4:

   ```
   <div id="hello" title="Hello World!">
     <p>This dialog box is actually a div, that's placed
        on the page using absolute positioning.</p>
     <p>Try dragging the dialog around the screen. You can!</p>
   </div>
   ```

   Because you need to tell jQuery UI to turn this <div> into a dialog box, you need to have some way of identifying it. Adding an ID—id="hello", for example—is a good approach.

   > **NOTE** The dialog box doesn't have to be a <div> tag. Any block level element like <article> or <p> will also work.

3. **Add jQuery's $(document).ready() function to your page:**

   ```
   $(document).ready(function() {

   }); // end ready
   ```

4. **Use jQuery to select the <div> and call the dialog function:**

   ```
   $(document).ready(function() {
     $('#hello').dialog();
   }); // end ready
   ```

   In this example, you're using $('#hello') because that's the ID you gave the <div> in step 2, but you can use any of jQuery's many ways of selecting elements (page 119) to select the dialog HTML and turn it into a dialog box.

These steps will make the dialog box appear as soon as the page loads. This setup is good for whenever you need to give your site's visitors an urgent notice like "This site will be offline for routine maintenance from 3:00–4:00 a.m.," or you want to pop up an ad before they can read the content on your site. In the next section, you'll see how to keep the dialog box hidden when the page loads and only open it based on an event. But first, here's how to create your first dialog box.

Mini-Tutorial: Creating a Dialog Box

Now that you know how the Dialog widget works, take it for a quick spin by adding a basic dialog box that appears when the page loads.

NOTE See the note on page 12 for information on how to download the tutorial files.

1. **In a text editor, open the file *hello_world.html* in the *chapter09* folder.**

   This file already contains a link to the jQuery file and the `$(document).ready()`
   function (page 160), but you have to link to the jQuery UI CSS and JavaScript files.

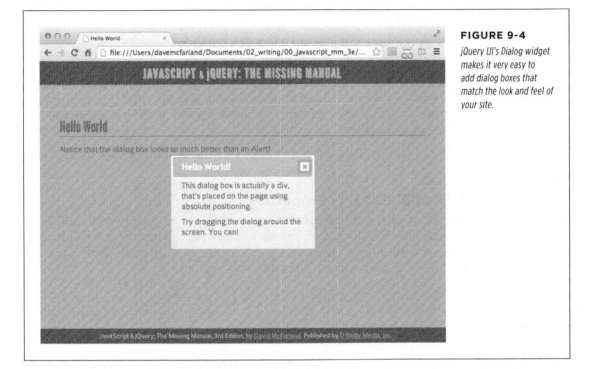

FIGURE 9-4

*jQuery UI's Dialog widget
makes it very easy to
add dialog boxes that
match the look and feel of
your site.*

2. **Add the lines in bold to the page's <head> section:**

```
<link href="../_css/ui-lightness/jquery-ui.min.css" rel="stylesheet">
<link href="../_css/site.css" rel="stylesheet">
<script src="../_js/jquery.min.js"></script>
<script src="../_js/jquery-ui.min.js"></script>
```

   Notice that jQuery UI's style sheet goes before the *site.css* file, and the jQuery
   UI file is linked *after* the jQuery file. Now it's time to add the HTML that makes
   up the dialog box.

3. **Locate the empty line, just below the HTML comment `<!-- add the dialog
   <div> here -->` and type:**

```
<div id="hello" title="Hello World!">
  <p>A jQuery UI Dialog Box</p>
</div>
```

   Next, you'll turn this div into a dialog box.

4. **In the empty line inside the $(document).ready() function, add the bolded line below:**

```
$(document).ready(function() {
 $('#hello').dialog();
}); // end ready
```

This selects the <div> you just added and turns it into a dialog box. It really *is* that simple.

5. **Save the page and preview it in a web browser.**

A dialog box appears. You can move the dialog box by clicking the orange title bar and dragging it around the screen. You can even drag any of the four corners of the dialog box to make the box larger or smaller. Grab the title area again and notice that the cursor changes to a four-way arrow. That's not your regular old browser behavior—it's one of the little details programmed right into jQuery UI.

You'll find the finished version of this tutorial in the *complete_hello_world. html* file.

Setting Dialog Box Properties

You can set various properties of the dialog box—like its height, width, and how it animates on and off the screen—by sending the dialog() function a list of property names and values in an object. As you read on page 136, an object literal is a group of name/value pairs enclosed in braces, like this:

```
{
  name : 'Dave',
  awesomeAuthor : true
}
```

You pass an object with options the plug-in understands when you call the dialog() function. For example, say you didn't want visitors to be able to either drag or resize a dialog box. You'd just pass an object literal with two dialog options, like this:

```
$('#hello').dialog({
  draggable : false,
  resizable : false
});
```

The Dialog widget is programmed to turn off the dragging ability when the draggable property is set to false, and prevent resizing of the dialog when the resizable property is set to false. Here are some of the most useful properties:

• **draggable.** Set this property to false to keep the dialog box locked in place on the screen and prevent visitors from dragging it around. (If you want to let visitors drag the dialog around, you don't have to do anything; that's the normal behavior of the Dialog widget.)

- **resizable.** Set this property to `false` to keep the dialog box at its default size and prevent visitors from making it bigger or smaller. (Again, if you want to let visitors resize the dialog, you don't have to do anything; that's the normal behavior.)

- **height and width.** Normally, jQuery UI makes a dialog box just big enough to display all of the content in it. But you can control this behavior by specifying an exact height and width in pixels. For example, if you wanted the dialog box to be 600 pixels wide and 400 pixels tall, you could add this code to the object literal you pass to the dialog:

```
width: 600,
height: 400
```

You can use only pixels (no percentage or em values), and you leave off the `px` you'd normally attach to a CSS pixel value. If you set the width and height and there's more content inside that dialog box than will fit, jQuery UI will add a scroll bar inside the dialog box. Visitors can then scroll down to see all of the content in the dialog box. (This is the kind of behavior you see on many "Terms and Conditions" pop-up windows, where you have to keep scrolling for a few days in order to read all of the fine print.)

You don't have to set both properties. Maybe you want to make sure that the dialog box is a certain width, but you don't care how tall it is. In that case, just set the `width` property.

- **Minimum width and heights.** You can tell the dialog widget to make a dialog *at least* a certain width and height by specifying values for the `minWidth` and `minHeight` properties. For example, if you wanted a dialog box to be at least 600 pixels wide and 400 pixels tall, you'd set the properties like this:

```
minWidth: 600,
minHeight: 400
```

When you set a minimum height and width, jQuery UI may make the dialog box bigger than those values but not smaller. In other words, if you put more content than will fit inside the dialog box, jQuery UI will expand the dialog enough to show all of the content.

- **Maximum width and heights.** You can also tell the dialog widget that it can't make the dialog box wider than a certain value or taller than a certain value with the `maxWidth` and `maxHeight` properties. For example, if you wanted a dialog box to be at most 600 pixels wide and 400 pixels tall, you'd set the properties like this:

```
maxWidth: 600,
maxHeight: 400
```

If you don't have much content inside the box, jQuery UI will make the dialog smaller than these values, but never bigger. If the content won't fit within the dialog box, jQuery UI adds a scrollbar so visitors can scroll down and read all of the content.

- **modal.** A *modal* dialog box is used to lock a visitor's attention on a message and prevent her from doing anything else until she's closed the dialog box. When a modal dialog box opens, the visitor can't click anywhere else on the page: in fact, a dark transparent overlay settles over the page, so it's difficult to even read. Use modal dialog boxes when you don't want a visitor to proceed until she's read the message and perhaps made an important decision: "Are you sure you want to delete every episode of *Dr. Who* from your video library?" To make a dialog box modal, just set the modal property to true:

```
modal: true
```

NOTE For a complete list of options as well as more information on how to use the dialog widget, visit *http://api.jqueryui.com/dialog/*.

- **show and hide.** A dialog box usually appears on the screen when it's opened and disappears when it's closed. But what fun is that? You can animate how the dialog box opens and closes by setting the show and hide properties. These properties can take many different values. If you set them to true, then the dialog box will fade in and out quickly:

```
show: true,
hide: true
```

You can also provide a number, which is the number in milliseconds it takes to either fade the dialog in or out. For example, say you wanted the dialog box to fade in really quickly—say 250 milliseconds—but take 2 seconds to fade out. You'd set those properties like this:

```
show: 250,
hide: 2000
```

You're not limited to just the fade effect either. You can pass the name of any jQuery effect (page 183) to these properties as a value. Just enclose the name of the effect in quotes—'slideDown'—for example. To make a dialog box slide in and out of view, use these settings:

```
show: 'slideDown',
hide: 'slideUp'
```

You can also use jQuery UI effects (page 438) like 'scale' or 'explode'. As if that weren't enough options, you can also pass *another* object literal specifying an effect name, a duration, a delay, and an easing value (page 442). For example, say, when a dialog is closed you want it to wait 250 milliseconds and then explode for 1 second, using an 'easeInQuad' easing function (please don't try this at home). You'd pass this line along with the properties object:

```
hide: { effect: 'explode',  delay: 250, duration: 1000, easing:
'easeInQuad' }
```

- **position.** Dialog boxes usually pop up right in the middle of the browser window. But they don't have to. You can set the position of the dialog box using the position property. Like show and hide, it can accept several different types of values. For simple x,y coordinates pass an array (page 44) containing two numbers. The first sets the left position of the dialog (the distance from the left edge of the browser window to the left edge of the dialog box) in pixels; the second is the top position in pixels. For example, say you wanted the dialog to open 100 pixels from the left side of the screen and very close to the top of the screen (say 10 pixels from the top). You'd set the position property like this:

```
position: [100,10]
```

You can also use keywords—center, left, top, right, bottom—to specify the dialog's position. For example, to place the dialog in the bottom-right corner of the screen, set the position property like this:

```
position: 'right bottom'
```

The first keyword must be the horizontal setting—left, center, or right—and the second keyword the vertical—top, center, or bottom. Separate the two keywords with a space.

Finally, you can give the position property a jQuery UI position object. This useful utility is discussed in the box on page 318.

Mini Tutorial: Passing Options to the Dialog Widget

You can combine any or all of the properties listed above when you call the dialog() function. You can see how properties work by building upon the dialog box code from the previous tutorial. Here you'll make the dialog modal, so the visitor can't do anything until the dialog is dismissed; you'll also prevent visitors from moving or resizing the dialog; and, lastly, you'll make it disappear in a flashy way:

1. **In a text editor, return to the *hello_world.html* file you worked on in the steps on page 306.**

   You'll start by passing an empty object literal to the dialog function.

2. **Click between the opening and closing parentheses in dialog(). Type {, press Return twice, then type }. The code should now look like this:**

```
$(document).ready(function() {
  $('#hello').dialog({

  });
}); // end ready
```

You can now plug in property and value pairs. First, you'll make the dialog modal.

3. **Inside the object literal, type** `modal:  true:`

```
$(document).ready(function() {
  $('#hello').dialog({
    modal: true
  });
}); // end ready
```

Save the file and open it in a web browser. The rest of the screen around the dialog box is darkened by a transparent, striped background. You have to close the dialog box to see the page clearly again.

4. **In the line you just typed, add a comma after** `true`**. Hit Return and add the lines in bold below:**

```
$(document).ready(function() {
  $('#hello').dialog({
    modal: true,
    resizable: false,
    draggable: false
  });
}); // end ready
```

Remember, you must separate name/value pairs with commas. Every line with a name/value pair should end in a comma, except for the last name/value pair in the object. These two new lines prevent a visitor from moving or resizing the dialog. Finally, it's time to close the dialog with a little flair.

5. **Add a comma after** `false` **in that last line you typed; hit Return and type** `hide:  'explode'` **like this:**

```
$(document).ready(function() {
  $('#hello').dialog({
    modal: true,
    resizable: false,
    draggable: false,
    hide: 'explode'
  });
}); // end ready
```

This code makes jQuery UI apply its explode effect when the visitor closes the dialog box. Save the page and preview it in a browser. Watch what happens when you close the dialog. Have fun with some of the other jQuery UI effects—replace `'explode'` above with one of these: `'bounce'`, `'blinds'`, or `'drop'`.

You'll find a completed version of this tutorial in the *complete_dialog_proper-ties.html* file in the *Chapter09* folder.

Opening Dialog Boxes with Events

jQuery UI dialog boxes are easy to use and are an excellent replacement for a browser's boring alert box. However, you probably won't want to see a dialog box every time you visit a web page. Dialog boxes are much more useful when they open in response to a visitor's interaction. For example, when a visitor clicks a "Sign up for our e-mail newsletter" button, instead of whisking the visitor off to another web page, the browser could open a dialog box with a sign-up form on it.

You can open dialog boxes in response to any of the events you learned about on page 152—a mouse click, a key press, or window resizing (but that would be weird). In addition, you can always open a dialog box with your own programming. For example, maybe you created a timed quiz. If the time runs out before the visitor finishes the quiz, you could open a dialog box that says "Time's up!"

There are a couple of things you need to do to open a dialog box. First, you must tell the dialog box to not open when it's first created—normally it pops right up (as in the previous tutorial). Second, you need a way to trigger the dialog box to open later; most commonly, you'll do this with an event handler (page 152).

To hide a dialog box immediately when it's created, you need to pass the `dialog()` function the property `autoOpen` with a value of `false`. For example, say you added a `<div>` to a page with the ID `login`. To turn that div into a jQuery UI dialog box but initially hide it, you'd add this JavaScript code:

```
$('#login').dialog({
  autoOpen: false
});
```

When the page loads, jQuery UI turns the div into a dialog box object and hides it on the page. To make it visible, you need to give the open argument to the dialog function. For example, say you had a button that said "Login to our site," and you want a dialog box to open when a visitor clicks that link. Assume the link has the ID of `loginLink`. You could select that link, add a click event handler, and give it a function that will open the dialog, like this:

```
$('#loginLink').click(function(evt) {
  evt.preventDefault();
  $('#login').dialog('open');
}); // end click
```

The second line of code—`evt.preventDefault();`—is needed to prevent the browser from following the link and loading a new web page (see page 165 for a description of the `preventDefault()` method).

In addition, while a visitor can always close a dialog box by clicking the Close button in its upper-right corner, you can also close the dialog programmatically. For example, if you include a dialog box with a form in it, you might want to close the dialog when the visitor submits the form, instead of making him submit the form and then close the dialog box himself.

NOTE You'll see an example of opening and closing dialogs in the next tutorial

Now suppose that the dialog box discussed in this section—a <div> tag with an ID login—has a form in it. You want to close the dialog when the visitor submits that form. Here's how you could do that:

```
$('#login form').submit(function() {
  $('#login').dialog('close');
}); // end submit
```

To close a dialog, just select the <div>, call the dialog() function, and pass 'close' as the argument. Easy peasy.

NOTE The above web form example is just part of the solution, however. When the form is submitted, you would need to do some other things as well. Because submitting a form exits the current web page and leads to a page that handles the form submission, you would need to stop the form from submitting and instead handle the whole submission with JavaScript alone using a technology called Ajax. You'll learn about that in Chapter 13.

Adding Buttons to a Dialog Box

Dialog boxes are good for more than just popping up messages for your visitors. They're also handy for receiving visitor input. For example, say you've built a web application that lets people create to-do lists (as you'll do in Chapter 14). If someone added a to-do list item but then wanted to remove it, he could click a button to delete the list item. To make sure she doesn't accidentally delete a to-do item, you could pop up a dialog box that asks her to confirm her choice (Figure 9-5).

jQuery UI's Dialog widget lets you add buttons to any dialog box. In addition, you can then run different programs based on which button the visitor clicks. For example, if the visitor clicks Delete, the to-do list item is removed from the list, but if he clicks Cancel, the list item is left alone.

To add buttons, you give the dialog() function a buttons property whose value is itself an object literal containing each button's name and action. For example, say you wanted to add Confirm and Cancel buttons to a dialog box. You could do that like this:

```
$('#dialog').dialog({
  buttons : {
    "Confirm" : function() {
      // code executed when "Confirm" button is clicked
    },
    "Cancel" : function() {
      // code executed when "Cancel" button is clicked
    }
  } // end buttons
}); // end dialog
```

That's a lot of code and a lot of { and } symbols. But keep in mind that each button you add is just an item inside an object literal with a name and a function value. For example, here's the code for just the Confirm button:

```
"Confirm" : function() {
  // programming when "Confirm" button is clicked
},
```

The first part of the object—the name—is what will appear as the text on the button. In this example, it's Confirm. The second part of the object is a function (page 138), which contains the code you want to run when that button is clicked. This could be anything you want, from removing an item from the web page to beginning a JavaScript-based game. In most cases, you'll also want to close the dialog box after the button is clicked. To do that, you can use the 'close' argument. For example, to close the confirm button after it's clicked and its code executes, you'd add $(this).dialog('close'); to the end of the anonymous function, like this:

```
"Confirm" : function() {
  // programming when "Confirm" button is clicked
  $(this).dialog('close');
},
```

Your read about $(this) on page 139. In the context of the dialog object, $(this) refers to the <div> that is the dialog box. You can then use the dialog() function on that div to close it. Time for some practice adding buttons to a dialog box.

Mini-Tutorial: Adding Buttons to a Dialog Box

In this tutorial, you'll let a visitor delete a photo from the web page by clicking it. To make sure the photo isn't accidentally removed, you'll add a dialog box that asks the visitor to confirm the action:

1. **In a text editor, open the *dialog_buttons.html* file.**

   In this example, you've already linked the jQuery UI CSS and JavaScript files to the page, so you'll start right in by adding a dialog box.

2. **Locate the empty line, just below the HTML comment `<!-- add dialog here -->` and type:**

   ```
   <div id="confirm" title="Confirm Destruction">
     <p>Are you sure you want to destroy the robot?</p>
   </div>
   ```

   Next, you'll turn this div into a dialog box.

3. **Click the empty line after the $(document).ready() function, and type:**

   ```
   $('#confirm').dialog({

   });
   ```

This code turns the div into a dialog box. The { and } indicate an empty object literal (page 136) which will hold the dialog box's options. First, you'll make it a modal dialog box so visitors can't do anything else until they dismiss this dialog box.

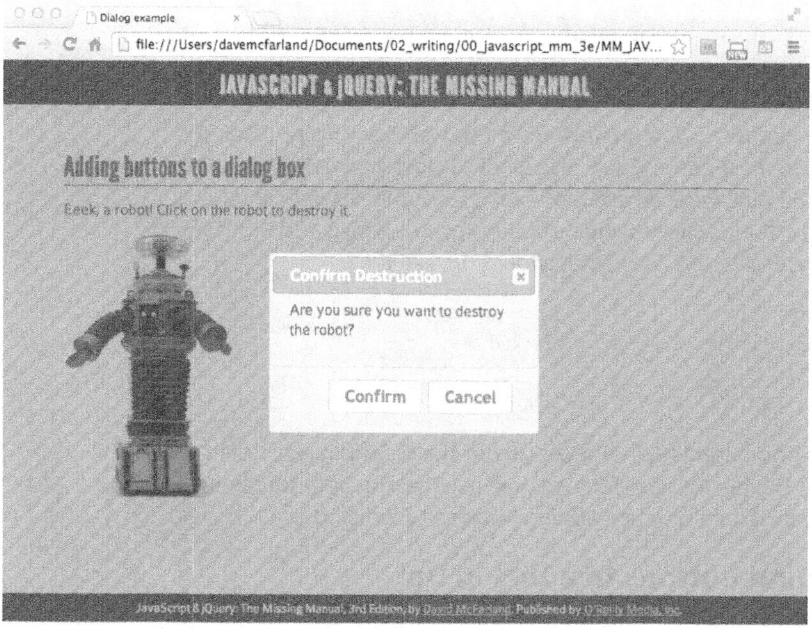

FIGURE 9-5

Want to make a dialog box interactive? Put a button on it! You can program a button to do anything you'd like when a visitor presses it. For example, the Confirm button pictured here will make the photo of the robot explode!

4. **Inside the object literal, type** modal: true:

```
$('#confirm').dialog({
    modal: true
});
```

You also want to make sure the dialog box is hidden at first. It'll only appear when the visitor clicks on the photo of the robot.

5. **Add a comma after** true **in that last line you typed, hit Return, and type the code in bold below:**

```
$('#confirm').dialog({
    modal: true,
    autoOpen: false
});
```

You need to separate name/value pairs with commas, so don't forget to add a comma after true. You'll add buttons to the dialog in a moment, but first you'll add the code required to open the dialog box when a visitor clicks the robot photo. The photo has an ID of robot, so you can easily select it and add a click event to it.

6. **After the dialog function add three new lines of code, so your program looks like this:**

```
$(document).ready(function() {
  $('#confirm').dialog({
    modal: true,
    autoOpen: false
  });
  $('#robot').click(function() {

  }); // end click
}); // end ready
```

This code selects the photo and adds an event handler to it (page 152). Now to open the dialog box: you simply select the dialog div, call the dialog() function, and pass it the value 'open'.

7. **Add one line of code to the click() function:**

```
$(document).ready(function() {
  $('#confirm').dialog({
    modal: true,
    autoOpen: false
  });
  $('#robot').click(function() {
      $('#confirm').dialog('open');
  }); // end click
}); // end ready
```

Now the dialog opens when the robot image is clicked.

8. **Save the file and preview it in a web browser. Click the robot picture to see your newborn dialog box.**

The dialog doesn't have any buttons on it yet. In the next few steps, you'll add them bit by bit, so you can really see how they work.

Precise Positioning with jQuery UI

The dialog and tooltip widgets let you control the placement of their boxes using a `position` property. The `position` property is an object (page 136) that defines where the box will be placed in relation to another element on the page. The way you write it is a little weird, but with a little experience it will seem pretty straightforward. There are several options, but the two most important are my and at.

For example, if you wanted to place the dialog box in the bottom-right corner of the window, you'd write this:

```
$('#dialog').dialog({
  position: {
    my: 'right bottom',
    at: 'right bottom'
  }
}); // end dialog
```

The my property refers to the dialog box; the at property refers to the window. So my defines which part of the dialog is placed at which position (at) on the window. In this example, it's saying put *my* (the dialog's) bottom-right corner *at* the window's bottom-right corner.

You use the CSS positioning syntax (same as that used in the background-position property). The first keyword is the horizontal position: left, right, or center. The second is vertical: top, center, or bottom.

Dialog boxes are placed in relation to the window. A tooltip (page 321), on the other hand, is placed in relation to the *triggering element*—that is, the element you mouse over to open the tooltip. However you can add a third property—of—to tell the dialog or tooltip to place itself in relation to another element on the page. This is handy for a "tour of the interface" type presentation, where you introduce a visitor to different elements of your web page. For example, you could pop up a dialog box near the Login box to show visitors where to log in.

The of property takes a selector (page 119) or a jQuery element. So, say the login box had an ID of login and you wanted the dialog box to display directly below it; you could write this code:

```
$('#dialog').dialog({
  position: {
    my: 'center top',
    at: 'center bottom',
    of: '#login'
  }
}); // end dialog
```

You can even provide an *offset* value to further control the placement of the dialog or tooltip. For example, if you wanted to place the dialog box so it overlaps the login box by 10 pixels, you could do this:

```
$('#dialog').dialog({
  position: {
    my: 'center top-10',
    at: 'center bottom',
    of: '#login'
  }
}); // end dialog
```

You can add or subtract using either a number (for pixel values) or a percentage (for example, my: 'center top+25%'. Make sure you don't add any spaces between the keyword (top, for example), the operator (+ or -) and the value (25%, for example), or the position object won't work.

Visit *http://api.jqueryui.com/position/* to learn more about jQuery UI's position utility.

9. **Return to your text editor and the *dialog_buttons.html* file. In the** `dialog()` **function, in the last line of options passed to the function, type a comma after** `false`**, hit Return, and then add the bolded code below:**

```
$(document).ready(function() {
  $('#confirm').dialog({
```

```
        modal: true,
        autoOpen: false,
        buttons: {

        }
    });
    $('#robot').click(function() {
        $('#confirm').dialog('open');
    }); // end click
}); // end ready
```

This passes another option to the dialog box—buttons. Its value is another object literal, which is made up of button items. First, you'll add a Confirm button.

10. **In the buttons object, add the code in bold:**

```
buttons : {
  "Confirm" : function() {

  }
}
```

The word Confirm will be the label on the first button. When a visitor clicks that button, the anonymous function runs. Save the file and try it out in a web browser: click the robot picture and you'll see the dialog box with a Confirm button. Unfortunately, it doesn't do anything yet. Return to your text editor.

11. **In the anonymous function for the Confirm button, add one line of code:**

```
buttons : {
  "Confirm" : function() {
    $('#robot').effect('explode');
  }
}
```

This code selects the robot image and then applies jQuery UI's explode effect to it, like the one you saw in action on page 312. (You'll also read more about it and other jQuery UI effects on page 438.)

Time for another button.

12. **Type a comma after the closing } for the Confirm button, press Return, and then type the code in bold:**

```
buttons : {
  "Confirm": function() {
    $('#robot').effect('explode');
  },
  "Cancel": function() {

  }
}
```

If you preview the page now, you'll see two buttons in the dialog box. The Cancel button doesn't do anything, and it shouldn't because it's meant to cancel other actions. However, you'll notice that clicking it doesn't even close the dialog box. It should at least do that.

13. **Inside the anonymous function for the Cancel button, type $(this).** dialog('close');:

```
buttons : {
  "Confirm": function() {
     $('#robot').effect('explode');
  },
  "Cancel": function() {
    $(this).dialog('close');
  }
}
```

Because the buttons are created inside the dialog() function which is applied to the dialog <div>, $(this) refers to the dialog box itself. So, in this case, $(this).dialog('close'); is the same as $('#confirm').dialog('close');.

Save the page and preview it in a web browser. Click the robot image to open the dialog box, then click the Cancel button—the dialog box closes! Click the robot image again, and this time, click Confirm: the robot image explodes and disappears. Unfortunately, the dialog box doesn't close. That's an easy fix.

14. **Add $(this).dialog('close'); as the last line of the anonymous function for the Confirm button. Your final code should look like this:**

```
$(document).ready(function() {
  $('#confirm').dialog({
    modal: true,
      autoOpen: false,
    buttons : {
      "Confirm" : function() {
        $('#robot').effect('explode');
        $(this).dialog('close');
      },
      "Cancel" : function() {
        $(this).dialog('close');
      }
    }
  });
  $('#robot').click(function() {
      $('#confirm').dialog('open');
  }); // end click
}); // end ready
```

Save and preview the page in a browser. Your finished page (when the dialog box is open) should look like Figure 9-5. Try both buttons and see what happens. You'll find a finished version of this tutorial in the *complete_dialog_buttons. html* file in the *chapter09* folder.

Providing Information with Tooltips

Sometimes you need to give your visitors a bit more information. For example, say you have a line of social media icons which lead off to different sites like Twitter, Facebook, Reddit, Instagram, and so on. Someone unfamiliar with any of those sites won't recognize the icons and won't know where clicking them will lead. To help them out, you could add tooltips that pop up when they mouse over an icon: "My Facebook Page," for example.

jQuery UI provides a simple way to add these types of tooltips to any page element (Figure 9-6). You can even add more elaborate tooltips that include entire chunks of HTML including text, images, and links. The following steps outline the most basic way to add tooltips to a page:

1. **Follow the steps on page 304 to attach the jQuery and jQuery UI files to your page.**

   You won't get very far without the needed CSS and JavaScript.

2. **Add a `title` attribute to any element you wish to have a tooltip:**

   ```
   <a href="https://twitter.com/OReillyMedia" title="Follow us on Twitter">
   <img src="twitter.png">
   </a>
   ```

   Some browsers already display a tooltip when you add a `title` attribute to an element. However, as with a browser's alert box, you can't style a browser's tooltips. In addition, not all browsers show tooltips, so using jQuery UI gives you maximum control and effectiveness.

3. **Select the elements and apply the `tooltip()` function:**

   ```
   $(document).ready(function() {
     $('[title]').tooltip();
   }); // end ready
   ```

   Here, you use a simple attribute selector (page 123) to find every element with a `title`, and then apply the `tooltip()` function to it. And, yes, you're done. jQuery UI takes care of the rest and creates attractive pop-up tooltips for every element with a title.

   You can be more specific if you'd like. For example, if you don't want all elements with a title to have tooltips, you could add a class—like `tooltip`—to each tag and then use a class selector to add tooltips to just those elements:

   ```
   $('.tooltip').tooltip();
   ```

Mini-Tutorial: Adding Tooltips Quickly

jQueryUI gives you the easiest way to add tooltips to elements on a web page (and your visitors will thank you for it):

1. **In a text editor, open the *tooltips.html* file.**

   The jQuery UI CSS and JavaScript files are already linked to this web page. You can start right in by adding `title` attributes to HTML tags. These titles will become the text of the tooltips.

2. **Locate the paragraph `<p>A paragraph</p>` and add *Yes, I am a paragraph.* as a title:**

   ```
   <p title="Yes, I am a paragraph.">A paragraph</p>
   ```

   You can add a title to any element in the body of a web page. (You can also get more creative with these titles if you wish.)

3. **Locate the image tag `<img src="images/map.png">` and add *I am a map!* as a title:**

   ```
   <img src="images/map.png" title="I am a map!">
   ```

   One more tag and you're done with the HTML edits.

4. **Locate the paragraph `<button>A button</button>` and add *Click this button!* as a title:**

   ```
   <button title="Click this button!">A button</button
   ```

   Now to add the jQuery code.

5. **In the $(document).ready() function, add $('[title]').tooltip(); so the code looks like this:**

   ```
   $(document).ready(function() {
     $('[title]').tooltip();
   }); // end ready
   ```

   Believe it or not, that's it. The `$('[title]')` part selects any tag with a `title` attribute, and `.tooltip()` adds tooltips to them. Save the page and preview it in a browser. Mouse over the paragraph, the image, and the button to see the results (Figure 9-6). The finished version *complete_tooltips.html* is located in the *chapter09* folder.

Tooltip Options

Like a dialog box, a tooltip simply appears on the screen when it opens. But you have several ways to modify how the tooltip widget works. Like the Dialog widget (page 305), tooltips can accept an object (page 136) containing properties that control how the tooltip behaves. Here are a few of the most useful:

- **show.** The show property lets you animate the tooltip's appearance. It works just like the show property for dialog boxes as described on page 310. In other words, you can make the tooltip fade into view, slide into view, or use one of jQuery UI's many effects (page 438) to add visual excitement to your tooltips.

- **hide.** Works just like show, but controls how the tooltip disappears from the screen.

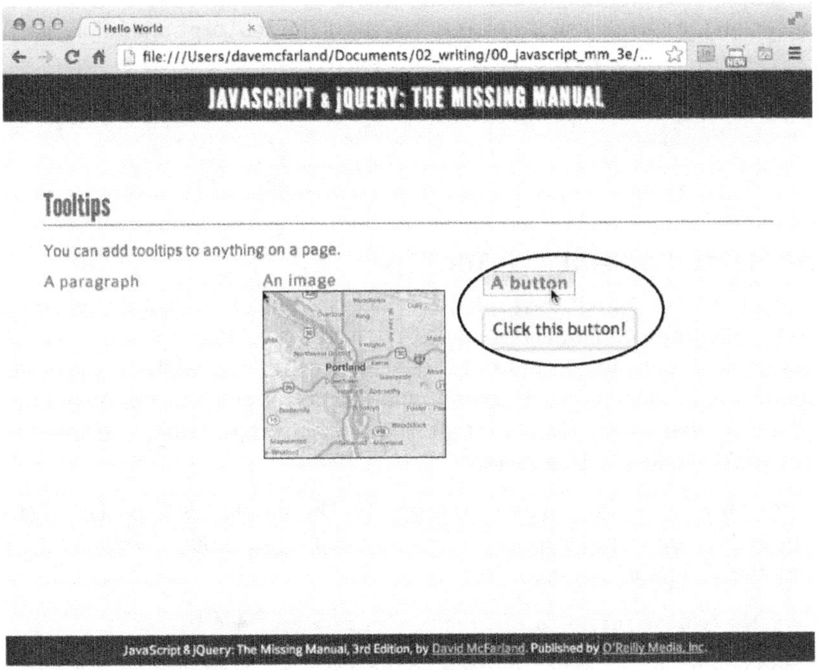

FIGURE 9-6

Provide extra information to your visitors with tooltips. You can make a small text box appear whenever someone hovers over an element (circled). Tooltips are a great way to explain what clicking an icon will do, provide a caption for a photo, or even display photos and other HTML content when a visitor hovers over something on a web page.

- **track.** Set this property to true, and the tooltip will follow the mouse around (as long as the mouse stays over the HTML tag that triggers the tooltip):

```
track: true
```

A moving tooltip definitely draws attention, but can be distracting and hard to read.

- **tooltipClass.** If you want to add a class name to your tooltips, you can supply a value for this property:

```
tooltipClass: 'tooltip'
```

This value lets you supplement the regular jQuery UI theme tooltip styles with some custom styling via a class you create.

- **position.** This property accepts a jQuery UI position object (see the box on page 318), and specifies where the tooltip should be placed in relation to the target element (the item on the page a visitor mouses over to see the tooltip).

Be careful with the `position` property. Tooltips disappear when you mouse over them. If you position the tooltip over the HTML element associated with that tooltip, you may run into a situation where the tooltip never appears. That's because mousing over the element that opens the tooltip also mouses over the tooltip, instantly closing it!

You use these options by passing them in an object literal to the `tooltip()` function. For example, say you wanted tooltips to fade into view, explode when they disappear, and track the visitor's mouse: you'd call the `tooltip()` function, like this:

```
$('[title]').tooltip({
  show: true,
  hide: 'explode',
  track: true
});
```

Using HTML Content in a Tooltip

As you can see, adding a tooltip with jQuery UI is simple. But what if you want the tooltip to have more content, like a photo, or several paragraphs of text? You can't just put HTML directly inside a tag's `title` attribute—it's not valid and will mess up your page. For longer chunks of content, the Tooltip widget provides an option for specifying another source for its content. The `content` property lets you specify the content you'd like to add to a tooltip.

There are a few ways you can use this property. The simplest is to provide a string with the HTML you want to appear in the tooltip. For example, say you had a link that pointed to a page about yourself:

```
<a href="coolest_person_on_earth.html" id="me">About Me</a>
```

Assuming you have a photo of yourself on the site, you could display that photo in a tooltip, when someone mouses over the link like this:

```
$('#me').tooltip({
  content: '<img src="me.png" alt="Look at me!">'
});
```

The `$('#me')` selects the link, and `.tooltip()` adds a tooltip to that link. The content property then defines what HTML should appear inside that tooltip—in this example, an `<img>` tag.

Another approach to adding HTML to a tooltip is to add the HTML to your page, then use the `content` property to suck it up into a tooltip. But how would that work? If you add HTML to a page, it shows up in the web browser, and you want that HTML to appear only in a tooltip. One way would be to use jQuery's `hide()` method to hide the HTML from view, and then use the `tooltip()` function to grab that hidden HTML and display it inside a tooltip.

But there's another, simpler way that many JavaScript programmers have started using: you can create a "template" by putting HTML inside of `<script>` tags. Because a browser considers anything inside of `<script>` tags to be JavaScript, it won't display the HTML. But you can use jQuery to access and use that HTML—in a tooltip, for instance! For example, say you wanted to print an `<h2>` tag and an unordered list in a tooltip. You could create a template with that HTML inside `<script>` tags, like this:

```html
<script id="tooltipTemplate" type="text/template">
  <h2>About Me</h2>
  <ul>
    <li>I'm super awesome.</li>
    <li>I brush my teeth 3 times daily</li>
    <li><img src="me.png" alt="Look at me!"></li>
  </ul>
</script>
```

Because you'll use it to select the template, the ID is important—but it doesn't have to be `tooltipTemplate`. Use any ID you'd like. Likewise, the `type="text/template"` is optional, but many programmers who use this template technique put the `type` attribute in to clarify the purpose of the script tags. It's also common practice to put these templates at the bottom of the page before the closing `</body>` tag.

Once the template is in place, you can select it, pull out its HTML, and hand that over to the Tooltip widget like this:

```javascript
$('#me').tooltip({
  content: $('#tooltipTemplate').html();
});
```

As you read on page 128, jQuery's `html()` method can extract the HTML from a selection. In this example, you're selecting the `<script>` tag that defines the HTML for the template, and then getting the HTML inside it. jQuery UI then uses this HTML as the content for the tooltip.

Mini-Tutorial: Add HTML to a Tooltip

Creating an HTML-formatted tooltip is a little more complicated than adding a plain old text one, but with the `<script>` tag trick, it's still pretty darn easy:

1. **In a text editor, open the *advanced_tooltips.html* file.**

   This web page is already linked to the jQuery UI CSS and JavaScript files. The next step is adding the HTML code you want to appear in the tooltip.

2. **Near the bottom of the page after the comment `<!-- put template here -->`, add the following HTML:**

   ```html
   <script id="contactInfo" type="text/template">
     <p>You can reach us at 555-555-5555</p>
     <p><img src="images/map.png" title="I am a map!"></p>
   </script>
   ```

   You're using the technique described on page 324 to hide HTML inside of `<script>` tags. The browser won't display this HTML, but you can still access it and use it with jQuery.

3. Inside the $(document).ready() function, add the following code:

```
$('#contact').tooltip({
    content: $('#contactInfo').html();
}); // end tooltip
```

This kind of function should look familiar by now: it selects an element on the page (in this case, a <p> tag with an ID of contact). It then applies the tooltip with the specified content. The $('#contactInfo') selects the <script> tag you add in the previous step, while the .html() extracts the HTML.

Save the file and open it in a web browser. Mouse over the Contact Us text, and you'll see the tooltip, as shown in Figure 9-7. A completed version of this file—*complete_advanced_tooltips.html*—is located in the *chapter09* folder.

■ Adding Tabbed Panels

Sometimes building a web page feels like a fight for the viewer's attention. You may need to cover so much information that the page becomes long, crowded, and difficult to read. One solution to an overcrowded page is tabbed panels. Tabbed panels let you divide content into separate sub-pages among which the visitor can switch by clicking a tab. E-commerce sites like Best Buy (Figure 9-8) use this technique all the time. When information is divided into tabs, visitors can find everything they need to know—like a product's technical specifications, reviews, and purchase options—without being overwhelmed by too much content at once.

jQuery UI's tabbed panels (like other widgets) are easy to implement. The key is in how you structure your HTML. jQuery UI has some specific ways that you need to insert the HTML for tabbed panels, but essentially, you need to include three components:

- **Container <div>.** The entire collection of tabs and panels must be wrapped in a containing element. It doesn't have to be a div, but that's the most common choice. You select this element with jQuery, and it then instructs jQuery UI where to find the tabbed panels. Provide an ID on the element so you can select it.

> **TIP** If you plan on using more than one set of tabbed panels on a single page, you could use the same class name on each container div—<div class="tabbedPanels">, for example. Then, you can select all those divs at once with $('.tabbedPanels') and create all the sets of tabbed panels on the page with one line of code:
>
> ```
> $('.tabbedPanels').tabs();
> ```

Tooltips

You can add tooltips to anything on a page.

Contact Us

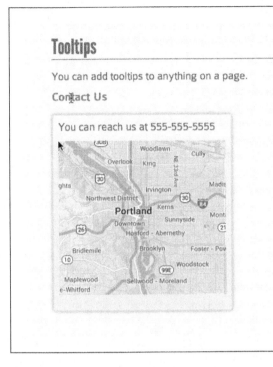

You can reach us at 555-555-5555

FIGURE 9-7

Tooltips aren't just limited to what you can stuff into a tag's title *attribute. You can put any HTML you'd like inside a tooltip including photos, text, and videos. One caveat though: mousing over a tooltip makes it disappear, so don't include anything that a user has to interact with, like links or form fields. For that type of interactivity, you're better off using a dialog box (page 305).*

- **Tabs.** Use either an unordered or ordered list for your tabs. Each tab is represented by one `<li>` tag. Inside the `<li>` you also need to include an `<a>` tag with an `href` value that points to an ID for the associated panel. For example, say you include three tabs pointing to three panels. The HTML for the tabs might look like this:

```
<ul>
  <li><a href="#details">Product Details</a></li>
  <li><a href="#reviews">Reviews</a></li>
  <li><a href="#order">Order</a></li>
</ul>
```

- **Panels.** Each panel is a single HTML block-level element. Most commonly it's a `<div>` tag, but you can use `<article>`, `<section>`, or any other block level tag. Include an ID on this `<div>` that matches the # link in the panel. For example:

```
<div id="details">
   <!-- HTML for panel goes in here -->
</div>
```

The ID is important. jQuery UI uses it to associate the tab with the proper panel. In addition, it's useful for browsers without JavaScript, because that named anchor acts as a way to navigate from the link in the unordered list to the associated div on the page. Inside the panel element, you can put any HTML you'd like—images, text, lists, videos, and so on. The panel's HTML will only be displayed when its tab is clicked.

Here's the basic HTML structure for a complete tabbed panel:

```html
<div id="tabbedPanel">
  <ul>
    <li><a href="#details">Product Details</a></li>
    <li><a href="#reviews">Reviews</a></li>

    <li><a href="#order">Order</a></li>
  </ul>
  <div id="details">
    <!-- HTML for panel 1 goes in here -->
  </div>
  <div id="reviews">
    <!-- HTML for panel 2 goes in here -->
  </div>
  <div id="order">
    <!-- HTML for panel 3 goes in here -->
  </div>
</div>
```

The names you use for the ID are up to you. You don't need to use *tabbedPanel* for the container element ID, and you can name the panels whatever you want instead of #details, #reviews, and #order. Just remember that whatever ID you do choose for a panel, the link in the associated tab—the <li> tag—matches.

NOTE jQuery UI's tabbed panels are fully keyboard navigable. Visitors can press the right arrow key to open the next panel to the right and the left arrow key to open the panel to the left.

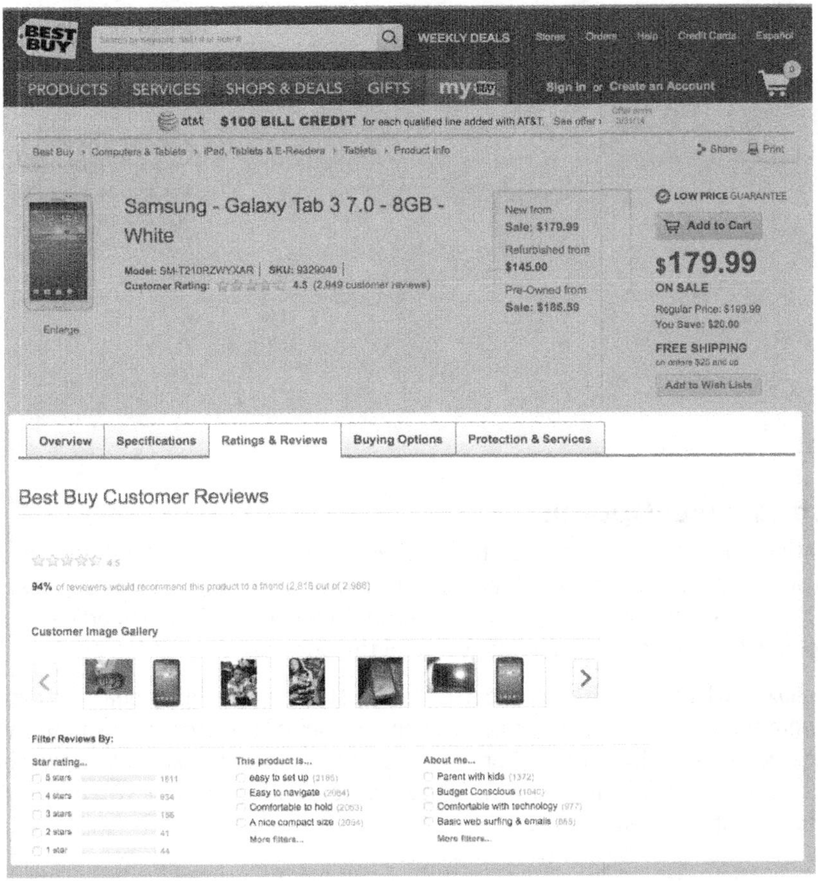

FIGURE 9-8

Tabbed panels are common on sites that need to present a lot of information. E-commerce sites use panels extensively on product pages, so potential buyers aren't overwhelmed by a sea of data, but can still quickly access the information they want.

To turn this collection of HTML into tabbed panels, you simply select the container and then call the tabs() function, like this:

```
$('#tabbedPanels').tabs();
```

This creates the basic tabbed panel you see in Figure 9-9.

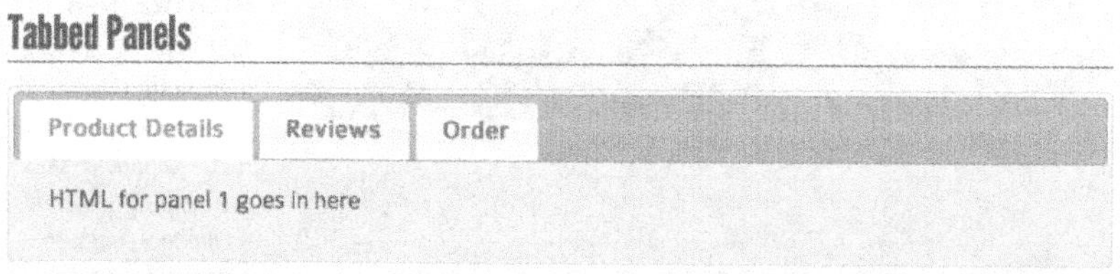

FIGURE 9-9

Tabbed panels are really easy with jQuery UI: just a little HTML and a dash of JavaScript. If you don't like the way the tabs or panels look, you can change their appearance with jQuery UI's ThemeRoller (page 385).

Tabbed Panel Options

As with other jQuery UI widgets, the Tabs widget provides many options for customizing how it works. To change the options for the tabbed panels, simply pass an object literal to the tabs() function containing the name of the property and the value you'd like to set it to. Here are some of the options:

- **show and hide.** These two properties control how the panels appear and disappear from the screen. They take the same values as the properties of the same name in the Dialog widget. For example, to make a panel slide into view when it opens and slide out of view when it's closed, you'd pass these two properties to the tabs() function:

```
show: 'slideDown',
hide: 'slideUp'
```

- **active.** Normally, when a page with tabbed panels loads, the first tab is selected and the first panel is visible. But you might want the second or last panel to be visible first. You can set which panel is visible by setting the active property:

```
active: 1
```

As with JavaScript arrays (page 44), you count the panels starting at 0—so setting panel 1 to active actually opens the second panel. Instead of a number, if you give this property a value of false—active: false—you hide *all* of the panels. A panel will only open when a visitor clicks one of the tabs. Note that this option only works if you also set the collapsible property to true.

- **collapsible.** Set the collapsible property to true if you want to let users hide all panels. Normally, at least one panel is visible at all times, but with this property set to true, if you click the tab of an already open panel, the panel itself closes completely and all you see are the tabs. You could use this option if space on the screen is really limited, but, in general, this is an unusual choice and won't be familiar to most visitors to your site. However, you must set this property to true if you set the active property (above) to false—this hides all panels when the page loads.

- **event.** When you click on a tab, its associated panel opens. At least that's how it normally works. If you want to make a different event trigger a panel, set the event property to the name of an event (page 148). For example, to make a panel appear when a visitor mouses over a tab, you could do this:

  ```
  event: 'mouseover'
  ```

  Be careful with this option, however. People are used to certain conventions on the Web, the most common being if you click something on a web page, something happens. If people have to double click on a tab (the dblclick event) to open a panel, they may never figure out how to access your panel's contents.

- **heightStyle.** The heightStyle property controls the height of each panel and has three possible values: content, auto, and fill. The normal setting is content, which makes each panel only as tall as the content inside it. If one panel has many paragraphs of text, and another panel has only a single sentence, when you switch between panels, the overall height of the panel widget changes. If there's a really big difference in the amount of content in your panels, your visitors might find this visual "yo-yo" effect distracting.

  The auto option sets the same height for every panel, based on the panel that has the most content. This option prevents the panel group from changing height, but it also means that a panel without much content will have a lot of empty space at the bottom. Finally, the fill option makes the panel group fill to match the available area of the panel's parent element. This option usually creates a lot of empty space in each panel and wastes valuable screen real estate, so it's best avoided.

Mini-Tutorial: Add Tabbed Panels

This tutorial will take you through the process of adding tabbed panels to a page. The most difficult part is getting the HTML in place; the JavaScript code is simple:

1. **In a text editor, open the *tabs.html* file.**

   The jQuery UI CSS and JavaScript files are already linked to this web page. As an added bonus, you won't have to type all the HTML required to create tabbed panels. (The required HTML components are described on page 327.) However, there are a few things missing from this example code. In particular, an ID for the tabbed panel container and the links that point from the tabs to the panels.

2. **In the page's HTML, locate `<h1>Tabbed Panels</h1>`. In the `<div>` tag following that headline, add `id="tabContainer"`:**

```
<h1>Tabbed Panels</h1>
<div id="tabContainer">
```

jQuery UI tabs are applied to an element that contains the tabs and panels—usually a `<div>` tag. By adding an ID, you've got a way to select that `<div>` using jQuery and apply the `tabs()` function. Now let's add links.

3. **Locate the unordered list (`<ul>`) tag just below the opening `<div>` you just edited. For each `<a>` tag, add a # link like this:**

```
<li><a href="#panel1">Tab 1</a></li>
<li><a href="#panel2">Tab 2</a></li>
<li><a href="#panel3">Tab 3</a></li>
```

These are named anchor links—links that point to other sections of the page that are identified with the matching ID. In other words, the first `<li>` tag will link to the `<div>` for the first panel, the second `<li>` tag to the second panel, and so on. In order to make these links work, you need to add the matching IDs to the panel divs.

4. **Locate the `<div>` below the `<ul>` tag you just edited (an HTML comment`<!-- panel 1 -->` above the `<div>` makes it easier to identify. Add `id="panel1"` to the div, like this:**

```
<!-- panel 1 -->
<div id="panel1">
```

You need to do this for the other panels as well.

5. **Repeat step 4 for the last two panel divs (they are identified with HTML comments as well).**

Make sure you give each div an ID that matches the link from step 3. For example, the second panel's div should be `<div id="panel2">`. Now let's turn them into tabbed panels.

6. **Inside the `$(document).ready()` function select the container and call the `tabs()` function:**

```
$(document).ready(function() {
  $('#tabContainer').tabs();
}); // end ready
```

Save the file and preview it in a web browser. The page should look like Figure 9-10. If it doesn't, check your browser's console (page 18) and see if there are any JavaScript errors. If you don't see any, check whether you typed the correct ID names for the container div and panels.

Next, you'll add some effects to the panel transitions by making them fade into view when they open and fade out when they close.

7. **Add the following object literal (in bold) to the tabs() function:**

```
document).ready(function() {
  $('#tabContainer').tabs({
    show: 'fadeIn',
    hide: 'fadeOut'
  });
}); // end ready
```

This applies an effect to the panel transitions. You can try other effects like `'slideDown'` and `'slideUp'`. Save the page and preview it in a web browser.

The tabbed panels work well, but there's one problem with tabbed panels: the page always opens to either the first tab or one you specify using the `active` property (page 330). But what if you wanted to e-mail a link to the page and have a particular tab open from that link? For example, imagine you're in customer service and a customer asks about the technical specs for a product your company sells. There's a page for that product with the technical specs in a tabbed panel; the problem is that the "About this Product" panel appears whenever that page loads.

What if you could just email a link like *http://mycompany.com/productA. html#specs*, and the tab with the technical specs opens when that link is followed. Well, you can, if you add a little JavaScript magic. The secret is pulling out that #specs from the URL and using it to trigger the panel.

8. **After the tabs() function, add a new line and type var hash = location.hash;.**

The browser window provides what's called a *location* object. This object holds lots of information about the URL of the current page, including the hostname (`location.hostname`), the entire URL (`location.href`), and other properties (visit *https://developer.mozilla.org/en-US/docs/Web/API/Location* for a complete list). The `location.hash` property returns just the part of the URL that includes the # part.

For example, say you visited *http://mycompany.com/productA.html#specs*. The `location.hash` property for this URL is #specs. You'll use the hash property to load a panel with a matching hash value.

9. **After the code you just added, add a conditional statement, so your final code looks like this:**

```
$(document).ready(function() {
  $('#tabContainer').tabs({
    show: 'fadeIn',
    hide: 'fadeOut'
  });
  var hash = location.hash;
  if (hash) {
    $('#tabContainer').tabs('load', hash)
  }
}); // end ready
```

This code first checks to see if a hash value exists—for example, if the visitor simply just visits the *tabs.html* page, there isn't any hash value, so you can skip the rest of the code and just let the first panel load normally. However, if there is a hash value like #panel1, then the next bit of code runs. It simply selects the container again ($('#tabContainer')), calls the tabs() function, and passes two arguments. The first, load, is a command built into the jQuery UI program that tells the tabs function to load a panel. The second argument—hash—is the panel that should be loaded, either #panel1, #panel2, or #panel3 in this example.

10. **Save the page and preview it in a web browser.**

The first panel should open. In the location bar, add #panel3 at the end of the URL (after the *tabs.html*). Then reload the page.

The third panel should display. (If it doesn't, try copying the URL in the location bar, opening a new tab or browser window and pasting it in.) A finished version of the file—*complete_tabs.html*—can be found in the *chapter09* folder.

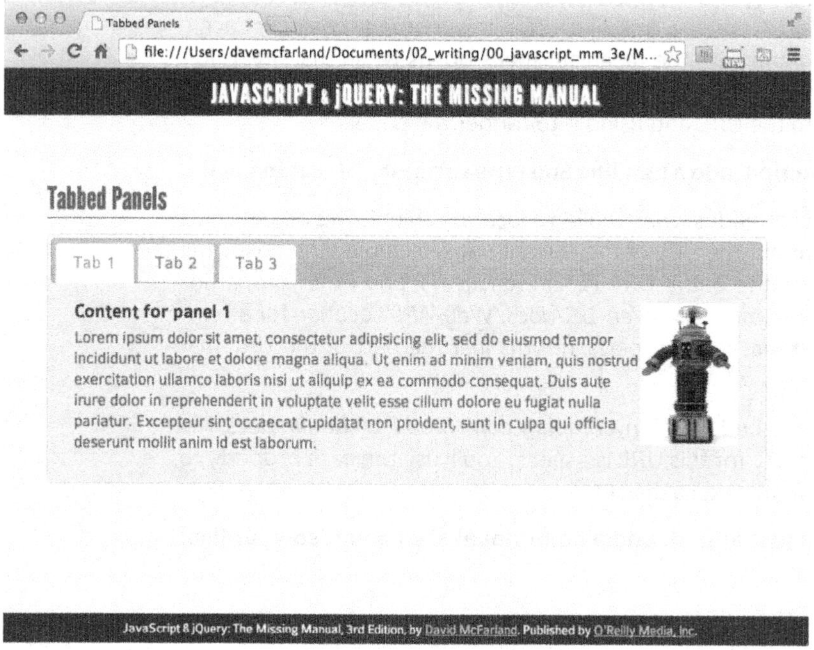

FIGURE 9-10

The final web page showing the three tabbed panels.

jQuery UI's Custom Events

You learned about browser events like click, mouseover, focus, and resize on pages 148-152. These events are built into browsers and triggered when visitors take certain actions on a page, like click a link or submit a form. Events are useful because they let you write programs that respond to things that are happening on the page.

jQuery UI widgets are programmed with their own custom events—they're not exactly like the kinds of browser events you're used to, however. Widget events are simply moments during the creation, execution, or completion of a widget component.

For example, the tabs widget provides a beforeActivate event that lets you run some code right before jQuery UI makes a hidden panel visible. This would come in handy if you wanted to trigger some other action each time a tab is clicked. For example, you could use the beforeActivate custom event to update the URL in the browser's location bar each time a tab is clicked, so the URL would add the # of the proper panel to the filename—*tabs.html#panel3*, for instance. Used in conjunction with a conditional statement like the one added in step 9 on page 333, you can provide a way for users to bookmark a custom URL that would display the proper panel each time that bookmark was loaded.

To do that, you'd add the beforeActivate property to the tabs() function with a function as a value, like this:

```
$('#tabContainer').tabs({
  beforeActivate: function(evt) {
    location.hash=$(evt.currentTarget).
attr('href');
  }
});
```

There's a lot going on here, but in a nutshell, you find the href attribute of the tab the visitor clicked (#panel, #panel2, or #panel3) and store it to the location's hash property (see step 8 on page 333 for more on the hash property). You can find a working copy of this code in a file named *complete_tabs_with_custom_event.html* in the *chapter09* folder.

Like the tabs widget, each jQuery UI widget gives you lots of ways to do things as the widget is being created, modified, or destroyed. Programmers call these *hooks* because they let you attach your own programming to the programming already existing in jQuery UI. This is a complex topic, but fun to explore.

The best way to learn about these custom events is to visit the API page for each widget (API stands for *application programming interface* and represents all the properties and functions that you can access as a programmer). At the top of each page there's a QuickNav box that lists all the custom events the widget supports. For example, the dialog widget's API page (*http://api.jqueryui.com/dialog/*) lists 11 different events you can hook into!

Tabs with Remote Panel Content

jQuery UI even lets you pull in content for tabbed panels from other web pages. In other words, instead of creating an unordered list of links which link to divs *within* the page, you can create an unordered list of links that point to *other* pages (or to content that's generated by a web server). You might want to take this approach if the content in each tab is constantly changing (stock prices, reviews, forum posts). By linking to dynamically created content—for example, information drawn from a frequently updated database using a technology like PHP, .NET, or Ruby On Rails—you can be assured that the content inside the panel is up-to-date.

To load panel content from other pages or web server requests, simply create a containing div, an unordered list with links to other pages, and call the tabs() function. For example, say you wanted each panel to include content from a separate web page. Those pages are named *panel1.html*, *panel2.html*, and *panel3.html*. You'd add this HTML to your page:

```
<div id="tabContainer">
  <ul>
    <li><a href="panel1.html">Tab 1</a></li>
    <li><a href="panel2.html">Tab 2</a></li>
    <li><a href="panle3.html">Tab 3</a></li>
  </ul>
</div>
```

If you're linking to dynamic data, you might not be pointing to a web page, but to content generated by a server-side language like PHP:

```
<div id="tabContainer">
  <ul>
    <li><a href="reviews.php?id=1298">Current Reviews</a></li>
    <li><a href="forum.php?id=1298">Forum Discussions</a></li>
  </ul>
</div>
```

When linking to external web pages, you don't need to include the panel divs as in step 3 on page 332. jQuery UI will automatically create those divs when the tabbed panels are created. To create the tabbed panels, simply select the container div and call the tabs() function:

```
$('#tabContainer').tabs();
```

When this code runs, jQuery UI will fetch the HTML from the web page that's linked to the first visible panel. For example, given the code on above, when the page loads, jQuery UI will load the HTML from the *panel1.html* file and display it in a panel below the tabs. When someone clicks the second tab, jQuery UI will request the HTML from the second link and create a new panel to place that HTML into.

In most cases, you can even link to an external website like Google, Wikipedia, or a server other than the one the tabbed panel page comes from. However, sites can block this process, and then content like web fonts, images, and videos won't load.

There's another problem with this approach: *all* of the content of the linked to the page will appear in the panel. So if you link to a *complete* HTML file with a <header>, <title> tag, and links to CSS and JavaScript files, all of that will be loaded as well. You end up with a page within a page. If all you want is a chunk of HTML content in a panel, there are two solutions.

The easiest way is to create page *fragments*—HTML files that contain *only* the HTML you wish to appear in the panel. You can easily make a fragment if you're loading data dynamically from the server—your server-side script only needs to spit out the content that should appear in the panel (and not all the other stuff like the <head> tag required by a full web page).

Alternatively, you can let the panel load a full web page and extract only the content you want to appear in the panel using a *custom event* (see the box on page 335). Here's how it works: jQuery UI tabbed panels include an event called load. This event lets you run a function immediately after jQuery UI loads content from a remote source. You can use jQuery to find just the content you want, extract it, and place it inside the panel. This method is a little complex, but it doesn't require a lot of code.

First, you need to make sure there's a way to select specific content from the remote page. An easy way to do this is to wrap the content you want in the panel in a <div> tag with an ID—<div id="panelContent">, for example. With that in place, you now have a way to select just that content and not unnecessary HTML like the <head> or <title> tags.

Then, you need to pass a load option to the tabs() function. The load option is the custom event, and you supply an anonymous function (page 138) that tells jQuery UI what to do when it's received content from the remote page and placed it into a panel. When the load event is triggered, jQuery UI has already created a new tab *and* inserted the HTML from the remote page into it. At this point, the new panel has all the extra HTML you don't want. However, you can use jQuery to quickly remove that new HTML and replace it with the stripped-down HTML. It happens so fast, this quick change of content isn't even displayed in the browser.

Here's an example:

```
$('#tabContainer').tabs({
  load: function(evt,ui) {
    var newHTML = ui.panel.find('#panelContent').html();
    ui.panel.html(newHTML);
  }
})
```

Lines 2-5 are the load option. jQuery UI provides two pieces of information to its custom events (those are evt and ui in line 2). The first, evt, is a regular jQuery event object (page 164). You can use any of the event properties and methods discussed on pages 165-167. In this case, you're interested in the second argument passed to the load event's anonymous function: ui. The ui object represents the currently updated user interface element. For tabbed panels, there's a ui.panel object and ui.tab object. The ui.panel object represents the newly created panel (the <div> that jQuery UI creates when it loads the external web page).

In line 3, you create a new variable—newHTML—to hold the final panel content (without the extra HTML like <head>). When jQuery UI creates the new panel, it loads the entire HTML content from the requested page, so you can look inside that panel and get just the HTML you're after. The ui.panel.find('#panelContent') part gets the new panel HTML and looks inside it for an element with the ID of panelContent (jQuery's find() method is described on page 531). Then, the html() method (page 119) kicks in and extracts the HTML from just that one part of the page. In other words, you've just collected the small amount of HTML you're interested in and stored it into a variable named newHTML.

NOTE You can find an example of using separate web pages for panel content in the *remote_tabs.html* file located in the *chapter09* folder. The file also uses the load custom event to strip out unwanted HTML.

In line 4, you simply replace the HTML in the panel (that's the old HTML, complete with <head>, <title>, and other unwanted tags) with the new HTML (only the HTML you need for the new panel). This code runs so quickly that the browser never even displays the full web page inside the panel—the visitor will only see the lean, stripped-down HTML you're after.

Saving Space with Accordions

jQuery UI accordions, like tabbed panels, are another space-saving user interface device. See the bottom image in Figure 9-11 for an example. But instead of being controlled by a line of tabs along the top, each accordion panel has a clickable headline used to hide and close the accordion panel. The accordion headlines open the panel directly below it and close any currently opened panel. In other words, only one accordion panel is opened at a time.

In general, accordions work much the same way as tabs. Most of the options are the same and work the same way as tabs, but the HTML structure is very different. With accordions, you need just three components:

• **Enclosing <div> that holds the accordion.** You need to select the div with jQuery, so add an ID or class to the div so you can select it and apply the Accordion widget to it.

• **Headline containing text.** This headline is the clickable control that opens and closes accordion panels (for example, the blue headline "What does the robot say" in Figure 9-11). It doesn't matter which level of headline you use—<h2>, <h3>, and so on. Just use the same one for each accordion group. (Technically you don't even have to use a headline tag—any block level tag works—but headlines are the most commonly used.)

• **Block-level element immediately following the headline.** Usually this is a <div> tag filled with the content you wish to show and hide. This div *must* go directly after the headline.

FIGURE 9-11

*Now you see it, now you don't.
jQuery UI can transform a simple
collection of headlines and `<div>`
tags (top) into an interactive
presentation of collapsible panels
(bottom).*

The headline and following div element represent one part of an accordion. To add more accordion elements, add more headline/div pairs. For example, the basic HTML structure of a three-panel accordion looks like this:

```html
<div id="accordion">
  <h3>Trigger for first accordion panel</h3>
  <div>
    <!-- content for first accordion -->
  </div>
  <h3>Trigger for second accordion panel</h3>
  <div>
    <!-- content for second accordion -->
  </div>
  <h3>Trigger for third accordion panel</h3>
  <div>
    <!-- content for third accordion -->
  </div>
</div>
```

Once you've set up your HTML, attached the jQuery UI CSS, and the jQuery and jQuery UI JavaScript files (page 104), turning on the accordion widget is as simple as selecting the containing element and calling the accordion() function, like this:

```javascript
$('#accordion').accordion();
```

As usual, jQuery UI takes care of all the heavy lifting and transforms your basic HTML structure into an accordion like the one pictured in Figure 9-11. As with tabbed panels, the jQuery UI accordion can accept an object with a variety of options (many of which work the same way as tabbed panels):

- active. The active option works just like the same option for tabbed panels (page 330). Provide a number, and that accordion panel will open when the page loads. For example, to open the second accordion panel, you'd supply this:

    ```
    active: 1
    ```

    Like arrays, you count from 0 when counting accordion panels. If you supply the value of false for this option, and set the collapsible property to true, you can load the page with all accordion panels closed.

- collapsible. Set this option to true, and the active option to false and all accordion panels will be closed when the page loads. In addition, if you set this option to true, then accordion headlines work like a toggle switch: click the headline, and if the panel below it is open, then that panel closes. If the panel is closed when you click the headline, the accordion panel opens.

- animate. Normally, accordion panels slide open and slide shut. You can turn this behavior off and make the panels just blink open and close instantly by setting this option to false:

    ```
    animate: false
    ```

You can also supply a few other values for different behaviors. If you supply a number, then you're telling jQuery UI how long the animation should take to complete (in milliseconds). For example, to really bug your site's visitors, you could force accordion panels to open and close painfully slowly over the course of 5 seconds, like this:

```
animate: 5000
```

You can also supply a string that matches the name of an easing function. As discussed on page 442, easing functions control how an animation plays out over its overall duration: you can make an animation start off very slowly, then finish really quickly. For example, to use the `easeInElastic` easing function, you'd set the `animate` property like this:

```
animate: 'easeInElastic'
```

However, anything but the default easing looks pretty awful.

- **event.** Set the event that causes an accordion panel to open. Works just like the tabbed panels event option described on page 331.

- **heightStyle.** Just like the tabbed panels option of the same name (page 331).

- **icons.** As you can see in Figure 9-11, jQuery UI attaches small icons on the left side of accordion headers. A small down arrow appears in headlines whose accordion panel is open; a right-pointing arrow appears in headlines whose panels are closed. jQuery UI includes a large selection of icons as part of each theme (see *http://api.jqueryui.com/theming/icons/* for a complete list). You can swap in new icons by supplying an `icons` option and a value that includes an object literal, like this:

```
icons : {
  header: "ui-icon-plus",
  activeHeader: "ui-icon-minus"
}
```

The object literal defines the two icons jQuery UI should use. The `header` property sets the icon used in headers whose accordion panels are closed, and the `activeHeader` property defines the icon used for headers of opened panels. The above example uses + and – symbols to indicate the different header states.

As with the other jQuery UI plug-ins, you can combine multiple options to the accordion widget to control how the accordion looks and functions. For example, say you wanted to change the event trigger so mousing over a headline opens an accordion panel, and you want to change the icons used in the headlines. You could do that when you call the `accordion()` function, like this:

```
$('#accordion').accordion({
  event: 'mouseover',
  icons : {
    header: 'ui-icon-circle-plus',
    activeHeader: 'ui-icon-circle-minus'
  }
});
```

Mini-Tutorial: Create a jQuery UI Accordion

Accordions are very much like tabbed panels. Most of the work required is formatting the HTML. But the HTML for accordions is even simpler than for tabbed panels. In this tutorial, you get to start with an already created HTML file and add an accordion to it:

1. **First take a look at the HTML to see what's there. In a web browser, open the *accordion.html* file.**

   The page contains a headline—jQuery UI Accordion—and a simple collection of headlines, text, and images (see the top image in Figure 9-11).

2. **Open the *accordion.html* page in a text editor and look at the HTML starting below the <h1> tag.**

   Notice that there's a <div> tag—that's a container element that holds the items for the accordion. Inside that div you'll see an <h3> tag followed by a <div> tag. The <h3> represents the accordion label and the <div>, the accordion panel. In the HTML for this page, there are three of these <h3>/<div> pairs, so once you add the programming, you'll have three accordion panels. First, you need to give jQuery a "hook" for selecting the accordion container.

3. **Locate the <div> tag below the <h1> tag and add an ID:**

   ```
   <div id="accordion">
   ```

   This is all the HTML you need to add accordions to the page. Now it's time to add the programming.

4. **Inside the $(document).ready() function, select the container and call the accordion() function:**

   ```
   $(document).ready(function() {
     $('#accordion').accordion();
   }); // end ready
   ```

   Save the file and preview it in a web browser. The page should look like the bottom image in Figure 9-11. See why it's called a "mini" tutorial? jQuery UI makes it that simple. But you're not done yet. You want to make it so that all of the accordion panels are closed when the page loads.

5. **Add the following object literal (in bold) to the tabs function:**

   ```
   $(document).ready(function() {
     $('#accordion').accordion({
   ```

```
    active: false,
    collapsible: true
  });
}); // end ready
```

Preview the page in a browser, and you'll see that all of the accordion panels begin in the closed position. Click one of the headers to open a panel; click that same header again to close the panel. Accordion panels only close when their associated headline is clicked if the collapsible option is set to true. Let's choose some different icons from jQuery UI's large selection of icon elements (*http://api.jqueryui.com/theming/icons/*).

6. **Add an** icons **property to the accordion options object. The value of this option will be another object literal with two properties:**

```
$('#accordion').accordion({
  active: false,
  collapsible: true,
  icons : {
    header: 'ui-icon-circle-plus',
    activeHeader: 'ui-icon-circle-minus'
  }
});
```

Don't forget to add a comma after true on line 3. As you can see, JavaScript lets you nest object literals inside of other object literals. Sometimes this kind of code can get a little hard to read, but keep in mind that you can just treat an object literal like any other object—a variable, number or string, for example— and use it as a single value for a variable or object property.

7. **Save the page and preview it in a web browser.**

The page should look like the bottom image in Figure 9-11. If it doesn't, double-check your code against what's printed in step 4 above. A finished version of the tutorial—*complete_accordion.html*—is located in the *chapter09* folder.

■ Adding Menus to a Page

jQuery UI also includes a Selectmenu widget that makes it very easy to convert an unordered, nested list of links into a menu with fly-out submenus. It's intended to present a vertical menu bar, with menu items listed on top of each other, and sub-menus appearing to the right (Figure 9-12). However, if you'll settle for a single set of submenus, it's possible to coax the Selectmenu widget to a horizontal orientation for the menu's top level.

As with all of the jQuery UI widgets, menus are really simple to use. The hardest part is structuring your HTML, and even that isn't hard. In fact, you've already seen the same structure in the SmartMenus plug-in on page 241. You start with a simple unordered list of links—these are your top-level menu buttons, the ones that you see when the page loads. If you want to add a pop-out menu to one of those buttons, simply nest another unordered list inside the top-level button's `<li>` tag. For example, here's the HTML for a menu with three top-level menus and a submenu that appears when you mouse over the last menu item:

```
<ul id="mainMenu">
  <li><a href="about.html">About Us</a></li>
  <li><a href="contact.html">Contact Us</a></li>
  <li><a href="products.html">Products</a>
    <ul>
      <li><a href="a.html">Product A</a></li>
      <li><a href="b.html">Product B</a></li>
      <li><a href="c.html">Product C</a></li>
    </ul>
  </li>
</ul>
```

When this HTML is converted into a menu, visitors can mouse over the Products menu item, and a submenu with the three product options will pop into view. As with other jQuery UI widgets, it's good to provide an ID to the widget's containing element. In this case, it's the first `<ul>` tag because that's the container for all of the menu items and submenus.

> **TIP** If you want to visually organize the options in your menus, you can add a divider to separate submenu buttons. Just insert a `<li>` tag with no link and a dash in it like this:
>
> `<li>-</li>`
>
> jQuery UI will draw a line (instead of adding a button) to the menu.

Using the menu widget is easy:

1. **Attach the jQuery UI CSS file, jQuery JavaScript file, and the jQuery UI JavaScript file.**

   These are the same basic steps for using any jQuery UI widget as described on page 104.

2. **Insert an unordered list of links, with additional unordered lists for submenus as described above.**

   It's a good idea to make sure your top-level menu items link to pages on your site.

3. **Add CSS to limit the size of the menu buttons and submenus.**

   The out-of-the-box CSS for jQuery UI menus doesn't limit the width of the menu buttons, so you can end up with extraordinarily wide buttons on your main navigation menu. To set a size for the main menu buttons, create a `.ui-menu` style with a `width` property, like this:

```
.ui-menu {
  width: 10em;
}
```

The ui-menu class is applied automatically by jQuery UI when it creates a menu widget. That class is applied to each <ul> tag within the menu—the main menu and any submenus.

You can use any measure you'd like—em, px, %—but be careful using percentage. A submenu takes its percentage value from its parent, so each submenu will get progressively thinner. To get around this, set the submenu (which is actually an <ul> inside an <ul>) to a 100% width (to match the parent menu). For example:

```
.ui-menu {
  width: 25%;
}
.ui-menu .ui-menu {
  width: 100%;
}
```

Add this CSS to your site's custom CSS file—not to the jQuery UI CSS file. If you decide to change the theme, or update jQuery UI to a newer version, any changes you make to the jQuery UI CSS file will be wiped out by the update. You'll learn more about styling jQuery UI widgets in Chapter 11.

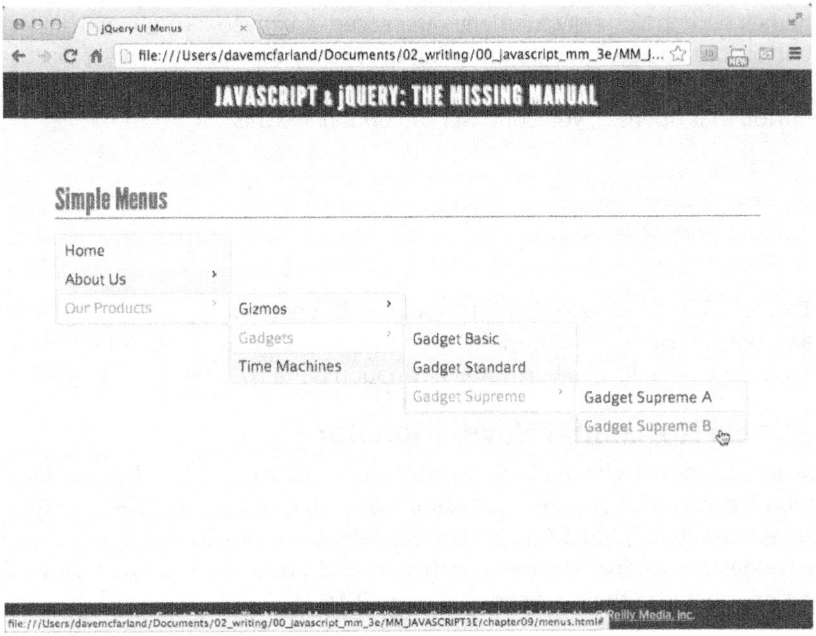

FIGURE 9-12

jQuery UI's menu widget makes it easy to create a multi-level menu that matches the look and feel of the other jQuery UI widgets. It's great for adding a menu to a web application to make the application feel more like desktop software.

4. **Select the outer `<ul>` tag and apply the `menu()` function:**

```
$('#mainMenu').menu();
```

> **NOTE** You'll find an example of the menu widget in the *complete_menu.html* file in the *chapter09* folder.

As with other jQuery UI widgets, the menu widget includes several options for customizing its behavior and appearance. Pass an object literal to the `menu()` function to control it:

- **icons.** As you can see in Figure 9-12, jQuery UI attaches small icons on the right side of any menu button that has an attached submenu. The icon indicates to visitors that there's another menu hidden away in that button. jQuery UI includes a large selection of icons as part of each theme (see *http://api.jqueryui.com/theming/icons/* for a complete list). You can swap in new icons by supplying an `icons` option and a value that includes an object literal, like this:

```
icons : {
  submenu: "ui-icon-circle-triangle-e"
}
```

  Unfortunately, you can only specify one icon, so the icon used for buttons on the main menu bar is also shared by submenus buttons that have their *own* submenus.

- **position.** The `position` option controls where submenus are placed in relation to their parent. Normally submenus are placed directly to the right of their parent button, but you can change this using the jQuery UI `position` object discussed on page 318. For example, if you want to place the submenu directly below the button that opens it, you could set the option like this:

```
position : {
  my: "center top",
  at: "center bottom"
}
```

  This translates to place "my" (the submenu) center and top, and "at" center and bottom of my parent menu button. This technique is useful for creating drop-down menus in a horizontal navigation bar as described on page 349.

Creating a Horizontal Navigation Bar

The jQuery UI menus weren't intended to create a classical navigation bar like the ones you see at the top of most websites. If that's what you're after, the SmartMenus plug-in discussed on page 241 is probably a better bet. However, you can coax the menu widget into a horizontal menu with a single drop-down menu with a little CSS like the one shown in the top image in Figure 9-13.

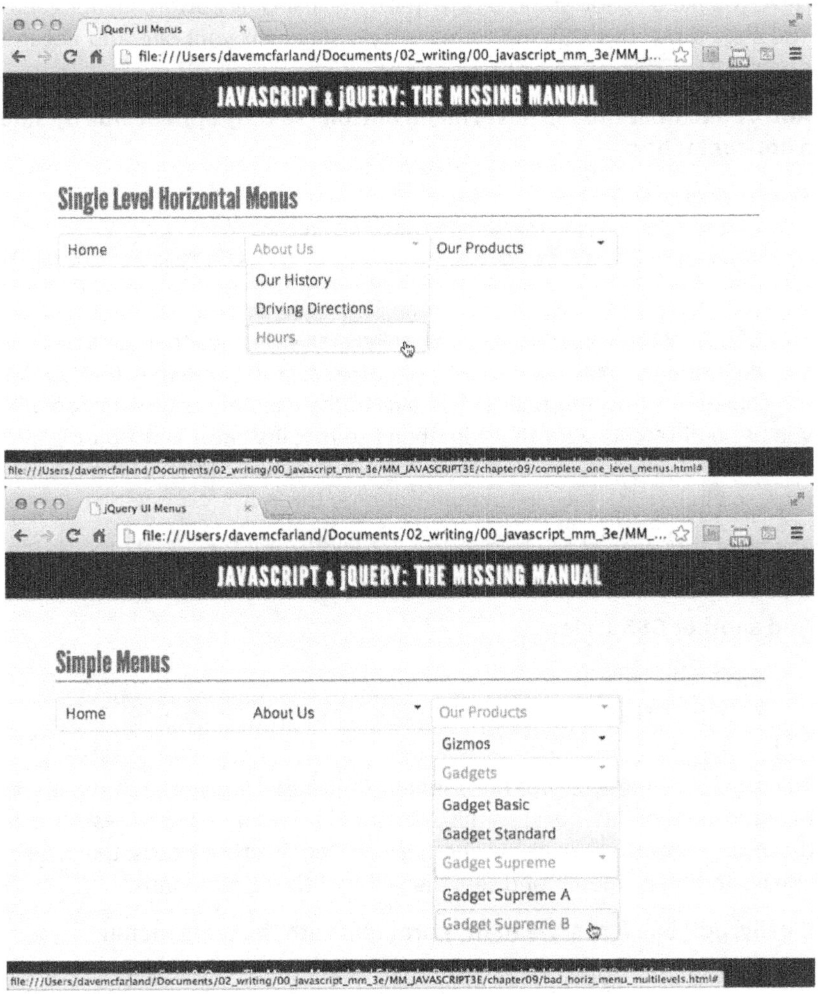

FIGURE 9-13

If you want to keep your site's user interface looking consistent by using jQuery UI's CSS and widgets throughout your site, you can get a fully functional horizontal jQuery UI menu if you're willing to settle for only one level of drop-down menus (top). jQuery UI's Selectmenu widget doesn't work very well if you're interested in a multilevel horizontal menu (bot-tom). Because all submenus are placed in the same relationship to their parent, you end up with overlapping submenus. You can see examples of both types of menus in the chapter09 *folder:* complete_ horiz_menus.html *and* bad_horiz_menu_multi-level.html.

Multi-level drop-down menus don't work well because the jQuery UI menu widget places all submenus in the same position relative to their parents. With a vertical menu (Figure 9-12), that works well: the submenus pop out to the right of their parent menu button. But with a horizontal menu bar, the first submenu usually appears *below* its parent button (Figure 9-13, top) and sub-submenus appear to the right of their parent. Unfortunately, with jQuery UI, if you place one submenu below its parent *all* submenus are placed that way, so you end up with a confusing overlapping mess of submenus, as pictured in the bottom image in Figure 9-13:

1. **To create a horizontal menu, start with an unordered list of links, but add only one level of nested unordered lists (the HTML example on page 344, for instance).**

   Next, you need to add some CSS to make the main nav buttons sit horizontally. You should put this CSS in the main style sheet for your site and not in the jQuery UI CSS file.

2. **Add CSS to float the top-level menu buttons so they appear side by side in a horizontal bar:**

   ```
   #mainMenu > li {
     width: 10em;
     float: left;
   }
   ```

   This CSS selector—#mainMenu > li—selects all <li> tags that are a direct descendant of an element with the ID of mainMenu. (This assumes that you gave the containing <ul> tag that ID name as in the example code on page 344. If you use a different ID for that tag, then use that instead.) The > part is a child selector and only selects <li> tags that are *directly* children of the main <ul> tags, so all the <li> tags in submenus ignore this rule.

   The style sets each menu button to a set width, and then floats them side by side. Then you need to set the width of the submenus.

3. **Add another CSS style:**

   ```
   .ui-menu .ui-menu {
     width: 10em;
   }
   ```

   This style sets the width of the submenus. jQuery UI gives each menu—<ul> tag—the class of .ui-menu, so this selector—.ui-menu .ui-menu—selects only those <ul> tags that are inside another <ul> tag. In other words, the style only applies to nested menus and sets the width of those submenus.

4. **Finally, add one last style to fix a problem with the main menu:**

   ```
   #mainMenu {
     float: left;
   }
   ```

   This style fixes what's called an *escaping float*—a situation where a parent element's height collapses when its child elements are floated. In plain English, it just means that the border and background of the main menu don't look right when all the buttons are floated. This is one technique for fixing the problem; just float the parent element.

   With the CSS out of the way, you can add the JavaScript.

5. **Call the `menu()` function as described on page 346, but add a few options to control the placement of the submenu and icon used on the main menu:**

```
$('#menu').menu({
  position: {
    my: 'center top',
    at: 'center bottom'
  },
  icons: {
    submenu: 'ui-icon-triangle-1-s'
  }
});
```

The `position` option (described on page 346) controls the placement of the submenu. In this case, it puts the menu directly below the menu button that opens it. In addition, the menu widget normally shows a right-pointing arrow icon on menu buttons that have submenus. However, because the menu bar is now horizontal, and the submenu opens up below the main menu bar, you must use a down-pointing arrow (`'ui-icon-triangle-1-s'`).

Forms Revisited

Forms are the original interactive web element, and they're a part of most web applications in one form or another. Forms can get input from visitors, let shoppers buy goods, let community members post their thoughts, and so on. Chapter 8 looked at ways to make web forms smarter and easier to use. jQuery UI lets you do even more with your forms and provides a consistent design to make your form elements look and function in similar ways.

This chapter will show you how to use four jQuery UI widgets—Datepicker, Auto-complete, Selectmenu, and Button—that can really make your forms look great and work well.

■ Picking Dates with Style

Many forms require date input. Forms for adding an event to a calendar, booking a plane flight, and making a dinner reservation all require you to specify a date for an activity. Many forms provide instructions, like "Type a date, like 12/10/2014," but simply asking visitors to type a date into a field can generate a wide variety of results. First of all, you're relying on your visitors never to make typos. In addition, because people often write dates in different ways (in the United States, for example, dates are specified in the order month, day, year, but many other places the order is day, month, year), hand-typed dates may be misleading or inaccurate.

Fortunately, jQuery UI's Datepicker widget makes selecting a date straightforward. Instead of typing a date, visitors just click a form field, and then use a visual calendar to pick the desired date (Figure 10-1). This widget is simple to use and customize.

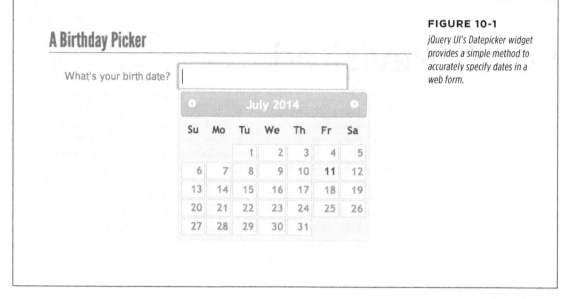

FIGURE 10-1

jQuery UI's Datepicker widget provides a simple method to accurately specify dates in a web form.

As with most jQuery UI widgets, Datepicker is extremely easy to use:

1. **Follow the steps on page 304 to attach jQuery UI's CSS and JavaScript files to your web page.**

   You'll need to attach the jQuery file as well, so that whenever you use a jQuery UI widget, you'll have the jQuery UI CSS, jQuery JavaScript, and jQuery UI JavaScript files attached to your page (in that order, too).

2. **Add a form to a page, and include a text <input> field for capturing a date.**

   Provide a way to identify that input field, so you can select it with jQuery. For example, you might give it an ID like this:

   ```
   <input type="text" name="birthdate" id="birthdate">
   ```

   Or, if the form has several fields for capturing dates (like fields for arrival and departure) you might use a class name to identify all fields that should use the datepicker widget like this:

   ```
   <input type="text" name="arrival" class="date">
   <input type="text" name="departure" class="date">
   ```

3. **Add jQuery's $(document).ready() function to your page:**

   ```
   $(document).ready(function() {

   }); // end ready
   ```

4. Use jQuery to select the input element(s) and call the `datepicker()` **function:**

```
$(document).ready(function() {
  $('#birthdate').datepicker();
}); // end ready
```

Or, if you've used a class to identify more than one input like in the example in step 2, you could write this:

```
$(document).ready(function() {
  $('.date').datepicker();
}); // end ready
```

These are the only steps you need to create a date picker like the one you can see in Figure 10-1. And if that's all the Datepicker widget did, it'd be good enough. But the Datepicker widget provides many different options for customizing its display and how it works.

> **NOTE** HTML5 includes a special `date` field that's intended to provide some of the functionality that Datepicker provides, but without any JavaScript. However, it's not supported that well on all browsers, and doesn't provide any way to customize the look of the pop-up calendar. In addition, jQuery UI's Datepicker provides many additional features that you won't get if you use the HTML5 `date` field.

Setting Date Picker Properties

You can set properties of the Datepicker widget—like the date format jQuery UI will use when writing the date into the form field—by passing an object to the `datepicker()` function. This object literal contains `datepicker` options and values to control those options.

For example, one option—`numberOfMonths`—lets you specify how many months should appear when the date picker opens. Normally that's just 1 as pictured in Figure 10-1, but it's possible to display three months at a time, as shown in Figure 10-2, by setting this value to 3:

```
$('.date').datepicker({
  numberOfMonths : 3
});
```

Here are some of the most useful options:

- **changeMonth.** Normally, visitors can change the month displayed by the Datepicker pop-up calendar by clicking either the left or right arrows in the top of the calendar (Figure 10-1). These buttons display either the previous (left) or next (right) month. However, this is a tedious way to select a date that's nine months away. Set the `changeMonth` option to `true`, and a drop-down menu appears in the calendar, letting visitors quickly choose a new month (Figure 10-2).

  ```
  changeMonth : true
  ```

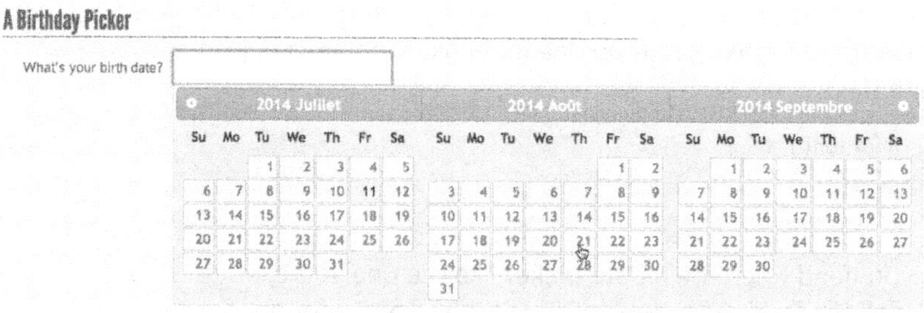

A Birthday Picker

What's your birth date?

FIGURE 10-2

jQuery UI's Datepicker widget is highly customizable. You can change the number of months visible at a time, place the year before the month name, and supply different names for months to match different languages.

- **changeYear.** Like changeMonth, this option, when set to true, tells jQuery UI to display a drop-down menu for selecting a new year for the calendar. You'll frequently use this option with the yearRange option (page 346) to set the number of years to display in the drop-down menu.

      changeYear : true

- **dateFormat.** Lets you supply a string that defines the format you want jQuery UI to use when writing the selected date to the input field. You use predefined codes to define different outputs. For example, dd is used to indicate day of the month, mm the month of the year, and yy the year. You can also insert characters like space, /, or - as part of the string. For example, say someone selects January 27, 2015 from the pop-up calendar, and you want this to appear in the actual form as 01-27-2015. You'd set the dateFormat option like this:

      dateFormat : 'mm-dd-yy'

  jQuery UI supplies many different codes for formatting the date. For some useful examples, see Table 10-1. You can find a complete list of formats jQuery UI's Datepicker widget accepts for the dateFormat option at *http://api.jqueryui.com/datepicker/#utility-formatDate*.

> **NOTE** There are other options, events, and methods for jQuery UI's datepicker widget. To see them all, visit *http://api.jqueryui.com/datepicker/*.

- **monthNames.** Provide an array of 12 strings to use names other than English months. For example, to make datepicker display French names of the month, you'd add this to the object literal passed to datepicker() function:

      monthNames: ["Janvier", "Février", "Mars", "Avril", "Mai", "Juin",
      "Juillet", "Août", "Septembre", "Octobre", "Novembre", "Décembre"]

- **numberOfMonths.** Assign a number to this option to determine the number of months visible in the pop-up date picker. Normally it's a single month, but you can specify whether you want to display more months. If you go beyond three months (pictured in Figure 10-2), the `datepicker` pop up begins to be a bit unwieldy. The months always appear side by side, so if there are more than three or four, you'll have to scroll sideways to see the other months and make a selection in them. Stick to 1, 2, or 3.

- **maxDate.** Sets the latest date that a visitor can select from the `datepicker` pop-up calendar. For example, you could use this for a hotel reservation system. Many hotels don't let you reserve a room more than one year in advance, so you could limit the `datepicker` to no further than one year from the current date. One way is to assign a number specifying a number of days in the future. For example, to limit a visitor from picking a day that's later than 30 days in the future, you could set the `maxDate` option like this:

```
maxDate : 30
```

Alternatively, you can give this option a string containing special characters that indicate amounts of time—y for years, m for months, w for weeks, and d for days. For example, to limit a selection to one year out or less, set the `maxDate` option like this:

```
maxDate : '+1y'
```

Separate each time character by a space. So, for example, if you want to limit the date selection to three months, two weeks, and five days into the future, you'd do this:

```
maxDate : '+3m +2w +5d'
```

You'll find an example of the `maxDate` option in action in the tutorial on page 359.

- **minDate.** The opposite of the `maxDate` option. It sets the *earliest* selectable date from the `datepicker`. This setting is very useful for a scheduling form—after all there's no point in letting a visitor schedule a reservation that's before today (unless time travel has been discovered since this book was written). You use the same characters as `maxDate` to specify the earliest date. For example, to prevent people from selecting a date earlier than today, set this option to 0, like this:

```
minDate : 0
```

Positive values for this option mean the visitor has to select a day in the future. For example, if the hotel is booked for the next three weeks, you can prevent a visitor from selecting a date in that time like this:

```
minDate : '+3w'
```

Use negative values to set the earliest selectable date in the past. For example, say you've created a form for searching your company's database of archived email. To keep the database from bursting at the seams, your company only stores the past two years' worth of email records, so there's not point in letting people search three, four, or five years in the past—those emails were erased a long time ago. Here's how to limit the search to just the past two years:

```
minDate : '-2y'
```

You can combine dates, months, and years as well. For example, here's how to specify a date that's one year, two months, and three days in the past:

```
minDate : '-1y -2m -3d'
```

NOTE The minDate and maxDate options also accept a JavaScript date object as an acceptable value. For example, say your company started business on March 13, 2010. You could set the minimum selectable date for a datepicker calendar to that date like this:

```
minDate : new Date(2010, 2, 13)
```

See page 568 to learn how to create date objects using JavaScript.

- **yearRange.** This option is used with the changeYear option (page 354), and determines how many years are displayed in the drop-down year menu. For example, say you want to collect someone's date of birth. You set the changeYear option to true so it's easy for a visitor to jump back 20, 30, or 50 years. Normally, the changeYear option forces that drop-down menu to show 10 years in the past and 10 years in the future. It would be better to list a lot of years in the past and no years in the future (unless, again, time travel has been perfected). To do that, you give the yearRange option a positive or negative number, followed by a colon, followed by another positive or negative number. The first number represents the first year listed in the menu, and the second number is the last year in the menu.

Back to the birth year example, you'd want to be able to list perhaps 120 years back, but no years in the future. Here's how:

```
yearRange : '-120:0'
```

This setting tells jQuery UI to display a drop-down menu to select a year, with the first year on the list 100 years before this year and the last year on the list the current year. If you're getting confused, check out the tutorial on page 359 for an example.

TABLE 10-1 *Useful strings for supplying to the* dateFormat *option.*

EXAMPLE	WHAT IT MEANS	EXAMPLE OUTPUT
'yy-mm-dd'	Complete year, dash, 2 digit month, dash, 2 digit day. This is the format used for a date in MySQL databases.	2015-02-05
'm/d/y'	1 or 2 digit month, forward slash, 1 or 2 digit day, forward slash, 2 digit year	2/5/15
'D, M d, yy'	Abbreviated day-of-the-week name, comma, space, abbreviated month name, space, 1 or 2 digit day, comma, space, complete year.	Thu, Feb 5, 2015
'DD, MM dd, yy'	Full day-of-the-week name, comma, space, full month name, space, 1 or 2 digit day, comma, space, complete year.	Thursday, February 5, 2015
'@'	Unix timestamp. The number of milliseconds since midnight on January 1, 1970 (see page 570).	1423123200000

Tutorial: Adding a Birthdate Picker

It's time to try out the Datepicker widget. In this tutorial, you'll turn a text field into an intelligent device for easily selecting a person's birthdate.

> **NOTE** See the note on page 12 for information on how to download the tutorial files.

1. **In your text editor, open the file *birthdate.html* in the *chapter10* folder.**

   This file already contains a link to all of the jQuery and jQuery UI files and the $(document).ready() function (page 160). The first step is selecting the input element.

2. **Inside the $(document).ready() function, type:**

   ```
   $('#dob')
   ```

   If you look at the HTML for this page, you'll see an input element for collecting a birthdate: <input type="text" id="dob" name="birthdate">. It has an ID of dob, so this code selects that form field. Now you need to apply the Datepicker widget.

3. **Type a period, followed by** `datepicker();` **so the code now looks like this:**

   ```
   $('#dob').datepicker();
   ```

   That's all there is to it!

4. **Save the file and preview it in a web browser. Click the input field.**

   A calendar pops up like magic. This calendar uses jQuery UI's UI Lightness theme, but you'll learn how to change the widget's appearance in the next chapter.

   If you try to select your birthdate, you'll see it's kind of a pain. You have to hit the left arrow button at the top of the calendar 12 times just to go back one year! So you'll make it easier to select an older date by adding drop-down menus for the month and year.

5. **Return to your text editor, and in the** `datepicker()` **function, add an object literal, like this:**

   ```
   $('#dob').datepicker({

   });
   ```

   To change options, you pass the `datepicker()` function an object—{ }—filled with options, names, and values. First, add a drop-down menu for selecting months.

6. **Add** `changeMonth : true` **to the object:**

   ```
   $('#dob').datepicker({
     changeMonth : true
   });
   ```

   If you save the page now, preview it in a web browser, and click inside the form field, you should see a drop-down menu in the calendar's header that lets you select any of the 12 months of the year. This menu provides a much faster way to select a date that happened 9 months ago.

   Next you'll create a drop-down for the year.

7. **Type a comma after the line you just typed, hit Return, and type** `changeYear : true`:

   ```
   $('#dob').datepicker({
     changeMonth : true,
     changeYear : true
   });
   ```

   This adds another drop-down menu to the calendar. Unfortunately, that menu only goes back 10 years and also includes the next 10 years, which isn't what you want. Unless your visitor is younger than 10 or owns a time machine, the choices in this drop-down menu aren't going to be of much use. Fortunately, you can change the range of years that appear in the menu.

8. **Type a comma after the line you just typed, hit return and type** yearRange
   : '-120:+0':

```
$('#dob').datepicker({
  changeMonth : true,
  changeYear : true,
  yearRange : '-120:+0'
});
```

This changes the years displayed in the year drop-down menu. It now goes back 120 years and doesn't display any years after the current one. Much better. However, if you give this latest change a try, you'll notice that it is possible to select tomorrow, or a date next week or next month. At the very least, you want to limit this form to babies that were born today.

9. **Type another comma after the line you just typed, hit return and type** maxDate **:** 0 **like this:**

```
$('#dob').datepicker({
  changeMonth : true,
  changeYear : true,
  yearRange : '-120:+0',
  maxDate : 0
});
```

Now you can't pick a date beyond the current one. Finally, you'll change the format of the date, so birthdates are written like this: 1-27-2015.

10. **Type another comma after the line you just typed, hit Return, and type** dateFormat **:** 'm-dd-yy' **like this:**

```
$('#dob').datepicker({
  changeMonth : true,
  changeYear : true,
  yearRange : '-120:+0',
  maxDate : 0,
  dateFormat : 'm-dd-yy'
});
```

Now you have a highly customized date picker, perfect for selecting birthdates.

11. **Save the file and preview it in a web browser.**

When you click in the input field the final date picker appears (see Figure 10-3). You can find a complete version of this tutorial in the *complete-birthdate.html* file in the *chapter10* folder.

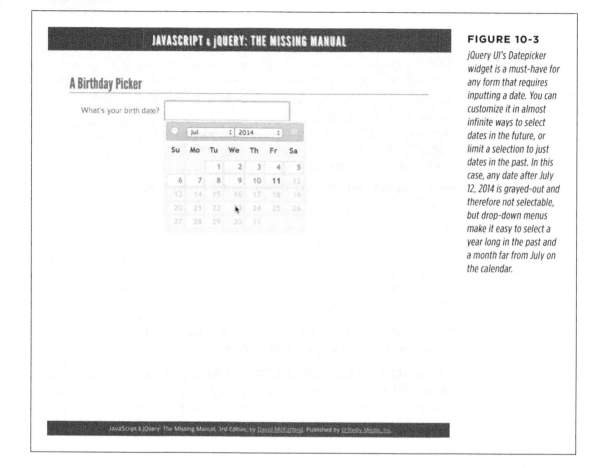

FIGURE 10-3

jQuery UI's Datepicker widget is a must-have for any form that requires inputting a date. You can customize it in almost infinite ways to select dates in the future, or limit a selection to just dates in the past. In this case, any date after July 12, 2014 is grayed-out and therefore not selectable, but drop-down menus make it easy to select a year long in the past and a month far from July on the calendar.

Stylish Select Menus

jQuery UI's themes let you add a unified design to your user interface elements. For example, the date picker looks similar to tabbed panels, which look similar to dialog boxes. Select menus—those form elements that let you pick an option from a drop-down menu—are notoriously hard to style with CSS. Each browser has its own way of displaying select menus—which is often dictated by the operating system (Windows, Mac, Linux)—and browsers don't let you apply every CSS property to select menus.

Fortunately, jQuery UI provides a handy Selectmenu widget which takes a regular HTML select menu and converts it into a much more attractive menu that matches the look of other jQuery UI widgets (see Figure 10-4). The Selectmenu widget literally re-creates the select menu as an unordered list and a series of <span> tags, which are more accepting of CSS styling. Using clever JavaScript programming, this widget hides the real menu, while letting visitors select an option from a JavaScript-powered drop-down menu. The visitor's selection is mirrored by the real form element, so when the visitor submits the form, the visitor's selection is correctly passed to the web server.

Behind the scenes, jQuery UI is performing some sophisticated programming magic, but for you, turning a select menu into a jQuery UI select menu couldn't be simpler:

1. **Follow the steps on page 304 to attach jQuery UI's CSS and JavaScript files to your web page.**

   You'll need to attach the jQuery file as well, so whenever you use a jQuery UI widget, you'll have the jQuery UI CSS, jQuery JavaScript, and jQuery UI JavaScript files attached to your page (in that order, too).

2. **Add a form to a page, and include a select menu: that's a <select> tag containing <option> tags:**

   ```
   <select name="meal" id="meal">
     <option>No meal</option>
     <option>Vegan</option>
     <option>Gluten Free</option>
     <option>Vegetarian</option>
     <option>Meat eater</option>
   </select>
   ```

   You should include a way to select the menu using jQuery. Either apply an ID to the menu, or if you have multiple select menus in a form, apply the same class to each: class="select", for example.

3. **Add jQuery's $(document).ready() function to your page:**

   ```
   $(document).ready(function() {

   }); // end ready
   ```

   You only need to do this if you're placing your JavaScript programming in your page's <head>, as described on page 161.

4. **Use jQuery to select the menu and call the selectmenu() function:**

   ```
   $(document).ready(function() {
     $('#meal').selectmenu();
   }); // end ready
   ```

   Or, if you've used a class to identify more than one menu, you could write this:

   ```
   $(document).ready(function() {
     $('.select').selectmenu();
   }); // end ready
   ```

Unless the options in the menu are very short, jQuery UI's Selectmenu widget often doesn't display the first option completely. In other words, the widget isn't wide enough to display the first option. This looks weird, so you should always set the width of the menu.

5. **Pass an object literal to the** `selectmenu()` **function with a** `width` **property:**

```
$(document).ready(function() {
  $('#meal').selectmenu({
    width: 200
  });
}); // end ready
```

As with other jQuery UI widgets (see the Datepicker on page 353, for example), you can set various options for the Selectmenu widget by passing an object literal containing option/value pairs. The `width` option is almost always required and accepts a numeric value that indicates the number of pixels wide the menu should be (see the next section for more options for the `width` property).

These are the only steps you need to create a menu like the one in Figure 10-4.

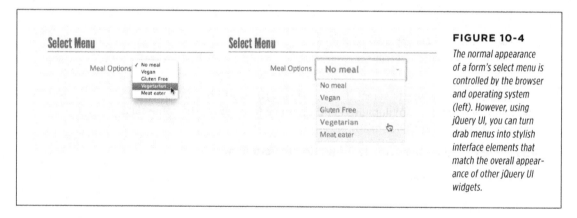

FIGURE 10-4

The normal appearance of a form's select menu is controlled by the browser and operating system (left). However, using jQuery UI, you can turn drab menus into stylish interface elements that match the overall appearance of other jQuery UI widgets.

Setting Select Menu Properties

The Selectmenu widget doesn't have many options. It's mainly a tool to make select menus look more like other jQuery UI widgets. However, there are a few options that you may find useful:

- **width.** This option is almost never optional. Normally, jQuery UI creates a menu that's not wide enough to display all of the text for a single select menu option. You'll want to set this wide enough that you can read an entire menu option. In addition, if the menu isn't wide enough to display an option that's more than one word long, then jQuery UI will display the option on two lines. You can use a number if you want to set the width in pixels like this:

```
width : 300
```

You can also specify a width in percentages or ems by using a string containing a number with either % or ems following. For example, to make the menu fit its parent element (like a containing div), you could set its width to 100% like this:

```
width : '100%'
```

Or, if you prefer em units, you could set the width of a menu to 6 ems like this:

```
width : '6em'
```

- **icons.** You can also display one of jQuery UI's icons to the right of the menu, like the triangle in Figure 10-4. jQuery UI includes a large selection of icons as part of each theme (see *http://api.jqueryui.com/theming/icons/* for a complete list). You can add an icons by supplying an icons option and a value that includes an object literal like this:

```
icons : {
  button: "ui-icon-circle-triangle-s"
}
```

> **NOTE** You may be wondering why the icons option requires another object literal with a name/value pair. After all, it would be a lot easier to assign the icon name to the icons property. That would make sense if selectmenu were the only widget you can assign an icon to. Other widgets also can display icons, and some widgets, like the accordion widget (page 338), let you assign *more* than one icon. For that widget, you have to pass an object literal containing multiple name/value pairs to display more than one icon. To remain consistent with other jQuery UI widgets, the Selectmenu widget also requires an object value for the icons option.

- **position.** You can control the position of the pop-up menu using this option. Normally, the menu appears directly under the menu control—that's how select menus normally work. However, you can make the pop-up list of menu options appear to the left or right of the control if you want. To do this, you can set the position option using jQuery UI's position object. Because positioning a select menu anywhere other than directly below the form control is unexpected behavior, be careful with this property as you might end up confusing visitors. (This specialized utility is discussed in the previous chapter in the box on page 318.)

Performing an Action When a Visitor Selects an Option

When a visitor makes a selection from a menu, usually something should happen as a result. For example, say you have an online clothing order form with a select menu listing all available colors. When a visitor selects a color from the menu, you may want to update the picture of the clothing item to show the item in that color. In other words, selecting an item from the menu changes an image on the page. jQuery UI lets you call a function whenever a new selection is picked from the menu.

To do so, you use the change option. It works like the other options discussed in this chapter in that you put it inside an object literal that you pass to the selectmenu() function. For the option value, you supply a function to the change option. For example, say you had a select menu with the ID `colors`. You would turn this menu into a jQuery UI Selectmenu widget and add a change option to it like this:

```
$('#colors').selectmenu({
  width : 300,
  change : function (event, ui) {
    // put your programming here
  }
});
```

Whenever a visitor makes a new selection from the menu (that is, *changes* the menu), the function will run. The function has two parameters—event and ui. The event parameter contains a jQuery UI event object (page 164). You probably won't need to use that parameter in the function—it only contains event information, like the mouse's X and Y positions and other things that aren't useful for working with menu selections.

However, the ui parameter contains useful information about the select menu. In particular, it can tell you the index value of the newly selected option; that is, its place in the menu, with the first option having an index of 0. The ui parameter also knows the label and value of the selected option. The ui parameter is an object itself, composed of different properties that you can access using dot notation (page 55).

- **ui.item.index** contains the index value of the selected menu option. Menu options are numbered like arrays: the first item in the menu is 0, the second is 1, and so on.

- **ui.item.label** contains the label of the selected menu option. The label is the word or words the visitor sees in the select menu. It appears in the HTML inside the <option> tag. So if you had this menu on a page:

```
<select id="colors">
  <option>Red</option>
  <option>Green</option>
  <option>Blue</option>
</select>
```

the labels for the items in this menu are "Red," "Green," and "Blue."

- **ui.item.value** contains the value of the selected menu option. The value is set using the option tag's value attribute. Often, the label and value are the same thing. If that's the case, you don't need to specify a value attribute in your HTML. But sometimes you want to submit a different value to the server that processes the form input. For example, a company might have special codes that indicate a precise stock color. A visitor might want a "red" shirt, but to the clothing company, which might have multiple shades of red for different clothing types, that red shirt color might have a special code like "R785".

In this case, the form will include values in addition to labels like this:

```html
<select id="colors">
  <option value="R785">Red</option>
  <option value="G101">Green</option>
  <option value="B498">Blue</option>
</select>
```

For this menu, the values are "R785", "G101", and "B498", while the labels are still "Red," "Green," and "Blue."

Now think about how you might change an image on a page when a visitor makes a change to a menu. Say you use the HTML for the menu above, with the three color options—Red, Green, and Blue. When a visitor makes a selection, the browser should load an image of a shirt that matches the color selected. Assume there's the following HTML on the page when it loads:

```html
<img src="red_shirt.jpg" id="shirt" alt="Buy our shirts!">
```

As you read on page 209, by changing an image's src attribute, you can tell a browser to load a new image in that spot. So for example, to load a picture of a blue shirt to the page, you could select this image and change its src attribute like this:

```javascript
$('#shirt').attr('src', 'blue_shirt.jpg');
```

Putting all of this together, you could then change the image each time a new menu option is selected like this:

```javascript
$('#colors').selectmenu({
  width : 300,
  change : function (event, ui) {
    var newImage;
    if (ui.item.label === 'Red') {
      newImage = 'red_shirt.jpg';
    } else if (ui.item.label === 'Green') {
      newImage = 'green_shirt.jpg';
    } else {
      newImage = 'blue_shirt.jpg';
    }
    $('#shirt').attr('src', newImage);
  }
});
```

You can do all sorts of things with the change option, like updating HTML, adding a second select menu with another set of options related to the original menu's selected option, and so on.

> **NOTE** There are other options, events, and methods for jQuery UI's Selectmenu widget. To learn them all, visit *http://api.jqueryui.com/selectmenu/*.

■ Styling Buttons

jQuery UI also includes a widget to make a variety of button-like form elements look and behave similarly. The Button widget can be used to style a submit button, a reset button, or an <input> element with the type of button: <input type="button">. In addition, you can use it to style the HTML <button> element to match the look of a jQuery UI CSS theme (Figure 10-5):

1. **Follow the steps on page 304 to attach jQuery UI's CSS and JavaScript files to your web page.**

   You'll need to attach the jQuery file as well, so that whenever you use a jQuery UI widget you'll have the jQuery UI CSS, jQuery JavaScript, and jQuery UI JavaScript files attached to your page (in that order).

2. **Add a button to the page. It can be either a reset, submit, or input button or <button> element. For example:**

   ```
   <input type="submit" id="submit" value="Submit form!">
   <input type="reset" id="reset" value="Reset form.">
   <input type="button" id="inputButton" value="An input button.">
   <button id="button">A button element</button>
   ```

   You also need to include a way to select the menu using jQuery. You can either apply an ID to the element, or if you have multiple buttons in a form, apply the same class to each: class="button", for example.

3. **Add jQuery's $(document).ready() function to your page:**

   ```
   $(document).ready(function() {

   }); // end ready
   ```

   You only need to do this if you're placing your JavaScript programming in the <head> of your page, as described on page 160.

4. **Use jQuery to select the button and call the button function:**

   ```
   $(document).ready(function() {
     $('#submit').button();
   }); // end ready
   ```

   Or, if you've used a class to identify more than one button, you could write this:

   ```
   $(document).ready(function() {
     $('.button').button();
   }); // end ready
   ```

   When applied, the widget simply styles the element to match the jQuery UI theme that's in use (Figure 10-5).

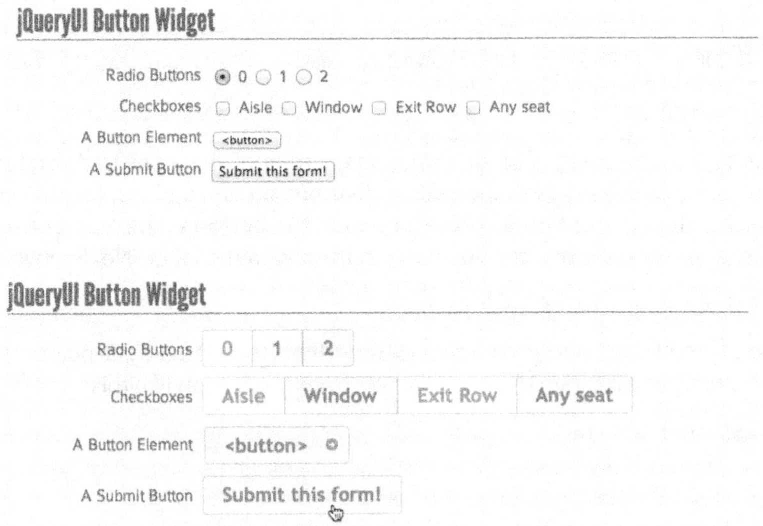

FIGURE 10-5

jQuery UI's button widget provides a quick and simple way to turn drab form elements like radio buttons, checkboxes, submit, and HTML buttons (top) into elegant looking interface elements that provide a consistent presentation (bottom).

Customizing Buttons

The jQuery UI button widget doesn't provide many options for customization. The text you see on the button is provided by the value attribute, in the case of <input> elements like the submit and reset buttons. In the case of the <button> element, which includes an opening and closing tag—<button>I'm a button</button>—the text you see in the button comes from the text between the tags. However, you can customize buttons in a few ways by passing option settings to the button() method.

- **icons.** You can also display one of jQuery UI's icons to the left of a button and another icon on the right (see the <button> element in Figure 10-5 for an example). jQuery UI includes a large selection of icons as part of each theme (see *http://api.jqueryui.com/theming/icons/* for a complete list). You can add an icon by supplying an icons option and a value that includes an object, like this:

```
icons : {
  primary: "ui-icon-gear",
  secondary: "ui-icon-triangle-1-s"
}
```

The "primary" icon appears on the left, while the "secondary" icon appears to its right. You don't have to specify two icons—in fact, that usually looks pretty weird. Usually, you'll just specify one of the two. For example, to display a right-pointing arrow on all <button> elements on a page, you could write this:

```
$('button').button({
  icons : { secondary: 'ui-icon-circle-arrow-e' }
});
```

NOTE You can't use the icons option on any button created using the <input> element—that is, submit or reset buttons—only on the <button> element.

- **text.** If you're using <button> elements, and applying icons to those buttons, you can completely hide the text on that button and just display the icon. By setting the text option to false, you hide the button's label and only display the icon. For example, say you had a button with the label "Next" on it:

```
<button id="next">Next</button>
```

You could turn that button into a jQuery UI button, add a right-pointing arrow icon to it, and remove the word "Next" from the button like this:

```
$('#next').button({
  icons : { secondary : 'ui-icon-arrowthick-1-e' },
  text : false
});
```

NOTE The jQuery UI button widget has a couple other options, methods, and events, which you can read about at *http://api.jqueryui.com/button/*.

■ Improve Radio Buttons and Checkboxes

Radio buttons and checkboxes are more form elements that don't look so great in their native format (see Figure 10-5, top). Browsers use the native look for operating system buttons and checkboxes, which don't allow the same amount of CSS customization as other HTML elements.

Fortunately, jQuery UI provides a widget to make radio buttons and checkboxes share the look and feel of other jQuery UI elements (see Figure 10-5, bottom). The really good news is that it takes almost no work on your part to take advantage of this improved appearance. The jQuery UI .buttonset() method does all of the work. In fact, it simply applies the .button() method to each radio button or checkbox in a group.

All you have to do is a little bit of HTML setup: wrap the group of buttons in some kind of container element like a <div> tag so you can select it with jQuery. For example, say you're creating an airline reservation form where customers can indicate the number of bags they will check—either 0, 1, or 2 bags. You might have HTML organized like this:

```
<div id="radio">
  <p class="label">Number of bags to check</p>

  <input type="radio" id="none" name="bags" checked="checked">
  <label for="none">0</label>

  <input type="radio" id="one" name="bags">
  <label for="one">1</label>

  <input type="radio" id="two" name="bags">
  <label for="two">2</label>
</div>
```

There are three radio buttons—`<input type="radio">`—which are enclosed by a div with an ID of radio. To turn these into a jQuery UI radio button group, just follow steps 1–3 on page 304 to download and attach the jQuery and jQuery UI CSS and JavaScript files, and add a `$(document).ready()` function to the page. Then add the following JavaScript code:

```
$('#radio').buttonset();
```

It's as easy as that. The `$('#radio')` part selects the div containing the radio buttons; the `.buttonset()` code looks for every radio or checkbox element inside the div and turns each of them into a button. The unique part about the `buttonset()` function is that it groups all of those elements so they appear as a unit (see Figure 10-6).

> **TIP** By default, jQuery UI's CSS formats a group of buttons or checkboxes as a single unit (Figure 10-6). That is, they sit side by side and touch each other. If you prefer to have the buttons not touch, and appear as separate buttons sitting side by side, just apply the `button()` function to each element individually. For example, given the HTML above and the group of radio buttons, you could add this JavaScript code to create individual buttons:
>
> ```
> $('#radio input').button();
> ```
>
> This applies the `button()` function individually to each radio button inside the div.

The same technique applies to checkboxes. Just group the adjoining checkboxes in some kind of selectable container like `<div id="check">`, select that container, and apply the `buttonset()` function. Whether it's a group of radio buttons or a group of checkboxes, jQuery UI formats them the same way, as shown in Figure 10-6. However, the two types of controls behave differently: With radio buttons, only one button in the group can be selected at a time. With checkboxes, you can select any number of checkboxes in the group (or none at all). jQuery UI highlights selected buttons or checkboxes.

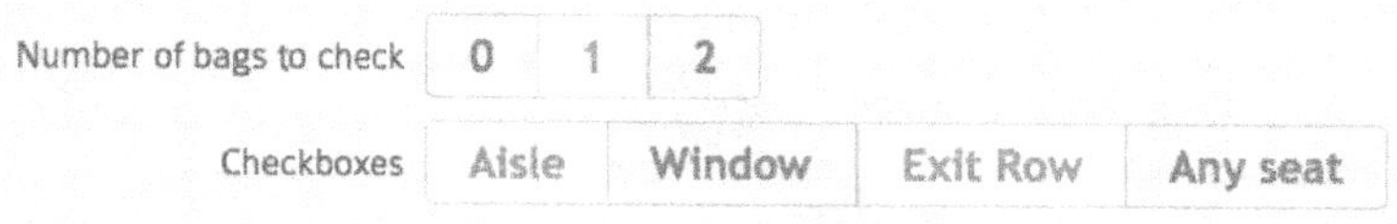

Number of bags to check	0	1	2		
Checkboxes	Aisle	Window	Exit Row	Any seat	

FIGURE 10-6

You can only select a single button in a group of radio buttons (top). In this example, the middle button—"1"—is selected (and highlighted by jQuery UI). You can, however, select any number of boxes among a group of checkboxes (bottom). Here, the first ("Aisle") and third ("Exit Row") checkboxes are selected.

The buttonset() function doesn't take any arguments. However, behind the scenes, it just applies the button() method to each button or checkbox in the group. This means you can customize the buttons further using the options discussed on page 366.

◼ Providing Hints with Autocomplete

Many sites with a search box provide a helpful feature that provides suggestions matching what you've started to type. For example, visit Amazon and type *light*, and a drop-down menu appears suggesting categories of products that include the word "light"—light bulbs, LED lights, light switch covers, and so on (Figure 10-7). Instead of typing the rest of the word, you can click one of the suggestions, or even use the keyboard up and down arrow keys to make a selection from the menu.

This suggestion feature is called *autocomplete*, and jQuery UI includes a helpful widget that lets you provide this feature on your own site. You can add autocomplete to any text field on a form. For example, say you're building an airline reservation system, and a customer needs to type the airport he's flying from. When he starts typing the name of her airport, a helpful drop-down menu appears suggesting airports that match the first few letters that he types. He can then just click one of the airports that appears in the menu instead of typing out the entire name.

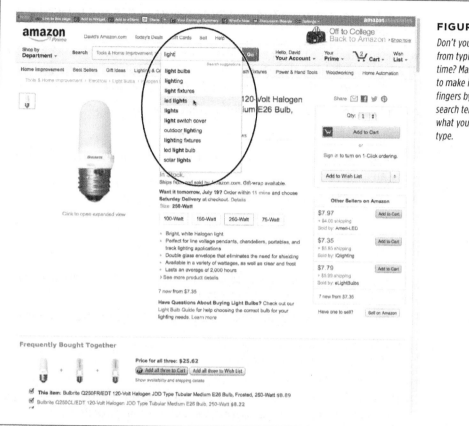

FIGURE 10-7

*Don't your fingers hurt
from typing all of the
time? Many websites try
to make it easier on your
fingers by suggesting
search terms that match
what you've begun to
type.*

Even better, you can use the autocomplete feature to place different content in the text field. Using the airline reservation example, a customer could type in the name of the city she's flying out of, and when she picks the name from the list, the airport *code* is added to the form instead. For example, typing *Portland* might provide a list of airport names including "Portland International Airport." When the customer picks that option, the airport code—PDX—is written in the text field instead. You could use this feature to locate the product number of an item in a catalog. When someone types the name of a product and selects that name from the pop-up autocomplete menu, the product number is added to the text field.

To use the Autocomplete widget, you need to provide data to jQuery UI that it can use to try to find matches to display in the pop-up autocomplete menu. For example, you need a list of airport names, so that jQuery UI can try to find a match to whatever the visitor types in the airport form field. There are two ways you can do this: provide an array of information using JavaScript, or send the search term to the web server using Ajax, and have the web server send back a list of matching terms. You'll see both approaches later in this chapter, but first here's the basic method for adding autocomplete to a form:

1. **Follow the steps on page 304 to attach jQuery UI's CSS and JavaScript files to your web page.**

   You'll need to attach the jQuery file as well, so that whenever you use a jQuery UI widget you'll have the jQuery UI CSS, jQuery JavaScript, and jQuery UI JavaScript files attached to your page (in that order, too).

2. **Add a form to the page, and include a text input field:**

   ```
   <input type="text" id="airport" name="airport">
   ```

   You should also include a way to select the menu using jQuery. For example, apply an ID to the field.

3. **Add jQuery's $(document).ready() function to your page:**

   ```
   $(document).ready(function() {

   }); // end ready
   ```

   You need to do this only if you're placing your JavaScript programming in your page's <head>, as described on page 160.

4. **Use jQuery to select the text field and call the autocomplete function:**

   ```
   $(document).ready(function() {
     $('#airport').autocomplete();
   }); // end ready
   ```

   At the very least, you need to pass the autocomplete() function an object containing a property named source, and either an array of items or a URL of a server-side program that can return a list of possible matches to the visitor's typed input. The following sections cover the two ways to do this—you'll either use an array or a server-side script.

Using Arrays for Autocomplete

The Autocomplete widget requires a list of terms that jQuery UI uses to search for matches to the visitor's typed input. The simplest way to do this is to provide an array of items that jQuery UI will use. For example, maybe you have a question like "What's your favorite shade of red?" You could provide an array of color names, and supply that to the autocomplete() function like this:

```
var colors = ['Barn Red', 'Beetroot', 'Brick', 'Bright Maroon', 'Burgundy'];
$('#redInput').autocomplete( { source : colors } );
```

In other words, you start by creating an array—colors. Then you pass an object to the autocomplete() function with a property named source and a value that's the array: { source : colors }.

After this code runs, and a visitor types the letter *B* into the text field, a menu appears listing all the items in the array: "Barn Red," "Beetroot," "Brick," "Bright Maroon," and "Burgundy" (Figure 10-8, top). However, if the visitor next types *r* so "Br" is listed in the field, he'd see only the two colors that have "Br" in their names: "Brick," and "Bright Maroon" (Figure 10-8, bottom).

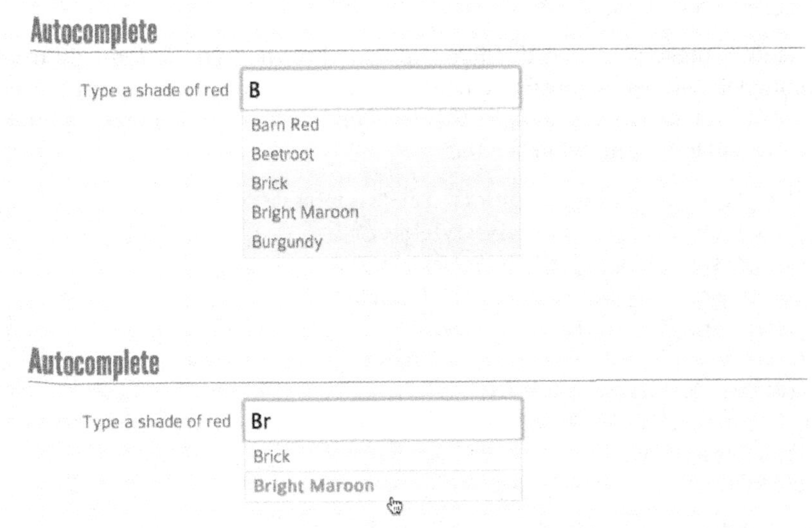

FIGURE 10-8

jQuery UI's Autocomplete widget makes typing common search terms easier by providing hints to words that match what the visitor types.

An array of only five items, however, doesn't really provide a lot of value. After all, if those were the only options, you might as well just use a select menu with those choices listed. Autocomplete is really most useful when you can provide your visitors *lots* of suggestions—more than would be comfortable in a normal drop-down menu. With lots of options, it's a good idea to create a separate JavaScript file that only contains the data you want to use as the source option for the widget. For example, say you wanted to provide autocomplete for a text field requiring an airport name. You could create a separate JavaScript file—*airports.js*, for example—that creates an array and assigns values to it, like this:

```
var airports = [
  'Aberdeen Regional Airport, Aberdeen, South Dakota',
  'Abilene Regional Airport, Abilene, Texas',
  'Abraham Lincoln Capital Airport, Springfield, Illinois',
  'Adak Airport, Adak Island, Alaska',
  'Adirondack Regional Airport, Saranca Lake, New York'
]; // lots more airports would go in here
```

This file would be large, and you wouldn't need to use this array on every page in your site, so it's best to put it into its own file and link to it only on the page that uses the autocomplete widget. You'd attach this file just as you would attach any JavaScript file to a page (page 15). For example:

```
<script src="airports.js"></script>
```

You need to make sure that this file is attached to the page *before* you use the autocomplete widget because you need to load the array before calling the auto-complete() function. For example, the JavaScript-related code in the web page's <head> would look something like this:

```
<link href="css/jquery-ui.min.css" rel="stylesheet">
<link href="css/site.css" rel="stylesheet">
<script src="js/jquery.min.js"></script>
<script src="js/jquery-ui.min.js"></script>
<script src="js/airports.js"></script>
<script>
$(document).ready(function() {
  $('#airport').autocomplete( { source : airports} );
}); // end ready
</script>
```

Notice that the *airports.js* file loads before the autocomplete() function runs so as to make sure the airports array is created first and can then be passed to the widget.

Using Separate Labels and Values

Choosing an option from the pop-up autocomplete menu instructs jQuery UI to write that item into the text field. For example, in the form pictured in Figure 10-8, if, after typing *B*, the visitor clicked "Bright Maroon" from the menu, then jQuery UI would fill out that text field with the words "Bright Maroon."

You can also instruct jQuery UI to write something *different* from what appears in the pop-up autocomplete menu. For example, with the airport example, say someone typed *Ab* in the text field. The Autocomplete widget would then display a list of three airports—Aberdeen Regional Airport, Abilene Regional Airport, and Abraham Lincoln Capital Airport. You can tell jQuery UI to write the airport code instead of the actual name, so if the visitor selected "Abilene Regional Airport," you could have jQuery UI write "ABI" in the text field.

To do this, you supply an array of *objects*. Each object contains two properties—label and value. The label is what the visitor sees in the pop-up autocomplete form, and the value is what jQuery UI actually adds to the form field after the visitor makes a selection. For example, in the airport example, the label will be the airport name, and the value is the airport code. For example, the object to identify the Abilene Airport would look like this:

```
{
  label : 'Abilene Regional Airport, Abilene, Texas',
  value : 'ABI'
}
```

And the array of airport values would start off like this:

```
var airports = [
  {
    label : 'Aberdeen Regional Airport, Aberdeen, South Dakota',
    value : 'ABR'
  },
  {
    label : 'Abilene Regional Airport, Abilene, Texas',
    value : 'ABI'
  },
  {
    label : 'Abraham Lincoln Capital Airport, Springfield, Illinois',
    value : 'SPI'
  },
  {
    label : 'Adak Airport, Adak Island, Alaska',
    value : 'ADK'
  },
  {
    label : 'Adirondack Regional Airport, Saranca Lake, New York',
    value : 'SLK'
  }
]; // lots more airports would go in here
```

NOTE Again, this is an incomplete list of U.S. airport names and codes. The actual *airports.js* file would be huge.

Each of the objects in this array has two properties. You still pass the array to the autocomplete() function the same way—jQuery UI is programmed to adjust how it works when it gets an array of objects like this.

```
$('#airport').autocomplete( { source : airports} );
```

When passed an array of objects, the Autocomplete widget now tries to match the visitor's input to a matching label in each object. However, when the visitor actually makes a choice from the drop-down menu, the second property in the selected object—the value property—is inserted into the form. You'll see an example of this on page 383 in step 12 of the tutorial.

Getting Autocomplete Data from the Server

The Autocomplete widget is most useful when you have lots of data that it can search through. Remember the example on page 372, where you supplied just six shades of red? That small number of options won't help a user's search much. Creating a file with a very large array isn't that easy, and in many cases, not realistic. For example, Amazon's autocomplete feature certainly doesn't rely on one large JavaScript file containing a list of every single product category and description on its site: that file would be immense, and loading it from the Web would take a really long time.

Many sites that include an autocomplete feature (like Google and Amazon) use server-side programming to send a much smaller list of autocomplete hints. Here's how it works:

1. **A visitor begins typing into a text field.**

2. **The visitor's input is sent to the server.**

   Using Ajax, the browser sends data to the server and waits for a response. In this case, the browser sends the text the visitor has typed so far.

3. **The server sends back an array of terms that match what the visitor has typed so far.**

   The server provides a list of matching terms. Usually, this is accomplished using server-side programming that searches a database, gets results, and formats those results into an array that's sent back to the browser.

4. **The list of matching terms appears in the autocomplete menu.**

As you can see, a lot of this magic happens thanks to Ajax, which lets you use JavaScript to send and receive information to a web server without needing to reload a new web page (you'll read all about Ajax in Chapter 13). The server-side programming part of this equation isn't what this book is about—to create server-side programs in PHP, Ruby, Python, and even in JavaScript (using Node.js), you'll need to turn to another source. However, here's how you use jQuery UI's autocomplete widget to talk to the server: instead of providing an array of possible search terms for the source property, you provide a URL pointing to a server-side script.

For example, say you had a text field that visitors use to search your company's catalog of 250,000 products. To make it easier for visitors to search, you want to add autocomplete to that field; however, your catalog of products is way too big to stuff into a single array in one JavaScript file. So instead, you set up a server-side program named *products.php* located in the root of your site. You could then specify the path to that file using the source property. Let's assume that you gave the input field an ID of "productSearch" like this:

```
<input type="text" id="productSearch" name="productSearch">
```

In the JavaScript for your page, you could then apply the autocomplete widget to this element and point to the server-side page like this:

```
$('#productSearch').autocomplete( { source : '/products.php'} );
```

You can also provide a complete URL including protocol and domain name like this:

```
$('#productSearch').autocomplete( { source : 'http://myCompany.com/products.
php'} );
```

When you supply an array of elements for the source option (described on page 372), jQuery UI filters that array to find items that contain the text the visitor has started typing; jQuery UI displays only those matching items from the array. The autocomplete widget behaves a little differently when supplying a URL for the source option. jQuery UI displays *all* of the data the server returns and doesn't filter that data for matches. For example, if a visitor typed *Light*, and the server returned an array containing "Dark," "Artichoke," and "Ostrich," jQuery UI would pop-up the autocomplete menu listing "Dark," "Artichoke," and "Ostrich."

In other words, it's entirely up to the server to return the correct data. That means you (or another programmer) needs to write all of the logic to generate the proper list and send it back to the browser. To help in that task, jQuery UI adds on a URL parameter to tell the server what it needs to search for. The parameter is named term, and its value is whatever the visitor has typed into the field. In the product search example, if the visitor typed *light*, jQuery UI would send a request to the server like this:

```
http://myCompany.com/products.php?term=light
```

It's up to the *products.php* page to then do something with that data—for example, search the database for products that somehow relate to light. This could be a literal search that displays only products with the name "light" in them: "light bulb," "lightning rod," and so on. Or, the program might be more complete and return products related to the concept of light, such as "fluorescent bulb," "antigravity machine," and so on. It's up to the programmer to decide how to process this search term and what data to send back.

> **NOTE** It's also possible to use the autocomplete feature to point to another domain and web server. However, due to Ajax's security limitations, that server must be set up to respond using a special format called JSONP. See page 483 for more about Ajax security and JSONP.

The server-side program needs to return this list of items formatted as an array:

```
[
  "lightbulb",
  "lighter",
  "lightning rod"
]
```

Alternatively, the server can return data as an array of objects containing a label and a value as described on page 374. However, the data must use the JSON format discussed on page 477; that is, all property names and strings must get double-quotes like this:

```
var airports = [
  {
    "label" : "Aberdeen Regional Airport, Aberdeen, South Dakota",
    "value" : "ABR"
  },
  {
    "label" : "Abilene Regional Airport, Abilene, Texas",
    "value" : "ABI"
  },
  {
    "label" : "Abraham Lincoln Capital Airport, Springfield, Illinois",
    "value" : "SPI"
  },
  {
    "label" : "Adak Airport, Adak Island, Alaska",
    "value" : "ADK"
  },
  {
    "label" : "Adirondack Regional Airport, Saranca Lake, New York",
    "value" : "SLK"
  }
];
```

Autocomplete Options

There aren't a lot of options for controlling how the Autocomplete widget works. The most important (and required) option is source, as discussed on pages 372-378. However, there are a couple of other options that can come in handy. As with other widget options, the autocomplete options should be passed as part of an object to the autocomplete() function. For example:

```
$('#airport').autocomplete({
  source : '/airportSearch.php',
  delay : 500,
  minLength : 2
});
```

Here are the most useful options:

- **source.** The most important and only required option. Used to pass either an array or a URL of a server-side page. The array is either an array of values or an array of objects with label and value properties (page 374). If it's a URL, the server-side program must return data formatted like an array (page 372).

- **delay.** When using a server-side program as the source for the autocomplete data, jQuery UI sends a request to the server each time a visitor types into the autocomplete field. Multiple, fast requests can slow down the server and the autocomplete widget's response. You can build in a slight delay, so your web server isn't hit by so many requests from the widget, by setting this option to a number in milliseconds. For example, to wait half a second before sending a request, you can set the delay option like this:

```
delay : 500
```

- **minLength.** This option specifies the minimum number of letters required before the autocomplete widget begins making suggestions. If the autocomplete data sources could be hundreds of thousands of records, you might want to set this minimum length to three characters. After all, if a visitor types *a* into the field, you could potentially get thousands of autocomplete suggestions from a large data source.

NOTE You can find a complete list of options, plus additional features for the autocomplete widget, by visiting *http://api.jqueryui.com/autocomplete/*.

◼ jQuery UI Form Widget Tutorial

In this tutorial, you'll start with a basic flight reservation form: it contains text fields, radio buttons, and the <button> element (Figure 10-9, top). By adding jQuery UI to the page and applying jQuery UI's form widgets to the page, we'll get a more attractive, interactive, and functional form (Figure 10-9, bottom).

NOTE See the note on page 12 for information on how to download the tutorial files.

1. **In your text editor, open the file *form.html* in the *chapter10* folder.**

    This file already contains a link to all of the jQuery and jQuery UI files and the $(document).ready() function (page 160). The HTML for the form on this page looks like this:

```
<form>
  <div>
    <label for="departure" class="label">Pick a departure date</label>
    <input type="text" id="departure" name="departure">
  </div>
  <div>
    <label for="airport" class="label">Find an airport</label>
    <input type="text" id="airport" name="airport">
  </div>
  <div>
    <label for="meal" class="label">Meal Options</label>
    <select name="meal" id="meal">
      <option>No meal</option>
      <option>Vegan</option>
      <option>Gluten Free</option>
```

```
      <option>Vegetarian</option>
      <option>Meat eater</option>
    </select>
  </div>
  <div id="bags">
    <p class="label">Number of bags to check</p>
    <input type="radio" id="none" name="bags" checked="checked">
    <label for="none">0</label>
    <input type="radio" id="one" name="bags">
    <label for="one">1</label>
    <input type="radio" id="two" name="bags">
    <label for="two">2</label>
  </div>
  <div id="seatTypes">
    <p class="label">Type of seat you'd like</p>
    <input type="checkbox" id="aisle" name="aisle">
    <label for="aisle">Aisle</label>
    <input type="checkbox" id="window" name="window">
    <label for="window">Window</label>
    <input type="checkbox" id="exit" name="exit">
    <label for="exit">Exit Row</label>
    <input type="checkbox" id="any" name="any">
    <label for="any">Any seat</label>
  </div>
  <div>
    <button id="next">Continue reservation process</button>
  </div>
</form>
```

The important form elements—the one's you'll apply jQuery UI to—are in bold. You'll start by adding a data picker to the first field. For the next step, note that the <input> element has the ID departure.

2. **Inside the $(document).ready() function, select the input element:**

   ```
   $('#departure')
   ```

   Now you need to apply the Datepicker widget.

3. **Type a period, followed by datepicker(); so the code now looks like this:**

   ```
   $('#departure').datepicker();
   ```

   That's all that's needed to add a pop-up calendar date picker to the page. However, if you save the file and view it in a web browser now, you'll see that you can pick dates prior to today. Obviously, you can't exactly get on a flight that happened last week, so you want to make sure you can't make a reservation earlier than today's date.

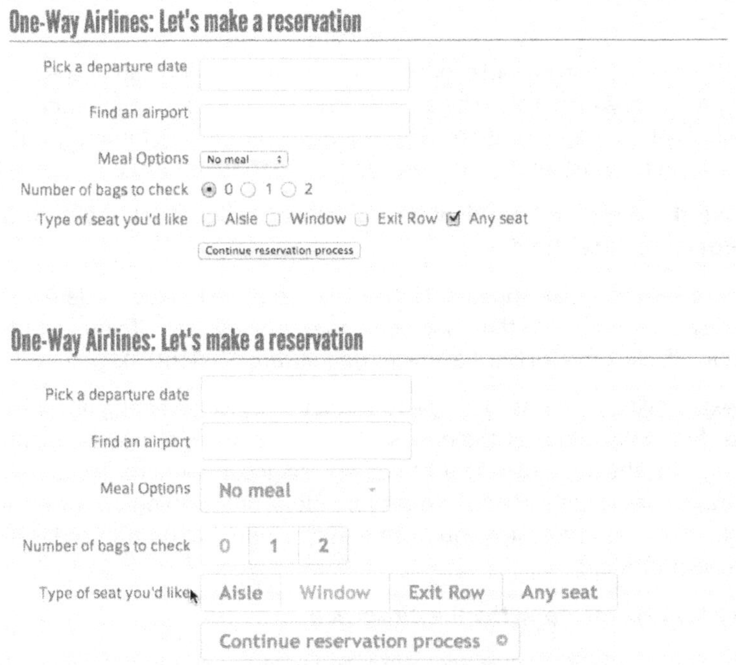

FIGURE 10-9

jQuery UI can make a drab form, match the look and feel of your entire application. It can transform form controls like select menus, radio buttons, and check boxes (which are normally styled by your browser) into attractive and attention-grabbing user interface elements.

FIGURE 10-9

jQuery UI can make a drab form, match the look and feel of your entire application. It can transform form controls like select menus, radio buttons, and check boxes (which are normally styled by your browser) into attractive and attention-grabbing user interface elements.

4. **Click inside the `datepicker()` function and type a `{`. Press return twice and type `}` so that the code looks like this:**

   ```
   $('#departure').datepicker({

   });
   ```

   The `{ }` is an empty object literal, and you'll specify options for the widget by adding properties inside it. First, set the minimum date for making a reservation.

5. **On the blank line, inside the object literal type `minDate : 0`.**

   The value for the `minDate` option indicates the number of days from today: 0 days from today *is* today; -7 days from today would be last week, and 7 days from today would be next week.

   You can also specify the *maximum* date allowable by the date picker. In this case, the airline doesn't keep track of flights past 1 year from the current day, so you'll prevent someone from selecting dates later than that.

6. **Type a comma at the end of the last line you typed, hit Return, and type maxDate : '+1y' so the code looks like this:**

```
$('#departure').datepicker({
  minDate : 0,
  maxDate : '+1y'
});
```

Both `minDate` and `maxDate` let you use a number to indicate a specific number of days, but you can also use a string value that includes a number and a letter to indicate a length of time: `'+1y'` means 1 year in the future, `'-2w'` means 2 weeks in the past, and `'+1m +10d'` means 1 month and 10 days in the future.

7. **Save the page and preview it in a web browser. Click inside the "Pick a departure date" field.**

A pop-up calendar appears. Notice that you can't select a date earlier than today's date or more than one year from today's date (if you want to see for yourself, click the forward arrow to go forward 12 months).

Next, you'll use the Autocomplete widget to make selecting an airport easier. But first, take a look at the data source you're going to use. As mentioned on page 372, the autocomplete() function can accept either a JavaScript array of data, or data sent back from a server-side script running on a web server. To keep this example easier, you'll use a small amount of data stored in a separate JavaScript file.

8. **In a text editor, open the file *airports.js*.**

This is a simple JavaScript file containing an array assignment: it creates an array named `airports` filled with objects made up of two properties: `label` and `value`. The label will appear in the pop-up autocomplete menu, while the value will be written to the text field when the visitor selects an item from the list.

Obviously this file is not a complete list, just a small amount of data to try this widget out. To access the data in this file, you'll need to link it to the page.

9. **In your text editor, open the *form.html* file. Below the last <script> line—<script src ="../_js/jquery-ui.min.js"></script>—add one other script tag linking to the data file:**

```
<script src="airports.js"></script>
```

This line loads the external JavaScript file, and once it's loaded, the JavaScript will run. In this case, the file just creates an array full of data, which you can then use in the autocomplete widget.

10. **Add an empty line after the datepicker widget code you added earlier, and type:**

```
$('#airport').autocomplete({ source : 'airports.json'});
```

The text field for collecting an airport name has an ID of `airport`, so `$('#airport')` selects that field, and `.autocomplete()` applies the widget to that fields.

11. **Save the page and preview it in a web browser. Click inside the "Find an airport" field and type *Port*.**

    An autocomplete menu appears listing suggestions for airports that might be what you're looking for. Notice that the widget matches items that have "Port" *anywhere* in their label: "La Guardia Air*port*," for example.

12. **Click the "Portland International Airport, Portland, OR" item.**

    Notice that "PDX" appears in the text field. That's because you supplied an array of objects with labels and values. The label that appears in the drop-down menu was "Portland International Airport, Portland, OR", but the value added to the text field by the jQuery UI widget is "PDX," the airport code.

    Next, you'll change that drop-down menu into a thing of user interface beauty.

13. **Return to your text editor and the *form.html* file. Add the following code after the last line of code you added in step 10:**

    ```
    $('#meal').selectmenu();
    ```

    You may have the urge to type more code, but that's all you need to do to transform the select menu. If you save and preview the page, however, you'll notice that the menu looks a bit weird. Actually, the first item on the menu isn't listed completely! Unless the labels in your select menu are very short, you'll need to set a width for this widget.

14. **Inside the parentheses for the `selectmenu()` function, type `{ width : 200 }` so the line of code looks like this:**

    ```
    $('#meal').selectmenu( { width : 200 } );
    ```

    The `selectmenu` widget's `width` option (page 362) lets you set the width of the menu on the page. In this case, 200 means 200 pixels wide, though you can use other dimensions and types of measurement such as percentages or ems, as described on page 363. Save the page and check it out in a web browser. Who says programming's hard?

    Next, you'll convert the radio buttons and checkboxes into something that more closely resembles the rest of your form.

15. **In your text editor, add the following two lines after the code you added in the last step:**

    ```
    $('#bags').buttonset();
    $('#seatTypes').buttonset();
    ```

    The `buttonset()` function works for both radio buttons and checkboxes. The last step is to convert the `<button>` element into a jQuery UI button.

16. **Add one more line of code to your program:**

```
$('#next').button();
```

This converts the drab HTML button to something that looks a lot more like this form and matches the look of the radio buttons and checkboxes. You can also add jQuery UI icons to <button> elements, as described on page 367. Let's do that next.

17. **Inside the parentheses in the button() function add:**

```
{
  icons : {
    secondary : 'ui-icon-circle-arrow-e'
  }
}
```

The final JavaScript code for the page should look like this:

```
$(document).ready(function() {
  $('#departure').datepicker({
    minDate : 0,
    maxDate : '+1y'
  });
  $('#airport').autocomplete({ source : airports});
  $('#meal').selectmenu({width : 200});
  $('#bags').buttonset();
  $('#seatTypes').buttonset();
  $('#next').button({
    icons : {
      secondary : 'ui-icon-circle-arrow-e'
    }
  });
}); // end ready
```

In just a few lines of code, you've completely transformed the look and functionality of a web form.

18. **Save the page and preview it in a web browser.**

The page should look like the bottom image in Figure 10-9. If your page doesn't look like this one, make sure the code you have matches the code in step 17. You can also check the JavaScript console (page 18) for any errors; however, be aware that jQuery often hides errors from the console, so it can make it harder to find errors in your jQuery code.

You can find a completed version of this tutorial in the *complete_form.html* file in the *chapter10* folder.

Customizing the Look of jQuery UI

jQuery UI widgets share a unified appearance—the date picker looks similar to tabbed panels, which looks similar to a dialog box, which looks similar to a tooltip. If you pieced together a bunch of separate jQuery plug-ins by different authors to get these same widgets, you'd spend a lot of time messing around with CSS to get the different plug-ins to look related. The consistent presentation throughout the different jQuery UI widgets means you can build a web application with a unified look without spending countless hours handcrafting CSS.

However, what if you already have a look for your site and you want to make jQuery UI fit in with your existing design? For this situation, the jQuery UI team has put together lots of helpful advice as well as a cool online tool for even more assistance. This chapter covers how to override or modify existing jQuery UI styles and how to create new ones.

■ Introducing ThemeRoller

There are a lot of moving pieces in jQuery UI: creating all of the CSS to make each widget look great (and visually related) is a big task. Fortunately, the jQuery UI team put together an online tool called ThemeRoller. This tool lets you choose among 24 themes developed by designers for use with jQuery UI. It also provides tools to modify an existing theme, letting you pick fonts and colors that match the look of your site.

To use ThemeRoller, visit *http://jqueryui.com/themeroller/* (Figure 11-1). You can look at the collection of pre-designed themes by clicking the Gallery tab in the lefthand sidebar (circled). The main body of the page provides demonstrations of the different jQuery UI widgets: selecting a theme from the lefthand list immediately applies that theme to the widgets on the page, providing an instant preview of their design.

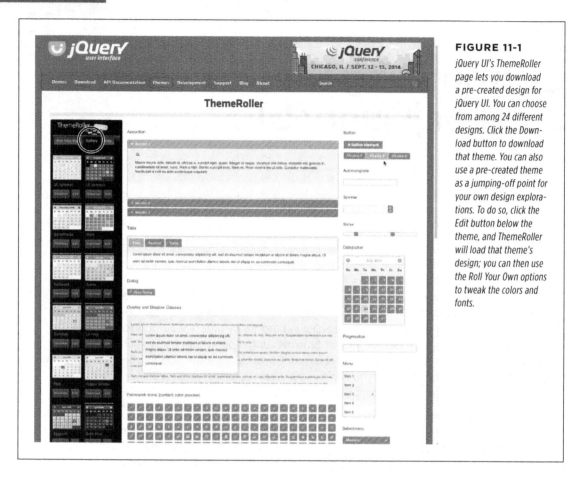

FIGURE 11-1

jQuery UI's ThemeRoller page lets you download a pre-created design for jQuery UI. You can choose from among 24 different designs. Click the Download button to download that theme. You can also use a pre-created theme as a jumping-off point for your own design explorations. To do so, click the Edit button below the theme, and ThemeRoller will load that theme's design; you can then use the Roll Your Own options to tweak the colors and fonts.

If you like the look of a theme in the gallery, click the Download button below its thumbnail preview in the sidebar at left to go to the jQuery Download Builder described on page 302. On that page, select the widgets, interactions, and effects you want to include and then click the Download button at the bottom of the page to download the files.

NOTE Turn to page 302 for a complete description of how to download and organize the jQuery UI files to use in your site.

If you want to add jQuery UI to a website you've already built, you can use ThemeRoller to create a custom theme that matches your site's design. Click the Roll Your Own tab in the left sidebar (circled in Figure 11-2): this tool provides access to settings for fonts, colors, and other options. Settings are grouped into categories, which you can open or close by clicking the disclosure arrow to the left of the category name. Here's a list of categories and their options:

- The **Font Settings** category lets you specify fonts, along with font size and weight. Type the name of the font(s) you want to use into the Family field. Fonts are usually specified as a group of three options: the font you want to load first, a fallback font, and then a fallback font type. If the first font isn't available on your visitor's computer, then the second font is used; if that font is unavailable, then a generic font type (serif, sans-serif, monospace, or fantasy) is picked.

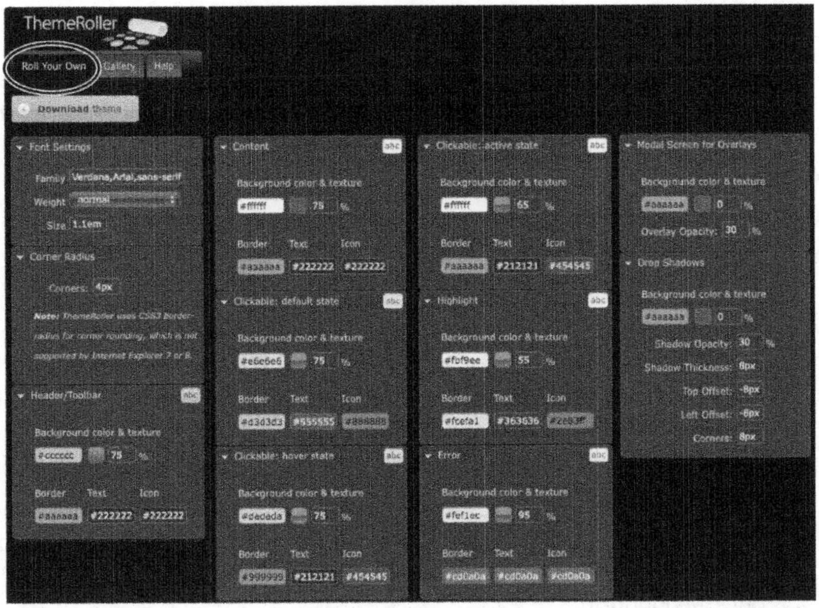

FIGURE 11-2

To open a category of settings, click the disclosure arrow next to the category name. Normally all of the categories are closed, but here they're shown open and (to fit on this page), side by side. On the ThemeRoller site, the categories are actually stacked on top of each other.

Use the same list of fonts that you're currently using on your site. For example, if your site uses Helvetica Neue as its primary font, you could type the following: *"Helvetica Neue", Arial, sans-serif.*" (When you use a font name with more than one word—Helvetica Neue, for example—you must place quotes around the font name.) jQuery UI applies the same font to all widgets and their parts, including the font used for tabs and panels. Otherwise, you can specify different fonts for different components, as described on page 392.

NOTE If you're using a web font that's on your site or delivered by a service like TypeKit or Google Fonts—or any font that's not on your computer—that font won't display in the ThemeRoller preview.

The font weight can be either "normal" or "bold." Selecting "bold" doesn't make all of the text inside jQuery UI widgets bold—it applies boldface to certain elements like the text in tabs, buttons, select menus, and accordion headers. Other text is left as "normal."

The font size is the base font for all jQuery UI widgets. Text inside some widgets will be larger. For example, the header text in dialog boxes and the text in tooltips are larger than the text in other widgets.

- **Corner Radius.** Most jQuery UI widgets have corners, and the corner radius setting lets you make these corners more or less rounded. Setting the value to 0 creates square corners; progressively higher values make the corners more rounded. Type different values in ThemeRoller until you find a look you like.

- The **Header/Toolbar** category lets you set colors and patterns for the header in a date picker or dialog box, or the color in a progressbar or slider. This category provides six different settings: background color, background texture, background texture opacity, border color, text color, and icon color. These same six settings appear in most of the other categories as well, so it's good to be familiar with them:

  - **Background color.** Click this box, and a color picker pops up. Use the color picker to select a hue (click on the outer wheel) and then a specific color (click inside the inner box). See Figure 11-3.

  - **Background texture.** jQuery UI can insert different patterns into the background of an element, such as horizontal or diagonal stripes. Click the text box to open a palette of textures. Click the one you like, or click the solid pattern in the upper-left corner to assign no texture. The texture is achieved by using a small image file in the background. See Figure 11-3.

  - **Background texture opacity** determines how strongly the pattern shows. Set the opacity to 0 and the pattern won't show at all; a value of 10 adds a very subtle pattern; and values above 75% make the pattern really stand out. See Figure 11-3.

  - **Border color** sets the color of the border that appears around the header or toolbar. Click the box for this setting, and a color picker appears. If you don't like having a border, just set this color to match the background color, and the border will blend into the background. (The same color picker that appears for all color settings, and it's shown in Figure 11-3.)

  - **Text color.** Click this button to open a color picker to select a color for the text inside in the header or toolbar.

  - **Icon color.** Some widgets display icons. For example, the datepicker widget includes "Previous month" and "Next month" icons in its pop-up calendar. To set the colors of those icons, click the icon color box and use the color picker to select a color that fits in well with your site.

NOTE For all color settings, you can also click inside the color setting box and type a hexadecimal color value, like #e64c4c.

- **Content.** The Content category lets you set background, border, and text colors for the content areas of widgets. These include the panels in accordions and tabbed panel widgets, the menu items in the Selectmenu widget, and the calendar in the datepicker widget. The options are the same as for the Header/Toolbar category—background color, background texture, background texture opacity, and border, text, and icon colors.

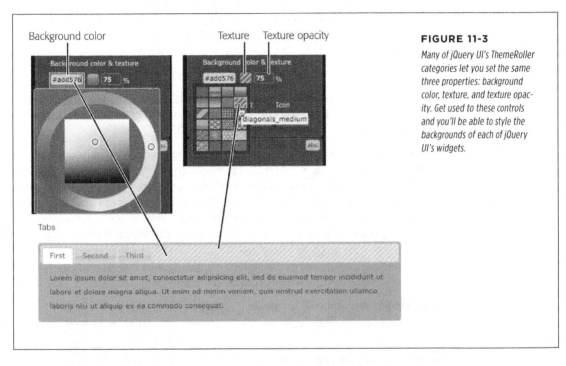

Background color Texture Texture opacity

FIGURE 11-3

Many of jQuery UI's ThemeRoller categories let you set the same three properties: background color, texture, and texture opacity. Get used to these controls and you'll be able to style the backgrounds of each of jQuery UI's widgets.

Tabs

- **Clickable items.** ThemeRoller provides three categories for clickable elements, which include any part of a widget that you click to make the widget work: accordion headers, tabs, buttons, dates on a Datepicker calendar, icons, buttons in a dialog box, and the select menu. The three categories map to the three states of a clickable item: the "default state" (this is how the clickable item looks when the page first loads), the "hover state" (when a visitor mouses over a clickable item), and the "active state." The active state refers to a selected tab in a group of tabbed panels, the currently selected accordion header in an accordion widget, the selected date in a datepicker widget, or a selected button widget (for example, a selected radio button on a form). You have the same six styling options for each category of clickable items: the same ones you'll use for the Header/Toolbar category as described on page 388: background color, background texture, background texture opacity, and border, text, and icon colors.

- The **Highlight** and **Error** categories don't actually format any of the widgets out of the box. However, they do create two CSS classes—`.ui-state-highlight` and `.ui-state-error`—that you can apply to widgets or to any element on a page. For example the dialog widget (page 305) lets you assign a class name to a dialog box. So if you wanted to open a special dialog box with the Highlight styling, you just pass the class name (without the period) to the dialog() function like this:

```
$('#dialogDiv').dialog({ dialogClass : 'ui-state-highlight' });
```

Likewise, you could use the .ui-state-error style to format an element on a page that you want to stand out. For example, if someone incorrectly filled out a form field, you could select the label for that field and dynamically apply the error class to it:

```
$('#userNameLabel').addClass('ui-state-error');
```

In this case, you're not even using a jQuery widget—just the class style created by ThemeRoller. In fact, you can apply any jQuery UI class to other elements on the page. (You'll read about that on page 392.)

- **Modal Screen for overlays.** You can use the Dialog widget (page 305) to create modal dialog boxes. A *modal* dialog prevents the visitor from interacting with anything else on the page until the modal box is closed. It's used for important messages and actions like "Are you sure you want to delete your Facebook profile forever?" jQuery UI darkens the rest of the screen when it opens a modal dialog by placing a semi-transparent "overlay" between the modal dialog and the rest of the page. You can control how that screen looks by changing the background color, texture, and opacity (the same settings used for the background of the Header/Toolbar category described on page 388).

- **Drop shadows.** Ignore this category: it isn't used for any of the jQuery UI widgets—even the Tooltip widget, which *does* have a drop shadow. Strange, but true.

> **TIP** As you use jQuery UI's ThemeRoller to create a new jQuery UI design, the URL in the location bar of the browser changes: each change you make to the theme is replicated by a change in the URL. Why? Because ThemeRoller is cleverly creating a URL that will exactly duplicate your custom theme. This means you can bookmark that URL so it's easy to return to ThemeRoller with all your theme's settings in place. You can also copy the URL and email it to a friend or colleague so he can quickly replicate the theme you designed.

■ Downloading and Using Your New Theme

Once you've crafted a new jQuery UI theme, click the Download Theme button at left on the ThemeRoller page. This button takes you to the Download Builder page (Figure 11-2). If you want *all* of the widgets and functionality that jQuery UI offers, simply click the download button at the bottom of the page. However, if you want just a subset—just the Dialog, Datepicker, and Tabs—then uncheck the widgets, effects, and interactions you're not interested in, and then click the Download button.

Adding a New Theme to an Existing Website

If you're already using jQuery UI on a site, and just want to update the look with a new theme, all you need are new styles. You can go through the same process described in the previous section to create and download the new theme. This time, however, when you get to the Download Builder page (Figure 11-2) make sure you select all the same options—widgets, interactions, and effects—that you're currently using. If you don't, you'll get either more or less CSS than you need.

For example, if you're using all of the jQuery UI widgets on your site, but turn off, say, dialog in the download builder, you won't download the CSS required to style the dialog widget. Likewise, if you're only using the dialog widget, but download the entire jQuery UI feature set, the new CSS you get will have way *more* CSS than you actually need, which means visitors will have to waste time downloading un-needed CSS.

Once you download the new copy of jQuery UI, you'll have files you don't need (for example, if you're already using jQuery UI, then you don't need to replace the JavaScript files already in place). The only things you need to replace are the *images* folder and the CSS files:

1. **Replace the old jQuery UI CSS file or files with the new theme.**

    As mentioned on page 304, jQuery UI includes six CSS files. Most of these are duplicates in different formats. In a nutshell, the only one you *really* need is the *jquery-ui.min.css* file. This file contains all of the CSS jQuery needs in a smaller (minified) file. In general, you should use files that have *.min* in their name, because they're the smallest. Place the new CSS file wherever you had the old one—in a *css* folder in the root of the site, for example.

2. **Replace the old jQuery UI *images* folder with the new *images* folder.**

    Different themes use different color icons, as well as different styles of background patterns. The icon and graphics for the new theme probably won't match your old theme so you need to replace the old images. The jQuery UI images folder should be located wherever you placed the jQuery UI CSS file or files—this could be in a *css* folder in the root of your site, or a *jquery-ui* folder. Regardless, whichever folder you place the jQuery CSS file in, place the images folder there too.

NOTE   When downloading a new theme, check to make sure the version of jQuery UI hasn't changed. jQuery UI changes frequently, so if you decide to update your theme, jQuery UI JavaScript might have changed. In this case, you *should* replace the CSS, images, and the jQuery UI JavaScript file (*jquery-ui.min.js*) in your site.

More About the jQuery UI CSS Files

When you download jQuery UI, you get six CSS files. These are actually two groups of three files: one group is a minified or compressed version (*jquery-ui.min.css*, for example), and the other set contains easy-to-read CSS files (*jquery-ui.css*, for example).

As mentioned earlier, the minified versions are the best for production (going onto your web server) because they download more quickly. The other files are great for opening in a text editor so you can see how the jQuery UI CSS is put together.

The largest of the three files—*jquery-ui.css*—is just a combination of the two others (*jquery-ui.structure.css* and *jquery-ui.theme.css*). The jQuery UI team split the full code into two separate files because there are certain CSS rules that apply to *all* widgets regardless of the font or colors used. These rules provide the "structure" of the jQuery UI widgets and interactions, including properties like the z-index of a dialog box, or position property of a tooltip. These rules are in a file named *jquery-ui-structure.css*.

But other styles change depending on the theme. For example, the font family used for widgets and the background color of an accordion header are specific to a particular theme. These styles are in the *jquery-ui-theme.css* file. You can open this file and see the specific properties that affect text and backgrounds.

Accordingly, you should link to the *jquery-ui.min.css* file on your site's pages, but use the *jquery-ui-theme.css* file as a way to investigate the style names and properties for the various jQuery UI widgets.

■ Overriding jQuery UI Styles

jQuery UI's themes look good, but they may not always work for you. For example, when you use ThemeRoller (page 385) to set up the font-family, you get just one choice for dialog boxes, date pickers, tabbed panels, and so on. What if you want to use one font for the tabs in a panel, and another for the panel content?

There are several different approaches to solving this problem, but there's one thing you should definitely *not* do—edit the jQuery UI CSS files themselves. The jQuery UI CSS styles change when new versions of jQuery UI come out, so if you edit the *jquery-ui.css* file, and then need to update jQuery UI, you'll have the difficult task of replicating every change you made to the original CSS file in the new *jquery-ui.css* file.

Even if you don't update jQuery UI, you won't be able to use the ThemeRoller to create a new design without again painstakingly copying over your original changes to the new theme file.

Instead, you should create new jQuery UI styles in a separate CSS file. This file could be a separate CSS file just for your updates to jQuery UI, or it could be the main style sheet for your site. It's probably easiest to just add new styles to your site's main style sheet. As you'll read in a moment, there are a few techniques for overriding jQuery UI styles, but they all rely on using the CSS *specificity* concept. You'll see more about that in a moment, but for now, keep this in mind: link the style sheet you'll use to override jQuery UI's styles *after* you load the jQuery UI style sheet:

```
<link href="css/jquery-ui.min.css" rel="stylesheet">
<link href="css/site.css" rel="stylesheet">
```

By placing your site-specific style sheet after the jQuery UI style sheet, you can freely create a style with the *exact* same name as a style in the jQuery UI style sheet. The style you create will take precedence because it's created after the same style in the jQuery UI style sheet.

Understanding Specificity

CSS styles often interact and conflict. You can have more than one style apply to the same page element and the browser determines which properties from which styles to apply. This is the cascade part of Cascading Style Sheets, and one really important concept in CSS is *specificity*. In CSS, the more specific rule always wins out. Here are some of the most important specificity rules:

- **ID selectors are more specific than classes, and classes are more specific than element selectors.** Here's an example:

  ```
  <p id="susan" class="person">Susan Jones: CSS Superstar</p>
  ```

  In this HTML, the <p> tag has an ID and a class. Now, suppose this is the CSS:

  ```
  #susan {
    color: green;
    font-size: 24px;
  }
  .person {
    color: blue;
    text-align: center;
    font-weight: bold;
  }
  p {
    color: orange;
    font-weight: normal;
    font-family: Arial, sans-serif;
  }
  ```

  All three styles apply to the paragraph, and all three have a `color` property. But, because ID selectors are more specific, this paragraph will use the color green, as the ID selector overrides the other two styles. However, when there is no conflict—for example, the `text-align` property in the `.person` class style—that property applies no matter which style it comes from.

  In this example, the paragraph's text will be 24px in size and have a green color (from the #susan selector), be bold and centered (from the `.person` selector), and use the font Arial (from the p selector).

  Because jQuery UI uses class styles to apply formatting, knowing how specificity works with different types of selectors is important.

- **Rules that are defined later win.** If the same rule name appears in two different style sheets (or even in the same style sheet), the one that's defined last wins. That's why you should link the jQuery UI style sheet first. You can add new styles with the same name as jQuery UI classes in a second style sheet and override those from jQuery UI. For example, in the jQuery UI style sheet, you'll find a style like this:

```
/* in jquery-ui stylesheet */
 .ui-widget-content a {
    color: #222222;
}
```

If you link your site-specific style sheet *after* the jQuery UI style sheet, you could add this style to that site-specific style sheet and completely override the jQuery UI styling for this element:

```
/* in the site-specific stylesheet */
.ui-widget-content a {
    color: #FF0;
}
```

- **Specificity adds up.** Using descendant selectors is a powerful way to create very specific styles. A browser adds up all of the selectors listed in a descendant selector to come up with a sum total for that rules specificity. A simple way to calculate this is to consider ID selectors as being worth 100 points, class selectors worth 10 points, and element selectors worth 1. For example, a style with the selector #main a will override a style named .ui-state-default a because the first is worth 101 points (one ID and one element) and the second just 11 points (one class and one element). In other words, you can override a jQuery UI rule by using a descendant selector that provides more points.

- **In dire times, use the !important rule.** CSS includes a sort of "nuclear option," called the *!important* rule. If you add !important after the value in a CSS declaration that value overrides any other style no matter how specific. For example, say in the CSS listed in the first bullet point above, you had another p style like this:

```
p {
    color: orange !important;
    font-weight: normal !important;
    font-family: Arial, sans-serif !important;
}
```

Because each of the properties in this style has the !important rule, those properties override the values in the more specific #susan and .person rules. Using !important should really just be used as a last resort. If you use it really frequently, you'll end up with styles full of !important rules, and it will be difficult for you to then sort out the specificity among your styles. (If every property in every style had an !important rule, then the normal specificity rules would apply: that is, IDs trump classes, which trump element selectors.)

How jQuery UI Styles Widgets

jQuery UI uses a modular approach to styling its widgets: instead of creating a single `.ui-dialog` style with all of the styling for jQuery dialog boxes, the look of a widget is built up from multiple class styles. For example, there's a `.ui-widget` style that's applied to all the widgets. It contains some very basic styling:

```
.ui-widget {
    font-family: Verdana,Arial,sans-serif;
    font-size: 1.1em;
}
```

Because this class is applied to all widgets, they all share the same basic font and font size. But for the dialog widget, jQuery applies many other classes as well. For example, for the dialog box alone, you'll find these classes applied to the outer container:

```
class="ui-dialog ui-widget ui-widget-content
ui-corner-all ui-front ui-draggable ui-resizable"
```

Each of those classes contributes one small aspect of the overall look of the dialog box. By combining multiple classes like this, jQuery UI is able to re-use them to build up the look of different widgets. For example, here are the classes used on the outer container for a jQuery UI menu (page 343):

```
class="ui-menu ui-widget ui-widget-content"
```

Notice that two of the classes—`ui-widget` and `ui-widget-content`—are also used in the dialog box. These two styles include some basic formatting shared by these two widgets.

As you've seen, it's really easy to turn a simple `<div>` element into a complex dialog box (page 305), or a nested list into a drop-down menu (page 343). Behind the scenes, jQuery UI takes your simple HTML and adds layers of divs, spans, and other HTML objects to create the final onscreen appearance. As a result, you can't tell how the styling occurs by looking at your HTML or even the jQuery UI style sheets. You have to dig into the *rendered* HTML (that is, the HTML, after jQuery UI has done its fancy magic on it) to see how jQuery UI formats its widgets.

The best way to analyze how jQuery UI applies classes to widgets is to use your browser's built-in inspection tools. Most browsers have a way to see the rendered HTML. In Chrome, for example, right-click a jQuery UI widget and choose Inspect Element. The console opens at the bottom of the browser window and displays the rendered HTML in the Elements tag (Figure 11-4).

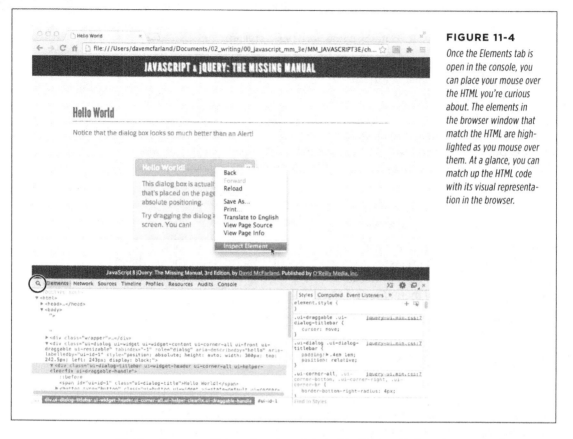

FIGURE 11-4

Once the Elements tab is open in the console, you can place your mouse over the HTML you're curious about. The elements in the browser window that match the HTML are highlighted as you mouse over them. At a glance, you can match up the HTML code with its visual representation in the browser.

Clicking the magnifying glass icon (circled in Figure 11-4) activates the inspection tool. With the magnifying glass selected, you can clik any element on the page and the corresponding HTML is selected in the Elements tab. This is a great way to identify the header in a dialog box, for example, and see which classes are applied to it.

Once you've identified the classes, you can create styles of the same name in your own style sheet. For example, using the inspector in Chrome, you can see that the HTML used to create the title of a dialog box includes a class named .ui-dialog-title (Figure 11-5). To change the headline in dialog boxes to red, you can add a style to your site's style sheet like this:

```
.ui-dialog-title {
  color: red;
}
```

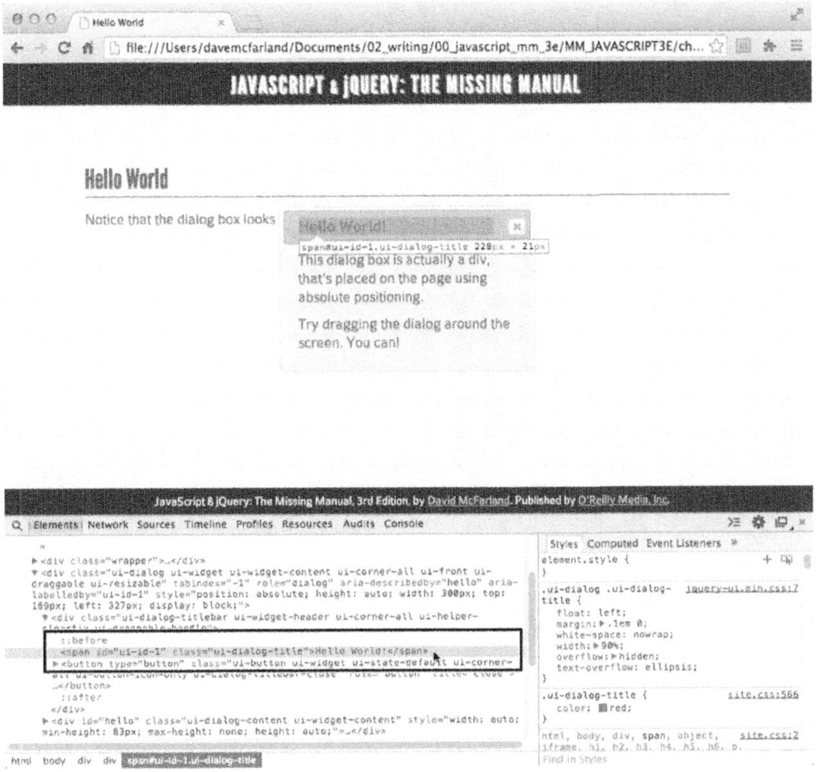

FIGURE 11-5

Using the Inspector tool (the magnifying glass), you can quickly identify the rendered HTML associated with elements in the browser window. Here's the HTML that jQuery UI produces to create the title for a dialog box.

jQuery UI Interactions and Effects

jQuery UI has more to offer than just user interface widgets. It also provides a handful of useful features for adding interactivity to your web pages and web applications. These jQuery UI *interactions* provide the tools to let visitors move elements on a page. For example, some widgets are draggable and droppable, which means visitors can drag an element and drop it onto another element—think dragging a file to the trash, or dragging a product to a shopping cart. You can also make lists of sortable items that the user can rearrange by simply dragging an item to a new position in the list—think to-do lists or music playlists.

In addition, jQuery UI includes a suite of effects that you can use to add visual flair to your site with high-quality animations. For example, you can grab a visitor's attention by making an element's background color flash, make a page element bounce, shake, scale, or explode. You'll learn about effects on page 438.

The Draggable Widget

Dragging is second nature when you're on a computer—dragging files into folders or the trash, dragging windows to make room for more windows, and so on. These interactions are natural for a generation who has grown up with personal computers and mice. jQuery UI brings this same type of interaction to web pages with its draggable widget and its companion, the droppable widget (discussed on page 412).

The Draggable widget lets you make any page element movable. You've already seen it in use in jQuery UI's dialog widget (page 305): jQuery UI's dialog boxes pop onto the screen but can be freely dragged to another spot. You can use the draggable widget in conjunction with the droppable widget to create an interactive shopping cart. Shoppers drag images of products onto a shopping cart on the page, and those items are added to the cart.

Adding the Draggable Widget to a Web Page

You can turn anything on a page into a draggable element. Of course, it should make sense that a visitor would move that element. For example, making paragraphs of text movable won't make a page more readable and won't benefit your visitors. But making pop-up dialog boxes movable makes sense, and movable game pieces are a must for any web-based checkers game.

Getting started with the draggable widget is easy:

1. **Follow the steps on page 304 to attach the CSS and JavaScript files.**

   Remember that jQuery UI has its own CSS and JavaScript files, and that the jQuery UI JavaScript file should be linked to *after* the jQuery JavaScript file.

2. **Add jQuery's $(document).ready() function to your page or to another external JavaScript file:**

   ```
   $(document).ready(function() {

   }); // end ready
   ```

   As discussed on page 160, this step is necessary only if you're putting your JavaScript code in the page's <head>, before the majority of the HTML. Some programmers put their JavaScript code at the bottom of the page, before the closing </body> tag; in that case, you can skip the $(document).ready() function.

3. **Use jQuery to select a page element and apply the draggable widget to it:**

   ```
   $(document).ready(function() {
     $('#dialog').draggable();
   }); // end ready
   ```

   In this example, you're selecting a single item using an ID selector. However, if you want to make a bunch of elements on the page draggable, you can apply a class to each of their HTML tags—<div class="draggable">, for example—and then use a class selector to apply the draggable function to all of those tags in one step:

   ```
   $('.draggable').draggable();
   ```

4. **Save your files and preview them in a browser.**

   That's all there is to it. However, you'll probably want to customize the dragging experience. Fortunately, jQuery UI provides many different options for configuring this widget. You'll learn about those on page 402.

Draggable Mini-Tutorial

Time to take this widget out for a spin, and see how easy it is to make any element on a page draggable.

NOTE See the note on page 12 for information on how to download the tutorial files.

1. **In a text editor, open the file *draggable.html* in the *chapter12* folder.**

   This file already contains a link to the required jQuery UI and jQuery files as well as the $(document).ready() function (page 160).

   Look at the HTML and find a <div> with an ID of note and a little bit of content. You'll turn this into a draggable item.

2. **In the empty line inside the $(document).ready() function add the bolded line below:**

   ```
   $(document).ready(function() {
     $('#note').draggable();
   }); // end ready
   ```

   This selects the <div> and makes it movable.

3. **Save the page and preview it in a web browser (Figure 12-1).**

   Click anywhere in the div with the headline "You can drag me" and drag it around the screen. There are many ways to configure this widget, which you'll look at next.

NOTE You'll find the finished version of this tutorial in the *complete_draggable.html* file.

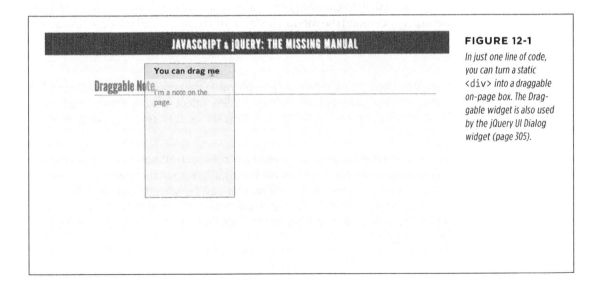

FIGURE 12-1

In just one line of code, you can turn a static <div> into a draggable on-page box. The Draggable widget is also used by the jQuery UI Dialog widget (page 305).

Draggable Widget Options

jQuery UI's draggable widget is very powerful and includes many options. You can control a dragged element's direction and distance, how it behaves when you drag it, and even what portion of the element you can grab. As with other jQuery UI widgets, you can set options by passing an object to the draggable() function. For example, to change the cursor to a pointing finger and to set the <h2> element inside the dragged item as the "handle" that a visitor must grab, you'd pass an object with those two options set like this:

```
$('#controls').draggable({
  cursor : 'pointer',
  handle : 'h2'
});
```

Here are the most common options:

- **axis.** You can limit the movement of a draggable element to just left and right or up and down using the axis property. For example, say you wanted to drag an item along a timeline. The dragged item needed to stay positioned along that line, so you wouldn't want someone to drag the element to the bottom of the page off the line. Use either 'x' (to constrain the dragged item to just left and right movement) or 'y' (to make sure the dragged item can only be moved up and down the page):

  ```
  axis : 'x'
  ```

- **cancel.** This option lets you prevent dragging when a specific element is clicked on. For example, say you created an announcement box that visitors could drag around the screen. The announcement has a headline, but also several paragraphs of text that includes important information like a street address and phone number. Normally, if a visitor tried to select the street address (to copy and paste into Google Maps, for instance), she'd end up dragging the announcement around the window instead. You could turn off the dragging action of those paragraphs, by setting the cancel option:

  ```
  cancel :  'p'
  ```

  Now, if someone clicked on a paragraph inside the announcement, she wouldn't trigger the dragging action and could freely select and copy text. The handle option discussed on page 405, can also let visitors select content within a draggable item.

- **connectToSortable.** Lets you specify a collection of sortable items that the dragged item can be added to. jQuery UI offers a sortable interaction which lets you group a collection of items that can be sorted, such as a To-do list (you'll learn about sortable items on page 426). To use this option, just specify an ID for an element you've already turned into a sortable group (as described on page 426):

  ```
  connectToSortable :  '#toDoList'
  ```

- **containment.** You can prevent a visitor from dragging an element outside a container element. For example, say you create a "Refrigerator magnet" activity where a visitor can drag words around to form a sentence. You can add a bunch of small, draggable divs with words in them and include an area of the page where the visitor can construct the sentence. You want to make sure that he doesn't drag words all over the place, like into the navigation bar, headline, or footer. The containment options let you limit the interaction to a smaller area of the page. It accepts several possible values:

  - **A selector.** If you provide a selector name, then jQuery UI will keep the draggable item confined to the boundaries of that element. For example, if you had a `<div>` on the page with an ID of `refrigerator`, you could keep the draggable element inside that div by setting the containment option like this:

    ```
    containment :  '#refrigerator'
    ```

  - **parent, document, or window.** To keep the draggable item contained inside its parent element, use `parent` as the value. For example, if the draggable item is a `<div>` inside another `<div>` and you want to limit the dragging to within that outer div, use `parent` like this:

    ```
    containment :  'parent'
    ```

    The `document` and `window` values are nearly the same, except `document` keeps the entire draggable area contained within the document area and `window` lets you drag the element partly outside the window.

  - **An array of coordinates.** Lastly, you can supply an array of coordinates that represent the top-left and bottom-right points of a containing box. You provide pixel values that are in relation to the top-left of the browser window. For example, say you wanted to limit dragging to an area that starts 50 pixels from the left and 100 pixels from the top and ends 500 pixels from the left and 600 pixels from the top. You'd assign those values like this:

    ```
    containment :  [50, 100, 500, 600]
    ```

    Because using coordinates like this requires precise values, it's not very good for a fluid design. You're better off using a containing element and specifying a selector.

- **cursor.** When an element is dragged, you can change the appearance of the cursor. Normally, the cursor will look like either an arrow (if you click on an empty space in an element) or a text selection bar (if you click on text in a headline, for example). However, you can tell jQuery UI to use a different cursor as the visitor drags an element by setting the cursor option with a valid CSS cursor value. You can find a list of values at *https://developer.mozilla.org/en-US/docs/Web/CSS/cursor,* but common cursors used when dragging include `pointer`, `crosshair`, and `default` (which is an arrow):

  ```
  cursor : 'pointer'
  ```

- **cursorAt.** You can control where the cursor appears as the visitor drags the element. Usually the cursor remains wherever the visitor first grabs the element. For example, if you grab a draggable div at the bottom, the cursor will remain at the bottom of the div as you drag it around the screen. However, maybe you want the cursor to appear in a specific spot—maybe a visual handle that you've added to the draggable element. To do so, provide an object for the cursorAt option. The object can contain values using left, right, top, and bottom properties. For example, to position the cursor at the top-left of an element as the visitor drags it, set the left and top properties like this:

```
cursorAt : {
  left : 5,
  top : 5
}
```

You can't set both left and right because they're different locations on the same axis; and you can't set both top and bottom for the same reason. However, you can use one value from each axis (left or right and top or bottom). Likewise, you can set just one value if you prefer. For example, if you only care that the cursor appears inside a bar at the top of a draggable element, you can set just the top value. The horizontal value will be set to the horizontal position from which the visitor grabbed the element in the first place:

```
cursorAt : { top : 5 }
```

- **disabled.** Determines whether the item is draggable. If this property is set to true, then you can't drag the item. You're probably thinking that if you wanted to *not* make an element draggable, you'd just avoid the draggable() function. True, you probably wouldn't use the disabled option when you first apply the draggable widget to an element.

  However, it can come in handy *after* someone has dragged the item. For example, you might want to let a visitor drag an item into a shopping cart, but not let them drag it out. In this case, you can apply this option after the dragging operation is complete (you'll see an example of this on page 418).

- **grid.** Normally, when you drag an element it moves freely across the window. However, you might want to force an element to move a specific number of spaces horizontally and vertically when dragged. For example, imagine an online checkers game. You have a grid of 8 squares by 8 squares. The checker pieces can be dragged around the border, but it would look sloppy if you could just drag those pieces anywhere. You want the pieces to move the same distance as a square on the board.

  jQuery UI lets you force an element to move in specific horizontal and vertical increments. The grid option takes an array of two numbers. The first number is the horizontal increment, and the second is the vertical increment. For example, say you wanted an element to move in increments of 50 pixels when dragged left or right. You also wanted the element to move in 100 pixel increments when dragged up or down. You can set the grid option to do that like this:

```
grid : [50, 100]
```

- **handle.** You can limit the area that a visitor clicks to drag an element. Normally, you can click anywhere inside a draggable element to drag it. However, you might want to limit that to just one area such as a headline or a visual drag bar in the element. Use the handle option to identify a selector within the draggable item that will act as the handle for dragging. For example, you can make it so you can only drag an element by clicking its headline—an <h2> element, for instance—like this:

```
handle : 'h2'
```

- **helper.** You may not want the user to move the actual draggable element on the page. For example, say you create a shopping cart page. Pictures of products appear on the page and visitors can add items to the cart by dragging a picture of a product onto a shopping cart icon. In this case, you don't want the shopper to actually move the product photo into the cart—that would move the picture on the page. You'd rather have the shopper just drag a copy of the picture while leaving the original photo unmoved. You can do this by setting the helper option to 'clone' like this:

```
helper : 'clone'
```

A more complex option is to pass the helper option a function that generates the HTML that jQuery UI should display as the user drags her mouse. For example, to display a generic helper div (instead of dragging the actual HTML element), you could set the helper like this:

```
helper: function( event ) {
  return $( "<div class='ui-widget-header'>I'm a custom helper</div>" );
}
```

Whatever you provide for the return statement is what jQuery UI will display under the user's mouse cursor. Note that you must return a jQuery object, so use the $() function to create the helper. A plain string of HTML won't work.

- **opacity.** When an element is dragged, you can make its opacity change. For example, you can fade the element to 50% opacity to give it a ghost-like appearance. This technique is a popular way to indicate that you're moving an item from one place to another. Use a value between 0 (completely invisible) to 1 (completely opaque). This works just like the CSS opacity property. For example, to make the dragged element appear 50% transparent, set the opacity value to 0.5:

```
opacity : 0.5
```

- **revert.** This option dictates whether the dragged item returns to its original position after the user stops dragging it. Normally, this is set to false, which means that when you drag the element and let go, it stays where you left it. For draggable windows or dialog boxes, that's generally a good approach: you drag the window out of the way of something else on the page.

However, there are times when you want to make the dragged element return to its starting position. For example, if you're using the droppable widget (page 412), you might want a dragged item that's not dropped in a specific spot to return to where it came from. For example, say you created an app for organizing images. You can drag thumbnails of the images into different folders on the page, or into a trashcan icon. However, a user might drag an image up into a headline on the page, or down into the footer, and not into one of the intended folders or the trashcan. In that case, you'd want the image to move back to where it was on the page and not sit there obscuring the headline or footer.

The revert option accepts several different values: true makes the dragged item always return back to its starting point (great for your next prank website); 'invalid' makes the dragged item return only if it's not dropped on a valid droppable item (page 412). In the case of the photo-organizing app mentioned above, you'd use the invalid option like this:

```
revert : 'invalid'
```

Lastly, you can pass a function to this option. If the function returns true, then the element reverts back to its original position. You could use a function in a JavaScript checkers game, for example: if a player moves his piece and drops it on another square on the board, a function could check if the move was invalid (if that square is already occupied by another piece, or if the piece moved farther than allowed, for instance). In that case, the function would return the value true, and jQuery UI would move the piece back to its original position.

```
revert : function() {
    // do some kind of test in this function and return either
    // true to make the element revert to its original position
    // or false if the element can stay where the user dropped it
}
```

- **revertDuration.** When jQuery UI reverts a dropped element (moves it backs to its original position), it animates this movement. The default value is 500 milliseconds or half a second. It looks really cool, but you can make the animation happen faster (a number less than 500) or slower (a number greater than 500). To do that, set the revertDuration option, which accepts a number indicating the number of milliseconds the animation should take. For example, for a quarter of a second animation (250 milliseconds) you'd set the revertDuration option like this:

```
revertDuration : 250
```

- **scope.** The scope option lets you group sets of draggable and droppable items. For example, say your page has a calendar. Users can drag an event from one day on the calendar to another. All the draggable events in the calendar belong to the calendar, so you can set the draggable item's scope to `calendar` like this:

```
scope : 'calendar'
```

The string `'calendar'` here doesn't refer to a selector or element on the page. It's just a name used to group draggable and droppable items together. You could use any term you want; just make sure you use the same name for the `scope` option on the droppable item (page 412).

You need to set the `scope` option only if there's a chance that a page has different types of draggable and droppable items. For example, if you have a jigsaw puzzle on the same page as the calendar, you wouldn't want people dragging events from the calendar onto the puzzle and puzzle pieces onto the calendar. By specifying different scopes for each group, you can control which draggable items can be dropped on what other elements (see page 412 for more on the droppable widget).

> **NOTE** You can try out these options on the tutorial file—*draggable.html*—you programmed on page 401. If you didn't complete that tutorial, open the *complete_draggable.html* file and add some of these options to the `draggable()` function in that file.

- **snap.** You can make a draggable item snap to another page element or another draggable item. For example, say you create a jigsaw puzzle game. A dozen square fragments of a photo need to be re-assembled to create the original photo. You can make one puzzle piece snap to another piece by setting this option. Use one of two possible values for this option:

  - `true` tells jQuery UI to make the dragged item snap to any other draggable item on the page. This is good in the case of a jigsaw puzzle because you'll have lots of individual tiles.

  - A selector name. The name of any selector on the page. For example, if you want the dragged item to snap to a div with the ID of `photoholder`, you could do this:

    ```
    snap : '#photoholder'
    ```

How the item snaps to another element is controlled by the `snapMode` and `snapTolerance` options, discussed next.

- **snapMode.** This option only works if you've also set the `snap` option. This option takes one of three keywords: `inner`, `outer`, or `both`. If you want the dragged element to snap only when its inside the element, use `inner`, which makes the dragged element snap to any of the inner edges of the element specified by the `snap` option.

Use `outer` when you want the element to snap to the outside edge of an item. This option is ideal for things like the jigsaw puzzle because you want the pieces to snap next to each other.

Finally, you can make the dragged item snap to *either* the outer or inner edges using the both option:

```
snapMode : 'both'
```

- **snapTolerance** determines how close the dragged item should be before it snaps to an element. The larger the number, the farther away the dragged item can be before it tries to snap to an element. Specify a pixel value for this option:

```
snapTolerance : 30
```

- **zIndex.** This option lets you set a z-index for the dragged element. The CSS z-index property determines the stacking order of elements on the page. An element with a higher z-index will appear on top of any page elements it over-laps. This property comes in handy when you want to make sure that, as the visitor drags an item around the page, that item appears on top of surrounding content. (You'll see an example of this option in the tutorial on page 423.)

```
zIndex : 100
```

NOTE You'll find even more options for the draggable widget at *http://api.jqueryui.com/draggable/*. See Figure 12-2.

Draggable Widget Events

The droppable widget supports several different events, each of which is triggered at a different moment of the dragging process. You add a function to an event to make your program do something in response to the item being dragged.

Say you've created a game that requires a player to quickly drag an item to a target. The faster he can drag the item, the higher the score. You could check the time when the player first starts to drag the item, then check the time when the player stops.

Three events deal with the various points in the dragging process.

■ THE CREATE EVENT

This event fires whenever you use the draggable() function to create a new drag-gable item. You could use this event to pop up a dialog box with the instructions "Drag this product to your shopping cart." It only runs once, when the draggable widget is created. You use this event by passing a create property with a function to the draggable method like this:

```
$('.product').draggable({
  create : function (event){
    // programming here
  }
});
```

FIGURE 12-2

*jQuery UI's documenta-
tion is extensive. The
page dedicated to the
draggable widget lists
multiple options, meth-
ods, and events that you
can tap into to customize
how this widget works.*

THE START EVENT

This event triggers as soon as a user begins dragging an element. You assign this
event as a property of the draggable widget's options object. The name of the
event—start—is the property name, and the value should be a function that runs
when the visitor starts dragging the item.

For example, say you have a <div> tag with an ID of raceCar. You turn that div into
a draggable item, and assign it a start event like this:

```
$('#raceCar').draggable({
  start : function (event, ui) {
    // programming goes here
  }
});
```

The function assigned to the start event has two parameters—event and ui. The event parameter is a jQuery event object and provides details about which element is receiving the event, the screen coordinates of the mouse, and other information. (You can read about the event object and how to use it on page 164.) The ui parameter is an object with three properties:

- The **ui.helper property** is a jQuery object containing a reference to the item that's visibly dragged across the screen. This is usually the same as the element to which you applied the draggable() method. However, that's not always the case. If you set the draggable widget's helper option to 'clone' or passed it a function to generate the helper HTML (page 405), ui.helper refers to an element other than the original draggable element: either a copy of that element or a jQuery object created as a helper (as described on page 405). This arrangement is helpful in a shopping cart, for example, when dragging a product from one place on the page to the shopping cart will disturb the page's layout. Instead, the shopper should drag a *copy* of the product into the cart.

Use the ui.helper property whenever you want to perform an action on the item that's visibly dragged across the page. For example, say you wanted to make an item double in size when the user starts to drag it. You could set a CSS property on the ui.helper object like this:

```
$('#photo').draggable({
  start : function (event, ui) {
    ui.helper.css('transform', 'scale(2)');
  }
});
```

This uses jQuery's css() method (page 134) and sets the CSS transform property to scale the element by 2 (doubling it size). You could also use jQuery's addClass() method to add a class to the item as the user starts dragging it—a style that highlights the item, for example. Then remove the class using removeClass() when the visitor stops dragging the item (see the stop event on page 411).

> **NOTE** To learn more about CSS transforms, visit *https://developer.mozilla.org/en-US/docs/Web/Guide/CSS/Using_CSS_transforms.*

- **ui.position** provides the x and y position of the top-left corner of the *helper* item (the item that is visibly dragged across the screen). This is the element's CSS position value, and it can be affected by the position of its parent element (or any other positioned ancestor). For example, if you have a draggable item inside a <div>, and that <div> is absolutely positioned on the page, the draggable element's left and top position values will be in relation to the left and top corner of the positioned ancestor.

The ui.position property is a JavaScript object composed of two properties top and left. The top property is the element's top position as measured in a number of pixels from the top of its nearest positioned ancestor (that is, a tag with either absolute or relative positioning that wraps around the dragged element). The left property is the helper's position relative to the left edge of the nearest positioned ancestor. Accessing this property can be useful for determining where the helper is when the visitor stops dragging (or while he's dragging the element) (see the drag and stop events next).

You can access those values like this: ui.position.top and ui.position.left.

- **ui.offset** also provides an object with two properties top and left. The position is calculated relative to the top left of the *browser window*. ui.position and ui.offset will be the same if the dragged element is not inside any other elements that have CSS position property of absolute or relative. The ui.offset.top property identifies how far the top of the helper element is from the top of the window. The ui.offset.left property identifies how many pixels the draggable item is placed from the left side of the browser window.

- **ui.originalPosition** contains the same two properties—top and left—as ui.position and ui.offset. However, ui.originalPosition indicates the draggable element's starting position—the spot the element was in just before the user started dragging it. Like the ui.position property, ui.originalPosition is based on any positioned ancestors.

■ THE DRAG EVENT

Draggable items also fire off a drag event as they are dragged around the screen. You can create a function that runs repeatedly while the object is being dragged. You could use this event to leave a trail of sparkles as the dragged object is moved across the window, for example. Because this event fires off numerous times while dragging an element, try to limit the amount of work the function does. If you perform lots of complicated operations in response to the drag event, the browser may slow to a crawl.

The drag event function accepts the same two parameters as the start event described on page 409—event and ui.

Say you wanted to display the current position of a dragged item as it's dragged across the screen. Assume the page has a couple of <span> tags with the ID of left and top to display these values. You could continuously update the values as the element is being dragged like this:

```
$('#raceCar').draggable({
  drag : function (event, ui) {
    $('#left').text(ui.position.left);
    $('#top').text(ui.position.top);
  }
});
```

■ THE STOP EVENT

The Draggable widget's stop event works just like the start event, except it's triggered when the user stops dragging the item and releases the mouse button. This doesn't necessarily mean that the user dropped the item on a droppable target (like the ones discussed in the next section). It doesn't even mean that the user has completely finished dragging the element. For example, a user could click a draggable element and begin moving it (the start event fires); keep moving it around the page (the drag event fires continuously); then stop dragging (the stop event fires); then click and drag the same element again repeating all of the same events.

You use the stop event following the same structure as the start event. For example, say you used the code above to make the draggable element scale up to twice its size while being dragged. You could return the element to normal size when the user stops dragging it using this code:

```
$('#photo').draggable({
  stop : function (event, ui) {
    ui.helper.css('transform', 'scale(1)');
  }
});
```

■ The Droppable Widget

The Draggable widget, by itself, is useful for dialog boxes or other page elements that you'd move around the screen (like tool palettes, for example). However, when you add the droppable widget to the mix, you can build highly interactive applications, where dragging one item onto another item can make something else happen.

For example, a photo sharing application might let a user drag a thumbnail image to a trashcan to delete that photo from the site. A language-learning website could test students by having them drag a word onto a corresponding picture to show their mastery of vocabulary.

Using the Droppable Widget

Droppable widgets aren't useful without draggable widgets. A droppable widget acts like a "drop zone" for draggable items. When an item is dropped on it, a droppable widget can also trigger additional programming. You can turn anything on a page into a droppable element. Of course, it should make sense that a visitor would drag something on to it: for example, icons of shopping carts and trashcans are visual metaphors that clearly indicate that items can be dropped into them. But you can also turn divs into droppable widgets as long as you clearly indicate to the visitor what they can drag and where they can drag it to.

Using the droppable widget is very easy:

1. **Follow the steps on page 304 to attach the CSS and JavaScript files.**

   Remember that jQuery UI has its own CSS and JavaScript files, and that the jQuery UI JavaScript file should be linked to *after* the jQuery JavaScript file.

2. **Add jQuery's $(document).ready() function to your page or to another external JavaScript file:**

```
$(document).ready(function() {

}); // end ready
```

As discussed on page 160, this step is only necessary if you're putting your JavaScript code in the page's <head>, before the majority of your HTML. Some programmers put their JavaScript code at the bottom of the page, before the closing </body> tag; in that case, you can skip the $(document).ready() function.

Droppable widgets don't make sense without something you can drag into them, so always add at least one draggable item to the page.

3. **Use jQuery to select one or more page elements and apply the Draggable widget to it:**

```
$(document).ready(function() {
  $('.product').draggable();
}); // end ready
```

In this example, you have a catalog page with a bunch of products on it. Each product photo has the class product applied to it, so this code will make each of those photos draggable.

4. **Use jQuery to select a drop zone and make it droppable:**

```
$(document).ready(function() {
  $('.product').draggable();
  $('#cart').droppable();
}); // end ready
```

The item on the page with an ID of cart is now a drop zone. But this is just the start. You have to set various options of the droppable element in order to make something happen: such as calculate a sales total each time a product is added to the cart. You do this by passing an object containing options and functions to the droppable() function.

5. **Add options to the droppable() function:**

```
$(document).ready(function() {
  $('.product').draggable();
  $('#cart').droppable({
    activeClass : 'highlight',
    drop : function (event,ui) {
      alert('Product added');
    }
  });
}); // end ready
```

You'll learn about the various options for this widget next, but as a sneak preview, you'll take a look at what the code above does. First, the `activeClass` option tells jQuery UI to add a class named `highlight` to the drop zone element, which you use to apply a CSS rule to the droppable element. The CSS can visually identify the drop zone by adding a bold background color to the drop zone, or outlining it with a bright red border.

The second option, `drop`, is an event handler. It lets you run a function when an item is dropped onto the drop zone. In this case, an alert box pops open with a message.

Droppable Widget Options

The droppable widget doesn't provide as many options as the draggable widget (the droppable widget's main role is to receive items, and, most importantly, run functions when that happens):

- **accept.** Dictates which draggable items can be added to the droppable widget. You can assign either a selector or a function. The selector indicates the selector for the draggable item. For example, if you had a bunch of images all with the class photo on them, and wanted to be able to drop them on a droppable item, you'd set the option like this:

      accept : '.photo'

- **activeClass.** You can highlight a droppable element when any acceptable draggable element is being dragged. For example, say you created a filesystem app that let users view files on the server, move them to different folders, rename the files, and so on. You could also drag a file to the trash to delete it. The trashcan would be a droppable widget, and a file a draggable widget. When a visitor started to drag a file, you could apply a class that highlights the trashcan in some way (for example, changes the background image to display a trashcan with an open lid, ready for the file). Just assign a class name (without a period) to this property, and jQuery UI will add the class to the droppable item, when an acceptable draggable item is dragged:

      activeClass : 'highlight'

- **disabled.** Determines whether the item is an active drop zone. If this property is set to `true`, then you can't drop anything on the element. You can use this property *after* creating the drop zone as a way to turn off the ability. For example, say you had a drop zone but you only wanted users to be able to drop 5 items into it. Once the five items were in place, you would then turn off the drop zone, so users could no longer drop anything into it (you can use the `drop` event described on page 416 to trigger a function that disables the drop zone):

      $('#dropZone').droppable({
        disabled : true
      });

You're probably thinking that if you wanted to turn an element into a drop zone, then just avoid the droppable() function altogether. True, you probably wouldn't use the disabled option when you first apply the droppable widget to an element.

However, it can come in handy *after* someone has dropped an item into the droppable widget. For example, you might want to let a visitor add only five items to a shopping cart. Once the shopper drops in the fifth item, you can disable the drop zone so he can no longer add items to the cart.

- **hoverClass.** You can also apply a class when an acceptable draggable item is dragged over a droppable item (Figure 12-3). For example, you could add a class to the trashcan element mentioned earlier *only* when the file is dragged on top of the trashcan:

```
hoverClass : 'openTrashcan'
```

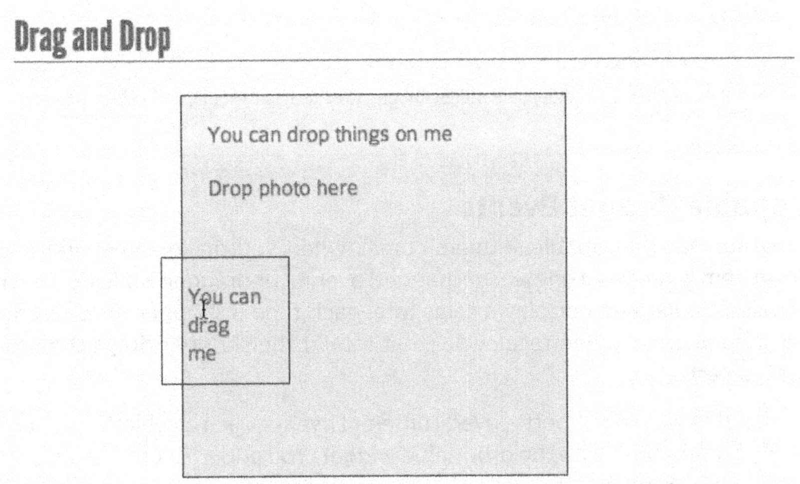

FIGURE 12-3

Using a Droppable widget's hoverClass option, you can apply a class to a droppable element when another element is dragged over it. Here, the large box lights up in bright yellow when the smaller box is dragged over it (the color change is provided by a CSS class style). The style adds both a background color and background image, but you could create a class style that added a bold outline to the drop zone, or even added a CSS animation to make the drop zone's color pulsate between white and another color.

- **scope.** Works like the draggable property of the same name (page 406). Lets you group related draggable and droppable widgets.

```
scope : 'calendar'
```

The name you use—'calendar' in this example—doesn't matter. Use any name that makes sense—just make sure to use the same scope name for the related Draggable widgets and Droppable widgets.

- **tolerance.** This option determines when a draggable item is considered to be hovering over a droppable item. There are four possible values for this option:

  - **'fit'**—the draggable item must fit entirely within the droppable item.

  - **'intersect'**—the draggable item must overlap the droppable item by at least 50% in both directions. In other words, the draggable item needs to be mostly inside the droppable item, but not entirely. This is the normal setting for droppables.

  - **'pointer'**—only the mouse cursor needs to be inside the droppable item.

  - **'touch'**—the draggable needs only to touch the droppable item on one side.

  The 'fit' option is good for confirming that the user really wants to place the draggable item onto the droppable item, but requires that the draggable item be smaller than the droppable item. The most common choice is 'intersect' because it doesn't require extreme precision on a user's part:

  ```
  tolerance : 'intersect'
  ```

> **NOTE** For a complete list of droppable widget options, methods, and events, visit *http://api.jqueryui.com/droppable/*.

Droppable Widget Events

The real fun with droppable widgets comes when you make something happen when an item is dropped onto it...or dragged over it...or dragged off it. For example, you could calculate and display a sales total each time a shopper drops a product into a shopping cart, then recalculate that total if the shopper drags the product out of the cart.

The droppable widget supports several different events, each of which is triggered by a different interaction with the droppable widget. You add a function to an event to make your program do something in response to dragging an item, moving an item over or out of the drop zone, or dropping an item onto the drop zone. For example, say you created a to-do list application: when a visitor drags an item from the list and drops it onto a trashcan icon, the item is removed from the to-do list and from the page. The event in this example is the drop event.

Next, we'll look at each event, starting with the most commonly used one.

■ THE DROP EVENT

This event triggers a function when an item is dropped onto the droppable item. The dropped item must be an *acceptable* item—that is, one that's specified by the accept option (page 414) or within the same scope (page 406) as the droppable widget.

The event is assigned as a property sent to the droppable widget as part of the options object. For example, say you have a <div> tag with an ID of trashcan. You turn that div into a droppable item, and assign it a drop event like this:

```
$('#trashcan').droppable({
  drop : function (event, ui) {
    // programming goes here
  }
});
```

The function assigned to the drop event has two parameters—event and ui. The event parameter is a jQuery event object (page 164) that provides details such as which element is receiving the event, the screen coordinates of the mouse, and other information. The ui parameter is like the parameter used in draggable widget events (page 408).

• The **ui.helper property** is a jQuery object containing a reference to the item that's visibly dragged across the screen and is the same as the ui.helper property described for draggable items on page 410.

Use the ui.helper property whenever you want to perform an action to the item that's visibly dragged across the page. For example, if you wanted to make an element "explode" when it was dropped onto a trashcan, you could use this code:

```
$('#trashcan').droppable({
  drop : function (event, ui) {
    ui.helper.hide('explode');
  }
});
```

The 'explode' value here is actually a cool jQuery UI effect, that you'll learn about on page 440.

• The **ui.draggable property** is a jQuery object containing a reference to the element the draggable() method is run on. In many cases, this is the same as ui.helper. However, if you've set the draggable item's helper property (page 405) to 'clone', the cloned item is dragged across the screen, while the original item is left in place.

This property could also come in handy in the case of a shopping cart page. Say you've built a shopping cart system that tracks inventory as well as products. A catalog page might show a photo of a product plus a label indicating how many of those products are in stock—10, for example. When a shopper clicked on the product, she'd drag a clone of that product to the cart. When she dropped the clone on the cart, the drop function could update the ui.draggable item to lower the stock number by one (and at the same time, use Ajax—Chapter 13—to send the shopping data to the server).

• **ui.position** provides the x and y positions of the top-left corner of the helper item when it's dropped onto the target. It's the same as the ui.position property described for draggable items on page 410.

- **ui.offset** provides the top and left position of the draggable item in relation to the browser window. It's the same as the draggable item's ui.offset property described on page 411.

- **ui.originalPosition** provides the top and left position of the draggable item just before a user starts dragging it. It's the same as the draggable item's ui.originalPosition property described on page 411.

When using drop zone, you'll probably end up using the drop event frequently. One task you might wish to perform is to prevent an item from being dragged out of the drop zone. Going back to the checkers example, you could make it so once a player moves a piece, she can't take the move back. In other words, you want to "lock" the piece in place when it's dropped onto a square. You could do that by disabling the dragged item, when it's dropped on the drop zone:

```
$('.square').drop({
  drop : function (event, ui) {
    ui.helper.draggable({
      disabled : true
    });
  }
});
```

You're using the ui parameter's helper object (the thing that was dragged onto the drop zone) and then calling the draggable() method to turn off dragging by setting that item's disabled property to true. Keep in mind this is the disabled property of the draggable item (page 404) not of the drop zone. You'll need to set the disable property of the draggable item back to false to make the element draggable again (see page 404).

■ THE ACTIVATE EVENT

When a user starts dragging an element that's acceptable to the drop target (see the droppable widget's accept and scope options above), an *activate* event is triggered. You can add programming to respond to this event. Say, for example, you're creating a web application that lets a user drag one or more photos into a div and then click a Send button to email those photos to a friend. You could add a label like "Drop photo here" to the drop zone, but only when the user starts dragging a photo.

You could add a function to the activate event to write "Drop photo here" to the drop zone. Assuming the droppable item is a div with an ID of photoZone, here's how you could add a message to the drop zone when the user started dragging a photo:

```
$('#photoZone').droppable({
  activate : function (event, ui) {
    $(this).append('<p id="dropMessage">Drop photo here</p>');
  }
});
```

The $(this) refers to the drop zone element (see page 139 if you need a refresher on what $(this) is and how it works). The append() method just adds HTML inside a tag as the last child of the element (page 127).

The activate function accepts the same two parameters—event and ui—as the drop event (page 416).

THE DEACTIVATE EVENT

The deactivate event is the flip side of the activate event. It triggers a function when a user *stops* dragging an acceptable item—meaning the user has released the mouse button. You could use this to undo an action performed by the activate event. For example, to add a message to the drop zone while the user drags an item and then remove that message when he stops dragging the item, you could use this:

```
$('#photoZone').droppable({
  activate : function (event, ui) {
    $(this).append('<p id="dropMessage">Drop photo here</p>');
  },
  deactivate : function (event, ui) {
    $('#dropMessage').remove();
  }
});
```

THE OVER EVENT

You can even run a function when a visitor drags an item over a droppable element. The over event is triggered as soon as a draggable item is over the drop zone, but before it's dropped. You could use this event, for example, to add an encouraging message as a hesitant shopper pauses before dropping a product into a shopping cart: "You know you'll look fabulous in those shoes. Just buy them!"

Or, say you've created a trashcan drop zone for users to delete photos from their page. The trashcan is normally closed, but when the droppable item is over the can, the can's lid comes off; when the item is dropped in the can, you could then use the drop event to replace the empty can with an image of a can full of trash.

You program the over event just like any other Droppable widget event—just assign a function to the over property:

```
$('#trashcan').droppable({
  over : function (event, ui) {
    $('#trashCanImage').attr('src','images/open-lid-can.png');
  }
});
```

In this example, you're just swapping out an image for another file, but you could make a much more elaborate function for this (or any) event.

NOTE The tolerance property (page 416) determines when jQuery UI thinks a draggable item is over, dropped on, or out of the droppable zone.

THE OUT EVENT

Finally, you can trigger a function when a visitor drags an item out of a drop zone. For example, say a shopper dragged a product into a shopping cart and you calculate the sales total when the product was dropped into the cart. Then, when the shopper decides he's no longer interested in the product, he drags it out of the cart. The out event gives you a chance to deduct the cost of the removed product from the sales total:

```
$('#shoppingCart').droppable({
  drop : function (event, ui) {
    // perform math to update sales total
  },
  out : function (event, ui) {
    // perform math to remove product cost from sales total
  }
});
```

These few examples demonstrate that you'll often use events in pairs to trigger opposite actions. For example, the out event with the drop event, and the deactivate event with the activate event.

Drag-and-Drop Tutorial

This example combines the draggable and droppable widgets into one program. You'll build a simple drag-and-drop application that demonstrates the basic components of each widget. The final project will let you drag a photo to a trashcan, removing the photo in a dramatic fashion, as shown in Figure 12-4.

> **NOTE** See the note on page 12 for information on how to download the tutorial files.

1. **In a text editor, open the file *to-the-trash.html* in the *chapter12* folder.**

   This file already contains a link to the proper CSS and JavaScript files as well as the $(document).ready() function (page 160).

   If you preview this page, you'll see that there's an image of a trashcan on the left and a row of photos on the right (Figure 12-4). The HTML for the trashcan and photos looks like this:

   ```
   <img src="../_images/trashcan-empty-icon.png" id="trashcan">
   <div id="photos">
     <img src="../_images/small/slide1_h.jpg">
     <img src="../_images/small/slide2_h.jpg">
     <img src="../_images/small/slide3_h.jpg">
     <img src="../_images/small/slide4_h.jpg">
     <img src="../_images/small/slide5_h.jpg">
     <img src="../_images/small/slide6_h.jpg">
   </div>
   ```

The trashcan image has an ID of trashcan, and the photos are all inside a div with an ID of photos. You'll start by making the photos draggable.

2. **In the empty line inside the $(document).ready() function, add the bolded line below:**

```
$(document).ready(function() {
 $('#photos img').draggable();
}); // end ready
```

This selects all the img elements inside the photos div and turns them into drag-gable items. Because the goal of this project is to add an image to the trashcan, you want to make sure that if the visitor drops the photo anywhere but in the trashcan, the photo snaps back to its original location.

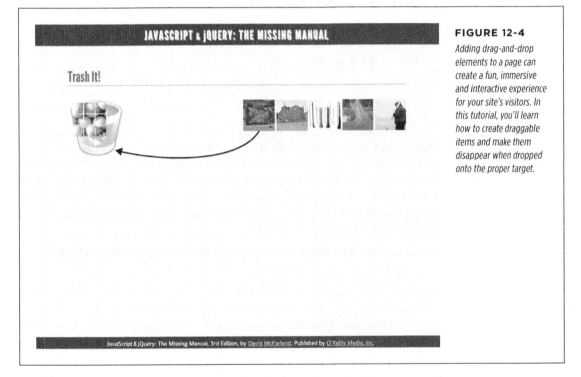

FIGURE 12-4

Adding drag-and-drop elements to a page can create a fun, immersive and interactive experience for your site's visitors. In this tutorial, you'll learn how to create draggable items and make them disappear when dropped onto the proper target.

3. **Add an object literal to the draggable() function, with the revert property set to 'invalid':**

```
$('#photos img').draggable({
 revert : 'invalid'
});
```

The revert option (page 405) can return a dragged item to its original starting place. By setting this option to 'invalid', you're basically saying "Return this item to its original spot (revert), if its dropped in an 'invalid' spot." What's invalid? Any element that isn't specified as a droppable widget. Because you haven't added a Droppable widget yet, the photos will always snap back to their original spot when dropped.

4. **Save the page and preview it in a browser. Drag a photo around the page and drop it.**

The photo should snap back to where it started. If it doesn't, double check your code and look in the JavaScript console for any errors (page 18).

Next, you'll use draggable events to make something happen when you start dragging a photo on the page. Specifically, you'll apply a CSS transformation to the dragged photo.

5. **Type a comma after** `invalid` **in the code you just added, hit Return and add a start event handler like this:**

```
$('#photos img').draggable({
  revert : 'invalid',
  start : function (event, ui) {


  }
});
```

The `start` option requires a function as its value. The function is an event handler just like the ones you used for jQuery's `click()` and `mouseover()` functions (page 152). "Start" isn't a real browser event, though. It's a custom event programmed by the jQuery UI team, and it fires the moment someone starts to drag an item. The function here is empty, so you'll need to add some programming to it next. In this case, you'll just apply some simple CSS using jQuery's `css()` function (page 134.)

6. **Inside the function you just added, type the following code (in bold):**

```
$('#photos img').draggable({
  revert : 'invalid',
  start : function (event, ui) {
    ui.helper.css('transform', 'rotate(5deg) scale(1.5)');
  }
});
```

As you read on page 409, the function assigned to draggable events accepts two parameters: an `event` object, and an object representing the draggable item—that's the `ui` parameter. You can use the `ui` parameter to select the dragged item and do something to it. The `ui.helper` (page 410) is the actual element the user drags across the screen, and because it's a jQuery object, you can apply any of jQuery's many functions to it. In this case, the `css()` function applies the CSS transform property to the element, rotating it slightly and enlarging it 1.5 times. In other words, the image will rotate and grow bigger when it's dragged.

Next, you'll make the photo return the photo back to normal when the visitor stops dragging it.

> **NOTE** To learn more about the CSS transform property, visit *www.sitepoint.com/css3-transformations-2d-functions/*.

7. **Add the stop event option to the option's object:**

```
$('#photos img').draggable({
 revert : 'invalid',
 start : function (event, ui) {
  ui.helper.css('transform', 'rotate(5deg) scale(1.5)');
 },
 stop : function (event, ui) {
  ui.helper.css('transform', 'rotate(0deg) scale(1)');
 }
});
```

Don't forget the comma after the start function.

This function simply undoes the CSS that was applied at the start of the drag, returning the photo to its regular size and removing the rotation. If you save the file and preview it in a browser, you'll notice something a little strange: if you click and start to drag a photo, you'll notice that it appears *underneath* the photo to the right of it (Figure 12-5). The reason for this phenomenon is explained in Figure 12-5. The solution is simple; just increase the z-index value of the dragged element.

8. **Add one last option, zIndex, to the options object.**

```
$('#photos img').draggable({
 revert : 'invalid',
 start : function (event, ui) {
  ui.helper.css('transform', 'rotate(5deg) scale(1.5)');
 },
 stop : function (event, ui) {
  ui.helper.css('transform', 'rotate(0deg) scale(1)');
 },
 zIndex : 100
});
```

Don't forget the comma after the stop function. The zIndex option (page 408) simply adjusts the dragged element's CSS z-index property. The higher the z-index value, the higher up the element is in the stacking order. A value of 100 is high enough to assure that the dragged element won't appear behind any other items on the page.

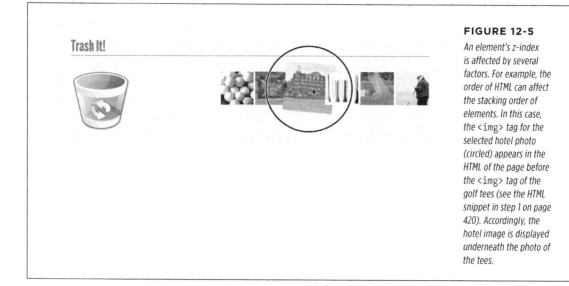

FIGURE 12-5

An element's z-index is affected by several factors. For example, the order of HTML can affect the stacking order of elements. In this case, the <img> tag for the selected hotel photo (circled) appears in the HTML of the page before the <img> tag of the golf tees (see the HTML snippet in step 1 on page 420). Accordingly, the hotel image is displayed underneath the photo of the tees.

9. **Save the file and preview it in a web browser. Drag a photo around the page.**

   The photo should rotate and grow slightly when you drag it, then snap back into place and revert to its normal size and rotation when released. In addition, when you first start to drag the photo, it should appear above any other photos around it.

   That's enough work on the photos. Next, you'll turn the trashcan image into a drop zone.

10. **After the draggable() function, create a new line and add the following code:**

    ```
    $('#trashcan').droppable();
    ```

    This turns the trashcan image into a droppable widget. If you save the page and preview it now, you'll see you can drop photos on the trashcan. The photos don't move back to their original spot on the screen, however, because the trashcan is a valid drop zone.

    To make things more exciting, you'll highlight the trashcan when a visitor starts to drag one of the photos. You'll also make the trashcan appear brighter, alerting visitors that they can drag the photo to the trash.

11. **Add an options object to the droppable() function:**

    ```
    $('#trashcan').droppable({
     activeClass : 'highlight'
    });
    ```

The activeClass option (page 414) simply adds a class name to the droppable widget as soon as someone drags a valid draggable on the screen. In this case, the highlight class, defined in the *interactions.css* file, changes the opacity of the trashcan image to 1 (100% opaque). Another rule in that CSS file sets the opacity of the trashcan to .6 (60% transparency) when the page loads. By changing the opacity from .6 to 1 with CSS, the trashcan appears brighter when a photo is dragged.

While this slight change looks cool and adds guidance for people viewing the page, you haven't yet done anything when the photo is dropped in the trash. To do that, you need to use the droppable widget's drop event.

12. **Type a comma after 'highlight' in the code you just added, hit Return, and add a drop event handler like this:**

```
$('#trashcan').droppable({
  activeClass : 'highlight',
  drop : function (event, ui) {

  }
});
```

The drop option requires a function as its value, just like the start and stop events on draggable items. This function is empty and doesn't do anything yet, but you can make it do something—like make the dropped photo explode!

13. **In the drop function, add the code in bold below:**

```
$('#trashcan').droppable({
  activeClass : 'highlight',
  drop : function (event, ui) {
    ui.helper.hide('explode');
  }
});
```

ui.helper refers to the dragged item (page 410). The hide() method is a jQuery function you've used earlier in this book (page 184); however, jQuery UI gives additional effects for hiding and showing elements. The explode option creates a fun, animated effect—a playful way to make the photo disappear from the page. (You'll read more about these effects on page 438.)

One last thing: swap in a new image for the trashcan after a photo has been dropped on it, showing a trashcan full of trash.

14. **Add one last line of code inside the drop function:**

```
$('#trashcan').droppable({
  activeClass : 'highlight',
  drop : function (event, ui) {
    ui.helper.hide('explode');
    $(this).attr('src','../_images/trashcan-full-icon.png');
  }
});
```

$(this) refers to the trashcan—the <img> element on the page with the ID of trashcan. You're simply changing that element's src attribute to point to a new graphic. (You learned how to do that back in Chapter 7.)

The finished code should look like this:

```
$(document).ready(function() {
  $('#photos img').draggable({
    revert : "invalid",
    start : function (event, ui) {
      ui.helper.css('transform', 'rotate(5deg) scale(1.5)');
    },
    stop : function (event, ui) {
      ui.helper.css('transform', 'rotate(0deg) scale(1)');
    },
    zIndex : 100
  });
  $('#trashcan').droppable({
    activeClass : 'highlight',
      drop : function (event, ui) {
          ui.helper.hide('explode');
          $(this).attr('src','../_images/trashcan-full-icon.png');
      }
  });
}); // end ready
```

15. **Save the file and preview it in a web browser.**

    You can drag photos onto the trashcan, and they explode and disappear from the page (Figure 12-4). There's a lot more programming you could add to the drop event in this example. For example, you could send an Ajax request to a server and instruct the server to remove the photo from the user's account (you'll learn about Ajax in Chapter 13). But this quick tour hopefully has you thinking of many possible uses for the draggable and droppable widgets.

> **NOTE** You'll find the finished version of this tutorial in the *complete-to-the-trash.html* file.

■ Sorting Page Items

jQuery UI also provides a widget for working with lists such as to-do lists, music playlists, and even lists within lists like folders inside of folders. The sortable widget makes it easy to re-order items within a group simply by dragging an item to a new position. This widget is useful for managing a list of songs, for example—users can create their own playlist by dragging songs into a playlist and even re-ordering those songs by dragging them to new spots in the list (Figure 12-6).

The sortable widget works with any grouped collection of items. While it's a natural option for an unordered or ordered list, you can also turn a group of divs, paragraphs, or images into a sortable group.

Using the Sortable Widget

Sortable widgets are a collection of elements that can be dragged into a different position within a group: for example, in a to-do list, each to-do item can be dragged to a different position in the list. The list, then, is the sortable widget, and the list items inside it are the elements you can sort. In other words, the sortable widget must be a container element such as an unordered list (<ul>), ordered list (<ol>), or a <div> element containing other items such as additional divs, paragraphs, or images.

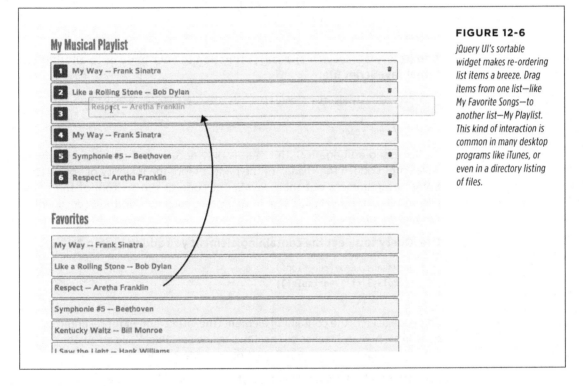

FIGURE 12-6

jQuery UI's sortable widget makes re-ordering list items a breeze. Drag items from one list—like My Favorite Songs—to another list—My Playlist. This kind of interaction is common in many desktop programs like iTunes, or even in a directory listing of files.

Using the sortable widget is easy:

1. **Follow the steps on page 304 to attach the CSS and JavaScript files.**

   Remember that jQuery UI has its own CSS and JavaScript files, and that the jQuery UI JavaScript file should be linked to *after* the jQuery JavaScript file.

2. **Add containing element to your web page.**

   This might be an unordered list or a <div> tag:

   ```
   <ul id="playlist">
   </ul>
   ```

It's a good idea to add an ID or class to the tag, so you have a way to select that item with jQuery.

3. **Add items inside the containing element.**

In the case of an unordered or ordered list, that would be a series of <li> tags. The items in the containing element represent the things that you can drag around and place in a new order within the list. In the case of a <div>, you could place images, paragraphs, or other divs inside (those items will be the sortable elements of the widget):

```
<ul id="playlist">
  <li>My Way -- Frank Sinatra</li>
  <li>Like a Rolling Stone -- Bob Dylan</li>
  <li>Respect -- Aretha Franklin</li>
</ul>
```

4. **Add jQuery's $(document).ready() function to your page or to another external JavaScript file:**

```
$(document).ready(function() {


}); // end ready
```

As discussed on page 160, this step is only necessary if you're putting your JavaScript code in the <head> of the page, before the majority of your HTML. Some programmers put their JavaScript code at the bottom of the page, before the closing </body> tag. In that case, you can skip the $(document). ready() function.

5. **Use jQuery to select the containing element you added in step 2:**

```
$(document).ready(function() {
  $('#playlist').sortable();
}); // end ready
```

This code selects the containing element (the <ul> element represented by the code in step 3) and makes all the items inside sortable. You can customize the sortable widget with many different options, described later.

6. **Add options to the sortable() function:**

```
$(document).ready(function() {
  $('#playlist').sortable({
    opacity : 0.5,
    placeholder : 'ui-state-highlight'
  });
}); // end ready
```

You'll learn about the various options for this widget next, but you can get a sneak preview by taking a look at what this code does. First, the opacity option tells jQuery UI to reduce the opacity of an element while it's being dragged. The second option, placeholder, tells jQuery to apply a style to the empty space where a dragged item can be dropped onto.

> **NOTE** You'll get to try out the Sortable widget in the web app you're going to build in Chapter 14.

Sortable Widget Options

jQuery UI's sortable widget includes many options. You can control a sortable item's direction and distance, how it behaves when you drag it, and even what portion of the element you can grab. Like other jQuery UI widgets, you can set options by passing an object to the sortable() function. For example, to change the cursor to a pointing finger and to set the <h2> element inside the item as the handle that a visitor must grab, you'd pass an object with those two options set:

```
$('#playlist').sortable({
  cursor : 'pointer',
  handle : 'h2'
});
```

Here are some commonly used options:

- **axis.** You can limit the movement of a sortable element to just left and right or up and down using the axis property. For example, say you created a horizontal group of divs that a visitor could re-order as part of a game (Figure 12-8). You could limit motion of those items to just left and right. Use either 'x' (to constrain the dragged item to just left and right movement) or 'y' (to make sure the dragged item can only be moved up and down the page):

  ```
  axis : 'x'
  ```

- **cancel.** This option lets you prevent dragging an item if a specific element is clicked on. For example, say you had a playlist of songs (an unordered list). Next to the name of each song is a trashcan icon; users could click this icon to remove the song from the list. However, if a user grabbed that icon, he could drag the song to new spot on the list instead of delete the song. To prevent an element *inside* a sortable item from acting as handle, provide a selector to the cancel option:

  ```
  cancel :  '.trashcan'
  ```

  Now, if someone clicked on the trashcan icon (assuming that icon had a class name of trashcan applied to it), she wouldn't trigger the dragging action. You can even specify multiple elements—just separate them by commas:

  ```
  cancel : '.trashcan, .addToFavorites'
  ```

  The handle option, discussed on page 431, lets you specify a particular element to act as the "grabbable" part of the item.

- **connectWith.** Lets you specify a selector of *other* sortable items—another list—that you can drag a list item to. For example, say you had two lists on a page: a wish list of products that you'd like to buy, and a shopping cart list that includes all the products you're going to buy. You might want to re-order your wish list—put your most desired products at the top of the list, for example— but also be able to drag an item from the wish list to the shopping cart list. In this case, you'd have two different lists, and apply the `sortable()` function separately to each. However, using the `connectWith` option, you can let users drag an item from one list to another:

```
$('#wishList').sortable({
  connectWith : '#shoppingCart'
});
```

The `connectWith` option is a one-way connection. In other words, in the above code, you could only drag items from the group of items within the wish list to the shopping cart, but not from the shopping cart to the wish list. To connect both lists, you need to use the `connectWith` option on both lists:

```
$('#shoppingCart').sortable({
  connectWith : '#wishList'
});
```

The value you supply the `connectWith` option should be a selector that matches an element to which you've applied the `sortable()` function.

- **containment.** You can prevent a visitor from dragging a list item outside a container element. This works just like the `containment` option for the draggable widget (page 403). In fact, a sortable item is really just a draggable item that you can insert within a list of items. The containment option accepts several possible values:

  - **A selector.** If you provide a selector name, then jQuery UI will keep the list item confined to the boundaries of that element. For example, if you had a `<div>` on the page with an ID of `mainContent`, you could keep the draggable element inside that div by setting the containment option like this:

    ```
    containment :  '#mainContent'
    ```

  - **parent, document, or window.** To keep the list item contained inside its parent element, use `parent` as the value. For example, if the list item is an unordered list and you want to limit the dragging to within that list:

    ```
    containment :  'parent'
    ```

    The `document` and `window` values are nearly the same, except `document` keeps the entire draggable area contained within the document area and `window` lets you drag the element partly outside the window (this doesn't look very good, so think twice before using `window`).

- **cursor.** Same as the `cursor` setting for draggable items (page 403)

- **cursorAt.** Same as the `cursorAt` setting for draggable items (page 404)

- **delay.** An amount in milliseconds to delay dragging the sortable item. This delay is handy if you find it easy to accidentally drag a list item as you're mousing around the page. The delay indicates how long someone needs to hold down the mouse button before the dragging is allowed:

  ```
  delay : 100
  ```

- **distance.** A pixel distance that a list item must be dragged before sorting begins. This is useful if visitors need to click on a sortable item other than to drag it. For example, if the sortable item includes a button to delete that item, you could set the `distance` option to prevent the item from being dragged when a visitor accidentally moves the mouse when clicking on the Delete button. Use a small number for this setting (otherwise, visitors will have to drag the item a fair distance before seeing the sortable behavior):

  ```
  distance : 10
  ```

- **grid.** Snaps the list item to a grid. This option could work well if you have a group of equally sized photos or divs: you can snap the list item to move exactly the width of the other list items when you drag it. It works just like the `grid` option for the draggable widget (page 404).

- **handle.** Indicates the part of the item the user must click to drag the item to another place in the list. Normally, users can drag by clicking on any spot of a sortable item. However, you might want to force users to click on a specific part of the item—like a tab. This option works like the `handle` option for draggable options described on page 405.

- **items.** You can limit which items within the sortable group can be sorted. For example, say you applied the sortable function to a nested list—a list containing indented lists or sublists (Figure 12-7). You don't want to make the top-level list items sortable (in Figure 12-7, the top-level list items are Folder A and Folder B). You do want nested list items to be sortable, so they can be dragged into other nested lists or rearranged in their current nested list.

  In this case, you can use the `items` option and set it to `'li li'`, which means only a list item inside another list item (a nested list item) can be sorted. The top-level lists aren't nested, so they can't be sorted:

  ```
  items : 'li li'
  ```

- **opacity.** When dragging an element you can make its opacity change. For example, you can fade the element to 50% opacity to give it a "ghost-like" appearance. Opacity is a common way to indicate that an item is moving from one place to another. Use a value between 0 (completely invisible) to 1 (completely opaque). This works just like the CSS `opacity` property. For example, to make the dragged element appear 50% transparent, set the value to 0.5:

  ```
  opacity : 0.5
  ```

- **placeholder.** A class name jQuery UI applies to the empty spot where a list item can be dragged to. You can use one of jQuery UI's own classes (page 395) to highlight this spot:

```
placeholder : 'ui-state-highlight'
```

FIGURE 12-7

You can create nested lists (lists within lists) in HTML by adding an unordered (`<ul>`) or ordered (`<ol>`) list tag inside a list item: `<li>Folder A <ul><li>Sublist</li></ul></li>`. jQuery UI lets you control which elements inside the sortable widget can be dragged and sorted, so you can limit sorting to just items inside nested lists.

> **NOTE** You'll find even more options for the sortable widget at *http://api.jqueryui.com/sortable/*.

Sortable Events

As a visitor interacts with a sortable list, jQuery UI fires off all sorts of events—like when a visitor starts dragging an item in the list and when he stops dragging that item. jQuery UI provides over a dozen different sortable widget events, each of which you can respond to with your own programming. Some of these events fire off very close to each other and, in practice, are indistinguishable.

As with the draggable and droppable widgets, you assign functions to a sortable event as part of the options object passed to the `sortable()` function. For example, to open an alert box after a user has moved an item in the list, you could write the following:

```
$('#playList').sortable({
  stop : function (event, ui) {
    alert('Well sorted, my friend!');
  }
});
```

Some events apply to all lists, and two only apply when you have two (or more) sortable lists on the same page and are dragging items between the lists. Suppose you start with a list of events that apply to all sortable widgets. These events are triggered in a specific order, so you'll list them that way:

- **create.** This event fires whenever you use the `sortable()` function to create a new sortable list. You could use this event to pop up a dialog box with instructions "Drag the songs around to re-order your playlist." It only runs once—when the sortable widget is created.

> **NOTE** Unlike all other Sortable widget events, the `create` event doesn't receive the `ui` object (described on page 409).

- **start.** Fired as soon as a user starts dragging a list item. The function you assign to this event accepts two arguments: an event object (page 164); and a `ui` object, which contains information about the widget. The `ui` object contains seven other objects, each with important information about the widget:

  - **ui.helper.** The helper object is a jQuery object that represents the item the user drags. jQuery UI makes a clone of the original item, so as you drag a sortable item, there are two different HTML elements in play: the helper clone and the actual element that's part of the list. When the visitor stops dragging the item, the helper element is removed from the document. Because helper is a regular jQuery object, you can use jQuery methods such as `css()`, `animate()`, or `find()` on it.

  - **ui.item.** Represents the actual sortable item that the visitor clicked to drag, like an `<li>` element. It's the real HTML element, and will be inserted into the proper spot in the list once the user has finished dragging the helper element. It's also a jQuery object, so all the regular jQuery methods apply to it.

  - **ui.position** provides the x and y position of the top-left corner of the helper item (the item that is visibly dragged across the screen) in relation its nearest positioned ancestor. If the sortable widget is inside a relative or absolutely positioned element, then the `ui.position` property will provide the top and left position values for the help in relation to the top-left of the positioned element.

    You can access those values like this: `ui.position.top` and `ui.position.left`.

  - **ui.originalPosition.** The original position of the sortable item; where it was before the user started to drag it. This is an object like `ui.position` with two properties—top and left.

  - **ui.offset** is an object with two properties top and left. But, in this case, the position is calculated relative to the top left of the browser window. The `ui.offset.top` property identifies how far the top of the helper element is from the top of the window.

    The `ui.offset.left` property identifies how many pixels the draggable item is placed from the left side of the browser window.

- **ui.sender.** This property only applies when dragging from one sortable widget to another. The ui.sender property contains a jQuery object for the sortable widget the dragged item is coming from.

- **placeholder.** A jQuery object representing the empty placeholder spot created when dragging a sortable item.

The ui object is available to all other sortable event handlers—activate, over, sort, and so on—except the create event.

- **activate.** Fires just after start, but at basically the same moment. You can use this to add a second function you want to run just after a function you've assigned to start.

- **sort.** The sort event fires each time the mouse is moved while a sortable item is being dragged. In other words, this event fires off continuously, so don't assign any time- or processor-intensive tasks to this event. If you do, the repeated calling of the function will slow the page's responsiveness and probably make dragging the Sortable widget difficult for your visitors.

- **change.** This event is fired as soon as sortable items change place. For example, when you drag an item from the top of a list down, and the second item jumps up to replace the first, the change event is triggered. You could use this event to highlight the two items that swapped position, for example.

- **beforestop.** The beforestop event fires just after the user lets go of a sortable item. It's the last event that still has access to the ui.helper object. After this event, the ui.helper (the clone of the dragged) item is deleted.

- **update.** When all of the sortable items are in place, and the DOM has been updated, the update event fires.

- **deactivate.** When sorting is done, the deactivate event always fires immediately after update.

- **stop.** After the sortable item is dropped into place, the stop event fires. This event is last of all, and always follows stop and deactivate. Assign a function to this event, when you want it to be the last thing to happen after a list item has been dropped. For example, you could use the stop event to check the status of the list to see if it matches some pre-defined order (Figure 12-7).

The events just listed fire in the order listed above. However, there are a few other events that are triggered at different times and for different types of Sortable widgets.

- **out.** The out event is trigged when a sortable item is moved out of a Sortable widget; for example, if you drag an item out of its Sortable widget to an empty spot on the page. It also fires when you move an item out of one Sortable widget into another.

- **over.** When you move a sortable item over a connected list. For example, if you have two connected lists and drag an item from the first list to the second, then the over event fires on that second list. This event also fires when you move an item off a group of sortable items and then back onto it.

- **receive.** Use the receive event when using multiple connected Sortable widgets (see the connectWith option on page 429). When a sortable widget receives an item from another sortable widget, the receive event fires. You can use this event in conjunction with the ui.sender object (page 434) to determine where the new sortable item came from.

- **remove.** This event fires when an item is removed from the current sortable widget. For example, say you had two sortable widgets: a wish list and a shopping cart. If a shopper dragged an item from the wish list to the shopping cart, the remove event would fire on the wish list (as well as the out event). (In this scenario, the over and receive events would fire on the shopping cart as well.)

Sortable Methods

The sortable widget includes several different methods, or functions that you can run on the widget. You don't call these methods as you would a normal jQuery method, like selecting a page element then applying the method to it like this: $('body'). hide(). Instead, you give the method name, as a string, to the sortable() method. Say you're using the destroy method, which completely removes the sortable widget—it returns a sortable set of list items, to regular list items that can't be dragged. The code to invoke the destroy method looks like this:

```
$('#sortableItems').sortable('destroy');
```

The selector—#sortableItems, in this example—should match the selector for a sortable widget on the page. You'll commonly use these methods in response to one of the sortable events discussed in the previous section. For example, if you created a game that required a player to place a set of blocks into a particular order, you could destroy the sortable after the player completed the game, keeping him from moving the blocks again.

You can find a complete list of sortable methods at *http://api.jqueryui.com/sortable/*, but here are a few of the most useful:

- **cancel.** This cancels any change in the current order of a sortable. In other words, it stops the re-ordering of the list. You could use this with the receive method (page 435), to reject a list item that was dragged to another sortable widget. Or as part of the stop event (page 434), you could create a function that checks the placement of the newly dropped item, and rejects that change if the item doesn't meet certain conditions. For example, in a to-do list application, you might make certain tasks dependent upon other tasks. For example, if a user tries to drag a task to the top of the to-do list, but another task must be completed first, you could cancel that user's action and pop up a dialog box with an explanation of why the move was rejected.

- **destroy.** To completely remove the sortable functionality of a sortable widget, use the destroy method.

- **disable.** To temporarily remove the sortable functionality of a widget, invoke the `disable` method. Use this when you want to prevent sorting temporarily, until some other condition is true. You can turn the sorting back on with the `enable` method (discussed next).

- **enable.** Turn sorting back on for a disabled sortable widget—a widget that previously had the `disable` method applied to it.

- **serialize.** This method is useful for sending the order of the list back to a web server via Ajax or a form post. You might want to do this if it's important to store this information on the server for later use. For example, if a manager was organizing a list of tasks for her employees, the order could be sent to the server, stored in a database, and retrieved when an employee logged in to see what tasks needed to be done (and in what order). You need to format your sortable items in a specific way:

  - Each list item must have an ID

  - Each ID should begin with the same word, which acts like a group identifier for the list, followed by an underscore (_) character.

  - After the _ character in the ID name must follow a unique identifier for the list item.

For example, say you had a playlist of songs. The HTML might look like this:

```
<ul id="playlist">
  <li id="song_1">My Way -- Frank Sinatra</li>
  <li id="song_2">Like a Rolling Stone -- Bob Dylan</li>
  <li id="song_3">Respect -- Aretha Franklin</li>
</ul>
```

Notice that the ID for each list item begins with "song_" and ends with a unique number. It doesn't have to be a number—it could be a word, or a unique ID from a database. The idea is to provide a way to let the server know the new order of the list.

You can use the `serialize` method to capture the current order of the list:

```
var listOrder = $('#playlist").sortable('serialize');
```

The `serialize` method returns a string that looks something like this:

```
song[]=2&song[]=3&song[]=1
```

The string indicates the order of the items in the list. In this case, the numbers are 2, 3, and 1, indicating that the first item in the list was dragged to the bottom of the list. You can tag the string value returned by `serialize` to a URL as part of an Ajax call (Chapter 13).

> **NOTE** The `serialize` method lets you provide options that control the format of the string returned by the method. You can read about those options at *http://api.jqueryui.com/sortable/#method-serialize.*

- **toArray.** The `toArray` method, like `serialize`, is a way to retrieve an ordered list of items in a sortable widget. To use it, you must add an ID to each item in the sortable list. But, unlike the `serialize` method, it doesn't require any special format. The method simply returns an array listing the ID of each item in the sortable widget in the order the items appear in the list. For example, say you had a sortable widget with an ID of `colorList`. Inside it are three list items, each with a different color:

```
<ul id="colorList">
  <li id="red">Red</li>
  <li id="green">Green</li>
  <li id="blue">Blue</li>
</ul>
```

Say a user dragged the colors into a different order so Blue was first, Red was second, and Green was last. You could use the `toArray` method at that point like this:

```
var colors = $('#colorList').sortable('toArray');
```

The color variable would then contain this array:

```
['blue', 'red', 'green']
```

The result is a basic JavaScript array (page 44). You can use any of the array methods discussed on pages 46-51 to manipulate it.

One use of the `toArray` method is to see the order of the list matches some predefined state. For example, say you created a game that showed a randomly assorted list of color blocks. The player is supposed to sort the blocks into the order they appear in the rainbow (remember, ROY G BIV?). You could add a function to the `stop` event (page 434) that gets the current order of the blocks using the `toArray` method and then compares it to another array containing the answer (Figure 12-8).

NOTE jQuery UI includes two other interaction widgets. The resizable widget is used by the dialog widget (page 305) to let users resize them by dragging a resize handle in the corner of the box. You can use this widget to make resizable floating windows. Learn more about this widget at *http://api.jqueryui.com/resizable/*.

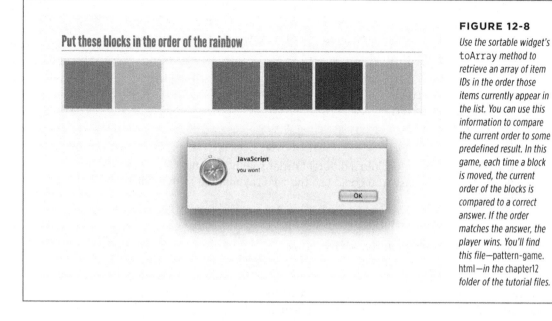

FIGURE 12-8

Use the sortable widget's toArray *method to retrieve an array of item IDs in the order those items currently appear in the list. You can use this information to compare the current order to some predefined result. In this game, each time a block is moved, the current order of the blocks is compared to a correct answer. If the order matches the answer, the player wins. You'll find this file—pattern-game. html—in the* chapter12 *folder of the tutorial files.*

NOTE The selectable widget lets a visitor select elements (highlight them) by clicking them. You could use it for a photo download page: "Select the photos that you'd like to download." Learn more at: *http://api.jqueryui. com/selectable/.*

jQuery UI Effects

jQuery UI includes a suite of visual, animated effects that you can use to enliven your web applications. For example, the explode effect, which you saw in action in the tutorial on page 425—makes an element break apart and fade out of view. You'll learn more about these kinds of effects in a moment, but first you need to know how to apply them.

Effects are intended to either bring an element into view, make the element disappear, or highlight the element in some way—for example, by making it light up or shake. To apply effects, you use either jQuery functions, as you've done so far in this book, or the jQuery UI-only effect() function. For example, to use the jQuery UI drop effect to make an element appear to drop onto the page, you could use the show() method with the name of the effect and a duration:

```
$('#pageElement').show('drop', 1000);
```

This would "drop" the element onto the page over the course of 1 second (1,000 milliseconds). The show() method should look familiar (page 184). It's a jQuery function that reveals a hidden element on the page. However, jQuery UI adds some new features to jQuery's show() function as well as to two other jQuery functions. jQuery UI offers four different functions for adding effects to elements:

- **show().** jQuery UI extends jQuery's show() function by letting you use one of 15 different effects to reveal an already hidden element. You should make sure the element is hidden (see the hide() method on page 184) before using show(); otherwise, you'll end up with the element quickly disappearing then reappearing.

- **hide().** To apply one of jQuery UI's effects while hiding an element, use the hide() method. It works like jQuery hide() function (page 184) in that it makes an element disappear from the page—but using a special effect. Make sure the element is visible on the page, before using this function.

- **toggle().** The toggle() method either shows or hides an element. If the element is hidden, the toggle() makes it appear using a specified effect. If the element is visible, then toggle() reveals the element.

- **effect().** Most of jQuery UI's effects are designed to reveal or hide an element with flair. A few effects—bounce, highlight, pulsate, and shake—can be used to highlight an already visible item without making it disappear. The highlight effect, for example, momentarily highlights an item by flashing a bright color, providing a great way to draw a visitor's attention to a specific spot on the page. The effect() function is unique to jQuery UI and isn't a normal jQuery function.

> **NOTE** You'll use the effect() function in the web app you're going to build in Chapter 14.

The Effects

The jQuery UI effects add powerful animated tools to your web design toolkit. You can pass each of these effects as an argument to the functions listed above. Each effect provides a different visual result.

The basic structure for using an effect with one of the above functions looks like this:

```
$('#element').hide('effectName', { optionName : optionValue }, duration, call-
BackFunction);
```

For example, if you wanted to hide an element with an ID of deleteThis on the page by making it explode into 16 pieces in half a second, and then pop up an alert box that says "Boom!" you'd write this code:

```
$('#deleteThis').hide('explode', { pieces : 16 }, 500, function () {
  alert('Boom!');
});
```

Most effects let you pass one or more additional options to control how the effect works. Options are passed as an object consisting of option names and values. In the previous example, the option is the number of pieces the explode effect should divide the element into:

```
{ pieces : 16 }
```

Each effect has different options, and some effects have no options at all. jQuery UI provides many effects:

- **blind.** The blind effect either shows or hides an element simulating a blind being lifted open or pulled closed. The effect accepts one option—direction—which indicates the direction the blind should move: up, down, left, or right. You pass the option as an object—option name and value—as second argument to the function. For example, to make a particular element disappear from the screen:

  ```
  $('#element').hide('blind', { direction : 'left'}, 1000);
  ```

- **bounce.** The bounce effect can be applied when hiding or showing an element. You can also use bounce with the effect() function to simply bounce a visible item up and down—a great way to make a page element say "look at me!!!!" The effect has two options:

  - **distance.** The farthest distance (in pixels) that the element will travel as it bounces. The higher the number, the farther it bounces, and the more attention it grabs.

  - **times.** The number of times the element will bounce.

  For example, to make an item bounce 20 times, at a distance of 100 pixels every time it's clicked, you could write this code:

  ```
  $('#theElement').click(function () {
    $(this).effect('bounce', {
        distance : 100,
        times : 20
      },
      1000
    );
  });
  ```

- **clip.** The clip effect applies the CSS clip attribute to an item to make it appear either vertically or horizontally. The effect accepts only one option—direction with a value of either vertical or horizontal:

  ```
  { direction : 'horizontal' }
  ```

- **drop.** The drop effect shows or hides an element by fading it into or out of view while sliding it up, down, left, or right. It has a single option, direction, which accepts one of the following four values: up, down, left, or right.

- **explode.** The explode effect divides an element into a bunch of pieces, animates them outward and fades them out of view. When used with the show() function, the element looks like an explosion in reverse: separate pieces coming together to form a whole. It only has one option—pieces—which indicates the number of pieces the element should be divided into. The number has to be a squared value: 1, 4, 9, 16, 25, and so on (but don't make the number any bigger than 25 or this effect slows down to a crawl):

```
{ pieces : 16 }
```

- **fade.** Works like jQuery's `fadeIn()` and `fadeOut()` functions. In other words, it's not a terribly exciting effect.

- **fold.** The `fold` effect shows or hides an element by folding it. You can set two options for this intriguing visual effect. `size` is the size in pixels (or percentages) that the item should reduce to before folding in the opposite direction and `horizFirst` accepts a Boolean value that determines whether the element should fold up vertically first (the default) or horizontally first:

```
{ size : '50%', horizFirst : true }
```

- **highlight.** The `highlight` effect momentarily changes the background color of an element to draw attention to it. It's another effect you can use on a visible element without hiding it. You can change the color of the background color by setting the `color` option. For example, to highlight an element by flashing a red background color for 1 second, you could apply the `effect()` method like this:

```
$('#element').effect('highlight', { color : '#ff0000' }, 1000);
```

- **puff.** This effect makes an element change size and fade out (or into) view. It has a single option, `percent`, which dictates the percentage the element should fade from (if showing the element) or fade to (if hiding the element):

```
{ percent : 200 }
```

- **pulsate.** Another effect that you can use to draw attention to an element without hiding it first. This effect hides and shows an element repeatedly. You can dictate the number of times the element pulsates by setting the `times` option like this:

```
$('#element').effect('pulsate', {times : 20}, 2000);
```

- **scale.** Use this effect to scale an element. You can use this effect with either the `hide()` or `show()` methods. Normally, if you use the `show()` method to reveal a hidden element, the element will scale up from a tiny spot on the page to its full size; if the element is visible and you use the `hide()` method, the element will shrink and disappear.

- **shake.** This effect can be applied to an element that's visible on the page using the `effect()` function (page 439). It simply shakes the element a specific direction, distance, and number of times. This is another one of those "Pay attention to me" type of effects, but it can serve a more important purpose, like indicating an error; for example, shaking a dialog box when a visitor hasn't checked the "Terms of service" box on a signup form. This effect has three options. The `direction` option dictates the direction to begin shaking the element: up, down, left, or right. Set the `distance` option to specify the number of pixels the element should move on each shake; the greater the number, the more obvious the shaking action. Finally, the `times` option indicates the number of times the element shakes. For example, to shake an element left (and keep shaking it horizontally) 10 times, 50 pixels each time, you'd pass this object containing these options to the `effect()` function:

```
{ direction : 'left' , distance : 50, times : 10 }
```

- **size.** This effect resizes an element to a specified width and height. It accepts three options: `to` is an object with `width` and `height` properties dictating the width and height the element should be resized to (when hiding the element) or the width and height to start at (when showing the element).

   The `origin` property dictates the vanishing point when using the `size` effect to hide an element. It's an array of two numbers: the first number indicates the top position, and the second the left position.

   The `scale` property is used to indicate what should be scaled. The possible values include both, box, and content. For example, to increase or decrease just the size of the outer box (the border, background, and width and height) use the box value. Doing so doesn't scale the content (like text) inside the element.

- **slide.** This effect slides an element out of the viewport (if hiding it) or slides the element into place (if it's showing). Provide a `direction` option—left, right, up, or down—to dictate the direction the `slide` effect moves:

```
$('#element').show('slide', { direction : 'right' }, 1000 );
```

> **NOTE** To learn more about jQueryUI effects, visit *http://api.jqueryui.com/category/effects/*.

Easing

jQuery UI includes a set of *easing* functions that control the speed of changes during an animation. Easing doesn't change the overall time an effect takes to animate, but does changes the speed at which individual parts of an animation occur. For example, if you use the bounce effect, you could apply an easing function that makes the bouncing start slowly then bounce really quickly before stopping.

> **NOTE** Visit the jQuery UI Easings page to see what each easing function looks like and to try them out: *http://api.jqueryui.com/easings/*.

To use an easing function with an effect, you need to pass it as a property of the options object. Its property name is `easing`, and the value should be one of the possible easing functions—easeInOutQuart, easeInSine, and so on (for a complete list of easing function names, visit *http://api.jqueryui.com/easings/*).

For example, say you want to use the bounce effect (page 440), to bounce an element each time it's clicked. You want the element to bounce 20 times with a maximum distance of 100 pixels (those are both options of the bounce effect). You also want to apply an easing function to make it look more realistic—a bouncing element slows down as it runs out of energy. You could add an easing property to the options object like this:

```
$('#theElement').click(function () {
  $(this).effect('bounce', {
      distance : 100,
      times : 20,
      easing : 'easeOutBounce'
    },
    1000
  );
});
```

You're not limited to using these easing functions only with jQuery UI's effects. As discussed on page 192, you can use these functions with jQuery UI animations as well.

Animating Changes Between Classes

jQuery UI includes several functions that animate changes to an element's CSS properties when a class is added or removed from the element. These functions are actually extensions of existing jQuery functions: addClass(), toggleClass(), and removeClass() (page 131). jQuery UI simply adds animation to the changes, so when you add or remove a class, jQuery UI animates the visual changes that occur because of the addition or removal of CSS properties.

> **NOTE** jQuery UI's class animations may sound a lot like CSS transitions. In fact, they're very similar: while CSS transitions depend on the browser's built-in CSS rendering engine, jQuery uses JavaScript to animate the changes. CSS transitions are actually a better way to go: they work more smoothly and don't require any work from the JavaScript interpreter. However, CSS transitions aren't supported by Internet Explorer 9 or earlier, therefore you may need to use jQuery UI's class animation feature to get the same effect in those browsers. However, if you don't need to support outdated versions of Internet Explorer, then use CSS transitions, and skip these jQuery UI functions. To learn more about CSS transitions, visit: *https://developer.mozilla.org/en-US/docs/Web/Guide/CSS/ Using_CSS_transitions.*

Each of jQuery UI's class animation features accept up to four arguments to modify how they work. The first argument is the class name you want to add or remove. The next three are composed of a duration, easing, and completion function—the same arguments you pass the effect() method (page 439). For example, to select an element with the ID of feature, add a class name highlight, and animate the visual changes caused by adding that class, you could write this:

```
$('#feature').addClass('highlight', 1000, 'easeOutBack', function () {
    alert('done animating');
});
```

This code adds the highlight class to the selected element and animates the visual changes to the element over the course of 1 second (1,000 milliseconds) using the easeOutBack easing method (page 442). After jQuery UI is finished animating the class change, a callback function is run opening an alert box with the words "done animating." Only a class name and duration are necessary to get the animated effect.

jQuery UI provides four functions for animating class changes:

- The **addClass() method** lets you add a class to one or more elements and animate the visual changes over a specified amount of time.

> **NOTE** If you don't pass a time argument to any of these methods, jQuery UI simply uses the standard jQuery form of the function, without animation. For example:
>
> ```
> $('#feature').addClass('highlight');
> ```
>
> This code adds the class highlight to the element, but doesn't animate the change.

- The **removeClass() method** works just like the addClass() method. You pass it a class name, animation duration, optional easing value, and optional callback function. However, this function *removes* the specified class and animates any visual changes caused by removing that class.

- The **toggleClass() method** removes a class from an element if that class is in place, or adds the specified class if it's missing. You could use this function in conjunction with a click event (page 149) to add a class the first time an element is clicked, then remove that class the next time it's clicked—in this way, you could create a "light switch" element that's either on or off. Of course, this function also animates the changes caused by adding or removing the class.

> **NOTE** jQuery UI's toggleClass() method has more advanced options as well. You can read about them at: *http://api.jqueryui.com/toggleClass/*.

- The **switchClass() method** is the only one of these jQuery UI class methods that has no jQuery equivalent. It takes two class names: the first is the class that jQuery UI removes from the selected elements, and the second is a class that jQuery UI adds. It's kind of like combining the removeClass() and addClass() methods together, but lets you animate the changes from the class you're removing to the class you're adding. For example, if you're removing a class with a red background color and adding a class with a green background color, jQuery UI will animate that background color change by transitioning from red to green:

  ```
  $('#feature').switchClass('defaultStyles','highlight',1000);
  ```

> **NOTE** To learn more about jQueryUI methods, visit the Effects Core page at *http://api.jqueryui.com/category/effects-core/*.

Advanced jQuery and JavaScript

Introducing Ajax

JavaScript is great, but it can't do everything. If you want to display information from a database, dash off an email with results from a form, or just download additional HTML, you need to communicate with a web server. For these tasks, you usually need to load a new web page. For example, when you search a database for information, you usually leave the search page and go to another page of results.

Of course, waiting for new pages to load takes time. If anything, people want websites to feel faster and more responsive, as if they were operating right on their own desktop, not on some far-off server. Sites like Facebook, Twitter, Google Docs, and Gmail are blurring the line between websites and desktop computer programs. The technology that makes this new generation of web applications possible is a programming technology called Ajax.

Ajax lets a web page ask for and receive a response from a web server and then update itself without ever having to load a new web page. The result is a website that feels more responsive. For example, when you visit Google Maps (Figure 13-1), you can zoom into the map; move north, south, east, or west; and even grab the map and drag it around. All of these actions happen without ever loading a new web page.

◾ What Is Ajax?

The term Ajax was originally coined in 2005 to capture the essence of new websites coming from Google—Google Maps (*http://maps.google.com*), and Gmail (*www.gmail.com*). Ajax stands for *Asynchronous JavaScript and XML*, but it isn't an "official" technology like HTML, JavaScript, or CSS. It's a term that refers to the interaction of a mix of technologies—JavaScript, the web browser, and the web server—to retrieve and display new content without loading a new web page.

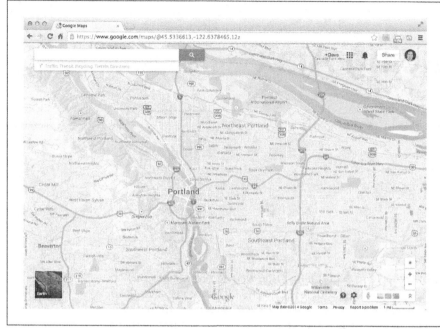

FIGURE 13-1

Google Maps (http://maps.google.com) was one of the first large sites to use Ajax to refresh page content without loading new web pages. The site's responsiveness is due to the fact that only the map data changes—the other parts of the page, like the search box, search results sidebar, and map controls, remain the same even as you request new map information.

Here's how Ajax works: you use JavaScript in your website to send a request from the web browser to a web server, which, in turn, sends some data back (called a *response*) to the web browser. The JavaScript program takes the response and does something with it. For example, if you're on a Google Maps page and click the "north" arrow button, the page's JavaScript code requests new map data from the Google server. Google sends back its response—new parts of the map—which the JavaScript then uses to update the map in the browser.

While you may not create the next Google Maps, there are many simple things that you can do with Ajax technologies:

- **Display new HTML content without reloading the page.** For example, on a page that lists news headlines and displays the article when a visitor clicks a headline, you can save her the tiresome wait for a new page to load. Instead, the news story could appear right on the same web page, without the banner, sidebar, footer, or other page content needing to reload. You'll learn how on page 455.

- **Submit a form and instantly display results.** For example, imagine a "sign up for our newsletter" form; when someone fills out and submits the form, the form disappears and a "you're signed up for our newsletter" message immediately appears. You'll learn how to make such forms using Ajax on page 471.

- **Log in without leaving the page.** Here's another form-related use of JavaScript—a page with a small "login" form. Fill out the form, hit the "login" button, and you're not only logged in, the page transforms to show your login status, username, and perhaps other information specific to you.

- **Star-rating widget.** On sites that list books, movies, and other products, you often see a star rating—usually 1 to 5 stars—to indicate how visitors have rated the item's quality. These rating systems usually let you voice your opinion by clicking a number of stars. Using Ajax, you can let your visitors cast votes without actually leaving the web page—all they have to do is click the stars. There's a cool jQuery plug-in that does just that: *www.wbotelhos.com/raty/*.

- **Browsing through database information.** Amazon is a typical example of an online database you can browse. When you search Amazon for books on, say, JavaScript, you get a list of the JavaScript books Amazon sells. Usually, there are more books than can fit on a single web page, so you need to jump from page to page to see "the next 10 items." Using Ajax, you can move through database records without having to jump to another page. Here's how Twitter uses Ajax: When you view your Twitter page, you see a bunch of tweets from the people you follow. If you scroll to the bottom of the page, Twitter loads more tweets. Scroll again and more tweets appear. It's like a never-ending web page!

There's nothing revolutionary about any of the tasks listed here—except for the "without loading a new page" part, you can achieve the same basic results using regular HTML and some server-side programming (to collect form data, or access database information, for example). However, Ajax makes web pages feel much more responsive, and lets you create a richer experience for your visitor.

■ Ajax: The Basics

Taken together, the technologies behind Ajax are pretty complicated. They encompass JavaScript, server-side programming, and the web browser all working together. However, the basic concept is easy to grasp, as long as you understand all of the steps involved. Figure 13-2 shows the difference between how HTML web pages and web pages with Ajax communicate with the web server.

Pieces of the Puzzle

Ajax isn't a single technology—it's a mixture of several different technologies that work together to make a more effective user experience. In essence, Ajax brings together three different components:

- **The web browser.** Obviously, you need a web browser to view web pages and run JavaScript, but there's a secret ingredient built into web browsers that makes Ajax possible: the XMLHttpRequest *object*. This odd-sounding term is what lets JavaScript talk to a web server and receive information in response.

The XMLHttpRequest object was actually introduced way back in Internet Explorer 5, but has made its way into all the major web browsers. You'll learn more about it on page 452.

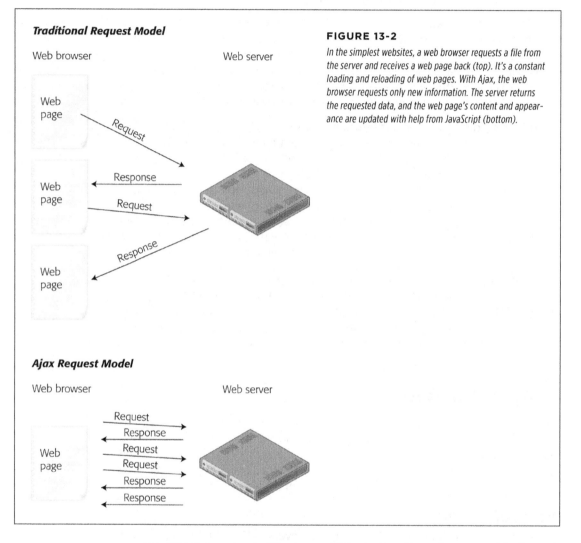

Traditional Request Model

Web browser   Web server

Web page

Request

Response

Web page

Request

Response

Web page

Ajax Request Model

Web browser   Web server

Web page

Request
Response
Request
Request
Response
Response

FIGURE 13-2

In the simplest websites, a web browser requests a file from the server and receives a web page back (top). It's a constant loading and reloading of web pages. With Ajax, the web browser requests only new information. The server returns the requested data, and the web page's content and appearance are updated with help from JavaScript (bottom).

- **JavaScript** does most of the heavy lifting in Ajax. It sends a request to the web server, waits for a response, processes the response, and (usually) updates the page by adding new content or changing the display of the page in some way. Depending upon what you want your program to do, you might have JavaScript send information from a form, request additional database records, or simply send a single piece of data (like the rating a visitor just gave to a book). After the data is sent to the server, the JavaScript program will be ready for a response back from the server—for example, additional database records or just a simple text message like "Your vote has been counted."

With that information, JavaScript will update the web page—display new database records, for example, or inform the visitor that he's successfully logged in. Updating a web page involves manipulating a page's DOM (Document Object Model, discussed on page 117) to add, change, and remove HTML tags and content. In fact, that's what you've been doing for most of this book: changing a page's content and appearance using JavaScript.

- **The web server** receives requests from and sends information back to the web browser. The server might simply return some HTML or plain text, or it might return an XML document (see the box on page 471) or JSON data (page 477). For example, if the web server receives information from a form, it might add that information into a database and send back a confirmation message (like "record added"). Or, the JavaScript code might send a request for the next 10 records of a database search, and the web server will send back the information for those next 10 records.

The web server part of the equation can get a bit tricky. It usually involves several different types of technologies, including a web server, application server, and database server. A web server is really kind of a glorified filing cabinet: It stores documents and when a web browser asks for a document, the web server delivers it. To do more complicated tasks such as putting data from a form into a database, you also need an *application server* and a *database server*. An application server is programmed in a language like PHP, Java, C#, Ruby, or Cold Fusion Markup Language and lets you perform tasks that aren't possible with only an HTML page, like sending email, checking Amazon for book prices, or storing information in a database. The database server lets you store information like the names and addresses of customers, details of products you sell, or an archive of your favorite recipes. Common database servers include MySQL, PostgreSQL, and SQL Server.

> **NOTE** The term *server* can refer either to a piece of hardware or software. In this book, the terms *application*, *web*, and *database* server refer to different pieces of software that can (and often do) run on the same machine.

There are many different combinations of web servers, application servers, and database servers. You might use Microsoft's IIS web server with ASP.NET (application server) and SQL server (a database server), for example. Or you can use Apache (a web server), PHP (an application server), and MySQL (a database).

> **NOTE** The combination of Apache, PHP, and MySQL (often referred to simply as AMP) is very common and available at no cost. You'll find that most web hosting companies provide these servers for you. This book's examples also use AMP (see the box on page 452).

Setting Up a Web Server

Ajax works with a web server—after all, its main purpose is to let JavaScript send and retrieve information from a server. While the Flickr tutorial in this following chapter will run on your local computer without a web server, the others won't. In addition, you'll need to have access to a web server if you want to further explore the world of Ajax. If you've already got a website on the Internet, one choice is to test your Ajax programs by moving your files to the web server. Unfortunately, this technique is cumbersome—you have to create the pages on your computer and then move them to your web server using a FTP program just to see if they work.

A better approach is to set up a *development server*, which involves installing a web server on your desktop computer so you can program and test your Ajax pages directly on your own computer. This task may sound daunting, but there are plenty of free programs that make installing all of the necessary components as easy as double-clicking a file.

On the Windows side, you can install Apache, PHP, and MySQL using WAMP (*www.wampserver.com/en/*). WAMP is a free installer that sets up all of the required elements needed to simulate a real website hosted on the Internet.

For Mac fans, MAMP (*www.mamp.info/en*) provides an easy-to-use program that includes Apache, PHP, and MySQL. It's also free. (There's even a version of MAMP for Windows.)

The tutorials on pages 458 and 471 require a web server. So if you want to follow along with that tutorial, you'll need to install a web server on your computer using one of the two programs just mentioned. If you already have a website that uses a different web server (for example, Microsoft's IIS), you'll probably want to install it on your computer if you plan to create Ajax applications that you'd like to use on your real website. *IIS* is already installed in Windows 8; you just need to turn it on. This video will show you how: *https://www.youtube.com/watch?v=mRm9-Xddt2w*.

Talking to the Web Server

The core of any Ajax program is the XMLHttpRequest object. Sometimes just referred to as *XHR*, the XMLHttpRequest object is a feature built into web browsers that allows JavaScript to send information to a web server and receive information in return. There are basically five steps, all of which can be accomplished with JavaScript:

1. **Create an instance of the XMLHttpRequest object.**

   This first step simply tells the web browser "Hey, I want to send some information to the web server, so get ready." In its most basic form, creating an XMLHttpRequest object in JavaScript looks like this:

   ```
   var xhr = new XMLHttpRequest();
   ```

   While this bit is simple, programming Ajax with plain JavaScript can be tough. Fortunately, jQuery provides an easier way to make Ajax requests. You'll learn the jQuery way on page 455.

2. **Use the XHR's `open()` method to specify a method for sending the data and where the data will go.**

You can send data in several ways. The two most common are GET and POST—these are the same options as used with HTML forms. The GET method sends any information to the web server as part of the URL—*shop.php?productID=34.* In this example, the data is sent as a "query string." The query string is the information that follows the ? (in this case, *productID=34*). This is a name/value pair, where *productID* is the name and *34* is the value. Think of the name like the name of a field on a form and the value as what a visitor would type into that field.

The POST method sends data separately from the URL. Usually, you use the GET method to get data back from the server, and the POST method to send information that the server needs to keep (for example, to add, update, or delete a database record). You'll learn how to use both methods on page 462.

You also use the `open()` method to specify the page on the server the data is sent to. That's usually a page on your web server that uses a server-side scripting language like PHP to retrieve data from a database or perform some other programming task, and you point to it by its URL. For example, the following code tells the XHR object what method to use (GET) and which page on the server to request:

```
xhr.open('GET', 'shop.php?productID=34');
```

> **NOTE** The URL you specify for the `open()` method must be on the same website as the page making the request. For security, web browsers won't let you make Ajax requests to other domains. JSONP provides one way around this security problem. You'll learn about it on page 483.

3. **Create a function to handle the results.**

When the web server returns a result like new database information, a confirmation that a form was processed, or just a simple text message, you usually want to do something with that result. That could be as simple as writing the message "form submitted successfully," or replacing an entire table of database records with a new table of records. In any case, you need to write a JavaScript function to deal with the results—this function (called a *callback function*) is often the meat of your program.

Usually, this function will manipulate the page's content (that is, change the page's DOM) by removing elements (for example, removing a form that was just submitted using Ajax), adding elements (a "form submitted successfully" message, or a new HTML table of database records), or changing elements (for example, highlighting the number of stars a visitor just clicked to rate a product).

There are a few other steps involved here, but you'll be using jQuery to handle the details, so the only thing you really need to understand about the callback function is that it's the JavaScript that deals with the server's response.

4. Send the request.

To actually send information to the web server, you use the XHR object's send()
method. Everything up to this point is just setup—*this* step is what tells the web
browser, "We're good to go...send the request!" If you're using the GET method,
this step is as simple as:

```
xhr.send();
```

The send() method can accept an argument—data that should be sent to the
server. In the case, of a GET request, the data is sent in the URL like this: *search.
php?q=javascript*, where the *q=javascript* is the data. With the POST method, on
the other hand, you must provide the data along with the *send()* method like this:

```
xhr.send('q=javascript');
```

Again, don't sweat the details here—you'll see how jQuery greatly simplifies
this process starting in the next section.

Once the request is sent, your JavaScript code doesn't necessarily stop. The "A"
in Ajax stands for *asynchronous*, which means that after the request is sent, the
JavaScript program can continue doing other things. The web browser doesn't
just sit around and wait for the server to respond.

5. Receive the response.

After the server has processed the request, it sends back a response to the
web browser. Actually, the callback function you created in step 3 handles the
response, but meanwhile, the XHR object receives several pieces of information when the web server responds, including the status of the request, a text
response, and possibly an XML response.

The status response is a number indicating how the server responded to the
request: You're probably familiar with the status number 404—it means the file
wasn't found. If everything went according to plan, you'll get a status of 200 or
possibly 304. If there was an error processing the page, you'll get a 500 Internal
Server Error status report, and if the file you requested is password protected,
you'll get a 403 Access Forbidden error. For a complete list of status codes,
visit *www.w3.org/Protocols/rfc2616/rfc2616-sec10.html*.

In addition, most of the time, you'll receive a text response, which is stored in the
XHR object's responseText property. This response could be a chunk of HTML, a
simple text message, or a complex set of JSON data (page 477). Finally, if the server
responds with an XML file, it's stored in the XHR object's responseXML property. Although XML is still used, it's more common for program server pages to return text,
HTML, or JSON data, so you may never have a need to process an XML response.

Whatever data the server returns, it's available to the callback function to use to
update the web page. Once the callback function finishes, the entire Ajax cycle is
over. (However, you may have multiple Ajax requests shooting off at the same time.)

■ Ajax the jQuery Way

Although the basic XMLHttpRequest process isn't too complicated, you do have to repeat the same set of steps each time you make an XHR request. Fortunately, the jQuery library provides several functions that greatly simplify the entire process. After all, if you look at the five steps in an Ajax request (page 452), you'll see that the interesting stuff—the programming that actually does something with the server's response—happens in just a single step (step 3 on page 453). jQuery simplifies all of the other steps so you can concentrate on the really fun programming.

Using the load() Method

The simplest Ajax method offered by jQuery is load(). This method loads an HTML file into a specified element on the page. For example, say you have an area of a web page dedicated to a short list of news headlines. When the page loads, the five most recent news stories appear. You may want to add a few links that let visitors choose what type of news stories are displayed in this area of the page: for example, yesterday's news, local news, sports news, and so on. You can do this by linking to separate web pages, each of which contain the proper news items—but that would force your visitors to move onto another web page (and wouldn't use Ajax at all!).

Another approach would be to simply load the selected news stories into the news headlines box on the page. In other words, each time a visitor clicks a different news category, the web browser requests a new HTML file from the server, and then places that HTML into the headlines box—without leaving the current page (Figure 13-3).

UP TO SPEED

Learning the Ways of the Server Side

Unless you're using jQuery's basic load() function (discussed above) to insert HTML from a page on the server into the page in the web browser, you'll need to have server-side programming to use Ajax. The main point of Ajax is to let JavaScript talk to and get information from the server. Most of the time, that means there's another script running on the web server that completes tasks JavaScript can't do, like reading information from a database, sending off an email, or logging a user in.

This book doesn't cover the server side, so you'll need to learn how to program using a server-side technology like PHP, Ruby on Rails, .NET, or JSP (or you'll need someone who can program the server-side bit for you). If you haven't picked a server-side language yet, PHP is a good place to start: It's one of the most popular web server programming languages, it's

free, and nearly every web hosting company offers PHP on its servers. It's a powerful language that's built for the web, and it's *relatively* easy to learn. If you want to get started learning server-side programming with PHP, check out *Learning PHP, MySQL, and JavaScript* (O'Reilly) and *Head First PHP & MySQL* (O'Reilly).

There are also plenty of free online resources for learning PHP. PHP 101 *(http://devzone.zend.com/6/php-101-php-for-the-absolute-beginner/)* from Zend (one of the main companies that supports the development of PHP) has plenty of basic (and advanced) information. The W3Schools website also has a lot of information for the beginning PHP programmer at *www. w3schools.com/PHP.*

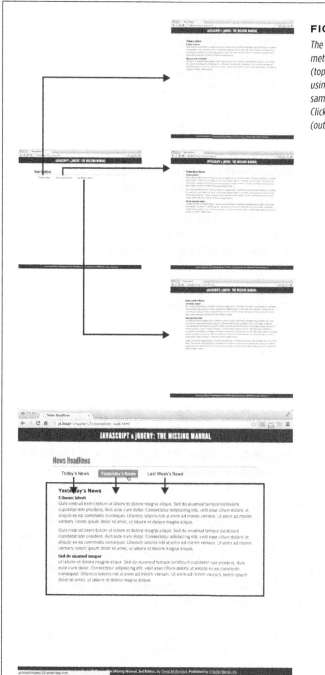

FIGURE 13-3

The top set of images shows how links work—the typical method of accessing additional HTML. Click a link on a page (top left) and it loads a brand new page (top right). However, using Ajax and jQuery's load() *function, you can access the same HTML without leaving the current web page (bottom). Clicking a link loads the HTML content into a* <div> *tag (outlined).*

To use the `load()` function, you first use a jQuery selector to identify the element on the page where the requested HTML should go; you then call the `load()` function and pass the URL of the page you wish to retrieve. For example, say you have a `<div>` tag with the ID `headlines` and you want to load the HTML from the file *todays_news.html* into that div. You can do that like this:

```
$('#headlines').load('todays_news.html');
```

When this code runs, the web browser requests the file *todays_news.html* from the web server. When that file is downloaded, the browser replaces whatever is currently inside the `<div>` with the ID `headlines` with the contents of the new file. The HTML file can be a complete web page (including the `<html>`, `<head>`, and `<body>` tags), or just a snippet of HTML—for example, the requested file might just have a single `<h1>` tag and a paragraph of text. It's OK if the file isn't a complete web page, as the `load()` function inserts only that HTML snippet into the current (complete) page.

NOTE   You can only load HTML files from the same site. For example, you can't load Google's home page into a `<div>` on a page from your site using the `load()` function.

When using the `load()` function, you must be careful with the file paths. First, note that the URL you pass to the `load()` function is in relation to the current page. In other words, you use the same path as if you were linking from the current page to the HTML file you wish to load. In addition, any file paths in the HTML don't get rewritten when the HTML is loaded into the document, so if you have a link or include images in the HTML file that's loaded, those URLs need to work in relation to the page using the `load()` function. In other words, if you're using document-relative paths (see the box on page 11) and the loaded HTML file is located in another folder on your website, images and links might not work when the HTML is loaded into the current page. Here's a simple workaround: Just use root-relative links, or make sure the file you load is located in the same directory as the page that's using the `load()` function.

The `load()` function even lets you specify which part of the downloaded HTML file you wish to add to the page. For example, say the page you request is a regular web page from the site; it includes all of the normal web page elements such as a banner, navigation bar, and footer. You may just be interested in the content from a single area of that page—for example, just a particular `<div>` and its contents. To specify which part of the page you wish to load, insert a space after the URL, followed by a jQuery selector. For example, say in the preceding example you want to insert the content only inside a `<div>` with the ID `news` in the *todays_news.html* file. You could do that with this code:

```
$('#headlines').load('todays_news.html #news');
```

In this case, the web browser downloads the page *todays_news.html*, but instead of inserting the entire contents of the file into the `headlines` div, it extracts just the `<div>` element (and everything inside it) with an ID of `news`. You'll see this technique in the following tutorial.

Tutorial: The load() Function

In this tutorial, you'll use jQuery to replace the traditional click-and-load method of accessing HTML (Figure 13-3, top) with a more responsive method that simply replaces content on the current page with new HTML (Figure 13-3, bottom).

■ OVERVIEW

To get a handle on what you'll be doing in this tutorial, you first need to understand the HTML of the page you're about to "Ajaxify." Take a look at Figure 13-4: The page has a bulleted list of links, each of which points to a different page containing different news headlines. The <ul> tag used to create the list has the ID newslinks. In addition, there's an empty <div> tag in the right sidebar (below the "News Headlines" header). That div has an ID of headlines and is, at this point, an empty placeholder. Eventually, once you use jQuery's load() function, clicking one of the links will load news stories into the <div>.

Currently, clicking a link just opens a web page with a series of news items. In other words, this page works the regular HTML way—it has links that point to other pages. In fact, without the nifty JavaScript you're about to add, the page works perfectly fine—it'll get any visitors to the news they're after. That's a good thing, because not everyone has JavaScript enabled in their browsers. In addition, if the only way to get to those news items is through JavaScript, search engines would skip over that valuable content.

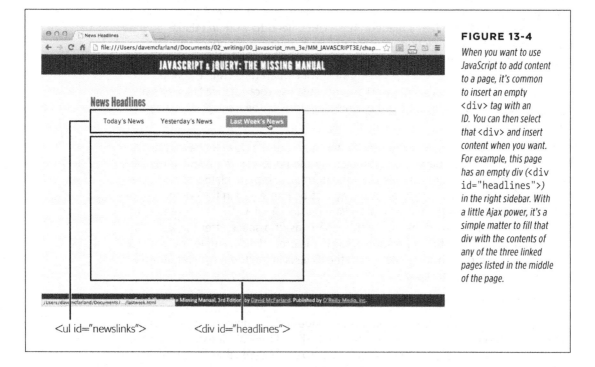

FIGURE 13-4

When you want to use JavaScript to add content to a page, it's common to insert an empty <div> tag with an ID. You can then select that <div> and insert content when you want. For example, this page has an empty div (<div id="headlines">) in the right sidebar. With a little Ajax power, it's a simple matter to fill that div with the contents of any of the three linked pages listed in the middle of the page.

> **NOTE** Most browsers don't let you use the load() method directly from your hard drive without a web server, so you need to set up a server on your computer (see the box on page 452) to follow along. At the time of this writing, Safari on the Mac *does* let you use the load() method without a web server.

This tutorial provides an example of *progressive enhancement*—it functions just fine without JavaScript, but works even better with JavaScript. In other words, everyone can access the content, and no one's left out.

> **NOTE** See the note on page 12 for information on how to download the tutorial files.

■ THE PROGRAMMING

To implement progressive enhancement, you'll add JavaScript to "hijack" the normal link function, then get the URL of the link, and then download the link to the page and put its contents into the empty <div>. It's as simple as that:

1. **In a text editor, open the file *load.html* in the *chapter13* folder.**

   You'll start by assigning a click event function to each of the links in the bulleted list in the main part of the page. The bulleted list (the <ul> tag) has an ID of newslinks, so you can easily use jQuery to select each of those links and assign a click() function to them.

   This file already links to the jQuery library, and it also has a <script> tag with the $(document).ready() function in it.

2. **Click in the empty line inside the $(document).ready() function, and type:**

   ```
   $('#newslinks a').click(function() {

   });
   ```

   The $('#newslinks a') is the jQuery way to select each of those links, and the .click() function lets you assign a function (an event handler) to the click event (page 152) if you need a refresher on events).

   The next step is to extract the URL from each link.

3. **Inside the click() function (the blank line in step 2) type var url=$(this).attr('href'); and press Return to create an empty line.**

   This line of code creates a new variable (url) and assigns it the value of the link's href attribute. As you'll recall from page 126, when you attach a function (like the click() function) to a jQuery selection ($('#newslinks a') in this case), jQuery loops through each element in the selection (each link) and applies the function to each one. The $(this) is just a way to get hold of the current element being worked on. In other words, $(this) will refer to a different link as jQuery loops through the collection of elements. The attr() function (discussed on page 137) can retrieve or set a particular element for a tag; in this case, the function extracts the href property to get the URL of the page the link points to. In the next step, you'll use that URL along with the load() function to retrieve the page's content and display it inside a <div> on the page.

4. **Type $('#headlines').load(url); so the script looks like this:**

```
$('#newslinks a').click(function() {
  var url=$(this).attr('href');
  $('#headlines').load(url);
});
```

Remember that the empty <div> tag on the page—where the downloaded HTML will go—has an ID of headlines, so $('#headlines') selects that <div>. The load() function then downloads the HTML at the URL that the previous line of code retrieved, and then puts that HTML in the <div> tag. Yes, there's actually *lots* of other stuff going on under the hood to make all that happen, but thanks to jQuery, you don't have to worry about it.

The page isn't quite done yet. If you save the file and preview it in a web browser, you'll notice that clicking one of the links doesn't load new content onto the page—it actually leaves the current page and loads the linked page instead! What happened to the Ajax? It's still there; it's just that the web browser is following its normal behavior of loading a new web page when a link is clicked. To stop that, you have to prevent the browser from following the link.

5. **Add a new empty line after the code you typed in the previous step and type return false; so the script now looks like this:**

```
$('#newslinks a').click(function() {
  var url=$(this).attr('href');
  $('#headlines').load(url);
  return false;
});
```

This simple step tells the web browser, "Hey, web browser, don't follow that link." It's one way of preventing a browser from following its normal behavior in response to an event. You can also use jQuery's preventDefault() function as described on page 165 to achieve the same effect.

6. **Save the file.**

If you have a web server set up on your machine, you can preview the page in a web browser. Click the links to test it out.

Now there's another problem, as you can see in Figure 13-5. The load() function is working, but the page doesn't look right. The load() function downloaded the entire web page and inserted it into the <div>. This caused some weird spacing issues and the banner "JavaScript & jQuery" is actually duplicated at the top of the page. What you really want is only a portion of that web page—the area containing the news items. Fortunately, the load() function can help here as well.

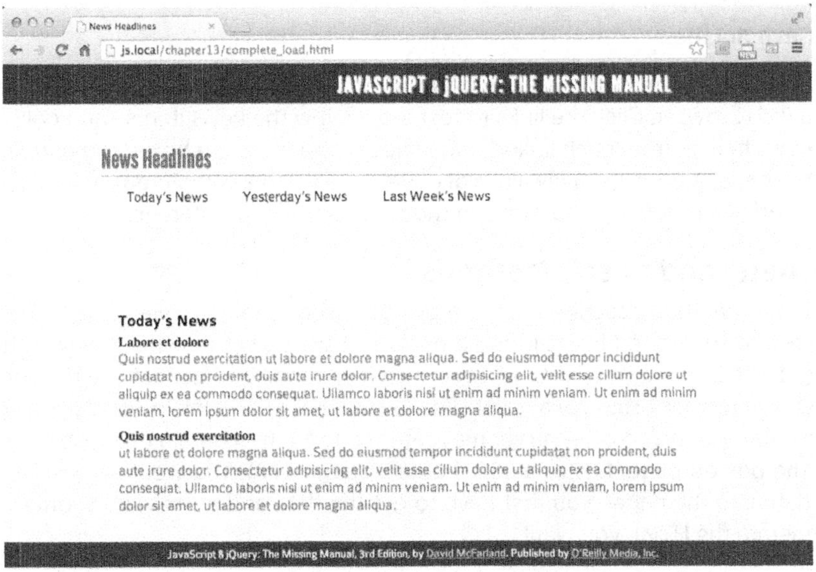

FIGURE 13-5

jQuery's load() function will download all of the HTML for a specified file and place it into an element on the current page. If the downloaded file includes unneeded HTML, like a duplicate banner, sidebar, and footer, the result can look like a page within a page. In this case, there's a lot of extra space above the headline "Today's News" and the banner at the top of the page has shifted—it is, in fact, a duplicate banner placed on top of the old banner!

7. **Locate the line with the load() function and add + ' #newsItem' after url. The finished code should look like this:**

```
$('#newslinks a').click(function() {
  var url=$(this).attr('href');
  $('#headlines').load(url + ' #newsItem');
  return false;
});
```

As described on page 457, you can specify which part of a downloaded file you want the load() function to add to the page. To do that, you add a space after the URL followed by a selector that identifies the part of the downloaded page you wish to display.

Here's how the code breaks down into bite-sized chunks: First, on each of the linked pages, there's a <div> tag with the ID newsItem. That div contains the HTML you want—the news items. So you can tell the load() function to only insert that part of the downloaded HTML by adding a space followed by #newsItem to the URL passed to load(). For example, if you want to load the file *today. html* and place just the HTML inside the newsItem div inside the headlines div, you can use this code:

```
$('#headlines').load('today.html #newsItem');
```

In this case, you need to combine two strings—the contents of the url variable and ' #newsItems' to get the proper code—so you use JavaScript's string concatenation operator (the + symbol) like this: load(url + ' #newsItems'). (See page 36 if you need a refresher on how to combine two strings.)

8. **Save the file.**

   If you have a web server set up on your computer, you can preview the page in a web browser. Click the links to test it out. Now the news items—and only the news items—from each linked page should appear in the box in the middle of the page. Ajax in just a few lines of code! (You'll find a completed version of the tutorial—*complete_load.html*—in the *chapter13* file for reference.)

The get() and post() Methods

The load() method described in the previous section is a quick way to grab HTML from a web server and inject it into a page. But the server may not always return straight HTML—it may return a message, a code number, or data that you then need to process further using JavaScript. For example, if you want to use Ajax to get some database records, the server may return an XML file containing those records (see the box on page 471) or a JSON object (page 477). You wouldn't just insert that data into the page—you first have to get the data and process it in some way to generate the HTML you want.

jQuery's get() and post() functions provide simple tools to send data to and retrieve data from a web server. As mentioned in step 2 on page 453, you need to treat the XMLHttpRequest object slightly differently when using either the GET or POST method. However, jQuery takes care of any differences between the two methods so the get() and post() functions work identically. (So which should you use? Read the box on page 464.)

The basic structure of these functions is:

```
$.get(url, data, callback);
```

Or:

```
$.post(url, data, callback);
```

Unlike most other jQuery functions, you don't add get() or post() to a jQuery selector—in other words, you'd never do something like this: $('#mainContent'). get('products.php'). The two functions stand by themselves and aren't connected to any element on the page, so you just use the $ symbol, followed by a period, followed by either get or post: $.get().

The get() and post() functions accept three arguments: url is a string that contains the path to the server-side resource that processes the data (for example, 'processForm.php'). The data argument is either a string or a JavaScript object literal containing the data you want to send to the server (you'll learn how to create this in the next section). Finally, callback is the function that processes the information returned from the server (see the page 194 for details on writing a callback function).

When either the get() or post() function runs, the web browser sends a request, using the specified method, to the specified URL, with the specified data. When the server sends data back to the browser, the browser hands that data to the callback function, which then processes that information and usually updates the web page in some way. You'll see an example of this in action on page 471.

Formatting Data to Send to the Server

Most of the time when writing a JavaScript program that uses Ajax, you'll be sending some information to the server. For example, if you want to get information about a particular product stored in a database, you could send a single number representing a product. When the web server gets the number from the XHR request, it looks for a product in the database that matches that number, retrieves the product information, and sends it back to the web browser. Or, you might use Ajax to submit an entire form's worth of information as part of an online order or a "sign up for our email newsletter" form.

In either case, you need to format the data for your request in a way that the get() and post() functions understand. The second argument sent to either function contains the data you wish to send the server—you can format this data either as a query string or as a JavaScript object literal, as described in the next two sections.

■ QUERY STRING

You've probably seen query strings before: They frequently appear at the end of a URL following a ? symbol. For example, in this URL *http://www.chia-vet.com/ products.php?prodID=18&sessID=1234*, the query string is *prodID=18&sessID=1234*. This query string contains two name/value pairs, *prodID=18* and *sessID=1234*. This string does basically the same as creating two variables, *prodID* and *sessID*, and storing two values into them. A query string is a common method for passing information in a URL.

You can also format data sent to the server using Ajax in this format. For example, say you've created a web page that lets visitors rate movies by clicking a number of stars. Clicking five stars, for instance, submits a rating of five to the server. In this case, the data sent to the server might look like this: rating=5. Assuming the name of the page processing these ratings is called rateMovie.php, the code to send the rating to the server using Ajax would look like this:

```
$.get('rateMovie.php','rating=5');
```

Or, if you're using the POST method:

```
$.post('rateMovie.php','rating=5');
```

> **NOTE** jQuery's get() and post() functions don't require you to define data or a callback function. You only need to supply the URL of the server-side page. However, you'll almost always provide data as well. For example, in this code $.get('rankMovie.php','rating=5'); only the URL and the data are supplied—no callback function is specified. In this case, the visitor is merely submitting a ranking, and there's no need for the server to respond or for a callback function to do anything.

GET or POST?

The two methods for submitting data to a web server, GET and POST, seem pretty much the same. Which should I use?

The answer really depends. In some cases, you don't have a choice. For example, suppose you're sending information to a server-side script that's already up and running on your server. In other words, the server-side programming is already done, and you just need to use JavaScript to talk to it. In that case, you use the method that the script is expecting. Most likely, the programmer set up the script to accept either GET or POST data. So you can either talk to the programmer or look at the script to see which method it uses, then use the jQuery function that matches—either get() or post().

If you (or another programmer) haven't yet written the server-side script that your JavaScript program will talk to, then you get to choose the method. The GET method is suited to requests that don't affect the state of a database or files on the server.

In other words, use it when you want to *get* information, like requesting the price of a particular product or obtaining a list of most popular products. The POST method is for sending data that will change information on the server, like a request to delete a file, update a database, or insert new information into a database.

In reality, you can use either method, and often programmers will use a GET method to delete database information, and the POST method just to retrieve information from the server. However, there is one situation where POST is required. If you're submitting a lot of form data to a server—for example, a blog post that might include hundreds of words—use POST. The GET method has a built-in limit on the amount of data it can send (this limit varies from browser to browser but Internet Explorer's limit is several thousand characters). Most of the time, web designers use POST for forms that include more than just a few fields.

If you need to send more than one name/value pair to the server, insert an & between each pair:

```
$.post('rateMovie.php','rating=5&user=Bob');
```

You need to be careful using this method, however, because some characters have special meaning when you insert them into a query string. For instance, you use the & symbol to include additional name/value pairs to the string; the = symbol assigns a value to a name. For example, the following query string isn't valid:

```
'favFood=Mac & Cheese' // incorrect
```

The & symbol here is supposed to be part of "Mac & Cheese," but when used as part of a query string, the & will be interpreted to mean a second name/value pair. If you want to use special characters as part of the name or value in a name/value pair, you need to *escape* or *encode* them so they won't be mistaken for a character with special meaning. For example, the space character is represented by %20, the & symbol by %26, and the = sign by %3D. So you need to write out the "Mac & Cheese" example like this:

```
'favFood=Mac%20%26%20Cheese' // properly escaped
```

JavaScript provides a method for properly escaping strings—the encodeURICompo-nent() method. You supply the encodeURIComponent() method with a string, and it returns a properly escaped string. For example:

```
var queryString = 'favFood=' + encodeURIComponent('Mac & Cheese');
$.post('foodChoice.php', queryString);
```

■ OBJECT LITERAL

For short and simple pieces of data (that don't include any punctuation symbols), the query string method works well. But a more foolproof method supported by jQuery's get() and post() functions is to use an object literal to store data. As you'll recall from page 136, an object literal is a JavaScript method for storing name/value pairs. The basic structure of an object literal is this:

```
{
  name1: 'value1',
  name2: 'value2'
}
```

You can pass the object literal directly to the get() or post() function. For example, this code uses the query string method:

```
$.post('rankMovie.php','rating=5');
```

To use an object literal, rewrite the code like this:

```
$.post('rankMovie.php', { rating: 5 });
```

You can either pass the object literal directly to the get() or post() functions, or first store it in a variable and pass that variable to get() or post():

```
var data = { rating: 5 };
$.post('rankMovie.php', data);
```

Of course, you can include any number of name/value pairs in the object that you pass to the get() or post() function:

```
var data = {
  rating: 5,
  user: 'Bob'
}
$.post('rankMovie.php', data);
```

Or, if you directly pass an object literal to $.post():

```
$.post('rankMovie.php',
  {
    rating: 5,
    user: 'Bob'
  }
); // end post
```

■ JQUERY'S SERIALIZE() FUNCTION

Creating a query string or object for an entire form's worth of name/value pairs can be quite a chore. You have to retrieve the name and value for each form element, and then combine them all to create one long query string or one large JavaScript object literal. Fortunately, jQuery provides a function that makes it easy to convert form information into data that the get() and post() functions can use.

You can apply the serialize() function to any form (or even just a selection of form fields) to create a query string. To use it, first create a jQuery selection that includes a form, then attach the serialize() function to it. For example, say you have a form with an ID of login. If you wanted to create a query string for that form, you can do so like this:

```
var formData = $('#login').serialize();
```

The var formData part just creates a new variable; $('#login') creates a jQuery selection containing the form; finally, .serialize() collects all of the field names and the values currently in each field and creates a single query string.

To use this with either the get() or post() functions, just pass the serialized results to the function as the second argument (the argument that follows the URL). For example, say you want to send the contents of the login form to a page named *login. php*. You can do so like this:

```
var formData = $('#login').serialize();
$.get('login.php',formData,loginResults);
```

This code sends whatever the visitor enters into the form to *login.php* using the GET method. The final argument for get() here—loginResults—is the callback function: the function that takes the data sent back from the server and does something with it. You'll learn how to create a callback function next.

Processing Data from the Server

Ajax is usually a two-way street—a JavaScript program sends some data to the server and the server returns data to the JavaScript program, which can then use that data to update the page. In the previous pages, you saw how to format data and send it to a server using the get() and post() functions. Now you'll learn how to receive and process the server's response.

When the web browser sends off a request to the server using the XMLHttpRequest object, it keeps listening for a response from the server. When the server responds, a callback function handles the server's response. That function is passed several arguments that can be used by the function. First, and most important, the data returned by the server is sent as the first argument.

You can format the data the server returns in any number of ways. The server-side script can return a number, a word, a paragraph of text, or a complete web page. In cases where the server is sending a lot of information (like a bunch of records from a database), the server often uses XML or JSON. (See the box on page 471 for more about XML; see page 477 for a discussion of JSON.)

The second argument to the callback function is a string indicating the status of the response. Most of the time, the status is "success," meaning that the server has successfully processed the request and returned data. However, sometimes a request doesn't succeed—for example, the request was made for a file that doesn't exist, or there was an error in the server-side programming. If a request fails, the callback function receives an "error" status message.

The callback function processes the information, and, most of the time, updates the web page in some way—replacing a submitted form with results from the server, or simply printing a "request successful" message on the page, for example. Updating the content of a web page is easy using jQuery's html() and text(), functions described on page 127. Other methods of manipulating a page's DOM are discussed in Chapter 4.

To get a handle on a complete request/response cycle, take a look at a basic movie-rating example (Figure 13-6). A visitor can rate a movie by clicking one of five links. Each link indicates a different rating. When the visitor clicks a link, the rating and ID of the movie being rated are sent to a server-side program, which adds the rating to the database, and then returns the average rating for that movie. The average rating is then displayed on the web page.

In order for this page to work without JavaScript, each of the links on the page points to a dynamic server-side page that can process the visitor's rating. For example, the five-star rating link (Figure 13-6) might be *rate.php?rate=5&movie=123*. The name of the server-side file that processes the ratings is called *rate.php*, while the query string (*?rate=5&movie=123*) includes two pieces of information for the server: a rating (*rate=5*) and a number that identifies the movie being rated (*movie=123*). You can use JavaScript to intercept clicks on these links and translate them into Ajax calls to the server:

```
1    $('#message a').click(function() {
2        var href=$(this).attr('href');
3        var querystring=href.slice(href.indexOf('?')+1);
4        $.get('rate.php', querystring, processResponse);
5        return false; // stop the link
6    });
```

Line 1 selects every link (<a> tag) inside of another tag with an ID of message (in this example, each link used to rate the movie is contained within a <div> with the ID message). A function is then applied to the click event for each of those links.

Line 2 extracts the href attribute of the link—so, for example, the href variable might hold a URL like *rate.php?rate=5&movie=123*. Line 3 extracts just the part after the ? in the URL using the slice() method (discussed on page 545) to extract part of the string, and the indexOf() method (page 543) to determine where the ? is located (this information is passed to the slice() method to determine where to start slicing).

Line 4 is the Ajax request. Using the GET method, a request containing the query string for the link is sent to the server resource *rate.php* (Figure 13-7). The results will then go to the callback function processResponse. Line 5 just stops the normal link behavior and prevents the web browser from unloading the current page and loading the linked-to page.

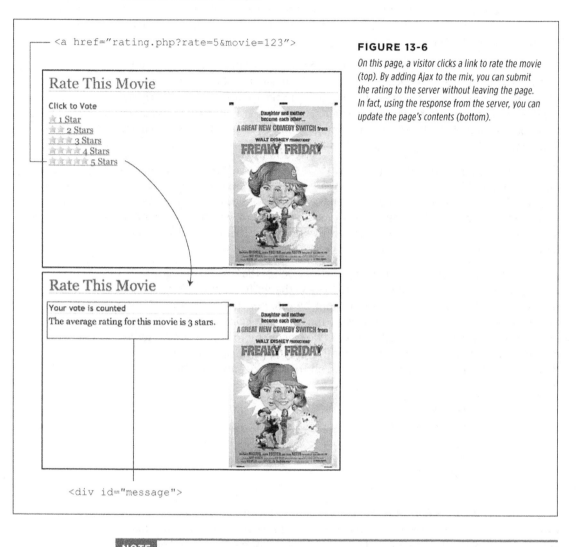

```
<a href="rating.php?rate=5&movie=123">
```

Rate This Movie

Click to Vote
★ 1 Star
★★ 2 Stars
★★★ 3 Stars
★★★★ 4 Stars
★★★★★ 5 Stars

Rate This Movie

Your vote is counted
The average rating for this movie is 3 stars.

```
<div id="message">
```

FIGURE 13-6

On this page, a visitor clicks a link to rate the movie (top). By adding Ajax to the mix, you can submit the rating to the server without leaving the page. In fact, using the response from the server, you can update the page's contents (bottom).

NOTE If you need a refresher on how functions work and how to create them, see page 85.

Finally, it's time to create the callback function. The callback function receives data and a string with the status of the response ('success' if the server sent information back). Remember the callback function's name is used in the request (see line 4 of the code on the previous page). So in this example, the function's name is processResponse. The code to deal with the server's response might look like this:

```
1   function processResponse(data) {
2     var newHTML;
3     newHTML = '<h2>Your vote is counted</h2>';
4     newHTML += '<p>The average rating for this movie is ';
5     newHTML += data + '.</p>';
6     $('#message').html(newHTML);
7   }
```

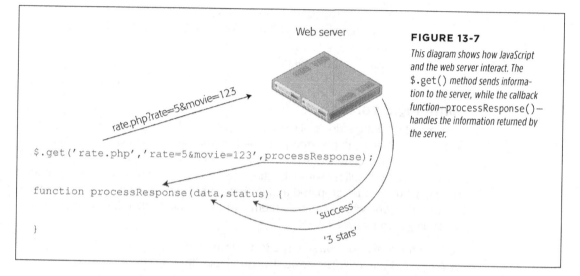

FIGURE 13-7

This diagram shows how JavaScript and the web server interact. The $.get() method sends information to the server, while the callback function—processResponse()—handles the information returned by the server.

The function accepts data arguments, which is the information returned by the web server. This data could be plain text, HTML, XML, or JSON. Line 2 creates a new variable that holds the HTML that will be displayed on the page (for example, "Your vote is counted"). In lines 3 and 4, the newHTML variable is filled with some HTML, including an <h2> tag and a <p> tag. The server's response doesn't come into play until line 5—there the response from the server (stored in the data variable) is added to the newHTML variable. In this case, the server returns a string with the average rating for the movie: for example, '3 stars'.

> **NOTE** If you want to add a star rating system to your site, there's a great jQuery plug-in that handles most of the details: *http://www.wbotelhos.com/raty/*.

Finally, line 6 modifies the HTML on the web page using jQuery's html() function (page 127) by replacing the contents of the <div> with the ID of message with the new HTML. The result is something like the bottom image in Figure 13-6.

In this example, the callback function was defined outside of the $.get() method; however, you can use an anonymous function (page 138) if you want to keep all of the Ajax code together:

```
$.get('file.php', data, function(data,status) {
    // callback function programming goes here
});
```

For example, you could rewrite line 4 on page 467 to use an anonymous function like this:

```
$.get('rate.php', querystring, function(data) {
    var newHTML;
    newHTML = '<h2>Your vote is counted</h2>';
    newHTML += '<p>The average rating for this movie is ';
    newHTML += data + '.</p>';
    $('#message').html(newHTML);
}); // end get
```

Handling Errors

Unfortunately, things don't always go as planned. When using Ajax to talk to a web server, things can go wrong. Maybe the web server is down for a moment, or a visitor's Internet connection drops momentarily. If that happens, the $.get() and $.post() methods will fail without letting the visitor know. While this type of problem is rare, it's best to be prepared and letting your visitors know that something has temporarily gone wrong can help them figure out what to do (like reload the page, try again, or come back later).

To respond to an error, you simply add a .error() function to the end of the $.get() or $.post() functions. The basic structure looks like this:

```
$.get(url, data, successFunction).error(errorFunction);
```

For example, you could rewrite line 4 on page 467 to look like this:

```
$.get('rate.php', querystring, processResponse).error(errorResponse);
```

Then create a new function named errorResponse that notifies the visitor that there was a problem. For example:

```
function errorResponse() {
    var errorMsg = "Your vote could not be processed right now. ";
    errorMsg += "Please try again later.";
    $('#message').html(errorMsg);
}
```

In this case, the function errorResponse runs only if there's some kind of error with the server or the server's connection.

> **NOTE** The .error() method doesn't work with jQuery's .load() method, or with a request to another website using JSONP (page 483).

Tutorial: Using the $.get() Method

In this tutorial, you'll use Ajax to submit information from a login form. When a visitor supplies the correct username and password, a message will appear letting her know she's successfully logged in. If the login information isn't correct, an error message will appear on the same page—without loading a new web page.

> **NOTE**   In order to successfully complete this tutorial, you'll need to have a running AMP (Apache, MySQL, and PHP) web server to test the pages on. See the box on page 452 for information on how to set up a testing server on your computer.

POWER USERS' CLINIC

Receiving XML from the Server

XML is a common format for exchanging data between computers. Like HTML, XML lets you use tags to identify information. Unlike HTML, you're free to come up with tags that accurately reflect the content of your data. For example, a simple XML file might look like this:

```
<?xml version="1.0" ?>
<message id="234">
  <from>Bob</from>
  <to>Janette</to>
  <subject>Lunch</subject>
  <content>Janette, let's grab lunch
today.</content>
</message>
```

As you can see, there's a main tag (called the *root element*) named <message>—the equivalent of HTML's <html> tag—and several other tags that define the meaning of each piece of data.

When using Ajax, you might have a server program that returns an XML file. jQuery has no problem reading and extracting data from an XML file. When you use the $.get() or $.post() methods, if the server returns an XML file, the data argument that's sent to the callback function will contain the DOM of the XML file. In other words, jQuery will read the XML file and treat it like another document. You can then use jQuery's selector tools to access the data inside the XML.

For example, say a server-side resource named *xml.php* returned the sample XML listed here, and you want to retrieve the text within the <content> tag. The XML file becomes the returned data, so the callback function can process it. You can use the jQuery find() function to search the XML to find a particular CSS element using any of the regular selectors you'd use with jQuery. For example, you can find an element, class, ID, descendant selector (page 122), or jQuery's filters (page 124).

For example:

```
$.get('xml.php','id=234',processXML);
function processXML(data) {
  var messageContent=$(data
find('content').text();
}
```

The key here is $(data).find('content'), which tells jQuery to select every <content> tag within the data variable. In this case, the data variable contains the returned XML file, so this code tells jQuery to look for the <content> tag within the XML.

To learn more about XML, visit *http://www.learn-xml-tutorial. com/xml-basics.cfm*. To learn more about jQuery's find() function, visit *http://api.jquery.com/find.*

OVERVIEW

You'll start with the form pictured in Figure 13-8. It includes fields for supplying a username and password to the server. When the form is submitted, the server attempts to verify that the user exists and the password matches. If the information supplied matches valid login credentials, then the server logs the visitor in.

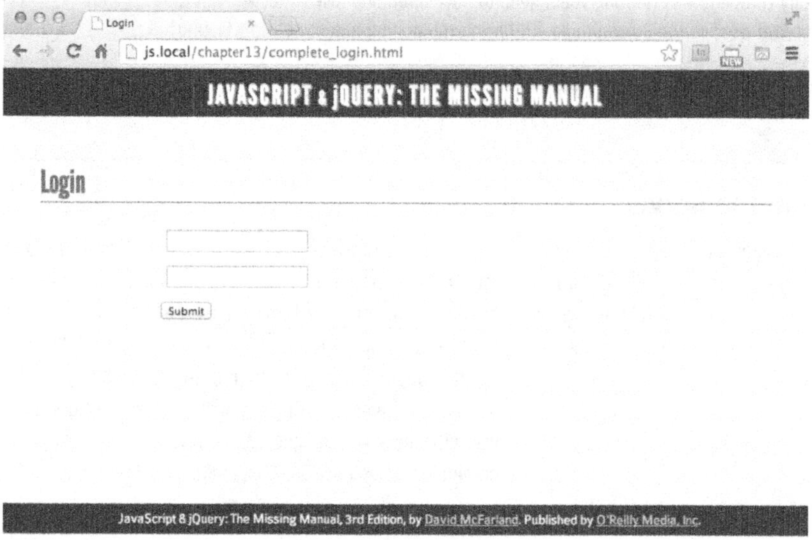

FIGURE 13-8

A basic login page is a simple affair: just a couple of fields and a Submit button. However, there's really no reason to leave the page when the user logs in. By adding Ajax, you can submit the visitor's credentials, then notify whether he logged in successfully or not.

You'll add Ajax to the form by sending the login information via an XMLHttpRequest. The server will send a message to the callback function, which removes the form and displays a "logged in" message if the login information is valid, or an error message if it's not.

THE PROGRAMMING

See the note on page 12 for information on how to download the tutorial files. The starting file contains the HTML form, ready for you to add some jQuery and Ajax programming:

1. **In a text editor, open the file *login.html* in the *chapter13* folder.**

   The link to the jQuery library file and the $(document).ready() function are already in place. You'll start by using jQuery to select the form and adding a submit event to it.

2. **Click in the empty line inside the $(document).ready() function and type:**

   ```
   $('#login').submit(function() {

   }); // end submit
   ```

The `<form>` tag has the ID login applied to it, so the jQuery selector—$('#login')—selects that form, while the submit() function adds an event handler to the submit event. In other words, when a visitor tries to submit the form, the function you're about to create will run.

The next step is to collect the information from the form and format it as a query string to submit to the server. You could do this by finding each form field, extracting the value that the visitor had typed in, then constructing a query string by concatenating those different pieces of information. Fortunately, jQuery's serialize() method takes care of all these details in one shot.

3. **Hit Return to create an empty line and type:**

```
var formData = $(this).serialize();
```

This line starts by creating a new variable to hold the form data, and then applies the serialize() method to the form. Recall that $(this) refers to the current element, so in this case it refers to the login form, and is the same as $('#login') (see page 139 for more on how $(this) works). The serialize() method (page 466) takes a form and extracts the field names and values and puts them in the proper format for submitting to the server.

Now you'll use the $.get() method to set up and send the XMLHttpRequest.

4. **Hit Return to create another empty line and type:**

```
$.get('login.php',formData,processData);
```

This code passes three arguments to the $.get() method. The first—'login.php'—is a string identifying where the data should be sent—in this case, a file on the server named *login.php*. The second argument is the query string containing the data that's being sent to the server—the login information. Finally, processData refers to the callback function that will process the server's response. You'll create that function now.

5. **Add another blank line below the last one and type:**

```
1   function processData(data) {
2
3   } // end processData
```

These lines form the shell of the callback function; there's no programming inside it yet. Notice that the function is set up to accept one argument (data), which will be the response coming from the server. The server-side page is programmed to return a single word—pass if the login succeeded, or fail if the login failed.

In other words, based on the response from the server, the script will either print a message letting the visitor know he's successfully logged on, or that he hasn't—this is the perfect place for a conditional statement.

NOTE The server-side page used in this tutorial isn't a full-fledged login script. It does respond if the proper credentials are supplied, but it's not something you could use to actually password-protect a site. There are many ways to effectively password protect a site, but most require setting up a database or setting up various configuration settings for the web server—these steps are beyond this basic tutorial. For a real, PHP-based login script, visit *http://www.wikihow.com/Create-a-Secure-Login-Script-in-PHP-and-MySQL.*

6. **Inside the `processData()` function, add the bolded code:**

```
1 function processData(data) {
2   if (data === 'pass') {
3       $('.main').html('<p>You have successfully logged on!</p>');
4   }
5} // end processData
```

Line 1 checks to see whether the information returned from the server is the string `'pass'`. If it is, the login was successful and a success message is printed (line 2). The form is inside a `<div>` tag with the class of `main`, so `$('.main').html('<p>You have successfully logged on!</p>')` will replace whatever's inside that `<div>` with a new paragraph. In other words, the form disappears and the success message appears in its place.

To finish up, you'll add an `else` clause to let the visitor know if he didn't supply the correct login information.

7. **Add an `else` clause to the `processData()` function so it looks like this (additions are in bold):**

```
1    function processData(data) {
2        if (data=='pass') {
3            $('#content').html('<p>You have successfully logged on!</p>');
4        } else {
5            $('#formwrapper').prepend('<p id="fail">Incorrect ↵
               login information. Please try again</p>');
6        }
7    } // end processData
```

Line 5 prints the message that the login failed. Notice that the `prepend()` function is used. As discussed on page 127, `prepend()` lets you add content to the beginning of an element. It doesn't remove what's already there; it just adds more content. In this case, you want to leave the form in place, so the visitor can try again to log in a second time.

8. **Save the file, and preview it in a web browser.**

You must view this page through a web browser using a URL, like *http://localhost/chapter13/login.html,* for this tutorial to work. See the box on page 452 for more information on how to set up a web server.

9. **Try to log into the site.**

"But wait—you haven't given me the username and password yet!" you're probably thinking. That's the point—to see what happens when you don't log in correctly. Try to log in a second time: You'll see the "Incorrect login information" message appear a second time (Figure 13-9). Because the prepend() function doesn't remove the first error message, it just adds the message a second time. That doesn't look right at all.

You have several ways to deal with this problem. You could, for example, insert an empty div—<div id="failMessage">—below the form. Then simply replace its HTML when the login fails. However, in this case, there's no empty div tag on the page. Instead, use a basic conditional statement to check whether the error message already exists—if it does, there's no need to add it a second time.

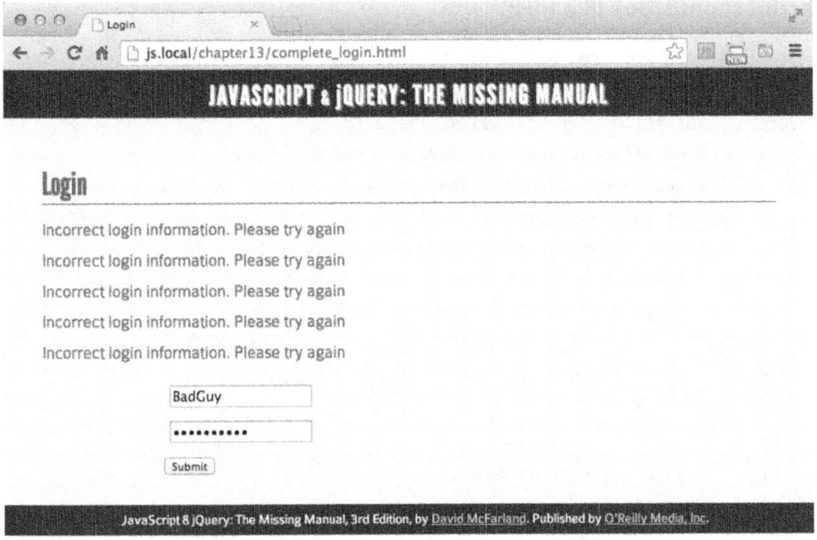

FIGURE 13-9

jQuery's prepend() *function adds HTML to an already existing element. It doesn't delete anything, so if you're not careful, you may end up adding the same message over and over again.*

10. **Add another conditional statement (lines 5 and 7):**

```
1    function processData(data) {
2        if (data=='pass') {
3            $('.main').html('<p>You have successfully logged on!</p>');
4        } else {
5            if ($('#fail').length === 0) {
6                $('#formwrapper').prepend('<p id="fail">Incorrect ↵
7                login information. Please try again</p>');
8            }
9        }
10    } // end processData
```

Notice that the error message paragraph has an ID—fail—so you can use jQuery to check to see if that ID exists on the page. If it doesn't, then the program writes the error message on the page. One way to check if an element already exists on the page is to try to use jQuery to select it. You can then check the length attribute of the results. If jQuery couldn't find any matching elements, the length attribute is 0. In other words, $('#fail') tries to find an element with the ID fail. If jQuery can't find it—in other words, the error message hasn't yet been written to the page—then the length attribute is 0, the conditional statement will be true, and the program writes the error message. Once the error message is on the page, the conditional statement always evaluates to false, and the error message doesn't appear again.

Finally, you need to tell the web browser that it shouldn't submit the form data itself—you already did that using Ajax.

11. **Add** return false; **at the end of the submit event (line 15). The finished script should look like this:**

```
1   $(document).ready(function() {
2   $('#login').submit(function() {
3     var formData = $(this).serialize();
4     $.post('login.php',formData,processData);
5     function processData(data) {
6       if (data=='pass') {
7         $('.main').html('<p>You have successfully logged on!</p>');
8       } else {
9         if ($('#fail').length === 0) {
10          $('#formwrapper').prepend('<p id="fail">Incorrect ↵
11          login information. Please try again</p>');
12        }
13      }
14    } // end processData
15    return false;
16  }); // end submit
17  }); // end ready
```

12. **Save the file and preview the page once again.**

Try to log in again: the username is 007 and the password is secret. A completed version of this tutorial, *complete_login.html,* is in the *chapter13* folder.

NOTE As mentioned on page 462, you use jQuery's $.post() and $.get() functions identically even though, behind the scenes, jQuery has to do two different set of steps to make the Ajax request work correctly. You can check this out yourself by just changing get to post in the script (see line 4 in step 11). The server-side script for this tutorial is programmed to accept either GET or POST requests.

■ JSON

Another popular format for sending data from the server is called JSON, which stands for *JavaScript Object Notation*. JSON is a data format that's structured like a JavaScript object. It's kind of like XML (see the box on page 471) in that it's a method for exchanging data. JSON is a string that's formatted just like a JavaScript object: browsers can quickly and easily convert JSON into real JavaScript. XML, on the other hand, needs to be parsed into a series of "nodes" that JavaScript needs to traverse to access the data inside the XML document: this process is generally slower and requires more programming. Because of this, JSON is a more common choice for exchanging data using Ajax.

In essence, JSON is very similar to a JavaScript object literal, or a collection of name/value pairs. Here's a simple example of JSON:

```
{
    "firstName" : "Frank",
    "lastName" : "Smith",
    "phone" : "503-555-1212"
}
```

The { marks the beginning of the JSON object, while the } marks its end. In between are sets of property name/value pairs; for example, "firstName": "Frank". The property name is separated from the property value by a colon. Unlike a regular JavaScript object, JSON property names must be quoted using double quotations, and all string values must be quoted with double quotes. In other words, the following is incorrect:

```
firstName : 'Frank'
```

While this is correct:

```
"firstName" : "Frank"
```

Like JavaScript objects, every property name/value pair is separated by a comma, but don't put a comma at the end of the last pair (otherwise, some versions of Internet Explorer will cough up an error).

Think of a name/value pair just like a variable—the name is like the name of the variable, and the value is what's stored inside that variable. In the above example, "lastName" acts like a variable, with the string "Smith" stored in it.

When the web server responds to an Ajax request, it doesn't actually send JavaScript: It just sends text that's formatted like a JavaScript object—that's what JSON is. It isn't actually real, usable JavaScript until the string is converted into an actual JavaScript object. Fortunately, jQuery provides a special function, $.getJSON(), that handles all of the details. The $.getJSON() method looks and works much like the $.get() and $.post() functions. The basic structure looks like this:

```
$.getJSON(url, data, callback);
```

The three arguments passed to the function are the same as for `$.post()` or `$.get()`—the URL of the server-side page, data to send to the server-side page, and the name of a callback function. The difference is that `$.getJSON()` will process the response from the server (which is just a JSON-formatted string) and convert it (through some JavaScript wizardry) into a usable JavaScript object.

In other words, `$.getJSON()` works just like `$.post()` or `$.get()`, but the data passed to the callback is a JSON string. To use the `$.getJSON()` function, then, you only need to learn how to process the JavaScript object with the callback function. For a basic example, say you want to use Ajax to request information on a single contact from a server-side file named *contacts.php*; that file returns contact data in JSON format (like the JSON example on the previous page). A basic request would look like this:

```
$.getJSON('contacts.php','contact=123',processContacts);
```

This code sends a query string—contact=123—to *contacts.php*. Say the *contacts.php* file uses that information to locate a single contact in a database and retrieve that contact's information. The result is sent back to the web browser and handed to the callback function `processContacts`. The basic structure of the callback, then, would look like this:

```
function processContacts(data) {

}
```

The `processContacts()` function has one argument—data—that contains the JavaScript object from the server. Next, you'll take a look at how the callback can access information from that object.

Accessing JSON Data

There are two ways to access data in the object converted from the JSON string: *dot syntax* or *array notation*. Dot syntax (page 56) is a way of indicating an object's property—specifically, by adding a period between the name of the object and the property you wish to access. You've seen this in use with properties of different JavaScript objects like strings and arrays. For example, `'abc'.length` accesses the string's length property, and, in this example, returns the number of letters in the string `'abc'`, which is 3.

For example, suppose you create a variable and store an object literal inside it like this:

```
var bdate = {
  "person" : "Raoul",
  "date" : "10/27/1980"
};
```

In this case, the variable bdate contains the object literal, so if you want to get the value of person in the object, use dot syntax like this:

```
bdate.person // "Raoul"
```

To get the birth date:

```
bdate.date // "10/27/1980"
```

The same is true with JSON data that's returned by the web server. For example, take the following $.getJSON() example and callback function:

```
$.getJSON('contacts.php','contact=123',processContacts);
function processContacts(data) {

}
```

Assuming that the server returned the JSON example on page 477, that JSON object is assigned to the variable data (the argument for the callback function process-Contacts()), just as if this code had been executed:

```
var data = {
  "firstName" : "Frank",
  "lastName" : "Smith",
  "phone" : "503-555-1212"
};
```

Now within the callback function, you can access the value of firstName like this:

```
data.firstName // "Frank"
```

And retrieve the last name of the contact like this:

```
data.lastName // "Smith"
```

So, say the whole point of this little Ajax program is to retrieve contact information and display it inside of a <div> with the ID info. All of the programming for that might look like this:

```
$.getJSON('contacts.php','contact=123',processContacts);
function processContacts(data) {
  var infoHTML='<p>Contact: ' + data.firstName;
  infoHTML+=' ' + data.lastName + '<br>';
  infoHTML+='Phone: ' + data.phone + '</p>';
  $('#info').html(infoHTML);
}
```

The final outcome would be a paragraph added to the page that looks something like this:

```
Contact: Frank Smith
Phone: 503-555-1212
```

Complex JSON Data

You can create even more complex collections of information by using object literals as the values inside a JSON-encoded string—in other words, object literals nested within object literals. Here's an example: Say you want the server to send back contact information for more than one individual using JSON. You'll send a request to a file named *contacts.php* with a query string that dictates how many contacts you wish returned. That code may look something like this:

```
$.getJSON('contacts.php','limit=2',processContacts);
```

The limit=2 is the information sent to the server, and indicates how many contacts should be returned. The web server would then return two contacts. Say the contact info for the first person matched the preceding example (Frank Smith), and a second set of contact information was another JSON object like this:

```
{
    "firstName" : "Peggy",
    "lastName" : "Jones",
    "phone" : "415-555-5235"
}
```

The web server may return a JSON string that represents a single object, which combines both of these objects like this:

```
{
    "contact1": {
        "firstName" : "Frank",
        "lastName" : "Smith",
        "phone" : "503-555-1212"
    },
    "contact2": {
        "firstName" : "Peggy",
        "lastName" : "Jones",
        "phone" : "415-555-5235"
    }
}
```

Assume that the callback function accepts a single parameter named data (for example, function processContacts(data)). The variable data would then be assigned that JSON object, just as if this code had been executed:

```
var data = {
    "contact1": {
        "firstName" : "Frank",
        "lastName" : "Smith",
        "phone" : "503-555-1212"
    },
    "contact2": {
        "firstName" : "Peggy",
        "lastName" : "Jones",
        "phone" : "415-555-5235"
    }
}
```

Now, you could access the first contact object within the callback function like this:

```
data.contact1
```

And retrieve the first name of the first contact like this:

```
data.contact1.firstName
```

But, in this case, because you want to process multiple contacts, jQuery provides a function that lets you loop through each item in an object—the $.each() method. The basic structure of the function is this:

```
$.each(JSON,function(name,value) {

});
```

You pass the JSON data, and a function to the $.each() method. That anonymous function receives the name and value of each item in the object. Here's how the JSON data would look in use in the current example:

```
1    $.getJSON('contacts.php','limit=2',processContacts);
2    function processContacts(data) {
3      // create variable with empty string
4      var infoHTML='';
5
6      //loop through each object in the JSON data
7      $.each(data,function(contact, contactInfo) {
8        infoHTML+='<p>Contact: ' + contactInfo.firstName;
9        infoHTML+=' ' + contactInfo.lastName + '<br>';
10       infoHTML+='Phone: ' + contactInfo.phone + '</p>';
11     }); // end of each()
12
13     // add finished HTML to page
14     $('#info').html(infoHTML);
15   }
```

Here's how the code breaks down:

1. **Line 1 creates the Ajax request with data (limit=2) and assigns the callback function (processContacts).**

2. **Line 2 creates the callback function, which accepts the JSON object sent back from the server and stores it in the variable data.**

3. **Line 4 creates a variable containing an empty string. The HTML that eventually gets added to the page will fill it.**

4. **Line 7 is the $.each() method, which will look through the objects in the JSON data.**

   The $.each() method takes the JSON data as its first argument (data) and an anonymous function as the second argument. The process is diagrammed in

Figure 13-10. Essentially, for each of the main objects (in this example, contact1 and contact2), the anonymous function receives the name of the object as a string (that's the contact argument listed in line 7) and the value for that object (that's the contactInfo argument). In this case, the contactInfo variable will hold the object containing the contact information.

5. **Lines 8–10 extract the information from one contact.**

Remember that the $.each() method is a loop, so lines 8–10 will run twice—once for each of the contacts.

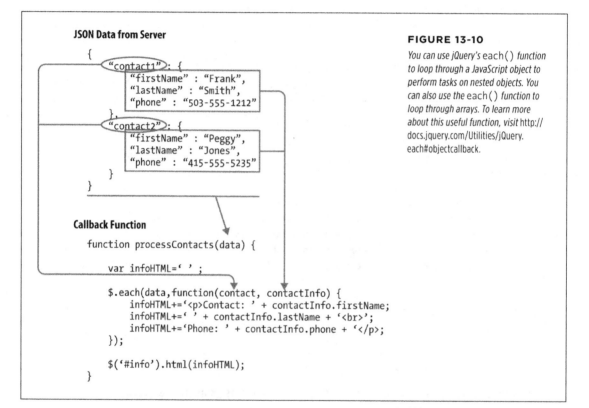

JSON Data from Server

Callback Function

FIGURE 13-10

You can use jQuery's each() function to loop through a JavaScript object to perform tasks on nested objects. You can also use the each() function to loop through arrays. To learn more about this useful function, visit http://docs.jquery.com/Utilities/jQuery.each#objectcallback.

6. **Line 14 updates the web page by adding the HTML to the page.**

The final result will be the following HTML:

```
<p>Contact: Frank Smith<br>
Phone: 503-555-1212</p>
<p>Contact: Peggy Jones<br>
Phone: 415-555-5235</p>
```

■ Introducing JSONP

For security reasons, Ajax requests are limited to requests to the *same origin*. That is, the page making an Ajax request must be on the same server as the page responding to the request. This policy is enforced by web browsers to keep one site from using JavaScript to maliciously contact another site (like your bank). There's one way around that, though. While a web browser can't send an XML HTTP request to a different website, it can download resources from other sites, including pictures, style sheets, and external JavaScript files.

JSONP (which stands for *JSON with padding*) provides one way to retrieve information from another site. Instead of making an Ajax request of the foreign site, you load a script that contains the JSON code in it. In other words, it's like linking to an external JavaScript file on another website.

You can't request just any bit of information that you'd like from another site, however. For JSONP to work, the foreign site must be set up to respond with JSONP. Most sites aren't set up to send information this way, but many of the big sites like Google Maps, Twitter, Flickr, Facebook, Netflix, and YouTube offer an API (*application programming interface*) that lets you request data like a map, a photo, movie review text, and so on, using jQuery's $.getJSON() method (Figure 13-11).

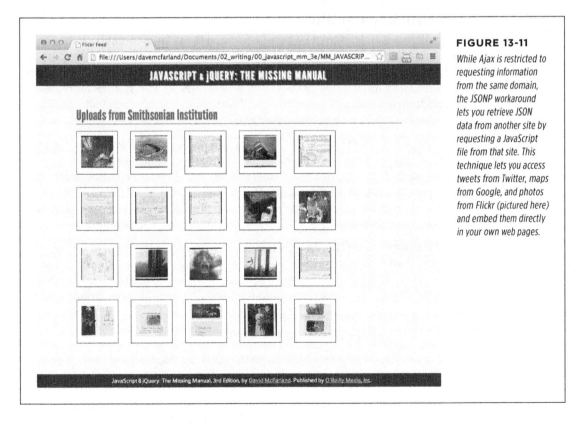

FIGURE 13-11

While Ajax is restricted to requesting information from the same domain, the JSONP workaround lets you retrieve JSON data from another site by requesting a JavaScript file from that site. This technique lets you access tweets from Twitter, maps from Google, and photos from Flickr (pictured here) and embed them directly in your own web pages.

■ Adding a Flickr Feed to Your Site

Flickr has been around for years, allowing people to share photographs—the site currently hosts billions of photos and counting. A lot of websites like to include photos either taken by the site owner or within a Flickr group (a collection of photos submitted by multiple people around a common subject like web design, landscape photography, cat yawns, and so on).

Flickr gives you a couple of ways to retrieve photos and related information. The most powerful, but also most complex, method is to use Flickr's API to search for photos. This method requires that you sign up at Flickr and get a special API *key* (a string of numbers and letters that identifies you). It also requires some fancy programming to work. The simplest way is to use the Flickr Feed Service. Feeds are a way to keep people up to date with a site's information. For example, you may have seen sites with RSS feeds that let you view the latest news and information from that website. Flickr offers a similar service for its photos—you can get a listing of the 20 most recent photos from a particular person or a particular group.

In this section, you'll use the feed method to get a collection of photos from Flickr and display them on a web page, and in the process, learn how to use jQuery's `$.getJSON()` method to retrieve JSONP data from another website.

Constructing the URL

Flickr offers several different URLs for accessing feeds for different types of photos (see *www.flickr.com/services/feeds/* for a full list). For example, you use *https://api. flickr.com/services/feeds/photos_public.gne* to access photos from specific Flickr accounts (such as your own account if you have one), as well as a link for retrieving photos from a particular group (like the Web Design group, which features photos and images to inspire awesome websites).

Once you know which type of photo feed you'd like and the basic URL that accompanies it, you need to add some additional information to retrieve the photos you're interested in. To do so, you add a query string with several pieces of information added on. (As you recall from page 463, a query string is a *?* mark at the end of a URL, followed by one or more name/value pairs: *https://api.flickr.com/services/ feeds/groups_pool.gne?id=25053835@N03&format=json*, for example.)

- **Add one or more IDs.** To select photos from a particular group or one or more individual accounts, you add `id`, plus an = sign followed by an individual or group account number. For example, to access a group photo feed for the Web Design group, you'd use this group photo feed and add the ID for the group, like this:

    ```
    https://api.flickr.com/services/feeds/ ↵
    groups_pool.gne?id=37996591093@N01
    ```

    For individual Flickr feeds, you'd use the public photos feed and use one or more IDs. For example, to retrieve photos from both the Smithsonian (which has its own Flickr account) and the Library of Congress, you can use the ids names and the public photo feed, like this:

```
https://api.flickr.com/services/feeds/ ↵
photos_public.gne?ids=8623220@N02,25053835@N03
```

To use multiple IDs, separate each with a comma. Note that you can only use multiple IDs for retrieving individual accounts: You can't use the group feed and retrieve photos from multiple groups.

> **TIP** If you know someone's Flickr username, you can get his Flickr ID using this website: *http://idgettr.com/*.

- **Add the JSON format.** The Flickr photo feed service is very flexible and can return photo information in many different formats from RSS to Atom, CSV, and JSON. To let Flickr know that you want data in JSON format, you need to add &format=json to the query string. For example, to get the a Flickr feed of the Smithsonian Museum's Flickr photos in JSON format, you'd use this URL:

```
https://api.flickr.com/services/feeds/ ↵
photos_public.gne?ids=25053835@N03&format=json
```

Go ahead and type the URL above into a web browser (if you're feeling lazy, you can copy and paste the URL from the *flickr_json.txt* file in the *chapter13* folder of the tutorial files). You'll see a bunch of data; actually, an object literal containing a bunch of information. That's what you receive from Flickr when you use the $.getJSON() method (discussed on page 477). You need to use JavaScript to dissect that object and then use it to build a neat little gallery of images. (The structure of Flickr's JSON feed is discussed on page 487, and taking apart the feed so you can use it is shown in the tutorial on page 488.)

- **Add a JSONP callback to the URL.** Finally, for a page on your site to success-fully request JSON data from another website, you need to add one last bit to the URL: &jsoncallback=?. Remember that for security reasons you can't just send an XMLHTTP request to a different domain. To get around that problem, the &jsoncallback=? piece notifies Flickr that you want to receive JSONP data and lets jQuery's $.getJSON() method treat this request as if the web browser were simply requesting an external JavaScript file. In other words, to receive a feed of the Smithsonian Museum's latest Flickr photos, you'd need to pass the $.getJSON() method a URL, like this:

```
https://api.flickr.com/services/feeds/ ↵ photos_public.gne?ids=25053835@
N03&format=json&jsoncallback=?
```

▓ FINDING PHOTOS OF SPECIFIC THINGS

On Flickr, you can *tag* any photo with one or more words; a tag is a word or short phrase that describes an element of the photo. For example, you might tag a particu-larly bright photo of a sunset with the word "sunset." Any photo can have multiple tags, so you might tag that sunset photo with the words "sunset, orange, beach."

Flickr's feed service provides options that let you search a feed for specific tags:

- **tags.** Add the `tags` keyword with one or more comma-separated keywords to the URL to specify a tag; for example: `tags=fireworks,night`. To search for photos of fireworks at night, you could then use this URL:

```
https://api.flickr.com/services/feeds/ ↵
photos_public.gne?tags=fireworks,night&format=json&jsoncallback=?
```

- **tagmode.** Normally when you search for a set of tags, Flickr retrieves photos that match all of the tags. For example, say you added `?tags=chipmunks,baseball,winter` to a feed. This code finds only photos of chipmunks playing baseball in the winter. If you wanted pictures of chipmunks, or baseball, or the winter (in other words, at least one of the tags), add `&tagmode=any` to the URL. For example:

```
https://api.flickr.com/services/feeds/ ↵
photos_public.gne?tags=chipmunk,baseball,winter ↵
&tagmode=any&format=json&jsoncallback=?
```

■ COMBINING OPTIONS

You can combine search options to refine the photo selection even more. For example, you can combine an ID with a tag, so you can find photos by a specific person and of a particular thing. For example, say you and a couple of friends like to take pictures of chipmunks and post them up on Flickr, and you want to get a feed of the 20 latest chipmunk photos you and your friends have taken. You can do this by filtering the feed by specifying one or more tags:

```
https://api.flickr.com/services/feeds/ ↵
photos_public.gne?ids=25053835@N03,8623220@N02 ↵
&tags=chipmunk&format=json&jsoncallback=?
```

Using the $.getJSON() Method

Using the `$.getJSON()` method to retrieve a photo feed from Flickr works the same way as retrieving JSON data from your own site. The basic structure for the function is the same. For example, here's the setup for retrieving the Smithsonian's Flickr feed:

```
1  var flickrURL = "https://api.flickr.com/services/feeds/ ↵    photos_public.
gne?ids=25053835@N03&format=json&jsoncallback=?";
2  $.getJSON(flickrURL, function(data) {
3    // do something with the JSON data returned
4  }); // end get
```

In this example, line 1 creates a variable named `flickrURL` and stores the URL (using the rules discussed in the previous section). Line 2 sends the Ajax request to the URL and sets up an anonymous function for processing that data. After sending an Ajax request, the code retrieves data back from the server—in this example, that data is sent to the anonymous function and is stored in the variable called `data`. You'll learn how to process the data in a few pages, but first, you need to understand what Flickr's JSON data looks like.

Understanding the Flickr JSON Feed

As discussed on page 477, JSON is simply a JavaScript object literal. It can be as simple as this:

```
{
  "firstName" : "Bob",
  "lastName" : "Smith"
}
```

In this code, firstName acts like a key with a value of Bob—a simple string value. However, the value can also be another object (see Figure 13-10 on page 482), so you can often end up with a complex nested structure—like dolls within dolls. That's what Flickr's JSON feed is like. Here's a small snippet of one of those feeds. It shows the information retrieved for two photos:

```
1 {
2    "title": "Uploads from Smithsonian Institution",
3    "link": "http://www.flickr.com/photos/smithsonian/",
4    "description": "",
5    "modified": "2011-08-11T13:16:37Z",
6    "generator": "http://www.flickr.com/",
7    "items": [
8       {
9          "title": "East Island, June 12, 1966.",
10          "link": "http://www.flickr.com/photos/smithsonian/5988083516/",
11          "media": {"m":"http://farm7.static.flickr.com/6029/5988083516_
   bfc9f41286_m.jpg"},
12          "date_taken": "2011-07-29T11:45:50-08:00",
13          "description": "Short description here",
14          "published": "2011-08-11T13:16:37Z",
15          "author": "nobody@flickr.com (Smithsonian Institution)",
16          "author_id": "25053835@N03",
17          "tags": "ocean birds redfootedbooby"
18       },
19       {
20          "title": "Phoenix Island, April 15, 1966.",
21          "link": "http://www.flickr.com/photos/smithsonian/5988083472/",
22          "media": {"m":"http://farm7.static.flickr.com/6015/5988083472_
   c646ef2778_m.jpg"},
23          "date_taken": "2011-07-29T11:45:48-08:00",
24          "description": "Another short description",
25          "published": "2011-08-11T13:16:37Z",
26          "author": "nobody@flickr.com (Smithsonian Institution)",
27          "author_id": "25053835@N03",
28          "tags": ""
29       }
30    ]
31 }
```

Flickr's JSON object has a bit of information about the feed in general: That's the stuff at the beginning—"title", "link", and so on. The "title" element (line 2) is the name of that feed. In this case, "Uploads from Smithsonian Institution"—the "link" element (line 3)—points to the main Flickr page for the Smithsonian Institution. You can use this information, for example, as a headline presented before displaying the photos.

To access that information, you use the dot syntax described on page 56. For example, say you used the code from the previous section (page 486): The anonymous function used to process the data stores the JSON response in a variable named data (see line 2 on page 486). Then, to access the title of the feed, you'd access the "title" property of the "data" object like this:

```
data.title
```

The most important part of the feed is the "items" property (line 7), which contains additional objects, each containing information about one photo. For example, lines 8–18 provide information for one photo, while lines 19-29 are about another photo. Within each item object, you'll find other properties like the title of the photo (line 9), a link to that photo's Flickr page (line 10), the date the photo was taken (line 12), a description (the "Short description here" on line 13 [the curators at the Smithsonian must have been feeling a little lazy that day]), and so on.

Another important element for each photo is "media"—it's another object. For example:

```
{
    "m":"http://farm7.static.flickr.com/6029/5988083516_bfc9f41286_m.jpg"
}
```

The "m" means "medium," and its value is a URL to the photo. Flickr photos are often available in different sizes, like medium, thumbnail, and small (which is a small square image). If you want to display the image on a page, then this URL is what you're after. You can use it to insert an <img> tag in the page and point to that photo on the Flickr server. You'll see how in the tutorial.

◼ Tutorial: Adding Flickr Images to Your Site

In this tutorial, you'll put together all the pieces to retrieve the photo feed from the Smithsonian Institution, display thumbnail images of the photos, and add links to each image, so a visitor can click the thumbnail to go to Flickr and see the photos page.

NOTE See the note on page 12 for information on how to download the tutorial files.

1. **In a text editor, open the file *flickr.html* in the *chapter13* folder.**

   You'll start by creating a few variables to store the components of the URL required to talk to Flickr.

2. **Click in the empty line inside the $(document).ready() function, and type:**

```
var URL = "https://api.flickr.com/services/feeds/photos_public.
gne?jsoncallback=?";
```

This URL points to the public feed and includes the magic little bit—?jsoncallback=?—that tells the Flickr website that it should send JSONP. In other words, this code tells Flickr to send a JavaScript file containing the photo information.

Next, you'll create an object to hold additional information to Flickr.

Each variable here is just part of that much longer URL discussed on page 484. Breaking each piece into a separate variable makes it easy to adjust this code. For example, if you want to get a photo feed from another Flickr user, just change the ID variable.

> **TIP** If you have a Flickr account, go ahead and plug in your ID number in here. If you don't know your Flickr ID, visit *http://idgettr.com/* to find out.

Next, you'll put these variables together to construct a complete URL:

1. **Add another line of code after the one you just typed:**

```
var searchInfo = {

};
```

This line is an empty JavaScript object literal. As you read on page 477, you can pass additional information along with an Ajax request. The server can then use that information to modify its response. In this case, you want to provide the a Flickr user's ID to find photos from just that user.

2. **Inside the object, add one name/value pair (bolded):**

```
var searchInfo = {
  id : "25053835@N03"
};
```

The Flickr API expects an ID for a particular user. In this case, the ID belongs to the Flickr account for the Smithsonian Institute. Note that you have to use lowercase—id—for the property name. If you want to get a photo feed from another Flickr user, just change the ID variable (again, if you have a Flickr account, you can use your own ID number).

You also need to tell Flickr to send back JSON data.

> **TIP** If you want to retrieve the photos from a Flickr group, like the Web Design group, change the URL in step 2 to: *https://api.flickr.com/services/feeds/groups_pool.gne?jsoncallback=?* and the ID in step 4 to the ID of the Flickr group.

3. **Add a comma after the line with the id, hit Return and type** `format : "json"`:

```
var searchInfo = {
  id : "25053835@N03",
  format : "json"
};
```

If you don't add this format part, you'll get data back in XML format.

Now it's time to get into the Ajax part of this and use jQuery `$.getJSON()` function.

4. **After the line you just added, type this:**

```
$.getJSON(ajaxURL, searchInfo, function(data) {


}); // end get JSON;
```

Here's the basic shell of the `$.getJSON()` method: It will contact the URL you specified in step 2, send the search criteria you created in steps 3–5, and receive data back from Flickr. That data is passed to an anonymous function and stored in a variable named data. You can then take that data and begin to use it on the page. First, you'll get the title of the feed and replace the `<h1>` tag that's currently on the page with it.

5. **Add the bolded line of code below to the code from the last step:**

```
$.getJSON(ajaxURL,function(data) {

  $('h1').text(data.title);
}); // end get JSON;
```

This line is a basic jQuery selector—`$('h1')`—and function—`.text()`—that selects the `<h1>` tag currently on the page and replaces the text inside it. The actual JSON feed is stored in the data variable. To access its components, you can use dot syntax (page 56), so `data.title` retrieves the title of the feed. If you save the page now and preview it in a web browser, you should see a bold headline reading "Uploads from Smithsonian Institution."

Next, you'll create a new variable, which will hold a string containing the HTML that you'll add to this web page.

6. **Add the bolded line of code below to the code from the last step:**

```
$.getJSON(ajaxURL,function(data) {
  $('h1').text(data.title);
  var photoHTML = '';
}); // end get JSON;
```

This string is empty now, but soon you'll add the HTML required to display the photos returned by Flickr. To create this HTML, you'll loop through the `items` array of objects returned by the Flickr feed. For each photo in the feed, you'll add more HTML to the `photoHTML` variable.

7. **Add the bolded lines of code below to the code from the previous step:**

```
$.getJSON(ajaxURL,function(data) {
  $('h1').text(data.title);
  var photoHTML = '';
  $.each(data.items,function(i,photo) {

  }); // end each
}); // end get JSON;
```

The `.each()` function (page 138) is used to loop through a jQuery selection. The `$.each()` method is different, but similar. It's a generic loop utility that you can use to loop through either an array (page 44) or a series of objects. You pass the `$.each()` method an array or an object literal and an anonymous function. The `$.each()` method then loops through the array or the object literal and runs the anonymous function once for each item. That anonymous function receives two arguments (`i` and `photo` in the code in this step), which are variables that contain the index of the item and the item itself. The index is the number of the item through the loop: This function works just like an index for an array (page 48). For example, the first item in the loop has an index of 0. The second argument (`photo` in this example), is the photo object containing the photo's name, description, URL, and so on, as described on page 488.

In the case of the Flickr feed, `data.items` represents the photo objects in the JSON feed, so the `$.each()` function passes the object for each photo to the anonymous function in the `photo` variable. In other words, this code loops through each of the photos in the feed and then does something. In this case, you'll create a series of thumbnail images that links to each photo's Flickr page. The goal is to create some basic HTML to display each image and include a link. For example:

```
<span class="image">
<a href="http://www.flickr.com/photos/smithsonian/5988083516/">
<img src="http://farm7.static.flickr.com/6029/5988083516_bfc9f41286_s.jpg">
</a>
</span>
```

To build this, you need only two pieces of information—the URL of the photo's Flickr page, and the path to the photo file. You'll just build up a long string that looks just like the HTML above, only replacing the URL and image path for each of the images.

8. **Inside the $.each() method, add the bolded code below:**

```
$.each(data.items,function(i,photo) {
    photoHTML += '<span class="image">';
    photoHTML += '<a href="' + photo.link + '">';
    photoHTML += '<img src="' + photo.media.m + '"></a></span>';
}); // end each
```

This code starts by adding an opening `<span>` tag to the variable `photoHTML`. Each subsequent line adds more to the variable (for a refresher on what `+=` means and how it works, see page 39). The key elements here are `photo.link` and `photo.media.m`. If you look at the JSON code on page 487, you can see that each photo has various properties like title (the name of the photo) and description (a short description of the photo). The link property points to the photo's page on Flickr.com, while the media object has a property named m, which contains the path to the medium-sized version of the graphic file. Altogether, this code builds up HTML like that pictured in step 6. Now you just need to add that code to the page.

9. **Add the bolded code below:**

```
$.each(data.items,function(i,photo) {
    photoHTML = '<span class="image">';
    photoHTML += '<a href="' + photo.link + '">';
    photoHTML += '<img src="' + photo.media.m + '"></a></span>';
}); // end each
$('#photos').append(photoHTML);
```

Note that this line goes *outside* of the loop. You don't want to add the HTML to the page until you've finished creating it inside of the loop. The `$('#photos')` part selects an already existing `<div>` tag on the page, while the `append()` function (discussed on page 127) adds the HTML to the end of that div.

10. **Save the page and preview it in a web browser.**

You should see 20 photos load on the page. (If you don't see anything, double-check your code and use your web browser's error console [page 18] to look for any syntax errors.) The problem is the photos all vary in size and don't form a nice grid on the page. That's because the Flickr feed only provides the path to medium-sized Flickr images.

Flickr does offer nice square thumbnails of all their photos as well. Displaying those identically sized photos together on a page makes a neat, orderly presentation. Fortunately, it's easy to request those thumbnail images. Flickr uses a consistent naming convention for their photos: If the path to a medium-sized image is *http://farm7.static.flickr.com/6029/5988083516_bfc9f41286_m.jpg,* the thumbnail path for that same image is *http://farm7.static.flickr.com/6029/5988083516_bfc9f41286_s.jpg.* The only difference is at the end of the filename: _m indicates a medium image, _s is a small square thumbnail image (75 pixels by 75 pixels), _t is a small image that's at most 100 pixels on the longest side, _o indicates the original image (the original size the file that the was uploaded to Flickr), and _b is a large image (at most, 1,024 pixels tall or wide). By simply adjusting the filename (replacing the _m with _s, for example), you can display a different size file. Fortunately, JavaScript provides a handy method of quickly swapping characters in a string.

11. **In the code, change `photo.media.m` to `photo.media.m.replace('m','s')`. The final code on the page should look like this:**

```
$(document).ready(function() {
  var URL = "https://api.flickr.com/services/feeds/photos_public.
gne?jsoncallback=?";
  var searchInfo = {
    id : "25053835@N03",
    format : "json"
  };
  $.getJSON(URL,searchInfo,function(data) {
    $('h1').text(data.title);
    var photoHTML = '';
    $.each(data.items,function(i,photo) {
      photoHTML += '<span class="image">';
      photoHTML += '<a href="' + photo.link + '">';
      photoHTML += '<img src="' + photo.media.m.replace('_m','_s') + '">
</a></span>';
    }); // end each
    $('#photos').append(photoHTML);
  }); // end get JSON
}); // end ready
```

JavaScript's `replace()` method (discussed on page 560) works with strings, and takes two arguments—the string to find ('_m' in this case) and the string to replace it with ('_s').

12. **Save the page and preview it in a web browser.**

Now you should see 20 neatly aligned, square thumbnails (Figure 13-11). Click a thumbnail to see a larger image on Flickr's site. A working version of this tutorial—*complete_flickr.html*—is available in the *chapter13* folder.

NOTE The Flickr feed only provides 20 images maximum. You can't retrieve more than 20 from any one feed. What if you only want to display 10 images from the feed? See the file *complete_flickr_limit_photos.html* in the *chapter13* folder for the solution.

Building a To-Do List Application

jQuery and jQuery UI provide the tools to build a professional-looking web application in just a few steps. jQuery takes care of the details regarding selecting page elements, adding new page elements, and updating the DOM. jQuery UI provides great-looking widgets, interactions, and effects that solve many common problems in user interface design. With both of these libraries working for you, you can skip time-consuming programming tasks and jump directly into coding a dynamic interactive application. This chapter walks you through the construction of a basic task manager.

▨ An Overview of the Application

Your to-do list application will let its users do the following:

- **Add a new task to the list of to-dos.** You'll achieve that by adding a jQuery UI button (#1 in Figure 14-1) that, when clicked, opens a jQuery UI dialog box.

- **Mark a task as complete.** Each to-do list item will have a checkbox to the left of the task name (#2 in Figure 14-1). Clicking this box will automatically remove the to-do list item from the To Be Done list and move it to the Completed Tasks list.

- **Drag items from the To Be Done list to the Completed Tasks list and vice versa** (#3 in Figure 14-1). While clicking a checkbox works, why limit your users to just one way of marking a task as complete? With jQuery UI's sortable widget, you can also let users just drag an item to the Completed Tasks list to mark it done. In addition, you can let users drag a completed task *back* to the To Be Done list.

• **Remove tasks from either list by clicking a Delete button** (#4 in Figure 14-1). To allow complete removal of a task, you'll supply a Delete button that removes it from the page. You'll also use a jQuery UI effect to make deleting the task look cool.

Because jQuery UI provides most of the user interface, you just need to work on the basic logic of the application. You'll tackle this task in small bits following the outline just presented. You'll start by adding a button, then a dialog box, and then build up the rest of the app. It's a good idea when taking on a programming task to break the task down into small, testable components, so in this tutorial you'll do one thing, make sure it works, and then continue to the next step.

FIGURE 14-1

jQuery and jQuery UI make it relatively simple to create a basic to-do list application. jQuery and jQuery UI solve the difficult user interface problems—like creating dialog boxes, creating sortable lists, and animating page elements—so you can concentrate on just coding the to-do list functionality.

■ Add a Button

First, you'll add a button and format it using jQuery UI. In this tutorial, you'll work on two different files supplied in the Chapter 14 folder: *index.html* and *todo.js*. You'll put all the JavaScript code into the *todo.js* file and add HTML code for the button and dialog box to the *index.html* file.

> **NOTE** See the note on page 12 for information on how to download the tutorial files.

1. **In a text editor, open the file *index.html* in the *chapter14* folder.**

   This file already contains links to the necessary CSS, jQuery, and jQuery UI files. However, it doesn't yet load the *todo.js* file—the file you'll add the programming to.

2. **In the line just below `<script src="js/jquery-ui.min.js"></script>`, add the following:**

   ```
   <script src="todo.js"></script>
   ```

   It's important that the *todo.js* file is listed last because it relies on both jQuery and jQuery UI. If you loaded it before either of those files, the browser would cough up a syntax error when the page loads.

   Next, you'll add a button. A visitor clicks this button to add a new task to the to-do list.

3. **Locate the HTML comment `<!-- add button here -->` and replace it with the following HTML:**

   ```
   <button id="add-todo">Add to-do item</button>
   ```

   There's nothing special about this code—it's just a basic HTML `<button>` element. If you previewed the page right now, you'd see that it looks like a basic Submit button on a form—drab and uninteresting. Next, you'll turn it into a jQuery UI button.

4. **Open the *todo.js* file in your text editor, and, inside the `$(document).ready()` function, type:**

   ```
   $('#add-todo').button();
   ```

   This code simply applies the button formatting supplied by the jQuery UI theme (page 385). You can spruce it up a little by adding a jQuery UI icon.

5. **Inside the `button()` function, add a JavaScript object literal that defines an icon for this button (additions in bold):**

   ```
   $('#add-todo').button({
     icons: {
       primary: "ui-icon-circle-plus"
     }
   });
   ```

   This adds a little + icon to the left of the text "Add to-do item" on the button. As discussed on page 367, jQuery UI lets you place two icons on a button one of the left (the `primary` icon) and one on the right (the `secondary` icon). One icon is enough for this button.

6. **Save both the *todo.js* and *index.html* files. Preview the *index.html* file in a browser.**

   The button should match the look of a jQuery UI button widget (Figure 14-1). If it doesn't, it's because the JavaScript isn't working. Double check your code and use your browser's JavaScript console to see if there are any errors.

Add a Dialog Box

Now there's a button, but it doesn't do anything. It's supposed to open a dialog box when clicked, so the next task is to add the dialog. First, you'll add the HTML for the dialog:

1. **Locate the comment `<!-- add dialog box here -->` in the *index.html* file and replace it with the following HTML:**

```
<div id="new-todo" title="Add to-do item">
  <form>
     <p>
       <label for="task">Task Name:</label>
       <input type="text" name="task" id="task">
    </p>
  </form>
</div>
```

As you learned on page 306, you can turn any chunk of HTML into a dialog box. In this case, there's a `<div>` element containing a form with a single text field. Users will type the name of their task into this field when adding a new to-do item.

To transform this HTML into a dialog box, you need to add some JavaScript.

2. **Return to the *todo.js* file. Below the code you added in step 5 on page 497, type:**

```
$('#new-todo').dialog();
```

Save the *index.html* and *todo.js* files and preview the *index.html* file in a browser. The dialog box should appear (see top image in Figure 14-2). However, it appears immediately, without clicking the button. That's the normal behavior of a jQuery UI dialog box. To hide the dialog, you need to pass the `dialog()` function some options.

3. **Add an object to the `dialog()` function with two properties:**

```
$('#new-todo').dialog({
  modal : true,
  autoOpen : false
});
```

As you read on page 310, the modal option requires a user to close the dialog box in order to do anything else with the web page. That's what you want—when the user clicks the "Add to-do item" button, the dialog should be the user's main focus.

By setting the autoOpen option to `false`, the dialog will no longer open as soon as the page loads. It's now hidden, and you need to open it programmatically—like when the button is clicked!

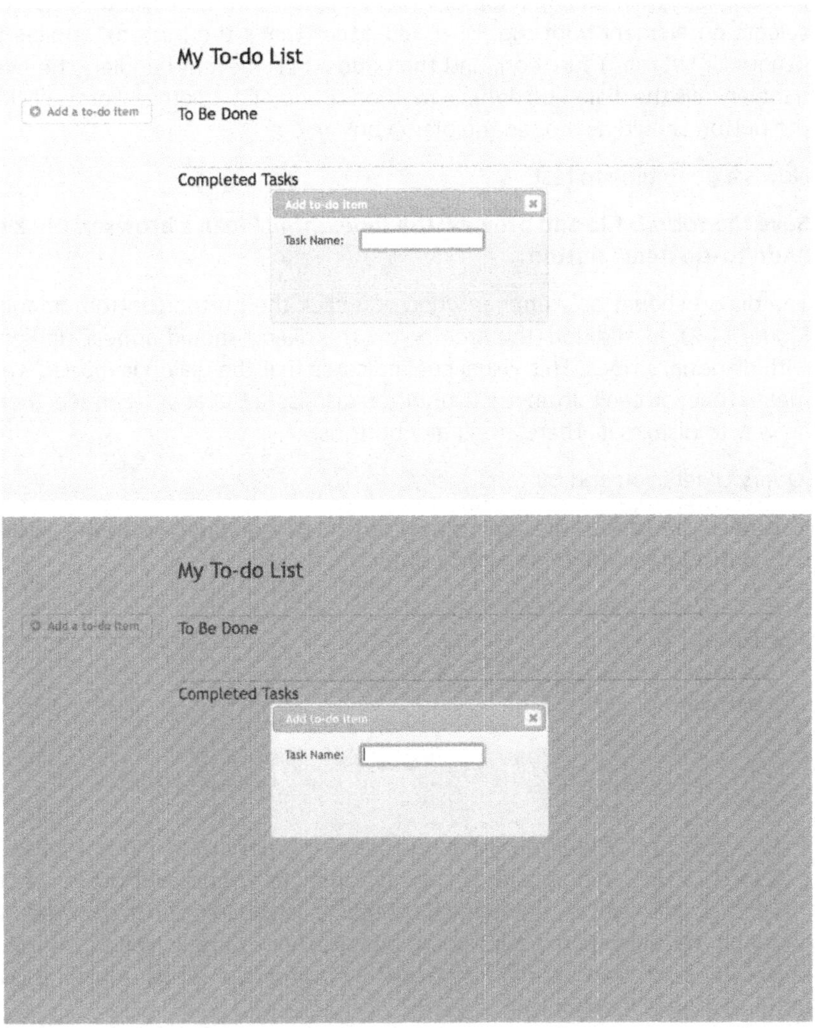

FIGURE 14-2

jQuery UI dialog boxes automatically open when the page loads. That's great for an important announcement that visitors should see when they visit the page, but not so useful for most other purposes, like adding a task to a to-do list. Most of the time, you'll want a dialog box to remain hidden until it's called into action by a visitor's request—like clicking an "Add to-do item" button.

4. **Add a click event handler to the button by chaining the click() function to the end of the button() function:**

```
$('#add-todo').button({
  icons: {
    primary: "ui-icon-circle-plus"
    }
}).click(function() {
```

```
    $('#new-todo').dialog('open');
  });
```

You can "chain" jQuery functions by simply adding a period at the end of one function and then adding another function after it. In this case, the code first selects an element with the ID of add-todo (that's the button), applies the jQuery UI button() function, and then adds a click event handler. The event handler calls the dialog box's open method (page 313). In other words, clicking the button should now open the dialog box.

Now's a good time to test.

5. **Save the *todo.js* file and preview the *index.html* file in a browser. Click the "Add to-do item" button.**

The dialog should only appear when you click the button (bottom image in Figure 14-2). In addition, the area below the dialog should appear darkened with diagonal stripes. This visual cue indicates that the dialog is *modal,* which means that you can't do anything until you dismiss it. But as you can see, there's no way to dismiss it. There aren't any buttons!

jQuery UI lets you add buttons easily.

6. **Return to the *todo.js* file. Add a new option named buttons to the options list, and set its value to an empty object:**

```
    $('#new-todo').dialog({
      modal : true,
      autoOpen : false,
      buttons : {

      }
    });
```

The buttons option lets you name buttons that jQuery UI dynamically adds to a dialog box. In addition, you can assign functions to each button, so when a visitor clicks the button, something happens. You're building up this code slowly, bit by bit, because there's a lot going on here. For example, you now have an object (the buttons property) inside another object (the options object passed to the dialog() function).

First, just add a button with an empty function.

7. **Add one property to the buttons object (additions in bold):**

```
    $('#new-todo').dialog({
      modal : true,
      autoOpen : false,
      buttons : {
        "Add task" : function () {
```

```
      }
    }
});
```

This code adds a button with a label reading "Add task". When a user clicks the "Add task" button, the function runs. Currently there's nothing in that function, so it won't do anything. You'll add functionality to the button in the next section of this tutorial. But for now, you'll add another button.

8. **Type a comma after the add task() function's closing } and add another button with a function:**

```
$('#new-todo').dialog({
  modal : true,
  autoOpen : false,
  buttons : {
    "Add task" : function () {

    },
    "Cancel" : function () {
       $(this).dialog('close');
    }
  }
});
```

This adds a second button with the label "Cancel." This time, the button does something. $(this) refers to the element that called the function—that's the dialog box itself. When the Cancel button is clicked, the jQuery UI Dialog widget's close method is called (page 315). This simply tells the dialog box to close without doing anything further.

Time to see how it works.

9. **Save the _todo.js_ file and preview the _index.html_ file in a browser. Click the "Add to-do item" button.**

The dialog should only appear with two buttons (Figure 14-3). Click the "Add task" button, and sure enough, nothing happens, because you haven't programmed it yet. However, you did add code to the Cancel button, so when you click it, the dialog box closes.

In the next section, you'll add the code to actually insert to-do list items onto the page.

FIGURE 14-3

With just a few lines of code, you have all the basic user interface components for adding to-do list items in place.

Adding Tasks

The to-do list application is looking good, but not doing much. It's time to add the code for adding tasks to the To Be Done list. All of this code is attached to the function assigned to the dialog box's "Add task" button—that empty function you added back at step 7 on page 500. The code breaks down into 4 steps:

1. **Retrieve the name of the task the user typed into the dialog box.**

   The value is stored in a form text input field, so you can easily use jQuery's val() function (page 255) to retrieve the task name.

2. **Build up a <li> item to add to the page.**

   Each task will be represented by a list item in an unordered list. The basic HTML for each list item looks like this:

   ```
   <li>
     <span class="done">%</span>
     <span class="delete">x</span>
     <span class="task">Bake cake</span>
   </li>
   ```

   The first <span> represents the area the visitor clicks to mark an item as done. The second <span> represents the delete button the visitor clicks to remove a task completely. The last <span> contains the task name the visitor types into the dialog box. You can build up this chunk of HTML by combining strings containing the literal tags just listed with the task name the visitor provides.

3. **Add the new <li> item to the To Be Done list.**

   jQuery makes it very easy to take a string, convert it to an actual DOM element, and add it to a web page (Chapter 4 discusses that thoroughly). Because you have jQuery UI's powerful effects at your disposal, you'll use them to add the new task in an eye-catching fashion.

4. **Close the dialog box.**

   This step's easy. You already programmed this same functionality for the dialog box's Cancel button in step 8 on page 501.

Now that you know the basic steps you need to code, it's time to get started. First, you'll capture the visitor's input—the task he types into the dialog box:

1. **Locate the function assigned to the "Add task" button (it's inside the buttons option for the dialog() function) and add the bolded code shown here:**

   ```
   "Add task" : function () {
     var taskName = $('#task').val();
   },
   ```

   This creates a new variable—taskName—and assigns the value of the dialog box's text field. Remember in step 1 on page 498, you added the HTML for the dialog box. That included an input field with the ID of task, so $('#task').val() retrieves the value of that field—in other words, what the visitor typed in as the task's name.

   It's possible that a visitor might leave the text field blank and click the "Add task" button anyway. Because you don't want to add an empty task to the to-do list, you should check to make sure the taskName variable isn't empty.

2. **Add three more lines of code below the one you added in the last step (additions in bold):**

   ```
   "Add task" : function () {
     var taskName = $('#task').val();
     if (taskName === '') {
       return false;
     }
   },
   ```

This code simply checks to make sure the `taskName` variable doesn't contain an empty string (that's two single quote marks next to each other like this ' ') and that the visitor didn't just click the "Add task" button without typing anything. The `return false` part just exits this function, with the result that the dialog box stays open. The visitor either has to type a task or click the Cancel button to close the dialog box (or click the little X button in the top right of all jQuery UI dialog boxes).

Next, you'll begin constructing the HTML for the task.

3. **Add a new variable and add string values to it by adding three more lines of code (additions in bold):**

```
"Add task" : function () {
  var taskName = $('#task').val();
  if (taskName === '') {
    return false;
  }
  var taskHTML = '<li><span class="done">%</span>';
  taskHTML += '<span class="delete">x</span>';
  taskHTML += '<span class="task"></span></li>';
},
```

You could have used just a single line of code to create the `taskHTML` variable and store one really long string in it. But that would create one very long, hard-to-read JavaScript statement. Building up a long string over the course of several lines like this makes the code more readable. The `+=` operator lets you combine a string with the string in an already existing variable (page 39).

Notice that you didn't add the visitor's task—the `taskName` variable—to this string. You'll see why in just a moment.

4. **Add another variable and assign to it a jQuery object created from the string of HTML (additions in bold):**

```
"Add task" : function () {
  var taskName = $('#task').val();
  if (taskName === '') {
    return false;
  }
  var taskHTML = '<li><span class="done">%</span>';
  taskHTML += '<span class="delete">x</span>';
  taskHTML += '<span class="task"></span></li>';
  var $newTask = $(taskHTML);
},
```

jQuery lets you take a string of text—'<h1>A headline</h1>', for example—and convert it to an actual DOM element. In other words, `taskHTML` is a variable that just holds a string—a series of characters. That string isn't "real" HTML, however; passing a string that's formatted like HTML to the $() function turns it into a

DOM element. Even better, it turns the string into a jQuery object so you can use all of the regular jQuery functions on it. While the $ at the beginning of the $newTask variable name isn't required, it's a common practice among JavaScript programmers who use jQuery. The $ is a visual way to remind the programmer that the variable holds a jQuery object and that all the various jQuery methods, like .show() and .addClass() can be used with that variable.

You'll add the task the visitor types in next.

5. **Add another line of code to the "Add task" function (additions in bold):**

```
"Add task" : function () {
  var taskName = $('#task').val();
  if (taskName === '') {
    return false;
  }
  var taskHTML = '<li><span class="done">%</span>';
  taskHTML += '<span class="delete">x</span>';
  taskHTML += '<span class="task"></span></li>';
  var $newTask = $(taskHTML);
  $newTask.find('.task').text(taskName);
},
```

jQuery's find() method looks for an element *inside* the current element (page 531). In this case, jQuery takes the <li> element contained inside $newTask and looks inside it for another element with the class name of task—that's the <span> tag where the task's name should go (look at step 3). jQuery's text() function then adds the contents of the taskName variable inside that span.

Why go to all this trouble, when you could just add taskName when creating the string in step 4 like this:

```
taskHTML += '<span class="task">' + taskName + '</span></li>';
```

If you did it that way, then a nefarious visitor could type something like <script>alert('ha, ha, ha, I am breaking your to-do list');</script> as the task's name. That code would be added as straight HTML to the page and the malicious JavaScript in this example would be run. However, jQuery's text() function converts all HTML tags into their HTML-safe equivalents—<script&gt instead of <script>.

Even if the visitor wasn't trying to be malicious, this step lets him type a perfectly reasonable task like "Add <h1> tag to the home page" without breaking the app.

Now it's time to add the new to-do item to the page.

6. **Add two more lines of code inside the "Add task" function (additions in bold):**

```
"Add task" : function () {
  var taskName = $('#task').val();
  if (taskName === '') {
    return false;
  }
  var taskHTML = '<li><span class="done">%</span>';
  taskHTML += '<span class="delete">x</span>';
  taskHTML += '<span class="task"></span></li>';
  var $newTask = $(taskHTML);
  $newTask.find('.task').text(taskName);
  $newTask.hide();
  $('#todo-list').prepend($newTask);
},
```

Because $newTask is a jQuery object, you can use jQuery functions on it. First, you hide it, so you can reveal it using some cool visual animations. After it's hidden, select the To Be Done list—an unordered list on the page with the ID todo-list—and then add the new (hidden) list item to the beginning of the list (see page 127 to learn how the prepend() method works).

Now, you'll reveal the new list item and close the dialog box.

7. **Add two more lines of code to complete the "Add task" button's functionality (additions in bold):**

```
"Add task" : function () {
  var taskName = $('#task').val();
  if (taskName === '') {
    return false;
  }
  var taskHTML = '<li><span class="done">%</span>';
  taskHTML += '<span class="delete">x</span>';
  taskHTML += '<span class="task"></span></li>';
  var $newTask = $(taskHTML);
  $newTask.find('.task').text(taskName);
  $newTask.hide();
  $('#todo-list').prepend($newTask);
  $newTask.show('clip',250).effect('highlight',1000);
  $(this).dialog('close');
},
```

The first new line selects the newly added and hidden list item and then uses jQuery's show() method to reveal it. For some added fun, you're using two jQuery UI effects: the clip effect (page 440) makes the new item appear to grow. After the item is visible, the effect() method applies the highlight effect to make the item flash yellow and draw attention to it (and get "ooohs" and "aaahhhs" from the people using this app).

The last line closes the dialog box (you already used this code with the Cancel button at step 8 on page 501). Time to check and see how it works.

8. **Save the *todo.js* file and open the *index.html* file in a browser. Click the "Add to-do item" button, type a task in the dialog box that appears, and then click "Add task."**

A new task should appear under the "To Be Done" headline. If it doesn't, check your code and use your browser's JavaScript console to see if there are any errors.

Try adding another task. You should see one small problem—the dialog box's text input field remembers the last task you typed. To add a new task, you first have to delete the old one from the text field. You can fix that easily.

9. **After the** buttons **option inside the object passed to the** dialog() **function, type a comma and add the following:**

```
close: function() {
  $('#new-todo input').val('');
}
```

The complete code for the dialog() function should look like this:

```
$('#new-todo').dialog({
  modal : true,
  autoOpen : false,
  buttons : {
    "Add task" : function () {
      var taskName = $('#task').val();
        if (taskName === '') {
          return false;
        }
        var taskHTML = '<li><span class="done">%</span>';
        taskHTML += '<span class="delete">x</span>';
        taskHTML += '<span class="task"></span></li>';
        var $newTask = $(taskHTML);
        $newTask.find('.task').text(taskName);
        $newTask.hide();
        $('#todo-list').prepend($newTask);
        $newTask.show('clip',250).effect('highlight',1000);
        $(this).dialog('close');
    },
    "Cancel" : function () {
        $(this).dialog('close');
    }
  },
```

```
    close: function() {
      $('#new-todo input').val('');
    }
  });
```

Wow, that's a lot of code. Make sure you add this new code outside the `buttons` object. jQuery UI's dialog widget's `close` option lets you run a function when the visitor closes the dialog box. In this case, you'll erase the text field, so next time the dialog is opened, the field will be empty and ready to receive a new task name. (You could also have erased the input field as part of the "Add task" function, but this example was intended to demonstrate the `close` option.)

Marking Tasks as Complete

One of the most satisfying actions you perform with a to-do list is checking off a completed task. Unfortunately, your to-do list is missing that most rewarding feature. In this section, you'll fix that. The basic process is pretty straightforward: the user checks the empty box to the left of the task name, and that task—the list item element—is moved from one unordered list to the other.

Event Delegation

To mark a task as complete, a user must click a box within the list item. Usually you assign an event handler using jQuery by selecting the element then adding an event handler, like this:

```
$('.done').click(function () {
  // do something when this element is clicked
});
```

However, there's something different about how you handle the items in this to-do list. When the web page first loads, there are no list items, and no boxes to mark a task as complete. If you applied the event handler when the page loaded, nothing would happen. Because there were no list items and no checkboxes when the page loaded, there's nothing to apply the handler to. Only after the visitor adds a task is there anything to click on. You could add the `click()` method each time a new list item is created, but jQuery provides a better method called event delegation (page 171).

In a nutshell, event delegation lets you select another page element—an already existing page element that will contain the items that are going to be added dynamically after the page loads. This container element will listen for the proper event—a click event, for example—anywhere inside of it. When it gets the event, it will see if the event was actually triggered on a particular element (the Done box on each task item, for instance), and if it was, the event handler runs.

In this case, an empty unordered list is already on the web page when it loads:

```
<ul id="todo-list">
</ul>
```

As the visitor adds tasks to the to-do list, your program dynamically adds list items:

```
<ul id="todo-list">
  <li>
    <span class="done">%</span>
    <span class="delete">x</span>
    <span class="task">Bake cake</span>
  </li>
</ul>
```

To respond to a click on the done span, you have to delegate the event handler to the existing unordered list:

1. **After the code for the dialog() function but still inside the $(document).ready() function, type the following:**

```
$('#todo-list').on('click', '.done', function() {

});
```

This is the basic outline for the event delegation routine. First, you select the unordered list. Then we use jQuery's on() method, which accepts three arguments. The first is a string containing the event name—'click'. The second is the element inside the unordered list that must be clicked on. In this case, it's the <span> tag with the class done. Finally, you add a function—the programming that should run when the visitor clicks the Done box.

2. **Inside the event handler function, add the following (in bold):**

```
$('#todo-list').on('click', '.done', function() {
  var $taskItem = $(this).parent('li');
});
```

Remember that the point of this function is to move the list item from the To Be Done list to the Completed Tasks list. At the point that the visitor clicks the Done box, jQuery is only aware of that one <span> in the list item, but we need to access the entire <li> tag. To do so, you'll use jQuery's parent() method, which lets you select the parent element of the current selection.

Here, $(this) refers to the element the visitor clicks the <span class="done">%</span>. So $(this).parent('li') selects the nearest ancestor that is an <li> tag; in other words, it selects the list item you're after!

That element is then stored in a variable named $taskItem, which you'll now make disappear.

NOTE For a more thorough discussion of what this and $(this) mean, turn to page 139.

3. **Inside the event handler function add the following (in bold):**

```
$('#todo-list').on('click', '.done', function() {
  var $taskItem = $(this).parent('li');
  $taskItem.slideUp(250, function() {

  });
});
```

jQuery's slideUp method is a fun way to hide a page element (page 186). It doesn't actually remove the element from the page, however. When the slideUp method is done, the item is still on the page; it's just hidden using some CSS. As you read on page 183, all jQuery animation functions (like hide(), show(), and slideUp()) can accept arguments. In this case, the first argument—250—is the amount of time the animation will take: 250 milliseconds.

The second argument here is a callback function. This is a function that runs *after* jQuery finishes the animation. Remember that after slideUp is finished, the list item is still in the To Be Done list—it's just hidden. You need to move it to the other unordered list. You can do that as part of the callback function.

4. **Inside the callback function, add the following (in bold):**

```
$('#todo-list').on('click', '.done', function() {
  var $taskItem = $(this).parent('li');
  $taskItem.slideUp(250, function() {
    var $this = $(this);
    $this.detach();
  });
});
```

The first new line just selects the list item—$(this)—and stores it inside another variable. You do this because each time you run the jQuery function—$( )—you're making the browser do work. You must perform several tasks on this list item, so instead of unnecessarily calling the jQuery function over and over, you can just run it once and keep the results in a variable. (This jQuery best practice is discussed in more detail on page 522.)

The second line uses jQuery's detach() method to remove the selected HTML element or elements from the page, but doesn't completely get rid of them. In other words, the list item is gone from the list, but it still exists in memory. In fact, it's still stored in the variable $this. You can then move the detached element to another place on the page—the other list!

NOTE Visit *http://api.jquery.com/detach/* to get the full scoop on jQuery's detach() method.

5. **Finish up the callback function by adding two more lines (in bold):**

```
$('#todo-list').on('click', '.done', function() {
  var $taskItem = $(this).parent('li');
  $taskItem.slideUp(250, function() {
    var $this = $(this);
    $this.detach();
    $('#completed-list').prepend($this);
    $this.slideDown();
  });
});
```

You've seen the prepend() method before (in step 6 on page 506). It inserts HTML inside another element. In this case, the detached list item—$this—is added inside the Completed Tasks list (another unordered list with the ID of completed-list). Lastly, because the slideUp() method hid the list item, you can now reveal it in its new location on the page with slideDown() (page 186).

6. **Save the *todo.js* file and preview the *index.html* file in a web browser. To test it out, add a few new to-do items, and then click the box to the left of the task name to mark the task as complete.**

You should be able to add tasks and mark them as complete (Figure 14-4). If it's not working, double check your code and look at your browser's JavaScript console for errors.

Now, wouldn't it be cool if you could reorder your tasks? For example, after you add a bunch of tasks to the list, you could put them in the order in which you should complete them: "Buy a cookbook," "Bake a cake," and "Eat a cake," for example. jQuery UI's sortable widget lets you add that feature easily. And while you're at it, you can make it so you can freely drag items between lists, so you can mark a to-do item "complete" simply by dragging it to the Completed Tasks list.

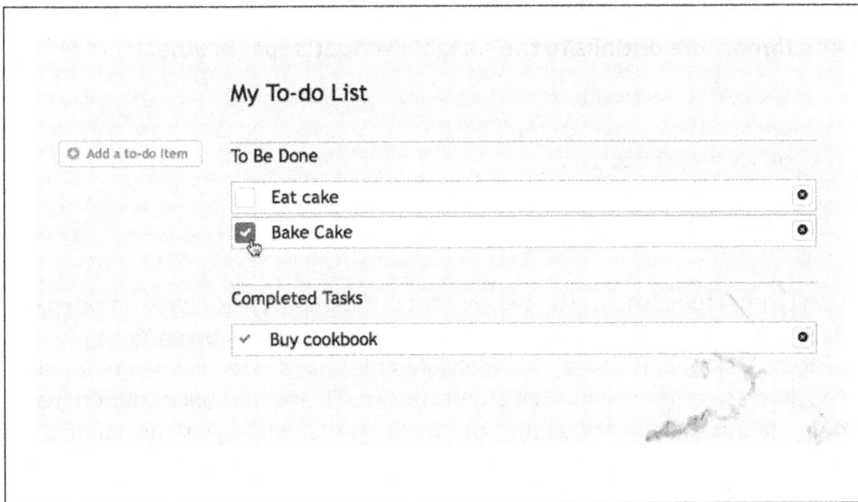

FIGURE 14-4

The buttons on the list items which let you mark a task as complete, or delete a task, change as you mouse over them. That's not JavaScript, that's CSS. In particular, it's the CSS :hover pseudo-class that lets you change how an element looks when you mouse over it. To see how this effect works, check out the todo.css file inside the css folder for this chapter.

7. **Open the *index.html* file in your text editor and locate the `<ul>` tags for the To Be Done and Completed Tasks lists. Add `class="sortlist"` to both so you'll end up with:**

```
<ul id="todo-list" class="sortlist">
```

and

```
<ul id="completed-list" class="sortlist">
```

By supplying the same class name to both lists, you can easily select both and make both sortable.

8. **Save the *index.html* file and open the *todo.js* file in your text editor. After the code for the delegated event handler you just added but still inside the $(document).ready() function, type the following:**

```
$('.sortlist').sortable();
```

Now the two lists are sortable. You can save the files and preview the *index.html* file if you want to try it out. But you'll notice that while you can re-order items in each list, you can't drag one list item into another list. You have to connect the two sortable widgets first.

9. **Inside the `sortable()` function you just added, insert an object with a property and value:**

```
$('.sortlist').sortable({
  connectWith : '.sortlist'
});
```

The sortable widget's `connectWith` option (page 429) lets you connect one list with another. Because you've supplied both lists with the same class name, you've connected both lists. Now you'll be able to drag items freely between lists, but you'll add just a few last user interface niceties before you're done with these sortable widgets.

10. **Add three more options to the sortable widget's option object:**

```
$('.sortlist').sortable({
  connectWith : '.sortlist',
  cursor : 'pointer',
  placeholder : 'ui-state-highlight',
  cancel : '.delete,.done'
});
```

Don't forget the comma after the `connectWith` option. The `cursor` option (page 403) changes the cursor to a pointer when a list item is being dragged; the `placeholder` option (page 432) highlights the space in the list where a visitor can drop an item as she drags it around the list. Finally, the `cancel` option (page 429) identifies elements on the sortable item that won't work as handles for dragging the item: in this case, a visitor can't drag a task by either its "delete this task" icon, or its "mark as done" box.

11. **Save the *index.html* and *todo.js* files, and preview the *index.html* file in a web browser.**

    Add lots of tasks. Drag tasks between the two lists. You should be able to mark an item as complete simply by dragging it from the To Be Done to the Completed Task list (Figure 14-1).

Deleting Tasks

There's just one last feature to add: the ability to delete a task. This feature is important because a user might accidentally add a task that shouldn't be there. Or if the Completed Tasks list starts getting too long, a user might want to delete those completed to-do items.

1. **After the code for the `sortable()` function but still inside the $(document). `ready()` function, type the following:**

   ```
   $('.sortlist').on('click', '.delete', function() {

   });
   ```

   It's event delegation again. When the page loads, there are no list items and no delete buttons, so you need to use event delegation to handle this situation. In this case, $('.sortlist') selects both of the unordered lists on the page (because users should be able to delete tasks from either list) and the on() method tells jQuery to be on the lookout for clicks on any element with the class delete. When that element is clicked, this event handler function is called.

   Next, you'll program the event handler.

2. **Inside the event handler function, add three lines of code (in bold):**

   ```
   $('.sortlist').on('click','.delete',function() {
     $(this).parent('li').effect('puff', function() {
       $(this).remove();
     });
   });
   ```

   There's a lot going on there, but you should be accustomed to this type of code by now. Here's how it breaks down:

   - `$(this).parent('li')` selects the element the user clicked on—$(this)—and then finds an ancestor that is an <li> tag. In other words, it selects the list item you want to delete.

   - jQuery UI's `effect()` method applies one of its many effects to the element. In this case, the puff effect makes an element grow in size, fade away, and disappear.

- The function inside the effect() method is a callback function that runs once the effect is done. In this case, it selects the item that the effect() method was applied to—that's the list item selected by $(this)—and removes it from the page using jQuery's remove() method (page 130). Unlike the detach() method discussed on page 510, the remove() method literally removes the selected elements from the page and disposes of them.

3. **Save the files and preview the *index.hml* file in a web browser.**

You should be able to add, move, and delete to-do list items. The page should look like Figure 14-1. If you have any problems, the complete code for this tutorial is shown here:

```
$(document).ready(function(e) {

$('#add-todo').button({
  icons: {
    primary: "ui-icon-circle-plus"
    }
  }).click(function() {
    $('#new-todo').dialog('open');
});

$('#new-todo').dialog({
  modal : true,
  autoOpen : false,
  buttons : {
    "Add task" : function () {
      var taskName = $('#task').val();
        if (taskName === '') {
            return false;
        }
        var taskHTML = '<li><span class="done">%</span>';
        taskHTML += '<span class="delete">x</span>';
        taskHTML += '<span class="task"></span></li>';
        var $newTask = $(taskHTML);
        $newTask.find('.task').text(taskName);
        $newTask.hide();
        $('#todo-list').prepend($newTask);
        $newTask.show('clip',250).effect('highlight',1000);
        $(this).dialog('close');
    },
    "Cancel" : function () {
        $(this).dialog('close');
    }
  },
  close: function() {
```

```
    $('#new-todo input').val('');
  }
});

$('#todo-list').on('click','.done', function() {
  var $taskItem = $(this).parent('li');
  $taskItem.slideUp(250, function() {
    var $this = $(this);
    $this.detach();
    $('#completed-list').prepend($this);
    $this.slideDown();
  });
});

$('.sortlist').sortable({
  connectWith : '.sortlist',
  cursor : 'pointer',
  placeholder : 'ui-state-highlight',
  cancel : '.delete,.done'
});

$('.sortlist').on('click','.delete',function() {
  $(this).parent('li').effect('puff', function() {
    $(this).remove();
  });
});

}); // end ready
```

NOTE For a complete, working copy of this tutorial look at the *complete-index.html* and *complete-todo.js* files in the *chapter14* folder.

■ Going Further

Congratulations—you've built your first web page application! But there's clearly some ways you can improve this to-do list manager. You may already have a list of additional features you'd like to add. This section will take a look at some possible improvements you could make to the app, including resources you could use to learn how to implement those changes.

Editing Tasks

Currently, the application has no way for a user to edit a typo in a task. If someone creates a new task named "Brake cake," he'd have to delete the task and create a new one to correct her mistake. There are two ways you could solve this problem.

The first solution is to add an Edit button on each task item. Clicking this button will open an edit dialog box with the text content of the task—that's contained inside a <span> element with the class of task.

You could add another dialog box to the page, like the one you added on page 498. Clicking the Edit button opens the dialog box and places the task name into an editable text field. Closing the box updates the task in the list.

Another method uses the HTML contentEditable property. This property makes any HTML element editable. For example, the HTML to make the task name editable in the example HTML you're using for this application would look like this:

```
<span class="task" contentEditable>
```

You can even apply this property dynamically with jQuery:

```
$('.task').prop('contentEditable', true);
```

There's one problem with using contentEditable in this application. jQuery UI's sortable widget prevents selections of text inside sortable items, so you can't select the text to edit it, even if the contentEditable property is enabled. You can get around this problem by telling jQuery UI to ignore the task elements when applying the sortable() function. You did something similar for the Delete and Done buttons in step 10 on page 512. You'd just need to add the .task selector to the list:

```
cancel : '.delete,.done,.task'
```

If you go this route, there won't be much of the list item left for a user to click on and drag. In this case, you should add a clearly identifiable handle that visitors could use to drag the tasks in the list. The sortable item's handle option can help with this (page 431).

Confirming Deletions

Currently, when a visitor clicks the Delete button, the task is gone forever. You could add a modal dialog box that asks the visitor to confirm the action. If the visitor clicks Yes, the task is removed; if No, the task stays as is.

Saving the Lists

The biggest problem with the to-do list application is that it doesn't remember the list when you close the browser window. The to-do list is completely temporary, and won't be remembered between browser visits or if the page is viewed on different computers. There are a few ways you can save the state of your to-do list.

■ LOCAL STORAGE

All current browsers include a feature called *local storage*, which lets you save data to the visitor's computer and call that data back up when the visitor returns to the page. You could use local storage to save a snapshot of the task items each time the to-do lists are updated. When a visitor returns to the page, you check to see if there is any local storage data, and if so, update the web page with that data.

You can learn more about local storage at the Mozilla Developer Network: *https://developer.mozilla.org/en-US/docs/Web/Guide/API/DOM/Storage*. There's even a jQuery plug-in to help make using local storage easy: *https://github.com/julien-maurel/jQuery-Storage-API*.

▓ SAVE TO A SERVER

Another approach is to save the to-do list to a web server. The benefit of this approach is that you could access the to-do list from any computer. The disadvantage is that you'd need to create some system for controlling access to the to-do list; otherwise, anyone could visit the to-do list page and see your tasks (and delete them).

This book doesn't cover server-side programming. However, you will need to use some JavaScript to send the to-do list items to the server. You'll use Ajax, covered in the previous chapter, to send the to-do list data to the server.

The best way would be to grab all of the list items with jQuery and use its `.each()` method to go over each of the list items and extract just the task name. You could build up a JavaScript object with a list of both the uncompleted and completed tasks. Finally, in order to be able to send the object containing the list of tasks to the server with Ajax, you'll need to *serialize* that object—convert it into a simple string that can be sent to the server. Here's a function that could do that:

```
function getData() {
  var todoData = {
    toDo : [],
    completed : []
  };
  $('#todo-list').each( function() {
    var task = $(this).find('.task').text();
    todoData.toDo.push(task);
  });
  $('#completed-list').each( function() {
    var task = $(this).find('.task').text();
    todoData.completed.push(task);
  });
  return $.param(todoData);
}
```

You could call this function whenever you wanted to retrieve the to-do list items in a form that could be sent to the server. It's up to the programming on your web server to decode this and do something with it.

More Ideas

If you have further ideas for improving this to-do list, explore them. This is a great project for trying out your new JavaScript, jQuery, and jQuery UI skills. You'll find an ever-evolving version of this project up on GitHub at *https://github.com/sawmac/jquery-todo*.

Tips, Tricks, and Troubleshooting

Getting the Most from jQuery

jQuery greatly simplifies JavaScript programming, and lets you quickly and easily give your websites sophisticated interactivity. This book has walked you through some examples, like using jQuery plug-ins for form validation and rollover effects. When you venture into jQuery on your own, you'll find it isn't always simple, and you need a certain amount of knowledge to use it to its full extent. In this chapter, you'll learn how to take jQuery further: how to use the documentation and how to take advantage of prepackaged interactivity with plug-ins, plus some useful tips and tricks.

Useful jQuery Tips and Information

jQuery makes programming easier, but on top of that, there are ways you can make programming jQuery easier. Here are a few bits of information that give you insight into jQuery so you can get the most from it.

$() Is the Same as jQuery()

In the many articles and blog posts on jQuery out there on the Web, you may encounter code like this:

```
jQuery('p').css('color','#F03');
```

While you're familiar with $('p'), which selects all the <p> tags on a page, you may be wondering about this jQuery() function. Actually, they are one and the same. The code above could also be written like this:

```
$('p').css('color','#F03');
```

$() is an alias for jQuery(), and the two are interchangeable. John Resig, the creator of jQuery, realized that programmers would be using the main jQuery function a lot, so rather than force people to type jQuery() over and over, he decided the shorter $() would be a good substitute.

In practice, you can use either jQuery() or $(); it's your choice. However, $() is faster to type, so you'll probably want to stick with it (as most programmers do).

NOTE Other JavaScript libraries, like Prototype (*www.prototypejs.org*), also use $(). If you happen to also use Prototype or another library that lays claim to the $ on your site, you might want to use jQuery() instead of $(). In addition, jQuery provides a special function to deal with this situation, named .noConflict(). You can read about it at *http://api.jquery.com/jQuery.noConflict/*.

Saving Selections into Variables

Every time you make a selection of page elements using $()—$('#tooltip'), for example—you're calling the jQuery function. And each time you do that, a visitor's browser has to run a bunch of code, which slows your programs down unnecessarily. For example, say you wanted to apply several jQuery functions to a selection like this:

```
$('#tooltip').html('<p>An aardvark</p>');
$('#tooltip').fadeIn(250);
$('#tooltip').animate({left : 100px},250);
```

This code selects an element with an ID of tooltip and inserts a <p> tag into it. It then selects the element again and fades it into view. Finally, it selects the element a third time and then animates its left property to 100px. Each of those selections—each $('#tooltip')—runs the jQuery function. These three lines of code affect the same element, so you really only need to select it once.

One approach (discussed earlier in the book on page 127) is to use jQuery's chaining abilities. You select the elements then add one function after another to it like this:

```
$('#tooltip').html('<p>An aardvark</p>').fadeIn(250).animate({left :
100px},250);
```

But sometimes chaining gets unwieldy and hard to read. One way to deal with that is by adding a line break after each chained method. Because JavaScript isn't that sensitive to the use of space and line breaks, you can do this:

```
$('#tooltip').html('<p>An aardvark</p>')
            .fadeIn(250)
            .animate({left:100px},250);
```

Even though .html, .fadeIn, and .animate are on separate lines, they're really part of one long statement of chained methods.

Another option is to only run the jQuery function a single time, and store its result in a variable that you reuse. Here's how you could do that with the preceding code:

```
1 var tooltip = $('#tooltip')
2 tooltip.html('<p>An aardvark</p>');
3 tooltip.fadeIn(250);
4 tooltip.animate({left : 100px},250);
```

Line 1 runs the jQuery function, creating a selection of an element with the ID of `tooltip` and stores it into a variable named `tooltip`. Once the selection is made and stored, you don't need to do it again. You can simply use that variable (which now contains a jQuery selection) and run jQuery functions on it.

When using this approach, many programmers like to add a $ before the variable name, which helps remind you that the variable is storing a jQuery selection as opposed to other data types like strings, variables, arrays, or object literals. For example:

```
var $tooltip = $('#tooltip');
```

Storing a selection into a variable is also very common when using events. As you recall from page 139, when you are inside an event function, the variable $(this) refers to the element the event is applied to. However, each time you use $(this) you are calling the jQuery function, so repeated use of $(this) inside an event function just wastes computer power. Instead, you can store $(this) into a variable at the beginning of the event function and use it repeatedly without needing to continually call the jQuery function:

```
$('a').click(function() {
  var $this = $(this); // store a reference to the <a> tag
  $this.css('outline','2px solid red');
  var href = $this.attr('href');
  window.open(href);
  return false;
}); // end click
```

Adding Content as Few Times as Possible

In Chapter 4, you learned about some jQuery functions that let you add content to page elements: The `.text()` function (page 129), for example, lets you replace the text inside an element, and the `.html()` function (page 128) lets you replace the HTML inside of an element. For example, if you wished to insert an error message inside a span tag with the ID of `passwordError`, you could write this code:

```
$('#passwordError').text('Passwords must by at least 7 characters long.');
```

Other functions let you add content after an element (append(); discussed on page 129) or before an element (prepend(); discussed on page 129).

Adding and changing content lets you add error messages, pop up tooltips (page 321), and insert pull quotes (page 141), but it does require a lot from a browser. Each time you add content, the browser needs to do a lot of work—you're basically changing the DOM (page 117) and when that happens, browsers do a lot of behind-the-scenes work. Changing the content a lot of times can significantly affect a web page's performance.

It's not the amount of content that matters—it's the number of times you change the page that affects performance. For example, say you wanted to create a tooltip effect: When someone mouses over a box, for example, a div would appear with some additional content. To do this, you need to add the box and the additional content to the page. Here's one way to add that div:

```
1 // add div to end of element
2 $('#elemForTooltip').append('<div id="tooltip"></div>');
3 // add headline to tooltip
4 $('#tooltip').append('<h2>The tooltip title</h2>');
5 // add contents
6 $('#tooltip').append('<p>The tooltip contents here</p>');
```

The code above will work just fine: Line 2 adds a div to the element the visitor will mouse over; line 4 adds a headline to the tooltip box; and line 6 adds a paragraph to the tooltip. However, the DOM is modified three times in the process with three different append operations. All of this processing is actually quite taxing on a web browser, and reducing the number of times you have to modify the DOM can significantly improve the performance of a page.

In this example, you can reduce the number of append operations to just one by building the entire tooltip HTML, storing it in a variable, and then appending that variable's contents to the page, like this:

```
1 var tooltip = '<div id="tooltip"><h2>The tooltip title</h2> ↵
  <p>The tooltip contents here</p></div>';
2 $('#elemForTooltip').append(tooltip);
```

NOTE The ↵ symbol at the end of a line of code indicates that the next line should really be typed as part of the first line. But because a *really* long line of JavaScript code won't fit on this book's page, it's broken up over two lines. Also note that a string is one case where JavaScript is sensitive about space and line breaks. You can't break a string over multiple lines like this:

```
var longString = "Now is the time for all good people
to come to the aid of their country";
```

You'll end up with a syntax error if you try.

In this code, line 1 creates a variable containing all of the HTML for the tooltip, and line 2 appends that HTML to a page element. There's only one append operation, and depending upon which browser the visitor views the page in, this code can be up to 20 times faster than using the three .append() functions.

The bottom line is that if you want to inject a chunk of HTML into a spot on the page, do it in one single operation (or at least in as few as you can get away with) rather than add the HTML in parts using multiple inserts.

Optimizing Your Selectors

jQuery's flexibility means you have many ways to achieve the same goal. For example, you can select a page element in a number of ways: you can use any CSS selector, or refine a jQuery selection using the DOM Traversal functions discussed on page 531. However, the following techniques will make your selections faster and your JavaScript programs more efficient:

- **Use ID selectors if at all possible.** The fastest way to select a page element is to use an ID selector. Browsers from the dawn of JavaScript have provided a method for selecting elements with IDs, and it's still the fastest way. If you're worried about performance, then you might want to slap an ID on each element that you plan on selecting rather than depending upon other methods like a descendant selector.

- **Use IDs first, as part of a descendant selector.** The problem with using just an ID selector is that you only ever retrieve a single element. What if you need to retrieve multiple elements like all the <a> tags inside a div, or the paragraphs on a page? If your page is structured in such a way that all the elements you wish to select are within an element with an ID, then use a descendant selector that includes the ID first. For example, say you want to select all the <a> tags on a page. It just so happens that all of those tags are also inside a div tag with an ID of main. It's faster to use this selector:

  ```
  $('#main a')
  ```

  than this selector:

  ```
  $('a')
  ```

- **Use the .find() function.** jQuery includes a function for finding elements within a selection. It works kind of like a descendant selector in that it locates tags inside of other tags. You'll read more about this function on page 531, but in a nutshell, you start with a jQuery selection, slap on .find(), and pass a selector to it. In other words, you could write $('#main a') like this:

  ```
  $('#main').find('a');
  ```

  In fact, in some situations, using .find() instead of a descendant selector is over two times as fast!

> **NOTE** You can try a speed test for the .find() function at *http://jsperf.com/sawmac-selector-test*.

- **Avoid too much specificity.** You may be used to using CSS's specificity rules to create CSS styles that target particular elements on a page. A rule like #main .sidebar .note ul.nav li a is very specific, but when you run it through the jQuery function, it can also perform slowly. If possible, either use a descendant selector that's shorter and more refined—$('.sidebar .nav a'), for example—or use the .find() function mentioned in the previous point: $('#main'). find('. sidebar').find('.nav a').

■ Using the jQuery Docs

The jQuery website provides very detailed documentation for jQuery at *http://api.jquery.com/* (Figure 15-1). You'll find useful links for how to get started with jQuery, where to seek help, tutorials, and more, but the most important section of the site deals with the jQuery API. API stands for application programming interface, and simply means the set of functions that jQuery lets you use, like the event handler functions you read about in Chapter 5 (.click(), .hover(), and so on), the CSS functions you learned about in Chapter 4 (.css(), .addClass(), and .removeClass()), and most importantly, the basic jQuery function itself—$()—which lets you select elements on a page.

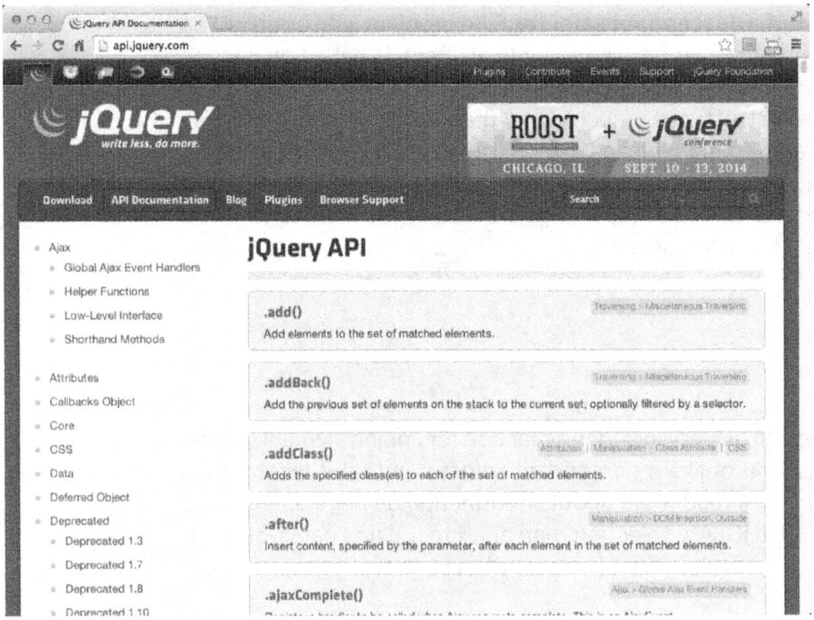

FIGURE 15-1

The main jQuery docs page contains links to lots of useful information. On the left side of the screen, you'll find a complete listing of each of jQuery's functions. In some cases, they're grouped into topics like the Ajax functions, the Event functions, the Manipulation functions, and so on.

The jQuery docs page provides information on every method available in jQuery. The main page actually lists all of them, which is useful if you know the name of the method, as the list is in alphabetical order, but otherwise it's a bit overwhelming. Instead, you'll probably want to select one of the categories in the lefthand navigation bar. Here are a few of the most useful categories:

- **Selectors** (*http://api.jquery.com/category/selectors/*) provides access to some of the most helpful jQuery functions. This page is worth visiting often, as it lists the many different ways to use jQuery to select page elements. You learned about many of these in Chapter 4, but you'll find even more ways when you visit this section of the jQuery documentation.

Because there are so many jQuery functions related to selectors, you'll see that the left sidebar provides sub-categories which group related selector functions such as basic selectors, form selectors, attribute selectors, and so on.

- **Attributes** (*http://api.jquery.com/category/attributes/*). Visit this page to find the various jQuery functions that get and set attributes of HTML elements such as adding a class to a tag, finding or setting the value of an attribute (like the href attribute on an <a> tag), or getting the value of a form element.

NOTE You'll often find the same function listed in more than one section of the jQuery documentation site. For example, the .val() function used to read and set the value of a form field is listed both under the Attributes and the Forms categories of the site.

- **Traversing** (*http://api.jquery.com/category/traversing/*) refers to functions used to manipulate a set of page elements. For example, the .find() function lets you find an element inside a jQuery selection: This is handy when you want to select a page element (a <ul> tag for example), perform an operation on it (like add a class, or fade it into view), and then find another element inside that page element to do something else (for example, find an <li> tag inside the original <ul> tag). jQuery provides lots of functions for traversing HTML elements, and you'll read about some of them later in this chapter.

- **Manipulation** (*http://api.jquery.com/category/manipulation/*). Whenever you want to add or remove something from a page, you need to manipulate the page's DOM. This page lists the many functions available for changing a page, including the ones you read about in Chapter 4 (page 127) like .html() to add HTML to a page, .text() to add text to a page, and so on. This category of functions is very important—a lot of JavaScript programming is about dynamically changing the content and appearance of a web page.

- The **CSS** page (*http://api.jquery.com/category/css/*) lists jQuery functions used for reading or setting CSS-related properties on elements including adding or removing classes, directly setting CSS properties, and controlling or reading the height, width, and position of an element. You'll learn about some of these functions on page 134.

- **Events** (*http://api.jquery.com/category/events/*). In Chapter 5, you learned how to use jQuery to respond to user interaction like the mouse moving over a link, or the visitor clicking a button on the page. You'll find a list of jQuery's many event-related functions on this page. On page 160, you'll learn about some advanced event functions.

- The **Effects** page (*http://api.jquery.com/category/effects/*) provides access to information on jQuery's effects-related functions like the .slideDown(), .fadeIn(), and .animate() functions you learned about in Chapter 6.

- The **Forms** category (*http://api.jquery.com/category/forms/*) lists functions related to—drum roll, please—forms. It mainly lists events used with form elements, but also includes the .val() function for reading or setting the value of a form field, as well as a couple of functions to make it easy to submit a form using Ajax (Chapter 13).

- The **Ajax** category (*http://api.jquery.com/category/ajax/*) lists functions related to dynamically updating a page based on information sent to or received from a web server. You read about Ajax in Chapter 13.

- **Utilities** (*http://api.jquery.com/category/utilities/*). jQuery also provides a handful of functions dedicated to simplifying common programming tasks like finding an element inside an array, acting on each item inside an array or object (the $.each() function discussed on page 138), and a bunch of other geeky niceties. You may not need any of these functions at this point in your programming career (they don't really tap into any cool effects, or help you update the content or appearance of a page), but as you get more advanced, it's worth visiting this page on the jQuery documentation site.

There are a few other categories of functions that are used less frequently, but still are worth knowing about:

- The **Data** category (*http://api.jquery.com/category/data/*) lists functions related to adding data to page elements. jQuery provides a .data() function to add data to an element—think of it as a way to add name/value pairs to any page element, kind of like a mini-database. This and the other data-related functions can come in handy when working on a web application where you need to store and track data. For an understandable introduction to using these data functions, check out *http://tutorialzine.com/2010/11/jquery-data-method/*.

- **Deferred Object** (*http://api.jquery.com/category/deferred-object/*). You don't need to look much further than the introduction to this category (which explains that a deferred object "is a chainable utility object that can register multiple callbacks into callback queues, invoke callback queues, and relay the success or failure state of any synchronous or asynchronous function") to understand that jQuery's Deferred Object is a complex beast. Basically, it helps with queuing up functions to control the order in which they run. If you want to learn more, visit the category page of the jQuery docs site.

- **Dimensions** (*http://api.jquery.com/category/dimensions/*) refers to functions used to determine the width and height of objects. These functions are also listed under the CSS category mentioned earlier.

- **Internals** (*http://api.jquery.com/category/internals/*) are a handful of functions of various degrees of usefulness. The .jquery property, for example, returns the version of jQuery in use on the page:

```
// open alert box with version number
alert($().jquery); // 1.6.2, for example
```

You can lead a long, happy life without using any of the functions here.

- The **Offset** category page (*http://api.jquery.com/category/offset/*) lists functions related to determining the position of an object relative to the screen or to its parent element. You'll use these functions when setting or getting the position of an element on the page.

Reading a Page on the jQuery Docs Site

Each jQuery function has its own page, documenting what it does and how it works. Figure 15-2 shows part of the page explaining jQuery's .css() function. The page lists the functions name (.css() in this case), as well as listing the category and subcategories the function falls under. You can click on the category and subcategory links to jump up to a page listing all functions that fit that category.

In some cases, a function serves double- or even triple-duty and acts differently based on the type and number of arguments you provide it. In that case, you'll see the function listed in several different ways under the function title. For example, in Figure 15-2, you'll see that the .css() function can accept one or two arguments (numbers 1 and 2 in the figure).

The first way, #1, is listed as css(propertyName). Here, propertyName indicates that you pass one argument to the function, which should be a CSS property name. jQuery then returns the value of that property for the specified element (notice "Returns: String" circled in Figure 15-2). The information listed on the page then lets you know that you pass one argument and receive a string in return. For example, say you want to determine the width of a <div> tag with the ID of tooltip; you can use this code:

```
var tipWidth = $('#tooltip').css('width'); // get the width value
```

In this code, 'width' is passed to the function, and a string value is returned. (However, in this case, because it's a width, the string will be the number of pixels wide; the element is—'300', for example.)

> **NOTE**   jQuery offers another variant—css(propertyNames)—which also returns the CSS property values of an element. But instead of accepting a single property name and returning a single value, it accepts an array (page 44) of property names and returns a JavaScript object (page 136) consisting of name/value pairs. The name is a CSS property name from the array and the value is the current value for that CSS property on the specified HTML element.

A second way to use the .css() function is listed (#2) as css(propertyName, value), indicating that you pass the function two arguments—the name of a CSS property and a value. Used this way, the .css() function sets the CSS property for the element. For example, if you wanted to set the width of a <div> tag with the ID of tooltip, you would pass width as the first argument, and the value you wish for the width as the second like this:

```
$('#tooltip').css('width',300); // set div to 300px wide
```

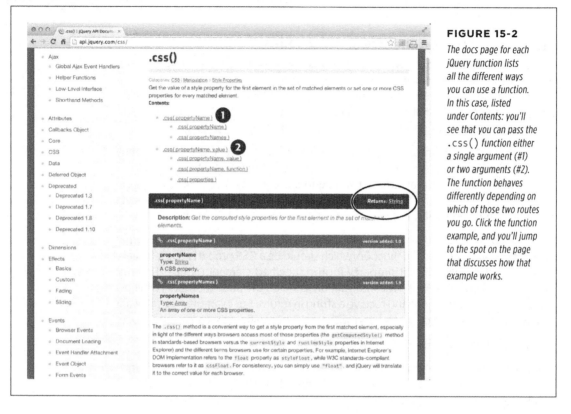

FIGURE 15-2

The docs page for each jQuery function lists all the different ways you can use a function. In this case, listed under Contents: you'll see that you can pass the .css() function either a single argument (#1) or two arguments (#2). The function behaves differently depending on which of those two routes you go. Click the function example, and you'll jump to the spot on the page that discusses how that example works.

The documentation also lists two other ways to use the .css() function to set CSS properties:

- **.css(propertyName, function)** indicates that you can set a CSS property using a function to dynamically generate a value. This is handy when you have a collection of page elements and you want to set slightly different values for each; for example, a series of divs that you wish to set the left property, but you want each div to be positioned next to each other at a different left position.

- **.css(properties)** is described on page 134, and means that you can pass an object literal in order to set several CSS properties and values in one step.

The important thing to understand is that the same jQuery function can and often does take different arguments and does different things. The .css() function, for example, can both retrieve a CSS value and set a CSS value. You'll frequently find jQuery functions working in this way as both "getters" (that is, they retrieve information about an element) and "setters" (that is, they set the value of a particular property for an element).

The docs page will describe each use of the function and usually provides working examples of how the function works. The jQuery docs are well-maintained, and as far as technical documentation goes, pretty easy to read and understand. You should spend some time visiting these pages and especially reading up on the functions you use most often.

Traversing the DOM

You've learned how to select page elements using jQuery and basic CSS syntax: $('p'), for example, selects all of the paragraphs on a page. Once you select elements, you can do stuff to them, such as add or remove a class, change a CSS property, or make the elements disappear. But sometimes you want to find *other* page elements in relationship to your original selection. In JavaScript-speak, this is called *Traversing the DOM* (Document Object Model).

Traversing the DOM happens frequently when you attach an event to an element but then want to do something to another element. For example, say you have a <div> tag with an ID of gallery; the div contains a series of thumbnail images. When a visitor clicks the div, you want the thumbnails to do something: shrink, grow, shake, or something like that. The event is attached to the <div> tag like this:

```
$('#gallery').click(function() {

}); // end click
```

Inside the function, you need to add the programming code to animate the images. So, although the user clicks the *div*, you want do something to the *images*. In the code above, you've merely selected the <div> tag, and inside the function $(this) will refer to that div (if that's news to you, turn to page 139 for a refresher on what $(this) means). So, although the <div> tag is the selected element inside the click function, you need to find the images inside that div. Fortunately, jQuery provides just such a solution: the .find() function. Its purpose is to generate a new selection of page elements by searching *inside* the current selection for other tags that match a given selector. So you can select the images inside the div by adding the bolded code below:

```
$('#gallery').click(function() {
  $(this).find('img');
}); // end click
```

The $(this).find('img') creates a new selection of elements; $(this) refers to the div, then .find('img') looks for every image inside that div. Of course, this code doesn't do anything to the new selection, but you could add any of the effects you learned about in the last chapter. For example, say you want the images to fade out temporarily and then fade back in. You could use this code:

```
$('#gallery').click(function() {
  $(this).find('img').fadeTo(500,.3).fadeTo(250,1);
}); // end click
```

As you read on page 185, the fadeTo() function takes a duration and an opacity value as arguments. So this code first fades all of the images to 30% opacity in 500 milliseconds, and then fades it back to 100% opacity in 250 milliseconds (see the file *find.html* in the *chapter15* tutorial folder to see this effect in action).

In fact, traversing the DOM is such a common task that jQuery provides many functions that help you take a selection of elements and then locate other elements in relationship to the first. To better understand how they work, you'll use a simple chunk of HTML represented in Figure 15-3: *http://api.jquery.com/category/manipulation/.* It's a <div> tag with an ID of gallery containing four links, each of which is wrapped around an image.

As discussed on page 122, you can use the relationships of a family to describe the relationships between tags on a page. For example, in Figure 15-3, the <div> tag is the parent of the <a> tags, and each <a> tag is the parent of the <img> tag inside it. Conversely, the <a> tags are children of the <div> tag, and each <a> tag is the sibling of the other <a> tags. Each <img> tag is the child of the <a> tag that wraps around them, and because there are no other tags inside each <a>, the <img> tags don't have siblings.

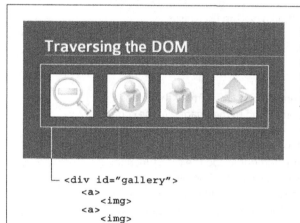

FIGURE 15-3

When you make a jQuery selection—for example, to add an event handler to an element, such as the <a> tags pictured here—you'll often want to act on another tag in relation to that selection (for example, add an outline to the div tag or alter the img tag). jQuery's DOM traversing functions can help.

```
<div id="gallery">
    <a>
        <img>
    <a>
        <img>
    <a>
        <img>
    <a>
        <img>
```

Here are a few of jQuery's most useful DOM traversing functions:

- **.find().** Finds particular elements inside the current selection. You start with a jQuery selection, add .find(), and pass it a CSS selector like this:

  ```
  $('#gallery').find('img')
  ```

  This code finds all of the images inside the gallery div. Of course, you could achieve the same goals with a descendant selector like this $('#gallery img'). As mentioned earlier, you're more likely to use .find() in a situation where you already have a selection that you've done something to—like attach a `click` event—to create a new selection to act on.

You use `.find()` to select a descendant (a tag inside another tag) of the current selection. So in the example pictured in Figure 15-3, you could use `.find()` on a selection including the div to select either the `<a>` tags or the `<img>` tags.

> **NOTE**   See page 531 to read about the huge performance benefits `.find()` offers. It's generally a faster way to select elements than using a descendant selector.

- **.children()** is similar to `.find()`. It also accepts a selector as an argument, but it limits its selection to immediate children of the current selection. For example, say you had a div tag that contains a series of other divs. When you click on the main div, it reveals previously hidden divs, and adds a red outline around them. Say you used the `.find()` function to achieve this goal like this:

```
$('#mainDiv').click(function() {
    $(this).find('div').show().css('outline','red 2px solid');
});
```

A problem arises if one of the divs inside the main div also has a div tags inside it. `.find('div')` locates all div tags, even divs inside other divs. You may end up with a page that has outlines around all the divs, when what you want is simply an outline around the immediate child divs of the main div. To solve that dilemma, you can rewrite the preceding code using `.children()` like this:

```
$('#mainDiv').click(function() {
    $(this).children('div').show().css('outline','red 2px solid');
});
```

Now this code finds only the divs that are immediate children of the main div and avoids any divs that might exist inside the child divs.

- **.parent().** Whereas `.find()` locates elements inside the current element, `.parent()` travels up the DOM locating the parent of the current tag. This could come in handy, for example, if you attach a hover event to the `<a>` tags pictured in Figure 15-3, but you want to perform an action on the `<div>` tag (for example, add a border or background color to the div. In this case, you'd use `.parent()` to locate the div and apply an action to it, like this:

```
$('#gallery a').hover(
    function() {
       var $this = $(this);
       // add outline to link
       $this.css('outline','2px solid red');
       // add background color to div
       $this.parent().css('backgroundColor','white');
    },
    function() {
```

```
      var $this = $(this);
      // remove outline from link
      $this.css('outline','');
      // remove background color from div
      $this.parent().css('backgroundColor','');
   }
); // end hover
```

In this example, hovering over a link adds an outline around that link, then selects the link's parent (the div) and applies a background color. Mousing off the link removes both the outline and background color (see page 162 for more information on the .hover() event). See the file *parent.html* in the *chapter15* tutorial folder for an example of this function in action.

- **.closest()** finds the nearest ancestor that matches a particular selector. Unlike .parent(), which finds the immediate parent of the current tag, .closest() accepts a selector as an argument and finds the nearest ancestor that matches. For example, in Figure 15-3, each image is inside an <a> tag; in other words, the <a> tag is the parent of the image. However, what if you wanted to select the <div> tag that surrounds the <a> tags (an ancestor further up the HTML chain)? You could then use .closest() like this:

```
1 $('#gallery img').click(function() {
2     var $this = $(this);
3     $this.css('outline','2px red solid');
4     $this.closest('div').css('backgroundColor','white');
5 }); // end click
```

In line 3, $(this) refers to the <img> tag; .closest('div') means find the nearest ancestor that's a <div> tag. The closest ancestor is the <a> tag, but because it isn't a div, jQuery skips it and finds the next ancestor, and so on and so on until it locates a <div>.

- **.siblings()** comes in handy when you wish to select an element that's at the same level as the current selection. Say you had the setup pictured in Figure 15-3; when a visitor clicks a link, you want all the other links to gently fade out and into view. In this case, the event—click—applies to a link tag, but the effect you wish to perform is to *all* the other links inside that div. In other words, you start with a link, but you want to select all that link's siblings. You could do that like this:

```
1 $('#gallery a').click(function() {
2     $(this).siblings().fadeTo(500,.3).fadeTo(250,1);
3 }); // end click
```

In the above code, $(this) refers to the clicked link, so .siblings() selects all of the other links in that div.

The .siblings() function also can take an argument—the name of a selector—to limit the selected siblings to a certain type of tag. For example, say inside the

<div> tag pictured in Figure 15-3, there's a headline and introductory paragraph prior to the links. The headline and paragraph are both inside the <div> tag along with all of the <a> tags, also making them siblings of the <a> tag. In other words, given the preceding code, clicking a link would also cause that headline and paragraph to fade out and back into view. To limit the effect to just other links, you could rewrite line 2 to look like the following:

```
$(this).siblings('a').fadeTo(500,.3).fadeTo(250,1);
```

The 'a' inside siblings('a') limits the selection to just siblings that are also <a> tags. See the *siblings.html* file in the *chapter15* tutorial folder to see how this function works.

- **.next()** finds the next sibling of the current selection. You already saw this function in action in the One Page FAQ tutorial on page 174. In that tutorial, clicking a question opens and then closes a <div> tag containing the answer to that question. Each question is represented by an <h2> tag, and each answer by a div tag immediately following that <h2> tag. The headline and div are siblings, but they are also the siblings of all the other questions and answers on that page. So when the headline is clicked, you must select the immediate sibling (in other words, the next sibling). Like .siblings(), .next accepts an optional selector so you can limit selection to the next sibling of a particular type. (See the *complete_faq.html* file in the *chapter15* tutorial folder for an example of .next() in action.)

- **.prev()** works just like .next(), except that it selects the immediately preceding sibling.

NOTE For more jQuery functions that let you traverse the DOM, visit *http://api.jquery.com/category/traversing/*.

■ More Functions for Manipulating HTML

You'll often want to add, remove, and change the HTML of a page dynamically. For example, when a visitor clicks a submit button on a form, you might want the text "Send form information. Please wait." to appear on the screen. Or when a visitor mouses over a photo, you want a box to appear on top of the photo with a caption and photo credits. In both cases, you need to add HTML to a page. You learned about the most common functions in Chapter 4 on page 127. Here's a quick recap:

- **.text()** replaces the text inside a selection with selection you pass to the function. For example:

```
$('#error').text('You must supply an e-mail address');
```

- **.html()** works like .text() but lets you insert HTML instead of just text:

```
$('#tooltip').html('<h2>Esquif Avalon</h2><p>Designed for canoe camping.
</p>');
```

Putting an .end() to DOM Traversal

In order to get the most done while writing the least amount of code, jQuery lets you chain functions together. Chaining is discussed on page 127, but in a nutshell it lets you select some pages elements, do one thing to them, then do another and another thing to them, simply by adding one function after another. For example, if you wanted to select all the paragraphs on a page and have them fade out of view then fade back into view, you could write this code:

```
$('p').fadeOut(500).fadeIn(500);
```

You can chain as many functions together as you'd like including the DOM Traversal methods discussed earlier. For example, you could select a <div> tag, add an outline around it, and then select all of the <a> tags inside that <div> and change the color of their text like this:

```
$('div').css('outline','2px red solid').
find('a').css('color','purple');
```

Broken into pieces, this means:

1. `$('div')` selects all <div> tags.

2. `.css('outline','2px red solid')` adds a 2-pixel red outline to the div.

3. `.find('a')` then changes the selection from the div to all of the <a> tags inside the div.

4. `.css('color','purple')` makes the text of all of the links (not the div tag) purple.

When adding one of the DOM Traversal functions to the chain, you alter the selection. For example, in the above code, jQuery first selects the div, then halfway through the chain, changes the selection to links inside the div. But sometimes when you want to return the selection to its original state. In other words, you want to select one thing, then select another thing in relation to the first selection, then return to the first selection. For example, say when a visitor clicks a div that has an opacity of 50%, you want to make the div fade to 100% opacity, change the color of the headline inside the div, add a background color to each p inside the div. One action—a click—needs to trigger several actions on different elements of the page. One way to do this would be like this:

```
$('div').click(function() {
    var $this = $(this);
    $this.fadeTo(250,1); // fade div in
    $this.find('h2').css('color','#F30');
    $this.find('p')
        .('backgroundColor','#F343FF');
}); // end click
```

Here's a case where chaining would be really helpful—instead of calling $(this) three times, you could call it once and chain together the functions. However, you'd run into trouble if you tried to chain the functions like this:

```
$('div').click(function() {
    $(this).fadeTo(250,1)
        .find('h2')
        .css('color','#F30')
        .find('p')
        .('backgroundColor','#F343FF');
}); // end click
```

This might look right, but the problem occurs after the .find('h2')—which changes the selection from the div to the h2 tag inside the div. When the next .find() function runs—.find('p')—jQuery tries to find p tags inside the h2 tag, not inside the div. Fortunately, you can use jQuery's .end() function to "rewind" a changed selection back to its original state. In the example above, you can use .end() to return the selection back to the div, and then find the <p> tags inside the div like this:

```
$('div').click(function() {
    $(this).fadeTo(250,1)
        .find('h2')
        .css('color','#F30')
        .end()
        .find('p')
        .('backgroundColor','#F343FF');
}); // end click
```

Notice the .end() after the .css('color', '#F30'); this code returns the jQuery selection back to the div, so the following .find('p') will find all <p> tags inside the div.

- **.append()** lets you add HTML to the end of an element (for example, at the end of a div just before the closing `</div>` tag. This function is perfect for adding items to the bottom of a list.

- **.prepend()** lets you add HTML to the beginning of an element (for instance, at the beginning of a div just after the opening `<div>` tag).

- **.before()** adds content before the selection.

- **.after()** works just like `.before()`, except that the content is added after the selection (after its closing tag).

Which of these you use really depends on what your final goal is. JavaScript is really just about automating the tasks web designers normally perform manually: adding HTML and CSS to create a web page. If you're writing a program to add content to a page dynamically—like a tooltip, an error message, a pull quote, and so on—just imagine what your finished product should look like and the HTML and CSS required to achieve it.

For example, if you want to create a special message on the page when a visitor mouses over a button, try building a web page that demonstrates that message without using JavaScript—just build it with CSS and HTML. Once you have the HTML/CSS mockup working, take a look at the HTML you used to achieve the effect: Is it placed before some other element? If so, use the `.before()` function. Is the HTML inside a specific tag? Then use the `.append()` or `.prepend()` functions.

jQuery also supplies some functions for removing content from a page:

- **.replaceWith()** completely replaces the selection (including the tag and everything inside it) with whatever you pass the function. For example, to replace a submit button on the page with the text "processing..." you could use this code:

```
$(':submit').replaceWith('<p>processing...</p>');
```

- **.remove()** removes the selection from the DOM; essentially erasing it from the page. For example, to remove a div with the ID of error from the page, you'd write this code:

```
$('#error').remove();
```

While you may only need the functions listed above and discussed in Chapter 4, jQuery provides other functions that provide additional ways of manipulating the HTML of a page:

- **.wrap()** wraps each element in a selection in a pair of HTML tags. For example, what if you want to create a fancy caption effect for images on a page? You can start by selecting images from the page and wrapping them in a `<div>` with a class like figure and adding a `<p>` tag inside that div with a class of caption. Then, using CSS, you can format the div and caption in whatever way you'd like. Here's one way to accomplish that:

```
1 // loop through the list of images
2 $('img').each(function() {
3     // save reference to current image
4     var $this = $(this);
5     // get the alt property for the caption
6     var caption = $this.attr('alt');
7     // add the HTML
8     $this.wrap('<div class="figure"></div>').after('<p>' + caption + '</
p>');
9 }); // end each
```

This code first selects all the images on the page and then loops through the list of images using the .each() function (page 138); on line 4, the current image in the loop is saved into a variable (a good practice, as described on page 522 in this chapter). In line 6, the alt attribute is retrieved from the image and stored in a variable named caption. Finally, line 8 wraps the image in a <div> tag, and adds a captions after the image using the .after() function described before.

NOTE You can see the .wrap() code listed on line 8 in action in the file *wrap.html* in the *chapter15* tutorial folder.

You pass a complete set of tags to the .wrap() function—$('p').wrap('<div></div>')—or even a nested set of tags like this:

```
$('#example').wrap('<div id="outer"><div id="inner"></div></div>');
```

In the above code, jQuery will wrap the selection with the two divs, leaving the HTML something like this:

```
<div id="outer">
  <div id="inner">
    <div id="example">This is the original code on the page</div>
  </div>
</div>
```

- **.wrapInner()** wraps the contents of each element in a selection in HTML tags. For example, say you had the following code in your HTML:

```
<div id="outer">
<p>This is the contents of outer</p>
</div>
```

If the browser encounters the code $('#outer').wrapInner('<div id="inner"></div>'); it transforms the HTML on the page into this:

```
<div id="outer">
<div id="inner">
<p>This is the contents of outer</p>
</div>
</div>
```

- **.unwrap()** simply removes the parent tag surrounding the selection. For example, say a page has the following HTML:

```
<div>
<p>a paragraph</p>
<div>
```

Running the code `$('p').unwrap()` changes the HTML to:

```
<p>a paragraph</p>
```

The outer <div> is simply removed. Note that unlike the other functions discussed here, `.unwrap()` takes no arguments—in other words, don't put anything inside the parentheses in `.unwrap()` or it won't work.

- **.empty()** removes all of the contents of a selection, but leaves the selection in place. For example, say you had a div on a web page with the ID of message-Box. Using JavaScript, you can dynamically add content to this div to display messages to a visitor as she interacts with the page. You might fill that div with lots of content headlines, images, and paragraphs to provide status messages to the visitor. You may want to empty that box at some point in the program (when there are no current messages to display, for example), but leave the box in place so you can later add status messages to it. To remove all the tags inside that box, you can use this code:

```
$('#messageBox').empty();
```

As with `.unwrap()`, `.empty()` takes no arguments.

> **NOTE** jQuery provides even more functions for manipulating HTML. You can read about all of them at *http://api.jquery.com/category/manipulation/.*

Going Further with JavaScript

This chapter covers various concepts that can help make you a better JavaScript programmer. You don't need most of the ideas here to write functioning JavaScript programs, so don't worry if you don't understand them all. The first few sections provide helpful tips and methods for working with strings, numbers, and dates, and once you've mastered the basics, these sections can really help you process visitor input in forms, work with HTML and HTML attributes, and generate dates for calendars. The section "Putting It All Together" on page 582 contains some good advice for beginners, but you can program happily for a long time without needing the information in the other sections in this chapter. But if you want to expand your skills, this chapter can point you in the right direction.

▦ Working with Strings

Strings are the most common type of data you'll work with: input from form fields, the path to an image, a URL, and HTML that you wish to replace on a page are all examples of the letters, symbols, and numbers that make up strings. You learned the basics of strings in Chapter 2, but JavaScript provides a lot of useful methods for working with and manipulating strings.

Determining the Length of a String

There are times when you want to know how many characters are in a string. For example, say you want to make sure that when someone creates an account on your top secret website, they create a new password that's more than 6 letters but no more than 15. Strings have a `length` property that gives you just this kind of information.

Add a period after the name of the variable, followed by `length` to get the number of characters in the string: `name.length`.

For example, assume you have a form with a text field. The field has the ID of password. To make sure the password has the proper number of characters, you could use a conditional statement (page 61) to test the password's length like this:

```
var password = $('#password').val();
if (password.length <= 6) {
  alert('That password is too short.');
} else if (password.length > 15) {
  alert('That password is too long.');
}
```

The code in this example uses jQuery to get the value of the password field—$('#password').val()—but the rest of the code is plain JavaScript. A great way to use this validation snippet would be to put it into its own function like this:

```
function verifyPassword() {
  var password = $('#password').val();
  if (password.length <= 6) {
    alert('That password is too short.');
  } else if (password.length > 15) {
    alert('That password is too long.');
  }
}
```

You could then call it as part of a submit event handler (page 258) to test whether the visitor entered a long enough password when submitting the form:

```
$('form').submit(verifyPassword);
```

You could also place this code inside a `blur()` event (page 260) placed on the password input, so when a visitor tabs or clicks outside of the password field, you could check immediately to see if the password was the correct length. For example, say the password field had an ID of password, you could then send the `verifyPassword` function as an event handler for the `blur` event like this:

```
$('#password').blur(verifyPassword);
```

Changing the Case of a String

JavaScript provides two methods to convert strings to all uppercase or all lowercase, so you can change "hello" to "HELLO" or "NOT" to "not". Why, you might ask? Converting letters in a string to the same case makes comparing two strings easier. For example, say you created a quiz program like the one from Chapter 3 (page 94) and one of the questions is, "Who was the first American to win the Tour de France?" You might have some code like this to check the quiz taker's answer:

```
var correctAnswer = 'Greg LeMond';
var response = prompt('Who was the first American to win the Tour de France?',
```

```
'');
if (response == correctAnswer) {
  // correct
} else {
  // incorrect
}
```

The answer is Greg LeMond, but what if the person taking the quiz typed *Greg Lemond*? The condition would look like this: `'Greg Lemond' == 'Greg LeMond'`. JavaScript treats uppercase letters as different than lowercase letters, so the lowercase `'m'` in Lemond wouldn't match the `'M'` in LeMond, so the quiz taker would have gotten this question wrong. The same would happen if her caps lock key was down and she typed *GREG LEMOND*.

To get around this difficulty, you can convert both strings to the same case and then compare them:

```
if (response.toUpperCase() == correctAnswer.toUpperCase()) {
  // correct
} else {
  // incorrect
}
```

In this case, the conditional statement converts both the quiz taker's answer and the correct answer to uppercase, so `'Greg Lemond'` becomes `'GREG LEMOND'` and `'Greg LeMond'` becomes `'GREG LEMOND'`.

To get the string all lowercase, use the `toLowerCase()` method like this:

```
var answer = 'Greg LeMond';
alert(answer.toLowerCase()); // 'greg lemond'
```

Note that neither of these methods actually alters the original string stored in the variable—they just return that string in either all uppercase or all lowercase. So in the above example, *answer* still contains `'Greg LeMond'` even after the alert appears. (In other words, these methods work just like a function that returns some other value as described on page 91.)

Searching a String: indexOf() Technique

JavaScript provides several techniques for searching for a word, number, or other series of characters inside a string. Searching can come in handy, for example, if you want to know which web browser a visitor is using to view your website. Every web browser identifies information about itself in a string containing a lot of different statistics. You can see that string for yourself by adding this bit of JavaScript to a page and previewing it in a web browser:

```
<script>
alert(navigator.userAgent);
</script>
```

Navigator is one of a web browser's objects, and userAgent is a property of the navigator object. The userAgent property contains a long string of information; for example, on Internet Explorer 10 running on Windows 8, the userAgent property is: Mozilla/5.0 (compatible; MSIE 10.0; Windows NT 6.2; Trident/6.0). So, if you want to see if the Web browser was IE 10, you can just search the userAgent string for "MSIE 10".

One method of searching a string is the indexOf() method. Basically, after the string you add a period, indexOf(), and supply the string you're looking for. The basic structure looks like this:

```
string.indexOf('string to look for')
```

The indexOf() method returns a number: If the search string isn't found, the method returns –1. So if you want to check for Internet Explorer, you can do this:

```
var browser = navigator.userAgent; // this is a string
if (browser.indexOf('MSIE') != -1) {
  // this is Internet Explorer
}
```

In this case, if indexOf() doesn't locate the string 'MSIE' in the userAgent string, it will return –1, so the condition tests to see if the result is not (!=) –1.

When the indexOf() method *does* find the searched-for string, it returns a number that's equal to the starting position of the searched-for string. The following example makes things a lot clearer:

```
var quote = 'To be, or not to be.'
var searchPosition = quote.indexOf('To be'); // returns 0
```

Here, indexOf() searches for the position of 'To be' inside the string 'To be, or not to be.' The larger string begins with 'To be', so indexOf() finds 'To be' at the first position. But in the wacky way of programming, the first position is considered 0, the second character (o) is at position 1, and the third character (a space in this case) is 2 (as explained on page 48, arrays are counted in the same way).

The indexOf() method searches from the beginning of the string. You can also search from the end of the string by using the lastIndexOf() method. For example, in the Shakespeare quote, the word 'be' appears in two places, so you can locate the first 'be' using indexOf() and the last 'be' with lastIndexOf():

```
var quote = "To be, or not to be."
var firstPosition = quote.indexOf('be'); // returns 3
var lastPosition = quote.lastIndexOf('be'); // returns 17
```

The results of those two methods are pictured in Figure 16-1. In both cases, if 'be' didn't exist anywhere in the string, the result would be –1, and if there's only one instance of the searched-for word, indexOf() and lastIndexOf() will return the same value—the starting position of the searched-for string within the larger string.

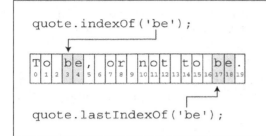

FIGURE 16-1

The indexOf() *and* lastIndexOf() *methods search for a particular string inside a larger string. If the search string is found, its position in the larger string is returned.*

Extracting Part of a String with slice()

To extract part of a string, use the slice() method. This method returns a portion of a string. For example, say you had a string like http://www.sawmac.com and you wanted to eliminate the http:// part. One way to do this is to extract every character in the string that follows the http:// like this:

```
var url = 'http://www.sawmac.com';
var domain = url.slice(7); // www.sawmac.com
```

The slice() method requires a number that indicates the starting index position for the extracted string (Figure 16-2). In this example—url.slice(7)—the 7 indicates the eighth character in the string (remember, the first letter is at position 0). The method returns all of the characters starting at the specified index position to the end of the string.

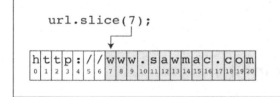

FIGURE 16-2

If you don't supply a second argument to the slice() *method, it just extracts a string from the specified position (7 in this example) all the way to the end of the string.*

You can also extract a specific number of characters within a string by supplying a second argument to the slice() method. Here's the basic structure of the slice() method:

```
string.slice(start, end);
```

The *start* value is a number that indicates the position of the first character of the extracted string. The *end* value is a little confusing—it's not the position of the last letter of the extracted string; it's actually the position of the last letter + 1. For example, if you wanted to extract the first five letters of the string 'To be, or not to be.', you would specify 0 as the first argument, and 5 as the second argument. As you can see in Figure 16-3, 0 is the first letter in the string, and 5 is the sixth letter, but the last letter specified is not extracted from the string. In other words, the character specified by the second argument is *never* part of the extracted string.

> **TIP** If you want to extract a specific number of characters from a string, just add that number to the starting value. For example, if you want to retrieve the first 10 letters of a string, the first argument would be 0 (the first letter) and the last would be 0 + 10 or just 10: `slice(0,10)`.

You can also specify negative numbers; for example, `quote.slice(-6,-1)`. A negative number counts backwards from the end of the string, as pictured in Figure 16-3.

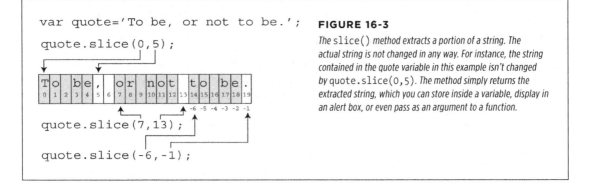

FIGURE 16-3

The `slice()` method extracts a portion of a string. The actual string is not changed in any way. For instance, the string contained in the quote variable in this example isn't changed by `quote.slice(0,5)`. The method simply returns the extracted string, which you can store inside a variable, display in an alert box, or even pass as an argument to a function.

> **TIP** If you want, say, to extract a string that includes all the last X number of characters in a string, just give `slice()` a single value—a negative number that matches the number of letter you want. For example, to extract the last 6 letters of the quote string you'd write this:
>
> ```
> var end_of_string = quote.slice(-6);
> ```

■ Finding Patterns in Strings

Sometimes you wish to search a string, not for an exact value, but for a specific pattern of characters. For example, say you want to make sure when a visitor fills out an order form, he supplies a phone number in the correct format. You're not actually looking for a specific phone number like 503-555-0212. Instead, you're looking for a general pattern: three numbers, a hyphen, three numbers, another hyphen, and four numbers. You'd like to check the value the visitor entered, and if it matches the pattern (for example, it's 415-555-3843, 408-555-3782, or 212-555-4828, and so on), then everything's OK. But if it doesn't match that pattern (for example, the visitor typed *823lkjxdfglkj*), then you'd like to post a message like "Hey buddy, don't try to fool us!"

JavaScript lets you use *regular expressions* to find patterns within a string. A regular expression is a series of characters that define a pattern that you wish to search for.

As with many programming terms, the name "regular expression" is a bit misleading. For example, here's what a common regular expression looks like:

```
/^[-\w.]+@([a-zA-Z0-9][-a-zA-Z0-9]+\.)+[a-zA-Z]{2,4}$/
```

Unless you're a super-alien from Omicron 9, there's nothing very *regular*-looking about a regular expression. To create a pattern, you use characters like *, +, ?, and \w, which are translated by the JavaScript interpreter to match real characters in a string like letters, numbers, and so on.

> **NOTE** Pros often shorten the name regular expression to *regex*.

Creating and Using a Basic Regular Expression

To create a regular expression in JavaScript, you must create a regular expression literal, which is a series of characters between two forward slashes. For example, to create a regular expression that matches the word "hello", you'd type this:

```
var myMatch = /hello/;
```

Just as an opening and closing quote mark creates a string, the opening / and closing / create a regular expression.

There are several string methods that take advantage of regular expressions (you'll learn about them starting on page 546), but the most basic method is the search() method. It works very much like the indexOf() method, but instead of trying to find one string inside another, larger string, it searches for a pattern (a regular expression) inside a string. For example, say you want to find 'To be' inside the string 'To be or not to be.' You saw how to do that with the indexOf() method on page 543, but here's how you can do the same thing with a regular expression:

```
var myRegEx = /To be/; // no quotes around regular expression
var quote = 'To be or not to be.';
var foundPosition = quote.search(myRegEx);  // returns 0
```

If the search() method finds a match, it returns the position of the first character matched, and if it doesn't find a match, it returns –1. So in the above example, the variable foundPosition is 0 because 'To be' begins at the very beginning (the first character) of the string.

As you'll recall from page 543, the indexOf() method works in the same way. You might be thinking that if the two methods are the same, why bother with regular expressions? The benefit of regular expressions is that they can find patterns in a string, so they can make much more complicated and subtle comparisons than the indexOf() method, which always looks for a match to an exact string. For example, you could use the indexOf() method to find out if a string contains the Web address *http://www.missingmanuals.com,* but you'd have to use a regular expression to find any text that matches the format of a URL—exactly the kind of thing you want to do when verifying if someone supplied a web address when posting a comment to your blog.

However, to master regular expressions, you need to learn the often confusing symbols required to construct a regular expression.

Building a Regular Expression

While a regular expression can be made up of a word or words, more often you'll use a combination of letters and special symbols to define a pattern that you hope to match. Regular expressions provide different symbols to indicate different types of characters. For example, a single period (.) represents a single character, any character, while \w matches any character (but not spaces, or symbols like $ or %). Table 16-1 provides a list of the most common pattern-matching characters.

> **NOTE** If this entire discussion of "regular" expressions is making your head hurt, you'll be glad to know this book provides some useful regular expressions (page 553) that you can copy and use in your own scripts (without really knowing how they work).

TABLE 16-1 *Common pattern-matching symbols for regular expressions*

CHARACTER	MATCHES
.	Any one character—will match a letter, number, space, or other symbol.
\w	Any word character including a–z, A–Z, the numbers 0–9, and the underscore character: _.
\W	Any character that's not a word character. It's the exact opposite of \w.
\d	Any digit 0–9.
\D	Any character except a digit. The opposite of \d.
\s	A space, tab, carriage return, or new line.
\S	The opposite of the \s. Anything but a space, tab, carriage return, or newline.
^	The beginning of a string. This is useful for making sure no other characters come before whatever you're trying to match.
$	The end of a string. Use $ to make sure the characters you wish to match are at the end of a string. For example, /com$/ matches the string "com", but only when it's the last three letters of the string. In other words, /com$/ would match "com" in the string "Infocom", but not 'com' in 'communication'.
\b	A space, beginning of the string, end of string, or any nonletter or number character such as +, =, or '. Use \b to match the beginning or ending of a word, even if that word is at the beginning or ending of a string.
[]	Any one character between the brackets. For example, [aeiou] matches any one of those letters in a string. For a range of characters, use a hyphen: [a-z] matches any one lower case letter; [0-9] matches any one number (the same as \d).

CHARACTER	MATCHES
[^]	Any character except one in brackets. For example, [^aeiouAEIOU] will match any character that isn't a vowel. [^0-9] matches any character that's not a number (the same as \D).
|	Either the characters before or after the | character. For example, a|b will match either *a* or *b*, but not both. (See page 557 for an example of this symbol in action.)
\	Used to escape any special regex symbol (*,.,\,/, for instance) to search for a literal example of the symbol in a string. For example, . in regex-speak means "any character," so you need escape a period -- like this \. -- if you want to really match a period in a string.

Learning regular expressions is a topic better presented by example, so the rest of this section walks you through a few examples of regular expressions to help you wrap your mind around this topic. Assume you want to match five digits in a row—perhaps to check if there's a U.S. Zip code in a string:

1. **Match one digit.**

   The first step is simply to figure out how to match one number. If you refer to Table 16-1, you'll see that there's a special regex symbol for this, \d, which matches any single number.

2. **Match five digits in a row.**

   Because \d matches a single number, a simple way to match five numbers is with this regular expression: \d\d\d\d\d. (page 552, however, covers a more compact way to write this.)

3. **Match only five digits.**

   A regular expression is like a precision-guided missile: It sets its target on the first part of a string that it matches. So, you sometimes end up with a match that's part of a complete word or set of characters. This regular expression matches the first five numbers in a row that it encounters. For example, it will match 12345 in the number 12345678998. Obviously, 12345678998 isn't a Zip code, so you need a regex that targets just five digits.

   The \b character (called the *word boundary* character) matches any non-letter or non-number character, so you could rewrite your regular expression like this: \b\d\d\d\d\d\b. You can also use the ^ character to match the beginning of a string and the $ character to match the end of a string. This trick comes in handy if you want the entire string to match your regular expression. For example, if someone typed "kjasdflkjsdf 88888 lksadflkjsdkfjl" in a Zip code field on an order form, you might want to ask the visitor to clarify (and fix) her Zip code before ordering. After all, you're really looking for something like 97213 (with no other characters in the string). In this case, the regex would be ^\d\d\d\d\d$.

NOTE   Zip codes can have more than five digits. The ZIP + 4 format includes a dash and four additional digits after the first five, like this: 97213-1234. For a regular expression to handle this possibility, see page 553.

4. Put your regex into action in JavaScript.

Assume you've already captured a user's input into a variable named *zip*, and you want to test to see if the input is in the form of a valid five-number Zip code:

```
var zipTest = /^\d\d\d\d\d$/; //create regex
if (zip.search(zipTest) == -1) {
  alert('This is not a valid zip code');
} else {
  // is valid format
}
```

The regex example in these steps works, but it seems like a lot of work to type \d five times. What if you want to match 100 numbers in a row? Fortunately, JavaScript includes several symbols that can match multiple occurrences of the same character. Table 16-2 includes a list of these symbols. You place the symbol directly *after* the character you wish to match.

For example, to match five numbers, you can write \d{5}. The \d matches one number, then the {5} tells the JavaScript interpreter to match five numbers. So \d{100} would match 100 digits in a row.

Let's go through another example. Say you wanted to find the name of any GIF file in a string. In addition, you want to extract the filename and perhaps use it somehow in your script (for example, you can use the match() method described on page 558). In other words, you want to find any string that matches the basic pattern of a GIF filename, such as *logo.gif*, *banner.gif*, or *ad.gif*. Here are the steps you should follow:

1. Identify the common pattern between these names.

To build a regular expression, you first need to know what pattern of characters you're searching for. Here, since you're after GIFs, you know all the filenames will end in *.gif*. In other words, there can be any number of letters or numbers or other characters before *.gif*. But there should be at least one character before the .gif: *a.gif* is a valid filename, but just *.gif* isn't

2. Find .gif.

You're after the literal string '.gif', so you might think that part of the regular expression would just be .gif. However, if you check out Table 4-3, you'll see that a period has special meaning as a "match any character" character. So .gif would match .gif, but it would also match "tgif." A period matches any single character so in addition to matching a period, it will also match the "t" in tgif. To create a regex with a literal period, add a slash before it; so \. translates to "find me the period symbol." So the regex to find .gif would be \.gif.

3. **Find one or more characters before .gif.**

   You want to match something like *a.gif, photo.gif,* but not just *.gif* (that wouldn't be a valid GIF file). To find at least one character, you can use `.+`, which translates to "find one character (.) zero at least once (+)." However, if you used that to create a regular expression like `.+\.gif`, you could end up matching more than just a filename: that regular expression matches all of the letters in any string. For example, if you have the string 'the file is logo.gif', the regex `.+\.gif` will match everything up to and including .gif. What you really want is just *logo.gif*. To do that, use the `\S` character, which matches any nonspace character: `\S+\.gif` translates to "find at least one non-space character (no tabs, spaces, carriage returns, or new lines) followed by .gif. That matches just *logo.gif* in the string.

4. **Make sure nothing follows `gif`.**

   The regular expression now finds just a filename...or does it? Regular expressions can be really tricky. For example, if you use the regex you've created so far on a string like "e-mail *alex.gifford@example*", you'd match "alex.gif," which isn't a filename at all. To make sure that doesn't happen, you should also check to make sure that nothing follows the gif part. You can do that by adding a word boundary (`\b`)—like this `\S+\.gif\b`–to make sure you don't match parts of a larger string that happens to include .gif in it.

5. **Make the search case-insensitive.**

   There's one last wrinkle in this regular expression: It only finds files that end in *.gif*, but *.GIF* is also a valid file extension, so this regex wouldn't pick up on a name like *logo.GIF*. To make a regular expression ignore the difference between upper and lowercase letters, you use the `i` argument when you create the regular expression:

   `/\S+\.gif\b/`**i**

   Notice that the `i` goes outside of the pattern and to the right of the `/` that defines the end of the regular expression pattern.

6. **Put it into action:**

   ```
   var testString = 'The file is logo.gif create by alex.gifford@example.com';
   // the string to test
   var gifRegex = /\S+\.gif\b/i; // the regular expression
   var results = testString.match(gifRegex);
   var file = results[0]; // logo.gif
   ```

   This code pulls out the filename from the string. (You'll learn how the `match()` method works on page 558.)

Grouping Parts of a Pattern

You can use parentheses to create a subgroup within a pattern. Subgroups come in very handy when using any of the characters in Table 16-2 to match multiple instances of the same pattern.

TABLE 16-2 *Characters used for matching multiple occurrences of the same character or pattern*

CHARACTER	MATCHES
?	Zero or one occurrences of the previous character (or group of characters), meaning the previous item is optional, but if it does appear, it can only appear once. For example, the regex colou?r will match both "color" and "colour", but not "colouur".
+	One or more occurrences of the previous item. The previous item must appear at least once.
*	Zero or more occurrences of the previous item. The previous item is optional and may appear any number of times. For example, .* matches any number of characters, or, no characters at all!
{n}	An exact number of occurrences of the previous item. For example, \d{3} only matches three numbers in a row.
{n, }	The previous item *n* or more times. For example, a{2,} will match the letter "a" two or more times, which would match "aa" in the word "aardvark" and "aaaa" in the word "aaaahhhh".
{n,m}	The previous item at least *n* times but no more than *m* times. So \d{3,4} will match three or four digits in a row (but not two digits in a row, nor five digits in a row).

For example, say you want to see if a string contains either "Apr" or "April"—both of those begin with "Apr", so you know that you want to match that, but you can't just match "Apr" because you'd also match the "Apr" in "Apricot" or "Aprimecorp." So, you must match "Apr" followed by a space or other word ending (that's the \b regular expression character described in Table 16-1) or April followed by a word ending. In other words, the "il" is optional. Here's how you could do that using parentheses:

```
var sentence = 'April is the cruelest month.';
var aprMatch = /Apr(il)?\b/;
if (sentence.search(aprMatch) != -1) {
  // found Apr or April
} else {
  //not found
}
```

The regular expression used here—/Apr(il)?\b/—makes the "Apr" required, but the subpattern—(il)—optional (that ? character means zero or one time). Finally, the \b matches the end of a word, so you won't match "Apricot" or "Aprilshowers." (See the box "Using Subpatterns to Replace Text" on page 561 for another use of subpatterns.)

To make this regular expression more foolproof, you could add a word boundary—\b—at the beginning of the regex as well:

```
var aprMatch = /\bApr(il)?\b/;
```

Adding the word boundary at the beginning of the regex would safeguard against encountering a mismatch like wApril, or SApr. (Granted, you aren't likely to encounter strings like those, but better safe than sorry.)

TIP You can find a complete library of regular expressions at *www.regexlib.com*. At this website, you'll find a regular expression for any situation.

Useful Regular Expressions

Creating a regular expression has its challenges. Not only do you need to understand how the different regular expression characters work, but you then must figure out the proper pattern for different possible searches. For example, if you want to find a match for a Zip code, you need to take into account the fact that a Zip code may be just five numbers (97213) or 5+4 (97213-3333). To get you started on the path to using regular expressions, here are a few common ones.

NOTE If you don't feel like typing these regular expressions (and who could blame you), you'll find them already set up for you in a file named *example_regex.txt* in the *chapter16* folder that's part of the tutorial download. (See page 12 for information on downloading the tutorial files.)

■ U.S. ZIP CODE

Postal codes vary from country to country, but in the United States they appear as either five numbers, or five numbers followed by a hyphen and four numbers. Here's the regex that matches both those options:

```
\d{5}(-\d{4})?
```

NOTE For regular expressions that match the postal codes of other countries, visit *http://regexlib.com/Search.aspx?k=postal+code.*

That regular expression breaks down into the following smaller pieces:

- \d{5} matches five digits, as in 97213.

- () creates a subpattern. Everything between the parentheses is considered a single pattern to be matched. You'll see why that's important in a moment.

- -\d{4} matches the hyphen followed by four digits, like this: -1234.

- ? matches zero or one instance of the preceding pattern. Here's where the parentheses come in: (-\d{4}) is treated as a single unit, so the ? means match zero or one instance of a hyphen followed by four digits. Because you don't have to include the hyphen + four, that pattern might appear zero times. In other words, if you're testing a value like 97213, you'll still get a match because the hyphen followed by four digits is optional.

U.S. PHONE NUMBER

U.S. phone numbers have a three-digit area code followed by seven more digits. However, people write phone numbers in many different ways, like 503-555-1212, (503) 555-1212, 503.555.1212, or just 503 555 1212. A regex for this pattern is:

```
\(?\d{3}\)?[ .-]\d{3}[ .-]\d{4}
```

This regex looks pretty complicated, but if you break it down (and have a good translation like the following), it comes out making sense:

- \(matches a literal opening parenthesis character. Because parentheses are used to group patterns (see the previous Zip code example), the opening parentheses has special meaning in regular expressions. To tell the JavaScript interpreter to match an actual opening parenthesis, you need to escape the character (just like escaping the quotes discussed on page 28) with the forward slash character.

- ? indicates that the (character is optional, so a phone number without parentheses like 503-555-1212 will still match.

- \d{3} matches any three digits.

- \)? matches an optional closing parenthesis.

- [.-] will match either a space, a period, or a hyphen. (Note that normally you have to escape a period like this \. in order to tell the JavaScript interpreter that you want to match the period character and not treat it as the special regular expression symbol that matches *any* character; however, when inside brackets, a period is always treated literally.)

- \d{3} matches any three digits.

- [.-] will match either a space, period, or hyphen.

- \d{4} matches any four digits.

EMAIL ADDRESS

Checking for a valid email address is a common chore when accepting user input from a form. A lot of people try to get away without trying to provide a valid email using a response like "none of your business," or people just mistype their email address (*missing@sawmac.commm*, for example). The following regex can check to see if a string contains a properly formatted email address:

```
[-\w.]+@([A-z0-9][-A-z0-9]+\.)+[A-z]{2,4}
```

> **NOTE** This regex doesn't check to see if an address is somebody's real, working email address; it just checks that it's *formatted* like a real email address.

This regex breaks down like this:

- `[-\w.]+` matches a hyphen, any word character, or a period one or more times. So it will match "bob," "bob.smith," or "bob-smith."

- `@` is the @ sign you find in an email address: *missing@sawmac.com*.

- `[A-z0-9]` matches one letter or number.

- `[-A-z0-9]+` matches one or more instances of a letter, number, or hyphen.

- `\.` is a period character, so it would match the period in sawmac.com (*http://www.sawmac.com*).

- `+` matches one or more instances of the pattern that includes the above three matches. This character allows for subdomain names like *bob@mail.sawmac.com*.

- `[A-z]{2,4}` is any letter 2, 3, or 4 times. This matches the com in .com, or uk in .uk.

> **NOTE** The email regex listed above doesn't match *all* technically valid email addresses. For example, `!#$%&'*+-/=?^_`.{|}~@example.com` is technically a valid email address, but the regex described here won't match it. It's designed to find email addresses that people would actually use. If you really want to be accurate, you can use the following regex. Type this expression on a single line:
>
> ```
> /^[\w!#$%&\'*+\/=?^`{|}~.-]+@(?:[a-z\d][a-z\d-]*(?:\.[a-z\d][a-z\d-]*)?)+\.(?:[a-z][a-z\d-]+)$/i
> ```

DATE

A date can be written in many different ways; for example, 09/28/2014, 9-28-2014, 09 28 2014, or even 09.28.2014. (And those are just formats for the United States. In other parts of the world, the day appears before the month, like 28.09.2014.) Because your visitors may enter a date in any one of these formats, you need a way to check to see if they supplied a validly formatted date. (In the box on page 570, you'll learn how to convert any of these formats into a single, standard format, so you can make sure all the dates you receive on a form are formatted correctly.)

Here's the regex that checks for a correctly entered date:

```
([01]?\d)[-\/ .]([0123]?\d)[-\/ .](\d{4})
```

- () surrounds the next two regex patterns to group them. Together they form the number for the month.

- [01]? matches either 0 or 1 and the ? makes this optional. This is for the first number in a month. Obviously it can't be bigger than 1—there's no 22 month. In addition, if the month is January through September, you might just get 5 instead of 05. That's why it's optional.

- \d matches any number.

- [-\/ .] will match a hyphen, a forward slash, a period, or a space character. These are the acceptable separators between the month and day, like 10/21, 10 21, 10.21, or 10-21.

- () is the next subpattern, which is meant to capture the day of the month.

- [0123]? matches either 0, 1, 2, or 3 zero or one time. There's no 40th day of the month, so you limit the first number of the month to one of these four digits. This pattern is optional (as determined by the ? character), because someone might just type 9 instead of 09 for the ninth day of the month.

- \d matches any digit.

- [-\/ .] is the same as above.

- () captures the year.

- \d{4} matches any four digits, like 1908 or 2880.

> **NOTE** While it's possible to write form validation yourself using some of the regex patterns discussed here, it's not your only alternative. Someone has already solved the problem, so why not use their hard work and free yourself to solve other problems? For an easier way to make sure your site's visitors are supplying the correct type of information to web forms, use a jQuery plug-in like the jQuery Form Validation plug-in discussed on page 273.

■ WEB ADDRESS

Matching a web address is useful if you're asking a visitor for his website address and you want to make sure he's supplied one, or if you want to scan some text and identify every URL listed. A basic regular expression for URLs is:

```
((\bhttps?:\/\/)|(\bwww\.))\S*
```

This expression is a little tricky because it uses lots of parentheses to group different parts of the expression. Figure 16-4 can help guide you through this regular expression. One set of parentheses (labeled 1) wraps around two other parenthetical groups (2 and 3). The | character between the two groups represents "or". In other words, the regular expression needs to match either 2 or 3.

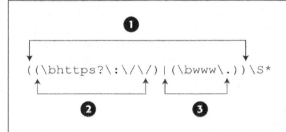

FIGURE 16-4

You can group expressions using parentheses and look for either one of two expressions by using the | (pipe) character. For example, the outer expression (1) will match any text that matches either 2 or 3.

- (is the start of the outer group (1 in Figure 16-4).

- (is the start of inner group (2 in Figure 16-4).

- \b matches the beginning of a word.

- http matches the beginning of a complete web address that begins with *http*.

- s? is an optional *s*. A web page may be sent via a secure connection, so a valid web address may also begin with *https*.

- :\/\/ matches *://*. Because the forward slash has meaning in regular expressions, you need to precede it by a backslash to match the forward slash character.

-) is the end of the inner group (2 in Figure 16-4). Taken together, this group will match either *http://* or *https://*.

- | matches either one or the other group (2 or 3 in Figure 16-4).

- (is the start of second inner group (3 in Figure 16-4).

- \b matches the beginning of a word.

- www\. matches *www.*.

-) is the end of the second inner group (3 in Figure 16-4). This group will capture a URL that is missing the *http://* but begins with *www*.

-) is the end of the outer group (1 in Figure 16-4). At this point, the regular expression will match text that begins with *http://*, *https://*, or *www*.

- \S* matches zero or more nonspace characters.

This expression isn't foolproof (for example, it would match a nonsensical URL like *http://#$*%&*@*), but it's relatively simple, and will successfully match real URLs like *http://www.sawmac.com/missing/js/index.html*.

TIP To see if a string only contains a URL (nothing comes before or after the URL), use the ^ and $ characters at the beginning and end of the regular expression and remove the \b characters: ^((https?:\/\/)|(www\.))\S*$.

Matching a Pattern

The search() method described on page 547 is one way to see if a string contains a particular regular expression pattern. The match() method is another. You can use it with a string to not only see if a pattern exists within the string, but to also capture that pattern so you can use it later in your script. For example, say you have a text area field on a form for a visitor to add a comment to your site. Perhaps you want to check if the comments include a URL, and if so, get the URL for further processing.

The following code finds and captures a URL using match():

```
// a string to test for a URL
var text='my website is www.missingmanuals.com';
// create a regular expression
var urlRegex = /((\bhttps?:\/\/)|(\bwww\.))\S*/
// find a match for the regular expression in the string
var url = text.match(urlRegex);
alert(url[0]); // www.missingmanuals.com
```

First, the code creates a variable containing a string that includes the URL *www.missingmanuals.com*. This variable is just for test purposes here (so you can see what the match() method does). If you actually wanted to test the contents of a text area on a form, you could use code like this:

```
var text = $('#comments').val() ;
```

Next, the code creates a regular expression to match a URL (see page 556 for the details on this regex). Finally, it runs the match() method on the string. The match() function is a string method, so you start with the name of a variable containing a string, add a period, followed by match(). You pass the match() method a regular expression to match.

In this example, the variable url holds the results of the match. If the regular expression pattern isn't found in the string, then the result is a special JavaScript value called null. If there is a match, the script returns an array—the first value of the array is the matched text. For instance, in this example, the variable url contains an array, with the first array element being the matched text. In this case, url[0] contains *www.missingmanuals.com* (see page 44 for more on arrays).

> **NOTE** In JavaScript, a null value is treated the same as false, so you could test to see if the match() method actually matched something like this:
>
> ```
> var url = text.match(urlRegex);
> if (! url) {
>   //no match
> } else {
>   //match
> }
> ```

The match() method also supplies some additional information. In addition to an array element whose first item is the matched string, match() also returns an index property that indicates the position within the string where the match begins. For example:

```
var string = 'To be or not';
ar regex = /be/;
var result = string.match(regex);
alert(result.index); //  alerts the number 3
```

The variable result stores the values returned from the match() method. In this case, there's an array, and the first and only item in the array is the matched string: result[0] contains the matched text "be". The match() method also adds the index property to the result. In this example, that property has the value 3 because "be" starts in the fourth position in the string (remember, JavaScript counts from 0). This is the same value that would be returned by the regular search() method (page 547) and is similar to how the indexOf() method (page 543) returns the starting position for a substring within a larger string. Also, it's the same value you'd use in the slice() method (page 545) to extract a substring from a larger string.

The match() method also returns additional array elements, if you've used ( ) to create subpatterns, as described in the box on page 561. The first item in the array is always the matched string, but if you've used subpatterns, each additional array element contains the matched value within the subpattern.

■ MATCHING EVERY INSTANCE OF A PATTERN

The match() method works in two different ways, depending on how you've set up your regular expression. In the preceding example, the method returns an array with the first matched text and an index property containing the starting position of the match (as well as additional array elements if you used subpatterns in your regular expression). In other words, if you had a long string containing multiple URLs, only the first URL would be found. However, you can also turn on a regular expression's global search property to search for more than one match in a string.

You make a search global by adding a g at the end of a regular expression when you create it (just like the i used for a case-insensitive search, as discussed on page 551):

```
var urlRegex = /((\bhttps?:\/\/)|(\bwww\.))\S*/g
```

Notice that the g goes outside of the ending / (which is used to enclose the actual pattern). This regular expression performs a global search; when used with the match() method, it searches for every match within the string and will return an array of all matched text—a great way to find every URL in a blog entry, for example, or every instance of a word in a long block of text.

You could rewrite the code from the top of this page using a global search, like this:

```
// create a variable containing a string with a URL
var text='there are a lot of great websites like ↵
        www.missingmanuals.com and http://www.oreilly.com';
```

```
// create a regular expression with global search
var urlRegex = /((\bhttps?:\/\/)|(\bwww\.))\S*/g
// find a match for the regular expression in the string
var url = text.match(urlRegex);
alert(url[0]); // www.missingmanuals.com
alert(url[1]); // http://www.oreilly.com
```

You can determine the number of matches by accessing the `length` property of the resulting array: `url.length`. This example would return the number 2 because two URLs were found in the tested string. In addition, you access each matched string by using the array's index number (as described on page 48); so in this example, `url[0]` is the first match and `url[1]` is the second.

Bear in mind, using a global regex search with the `match()` method doesn't return an index value for string matches, nor will it return any information on subpatterns. A global search only returns an array containing each match within the searched string.

Replacing Text

You can also use regular expressions to replace text within a string. For example, say you have a string that contains a date formatted like this: 10.28.2014. However, you want the date to be formatted like this: 10/28/2014. The `replace()` method can do that. It takes this form:

```
string.replace(regex,'replacement string');
```

The `replace()` method takes two arguments: The first is a regular expression that you wish to find in the string; the second is a string that replaces any matches to the regular expression. So, to change the format of 10.28.2008 to 10/28/2008, you could do this:

```
1   var date='10.28.2014'; // a string
2   var replaceRegex = /\./g // a regular expression
3   var date = date.replace(replaceRegex, '/'); // replace . with /
4   alert(date); // 10/28/2014
```

Line 1 creates a variable and stores the string `'10.28.2014'` in it. In a real program, this string could be input from a form. Line 2 creates the regular expression: The / and / mark the beginning and end of the regular expression pattern; the \. indicates a literal period; and the g means a global replace—every instance of the period will be replaced. If you left out the g, only the first matched period would be replaced, and you'd end up with `'10/28.2008'`. Line 3 performs the actual replacement—changing each . to a /, and stores the result back into the date variable. Finally, the newly formed date—10/28/2014—is displayed in an alert box.

Using Subpatterns to Replace Text

The replace() method not only can replace matched text (like the . in 10.28.2008) with another string (like /), but it can also remember subpatterns within a regular expression and use those subpatterns when replacing text. A subpattern is any part of a regular expression enclosed in parentheses. For example, the (il) in the regular expression /Apr(il)?\b/ is a subpattern.

The use of the replace() method demonstrated on page 560 changes 10.28.2008 to 10/28/2008. But what if you also want to put other formatted dates like 10 28 2008 or 10-28-2008 into the same 10/28/2008 format? Instead of writing multiple lines of JavaScript code to replace periods, spaces, and hyphens, you can create a general pattern to match any of these formats:

```
var date='10-28-2008';
var regex = /([01]?\d)[-\/ .]([0123]?\d)
```

```
[-\/ .](\d{4})/;
date = date.replace(regex, '$1/$2/$3');
```

This example uses the regular expression described on page 555 to match a date. Notice the groups of patterns within parentheses—for example, ([01]?\d). Each subpattern matches one part of the date. The replace() method remembers matches to those subpatterns, and can use them as part of the replacement string. In this case, the replacement string is '$1/$2/$3'. A dollar sign followed by a number represents one of the matched subpatterns. $1, for example, matches the first subpattern—the month. So this replacement string translates to "put the first subpattern here, followed by a /, followed by the second subpattern match, followed by another /, and finally followed by the last subpattern."

Trying Out Regular Expressions

You'll find sample regular expressions in the *example_regex.txt* file in the *testbed* folder in the tutorial files. In addition, you'll find a file named *regex_tester.html* in the *testbed* folder. You can open this web page in a browser and try your hand at creating your own regular expressions (Figure 16-5). Just type the string you'd like to search in the "String to Search" box, and then type a regular expression in the box (leave out the beginning and ending / marks used when creating a regex in JavaScript and just type the search pattern). You can then select the method you'd like to use—Search, Match, or Replace—and any options, like case-insensitivity or global search. Click the Run button and see how your regex works.

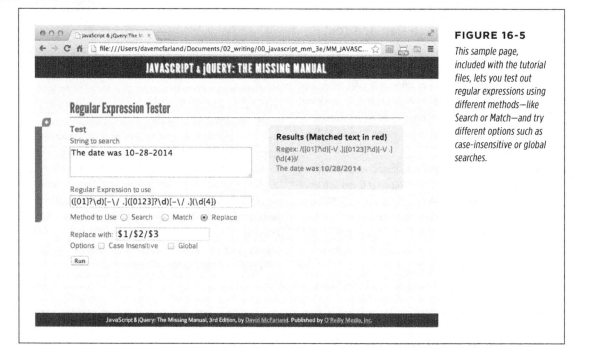

FIGURE 16-5

*This sample page,
included with the tutorial
files, lets you test out
regular expressions using
different methods—like
Search or Match—and try
different options such as
case-insensitive or global
searches.*

■ Working with Numbers

Numbers are an important part of programming. They let you perform tasks like
calculating a total sales cost, determining the distance between two points, or
simulating the roll of a die by generating a random number from 1 to 6. JavaScript
gives you many different ways of working with numbers.

Changing a String to a Number

When you create a variable, you can store a number in it like this:

```
var a = 3.25;
```

However, there are times when a number is actually a string. For example, if you use
the prompt() method (page 42) to get visitor input, even if someone types *3.25*,
you'll end up with a string that contains a number. In other words, the result will be
'3.25' (a string) and not 3.25 (a number). Frequently, this method doesn't cause a
problem—the JavaScript interpreter usually converts a string to a number when it
seems like a number is called for. For example:

```
var a = '3';
var b = '4';
alert(a*b); // 12
```

In this example, even though the variables *a* and *b* are both strings, the JavaScript interpreter converts them to numbers to perform the multiplication (3 x 4) and return the result: 12.

However, when you use the + operator, the JavaScript interpreter won't make that conversion, and you can end up with some strange results:

```
var a = '3';
var b = '4';
alert(a+b); // 34
```

In this case, both a and b are strings; the + operator not only does mathematical addition, it also combines (concatenates) two strings together (page 36). So instead of adding 3 and 4 to get 7, in this example, you end up with two strings fused together: 34.

When you need to convert a string to a number, JavaScript provides several ways:

- Number() converts whatever string is passed to it into a number, like this:

```
var a = '3';
a = Number(a); // a is now the number 3
```

So the problem of adding two strings that contain numbers could be fixed like this:

```
var a = '3';
var b = '4';
var total = Number(a) + Number(b); // 7
```

A faster technique is the + operator, which does the same thing as Number(). Just add a + in front of a variable containing a string, and the JavaScript interpreter converts the string to a number.

```
var a = '3';
var b = '4';
var total = +a + +b // 7
```

The downside of either of these two techniques is that if the string contains anything except numbers, a single period, or a + or – sign at the beginning of the string, you'll end up with a non-number, or the JavaScript value NaN, which means "not a number" (page 564).

- parseInt() tries to convert a string to a number as well. However, unlike Number(), parseInt() will try to change even a string with letters to a number, as long as the string begins with numbers. This command can come in handy when you get a string like '20 years' as the response to a question about someone's age:

```
var age = '20 years';
age = parseInt(age); //20
```

The parseInt() method looks for either a number or a + or – sign at the beginning of the string and continues to look for numbers until it encounters a non-
number. So in the preceding example, it returns the number 20 and ignores the
other part of the string, ' years'.

In addition to a string value, the parseInt() method takes a second argument,
called a radix value, which determines which numbering system to use. In most
cases, you will use a base 10 system, which is the decimal system you're used
to. But that's not the only way to count numbers; there are also base 8 or *octal*
numbers and base 16 or *hexadecimal* numbers.

NOTE Octal numbers begin with 0, so it's possible to run into a situation where you're using parseInt()
on the string "010" and because the string begins with 0, the browser may think it's an octal number and give
you a weird result. In this case, the octal number 10 is the decimal value of 8. Some browsers default to octal
numbers in this type of case, and other browsers (and the current JavaScript standard) default to decimal. In
other words, you may end up with different results in different browsers.

The upshot is, it's always a safe practice to specify a decimal method for the parseInt() method:

```
var age = '010' years;

age = parseInt(age,10); // 10
```

- parseFloat() is like parseInt(), but you use it when a string might contain a
  decimal point. For example, if you have a string like '4.5 acres', you can use
  parseFloat() to retrieve the entire value including decimal places:

  ```
  var space = '4.5 acres';
  space = parseFloat(space); // 4.5
  ```

  If you used parseInt() for this example, you'd end up with just the number 4
  because parseInt() only tries to retrieve whole numbers (integers).

Which of these methods you use depends on the situation: If your goal is to add
two numbers, but they're strings, then use Number() or the + operator. However, if
you want to extract a number from a string that might include letters, like '200px'
or '1.5em', then use parseInt() to capture whole numbers (200, for example) or
parseFloat() to capture numbers with decimals (1.5, for example).

Testing for Numbers

When using JavaScript to manipulate user input, you often need to verify that the
information supplied by the visitor is of the correct type. For example, if you ask for
people's years of birth, you want to make sure they supply a number. Likewise, when
you're performing a mathematical calculation, if the data you use for the calculation
isn't a number, then your script might break.

To verify that a string is a number, use the isNaN() method. This method takes a string as an argument and tests whether the string is "not a number." If the string contains anything except a plus or minus (for positive and negative numbers) followed by numbers and an optional decimal value, it's considered "not a number," so the string '-23.25' is a number, but the string '24 pixels' is not. This method returns either true (if the string is not a number) or false (if it is a number). You can use isNaN() as part of a conditional statement like this:

```
var x = '10'; // is a number
if (isNaN(x)) {
  // won't run
} else {
  // will run
}
```

Rounding Numbers

JavaScript provides a way to round a fractional number to an integer—for example, rounding 4.5 up to 5. Rounding comes in handy when you're performing a calculation that must result in a whole number. For example, say you're using JavaScript to dynamically set a pixel height of a <div> tag on the page based on the height of the browser window. In other words, the height of the <div> is calculated using the window's height. Any calculation you make might result in a decimal value (like 300.25), but because there's no such thing as .25 pixels, you need to round the final calculation to the nearest integer (300, for example).

You can round a number using the round() method of the Math object. The syntax for this looks a little unusual:

```
Math.round(number)
```

You pass a number (or variable containing a number) to the round() method, and it returns an integer. If the original number has a decimal place with a value below .5, the number is rounded down; if the decimal place is .5 or above, it is rounded up. For example, 4.4 would round down to 4, while 4.5 rounds up to 5. Here's an example:

```
var decimalNum = 10.25;
var roundedNum = Math.round(decimalNum); // 10
```

> **NOTE** JavaScript provides two other methods for rounding numbers: Math.ceil() and Math.floor(). You use them just like Math.round(), but Math.ceil() always rounds the number up (for example, Math.ceil(4.0001) returns 5), while Math.floor() always rounds the number down: Math.floor(4.99999) returns 4. To keep these two methods clear in your mind, think a *ceiling* is up, and a *floor* is down.

Formatting Currency Values

When calculating product costs or shopping cart totals, you'll usually include the cost, plus two decimals out, like this: 9.99. But even if the monetary value is a whole number, it's common to add two zeros, like this: 10.00. And a currency value like 8.9 is written as 8.90. Unfortunately, JavaScript doesn't see numbers that way: It leaves the trailing zeros off (10 instead of 10.00, and 8.9 instead of 8.90, for example).

Fortunately, there's a method for numbers called toFixed(), which lets you convert a number to a string that matches the number of decimal places you want. To use it, add a period after a number (or after the name of a variable containing a number), followed by toFixed(2):

```
var cost = 10;
var printCost = '$' + cost.toFixed(2); // $10.00
```

The number you pass the toFixed() method determines how many decimal places to go out to. For currency, use 2 to end up with numbers like 10.00 or 9.90; if you use 3, you end up with 3 decimal places, like 10.000 or 9.900.

If the number starts off with more decimal places than you specify, the number is rounded to the number of decimal places specified. For example:

```
var cost = 10.289;
var printCost = '$' + cost.toFixed(2); // $10.29
```

In this case, the 10.289 is rounded up to 10.29.

> **NOTE** The toFixed() method only works with numbers. So if you use a string, you end up with an error:
>
> ```
> var cost='10';//a string
> var printCost='$' + cost.toFixed(2);//error
> ```
>
> To get around this problem, you need to convert the string to a number as described on page 37, like this:
>
> ```
> var cost='10';//a string
> cost = +cost; // or cost = Number(cost);
> var printCost='$' + cost.toFixed(2);//$10.00
> ```

Creating a Random Number

Random numbers can help add variety to a program. For example, say you have an array of questions for a quiz program (like the quiz tutorial on page 94). Instead of asking the same questions in the same order each time, you can randomly select one question in the array. Or, you could use JavaScript to randomly select the name of a graphic file from an array and display a different image each time the page loads. Both of these tasks require a random number.

JavaScript provides the Math.random() method for creating random numbers. This method returns a randomly generated number between 0 and 1 (for example, .9716907176080688 or .10345038010895868). While you might not have much need for numbers like those, you can use some simple math operations to generate a whole number from 0 to another number. For example, to generate a number from 0 to 9, you'd use this code:

```
Math.floor(Math.random()*10);
```

This code breaks down into two parts. The part inside the `Math.floor()` method—
`Math.random()*10`—generates a random number from 0 up to 10. That will generate
numbers like 4.190788392268892; however, when using `floor()` the random number
is never 10 (though it can be 0). To get a whole number, the random result is passed
to the `Math.floor()` method, which rounds any decimal number down to the nearest whole number, so 3.4448588848 becomes 3 and .1111939498984 becomes 0.

If you want to get a random number between 1 and another number, just multiply
the `random()` method by the uppermost number, and use the `Math.ceil()` method
(which rounds a number up to the nearest integer). For example, if you want to
simulate a die roll to get a number from 1 to 6:

```
var roll = Math.ceil(Math.random()*6); // 1,2,3,4,5 or 6
```

■ RANDOMLY SELECTING AN ARRAY ELEMENT

You can use the `Math.random()` method to randomly select an item from an array. As
discussed on page 48, each item in an array is accessed using an index number. The
first item in an array uses an index value of 0, and the last item in the array is accessed
with an index number that's 1 minus the total number of items in the array. Using
the `Math.random()` method makes it really easy to randomly select an array item:

```
var people = ['Ron','Sally','Tricia','Bob']; //create an array
var random = Math.floor(Math.random() * people.length);
var rndPerson = people[random]; //
```

The first line of this code creates an array with four names. The second line does
two things: First, it generates a random number from 0 up to (but not including) the
number of items in the array (`people.length`)—in this example, a number *from* 0 up
to 4. Then it uses the `Math.floor()` method to round down to the nearest integer,
so it will produce the number 0, 1, 2, or 3. Finally, it uses that number to access one
element from the array and store it in a variable named `rndPerson`.

■ A FUNCTION FOR SELECTING A RANDOM NUMBER

Functions are a great way to create useful, reusable snippets of code (page 85).
If you use random numbers frequently, you might want a simple function to help
you select a random number between any two numbers—for example, a number
between 1 and 6, or 100 and 1,000. The following function is called using two arguments—the first is the lowest possible value (1 for example), and the second is the
largest possible value (6 for example):

```
function rndNum(from, to) {
  return Math.floor((Math.random()*(to - from + 1)) + from);
}
```

To use this function, add it to your web page (as described on page 85), and then
call it like this:

```
var dieRoll = rndNum(1,6); // get a number between 1 and 6
```

▇ Dates and Times

If you want to keep track of the current date or time, turn to JavaScript's Date object. This special JavaScript object lets you determine the year, month, day of the week, hour, and more. To use it, you create a variable and store a new Date object inside it like this:

```
var now = new Date();
```

The new Date() command creates a Date object containing the current date and time. Once created, you can access different pieces of time and date information using various date-related methods as listed in Table 16-3. For example, to get the current year, use the getFullYear() method like this:

```
var now = new Date();
var year = now.getFullYear();
```

> **NOTE** new Date() retrieves the current time and date as determined by each visitor's computer. In other words, if someone hasn't correctly set his computer's clock, then the date and time won't be accurate.

TABLE 16-3 *Methods for accessing parts of the Date object*

METHOD	WHAT IT RETURNS
getFullYear()	The year: 2014, for example.
getMonth()	The month as an integer between 0 and 11: 0 is January and 11 is December.
getDate()	The day of the month—a number between 1 and 31.
getDay()	The day of the week as a number between 0 and 6. 0 is Sunday, and 6 is Saturday.
getHours()	Number of hours on a 24-hour clock (a number between 0 and 23). For example, 11p.m. is 23.
getMinutes()	Number of minutes between 0 and 59.
getSeconds()	Number of seconds between 0 and 59.
getTime()	Total number of milliseconds since January 1, 1970 at midnight (see the box on page 570).

Getting the Month

To retrieve the month for a Date object, use the getMonth() method, which returns the month's number:

```
var now = new Date();
var month = now.getMonth();
```

However, instead of returning a number that makes sense to us humans (as in 1 meaning January), this method returns a number that's one less. For example, January is

0, February is 1, and so on. If you want to retrieve a number that matches how we think of months, just add 1 like this:

```
var now = new Date();
var month = now.getMonth()+1; //matches the real month
```

There's no built-in JavaScript command that tells you the name of a month. Fortunately, JavaScript's strange way of numbering months comes in handy when you want to determine the actual name of the month. You can accomplish that by first creating an array of month names, then accessing a name using the index number for that month:

```
var months = ['January','February','March','April','May',
              'June','July','August','September',
              'October','November','December'];
var now = new Date();
var month = months[now.getMonth()];
```

The first line creates an array with all twelve month names, in the order they occur (January–December). Remember that to access an array item you use an index number, and that arrays are numbered starting with 0 (page 47). So to access the first item of the array months, you use months[0]. So, by using the getMonth() method, you can retrieve a number to use as an index for the months array and thus retrieve the name for that month.

Getting the Day of the Week

The getDay() method retrieves the day of the week. And as with the getMonth() method, the JavaScript interpreter returns a number that's one less than what you'd expect: 0 is considered Sunday, the first day of the week, while Saturday is 6. The name of the day of the week is usually more useful for your visitors, so you can use an array to store the day names and use the getDay() method to access the particular day in the array, like this:

```
var days = ['Sunday','Monday','Tuesday','Wednesday',
            'Thursday','Friday','Saturday'];
var now = new Date();
var dayOfWeek = days[now.getDay()];
```

Getting the Time

The Date object also contains the current time, so you can display the current time on a web page or use the time to determine if the visitor is viewing the page in the a.m. or p.m. You can then do something with that information, like display a background image of the sun during the day, or the moon at night.

The Date Object Behind the Scenes

JavaScript lets you access particular elements of the Date object, such as the year or the day of the month. However, the JavaScript interpreter actually thinks of a date as the number of *milliseconds* that have passed since midnight on January 1, 1970. For example, Wednesday, December 1, 2014, is actually 1417420800000 to the JavaScript interpreter.

That isn't a joke: As far as JavaScript is concerned, the beginning of time was midnight on January 1, 1970 at UTC (what used to be called "Greenwich Mean Time"). That date (called the "Unix epoch") was arbitrarily chosen in the 70s by programmers creating the Unix operating system, so they could all agree on a way of keeping track of time. Since then, this way of tracking a date has become common in many programming languages and platforms.

Whenever you use a Date method like getFullYear(), the JavaScript interpreter does the math to figure out (based on how many seconds have elapsed since January 1, 1970) what year it is. If you want to see the number of milliseconds for a particular date, you use the getTime() method:

```
var sometime = new Date();
var msElapsed = sometime.getTime();
```

Tracking dates and times as milliseconds makes it easier to calculate differences between dates. For example, you can determine the amount of time until next New Year's Day by first getting the number of milliseconds that will have elapsed from 1/1/1970 to when next year rolls around and then subtracting the number of milliseconds that have elapsed from 1/1/1970 to today:

```
// milliseconds from 1/1/1970 to today
var today = new Date();
// milliseconds from 1/1/1970 to next new year
var nextYear = new Date(2015,0,1);
// calculate milliseconds from today to next year
var timeDiff = nextYear - today;
```

The result of subtracting two dates is the number of milliseconds difference between the two. If you want to convert that into something useful, just divide it by the number of milliseconds in a day (to determine how many days) or the number of milliseconds in an hour (to determine how many hours), and so on:

```
var second = 1000; // 1000 milliseconds in a second
var minute = 60*second; // 60 seconds in a minute
var hour = 60*minute; // 60 minutes in an hour
var day = 24*hour; // 24 hours in a day
var totalDays = timeDiff/day; // total number of days
```

(In this example, you may have noticed a different way to create a date: new Date(2015,0,1). You can read more about this method on page 573.)

You can use the getHours(), getMinutes(), and getSeconds() methods to get the hours, minutes, and seconds. So to display the time on a web page, add the following in the HTML where you wish the time to appear:

```
var now = new Date();
var hours = now.getHours();
var minutes = now.getMinutes();
var seconds = now.getSeconds();
document.write(hours + ":" + minutes + ":" + seconds);
```

This code produces output like 6:35:56 to indicate 6 a.m., 35 minutes, and 56 seconds. However, it will also produce output that you might not like, like 18:4:9 to indicate 4 minutes and 9 seconds after 6 p.m. One problem is that most people reading this book, unless they're in the military, don't use the 24-hour clock. They don't recognize 18 as meaning 6 p.m. An even bigger problem is that times should be formatted with two digits for minutes and seconds (even if they're a number less than 10), like this: 6:04:09. Fortunately, it's not difficult to adjust the script to match those requirements.

■ CHANGING HOURS TO A.M. AND P.M.

To change hours from a 24-hour clock to a 12-hour clock, you need to do a couple of things. First, you need to determine if the time is in the morning (so you can add 'am' after the time) or in the afternoon (to append 'pm'). Second, you need to convert any hours greater than 12 to their 12-hour clock equivalent (for example, change 14 to 2 p.m.).

Here's the code to do that:

```
1   var now = new Date();
2   var hour = now.getHours();
3   var am_pm;
4   if (hour < 12) {
5       am_pm = 'am';
6   } else {
7       am_pm = 'pm';
8   }
9   hour = hour % 12;
10  if (hour==0) {
11      hour = 12;
12  }
13  hour = hour + ' ' + am_pm;
```

NOTE The column of numbers at the far left is just line numbering to make it easier for you to understand the following discussion. Don't type these numbers into your own code!

Lines 1 and 2 grab the current date and time and store the current hour into a variable named hour. Lines 3–7 determine if the hour is in the afternoon or morning; if the hour is less than 12 (the hour after midnight is 0), then it's the morning (a.m.); otherwise, it's the afternoon (p.m.).

Line 8 introduces a mathematical operator called modulus and represented by a percent (%) sign. It returns the remainder of a division operation. For example, 2 divides into 5 two times (2 x 2 is 4), with 1 left over. In other words, 5 % 2 is 1. So in this case, if the hour is 18, 18 % 12 results in 6 (12 goes into 18 once with a remainder of 6). 18 is 6 p.m., which is what you want. If the first number is smaller than the number divided into it (for example, 8 divided by 12), then the result is the original number. For example, 8 % 12 just returns 8; in other words, the modulus operator doesn't change the hours before noon.

Lines 9–11 take care of two possible outcomes with the modulus operator. If the hour is 12 (noon) or 0 (after midnight), then the modulus operator returns 0. In this case, hour is just set to 12 for either 12 p.m. or 12 a.m.

Finally, line 12 combines the reformatted hour with a space and either "am" or "pm", so the result is displayed as, for example, "6 am" or "6 pm".

▓ PADDING SINGLE DIGITS

As discussed on the previous page, when the minutes or seconds values are less than 10, you can end up with weird output like 7:3:2 p.m. To change this output to the more common 7:03:02 p.m., you need to add a 0 in front of the single digit. It's easy with a basic conditional statement:

```
1  var minutes = now.getMinutes();
2  if (minutes < 10) {
3    minutes = '0' + minutes;
4  }
```

Line 1 grabs the minutes in the current time, which in this example could be 33 or Line 2 simply checks if the number is less than 10, meaning the minute is a single digit and needs a 0 in front of it. Line 3 is a bit tricky because you can't normally add a 0 in front of a number: 0 + 2 equals 2, not 02. However, you can combine strings in this way so '0' + minutes means combine the string '0' with the value in the *minutes* variable. As discussed on page 37, when you add a string to a number, the JavaScript interpreter converts the number to a string as well, so you end up with a string like '08'.

You can put all of these parts together to create a simple function to output times in formats like 7:32:04 p.m., or 4:02:34 a.m., or even leave off seconds altogether for a time like 7:23 p.m.:

```
function getTime(secs) {
    var sep = ':'; //separator character
    var hours, minutes, seconds, time;
    var now = new Date();
    var am_pm;
    hours = now.getHours();
    if (hours < 12) {
        am_pm = 'am';
    } else {
        am_pm = 'pm';
    }
    hours = hours % 12;
    if (hours == 0) {
        hours = 12;
    }
    time = hours;
    minutes = now.getMinutes();
```

```
        if (minutes<10) {
            minutes = '0' + minutes;
        }
        time += sep + minutes;
        if (secs) {
            seconds = now.getSeconds();
            if (seconds < 10) {
                seconds = '0' + seconds;
            }
            time += sep + seconds;
        }
        return time + ' ' + am_pm;
    }
```

You'll find this function in the file *getTime.js* in the *chapter16* folder in the Tutorials. You can see it in action by opening the file *time.html* (in that same folder) in a web browser. To use the function, either attach the *getTime.js* file to a web page, or copy the function into a web page or another external JavaScript file. To get the time, just call the function like this: getTime(), or, if you want the seconds displayed as well, getTime(true). The function will return a string containing the current time in the proper format.

Creating a Date Other Than Today

So far, you've seen how to use new Date() to capture the current date and time on a visitor's computer. But what if you want to create a Date object for next Thanksgiving or New Year's? JavaScript lets you create a date other than today in a few different ways. You might want to do this if you'd like to do a calculation between two dates: for example, "How many days until the new year?"

When using the Date() method, you can also specify a date and time in the future or past. The basic format is this:

```
new Date(year,month,day,hour,minutes,seconds,milliseconds);
```

For example, to create a Date for noon on New Year's Day 2015, you could do this:

```
var ny2015 = new Date(2015,0,1,12,0,0,0);
```

This code translates to "create a new Date object for January 1, 2015, at 12 o'clock, 0 minutes, 0 seconds, and 0 milliseconds." You must supply at least a year and month, but if you don't need to specify an exact time, you can leave off milliseconds, seconds, minutes, and so on. For example, to just create a date object for January 1, 2015, you could do this:

```
var ny2015 = new Date(2015,0,1);
```

NOTE Remember that JavaScript uses 0 for January, 1 for February, and so on, as described on page 568.

CREATING A DATE THAT'S ONE WEEK FROM TODAY

As discussed in the box on page 570, the JavaScript interpreter actually treats a date as the number of milliseconds that have elapsed since midnight, Jan 1, 1970, UTC. Another way to create a date is to pass a value representing the number of milliseconds for that date:

```
new Date(milliseconds);
```

So another way to create a date for January 1, 2015, would be like this:

```
var ny2015 = new Date(1420099200000);
```

Of course, because most of us aren't human calculators, you probably wouldn't think of a date like this. However, milliseconds come in very handy when you're creating a new date that's a certain amount of time from another date. For example, when setting a cookie using JavaScript, you need to specify a date at which point that cookie is deleted from a visitor's browser. To make sure a cookie disappears after one week, you need to specify a date that's one week from today.

> **NOTE** The example code just shown—new Date(1420099200000);—won't work for everyone. It only applies to the UTC-8 time zone, the Pacific time zone on the west coast of the United States. That's because web browsers take time zone into account and adjust the browser's clock based on the difference in UTC time as described in the box on page 570.

To create a date that's one week from now, you could do the following:

```
var now = new Date(); // today
var nowMS = now.getTime(); // get # milliseconds for today
var week = 1000*60*60*24*7; // milliseconds in one week
var oneWeekFromNow = new Date(nowMS + week);
```

The first line stores the current date and time in a variable named now. Next, the getTime() method extracts the number of milliseconds that have elapsed from January 1, 1970, to today. The third line calculates the total number of milliseconds in a single week (1000 milliseconds/sec * 60 seconds/min * 60 minutes/hr * 24 hours/day * 7 days/week). Finally, the code creates a new date by adding the number of milliseconds in a week to today.

> **NOTE** JavaScript's Date object has many different functions to help with computing dates and dealing with different locations. You can find a complete reference for the Date object at *https://developer.mozilla.org/en-US/docs/Web/JavaScript/Reference/Global_Objects/Date.*

Dealing with Different Time Zones

Computers do more than just keep track of seconds, minutes, and days. They also need to coordinate their time with the time of other computers located around the world in different time zones. After all, 8:00 p.m. in Moscow is not the exact same moment as 8:00 p.m. in San Francisco. Because those two cities are across the globe from each other, and the sun sets and rises at nearly the exact opposite time, 8:00 p.m. in Moscow is 8:00 a.m. in San Francisco and vice versa. (Or, if Daylight Saving Time is in effect, 8:00 p.m. in Moscow is 9:00 a.m. in San Francisco.)

To help computers (and people) in different time zones keep in sync, software developers use a convention called UTC or *Coordinated Universal Time*. This time zone used to be called Greenwich Mean Time and is marked by the 0° longitude meridian. Unless you live in England, France, Spain, or the African nations that are vertically in line with Greenwich, England, you live in a time zone that is *offset* from UTC.

San Francisco is UTC -8, which makes it is 8 hours behind UTC time. When it's 9:15 p.m. in London, it's 1:15 p.m. in San Francisco. Moscow is UTC +4, so when it's 9:15 p.m. in London,

it's 1:15 a.m. in Moscow. (Again, these times will vary depending on whether Daylight Saving or Summer Time is in effect).

JavaScript's Date object provides a function for determining your local time offset (that is, how many hours your time differs from UTC time):

```
var now = new Date();
var offset = now.getTimezoneOffset();
```

If you're on a computer in San Francisco, and you check the offset, you'll get a value of either 480 or 420. The number represents the total number of minutes different your computer is from UTC time, so 480 is 8 hours, and 420 is 7 hours (if it's Daylight Saving time). If your region participates in Daylight Saving time, your computer and web browser keep track of that, too (aren't computers smart?).

In general, you don't need to worry about converting time zones. JavaScript runs on your web visitors' computers, so when you do time computations, like spitting out the current time, the browser will adapt to the visitor's time zone and print a time that's right for them.

■ Writing More Efficient JavaScript

Programming is a lot of work. Programmers are always looking for ways to do things faster and with fewer lines of code. While there are lots of tips and tricks, the following techniques are especially useful for working with JavaScript and jQuery.

Putting Preferences in Variables

One important lesson that programmers learn is how to extract details from scripts so they are more flexible and easier to update. For example, say you want to change the color of a paragraph of text to orange when a visitor clicks on it. You could do that with jQuery using the css() function (page 134) like this:

```
$('p').click(function() {
  $(this).css('color','#F60');
});
```

In this case, the color orange (#F60) is hard-coded into this step. Say you apply this same color in other steps (maybe to add a background color when the visitor mouses over a table cell). You might be tempted to write #F60 into those steps as well. A better approach is to place the color into a variable at the beginning of your script and then use that variable throughout your script:

```
1   $(document).ready(function() {
2     var hColor='#F60';
3     $('p').click(function() {
4       $(this).css('color',hColor);
5     });
6     $('td').hover(
7       function() {
8         $(this).css('backgroundColor',hColor);
9       },
10      function() {
11        $(this).css('backgroundColor','transparent');
12      }
13    );
14  }); //end ready()
```

In this example, the variable hColor now holds a hexadecimal color value—that variable is used both in the click event for the <p> tags, and in a hover event for the <td> tags. If you later decide orange isn't your thing, you can change the value stored in the variable—var hColor='#F33';—and now the script will use that color.

You could make the above code even more flexible by uncoupling the connection between the color used for the <p> tags and <td> tags. Currently, they're both set to the same color, but if you want to make it so you could eventually assign different colors to each, you could add an additional variable to your code:

```
1   $(document).ready(function() {
2     var pColor='#F60';
3     var tdColor=pColor;
4     $('p').click(function() {
5       $(this).css('color',pColor);
6     });
7     $('td').hover(
8       function() {
9         $(this).css('backgroundColor',tdColor);
10      },
11      function() {
12        $(this).css('backgroundColor','transparent');
13      }
14    );
15  }); //end ready()
```

Now, the click and hover events use the same color—#F60 (because the tdColor variable is set to the value of pColor in line 3). However, if you later decide that you want the table cells to have a different color, just change line 3 like this:

```
var tdColor='#FF3';
```

When writing a JavaScript program, identify values that you explicitly name in your code and turn them into variables. Likely candidates are colors, fonts, widths, heights, times (such as 1,000 milliseconds), filenames (such as image files), message text (such as alert and confirmation messages), and paths to files (such as the path for a link or an image). For example:

```
var highlightColor = '#33A';
var upArrow = 'ua.png';
var downArrow='da.png';
var imagePath='/images/';
var delay=1000;
```

Put these variable definitions at the beginning of your script (or if you're using jQuery, right inside the .ready() function).

> **TIP** It's particularly useful to put text that you plan on printing to a page into variables. For example, error messages like "Please supply a valid email address," or confirmation messages like "Thank you for supplying your mailing information" can be variables. When these messages are grouped together as variables at the beginning of a script, it's easier to edit them later (and to translate the text if you ever need to reach an international audience).

Putting Preferences in Objects

There's a slightly more advanced way to store options: using a JavaScript object. As you read on page 136, a JavaScript object literal is a way to store data into a single object using name/value (or key/value) pairs. The example at the top of this page used lots of individual variables to store commonly used values like colors, image paths, icon names, and so on. There's nothing wrong with this approach, but you can group all of these values into a single object, and then reference individual properties using the *dot syntax* (page 56).

For example, the list of 5 variables in the previous section could be stored in a single object, like this:

```
var siteSettings = {
  highlightColor: '#33A',
  upArrow: 'ua.png',
  downArrow: 'da.png',
  imagePath: '/images/',
  delay: 1000
}
```

When you use dot syntax, you don't use an equals sign to assign a value to a name, so you write upArrow: 'ua.png', not upArrow='ua.png', and you add a comma after each name/value pair except the last one. To then use these settings in your program, use the dot syntax to access all of the object's individual properties. For example, to retrieve the value of the highlightColor property, you'd write this:

```
siteSettings.highlightColor
```

There are a couple of benefits to this approach. First, it's more organized than repeating a big bunch of variables. Instead, you put all of your settings into a single object in one spot in your code. Second, it helps you avoid running into a problem where you use the same name for two different variables. For example, the name "delay" is pretty generic. If you create a `delay` variable in your programming and you had defined a `delay` variable at the beginning of your program to store a preference, the first version of `delay` would be wiped out. However, when you store your site-wide delay setting in an object—`siteSettings.delay`—it won't conflict with another `delay` variable you might add to your program.

> **NOTE** You may recall from the discussion of jQuery plug-ins on page 236 that many jQuery plug-ins used object literals to pass information to the plug-in. The jQuery UI widgets (Chapters 10 and 11) use object literals to control how the widgets look and work.

Ternary Operator

It's a common programming task to set the value of a variable based on some kind of condition. For example, say you want to set up a variable that contains text with the login status of a user. In your script there's a variable named `login`, which contains a Boolean value—`true` if the user is logged in, or `false` if she isn't. Here's one way to create a new variable for this situation:

```
var status;
if (login) {
 status='Logged in';
} else {
 status='Not logged in';
}
```

In this case, a basic conditional statement (page 61) sets the value of a variable named `status` based on whether the user is logged in or not. JavaScript offers a shortcut for this common procedure, called a *ternary operator*. A ternary operator provides a one-line approach to creating a simple conditional statement. The basic format of the ternary operator is:

```
condition ? A : B
```

Depending upon the result of the condition, either A (if the condition is *true*) or B (if the condition is *false*) is returned. The ? precedes the *true* result, while the : precedes the *false* result. So, for example, the above code could be rewritten like this:

```
var status = login ? 'Logged in' : 'Not logged in';
```

What was once six lines of code is now a single line of code. Figure 16-6 diagrams how this code works.

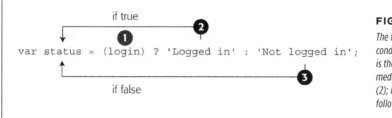

FIGURE 16-6

The ternary operator lets you write one-line conditional statements. In this example, 1 is the condition. If it's true, the code immediately following the ? mark is returned (2); if the condition is false, then the code following the : is returned (3).

The ternary operator is simply a shortcut—you don't have to use it, and some programmers find it too dense to easily understand and prefer the easier-to-read if/else statement. In addition, the best use of the ternary operator is for setting the value of a variable based on a condition. It doesn't work for every type of conditional statement; for example, you can't use it for multiple-line statements where many lines of code are executed based on a particular condition. But even if you don't use ternary operators, recognizing how they work will help you understand other peoples' programs, as you'll probably encounter them frequently.

The Switch Statement

There's more than one way to skin a conditional statement. While the ternary operator is great for assigning a value to a variable based on the results of a condition, the switch statement is a more compact way of writing a series of if/else statements that depend on the value of a single variable.

For example, say you ask visitors to your site to type their favorite color into a form field and then print a different message based on the color they submit. Here's how you might write part of this code using the typical conditional statement.

```
if (favoriteColor == 'blue') {
 message = 'Blue is a cool color.';
} else if (favoriteColor == 'red') {
 message = 'Red is a warm color.';
} else if (favoriteColor == 'green') {
 message = 'Green is the color of the leaves.';
} else {
 message = 'What kind of favorite color is that?';
}
```

Notice that there's an awful lot of favoriteColor == 'some value' in that code. In fact, 'favoriteColor ==' appears three times in just nine lines of code. If all you're doing is testing the value of a variable repeatedly, then the switch statement provides a more elegant (and easy to read) solution. The basic structure of a switch statement is diagrammed in Figure 16-7.

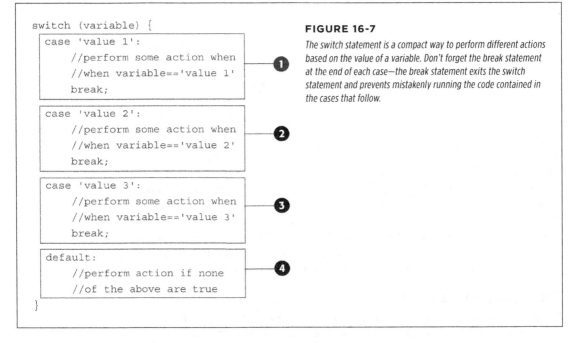

```
switch (variable) {
    case 'value 1':
        //perform some action when
        //when variable=='value 1'
        break;

    case 'value 2':
        //perform some action when
        //when variable=='value 2'
        break;

    case 'value 3':
        //perform some action when
        //when variable=='value 3'
        break;

    default:
        //perform action if none
        //of the above are true
}
```

FIGURE 16-7

The switch statement is a compact way to perform different actions based on the value of a variable. Don't forget the break statement at the end of each case—the break statement exits the switch statement and prevents mistakenly running the code contained in the cases that follow.

The first line of a switch statement begins with the keyword switch, followed by a variable name inside parentheses, followed by an opening brace symbol. Essentially, this code says, "Let's get the value of this variable and see if it matches one of several other values." Each test is called a case, and a switch statement has one or more cases. In Figure 16-7, there are three cases, numbered 1–3. The basic structure of a case looks like this:

```
case value1:
    // do something
    break;
```

The case keyword indicates the beginning of a case; it's followed by some value and then a colon. This line is shorthand for the longer if (variable=='value1'). The value can be a number, string, or Boolean (or a variable containing a number, string, or Boolean), so if you want to test whether the variable is equal to 37, for example, then the case would look like this:

```
case 37:
    //do something
    break;
```

To test whether the variable is true or not, you'd write this:

```
case true:
 //do something
 break;
```

After the first line, you add the statements you want to execute if the variable matches the test case value. Finally, you add a `break;` statement. This step is important—the `break;` statement exits the switch statement. If you leave out `break`, the JavaScript interpreter will actually run all the programming in all of the other cases that follow! In other words, once one case is matched, the JavaScript interpreter stops trying to find any other matches and just runs all the remaining code in the switch block.

Here's how the switch statement can help with the if/else if code from page 579:

```
switch (favoriteColor) {
 case 'blue':
   message = 'Blue is a cool color.';
   break;
 case 'red':
   message = 'Red is a warm color.';
   break;
 case 'green':
   message = 'Green is the color of the leaves.';
   break;
 default:
   message = 'What kind of favorite color is that?';
}
```

This code is the equivalent to the if/else if code, but is easier to read and doesn't require repeated conditions (`if (favoriteColor === blue)`, for example).

You can also put multiple `case` statements right after one another (if you want to run the same code for several values). For example:

```
switch (favoriteColor) {
 case 'navy':
 case 'blue':
 case 'indigo':
   message = 'Blue is a cool color.';
   break;
 case 'red':
   message = 'Red is a warm color.';
   break;
 case 'green':
   message = 'Green is the color of the leaves.';
   break;
 default:
   message = 'What kind of favorite color is that?';
}
```

This is similar to using if (favoriteColor == 'navy' || favoriteColor == 'blue' || favoriteColor == 'indigo') in an if/else statement.

Joining Arrays and Splitting Strings

A JavaScript array is sort of like a shopping list. It's a collection of values stored in a single variable. For example, you can create an array to hold the days of the week, like this:

```
var days = ['Monday','Tuesday','Wednesday','Thursday','Friday','Saturday',
'Sunday'];
```

Each item in the list is a separate value, and you can access them using the array notation described on page 47. To access the first item in the list, you'd type days[0]. But occasionally you want to get all of the items out of the list into a string, which is useful if you just want to print out everything that's in the array. You can do that with the .join() method. This array method takes all of the items in the array and turns them into a single string. Each item in the array is separated by either a comma or another separator you specify. For example:

```
var weekdays = days.join(); // Monday,Tuesday,Wednesday…
```

If you don't provide any arguments to the join() method, it uses a comma to separate each item in the string. However, you can supply any separator you'd like:

```
var weekdays = days.join(':'); // Monday:Tuesday:Wednesday…
```

JavaScript doesn't insert any spaces between the list items and separators, so if you wanted, say, one item, followed by a comma and a space, you'd need to pass the string ', ' to the join() method:

```
var weekdays = days.join(', '); // Monday, Tuesday, Wednesday…
```

On the other hand, you can take a string and turn it into an array using the split() method as long as the string has some kind of separator (or delimiter) that indicates where one item ends the next begins. For example, say you have this string:

```
var weekdays = 'Monday,Tuesday,Wednesday,Thursday,Friday,Saturday,Sunday';
```

You could take that string and break it up into an array like this:

```
var dayList = weekdays.split(','); // dayList now is array of 7 items
```

■ Putting It All Together

So far, you've seen lots of tasks that JavaScript can accomplish: form validation, image rollovers, photo galleries, user interface improvements like tabbed and accordion panels, and more. But you might be wondering, how do you put them together to work with your site? After all, once you start using JavaScript, you'll probably want to use it to improve every page of your site. Here are some tips for working with multiple scripts on a site.

Using External JavaScript Files

As mentioned on page 15, external JavaScript files are an efficient way to share the same JavaScript code among web pages. An external file makes updating your JavaScript easier—there's just one file to edit if you need to enhance (or fix) your JavaScript code. In addition, when an external JavaScript file is downloaded, it's stored in the browser's cache, so it doesn't need to be downloaded a second time, making web pages feel more responsive and load more quickly.

In the case of a JavaScript library like jQuery, external JavaScript files are a necessity. After all, your web pages would be unnecessarily large and difficult to maintain if you put the actual jQuery JavaScript code into each page. Furthermore, jQuery plug-ins are supplied as external files, so you need to link them to a web page if you want to use them. Linking to an external JavaScript file is as easy as this:

```
<script src="js/jquery-ui.min.js"></script>
```

Putting your own JavaScript code into external JavaScript files can also help make your code more reusable and your site feel faster—but only if you actually share that code among web pages. For example, with the form validation script you created on page 286, it doesn't make sense to put the code used to create the validation rules and error messages into an external file because all of those rules and error messages are specific to the form elements on that page, and wouldn't work on a form that has different form fields. In that case, it's best to just use the JavaScript to validate the form within the web page itself.

However, the validation plug-in file you learned about on page 273 can be used for any form, so it makes sense to have that in a separate file. The same is true for any code that you'll use in multiple pages. For example, on page 262 you learned how to focus the first field of a form using JavaScript—that's something you might want to do for every form. Likewise, the box on page 266 presents the JavaScript necessary to prevent a visitor from hitting the submit button multiple times (and thus submitting the form data more than once), which is also useful for any form page. So, you might want to combine these two scripts into a single external file named something like *forms.js*. The JavaScript code would look something like this:

```
1  $(document).ready(function() {
2    // focus first text field
3    $(":text")[0].focus();
4
5    // disable submit button on submit
6    $('form').submit(function() {
7      var subButton = $(this).find(':submit');
8      subButton.attr('disabled',true);
9      subButton.val('...sending information...');
10   });
11 }); //end ready
```

NOTE As mentioned on page 160, any scripts you place in the <head> of a web page and which use jQuery require a $document.ready() function. jQuery can handle multiple $(document).ready() functions without a problem. For example, you can have several external JavaScript files that do various things to the page, and each file can have a $(document).ready() function, and you can include a $(document). ready() function within <script> that appears only on that page. That's perfectly fine with jQuery. You can avoid the $(document).ready() function altogether by placing your <script> tags at the bottom of the web page, just before the closing </body> tag.

Using the same script across multiple pages requires a little planning. For example, line 3 places the cursor into the first text field on a web page. In most cases, that makes sense—you want the focus to be on the first field so a visitor can start filling out the form. However, if the page has more than one form, this code might not work as you want it to.

For example, if you have a search box at the top of the page and a separate form for submitting a product order, the code in line 3 will put the focus on the search box and *not* the first text field in the order form. In a case like that, you need to think through the problem and come up with a way of making sure the proper text field has the focus when the page loads. Here are two possible solutions:

- Add a class name to the field you want the focus on when the page loads. For example, say you add the class name focus to the text field, like this:

  ```
  <input type="text" class="focus" name="firstName">
  ```

  You could then you use this JavaScript to make sure that field is focused:

  ```
  $('.focus').focus();
  ```

  To use this code, you just need to make sure that you add the focus class to a text field on each form page, and make sure you link the external JavaScript file containing this code to each of those form pages.

- You can get the same effect by adding a class name to the <form> tag itself, using this JavaScript:

  ```
  $('.focus :text')[0].focus();
  ```

  This code automatically focuses the first text field of a form with the class focus. The benefit of this approach is that the first text field always gets the focus, so if you reorganize your form (add a few more text fields to the beginning, for example), you know that the first text field will get focus and not some other field (with the focus class) further down the page.

Once you start using JavaScript, you might end up using several scripts on all (or nearly all) of your web pages. For example, you might have some rollover images (page 209), and use JavaScript to make sure links outside your site open in a new window (page 231). In this situation, it's useful to create an external JavaScript file with all of the scripts you share among your site—you could call the file something like *site_scripts.js* or simply *site.js*.

> **NOTE** jQuery has a built-in mechanism to protect you from producing unwanted JavaScript errors. JavaScript usually spits out an error if you try to perform an action on something that doesn't exist—for example, trying to select a text field on a page that doesn't have a text field. Fortunately, jQuery ignores these kinds of errors.

Creating Fast-Loading JavaScript

Once you starting using external JavaScript files for your scripts, your visitors should start to feel like your site is faster. Thanks to a browser's cache, once your external JavaScript files download for one page of your site, they don't have to be downloaded a second time for a different page. However, there's still another way to make your site download more quickly: compressing your external JavaScript files.

> **NOTE** Files sent securely via SSL (secure socket layer) aren't *usually* cached. So if people access the pages of your site using *https://* as the protocol (for example, *https://www.oreilly.com*), then any files they download, including external JavaScript files, will most like be downloaded every time they're needed. (You can change settings on the web server to allow caching of securely sent files.)

To make a script more understandable, programmers usually insert empty spaces, carriage returns, and comments to explain what the script does. These are all important additions for the programmer, but not necessary for the web browser, which can happily understand JavaScript without carriage returns, tabs, extraneous spaces, or comments. Using a compression program, you can minimize the space your JavaScript takes up. The version of jQuery recommended in this book, for example, is *minified*, and is nearly half the file size of the uncompressed version.

There are several programs aimed at making JavaScript more petite. Douglas Crockford's JSMin (*http://crockford.com/javascript/jsmin.html*) is one example, and Dean Edward's Packer (*http://dean.edwards.name/packer*) is another. However, it's a good idea to use the same compressor Yahoo! (and jQuery) use, because it achieves great file size savings without changing your code (some compressors actually rewrite your code and in some cases can break your scripts!).

Yahoo!'s JavaScript compressor, *YUI Compressor*, lives at *http://developer.yahoo.com/yui/compressor*. Fortunately, there's an easy to use online tool that lets you use the YUI compressor without installing it on your own computer:

1. **Launch a web browser and visit *http://www.refresh-sf.com/yui/.***

   This is the site for the Online YUI Compressor.

2. **Click the File(s) link.**

   Alternatively, you can just copy the JavaScript code from your text editor and paste it into the large text box at the site's homepage; you can then skip to step 4.

3. **Click the Choose File button and locate the external JavaScript file on your computer.**

   The file must contain only JavaScript. For example, you can't select a HTML file that also has JavaScript programming in it.

4. **Select the "Redirect to gzipped output" box (just above the Compress button).**

   This option lets you download the minimized code in a new, zipped file. This will be your new, compressed, external JavaScript file, which you can save to your site.

5. **Click the Compress button.**

   The website processes your code and downloads the compressed file to your computer. You can then rename this file (because it's always saved as *min.js*), and put it into your site for use. The Online YUI Compressor site provides a nice report after you compress a file, listing the original file size, the new, compressed file size, and a percentage that represents how much smaller the new file is.

WARNING Make sure you keep the original JavaScript file on hand after using the Online YUI Compressor because the new, compressed version is unreadable and you'll never be able to edit it if you wish to make changes to your original code.

Troubleshooting and Debugging

Everybody makes mistakes, but in JavaScript, mistakes can keep your programs from running correctly—or at all. When you first start out with JavaScript, you'll probably make a lot of mistakes. Trying to figure out why a script isn't behaving the way it should can be frustrating, but it's all a part of programming. Fortunately, with experience and practice, you'll be able to figure out why an error has occurred and how to fix it.

This chapter describes some of the most common programming mistakes, and, more importantly, teaches you how to diagnose problems in your scripts—*debug* them, as programmers say. In addition, the tutorial will take you step by step through debugging a problematic script.

■ Top JavaScript Programming Mistakes

There are countless ways a program can go wrong, from simple typos to more subtle errors that only pop up every now and again. However, there are a handful of mistakes that routinely plague beginning (and even advanced) JavaScript programmers. Go over the list in this section, and keep it in the back of your mind when programming. You'll probably find that knowing these common mistakes makes it a lot easier to identify and fix problems in your own programs.

Non-Closed Pairs

As you've noticed, JavaScript is filled with endless parentheses, braces, semicolons, quotation marks, and other punctuation. Due to the finicky nature of computers, leaving out a single punctuation mark can stop a program dead in its tracks. One of the most common mistakes is simply forgetting to include a closing punctuation mark. For example, `alert('hello' ;` will produce an error because the closing parenthesis is missing: `alert('hello');`.

Leaving off a closing parenthesis will cause a syntax error (see page 21). This kind of "grammatical" error prevents scripts from running at all. When you give your script a test run, the browser lets you know if you've made a syntax error, but, confusingly, they all describe the problem differently. In the Firefox error console (page 22), you get an error message "SyntaxError: missing) after argument list"; Internet Explorer's console (page 21) reports this error as "Expected ')'"; Chrome's error console provides a misleading "SyntaxError: Unexpected token ;" message; and Safari's error console (page 23) gives you the helpful message "SyntaxError: Expected token ')'." Firefox tends to provide the most understandable error messages, so it's a good browser to start with when trying to figure out why a script isn't working (Figure 17-1).

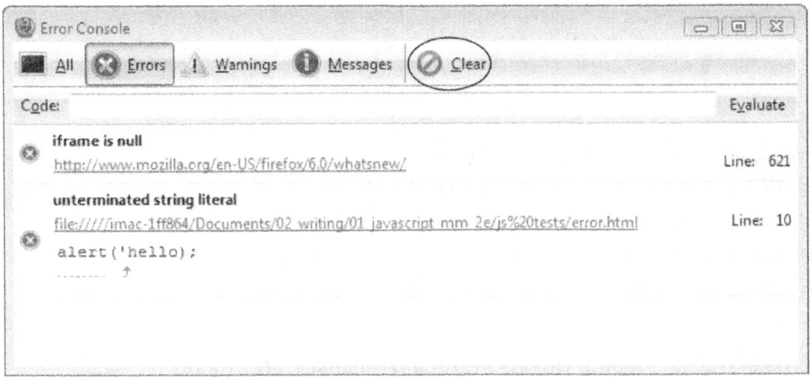

FIGURE 17-1

Firefox's Error Console lists all JavaScript errors that the browser encounters. You can display the console by choosing Web Developer→Error Console (Ctrl+Shift+K) on Windows, or Tools→Web Developer→Error Console (⌘-Option-K) on Macs. The console lists the errors it has encountered on all pages, so you'll want to frequently erase the list by clicking the Clear button (circled).

The syntax error in `alert('hello' ;` is pretty easy to spot. When you've got a nest of parentheses, though, it's very easy to leave off a closing parenthesis and difficult to spot that error at a glance. For example:

```
if ((x>0) && (y<10) {
    // do something
}
```

In this example, the final closing parenthesis for the conditional statement is missing—the one that goes directly after (y<10). The first line should really be: `if ((x>0) and (y<10)) {`. Again, Firefox provides the clearest description of the problem: "missing) after condition." Table 17-1 provides a list of Firefox's error console syntax error messages.

You'll encounter a syntax error when you forget to include the second quote mark as well. For example, `alert('hello);` produces an error because the final single quote is missing: `alert('hello');`. In Firefox, if you forget to include one of the quote marks, you'll get an "unterminated string literal" error, while Internet Explorer reports an "unterminated string constant"; and both Chrome and Safari calls this a "SyntaxError: Unexpected token ILLEGAL".

Braces also come in pairs, and you'll use them in conditional statements (page 61), in loops (page 78), when creating functions (page 85), and with JSON (page 477):

```
if (score==0) {
    alert('game over');
```

In this example, the closing } is missing, and the script will produce a syntax error.

One approach to overcome the problem of missing closing punctuation marks is to always add them before adding other programming. For example, say you want to end up with the following code:

```
if ((name=='bob') && (score==0)) {
    alert('You lose, but at least you have a great name');
}
```

> **NOTE** Many good text editors include syntax highlighting that highlights matching pairs of parentheses, brackets, and braces. Some editors even identify missing punctuation, so you can quickly fix errors.

Start by typing the outside elements first, creating a basic skeleton for the condition like this:

```
if () {

}
```

At this point, there's not much code, so it's easy to see if you've mistakenly left out any punctuation. Next, add more code, bit by bit, until the program is in place. The same is true when creating a complex JavaScript object literal like the one used to set the options for the Validation plug-in described on page 273, or like a JSON object described on page 477. Start with the basic structure:

```
var options = {

};
```

Then add more structure:

```
var options = {
    rules : {

    },
    messages : {

    }
};
```

Then finish the object:

```
var options = {
  rules : {
    name : 'required',
    email: 'email'
  },
  messages : {
    name : 'Please type your name',
    email: 'Please type your e-mail address.'
  }
};
```

This approach lets you check your work through various steps and makes it a lot easier to identify any mistakes in punctuation. Firefox's Error Console (discussed on page 22) provides the clearest description of syntax error messages. When a script isn't working, preview it in Firefox and review the Error Console. Table 17-1 shows a few of the most common error messages and what they mean.

TABLE 17-1 *Firefox's Error Console's most common error messages and what they mean.*

FIREFOX ERROR MESSAGE	EXPLANATION

Unterminated string literal	Missing opening or closing quote mark:
	`var name = Jane';`
	
	Error also appears with mismatched quote marks:
	`var name = 'Jane";`

Missing) after argument list	Missing closing parenthesis when calling a function or method: `alert('hello" ;`
Missing) after condition	Missing closing parenthesis within a conditional statement: `if (x==0`
Missing (before condition	Missing opening parenthesis within a conditional statement: `if x==0)`

Missing } in compound statement	Missing closing brace as part of conditional loop:
	`if (score == 0) { alert('game over'); // missing`
	`} on this line`

Missing } after property list	Missing closing brace for JavaScript object:
	`var x = { fName: 'bob', lName: 'smith' // miss-`
	`ing } on this line`

Syntax Error	General problem that prevents JavaScript interpreter from reading the script.

FIREFOX ERROR MESSAGE	EXPLANATION
Missing ; before statement	Lets you know when you've run two statements together on a single line, without separating them with a semicolon. You'll also see this when you incorrectly nest quotation marks: `var message='There's an error here.';`
Missing variable name	Appears if you attempt to use a JavaScript reserved word (page 31) for a variable name: `var if="Syntax error.";`

Quotation Marks

Quote marks often trip up beginning programmers. Quote marks are used to create strings of letters and other characters (called "string literals") to use as messages on the page, or as variables in a program. JavaScript, like other programming languages, lets you use either *double* or *single* quote marks to create a string literal. So,

```
var name="Jane";
```

is the same as:

```
var name='Jane';
```

As you read in the previous section, you must include both the opening and closing quote marks, or you'll end up with an "Unterminated string literal" error in Firefox (and all other browsers will give up on your script as well). In addition, as you read on page 28, you must use the same type of quote mark for each pair—in other words, both single quotes or both double quotes. So `var name='Jane"` will also generate an error.

Another common problem can arise with the use of quotations within a string. For example, it's very easy to make the following mistake:

```
var message='There's an error in here.';
```

Notice the single quote in `There's`. The JavaScript interpreter treats that quote mark as a closing quote, so it actually sees this: `var message='There'`, and the rest of the line is seen as an error. In the Firefox error console, you'll get the message "Missing ; before statement," because Firefox thinks that second quote is the end of a simple JavaScript statement and what follows is a second statement.

You can get around this error in two ways. First, you can mix and match double and single quotes. In other words, you can put double quotes around a string with single quotes, or you can put single quotes around a string containing double quotes. For example, you can fix the above error this way:

```
var message="There's no error in here.";
```

Or, if the string contains double quotes:

```
var message='He said, "There is no problem here."';
```

Another approach is to *escape* quote marks within a string literal. Escaping quote marks is discussed in greater detail in the box on page 28, but here's a recap. To escape a character, precede it with a forward slash, like this:

```
var message='There\'s no error here.';
```

The JavaScript interpreter treats \' as a single quote character and not as the symbol used to begin and end strings.

Types of Errors

There are three basic categories of errors that you'll encounter as you program JavaScript. Some of these errors are immediately obvious, while others don't always rear their ugly heads until the script is up and running:

- **Syntax Errors.** A syntax error is essentially a grammatical mistake that makes a web browser's JavaScript interpreter throw up its hands and say, "I give up." Any of the errors involving a missing closing parenthesis, brace, or quote mark generates a syntax error. The web browser encounters syntax errors immediately, as it reads the script, so the script never has a chance to run. An error message for a syntax error always appears in a web browser's error console.

- **Runtime errors.** After a browser reads a script's code successfully and the JavaScript interpreter interprets it, it can still encounter errors. Even if the program's syntax is fine, other problems might pop up as the program runs—called *runtime* errors. For example, say you define a variable named message at the beginning of a script; later in the script, you add a click function to an image so an alert box appears when the image is clicked. Say the alert code for this example looks like this: alert(MESSAGE); . There's nothing wrong with this statement's syntax, but it references the variable MESSAGE instead of lowercase message. As mentioned on page 30, JavaScript is case-sensitive, so MESSAGE and message refer to two different variables. When a visitor clicks the image, the JavaScript interpreter looks for the variable MESSAGE (which doesn't exist) and generates a runtime error.

Another common runtime error occurs when you try to access an element on a page that either doesn't exist

or the browser hasn't yet read into its memory. See the discussion of jQuery's $(document).ready() function on page 160 for more detail on this problem.

- **Logic errors.** Sometimes even though a script seems to run, it doesn't produce the results you're after. For example, you may have an if/else statement (page 61) that performs step A if a condition is true or step B if it's false. Unfortunately, the program never seems to get to step B, even if you're sure the condition is false. This kind of error happens when you use the equality operator incorrectly (page 33). From the JavaScript interpreter's perspective, everything is technically correct, but you've made a mistake in the logic of your programming that prevents the script from working as planned.

Another example of a logic error is an infinite loop, which is a chunk of code that runs *forever*, usually causing your programming to hang up and sometimes even crashing the web browser. Here's an example of an infinite loop:

```
for (var i=1; i>0; i += 1) {
    // this will run forever
}
```

In a nutshell, this loop will run as long as the test condition (i>0) is true. Since i starts out with a value of 1 (var i=1), and each time it goes through the loop i is increased by 1 (i += 1), the value of i will always be greater than 0. In other words, the loop never stops. (Turn to page 78 if you need a refresher on for loops.)

Logic errors are among the most difficult to uncover. However, with the debugging techniques described on page 597, you should be able to uncover many common problems.

Using Reserved Words

As listed on page 31, the JavaScript language has many words that are reserved for its private use. These words include words used in the language's syntax like `if`, `do`, `for`, and `while`, as well as words used as part of the browser object, like `alert`, `location`, `window`, and `document`. These words are not available to use as variable names.

For example, the following code generates a syntax error:

```
var if = "This won't work.";
```

Since *if* is used to create conditional statements—as in `if (x==0)`—you can't use it as a variable name. Some browsers, however, won't generate an error if you use words that are part of the Browser Object Model for your variable names. For example, `document` refers to the HTML document. For example, look at the following code:

```
var document='Something strange is happening here.';
alert(document);
```

Browsers don't generate an error, but instead pop up an alert with the text "[object HTMLDocument]," which refers to the HTML document itself. In other words, those browsers won't let you overwrite the document object with a string.

Single Equals in Conditional Statements

Conditional statements (page 61) provide a way for a program to react in different ways depending upon a value of a variable, the status of an element on a page, or some other condition in the script. For example, a conditional statement can display a picture *if* it's hidden or *else* hide it if it's visible. Conditional statements only make sense, however, if a particular condition can be `true` or `false`. Unfortunately, it's easy to create a conditional statement that's always true:

```
if (score=100) {
    alert('You win!');
}
```

This code is supposed to check the value stored in the variable `score`—if the value is 100, then an alert box with the message "You win!" should appear. However, in this case, the alert message will *always* display, no matter what value is stored in `score` prior to the conditional statement. That's because a single equals sign is an *assignment* operator, so `score=100` stores the value 100 in `score`. The JavaScript interpreter treats an assignment operation as `true`, so not only does the code above always pop up the alert box, it also rewrites the value of `score` to 100.

To avoid this error, make sure use the comparison equality operator when testing whether two values are the same:

```
if (score===100) {
  alert('You win!');
}
```

Case-Sensitivity

Remember that JavaScript is case-sensitive, meaning that the JavaScript interpreter tracks not only the letters in the names of variables, functions, methods, and keywords, but also whether the letters are uppercase or lowercase. So `alert('hi')` is not the same as `ALERT('hi')` to the JavaScript interpreter. The first, `alert('hi')`, calls the browser's built-in `alert()` command, while the second `ALERT('hi')` attempts to call a user-defined function named `ALERT()`.

You can run into this problem if you use the long-winded DOM selection methods—`getElementsByTagName()` or `getElementById()`—because they use both upper and lowercase letters (another good reason to stick with jQuery). Likewise, if you include both upper and lowercase letters in variable and function names, you may run into this problem from time to time.

If you see an "x is not defined" error message (where x is the name of your variable, function, or method), mismatched case may be the problem.

Incorrect Path to External JavaScript File

Another common mistake is incorrectly linking to an external JavaScript file. Page 15 discusses how to attach an external JavaScript file to a web page. Basically, you use the `<script>` tag's `src` property to point to the file. So in the HTML page, you'd add the `<script>` tag to the `<head>` of the document like this:

```
<script src="site_js.js"></script>
```

The `src` property works like a link's `href` property—it defines the path to the JavaScript file. As mentioned in the box on "URL Types", there are three ways you can point to a file: absolute links (*http://www.site.com/site_js.js*), root-relative links (*/site_js.js*), and document-relative links (*site_js.js*).

A document-relative path describes how a web browser gets from the current page (the web page) to a particular file. Document-relative links are commonly used because they let you test your web page and JavaScript file right on your own computer. If you use root-relative links, you'll need to set up a web server on your own computer to test your pages (or move them up to your web server to test them).

You can read more about how link paths work on page 11. But, in a nutshell, if you find that a script doesn't work and you're using external JavaScript files, double check to make sure you've specified the correct path to the JavaScript file.

> **TIP** If you're using the jQuery library and you get the error "$ is not defined" in the error console, you probably haven't correctly linked to the *jquery.js* file (see page 107 for more).

Incorrect Paths Within External JavaScript Files

Another problem related to file paths occurs when using document-relative paths in an external JavaScript file. For example, you might create a script that displays images on a page (like a slideshow or just a "random image of the day" script). If the script uses document-relative links to point to the images, you can run into trouble if you put that script into an external JavaScript file. Here's why: When an external JavaScript file is loaded into a web page, its frame of reference for document-relative paths is the location of the web page itself. So, any document-relative paths you include in the JavaScript file must be relative to the *web page* and not the JavaScript file.

Here's a simple example to illustrate this problem. Figure 17-2 represents the structure of a very simple website. There are two web pages (*page.html* and *about.html*), four folders (*libs*, *images*, *pages*, and *about*), an external JavaScript file (*site_js.js* inside the *libs* folder) and an image (*photo.jpg* in the *images* folder.) Say the *site_js.js* file references the *photo.jpg* file—perhaps to preload the image (page 212), or display it dynamically on a web page.

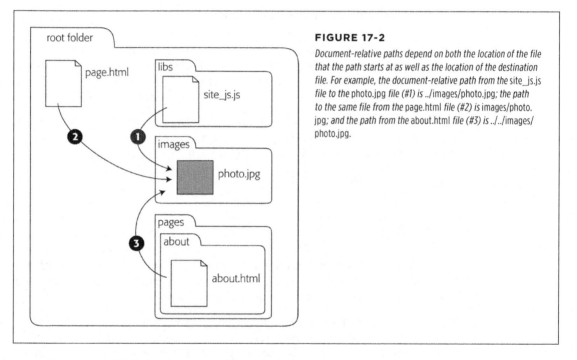

FIGURE 17-2

Document-relative paths depend on both the location of the file that the path starts at as well as the location of the destination file. For example, the document-relative path from the site_js.js file to the photo.jpg file (#1) is ../images/photo.jpg; the path to the same file from the page.html file (#2) is images/photo.jpg; and the path from the about.html file (#3) is ../../images/photo.jpg.

From the *site_js.js* file's perspective, a document-relative path to the *photo.jpg* file is *../images/photo.jpg* (#1 in Figure 14-2). The path tells the browser to exit the *libs* folder (*../*), enter the *images* folder (*images/*), and select the *photo.jpg* file. However, from the perspective of the *page.html* file, the path to the *photo.jpg* file (#2 in Figure 14-2) is just *images/photo.jpg*. In other words, the path to the same photo differs between the two files.

If you want to use the *site_js.js* script within the *page.html* file, then, you have to use path #2 in the *site_js.js* file to reference the location of *photo.jpg* (that is, specify a path relative to *page.html*). By the same token, you can't use the *site_js.js* file in a web page located in another directory in your site because the relative path would be different for that file (#3 in Figure 17-2).

There are a few ways around this problem. First, well, you may never encounter it—you may not find yourself listing paths to other files in your JavaScript files. But if you do, you can use site root-relative paths (page 11), which are the same from any page in the site. Alternatively, you can define the path to the files within each web page. For example, you can link to the external JavaScript file, and then, in each web page, define variables to hold document-relative paths from the current web page to the correct file.

Finally, you could use an approach like the one used in the photo gallery on page 220. The paths come from the web page and are embedded within links on the page—the JavaScript simply pulls the paths out of the HTML. As long as those paths work in the HTML, they'll work in a script as well.

Disappearing Variables and Functions

You may occasionally encounter an "*x* is not defined" error, where *x* is either the name of a variable or a function you're trying to call. The problem may just be that you mistyped the name of the variable or function, or used the wrong case. However, if you look through your code and can clearly see that the variable or function is defined in your script, then you may be running into a "scope" problem.

Variable and function scope is discussed in greater detail on page 92, but in a nutshell, if a variable is defined inside of a function, it's only available to that function (or to other functions defined inside that function). Here's a simple example:

```
1  function sayName(name) {
2    var message = 'Your name is ' + name;
3  }
4  sayName();
5  alert(message); // error: message is not defined
```

The variable message is defined within the function sayName(), so it only exists for that function. Outside the function, message doesn't exist, so an error is generated when the script tries to access the variable outside the function (line 5).

You may also encounter this error when using jQuery. On page 160, you read about the importance of the $(document).ready() function for jQuery. Anything inside that function only runs once the page's HTML is loaded. You'll run into problems if you define variables or functions within the $(document).ready() function and try to access them outside of it, like this:

```
$(document).ready(function() {
  var msg = 'hello';
});
alert(msg); // error: msg is not defined
```

So, when using jQuery, be sure to put all of your programming inside the $(document).ready() function:

```
$(document).ready(function() {
  var msg = 'hello';
```

```
    alert(msg); // msg is available
});
```

Programming Tips to Reduce Errors

The best way to deal with errors and bugs in your programs is to try to stop them as early as possible. It can be really difficult to track down the cause of errors in a program if you wait until you've written a 300-line script before testing it in a web browser. The two most important tips to avoiding errors are:

- **Build a script in small chunks.** As you've probably figured out by now, JavaScript programs can be difficult to read, what with all of the },), ', ifs, elses, functions, and so on. Don't try to write an entire script in one go (unless you're really good, the script is short, or you're feeling lucky). There are so many ways to make a mistake while programming, and you're better off writing a script in bits.

  For example, say you want to display the number of letters typed into a form field, right next to the field. In other words, as a visitor types into the field, a running total of the number of letters typed appears next to the box. (Some sites do this when they limit the amount a visitor can type into a field—say, 300 letters.) This task is pretty easy JavaScript, but it involves several steps: responding to the keydown event (when a visitor types a letter in the field), reading the value of that field,

counting the numbers of characters in the field, and then displaying that number on the page. You can try to write this script in one go, but you can also write the code for step 1 (responding to a keydown event) and then test it immediately in a web browser (using the `alert()` command or `console.log()` function, described on the next page, can help you see the results of a keydown event). If it works, you can then move on to step 2, test it, and so on.

  As you gain more experience, you won't need to test such small steps. You can write a few steps at once, and then test that chunk.

- **Test frequently.** You should also test your script in a web browser frequently. At a minimum, test after you complete each chunk of the program, as suggested in the previous point. In addition, you should test the script in different browsers—preferably Internet Explorer 8, and above; the latest versions of Chrome, Firefox, and Safari; and whatever other browsers you think your site's visitors might be using.

▮ Debugging with the Console

If you haven't been using your web browser's JavaScript console, you've been missing out on one of the best tools a web designer could have. All major web browser have a built-in JavaScript console that can help you improve your HTML, CSS, and JavaScript.

Opening the Console

To use the console, open a web page in your browser. Then use one of these methods:

- **Google Chrome.** Click the Chrome settings button (circled in Figure 17-3) and choose Tools→JavaScript Console. Or use the keyboard shortcut, Ctrl-Shift-J (Windows) or ⌘-Option-J (Mac).

- **Internet Explorer.** Press the F12 key to open the Developer Tools panel. Click the Console tab to display the JavaScript console.

- **Firefox.** To open the console, on Windows, click the Firefox tab in the top left of the browser window and choose Web Developer→Web Console. On a Mac, select Tools→Web Developer→Web Console. Or use the keyboard shortcuts Ctrl+Shift+I (Windows) and ⌘-Option-K (Mac).

- **Safari.** Safari's error console is available from the Develop menu: Develop→Show Error Console (⌘-Option-C). However, the Develop menu isn't normally turned on when Safari is installed, so you need to turn it on in Preferences. Choose Safari→Preferences. Once the Preferences window opens, click the Advanced button. Turn on the "Show Develop menu in menu bar" checkbox and then close the Preferences window.

  When you restart Safari, the Develop menu will appear between the Bookmarks and Window menus in the menu bar at the top of the screen on a Mac; and on Windows, you'll find it under the page icon in the top right of the browser. Select Develop→Show Error Console to open the console.

Viewing Errors with the Console

The console lists any errors that occur in your JavaScript. First, it identifies the first syntax error on the page. As you read on page 18, syntax errors are like grammatical mistakes. When the browser's JavaScript interpreter encounters a syntax error, it just throws up its hands and quits. It lets you know about that error, but, if there are more syntax errors on the page, you won't know about them until you fix the first one.

Once the syntax errors are fixed, you may begin encountering *runtime* errors (page 582)—errors that the browser tells you about as the program is running. For example, trying to access a variable that was never created causes an error. The console should be your first line of defense when you need to track down errors in your code (Figure 17-3).

Using console.log() to Track Script Progress

Once a script begins to run, it's kind of like a black box. You don't really know what's going on inside the script and only see the end result, like a message on the page, a pop-up window, and so on. You can't always tell exactly whether a loop is working correctly or see the value of a particular variable at any point in time.

JavaScript programmers have long used the alert() method (page 12) to pop up a window with the current value of a variable. For example, if you want to know what value is being stored in the variable elementName as a loop is running, you can insert an alert command inside the loop: alert(elementName);. That's one way to look into the "black box" of the script. However, the alert box is pretty intrusive: You have to click it to close it, and in a loop that might run 20 times, that's a lot of pop-up alerts to close.

The JavaScript console provides a better way to look into your program. It not only lists errors (see previous section), but can also be used to output messages from the program. The console.log() function works similar to the document.write()

function (page 15), but instead of printing a message to the web page, `console.log()` prints a message to the console.

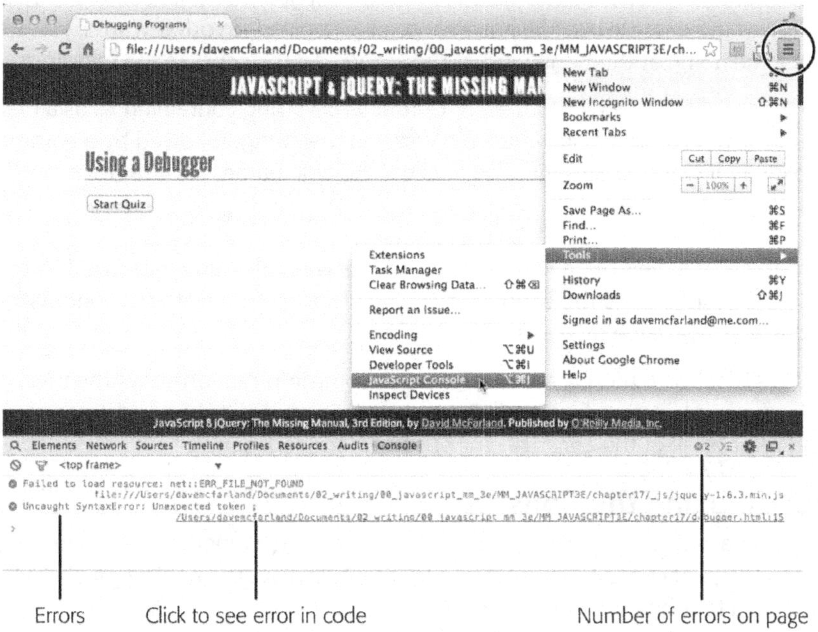

FIGURE 17-3

The JavaScript console lists any JavaScript errors the browser has encountered on the current page. In Chrome, pictured here, you can open the console by clicking the Chrome Setting button (circled) and choosing Tools→JavaScript Console. To see the exact line of code on which the error was encountered, click the code snippet under the error. The browser then switches from the console tab to the Sources tab and highlights the line where the error happened.

Errors   Click to see error in code   Number of errors on page

TIP All current browsers support the `console.log()` method. So you can use it in Chrome, Safari, Internet Explorer, Firefox, and Opera's consoles.

For example, you could print the current value of the variable `elementName` to the console using this code:

```
console.log(elementName);
```

Unlike the `alert()` method, this method won't interrupt your program's flow—you'll just see the message in the console.

To make the log message more understandable, you can include a string with additional text. For example, if you have a variable named `name` and you want to determine what value is stored in `name` at some point in your program, you can use the `console.log()` function like this:

```
console.log(name);
```

But if you wanted to precede the name with a message, you can write this:

```
console.log('User name:', name);
```

This line would print a single line to the console with "User name:" followed by the value stored in the name variable.

But what if you wanted to place variable values somewhere *within* the string? For example, say you're tracking a user's name and score. You'd like to write a clear message to the console like "Jill has a score of 50 points." In other words, you want to place the name at the beginning of the string and the score in the middle.

To do this, you'd pass the console.log() function a string containing %s as a place-holder for each variable you wanted to insert in the string, followed by a comma, a variable name, another comma, and another variable name. For example:

```
console.log('%s has a score of %s points', name, score);
```

The special %s is way of saying "substitute the variable value with me." In other words, the first %s gets replaced with the value of name, and the second %s gets replaces with the value of score.

The log() function is merely a way to give you some information about the function-ing of your script as you *develop* it. Once your program is finished and working, you should remove all of the console.log() code from your script.

Tutorial: Using the Console

In this tutorial, you'll learn how to use the console.log() function to see what's go-ing on inside your code. You'll create a script that displays the number of characters typed into a text box on a form.

> **NOTE** See the note on page 12 for information on how to download the tutorial files.

This tutorial is shown in the Google Chrome browser. You can follow along in your favorite browser, but it may behave a bit differently from Chrome.

1. **Open the file *console.html* in a text editor.**

   This script uses the jQuery library. The external jQuery file is already attached to the page, and the opening and closing <script> tags are in place. You'll start by adding jQuery's $(document).ready() function.

2. **Between the <script> tags near the top of the page, add the code in bold below:**

   ```
   <script>
   $(document).ready(function() {

   }); // end ready
   </script>
   ```

   You learned about the basic $(document).ready() function on page 160, which makes the browser load all of the page's code before starting to run any JavaScript. You'll first use the `console.log()` function to simply print out a message that the script has executed the `.ready()` function.

3. **Add the bolded code below to the script:**

```
<script>
$(document).ready(function() {
  console.log('READY');
}); // end ready
</script>
```

The `console.log()` function runs wherever you place it in the script. In other words, after this page's HTML is loaded (that's what the `ready()` function waits for), the browser writes "READY" to the console. Adding the `ready()` function is a pretty common and basic move, so you may not always add a `console.log()` function here, but for this tutorial, you'll add one to see how the `log()` function works. In fact, you'll be adding a lot of log messages to this page to get the hang of the `console.log()` function.

4. **Save the file, and open it in Chrome. If the console isn't already open, type Ctrl+Shift+J (Windows) or ⌘-Option-J (Macs).**

The word READY should appear in the console (circled in Figure 17-4). The script you're creating will display the number of characters typed into a form's text field each time your visitor types a character. To accomplish this, you'll add a keyup event (page 152) to that text box. During each step of this script, you'll also add a *console.log()* function, to clue you in to what's happening.

5. **After the line of code you added in step 3, add the following:**

```
$('#comments').keyup(function() {
  console.log('Event: keyup');
}); // end keyup
```

Make sure you place this code inside the `$(document).ready()` function.

The `<textarea>` tag on this page has an ID of comments, so you can select that element using jQuery (`$('#comments')`) and add a function to the keyup event (see page 152 if you need a refresher on adding events). In this case, the console.log() function is just printing a status message to the JavaScript console telling you each time the keyup event is triggered. This function is an easy way to see whether an event function is actually running or something's preventing the event from happening.

Save the page; reload it in the browser and type a few characters into the text box. Make sure the JavaScript console is open, and you should see "Event: keyup" in the console. A number will also appear near this message (on the left of the log message in some cases and to the right in others). The number indicates how many times this particular console.log() message has been printed.

Now that the keyup event is working, you might want to retrieve the contents of the text box and store it in a variable. To be sure you're getting the information you're after, you'll print the contents of the variable to the console.

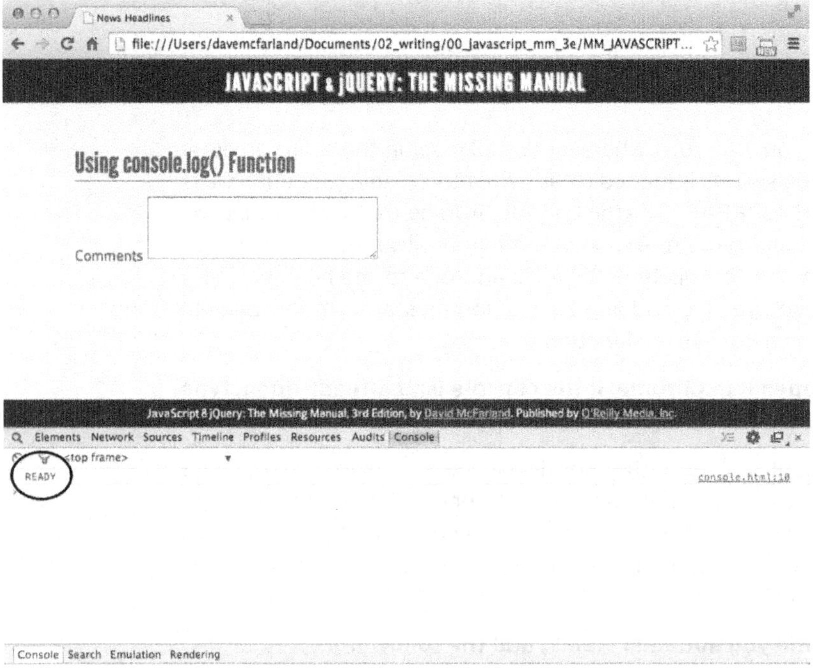

FIGURE 17-4

You can use the browser's console to write secret messages. But, it's more useful for displaying notes as you debug a program. In this case, a simple message—"Ready"—indicates that the program has successfully run jQuery's $(document). ready() *function.*

6. **Add lines 3 and 4 to the code you typed in step 5:**

```
1   $('#comments').keyup(function() {
2       console.log('Event: keyup');
3       var text = $(this).val();
4       console.log('Contents of comments:',text);
5   }); // end keyup
```

Line 3 retrieves the value from the text box and stores it inside a variable named text (see page 255 for more information on extracting the value from a form field). Line 4 writes a message to the console. In this case, it combines a string 'Contents of comments:' and the value currently stored in the text box. When a program isn't working correctly, a very common diagnostic step is to print out the values of variables in the script to make sure the variable contains the information you're expecting it to have.

7. **Save the file, reload it in your browser, and type some text into the comments box.**

   The console should now display the contents in the comments box each time you type a letter into the field. By now you should be getting the hang of the console, so you'll add one more message, and then finish this script.

8. **Edit the keyup event function by adding two more lines (5 and 6):**

```
1  $('#comments').keyup(function() {
2    console.log('Event: keyup');
3    var text = $(this).val();
4    console.log('Contents of comments:',text);
5    var chars = text.length;
6    console.log('Number of characters:',chars);
7  }); // end keyup
```

   Line 5 counts the number of characters stored inside the text variable (see page 541 for more on the length property) and stores it inside the variable chars. Just to make sure the script is correctly calculating the number of characters, use the log() function (line 6) to print a message to the console.

   There's just one last thing to do: Finish the script so it prints the number of characters typed so your visitor can see it.

9. **Add one last line to the end of the keyup event function (line 10), so the completed script for the page looks like this:**

```
1  <script>
2  $(document).ready(function() {
3    console.log('READY');
4    $('#comments').keyup(function() {
5      console.log('Event: keyup');
6      var text = $(this).val();
7      console.log('Contents of comments: %s',text);
8      var chars = text.length;
9      console.log('Number of characters: %s',chars);
10     $('#count').text(chars + " characters");
11   }); // end keyup
12  }); // end ready
13  </script>
```

10. **Save the file, and preview it in your browser.**

    The console should now look something like Figure 17-5. You'll find a finished version of this tutorial—*complete_console.html*—in the *chapter17* folder in this chapter's tutorial files.

NOTE Once you have functioning code, you should remove all console.log() code from your script. The log() function will generate errors in some browsers.

More Powerful Debugging

The JavaScript console is a great way to print out messages so you can see what's going on when a program runs. But sometimes a program zips by so quickly it's hard to see what's going on during each step. You need a way to slow things down. Fortunately, browsers contain powerful JavaScript debuggers, which let you step through a script line by line so you can see what's happening at each step of the program.

> **NOTE** The Chrome is shown in this section, but you'll find similar JavaScript debuggers in Firefox, Opera, Safari, and Internet Explorer.

Debugging is the process of fixing an incorrectly functioning program—getting the bugs out. To really understand how a program is functioning (or malfunctioning), you need to see how the program works, step by step.

To use the debugger, you mark certain lines of code as *breakpoints*. A breakpoint is a spot where the JavaScript interpreter stops running and waits. You can then use controls inside the debugger that let you run a program one line at a time. In this way, you can see exactly what's happening at any particular line. Here's the basic process.

1. **Open a web page in a web browser.**

   Remember, these instructions are shown in the Chrome web browser and its debugger. In other browsers' debuggers, the exact steps and panels will differ.

2. **Open the JavaScript console.**

   Follow the instructions on page 18 for opening your browser's developer tools. In Chrome, you can open the JavaScript console with the keyboard shortcuts Ctrl+Shift+J (Windows) or ⌘-Option-J (Mac).

3. **Click the Sources tab and, from the files list, select the file containing the JavaScript you wish to debug (Figure 17-6).**

   In Chrome, the Sources tab lists the source code for the file you wish to debug. In the case of a script that's written into a web page, you see the source code for the entire web page (including the HTML). For an external JavaScript file, you see just the JavaScript in that file.

4. **Select the file with the script you wish to debug from the list of files on the left of the debugger (Figure 17-6).**

   It's common to have scripts placed in different files: the web page itself, or one or more external JavaScript files. If your page uses scripts from multiple files, you need to select the file containing the script you wish to debug.

5. **Add breakpoints.**

   To add a breakpoint, click to the left of the line's number. A marker appears around the line number.

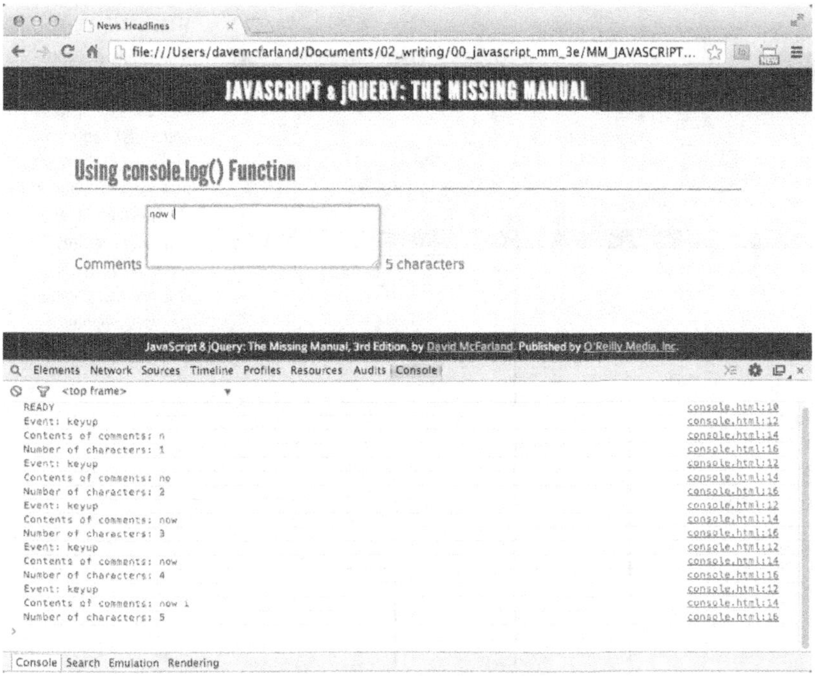

FIGURE 17-5

The JavaScript console is a great way to print out diagnostic information as a program is running. You can also group together a series of log entries (for example, to group all the log messages printed during a loop) by adding console.group() *before the first* console.log() *message in the group, and* console.groupEnd() *after the last message.*

> **NOTE** Adding a breakpoint to a line that only contains a comment has no effect—the debugger won't stop on that line. Only add breakpoints to lines containing actual JavaScript code.

6. **Reload the web page.**

   Because you have to view your web page in the browser to add breakpoints, the JavaScript you want to debug may have already run (before you added any breakpoints). In this case, you need to reload the page so you can start the JavaScript over again.

   If you added a breakpoint in a function that responds to an event (for example, you want to debug the code that runs when you click a button or mouse over a link), then you need to trigger that event—click the button, mouse over the link, or whatever—to reach the breakpoint and start the debugging process.

   After the script begins to run, as soon as a breakpoint is reached, the script stops. The program is frozen in time, waiting to execute the line from the first breakpoint.

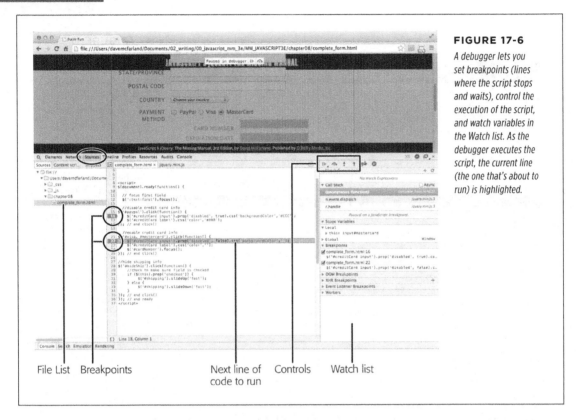

FIGURE 17-6

A debugger lets you set breakpoints (lines where the script stops and waits), control the execution of the script, and watch variables in the Watch list. As the debugger executes the script, the current line (the one that's about to run) is highlighted.

File List   Breakpoints   Next line of   Controls   Watch list
                                            code to run

7. **Use the debugger's controls to step through the execution of the program.**

   Most debuggers provide four controls (Figure 17-7) that dictate how the program runs after stopping at the breakpoint. You can read about these controls in the next section.

8. **Monitor program conditions in the watch list (Figure 17-7).**

   The point of stepping through a program is to see what's going on inside the script at any particular line. The watch list provides basic information about the program's condition and lets you add additional variables you want to watch. For example, if you wanted to track the value of the variable score as the script runs, you can do that in the watch list. You'll find out how to use the watch list on page 608.

9. **Fix your script in a text editor.**

   Hopefully, in stepping through your script you'll find out what's going wrong—for example, why the value of a particular variable never changes, or why a conditional statement never evaluates to false. With that information, you can then jump to your text editor and modify your script (you'll run through an example of fixing a script in the tutorial on page 609).

10. **Test the page in the browser, and, if necessary, repeat the previous steps to keep debugging your script.**

■ CONTROLLING YOUR SCRIPT WITH THE DEBUGGER

Once you've added breakpoints to the script and reloaded the page, you're ready to step through the script line by line. If you added a breakpoint to part of the script that runs when the page loads, the script will stop at the breakpoint; if you added a breakpoint to a line that only runs after an event (like clicking a link), you need to trigger that event before you can get to the breakpoint.

When the debugger stops the program at a breakpoint, it doesn't run that line of code; it stops just *before* running it. You can then click one of the four buttons on the debugger to control what the debugger does next (Figure 17-7):

- **Play.** The Play button simply starts the script running. The script won't stop again until the JavaScript interpreter encounters another breakpoint, or until the script has finished running. If there's another breakpoint, the script stops again and waits for you to click one of the four debugger controls.

  Use the Play button if you just want run the program through or skip to the next breakpoint.

- **Step Over.** This useful option runs the current line of code, then stops at the next line in the script. It's named Step Over because if the current line of code includes a call to a function, it won't display the function's code or stop at the first line inside the function—it simply runs the function (*steps over* it) and stops at the next line of code. This option is great if you know the function that's being called works flawlessly. For example, if your script calls a jQuery function, you'll want to step over the call to that function—otherwise, you'll be spending a lot of time viewing the scary jQuery programming line by line. You'll choose the Step Over option, unless you're at a line of code that calls a function you've created—then you'll probably want to see what happens inside that function using the Step Into option described next.

- **Step Into.** Step Into takes the debugger into a function call. That is, if you're on a line that includes a call to a function, the debugger enters the function and stops at the first line of that function. This option is the way to go when you're not sure if the problem is in the main script or within a function you wrote.

  Skip this option if you're sure that the function being called works—for example, if the function is one you've used dozens of times before. You also want to use Step Over instead of Step Into when you're debugging a line of code that includes a jQuery selector or command. For example, $('#button') is a jQuery way to select an element on the page. However, it's also a function of the jQuery library, so if you click the Step Into button when you encounter a jQuery function, you'll jump into the complex world of the jQuery library. (And if that happens, you'll know because the script tab will change to show all of the JavaScript code for the jQuery file.)

If, when using the debugger, you find yourself lost within a function, or in the code of a JavaScript library like jQuery, you can use the control described next to get out.

- **Step Out.** The Step Out button gets the debugger out of a function call. You'll usually use it after using Step Into. When you do, the function runs as normal, but you won't stop at each line of the function as you would if you clicked the Step Over or Step Into buttons. When you click this button, the debugger returns to the line where the function was originally called and then stops.

■ WATCHING YOUR SCRIPT

While the buttons at the top of the debugger let you control how the script executes, the whole point of a debugger is to see what's going on inside the script. That's where the watch list comes in (Figure 17-7). The watch list provides a listing of variables and functions within the context of the current executing line of code. All that means is if you put a breakpoint within a function, you'll see a list of all of the variables that are defined within that function; if you put a breakpoint in the main body of your script, you'll see a list of all variables that are defined there. You'll also see any functions that you've created listed in the watch list.

You can add your own variables and expressions using the yellow bar with the label "New watch expression…". Just click the yellow bar, and a text field appears. Type the name of a variable you'd like to track, or even a JavaScript statement you'd like to execute. For example, because the debugger doesn't keep track of a counter variable in a for loop (page 82), you can add this variable, and as you go step by step through the loop, you can see how the counter changes each time through the loop.

You can think of this watch list as a kind of a continual `console.log()` command. It prints out the value of a particular variable or expression at the time a particular line of code is run.

The watch list offers valuable insight into your program, providing a kind of freeze-frame effect so you can find exactly where in your script an error occurs. For example, if you know that a particular variable holds a number value, you can go step by step through the script and see what value gets stored in the variable when it's first created and see how its value gets modified as the program runs. If, after you click the Step Through or Step Into buttons, you see the variable's value change to something you didn't expect, then you've probably found the line where the error is introduced.

> **NOTE** Keep in mind that when the program is paused, the debugger highlights the line of code that's going to run next. So if that line sets the value of a variable, you won't see that new value in the watch list until you click the Step Through button.

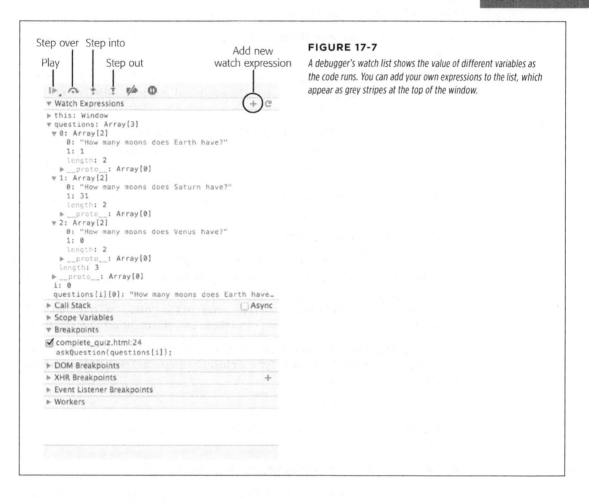

FIGURE 17-7

A debugger's watch list shows the value of different variables as the code runs. You can add your own expressions to the list, which appear as grey stripes at the top of the window.

▊ Debugging Tutorial

In this tutorial, you'll use Firebug to debug a file that's filled with various types of errors (syntax errors, runtime errors, and logic errors). The page is a simple quiz program that poses three questions and prints quiz results. (Open the *complete_debugger.html* file in the *chapter17* folder in any web browser to see how the page is supposed to work.)

NOTE   See the note on page 12 for information on how to download the tutorial files.

Like the other tutorials in this chapter, this one is run in Chrome. You can try it with another web browser, but the JavaScript Console and debugger may look different than what you see on these pages.

1. **Start Chrome and open the file *debugger.html* from the *chapter17* tutorials folder.**

   Open the JavaScript console: click the Chrome settings button and choose Tools→JavaScript Console. Or, use the keyboard shortcut, Ctrl+Shift+J (Windows) or ⌘-Option-J (Mac).

   The Console reports two errors on this page. You'll tackle the second one first. That error is listed as an "Uncaught SyntaxError: Unexpected token ; " error. The meaning is not immediately obvious, but it says that the browser didn't expect to run into a ; at this point. Given that the semicolon marks the end of a statement, there must be something wrong with that statement. Notice, also, that the line number of the error is listed (circled in Figure 17-8).

2. **Click the line number (circled at top in Figure 17-8).**

   Chrome opens the Sources panel, and highlights the line with the problem. Remember that a lot of bugs are often simple typos. One common mistake is forgetting to add a closing, matching punctuation mark like a), ",] or }, so you may be able to spot the problem right away. In this case, you've got an array that starts on line 11—var quiz = [—but there's no end to the array, no closing].

3. **Launch your text editor and open the file *debugger.html*. Locate line 15 (it's a single ; on a line by itself). Type a closing square bracket before the ; so the line looks like this:**

   ```
   ];
   ```

   This bracket ended a nested array that contained all of the questions and answers for the quiz.

4. **Save the file; return to Chrome, and reload the page.**

   One of the original errors is still there. And, there's another error! This time the error console says "$ is not defined" and points to line 8 containing jQuery's $(document).ready() function. When a browser reports that something's "not defined," it means the code is referring to something that doesn't exist, which could be the name of a variable or a function that hasn't yet been created. Or you might just have a typo in the code. In this case, the code looks OK. The culprit is actually earlier on the page, in this code:

   ```
   <script src="_js/jquery.min.js"></script>
   ```

   A common problem when working with external scripts is accidentally typing the wrong path to the script. In this case, the *jquery.min.js* file is located inside a folder named *_js* that's *outside* this file's folder. The code here says that the file should be inside a folder named *_js* that's in the same folder as this web page;

because the browser can't find the *jquery.min.js* file (where jQuery's special $( ) function is defined), it spits out an error.

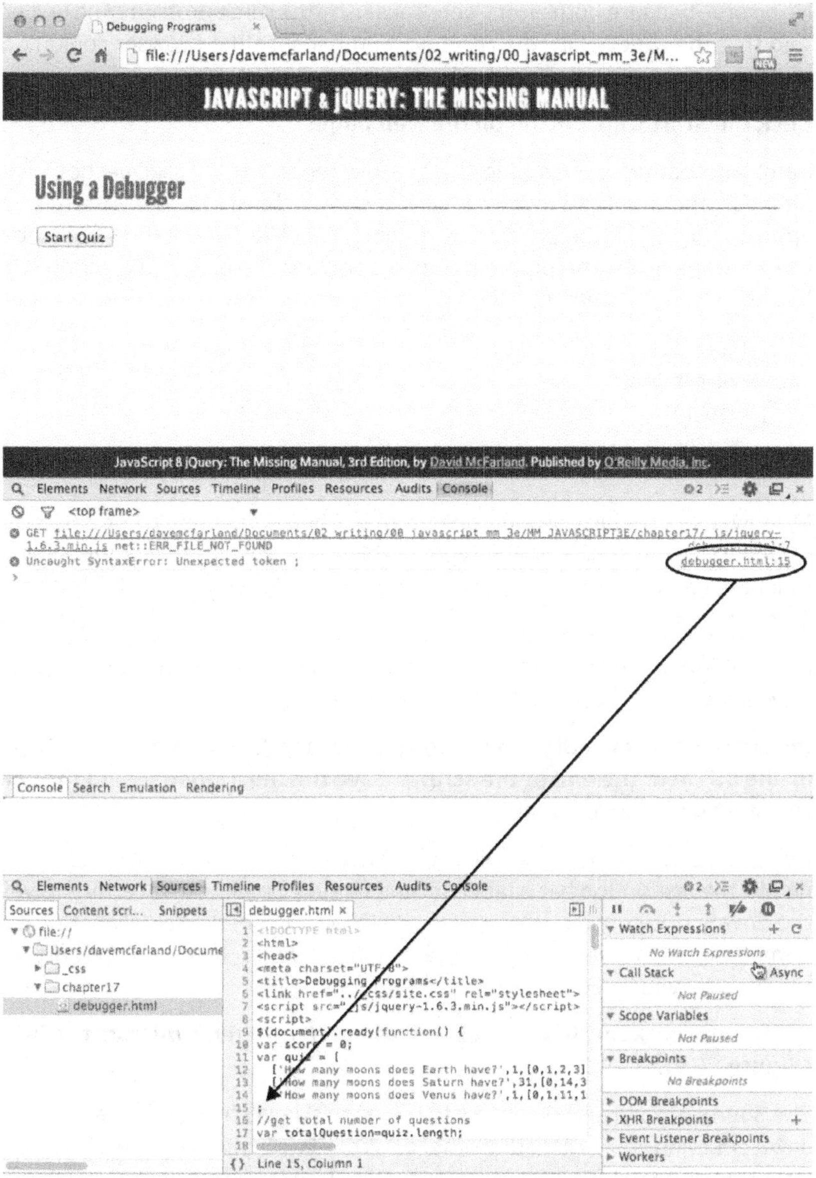

FIGURE 17-8

You can jump from the console to the spot in your code where an error occurs by clicking the line number listed next to the error in the console (circled). The Sources panel appears, and the spot where the error was found is highlighted.

5. **Change the `<script>` tag to read:**

```
<script src="../_js/jquery.min.js"></script>
```

The ../ indicates that the *js* folder is outside this folder, and the path is now correctly pointing to the jQuery file. What else could be wrong with this program?

6. **Save the file; return to the browser and reload the page.**

No errors—because both errors were caused by the same problem. The first error said that the jQuery file wasn't found, and because the browser couldn't find that file, it didn't know what the $ meant. Looks like the page is fixed...or is it?

7. **Click the Start Quiz button on the web page.**

Bam! Another error. This time the console reports that "askQuestions is not defined" and points to line 69 near the end of the script. Because this error appears only while the program is running, it's called a runtime error (see the box on page 592). The problem appears toward the end of the script, within this conditional statement:

```
if (quiz.length>0) {
  askQuestions();
} else {
  giveResults();
}
```

By now it's probably dawning on you that when something's not defined, it's often just because of a simple typo. In this case, askQuestions() is a call to a function, so take a moment now to look through the code and try to find this function.

Did you find it? While there isn't an askQuestions() function, you should have noticed an askQuestion() function (without an *s*).

8. **Return to your text editor, and then remove the last *s* from askQuestions() in line 69 (near the end of the script). Save the file, reload it, and then click the Start Quiz button again.**

Now, a quiz question appears along with five multiple-choice options. Unfortunately, the last option has a label of "undefined." Smells like an error. However, the JavaScript console is empty, so technically there's no JavaScript error. Something must be wrong with the program's *logic.* To get to the bottom of the trouble, you'll need to use the debugger.

9. **In Chrome, click the Sources tab and select *debugger.html* from the file list (Figure 17-9).**

The Sources tab gives you access to the page's JavaScript. If the page includes JavaScript and you've linked to other external JavaScript files, the Source menu lets you choose which JavaScript code you wish to debug.

Because the "undefined" radio button seems to be out of place, the code that creates the radio buttons is a good place to start looking for this bug. If you had written this script, you'd probably know just where to look in your code;

however, if you were just handed this buggy script, you'd have to hunt around until you found that part of the script.

In this case, the radio buttons are created within a function named `buildAnswers()`, whose purpose is to build a series of multiple choice options represented by radio buttons. That function is passed an array that includes a list of values for each radio button. When the function is done, it returns a string containing the HTML for the radio buttons. So this function's a good place to start debugging.

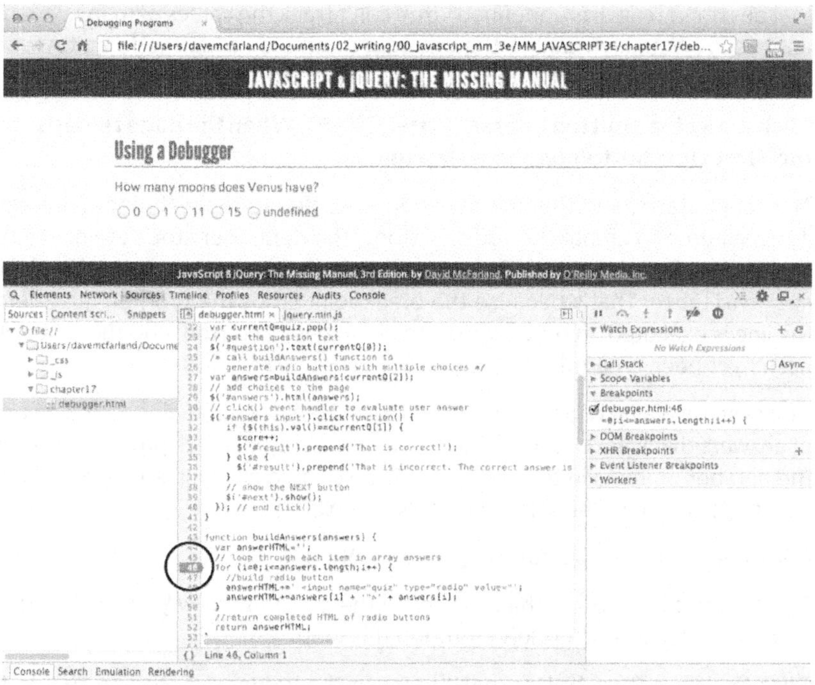

FIGURE 17-9

In Firebug, you can debug any scripts that the current page uses. The Source menu lets you select the JavaScript embedded in the current web page or from any attached external JavaScript file.

10. **In the middle pane of the Sources tab (the part listing the HTML and JavaScript for the page) scroll down until you see line 47. Click to the left of 46 to insert a breakpoint (circled in Figure 17-9).**

   That line number is highlighted, indicating a breakpoint, or a spot in the code, where the JavaScript interpreter stops running the script. In other words, when this script runs again, the moment the JavaScript interpreter hits that line, it stops, and you'll be able to step line by line through the code to see what's happening under the hood.

   The debugger also lets you look at the values of variables as the program runs, much as you used the `console.log()` function on page 598. You'll tell the debugger what variables you want to track next.

---

11. **In the right side of the window, click the + button (just to the right of "Watch Expressions"), type i, and then press the Return (or Enter) key.**

    This step adds the variable i to the Watch list. That variable is used in the for loop as a counter to track how many times the loop runs (see page 78 for more on for loops). As the script runs, you'll be able to see how that value changes. Next, you'll add another variable to watch.

12. **Click the New Watch Expression bar again, type answers.length, and then hit Return.**

    Don't worry about the value the debugger displays at this point (it probably says that answers.length is undefined). You can't track the values of many variables until you're actually running the debugger and are inside the function where the variable lives. Now it's time to take a look inside the script.

13. **Click the Reload button or press Ctrl+R (⌘-R). When the page reloads, click the Start Quiz button on the web page.**

    The script starts, and the first question is written to the web page. But when it comes time to create the radio buttons, the debugger stops at line 46 (see the top image in Figure 17-10). Notice that in the Watch tab, the value for i is not available. That's because the breakpoint stops the program just before the line is executed. In other words, the loop hasn't started, and the i variable hasn't yet been created.

    However, the value of answers.length is set to 4. The array answers is an array of answers that was passed to the function. An array's length property indicates the number of items in the array; in this case there are four, so you should get four radio buttons when the function's completed.

14. **Click the Step Over button (Figure 17-10).**

    This button takes you to the next line in the program. Now you can see that i is set to 0. You'll keep clicking through this loop.

15. **Click the Step Over button until you see the value of i change to 5 in the watch list (bottom image in Figure 17-10).**

    Although there are only four items in the answers array, you can see that the for loop is actually running five times (the value of i). So something's funny about how the loop is terminated. Remember that in a for loop, the middle expression in the for statement is the condition that must be true for the loop to run (page 82). In this case, the condition is i<=answers.length;. In other words, the loop starts out with i containing 0 and continues to run as long as i is less than or equal to the number of items in the answers array. In other words, i will be 0, 1, 2, 3, and 4 before it terminates—that's five times. However, because there are only four items in the answers array, the fifth time through the loop there are no more answers to print: "undefined" is printed because there is no fifth item in the answers array.

16. **Return to your text editor, and change the for loop at line 46 to read:**

```
for (i=0;i<answers.length;i++) {
```

Now the loop only runs for the number of items in the answers array, creating one radio button for each possible answer.

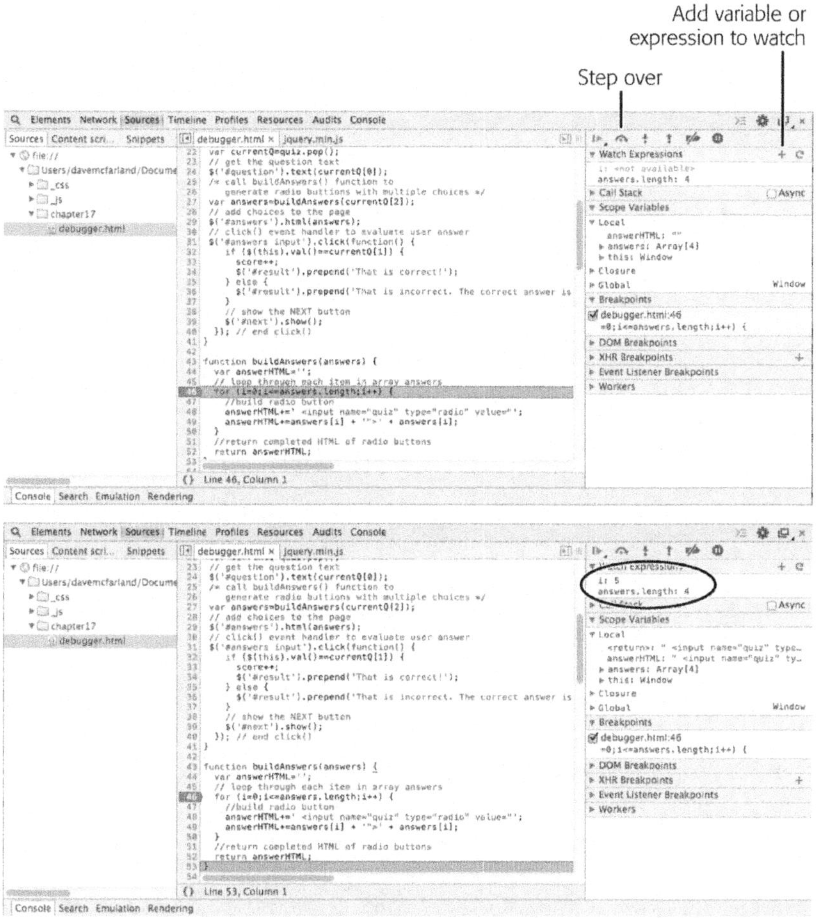

Add variable or
expression to watch

Step over

FIGURE 17-10

The watch list can display more than just the variables or expressions that you add. The Scope Variables section, for example, lists all of the variables inside the "scope" of the current function. In this example (top image) you can see that the variable answerHTML and answers are both variables accessible within the buildAnswers() function.

17. **Save the file, and preview it in the browser.**

You can turn off the breakpoint by clicking its highlighted line number in the Sources panel to see the finished page run without interruption.

The page *complete_debugger.html* contains the completed version of this tutorial. As you can see, finding bugs in a program can take a lot of work. But a debugging tool makes it a lot easier to see inside a program's "guts" and find out what's going wrong.

Appendix

APPENDIX A:
JavaScript Resources

JavaScript Resources

This book provides enough information and real-world techniques to get your JavaScript career off to a great start. But no one book can answer all of your JavaScript or jQuery questions. There's plenty to learn when it comes to JavaScript programming, and this appendix gives you taking-off points for further research and learning.

References

Sometimes you need a dictionary to read a book. When programming in JavaScript, it's great to have a complete reference to the various keywords, terms, methods, and other assorted bits of JavaScript syntax. You can find references both online and in books.

Websites

- The **ECMAScript** site (*www.ecmascript.org*) houses documentation and information about ECMAScript (the official name for JavaScript). It's where to learn about the current state (and future) of JavaScript.

- **Mozilla Developer Center Core JavaScript Reference** (*https://developer.mozilla.org/en-US/docs/Web/JavaScript/Reference*) provides a complete reference to JavaScript. It's very detailed, but sometimes hard to understand because it's aimed at a technical audience.

- **WebPlatform.org** (*http://www.webplatform.org*) covers JavaScript, DOM, and CSS and tells you which features are supported by each browser. It's a kind of encyclopedia for Web developers.

- **MSDN JavaScript Language Reference** (*http://msdn.microsoft.com/en-us/library/d1et7k7c(v=VS.94).aspx*) from Microsoft is an excellent resource if you're developing with Internet Explorer. While it provides technical information on the JavaScript used in other browsers, this resource provides a lot of IE-only information.

Books

- ***JavaScript: The Definitive Guide*** by David Flanagan (O'Reilly) is the most thorough printed encyclopedia on JavaScript. It's a dense, heavy tome, but it has all the details you need to thoroughly understand JavaScript.

◼ Basic JavaScript

JavaScript isn't easy to learn, and it never hurts to use as many resources as possible to learn the ins and outs of programming for the Web. The following resources provide help with the basics of the JavaScript language (which can sometimes be quite difficult).

Websites

- **The W3 Schools JavaScript tutorial** (*www.w3schools.com/js*) is a thorough (though not always thoroughly explained) tutorial that covers most aspects of JavaScript programming.

- **An Introduction to JavaScript** from howtocreate.co.uk (*www.howtocreate.co.uk/tutorials/javascript/introduction*) provides a free, detailed discussion of JavaScript. Of course, since you're using jQuery you won't need a lot of the information on this site; it covers much of the traditional methods of selecting and manipulating DOM elements.

Books

- ***Head First JavaScript Programming*** by Eric Freeman and Elisabeth Robson (O'Reilly) is a lively, highly illustrated introduction to JavaScript programming. It provides lots of information on JavaScript and is presented in a playful style.

◼ jQuery

Much of this book covered the jQuery JavaScript library, but there's still lots to learn about this powerful, timesaving, and fun programming library.

Websites

- **The jQuery Blog** (*http://blog.jquery.com*) keeps you up to date on all things jQuery.

- **jQuery's documentation** is a go-to resource for all aspects of jQuery (*http://api.jquery.com*). Every feature, function, and facet of jQuery is well documented.

Working examples demonstrate each jQuery function so you can see how a function is supposed to be used and how it works.

- **jQuery Fundamentals** (*http://jqfundamentals.com*) provides a unique hands-on instructional approach to jQuery. Not only does the site explain basic jQuery concepts, but it also provides a JavaScript "sandbox" built into each page of the site, so you can fiddle with code and watch the results live.

Books

- ***jQuery in Action*** by Bear Bibeault and Yehuda Katz (Manning) covers jQuery thoroughly with lots of example programming. It assumes some JavaScript and programming knowledge.

- ***jQuery Cookbook*** (O'Reilly) features tons of "recipes" for some of the most common tasks and problems you'll face as a programmer. It's written by a cast of characters, many of them the brilliant minds behind jQuery.

■ Advanced JavaScript

Oh yes, JavaScript is even *more* complicated than this book leads you to believe. Once you become proficient in JavaScript programming, you may want to expand your understanding of this complex language.

Articles and Presentations

- **JS-Must-Watch** (*https://github.com/bolshchikov/js-must-watch/*) is a GitHub repository dedicated to listing the best JavaScript presentations and videos on the Web.

Websites

- **Eloquent JavaScript** (*http://eloquentjavascript.net*) is an online JavaScript book. It's organized well, with creative ways of teaching lessons. Although it's supposed to be a beginner JavaScript tutorial site, the author writes as though he's talking to a bunch of computer scientists, so it's not the best place to start if you're new to JavaScript or programming. It's also available as a print book.

- **The JavaScript section of Douglas Crockfords' World Wide Web** (*http://javascript.crockford.com*) provides a lot of (complex) information about JavaScript. There's a lot of information on the site, some of it requiring a computer science degree just to understand.

- **Mozilla Developers Network JavaScript section** (*https://developer.mozilla.org/en-US/docs/Web/JavaScript*) contains tons of JavaScript information including the JavaScript reference mentioned at the beginning of this appendix, but also a detailed guide that covers the different versions of JavaScript as well as detailed tutorials for beginner to advanced JavaScript programmers.

Books

- **The Principles of Object-Oriented JavaScript** by Nichola Zakas is a short book (fewer than 100 pages) dedicated to advanced methods of organizing code. This is pro stuff, and worth a read.

- **JavaScript Patterns** by Stoyan Stefanov (O'Reilly). This book is a bit dated, but still full of great information for pushing your JavaScript programming forward. This book provides programming "patterns" that solve common tasks including how best to work with object literals, JSON, and arrays. Heavy duty programming; not for beginners.

- **JavaScript: The Good Parts** by Douglas Crockford (O'Reilly) is an oldie but a goodie. It uncovers the most useful parts of JavaScript, sidestepping bad programming techniques. Douglas should know what he's talking about, as he's a Senior JavaScript Architect at Yahoo! and the inventor of JSON. The book is short and dense, but contains a lot of wisdom about how to use JavaScript well.

CSS

If you're tackling this book, you're probably already pretty comfortable with CSS. JavaScript can really take advantage of the formatting power of CSS to control not only the look of elements, but even to animate them across the screen. If you need a CSS refresher, here are a few helpful resources.

Websites

- **The Complete CSS Guide** from WestCiv (*www.westciv.com/style_master/ academy/css_tutorial*) covers pretty much every part of Cascading Style Sheets. You won't learn a lot of different techniques here, but the basics of what CSS is and how to create styles and style sheets are thoroughly covered.

- **The Mozilla Developer Network CSS Reference** (*https://developer.mozilla. org/en-US/docs/Web/CSS/Reference*) is an A to Z guide to CSS properties.

- **Selectutorial** (*http://css.maxdesign.com.au/selectutorial*) is a great way to learn CSS selector syntax. jQuery is pretty much founded on the idea of using CSS selectors to manipulate the HTML of a page, so it pays to have a very good understanding of this concept.

Books

- **CSS3: The Missing Manual** by David Sawyer McFarland (O'Reilly) is a thorough, tutorial-driven book on Cascading Style Sheets. It includes in-depth coverage of CSS as well as real-world examples and troubleshooting tips for making sure your CSS works in a cross-browser world.

- **CSS: The Definitive Guide** by Eric Meyer (O'Reilly). The name says it all; this book covers CSS in such detail that your brain will definitely hurt if you try to read it all in one sitting.

Index

JavaScript & jQuery

THE MISSING CD

There's no
CD with this book;
you just saved $5.00.

Instead, every single Web address, practice file, and
piece of downloadable software mentioned in this
book is available at *missingmanuals.com*
(click the Missing CD icon).
There you'll find a tidy list of links,
organized by chapter.

CPSIA information can be obtained at www.ICGtesting.com
Printed in the USA
LVOW03s1605060115

421724LV00004B/5/P

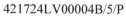